AF362042

Statistical Data Modeling and Machine Learning with Applications II

Statistical Data Modeling and Machine Learning with Applications II

Editors

Snezhana Gocheva-Ilieva
Atanas Ivanov
Hristina Kulina

MDPI • Basel • Beijing • Wuhan • Barcelona • Belgrade • Manchester • Tokyo • Cluj • Tianjin

Editors

Snezhana Gocheva-Ilieva
University of Plovdiv Paisii
Hilendarski
Plovdiv, Bulgaria

Atanas Ivanov
University of Plovdiv Paisii
Hilendarski
Plovdiv, Bulgaria

Hristina Kulina
University of Plovdiv Paisii
Hilendarski
Plovdiv, Bulgaria

Editorial Office
MDPI
St. Alban-Anlage 66
4052 Basel, Switzerland

This is a reprint of articles from the Special Issue published online in the open access journal *Mathematics* (ISSN 2227-7390) (available at: https://www.mdpi.com/si/mathematics/Statistica_Data_Machine_Learning_2021).

For citation purposes, cite each article independently as indicated on the article page online and as indicated below:

LastName, A.A.; LastName, B.B.; LastName, C.C. Article Title. *Journal Name* **Year**, *Volume Number*, Page Range.

ISBN 978-3-0365-8200-9 (Hbk)
ISBN 978-3-0365-8201-6 (PDF)

Contents

About the Editors . . . . **vii**

Snezhana Gocheva-Ilieva, Atanas Ivanov and Hristina Kulina
Special Issue "Statistical Data Modeling and Machine Learning with Applications II"
Reprinted from: *Mathematics* **2023**, *11*, 2775, doi:10.3390/math11122775 . . . . **1**

Michal Pavlicko, Mária Vojteková and Oľga Blažeková
Forecasting of Electrical Energy Consumption in Slovakia
Reprinted from: *Mathematics* **2022**, *10*, 577, doi:10.3390/math10040577 . . . . **5**

Snezhana Gocheva-Ilieva, Antoaneta Yordanova and Hristina Kulina
Predicting the 305-Day Milk Yield of Holstein-Friesian Cows Depending on the Conformation
Traits and Farm Using Simplified Selective Ensembles
Reprinted from: *Mathematics* **2022**, *10*, 1254, doi:10.3390/math10081254 . . . . **25**

Saddam Aziz, Muhammad Talib Faiz, Adegoke Muideen Adeniyi, Ka Hong Loo, Kazi Hasan, Linli Xu, et al.
Anomaly Detection in the Internet of Vehicular Networks Using Explainable Neural Networks (xNN)
Reprinted from: *Mathematics* **2022**, *10*, 1267, doi:10.3390/math10081267 . . . . **45**

Yunquan Song, Zitong Li and Minglu Fang
Robust Variable Selection Based on Penalized Composite Quantile Regression for
High-Dimensional Single-Index Models
Reprinted from: *Mathematics* **2022**, *10*, 2000, doi:10.3390/math10122000 . . . . **69**

Michail Tsagris
The FEDHC Bayesian Network Learning Algorithm
Reprinted from: *Mathematics* **2022**, *10*, 2604, doi:10.3390/math10152604 . . . . **87**

Claudia Angelini, Daniela De Canditiis and Anna Plaksienko
Jewel 2.0: An Improved Joint Estimation Method for Multiple Gaussian Graphical Models
Reprinted from: *Mathematics* **2022**, *10*, 3983, doi:10.3390/math10213983 . . . . **115**

Oksana Mandrikova, Yuryi Polozov, Nataly Zhukova and Yulia Shichkina
Approximation and Analysis of Natural Data Based on NARX Neural Networks Involving
Wavelet Filtering
Reprinted from: *Mathematics* **2022**, *10*, 4345, doi:10.3390/math10224345 . . . . **135**

Slavi Georgiev and Venelin Todorov
Efficient Monte Carlo Methods for Multidimensional Modeling of Slot Machines Jackpot
Reprinted from: *Mathematics* **2023**, *11*, 266, doi:10.3390/math11020266 . . . . **151**

Ivan De Boi, Carl Henrik Ek and Rudi Penne
Surface Approximation by Means of Gaussian Process Latent Variable Models and Line Element
Geometry
Reprinted from: *Mathematics* **2023**, *11*, 380, doi:10.3390/math11020380 . . . . **169**

Aleksandar Aleksić, Milan Ranđelović and Dragan Ranđelović
Using Machine Learning in Predicting the Impact of Meteorological Parameters on Traffic
Incidents
Reprinted from: *Mathematics* **2023**, *11*, 479, doi:10.3390/math11020479 . . . . **189**

Snezhana Gocheva-Ilieva, Atanas Ivanov, Hristina Kulina and Maya Stoimenova-Minova
Multi-Step Ahead Ex-Ante Forecasting of Air Pollutants Using Machine Learning
Reprinted from: *Mathematics* **2023**, *11*, 1566, doi:10.3390/math11071566 . . . . **219**

**Jay Raval, Pronaya Bhattacharya, Nilesh Kumar Jadav, Sudeep Tanwar, Gulshan Sharma,
Pitshou N. Bokoro, et al.**
RaKShA: A Trusted Explainable LSTM Model to Classify Fraud Patterns on Credit Card
Transactions
Reprinted from: *Mathematics* **2023**, *11*, 1901, doi:10.3390/math11081901 . . . . **245**

Zhanlin Ji, Jianyong Zhao, Jinyun Liu, Xinyi Zeng, Haiyang Zhang, Xueji Zhang, et al.
ELCT-YOLO: An Efficient One-Stage Model for Automatic Lung Tumor Detection Based on CT
Images
Reprinted from: *Mathematics* **2023**, *11*, 2344, doi:10.3390/math11102344 . . . . **273**

Qiyan Wang and Yuanyuan Jiang
Leisure Time Prediction and Influencing Factors Analysis Based on LightGBM and SHAP
Reprinted from: *Mathematics* **2023**, *11*, 2371, doi:10.3390/math11102371 . . . . **295**

Oksana Mandrikova, Bogdana Mandrikova and Oleg Esikov
Detection of Anomalies in Natural Complicated Data Structures Based on a Hybrid Approach
Reprinted from: *Mathematics* **2023**, *11*, 2464, doi:10.3390/math11112464 . . . . **317**

About the Editors

Snezhana Gocheva-Ilieva

Snezhana Gocheva-Ilieva, D.Sc., Ph.D., is currently a Guest Professor in the Department of Mathematical Analysis at the University of Plovdiv Paisii Hilendarski, Bulgaria. She received her M.Sc. degree and B.Sc. degree in Computational Mathematics from Sofia University "St. Kliment Ohridski" and received her Ph.D. degree in Physics and Mathematics from Taras Shevchenko National University of Kyiv. She received her Doctor of Sciences degree in Mathematics in 2016. From 1985 to 2011, Prof. Gocheva-Ilieva was an Associate Professor at the University of Plovdiv Paisii Hilendarski and has been a Full Professor here since 2011. She is a member of the Union of Bulgarian Mathematicians, and American Mathematical Society and is also a reviewer of Mathematical Reviews, Zentralblatt für Mathematik, and ACM. Her primary research interests lie in modeling and simulations of plasma and laser physics and engineering, modeling in environmental science, theories and applications of finite difference methods for ordinary and partial differential equations, singular problems, applied computational statistics, applications of predictive data mining techniques, and machine learning. Her secondary interests fall into scientific computing, ICT, programming, and innovative technologies in mathematics education.

Atanas Ivanov

Atanas Ivanov, Ph.D., is currently an Associate Professor in the Department of Mathematical Analysis at the University of Plovdiv Paisii Hilendarski, Bulgaria. He received his Ph.D. degree from the same University in 2016. Dr. Ivanov researches data analysis, predictive modeling, time series analysis, and their applications in various areas.

Hristina Kulina

Hristina Kulina, Ph.D., is an Associate Professor in the Department of Mathematical Analysis at the University of Plovdiv Paisii Hilendarski, Bulgaria. She received her M.Sc. degree in 1993 from the University of Plovdiv Paisii Hilendarski and her Ph.D. degree in 2013 from the Bulgarian Academy of Sciences. Dr. Kulina has been an Associate Professor since 2016. She is currently a member of the Union of Bulgarian Mathematicians. Her primary research interests are in algebra, especially of orthogonal arrays and spherical designs. Her the current interests are focused on data analyses and applications of predictive machine learning techniques.

Editorial

Special Issue "Statistical Data Modeling and Machine Learning with Applications II"

Snezhana Gocheva-Ilieva *, Atanas Ivanov and Hristina Kulina

Department of Mathematical Analysis, University of Plovdiv Paisii Hilendarski, 4000 Plovdiv, Bulgaria; aivanov@uni-plovdiv.bg (A.I.); kulina@uni-plovdiv.bg (H.K.)
* Correspondence: snow@uni-plovdiv.bg

Citation: Gocheva-Ilieva, S.; Ivanov, A.; Kulina, H. Special Issue "Statistical Data Modeling and Machine Learning with Applications II". *Mathematics* **2023**, *11*, 2775. https://doi.org/10.3390/math11122775

Received: 15 June 2023
Accepted: 16 June 2023
Published: 20 June 2023

Currently, we are witnessing rapid progress and synergy between mathematics and computer science. This interaction leads to a greater effect in solving theoretical and applied problems. In this context, and following the good results of the first Special Issue, "Statistical Data Modeling and Machine Learning with Applications", a second edition covering the same 15 topics was announced at the end of 2021. The present Special Issue (SI), like the first, concerns the section "Mathematics and Computer Science". In total, 35 manuscripts were submitted for review. Of these, after a strict peer-review process by at least three anonymous reviewers, 15 articles were accepted and published.

Study [1] proposes effective models for forecasting the maximum hourly electricity consumption per day in Slovakia. Four types of models were built: gray models (GM(1,1)), nonlinear gray Bernoulli models (NGBM(1,1)), one ANN (based on a multi-layer feed-forward back-propagation (MLPFFBP) network), and a hybrid model. This approach includes a pre-processed data series that is used to build the transverse set of gray models, construct a special validation process for the MLPFFBP-ANN, and create a weighted hybrid model with GM(1,1) and the ANN. According to the three criteria, the models of the GM(1,1) set, ANN, and hybrid model reported better accuracy in forecasting values than officially provided forecasts, as the hybrid model has the best indicators.

In [2], a new simplified selective algorithm is proposed to increase the efficiency of ensemble methods based on decision trees and the index of agreement. This approach was demonstrated on real-world data to predict the 305-day milk yield of Holstein–Friesian cows. Using rotated principal components, classification and regression tree (CART) ensembles and bagging, and Arcing methods, a 30% reduction in the number of trees of the constructed selective ensembles was achieved. In addition, hybrid linear stacked models were built, yielding a 13.6% reduction in test set prediction errors compared to hybrid models with the nonselective ensembles.

The aim of paper [3] was to create an effective approach to detect and counter cyberattacks on Internet of Vehicular networks (IoV). An innovative, explainable neural network (xNN) model based on deep learning (DL), and in particular, Denial of Service (DoS) assaults, has been developed. To build the model, K-means was first applied for clustering, classification, and extraction of the best features for anomaly detection. After that, the xNN model was built to classify attacks. The model was tested on the two known empirical datasets, CICIDS2019 and UNSW-NB15. The calculated statistical indicators showed that the proposed feature-scoring approach outperforms the known published results in this field.

Publication [4] deals with single-index quantile regression (SIQR), a type of semi-parametric quantile regression for analyzing heterogeneous data. The quantile regression method with the SCAD penalty and Laplace error penalty were used to construct two sparse estimators for the considered SIQR. This leads to an efficient procedure for variable selection and parameter estimation. Theorems were proved for the N-consistency and oracle properties of the proposed estimators. Computer simulations with benchmark data samples were performed. The method was shown to exhibit some resistance to heavy-tail errors and outliers while increasing the accuracy of parameter estimates.

Paper [5] presents a new computationally and highly efficient hybrid Bayesian network training algorithm called Forward with Early Dropping Hill Climbing (FEDHC), which is applicable to continuous or categorical variables. The algorithm applies the forward–backward-with-early-dropout (FBED) variable selection to each variable as a means of skeleton identification, followed by a hill-climb (HC) scoring phase. Another advantage of the proposed version of FEDHC is its robustness against outliers. FEDHC, PC Hill Climbing (PCHC), and Max–Min Hill Climbing (MMHC) were illustrated on two real cross-sectional datasets. A new, computationally efficient implementation of MMHC was also suggested.

In [6] the problem of estimating the graphs of conditional dependencies between variables under Gaussian settings is investigated. The authors present an improved Jewel 2.0 version of their previous Jewel 1.0 method. This was achieved on the basis of regression-based problem formulation with the appropriate minimization algorithm. Other contribution of the work is the proposed stability selection procedure that reduces the number of false positive scores in the estimated graphs. Simulation experiments were conducted.

The authors of [7] applied nonlinear autoregressive exogenous (NARX) networks coupled with an optimizing algorithm for wavelet filtering for modeling long-term dependencies and anomaly detection in noisy and nonstationary time series. A procedure using wavelet packets and stochastic thresholds was developed to approximate the decomposed components of the original data. The suggested wavelet filtering allows for the construction of a more accurate predictive NARX model. In addition, the NARX model was applied for anomaly detection. The results are demonstrated for ionospheric parameter time series prediction and ionospheric anomaly detection.

In paper [8], a method was developed for estimating the consolation prize of a slot machine jackpot using multidimensional integrals. Various modifications of the stochastic quasi-Monte Carlo approaches, such as lattice and digital sequences, Halton and Sobol sequences, and Latin hypercube sampling, were used to calculate the integrals. The expectations of the real consolation prize were evaluated, depending on the distribution of time and the number of players. The method was generalized for a multidimensional case. Computational experiments were performed.

Article [9] presents new theoretical and applied results in stochastic processes in spatial kinematics and line geometry for modeling some characteristics of 3D surfaces. The authors introduced theoretical principles on line-element geometry, kinematic surfaces, and the Gaussian process latent variable model (GPLVM). A method for surface approximation, unsupervised surface segmentation, and surface denoising in 3D modeling was described, which was based on the Bayesian GPLVM and the GPLVM with back constraints. The results were illustrated on sets with artificial and real-world objects.

In [10], a new method that aggregates five machine learning (ML) methods from different classification groups and a binary regression algorithm is proposed. The real-world task of predicting the impact of meteorological factors on the appearance of traffic accidents was solved. The most significant meteorological factors for road accidents were identified. The model was implemented as one of the agents in a two-agent system: agent 1 draws knowledge through ML from historically available data, and agent 2 deals with the same parameters, but in real-time. The suggested two-agent system can be implemented for providing early-warning alerts to citizens and traffic police, including through social media platforms.

The authors of [11] developed a novel, general multi-step-ahead strategy to forecast time series of air pollutants, extending the known multiple-input multiple-output (MIMO) strategy. The suggested strategy presupposes the availability of external independent forecasts for meteorological, atmospheric, and other variables, and continuously updated datasets. A new computational scheme was proposed for h-vector horizon prediction for each forward step. The strategy was applied to forecast the daily concentrations of pollutants PM_{10}, SO_2, and NO_2 17 horizons ahead, with h = 10 days. Random forest (RF) and arcing (Arc-x4) ML algorithms were used for modeling. The comparison with the existing strategies showed the advantage of the proposed one.

Paper [12] presents a novel credit card fraud detection scheme, RaKShA, which is integrated with explainable artificial intelligence (XAI) and long short-term memory (LSTM), i.e., the X-LSTM model, and the output is verified via a smart contract (SC). The results are stored in the InterPlanetary File System (IPFS), which is referenced on the public blockchain network. The proposed approach addressed the limitation of traditional fraud detection by providing model interpretability, improved accuracy, security, and transparency. The X-LSTM model was found to increase the power of the LSTM model in detecting credit card financial fraud (FF) and to make the scheme scalable and adaptable, which helps users to protect themselves from FF.

Paper [13] presents an efficient one-stage model for automatic lung tumor detection in computed tomography (CT) images, called ELCT-YOLO. It was designed to solve the problem of scales and meet the requirements of real-time tumor detection. The ELCT-YOLO model implemented a specially designed neck structure and a novel Cascaded Refinement Scheme (CRS) to process context information. The results of empirical tests showing the advantages of the model were presented.

In [14] a Light Gradient Boosting Machine (LightGBM) model is utilized to classify and predict leisure time. The SHapley Additive exPlanation (SHAP) approach was applied to conduct feature importance analysis and influence mechanism analysis of factors from four perspectives: time allocation, demographics, occupation, and family characteristics. The results verified that the LightGBM model effectively predicts personal leisure time.

A two-layer autoencoder neural network architecture, singular-spectrum analysis (SSA) decomposition, and an adaptive anomaly detection algorithm (AADA) were used in [15] to process natural data of a complex, noisy nature. The AADA includes wavelet transforms whose accuracy is set with appropriate thresholds. These methods were applied for the analysis and detection of anomalous decreases that occurred before the geomagnetic disturbances. High-performance hybrid models were built for the study of cosmic ray data. The hybrid SSA-AADA models reach about 84% efficiency in anomaly detection, while the Autoencoder-AADA models reach about 87%.

To summarize, we should emphasize that the results of the published articles fully correspond to the formulated goal and topics of the SI, "Statistical Data Modeling and Machine Learning with Applications II". Their main contributions are classified in Table 1. We can note that the selected 15 topics are well covered. The hybrid models, machine learning algorithms, and nonparametric statistical modeling received the greatest interest.

Table 1. Classification by topics of the main contributions of the articles published in the SI.

Topic	Paper
Computational statistics	[4,6,10]
Dimensionality reduction and variable selection	[4–6]
Nonparametric statistical modeling	[4–6,8–10]
Supervised learning (classification, regression)	[10,12,13]
Clustering methods	[3,12]
Financial statistics and econometrics	[1,12]
Statistical algorithms	[4,8,9]
Time series analysis and forecasting	[1,7,10,11]
Machine learning algorithms	[2,5,7,10–13]
Decision trees	[2,14]
Ensemble methods	[2,10,11]
Neural networks	[1,3,5,7,12,15]
Deep learning	[3,7,12–14]
Hybrid models	[1,2,5,7,12–15]
Data analysis	[4,7,10,14,15]

In conclusion, new mathematical methods and approaches, new algorithms and research frameworks, and their applications aimed at solving diverse and nontrivial practical problems are proposed and developed in this SI. We believe that the chosen topics and results are attractive and useful for the international scientific community and will contribute to further research in the field of statistical data modeling and machine learning.

Funding: This research received no external funding.

Acknowledgments: The research activity of the first Guest Editor of this Special Issue was conducted within the framework of and was partially supported by the MES (Grant No. D01-168/28.07.2022) for NCDSC, as part of the Bulgarian National Roadmap on RIs.

Conflicts of Interest: The authors declare no conflict of interest.

References

1. Pavlicko, M.; Vojteková, M.; Blažeková, O. Forecasting of Electrical Energy Consumption in Slovakia. *Mathematics* **2022**, *10*, 577. [CrossRef]
2. Gocheva-Ilieva, S.; Yordanova, A.; Kulina, H. Predicting the 305-Day Milk Yield of Holstein-Friesian Cows Depending on the Conformation Traits and Farm Using Simplified Selective Ensembles. *Mathematics* **2022**, *10*, 1254. [CrossRef]
3. Aziz, S.; Faiz, M.T.; Adeniyi, A.M.; Loo, K.-H.; Hasan, K.N.; Xu, L.; Irshad, M. Anomaly Detection in the Internet of Vehicular Networks Using Explainable Neural Networks (xNN). *Mathematics* **2022**, *10*, 1267. [CrossRef]
4. Song, Y.; Li, Z.; Fang, M. Robust Variable Selection Based on Penalized Composite Quantile Regression for High-Dimensional Single-Index Models. *Mathematics* **2022**, *10*, 2000. [CrossRef]
5. Tsagris, M. The FEDHC Bayesian Network Learning Algorithm. *Mathematics* **2022**, *10*, 2604. [CrossRef]
6. Angelini, C.; De Canditiis, D.; Plaksienko, A. Jewel 2.0: An Improved Joint Estimation Method for Multiple Gaussian Graphical Models. *Mathematics* **2022**, *10*, 3983. [CrossRef]
7. Mandrikova, O.; Polozov, Y.; Zhukova, N.; Shichkina, Y. Approximation and Analysis of Natural Data Based on NARX Neural Networks Involving Wavelet Filtering. *Mathematics* **2022**, *10*, 4345. [CrossRef]
8. Georgiev, S.; Todorov, V. Efficient Monte Carlo Methods for Multidimensional Modeling of Slot Machines Jackpot. *Mathematics* **2023**, *11*, 266. [CrossRef]
9. De Boi, I.; Ek, C.H.; Penne, R. Surface Approximation by Means of Gaussian Process Latent Variable Models and Line Element Geometry. *Mathematics* **2023**, *11*, 380. [CrossRef]
10. Aleksić, A.; Ranđelović, M.; Ranđelović, D. Using Machine Learning in Predicting the Impact of Meteorological Parameters on Traffic Incidents. *Mathematics* **2023**, *11*, 479. [CrossRef]
11. Gocheva-Ilieva, S.; Ivanov, A.; Kulina, H.; Stoimenova-Minova, M. Multi-Step Ahead Ex-Ante Forecasting of Air Pollutants Using Machine Learning. *Mathematics* **2023**, *11*, 1566. [CrossRef]
12. Raval, J.; Bhattacharya, P.; Jadav, N.K.; Tanwar, S.; Sharma, G.; Bokoro, P.N.; Elmorsy, M.; Tolba, A.; Raboaca, M.S. RaKShA: A Trusted Explainable LSTM Model to Classify Fraud Patterns on Credit Card Transactions. *Mathematics* **2023**, *11*, 1901. [CrossRef]
13. Ji, Z.; Zhao, J.; Liu, J.; Zeng, X.; Zhang, H.; Zhang, X.; Ganchev, I. ELCT-YOLO: An Efficient One-Stage Model for Automatic Lung Tumor Detection Based on CT Images. *Mathematics* **2023**, *11*, 2344. [CrossRef]
14. Wang, Q.; Jiang, Y. Leisure Time Prediction and Influencing Factors Analysis Based on LightGBM and SHAP. *Mathematics* **2023**, *11*, 2371. [CrossRef]
15. Mandrikova, O.; Mandrikova, B.; Esikov, O. Detection of Anomalies in Natural Complicated Data Structures Based on a Hybrid Approach. *Mathematics* **2023**, *11*, 2464. [CrossRef]

Article

Forecasting of Electrical Energy Consumption in Slovakia

Michal Pavlicko *, Mária Vojteková and Oľga Blažeková

Department of Quantitative Methods and Economic Informatics, Faculty of Operation and Economics of Transport and Communications, University of Žilina, Univerzitná 1, 01026 Žilina, Slovakia; maria.vojtekova@uniza.sk (M.V.); olga.blazekova@uniza.sk (O.B.)
* Correspondence: michal.pavlicko@uniza.sk; Tel.: +421-41-513-3274

Abstract: Prediction of electricity energy consumption plays a crucial role in the electric power industry. Accurate forecasting is essential for electricity supply policies. A characteristic feature of electrical energy is the need to ensure a constant balance between consumption and electricity production, whereas electricity cannot be stored in significant quantities, nor is it easy to transport. Electricity consumption generally has a stochastic behavior that makes it hard to predict. The main goal of this study is to propose the forecasting models to predict the maximum hourly electricity consumption per day that is more accurate than the official load prediction of the Slovak Distribution Company. Different models are proposed and compared. The first model group is based on the transverse set of Grey models and Nonlinear Grey Bernoulli models and the second approach is based on a multi-layer feed-forward back-propagation network. Moreover, a new potential hybrid model combining these different approaches is used to forecast the maximum hourly electricity consumption per day. Various performance metrics are adopted to evaluate the performance and effectiveness of models. All the proposed models achieved more accurate predictions than the official load prediction, while the hybrid model offered the best results according to performance metrics and supported the legitimacy of this research.

Keywords: forecasting model; electricity energy consumption; grey model; artificial neural network

Citation: Pavlicko, M.; Vojteková, M.; Blažeková, O. Forecasting of Electrical Energy Consumption in Slovakia. *Mathematics* **2022**, *10*, 577. https://doi.org/10.3390/math10040577

Academic Editor: Snezhana Gocheva-Ilieva

Received: 14 January 2022
Accepted: 10 February 2022
Published: 12 February 2022

Publisher's Note: MDPI stays neutral with regard to jurisdictional claims in published maps and institutional affiliations.

1. Introduction

Precise electrical energy consumption (EEC) forecasting is of great importance for the electric power industry. Electricity consumption can be directly or indirectly affected by various parameters. Such parameters include previous data of consumption, weather, population, industry, transportation, gross domestic product, and so on. Electricity consumption generally has a stochastic behavior that makes it hard to predict. Consumption overestimation would lead to redundant idle capacity, which would be a waste of funds. Underestimating, on the other hand, would lead to higher operating costs for energy suppliers and potential energy outages. Hence, precise forecasting of electricity consumption is crucial to avoid costly errors.

Another specificity of energy is its liberalization, which has led to a gradual separation of electricity generation, its distribution, and trading of this commodity. Thus, the ability to predict for most electricity market participants has become absolutely crucial for their functioning in a market environment.

For electricity producers, the essential information is how much electricity they will be able to deliver in the future, what their production costs will be, and at what price they will sell electricity on the market. The production of conventional sources is easier to plan and predict compared to the not entirely stable and intermittent production of photovoltaic and wind power plants.

Energy Profile of Slovakia

As the standard of living increases, the need for electricity grows not only in Slovakia but throughout the European Union. A significant share of the increase in consumption is due to the industry, which by introducing automation and robotization, has higher demands on electricity. Communal household consumption is also increasing due to the purchase of new electrical appliances. In forecasting the development of electricity consumption in the coming years, it will be necessary to consider the increase in transport consumption (expected by the massive production of electric vehicles), but at the same time consumption trends in electrical appliances and light sources in line with EU objectives.

In 2019, approximately 53.7% of the total production of electricity in Slovakia was obtained from nuclear power stations. The second biggest share was from fossil fuels (21.7%), and the third one was from waterpower (16.1%). The share from renewable sources (RES) was only 8.1%. Natural gas has the largest share (49.6%) in the production of electricity from fossil fuels, followed by brown coal (22.8%), and black coal (14.2%). The electricity production from RES was mostly from biomass (48.6%) and biogas and photovoltaic power plants participated by one-fourth (24.5% and 25.2%). The decrease in electricity production from RES in 2019 compared to 2018 was recorded in the case of biomass (95.3%) and biogas (95.2%). A similar decrease was documented for photovoltaic power plants (100.2%). Hydropower plants, on the other hand, recorded a significant increase in electricity production (117.7%) [1]. Electricity production by source in the period 2000–2020 is illustrated in Figure 1.

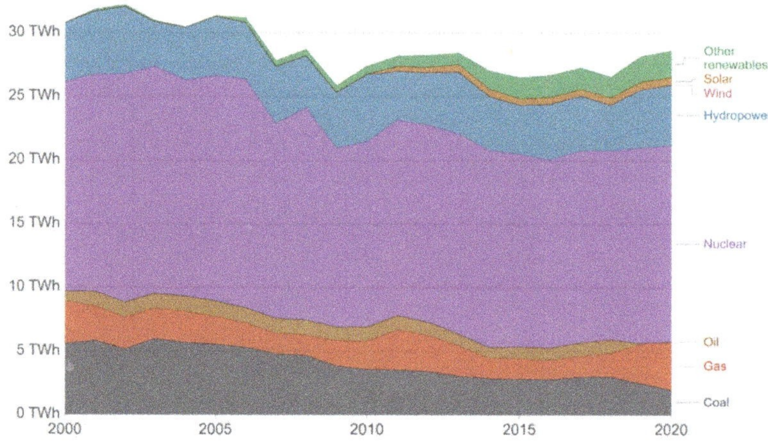

Figure 1. Electricity production by source in Slovakia [2].

After a significant decrease in electricity production in 2018, its production grew substantially in 2019. The amount of electricity produced from Slovak sources increased by 1460 GWh compared to 2018 and achieved 28,610 GWh in 2019. In 2016, electricity consumption crossed 30,000 GWh for the first time in history. In the following years, the consumption grew continuously until the culmination in 2018. However, in 2019 electricity consumption achieved 30,309 GWh, which means a considerable decrease compared to the previous year (−637 GWh, year-to-year index of 97.9%) and in 2020 the value was again below the level of 30,000 GWh [1]. The amounts of electricity production and consumption in Slovakia during the years 2000–2020 are listed in Figure 2.

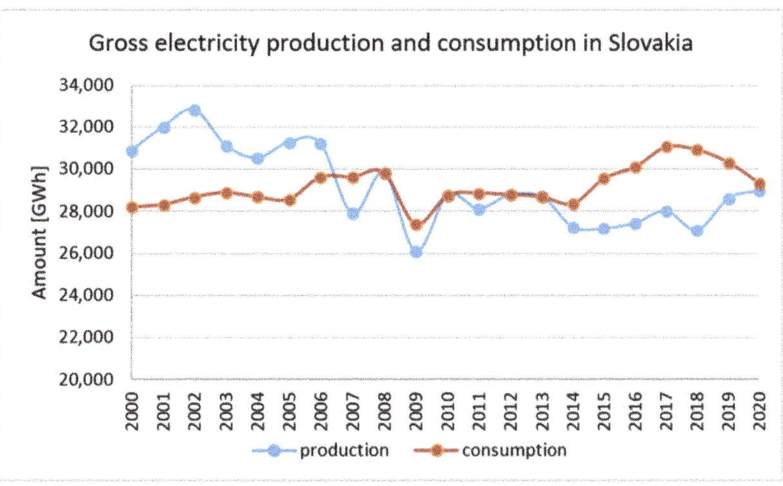

Figure 2. Gross electricity production and consumption in Slovakia [3].

The electricity system of the Slovak Republic (ES SR) is operated in parallel within the European Network of Transmission System Operators (ENTSO-E). Since 2015, SEPS (Slovenská Elektrizačná Prenosová Sústava, a. s.) is the only operator of the transmission system in the Slovak Republic. SEPS is the national provider of transmission and system services. Other key activities include providing auxiliary services and controlling the transmission system components as a dispatcher. It also serves as a facility providing support services and supplies of regulating electricity obtained within the Grid Control Cooperation (GCC) [1].

By initiation of auxiliary services, SEPS ensures a balance between the electricity production and consumption in Slovakia. This endeavor has to consider various circumstances and consider concluded agreements in the field of international electricity exchange.

Since 2011, company OKTE, a. s. serves as a coordinator of the short-term electricity market. It participates in all activities associated with the development, implementation, and operation of the single coupling of cross-border, day-ahead, and intraday markets in electricity within the European Union. Additionally, OKTE, a. s., evaluates and resolves disparities between demand aggregated and local distribution system deliveries [1].

The cross-border flows balance of ES SR has been in favor of import direction since 2007. In 2020, a substantial decrease in cross-border transmissions was measured compared to 2019. In the import direction, they were lower in total by 250 GWh, but in the export direction they dropped by 1132 GWh, and the import balance from 2014 achieved the lowest value (318 GWh) [1]. The amounts of imports, exports, and the differences between imports and exports of electricity in Slovakia during the years 2000–2020 are shown in Figure 3.

Electricity cannot be stored in significant quantities, nor is it easy to transport, and production units often face flexibility constraints. This implies an accurate estimate of electricity consumption on an hourly and daily basis.

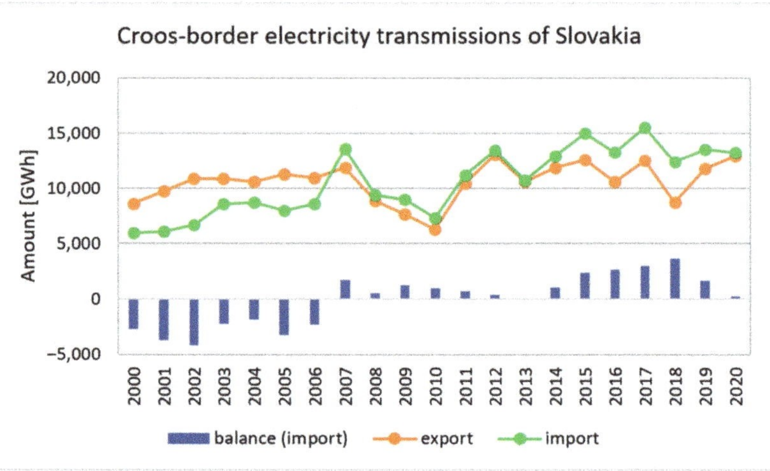

Figure 3. Cross-border electricity transmissions of Slovakia [4].

2. Literature Review

Various prediction models and methods are broadly explored to accurately forecast the electrical energy consumption because of economic, environmental, and technical reasons. In the field of energy consumption prediction, a variety of different methods have been proposed based on data analysis, including Box–Jenkins models, grey prediction models (GM), fuzzy logic methods, artificial neural networks (ANN), vector regressions, etc. Hybrid models combine features and benefits of parental methods to improve the accuracy of their predictions and help capture different data properties and avoid the limitations of a single method.

The GM's popularity in time series forecasting is probably due to its relative simplicity and capacity to model an unknown system by utilizing a small dataset. In addition to the basic GM(1,1) model, various variants of grey models to improve the accuracy of predicting energy consumption in China were used in [5–16].

Ayvaz in [17] introduced three different grey forecasting models for modeling and predicting yearly net electricity consumption in Turkey. A comparison of ARIMA and GM for electricity consumption demand forecasting in Turkey was applied in [18].

A gross final energy consumption, the energy consumption of renewable energy sources, and its share in France, Germany, Italy, Spain, Turkey, and the United Kingdom were forecasted using optimized fractional nonlinear grey Bernoulli model in [19].

The use of machine learning techniques, especially ANN, has become increasingly popular in many forecasting models, i.e., electricity demand prediction in Spain [20]; short-term electricity consumption in Spain [21]; an accurate forecast of the exploitable energy from renewable energy sources in Milan, Italy [22]; and a prediction of the 24-h electricity power demand in Poland [23].

Model hybridization or combining several similar or different methods has become a widespread practice to improve prediction accuracy. For example, Hu in [24] combined GM and neural networks to demonstrate the hybrid method effectiveness and forecasted EEC in Turkey. The grey and vector autoregressive models were coupled to improve their accuracy in [25]. The hybridizing support vector regression model with evolutionary algorithms was described in [26]. A comparison of statistical and machine learning models was given, and the use of hybrid models in electric power forecasting was identified in [27].

Regarding literature about forecasting EEC in the Slovak Republic, there are only a few articles. In [28], a comprehensive overview of energy consumption of six Central European countries, including Slovakia, was given. Avdakovic in [29] studied the correlation between air temperature and electricity demand using a linear regression and wavelet coherence approach in UK, Slovakia, and Bosnia and Herzegovina. Laurinec, in [30], presented a method for forecasting a load of individual electricity consumers using smart grid data and clustering. A time series prediction methodology based on deep neural networks was presented in Jarabek's research [31]. A long, short-term memory algorithm with a sequence-to-sequence architecture was used to improve the prediction accuracy of electricity consumption of Slovak enterprises. Oudjana, in [32], proposed a model employing neural networks and particle swarm optimization for a long-term forecast based on historical loads databases of Slovak power systems. Halaš, in [33], used biologically inspired algorithms and compared prediction accuracy of the ensemble learning model to base forecasting methods. Brozyna in [34] focused on the renewable energy and EU 2020 target for energy efficiency in the Czech Republic and Slovakia.

The rest of the paper is organized as follows: the description of data and the basic knowledge of proposed grey models, ANN, and hybrid model is in Section 3; Section 4 focuses on achieved results and introduces all the experimentation implemented; a discussion about the obtained outcomes is detailed in Section 5; and finally, Section 6 compiles the conclusions achieved from this research.

3. Methodology

The research was developed in three main stages: first, data collection and pre-processing for considered models; second, modeling the problem and implementation of the proposed models; and finally, validation and analysis of the results.

3.1. Data

The data were acquired via the Damas Energy information system (Damas) provided by SEPS [35]. The data of the official system load prediction was provided also by SEPS and can be found in [35]. It is worth note that the official load prediction is a one-year-ahead prediction usually published at the beginning of the forecasted year. The data provided by Damas contains all hourly consumptions in Slovakia, but the official load predictions contain only values for Wednesdays. For comparison, it was decided to make a prediction model only for Wednesdays. Hence, the maximum hourly electricity consumption for each Wednesday was extracted from the data.

The data from 2010 to 2018 were used for training purposes and the data from 2019 and 2020 were used for evaluation of prediction power, i.e., testing. However, the year 2019, which was not affected by COVID lockdown, was evaluated separately from the year 2020, which was affected by the pandemic. Note that the learning sample was divided into a training and validation subsample in the case of ANN, which is described in detail later in Section 3.3.1.

Electricity consumption is heavily influenced by various individual factors that can be easily determined, such as the time of day, day in the week, season of the year, or whether it is working day or weekend, etc. Therefore, the data were pre-processed for the use of individual models as follows.

3.1.1. Data Pre-Processing for Grey Models GM(1,1) and NGBM(1,1)

Normally, the data for prediction models are inputted in chronological order as measured. The grey theory is aimed at predicting the trend in data, such as a series of annual maxims or annual averages of energy consumption in a multiannual time series. The grey models are not meant to predict the periodically changing data series. However, the theory can be used, for example, to find out the trend of the first Wednesdays in the consecutive years, then the second one, etc. The data series were pre-processed accordingly, i.e., a matrix of 53 rows and 9 columns was constructed. Each row represents the input for the self-standing grey model, which in the final gives 53 grey models for respective Wednesdays in the year. There are usually 52 Wednesdays a year and only occasionally it is 53, therefore in the 53rd row the missing values were duplicated by the values from the 52nd row. In our case, there are just two years with 53 Wednesdays, one of which is situated in training data and one in the testing data.

3.1.2. Data Pre-Processing for ANN

As explained above, our data concern only Wednesdays, because of the comparison with the official prediction. For this purpose, the data were pre-processed for the ANN model as follows. Except for the target values of the maximum hourly electricity consumption per day, the following variables were added:

- serial number of Wednesday as a dummy variable,
- corresponding month as a dummy variable,
- the order of the individual Wednesday in the month as a dummy variable,
- public holiday or working day as a dummy variable,
- the day number where 1/1/1900 is equal to 1 and the next day is incremented by one.

3.2. Grey Models

The grey prediction is based on the grey systems theory. The methodology was created by Julong Deng in 1982, and it concentrates mainly on the study of problems concerning small samples and poor information [36]. The name "grey" was taken from control theory where the color shade has been usually used to specify the certain degree of information clarity. The adjective "grey" means that information is partially known and partially unknown. The methodology exhibits in systems with partially known information acquired via various means, such as generating, excavating, or extracting available information. Liu and Yang compared grey systems with other models dealing with some degree of uncertainty, such as stochastic probability, rough set theory, and fuzzy mathematics [37], and one can find in this study the discussion about the progress that grey systems theory has made in the world of learning and its wide-ranging applications in the entire spectrum of science.

3.2.1. Grey Model GM(1,1)

The grey models have become very popular among scholars due to its simple principle and high forecast accuracy. The forecasting via grey models is based on the grey generating function GM(1,1) which utilizes the variation within the system in order to discover the relationships between sequential data. The prediction of the model is based on this relationship. The grey model incorporates a system of first-order differential equations to forecast a time series prediction. The algorithm of forecasting based on the GM(1,1) grey prediction model can be summarized as follows [36].

1. Establish the initial non-negative sequence $X^{(0)} = \left\{ x^{(0)}(1),\ x^{(0)}(2),\ \dots,\ x^{(0)}(n) \right\}$, where the member $x^0(i)$ represents the original data with respect to time i.

2. Generate the first-order accumulated generating operation (AGO) sequence $X^{(1)}$ based on the initial sequence $X^{(0)}$ (to reduce the randomness of raw data to a monotonically increasing series) $X^{(1)} = \left\{ x^{(1)}(1),\ x^{(1)}(2),\ \dots,\ x^{(1)}(n) \right\}$, where the element $x^{(1)}(k)$ is derived as

$$x^{(1)}(k) = \sum_{i=1}^{k} x^{(0)}(i). \tag{1}$$

3. Compute the mean value of the first-order AGO sequence members

$$z^{(1)}(k) = 0.5 \left[x^{(1)}(k) + x^{(1)}(k-1) \right], \quad k = 2,\ 3, \dots, n. \tag{2}$$

4. Define the first-order differential equation for the sequence $X^{(1)}$ as

$$\frac{d\hat{X}^{(1)}}{dt} + a\,\hat{X}^{(1)} = b, \tag{3}$$

where a and b express the estimated parameters of the forecasting model.

5. Using the least squares estimate, it is possible to derive the estimated first-order AGO sequence

$$\hat{x}^{(1)}(k+1) = \left(x^{(0)}(1) - \frac{b}{a} \right) e^{-ak} + \frac{b}{a}. \tag{4}$$

Parameters a and b can be calculated using the following (5)–(7).

$$\begin{bmatrix} a \\ b \end{bmatrix} = \left(B^T B \right)^{-1} B^T Y_N, \tag{5}$$

$$B = \begin{bmatrix} -z^{(1)}(2) & 1 \\ -z^{(1)}(3) & 1 \\ \vdots & \vdots \\ -z^{(1)}(n) & 1 \end{bmatrix}, \tag{6}$$

$$Y_N = \left(x^{(0)}(2), \ x^{(0)}(3), \ \ldots, \ x^{(0)}(n) \right)^T. \tag{7}$$

6. The estimated members $\hat{x}^0_{k+1}$ can be obtained from the listed sequence by the inverse accumulated generating operation (IAGO)

$$\hat{x}^{(0)}(k+1) = \hat{x}^{(1)}(k+1) - \hat{x}^{(1)}(k). \tag{8}$$

3.2.2. Nonlinear Grey Bernoulli model NGBM(1,1)

To adjust the traditional grey model to obtain the higher prediction precision, professor Chen [38] (Z Application of the novel nonlinear) firstly proposed the Nonlinear Grey Bernoulli Model (NGBM(1,1) model) which combines GM(1,1) with the Bernoulli differential equation. The difference of NGBM(1,1) lies in the greater curvature compared to the GM(1,1) solution.

The Bernoulli differential equation for the sequence $X^{(1)}$ is defined as follows:

$$\frac{d\hat{X}^{(1)}}{dt} + a\,\hat{X}^{(1)} = b\left[\hat{X}^{(1)} \right]^i, \ i \in R. \tag{9}$$

If the exponent i was set to 0, the model would be equal to the GM(1,1) definition. Thus, the iterative approach with aspect to the minimal mean absolute percentage error (MAPE) should be applied to find the optimal exponent value i.

$$\hat{x}^{(1)}(k+1) = \left[\left(\left(x^{(0)}(1) \right)^{1-i} - \frac{b}{a} \right) e^{-a(1-i)k} + \frac{b}{a} \right]^{\frac{1}{1-i}}, \ i \neq 1. \tag{10}$$

Parameters a and b can be calculated by following (5) with vector Y_N (7), but with different matrix B:

$$B = \begin{bmatrix} -z^{(1)}(2) & \left[z^{(1)}(2) \right]^i \\ -z^{(1)}(3) & \left[z^{(1)}(3) \right]^i \\ \vdots & \vdots \\ -z^{(1)}(n) & \left[z^{(1)}(n) \right]^i \end{bmatrix}. \tag{11}$$

By performing IAGO, the predicted values $\hat{x}^{(0)}(k+1)$ can be calculated following (8).

3.2.3. Creating the Set of Grey Models

As mentioned above in the section concerning data pre-processing for GM models, the grey theory is used to find a trend in data. However, the result is a curve, which is almost straight in the case of GM(1,1). Therefore, it is not suitable for predicting periodically changing events, such as, daily energy consumption per year.

Electricity consumption is heavily affected by several factors, some of which were already mentioned. We observed that if annual electricity consumption is higher, it is usually dispersed within the year keeping the consumption pattern and the increment is dispersed proportionally. Concerning the maximal hourly consumption per day, the most affecting parameter is what kind of a day in the week it is and in what part of the year it is situated. Hence, the decision was made to create a set of transverse GM(1,1) models. Instead of predicting a standard time series, the first model of a set could forecast the consumption of the first Monday of a year based on data of the first Monday of previous years, etc. Therefore, the time series of data must be decomposed for this purpose and at the end results of the GM(1,1) set have to be recomposed to a regular time series. Provided that the annual consumption is rising, and the consumption pattern is preserved and not harmed by some unpredictable event, such as the pandemic lockdown, the forecast would disperse increased consumption among individual days effectively and vice versa.

Such a traverse set of grey models can be made for any day of the week or even for all days. However, due to the comparison with the official SEPS load consumption forecast, which publishes forecasts only for Wednesdays, we decided to construct the transverse grey model set for the same day of the week. Moreover, Wednesday is considered to be the day that best reflects the average consumption of a standard working day.

3.3. Artificial Neural Network (ANN)

An artificial neural network works similarly to a brain; it is a complex system of entities called neurons, with connections to other such entities. Each neuron somehow processes the incoming signal/s to an output signal/s. The interconnections, i.e., memory paths, consist of axons, dendrites, and synapses, and electrochemical media, the so-called neurotransmitters, are used for transmission. Some interconnections become stronger than others in the learning process. It is estimated that the human brain has around 100 billion interconnected neurons and each neuron may receive stimuli from as many as 10,000 other neurons. [39].

In the case of the ANN, artificial neurons act in the same way, but they are processing computer data, and their interconnections are called weights. Once the learning process and weight settings have been completed, ANN can be used to solve similar problems. Schematically, the whole layout of the neural network is usually divided into an input layer, a hidden layer/s, and a final output layer as is shown in Figure 4.

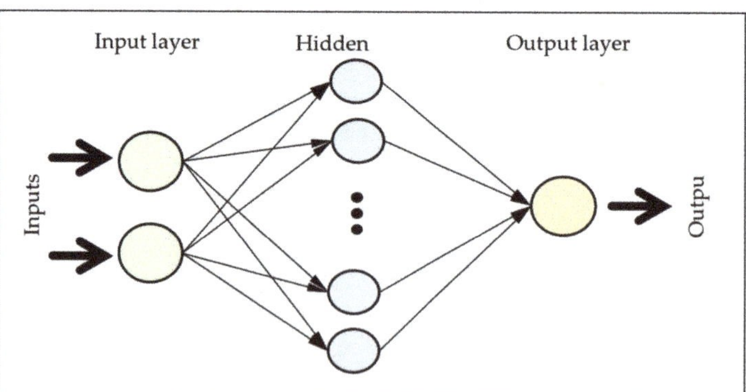

Figure 4. Shallow neural network.

3.3.1. Multi-Layer Feed-Forward Back-Propagation Network

A multi-layer feed-forward back-propagation network was designed via MATLAB's neural network fitting tool (nftool). Originally, nftool provided a shallow neural network, e.g., a network with just one hidden layer, that can be programmatically changed.

Nftool is the name of a tool that provides a graphic user interface to design, train, and validate a feedforward neural network to solve approximation problems. Default network settings of nftool are pre-set as follows:

- One hidden layer with 10 preset neurons (the number of neurons can be changed in the interface; other changes to layer design can be done in the corresponding block of the program code).
- The activation function of hidden units has a sigmoidal form (tansig or logsig) and the output units utilize a linear activation function.
- The default training algorithm is the backpropagation algorithm based on a Levenberg–Marquardt minimization method (the corresponding MATLAB function is trainlm) [40].
- The standard learning process is controlled by a cross-validation procedure that randomly divides the initial set of data into three subsets while the proportional amount is adjustable via the interface. One subset is used for weights adjustment in the training process, the other for validation, and the last for evaluating the quality of the final model (testing). By default, the approximation quality evaluation is measured by Mean Squared Error (MSE) [41].

Several changes have been made to the needs of this research and are as follows:

- The Quasi-Newton Backpropagation (BFGS) was used as a training method. The theory of quasi-Newton methods is based on the fact that an approximation to the curvature of nonlinear function can be computed without explicitly forming the Hessian Matrix. Newton's method is an alternative to the conjugate gradient methods for fast optimization. Backpropagation is used to calculate derivatives of performance with respect to the weight and bias variables. The variables are adjusted in the iteration process and a special parameter is estimated to minimize the performance along with the search direction dX. The line search function is used to locate the minimum point. The first search direction is the negative of the gradient of performance. In succeeding iterations, the search direction is computed according to the following formula:

$$dX = H^{-1}gX, \tag{12}$$

  where gX is the gradient and H is an approximate Hessian matrix [41,42].
- The number of hidden layers and neurons was one of the research goals of our investigation, thus the final configuration is revealed in the result section.
- The learning dataset (data from 2010 to 2018) was divided into two datasets, one for training and one for validation. Indices of both datasets were randomly chosen in each training process. The ratio was set to 85% for training and 15% for validation. However, the process of validation was altered and was programed as depicted in Figure 5 and described below.
- The Sum squared error (SSE) method was used instead of the MSE network performance function. This metric was chosen mainly due to the fact that the values of the maximum hourly electricity consumption per day fluctuate significantly within the observed period (from about 2500 to 5000). We decided to prefer absolute over relative deviations. Moreover, the resulting curve has a significantly smoother course.

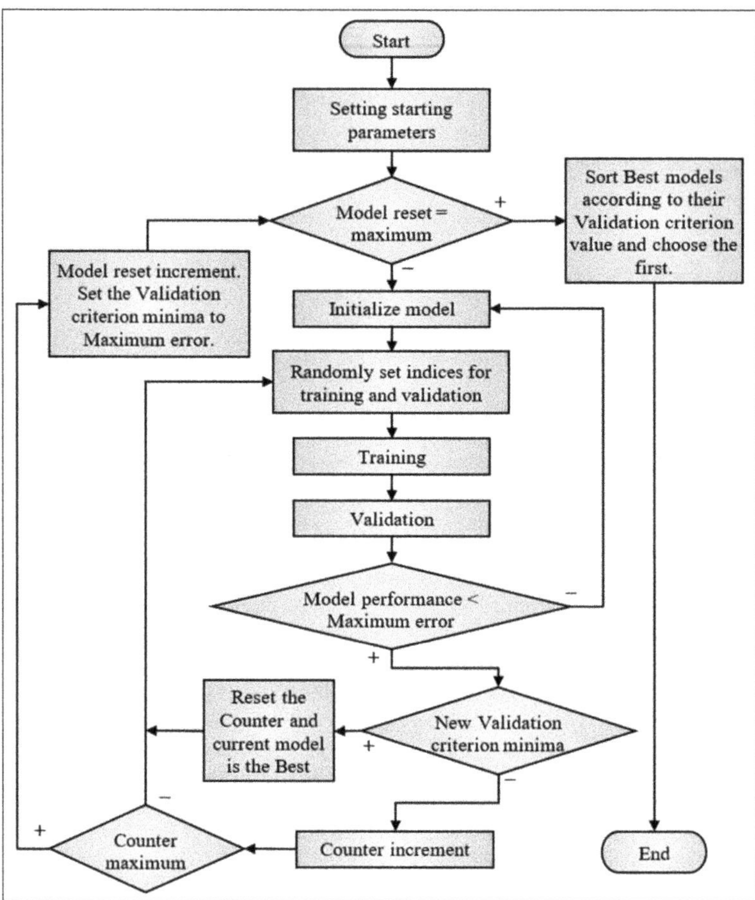

Figure 5. Validation process.

3.3.2. Validation Process

The actual, used network adjusts its weights and biases matrixes when the training process is repeated without network reinitialization. While continuous re-education of the network may lead to a higher prediction accuracy, it can also lead to an overfitting problem. On the other hand, learning process abortion immediately after performance decrement may lead to premature finalization because of local minima.

Therefore, the validation process was set as follows. Each training process increases the counter by one. If the validation criterion value achieves a lower value in less than 6 consecutive runs, the counter is restarted and the training process continues with the current network setting; otherwise, the network is reinitialized to default weights and biases. The validation criterion value was set as the sum of equalized training and validation performance, i.e., the training SSE was multiplicated by 0.15 and the validation SSE was multiplied by 0.85. The maximum number of reinitializations was set to 10 resets apart from the reinitialization due to the inappropriate initialization. The inappropriate initialization may occur after network reset and the network may get stuck in the local minima. This behavior is associated with a large performance error. In such a case, the network was reinitialized without increment of the reset counter. In the end, the model with the lowest validation criterion value was chosen for the evaluation of model performance on the testing sample.

3.4. Hybrid Model

Examples of combining different models can be found in the literature, e.g., [24,26,43]. The main idea for the hybridization is to deduce if a hybrid model may lead to further improvement of prediction performance. Therefore, here the process is not standard, i.e., to find the appropriate weight distribution on the training sample and then to validate it on the testing sample, but iteration runs straight on the testing sample. The process serves as a starting point for future research. In this case, all proportion weight combinations of the predictions of ANN and GM(1,1) set were searched. The step for this iteration was set to 5%. The RMSE (12) and the MAPE (13) metrics were monitored throughout all the component combinations of the potential hybrid model.

3.5. Performance Criteria

In order to reflect the performance and the effectiveness of models, some indicators are adopted to evaluate the result. The definitions of the forest accuracy indicators are shown respectively, as follows:

(a) RMSE—Root Mean Squared Error

$$RMSE = \sqrt{\frac{1}{n}\sum_{i=1}^{n}(x_i - \hat{x}_i)^2}. \tag{13}$$

(b) MAPE—Mean Absolute Percentage Error

$$MAPE = \frac{1}{n}\sum_{i=1}^{n}\left|\frac{x_i - \hat{x}_i}{x_i}\right|100\%. \tag{14}$$

(c) RMSPE—Root Mean Squared Percentage Error

$$RMSPE = \sqrt{\frac{1}{n}\sum_{i=1}^{n}\left(\frac{x_i - \hat{x}_i}{x_i}\right)^2}100\%. \tag{15}$$

In the formulations, the x_i is the real value and $\hat{x}_i$ is the predicted value, and n is the number of samples. Lower forecast indicators indicate more satisfactory predictive ability and higher accuracy.

4. Results

The results are divided into three parts, namely the prediction of grey models, the results of artificial neural networks, and finally the potential of hybridization. The results were maintained separately for the year 2019, which was not affected by pandemic lockdown, and the year 2020, which was affected in all provided results. However, in the part concerning the search of hybridization proportion, just the 2019 results were considered. All the prediction charts also contain the official SEPS prediction due to easier assessment of the prediction performance provided by the respective models. As a reminder, all provided models serve as two-year-ahead forecasting models and the official SEPS load consumption predictions are one-year-ahead predictions.

4.1. Grey Models Prediction

At first, the prediction of the model using the set of standard grey models is provided.

Figure 6 shows good results and supports the used methodology to construct the GM(1,1) set for prediction of periodic trend. Even the two-year-ahead prediction (for 2020) shows comparable or better results with the official one-year-ahead forecast and supports the viability of the proposed methodology.

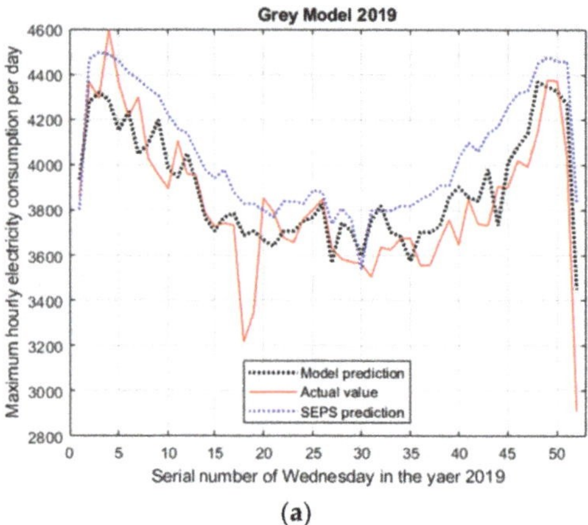
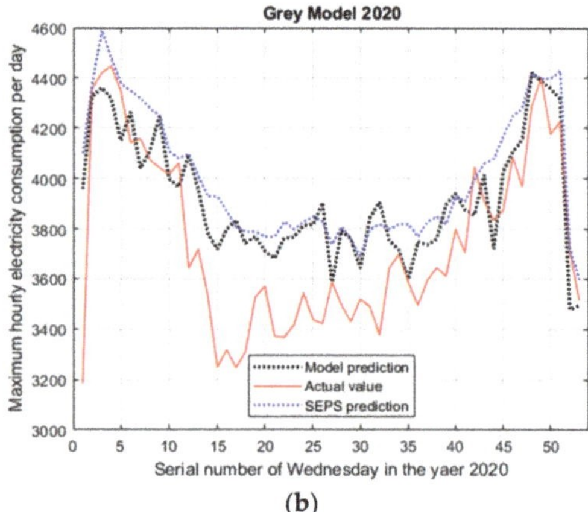

Figure 6. Prediction of Grey Model set. (**a**) Prediction of GM(1,1) set for 2019, (**b**) Prediction of GM(1,1) set for 2020.

Figure 7 shows the results for the NGBM(1,1) set. As can be observed in the charts, while one-year-ahead prediction achieved good results (but was worse than the GM(1,1) set), the two-year-ahead forecast falls considerably behind even the SEPS forecast. The main advantage of better curvature seems to be ineffective in such a transverse approach; thus, the NGBM(1,1) was not used for hybridization.

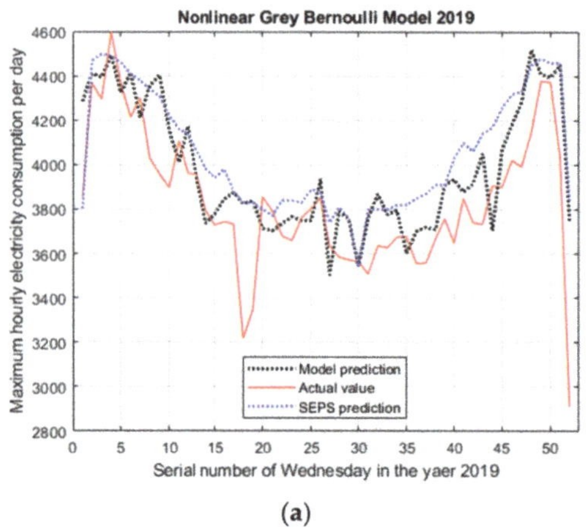
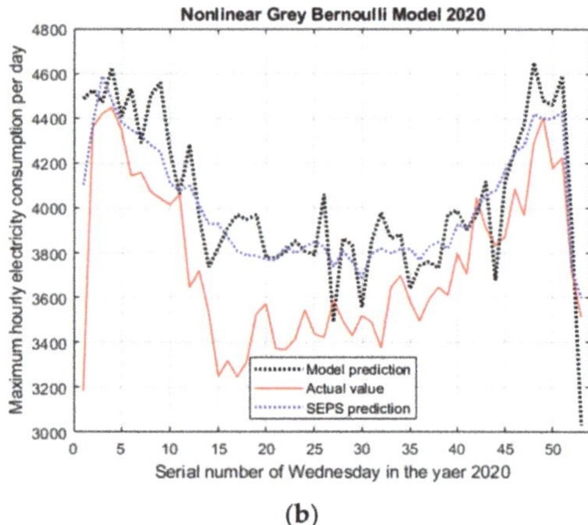

Figure 7. Prediction of Nonlinear Grey Bernoulli Model set. (**a**) Prediction of NGBM(1,1) set for 2019, (**b**) Prediction of NGBM (1,1) set for 2020.

4.2. Neural Network Prediction

4.2.1. Hidden Layers Composition

During our search for the optimal hidden layers layout, various combinations of the following numbers resulting from data composition were inspected:

- 53: maximal number of Wednesdays in the year,
- 12: number of the months,
- 5: maximal number of Wednesdays in the month,
- 3: other inputs.

Throughout the process, only the number of neurons and layers were changed, but not the layer types. Shallow NN with just one hidden layer composed of 3 or 5, ... or 53 and even 73 neurons were very fast, but the results were unsatisfying. The shallow NN with 9540 ($53 \times 12 \times 5 \times 3$) neurons gave a satisfactory result, but the time consumption for training was enormous. Interim results showed that more layers with a lower number of neurons gave comparable or even better results than the one shallow NN with a huge hidden layer. The composition of 53, 12, 5, and 3 neurons in 4 hidden layers achieved a satisfactory result. When the number of neurons was increased by multiplication with various integer multiplicators, the results were of comparable quality, but the learning time was rising significantly. Therefore, the decision on the minimal satisfactory composition was made as follows.

The final layout of the hidden layers was divided into 4 hidden layers with 53, 12, 5, and 3 neurons in the listed order, as depicted in Figure 8.

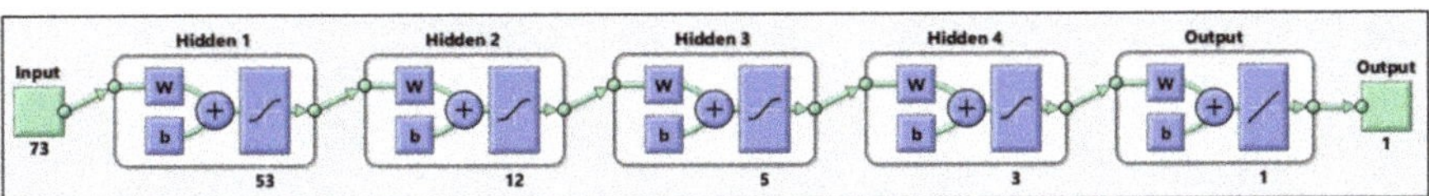

Figure 8. Neural network layout.

4.2.2. Validation Process

Data from the validation process can be seen in Figure 9. As it can be observed, all iterations brought relatively similar results in terms of performance measured via sum squared error. Probably, fewer resets were needed, but the figure shows another way of future research in creating a set of shallow NN components via bagging, boosting, or stacking to further improve the prediction power of ANN.

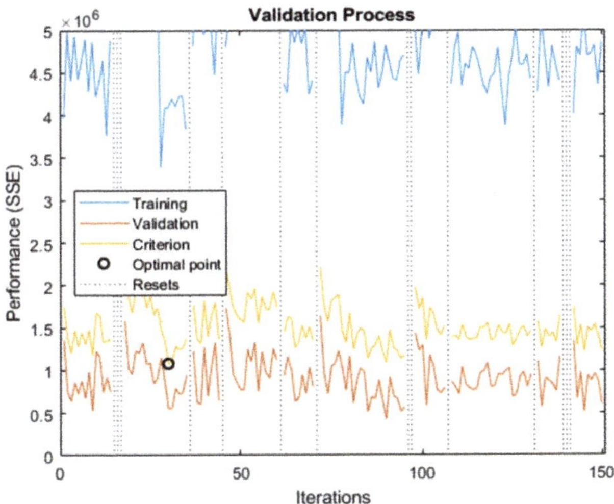

Figure 9. Validation process log.

Predictions achieved by the ANN are depicted in Figure 10. It is obvious, especially in one-year-ahead predictions, that the results are the best among provided models and the weight of this component would play the main role in the potential hybrid model.

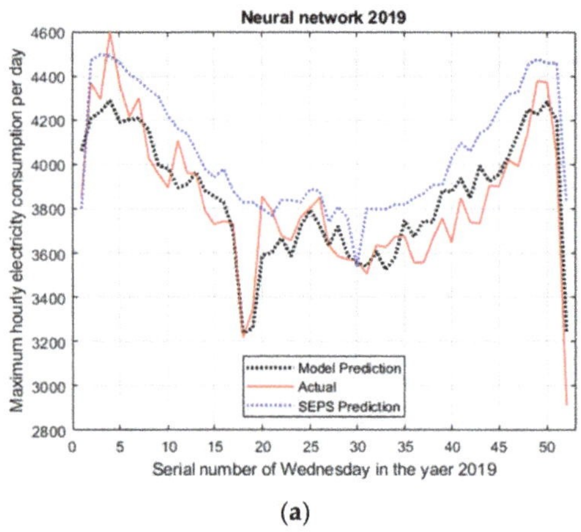

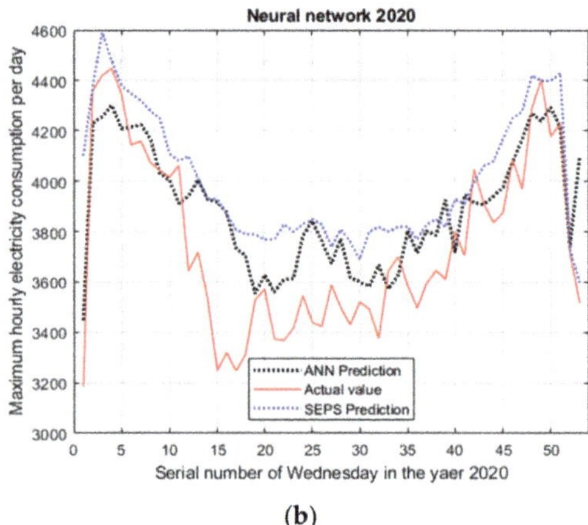

(a)

(b)

Figure 10. Prediction of ANN. (**a**) Prediction of ANN for 2019, (**b**) Prediction of ANN for 2020.

4.3. Hybridization

A comparison of the prediction performance metrics of the potential hybrid model is provided in this part of the results. The objective here is not to find the best score weight distribution of individual elements in the optimization or validation process, but to find out if such a process may lead to improvement. Deducing what period to take into consideration in the optimization process is a theme for future research. However, the weight distribution can be optimized via nonlinear programming with the objective function, Equation (16):

$$\min MAPE = \frac{1}{n} \sum_{i=1}^{n} \left| \frac{x_i - (w_A \hat{x}_{iA} + w_G \hat{x}_{iG})}{x_i} \right| \cdot 100\% \tag{16}$$

and the constrains of Equations (17) and (18):

$$w_A + w_G = 1 \tag{17}$$

$$w_A, w_G \geq 0 \tag{18}$$

where w_A, w_G are wanted weights of particular models and $\hat{x}_{iA}, \hat{x}_{iG}$ are estimated values by these models.

Nevertheless, Figure 11 shows a comparison of RMSE and MAPE metrics on different weight distributions based solely on the testing sample, i.e., predictions for 2019. The optimal point, in this case, is situated between near 85% weight for the ANN and 15% for the GM(1,1). We assume that the closer the prediction power is, the better the results could be achieved by hybridization. Figure 11 shows that the use of two components bring small but measurable improvements. We presume that the inclusion of another similarly performing method could potentially further improve the results.

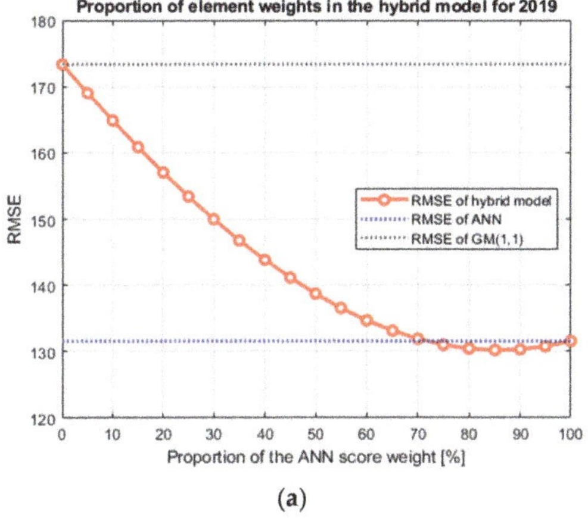
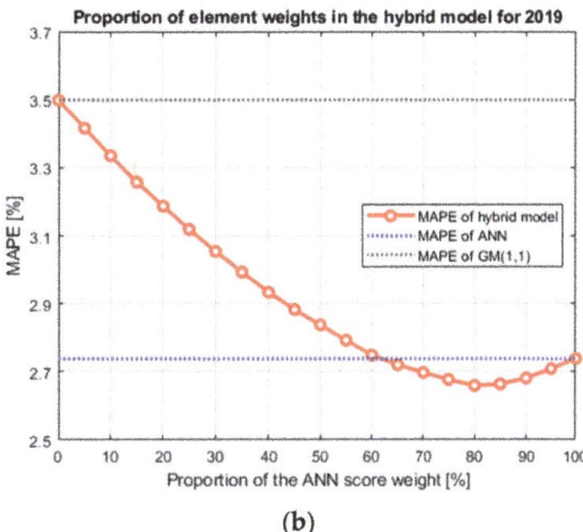

Figure 11. Performance metrics of prediction of potential hybrid models with different weights. (a) RMSE of the potential hybrid model for 2019, (b) MAPE of the potential hybrid model for 2019.

5. Discussion

There are many works incorporating grey models to forecast annual energy consumption, e.g., [5,7,9–13], but we have not found works concerning daily based forecasts via grey models. As far as we know, more sophisticated methods, such as random forests, NN, or SVM are used to forecast energy consumption, similar to [44]. Our experimentation is focused on the prediction of maximum hourly electricity consumption per day in Slovakia by two Grey model types (GM(1,1), NGBM(1,1)) as a transverse set and one ANN. Moreover, the fourth potential hybrid model, as an example of the future path of our research, was presented in the manuscript.

A traverse set of grey models or ANN can be constructed for any day of the week or for all days. However, due to the comparison with the official SEPS load consumption forecast, which publishes forecasts only for Wednesdays, the models and extracted data are focused on the same day. Wednesday is considered to be the day with the average working day consumption. In our study, all three mentioned models used the same sample of acquired data (maximum hourly electricity consumption per each Wednesday from 2010 to 2018) for training. Equally, the same sample of acquired data was used for testing, i.e., for comparison of the real data with predicted ones (maximum hourly electricity consumption per each Wednesday in years 2019 and 2020). Though, the whole training dataset cannot be denoted as equal for grey models and ANN due to the different data pre-processing as described in Section 3.1. However, these differences do not prevent relevant comparison of model performance.

Although we have no information about the indicators or method used in the official prediction (marked as SEPS), the predicted data are also involved in our comparison for the relevant purpose of our findings.

The prediction performance of our results altogether with official prediction is shown in Table 1.

As can be seen from Table 1, all our models performed better than SEPS in 2019. From the grey models, the GM(1,1) set is more accurate than the NGBM(1,1) set. The ANN model outperformed the official SEPS predictions as well as the grey model forecasts in both 2019 and 2020. This is probably caused by additional information added in the data pre-processing phase. Namely, it is information of whether the public holiday falls on a specific Wednesday or not. The importance of public holiday information can be observed in Figure 10, where the steep decrease can be monitored in the ANN prediction. There is a public holiday in Slovakia on the 1st and 8th of May (18th and 19th Wednesday in 2019) and maximal electricity consumption was reasonably lower as surrounding points in the chart. The only model that reflects these circumstances was the ANN. On the other hand, the 53rd Wednesday in 2020 (30 December 2020) is not a public holiday and the network predicted a higher value than it should.

Table 1. Prediction performance comparison.

Model	RMSE		MAPE [%]		RMSPE [%]	
	2019	2020	2019	2020	2019	2020
SEPS	273.32	311.56	6.03	7.22	7.88	9.09
GM(1,1)	173.38	275.31	3.49	6.27	4.95	8.05
NGBM(1,1)	244.21	390.16	4.99	9.03	7.05	11.29
ANN	131.58	243.09	2.74	5.32	3.51	7.04
Hybrid(85/15)	130.21	240.96	2.66	5.30	3.50	7.00

As mentioned before, there is various research that uses various types of grey models to forecast whole year consumption, but we are not aware of any using them as a transverse set for daily forecasting. Nevertheless, our results are of comparable quality in the terms of MAPE metrics despite the different usage. For example, the results of the improved grey models achieved 2.78% to 3.10% in consumption of the APEC countries in [5]. The results of backpropagation neural network in the mentioned research achieved 5.10% and 9.97% for support vector machine regression. Another research of this type was used to forecast energy consumption in China and India and compares 5 types of the grey models with various results ranging from 3.98% to 14.79% for Beijing consumption and from 3.46% to 35.02% for India in [9].

In the case of daily based forecasting of energy consumption in [44], more demanding methods compared to grey models were used. The results of the case study for two companies achieved from 8.75% to 19.23% for one company and from 4.45% to 6.07% for the second case. The Functional Principal Component Analysis was used to decompose the electric consumption patterns in [45]. The method was used to investigate and predict consumption patterns in the Milan metropolitan area on special contractual characteristic groups with MAPE ranging from 7.63% to 39.19%. Forecasting the daily night peak electric power demand of the Sri Lankan power system by using past daily data in time series analysis was used in [46]. The prediction model based on ARIMA achieved a month-ahead forecast with MAPE of 4.195% and a week-ahead MAPE of 1.855%. Modelling and forecasting hourly electricity demand in West African countries by using multiple regression analysis was introduced in [47] with an average relative error of less than 15%, except for Sierra Leone, which had a relative error of 38.5% due to civil war in the country. Research with a very different approach to forecasting daily electricity consumption can be found in [48]. The meteorological factors played a major role in the one-week-ahead prediction, and the relative errors of their models ranged from 2.36% to 10.40%.

All predictions for the year 2020 show worse results in comparison with the year 2019. This is because of the pandemic lockdown in spring 2020. However, the prediction of the NGBM(1,1) set starts to fall behind even the SEPS prediction and thus it seems to not be the right component in the hybridization, or at least with the used dataset. All possible combinations of the component weights with the step of 5% were checked to find out the potential of hybridization. This approach shows the potential to further improve the prediction power, where one component may improve the weaknesses of the other one. Finding out the optimum in an appropriate way and searching for suitable components are the objective for future research. However, Figure 12 is provided to show the comparison of predictions in the test period from January 2019 to December 2020, i.e., evaluation of the prediction power for the hybrid model with proportion 85/15 (ANN to GM(1,1)).

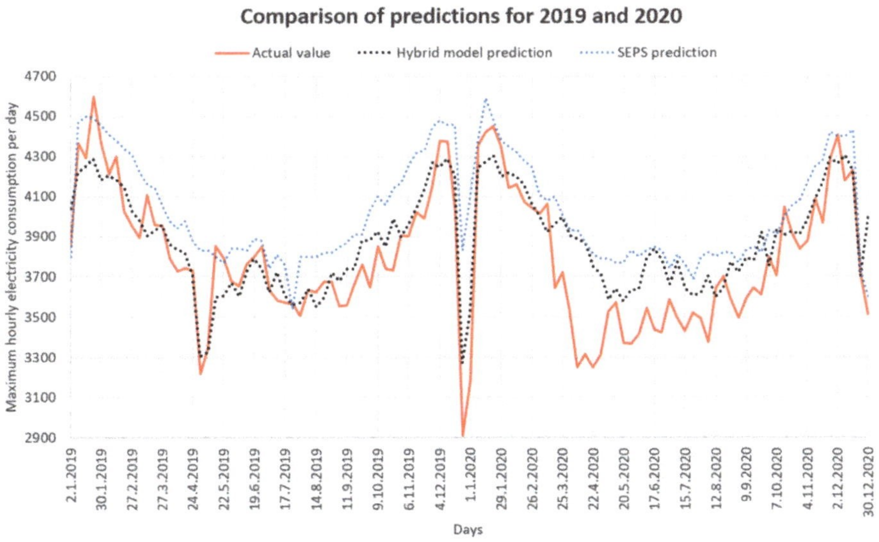

Comparison of predictions for 2019 and 2020

Figure 12. Comparison of predictions for the years 2019 and 2020.

We identify several limitations of our study. The difficulty was in acquiring the data of the official system load prediction provided by SEPS [35]. Electric energy consumption is influenced by many factors, as the impact of weather fluctuations and economic decisions (lockdown during COVID-19) are hard to consider in prediction. One way to overcome this obstacle is to focus on interval prediction instead of point prediction. Another possibility is to improve the prediction accuracy by looking for another component in a hybrid model, finding the optimal weight proportion, or stacking or bagging shallow neural networks.

6. Conclusions

Electrical energy consumption forecasting is important for planning and facility expansion in the electric industry. Accurate forecasts can save operating and maintenance costs, increase the reliability of power supply and delivery systems, and correct decisions for future development. Forecasting is also important for the sustainable development of the electric power industry. Much presented research and also our results show that is very problematic to predict an exact electricity consumption pattern. The reasons lie in the substantial impact of various factors, such as weather conditions, economic situation, population growth, pandemic outbreak, etc.

The main goal of the article was to offer more accurate models to predict electrical energy consumption in Slovakia than officially provided. The contributions of the proposed article can be summarized as follows:

(a) Three models, the (GM(1,1) set, NGBM(1,1) set and ANN) and the fourth hybrid model were suggested to improve forecasts of maximum hourly electricity consumption per day in Slovakia.

(b) The usual chronological time series was not used as the data set for grey models, but data series were pre-processed. The set of transverse models was created, i.e., the matrix of 53 rows and 9 columns was constructed. Each row represents the input for the self-standing grey model, which in the final gives 53 grey models for respective weekdays in the year and then is reconstructed to chronological order. The multi-layer feed-forward back-propagation network with the special validation process was designed.

(c) According to the three criteria (RMSE, MAPE, RMSPE) the models of GM(1,1) set, ANN, and the hybrid model reported better accuracy in forecasting values for 2019 and 2020 than SEPS officially provided forecasts.

(d) A gap in the available literature regarding forecasting of EEC in the Slovak Republic was filled and an overview of the energy situation in Slovakia was provided.

Author Contributions: Conceptualization: M.V., M.P. and O.B.; methodology: M.V. and M.P.; software: M.P.; validation: O.B.; formal analysis: M.P. and O.B.; investigation: O.B.; resources: M.V. and M.P.; data curation: O.B. and M.P.; writing—original draft preparation: M.P. and M.V.; writing—review and editing: M.V. and O.B.; visualization: M.P. and O.B.; supervision: M.V. and M.P.; project administration: M.V. and. M.P. All authors have read and agreed to the published version of the manuscript.

Funding: This research received no external funding.

Data Availability Statement: Publicly available datasets were analyzed in this study. This data can be found here: [1–4].

Acknowledgments: This research has been supported by Slovak Grant Agency for Science (VEGA), Grant No. 1/0157/21.

Conflicts of Interest: The authors declare no conflict of interest.

References

1. Slovenská Elektrizačná Prenosová Sústava, a.s. Available online: https://www.sepsas.sk/sk/sluzby/damas-energy/seps-vs2019.pdf (accessed on 6 July 2021).
2. Electricity Production by Source. Available online: https://ourworldindata.org/grapher/electricity-prod-source-stacked (accessed on 1 July 2021).
3. SAES.SK. Slovenske Elektrárne (Energetika Na Slovensku). Available online: https://www.seas.sk/energetika-na-slovensku/ (accessed on 17 June 2021).
4. Database—Eurostat. Available online: https://ec.europa.eu/eurostat/web/main/data/database (accessed on 1 July 2021).
5. Li, K.; Zhang, T. Forecasting Electricity Consumption Using an Improved Grey Prediction Model. *Information* **2018**, *9*, 204. [CrossRef]
6. Li, K.; Zhang, T. A Novel Grey Forecasting Model and Its Application in Forecasting the Energy Consumption in Shanghai. *Energy Syst.* **2021**, *12*, 357–372. [CrossRef]
7. Li, J.; Wang, Y.; Li, B. An Improved Grey Model WD-TBGM (1, 1) for Predicting Energy Consumption in Short-Term. *Energy Syst.* **2020**, *13*, 167–189. [CrossRef]
8. Wang, Z.-X.; Jv, Y.-Q. A Non-Linear Systematic Grey Model for Forecasting the Industrial Economy-Energy-Environment System. *Technol. Forecast. Soc. Chang.* **2021**, *167*, 120707. [CrossRef]
9. Liu, C.; Wu, W.-Z.; Xie, W.; Zhang, J. Application of a Novel Fractional Grey Prediction Model with Time Power Term to Predict the Electricity Consumption of India and China. *Chaos Solit. Fractals* **2020**, *141*, 110429. [CrossRef]
10. Chen, H.; Tong, Y.; Wu, L. Forecast of Energy Consumption Based on FGM(1, 1) Model. *Math. Prob. Eng.* **2021**, *2021*, e6617200. [CrossRef]
11. Huang, L.; Liao, Q.; Zhang, H.; Jiang, M.; Yan, J.; Liang, Y. Forecasting Power Consumption with an Activation Function Combined Grey Model: A Case Study of China. *Int. J. Electr. Power Energy Syst.* **2021**, *130*, 106977. [CrossRef]
12. Zeng, L. Forecasting the Primary Energy Consumption Using a Time Delay Grey Model with Fractional Order Accumulation. *Math. Comput. Model. Dyn. Syst.* **2021**, *27*, 31–49. [CrossRef]
13. Jiang, P.; Hu, Y.-C.; Wang, W.; Jiang, H.; Wu, G. Interval Grey Prediction Models with Forecast Combination for Energy Demand Forecasting. *Mathematics* **2020**, *8*, 960. [CrossRef]
14. Zeng, B.; Ma, X.; Shi, J. Modeling Method of the Grey GM(1,1) Model with Interval Grey Action Quantity and Its Application. *Complexity* **2020**, *2020*, e6514236. [CrossRef]
15. Yuan, C.; Liu, S.; Fang, Z. Comparison of China's Primary Energy Consumption Forecasting by Using ARIMA (the Autoregressive Integrated Moving Average) Model and GM(1,1) Model. *Energy* **2016**, *100*, 384–390. [CrossRef]
16. Wang, Z.-X.; Li, Q.; Pei, L.-L. A Seasonal GM(1,1) Model for Forecasting the Electricity Consumption of the Primary Economic Sectors. *Energy* **2018**, *154*, 522–534. [CrossRef]
17. Ayvaz, B.; Kusakci, A.O. Electricity Consumption Forecasting for Turkey with Nonhomogeneous Discrete Grey Model. *Energy Sources Pt. B Econ. Plann. Policy* **2017**, *12*, 260–267. [CrossRef]
18. Şişman, B. A Comparison of arima and grey models for electricity consumption demand forecasting: The case of Turkey. *Kastamonu Üniversitesi İktisadi ve İdari Bilimler Fakültesi Dergisi* **2016**, *13*, 234–245.

19. Sahin, U. Future of Renewable Energy Consumption in France, Germany, Italy, Spain, Turkey and UK by 2030 Using Optimized Fractional Nonlinear Grey Bernoulli Model. *Sustain. Prod. Consump.* **2021**, *25*, 1–14. [CrossRef] [PubMed]

20. Pegalajar, M.C.; Ruiz, L.G.B.; Cuéllar, M.P.; Rueda, R. Analysis and Enhanced Prediction of the Spanish Electricity Network through Big Data and Machine Learning Techniques. *Int. J. Approx. Reason.* **2021**, *133*, 48–59. [CrossRef]

21. Divina, F.; Gilson, A.; Goméz-Vela, F.; García Torres, M.; Torres, J.F. Stacking Ensemble Learning for Short-Term Electricity Consumption Forecasting. *Energies* **2018**, *11*, 949. [CrossRef]

22. Ogliari, E.; Niccolai, A.; Leva, S.; Zich, R.E. Computational Intelligence Techniques Applied to the Day Ahead PV Output Power Forecast: PHANN, SNO and Mixed. *Energies* **2018**, *11*, 1487. [CrossRef]

23. Ciechulski, T.; Osowski, S. Deep Learning Approach to Power Demand Forecasting in Polish Power System. *Energies* **2020**, *13*, 6154. [CrossRef]

24. Hu, Y.-C. Electricity Consumption Prediction Using a Neural-Network-Based Grey Forecasting Approach. *J. Oper. Res. Soc.* **2017**, *68*, 1259–1264. [CrossRef]

25. Guefano, S.; Tamba, J.G.; Azong, T.E.W.; Monkam, L. Methodology for Forecasting Electricity Consumption by Grey and Vector Autoregressive Models. *MethodsX* **2021**, *8*, 101296. [CrossRef] [PubMed]

26. Dong, Y.; Zhang, Z.; Hong, W.-C. A Hybrid Seasonal Mechanism with a Chaotic Cuckoo Search Algorithm with a Support Vector Regression Model for Electric Load Forecasting. *Energies* **2018**, *11*, 1009. [CrossRef]

27. Vivas, E.; Allende-Cid, H.; Salas, R. A Systematic Review of Statistical and Machine Learning Methods for Electrical Power Forecasting with Reported MAPE Score. *Entropy* **2020**, *22*, 1412. [CrossRef] [PubMed]

28. Magda, R.; Bozsik, N.; Meyer, N. An Evaluation of Gross Inland Energy Consumption of Six Central European Countries. *J. Eur. Cent. Asian Res.* **2019**, *6*, 270–281. [CrossRef]

29. Avdakovic, S.; Ademovic, A.; Nuhanovic, A. Correlation between Air Temperature and Electricity Demand by Linear Regression and Wavelet Coherence Approach: UK, Slovakia and Bosnia and Herzegovina Case Study. *Arch. Electr. Eng.* **2013**, *62*, 521–532. [CrossRef]

30. Laurinec, P.; Lucká, M. New clustering-based forecasting method for disaggregated end-consumer electricity load using smart grid data. In Proceedings of the 2017 IEEE 14th International Scientific Conference on Informatics, Poprad, Slovakia, 14–16 November 2017; pp. 210–215.

31. Jarábek, T.; Laurinec, P.; Lucká, M. Energy load forecast using S2S deep neural networks with K-shape clustering. In Proceedings of the 2017 IEEE 14th International Scientific Conference on Informatics, Poprad, Slovakia, 14–16 November 2017; pp. 140–145.

32. Oudjana, S.H.; Hellal, A. New Particle Swarm Neural Networks Model Based Long Term Electrical Load Forecasting in Slovakia. *WSEAS Trans. Bus. Econ.* **2018**, *15*, 13–17, Corpus ID: 55081487.

33. Halaš, P.; Lóderer, M.; Rozinajová, V. Prediction of electricity consumption using biologically inspired algorithms. In Proceedings of the 2017 IEEE 14th International Scientific Conference on Informatics, Poprad, Slovakia, 14–16 November 2017; pp. 98–103.

34. Brozyna, J.; Strielkowski, W.; Fomina, A.; Nikitina, N. Renewable Energy and EU 2020 Target for Energy Efficiency in the Czech Republic and Slovakia. *Energies* **2020**, *13*, 965. [CrossRef]

35. Slovenská Elektrizačná Prenosová Sústava, a.s. Available online: https://www.sepsas.sk/sk/sluzby/damas-energy/ (accessed on 6 July 2021).

36. Deng, J.L. Introduction to Grey System Theory. *J. Grey Syst.* **1989**, *1*, 1–24.

37. Liu, S.; Yang, Y. A brief introduction to grey systems theory. In *Grey Systems Theory Applications*; Springer: Berlin/Heidelberg, Germany, 2011; Volume 2. [CrossRef]

38. Chen, C.-I. Application of the Novel Nonlinear Grey Bernoulli Model for Forecasting Unemployment Rate. *Chaos Solit. Fractals* **2008**, *37*, 278–287. [CrossRef]

39. Kalogirou, S.A. Applications of Artificial Neural-Networks for Energy Systems. *Appl. Energy* **2000**, *67*, 17–35. [CrossRef]

40. Islam, M.S.; Kabir, M.M.; Kabir, N. Artificial Neural Networks Based Prediction of Insolation on Horizontal Surfaces for Bangladesh. *Procedia Technol.* **2013**, *10*, 482–491. [CrossRef]

41. MATLAB Documentation. Available online: https://www.mathworks.com/help/matlab/ (accessed on 29 June 2021).

42. Gill, P.E.; Murray, W.; Wright, M.H. *Practical Optimization*; Academic Press: Cambridge, MA, USA, 1981.

43. Han, X.; Chang, J. A Hybrid Prediction Model Based on Improved Multivariable Grey Model for Long-Term Electricity Consumption. *Electr. Eng.* **2021**, *103*, 1031–1043. [CrossRef]

44. Li, C.; Tao, Y.; Ao, W.; Yang, S.; Bai, Y. Improving Forecasting Accuracy of Daily Enterprise Electricity Consumption Using a Random Forest Based on Ensemble Empirical Mode Decomposition. *Energy* **2018**, *165*, 1220–1227. [CrossRef]

45. Beretta, D.; Grillo, S.; Pigoli, D.; Bionda, E.; Bossi, C.; Tornelli, C. Functional Principal Component Analysis as a Versatile Technique to Understand and Predict the Electric Consumption Patterns. *Sustain. Energy Grids Netw.* **2020**, *21*, 100308. [CrossRef]

46. Ananthasingam, A.; Atputharajah, A. Forecast daily night peak electric power demand in Sri Lankan power system. In Proceedings of the 2015 IEEE 10th International Conference on Industrial and Information Systems (ICIIS), Peradeniya, Sri Lanka, 17–20 December 2015; pp. 238–243.

47. Adeoye, O.; Spataru, C. Modelling and Forecasting Hourly Electricity Demand in West African Countries. *Appl. Energy* **2019**, *242*, 311–333. [CrossRef]
48. Wang, R.; Yao, X.; Li, C.; Hu, B.; Xie, K.; Niu, T.; Li, M.; Fu, J.; Sun, Q. Combination Forecasting Model of Daily Electricity Consumption in Summer Based on Daily Characteristic Meteorological Factors. *IOP Conf. Ser. Mater. Sci. Eng.* **2020**, *853*, 012024. [CrossRef]

mathematics

MDPI

Article

Predicting the 305-Day Milk Yield of Holstein-Friesian Cows Depending on the Conformation Traits and Farm Using Simplified Selective Ensembles

Snezhana Gocheva-Ilieva [1,*], **Antoaneta Yordanova** [2] **and Hristina Kulina** [1]

1   Department of Mathematical Analysis, University of Plovdiv Paisii Hilendarski, 24 Tzar Asen St., 4000 Plovdiv, Bulgaria; kulina@uni-plovdiv.bg
2   Medical College, Trakia University, 9 Armeyska St., 6000 Stara Zagora, Bulgaria; antoaneta.yordanova@trakia-uni.bg
*   Correspondence: snow@uni-plovdiv.bg

Abstract: In animal husbandry, it is of great interest to determine and control the key factors that affect the production characteristics of animals, such as milk yield. In this study, simplified selective tree-based ensembles were used for modeling and forecasting the 305-day average milk yield of Holstein-Friesian cows, depending on 12 external traits and the farm as an environmental factor. The preprocessing of the initial independent variables included their transformation into rotated principal components. The resulting dataset was divided into learning (75%) and holdout test (25%) subsamples. Initially, three diverse base models were generated using Classifiction and Regression Trees (CART) ensembles and bagging and arcing algorithms. These models were processed using the developed simplified selective algorithm based on the index of agreement. An average reduction of 30% in the number of trees of selective ensembles was obtained. Finally, by separately stacking the predictions from the non-selective and selective base models, two linear hybrid models were built. The hybrid model of the selective ensembles showed a 13.6% reduction in the test set prediction error compared to the hybrid model of the non-selective ensembles. The identified key factors determining milk yield include the farm, udder width, chest width, and stature of the animals. The proposed approach can be applied to improve the management of dairy farms.

Keywords: machine learning; rotation CART ensemble; bagging; boosting; arcing; simplified selective ensemble; linear stacked model

MSC: 62-11; 62P30

Citation: Gocheva-Ilieva, S.; Yordanova, A.; Kulina, H. Predicting the 305-Day Milk Yield of Holstein-Friesian Cows Depending on the Conformation Traits and Farm Using Simplified Selective Ensembles. *Mathematics* **2022**, *10*, 1254. https://doi.org/10.3390/math10081254

Academic Editor: Ripon Kumar Chakrabortty

Received: 28 February 2022
Accepted: 6 April 2022
Published: 11 April 2022

Publisher's Note: MDPI stays neutral with regard to jurisdictional claims in published maps and institutional affiliations.

1. Introduction

Numerous studies have found associative connections between external characteristics of dairy cows and their milk production [1–3]. The 305-day milk yield is dependent on many other factors, such as the genetic potential of the animals, fertility, health status, environmental comforts, etc. Therefore, establishing which connections between the various factors determine a given productive trait and predicting its values, including milk yield, is an important research issue for improving economic profitability and dairy farm management.

In dairy science, many studies are based on modeling of collected empirical data using modern computer-based statistical techniques. These techniques enable determination of not only linear-type dependencies using standard statistical approaches, such as multiple linear regression (MLR), but also complex and hidden local dependencies between examined variables with significantly better predictive ability. A review paper [4] showed that the health and productivity of milk cows depend on various parameters and that numerous researchers have recognized the potential of machine learning (ML) as a powerful tool in this field. In [5], MLR, random forest (RF), and artificial neural networks (ANN) were used to determine dairy herd improvement metrics, with the highest impact on the first-test-day milk yield of primiparous dairy Holstein cows. MLR and ANN were used in [6] for 305-day milk yield prediction. In [7], the decision tree (DT) method was used to study lactation milk yield for Brown Swiss cattle, depending on productivity and environmental factors. The live body weight of Pakistani goats was predicted in [8] depending on morphological measurements using classification and regression trees (CART), Chi-square Automatic Interaction Detector (CHAID), and multivariate adaptive regression splines (MARS). In [9], DT was used to assess the relationship between the 305-day milk yield and several environmental factors for Brown Swiss dairy cattle. Fenlon et al. [10] applied logistic regression, generalized additive models, and ensemble learning in the form of bagging to model milk yield depending on age, stage of suckling, calving, and energy balance measures related to the animals. Four ML methods were tested by Van der Heide et al. [11]: majority voting rule, multiple logistic regression, RF, and Naive Bayes for predicting cow survival as a complex characteristic, which combines variables such as milk production, fertility, health, and environmental factors. The authors of [12] studied cattle weight using active contour models and bagged regression trees.

Other publications in the field of study related to dairy cows and the use of data mining and ML methods are [13–16]. In a broader aspect, predictive ML models and algorithms are essential to make intelligent decisions for efficient and sustainable dairy production management using information, web information, and expert systems [17]. As stated in [17], modern dairy animals are selected for physical traits that directly or indirectly contribute to high milk production. In particular, this motivates the development of models and tools for assessing and forecasting expected milk based on a limited number of easily measurable factors, such as the main external characteristics of the animals.

A new approach based on ensemble methods using bagging, boosting, and linear stacking of their predictions was developed in this paper to increase the predictive ability of the models. The essential part of modeling is the construction of selective ensembles, which reduce the number of trees in the ensemble and, at the same time, improve the performance of the model. Many researchers are actively studying this problem. The complete solution to the problem of choosing a subset of trees in the ensemble to minimize generalization errors comes down to $2^{tn} - 1$ possibilities, where tn is the number of trees. Such an algorithm is NP-complete [18]. For this reason, various heuristic algorithms for pruning and building selective ensembles are being developed. Some of the well-known results on selective ensembles of decision trees and ANN are based on genetic algorithms [19,20]. In [19], the resulting ensemble model is a weighted combination of component neural networks, the weights of which are determined by the developed algorithm so as to reduce the ensemble size and improve the performance. The algorithm selects the trees with weights greater than a preset threshold to form an ensemble with a reduced number of trees. This algorithm was further modified and applied to build decision tree selective ensembles in [20]. A significant reduction in the number of trees was achieved, from 20 to an average of 8 trees for 15 different empirical datasets. It is also believed that to obtain more efficient models, the components of an ensemble must be sufficiently different [21–23]. Applied results in this area can be found in [24–26] and others.

This paper contributes to statistical data modeling and machine learning by developing a framework based on a new heuristic algorithm for constructing selective decision tree ensembles. The ensembles are built with rotation CART ensembles and bagging (EBag), as well as rotation-adaptive resampling and combining (Arcing) algorithms. The simplified selective ensembles are built from the obtained models based on the index of agreement. This approach not only reduces the number of trees in the ensemble but also increases the index of agreement and the coefficient of determination and reduces the root mean square error (RMSE) of the models. In addition, combinations by linear stacking of models were obtained that satisfy four diversity criteria. The proposed approach was applied to predict the 305-day milk yield of Holstein-Friesian cows depending on the conformation traits of the animals and their breeding farm. Comparative data analysis with the used real-world datasets showed that constructed selective ensembles have higher performance than models with non-selective ensembles.

2. Materials and Methods

All measurements of the animals were performed in accordance with the official laws and regulations of the Republic of Bulgaria: Regulation No. 16 of 3 February 2006 on protection and humane treatment in the production and use of farm animals, the Regulation amending of the Regulation No. 16 (last updated 2017), and the Veterinary Law (Chapter 7: Protection and Human Treatment of Animals, Articles 149–169). The measurement procedures were carried out in compliance with Council Directive 98/58/EC concerning the protection of animals kept for farming purposes. All measurements and data collection were performed by qualified specialists from the Department of Animal Husbandry—Ruminants and Dairy Farming, Faculty of Agriculture, Trakia University, Stara Zagora, Bulgaria, with methodologies approved by the International Committee for Animal Recording (ICAR) [27]. The data do not apply to physical interventions, treatments, experiments with drugs, or other activities harmful or dangerous to animals.

2.1. Description of the Analyzed Data

In this study, we used measurements from n = 158 Holstein-Friesian cows from 4 different farms located within Bulgaria. One productive characteristic was recorded: 305-day milk yield. Table 1 provides a description of the initial variables used. The collection of data and the choice of variables were based on the following considerations. It is well known from practice and research that the form and level of development of conformation traits depend on heritability and phenotypic characteristics of animals and influence their productivity, health, and longevity. The linear traits used were measured and evaluated for the animals according to the recommendations of the International Agreement on Recording Practices for conformation traits of ICAR (pp. 199–214, [27]). Our dataset of approved standard traits includes stature, chest width, rump width, rear leg set, rear legs (rear view), foot angle, and locomotion. Hock development and bone structure are representatives of the group of common standard traits. In addition, three other traits eligible under ICAR rules were recorded: foot depth, udder width, and lameness. For the present study, from each group, we selected those traits that have the highest coefficient of heritability and correlation with the 305-day milk yield, established as per Bulgarian conditions in [28,29]. The dataset includes the variable *Farm* to account for growing conditions, the environment, the influence of the herd, and other implicit and difficult-to-measure factors.

Table 1. Description of the variables used in statistical analyses.

Variable	Description	Type	Measure
Milk305	305-day milk yield	Scale	kg
Stature	Stature	Ordinal	1, 2, … , 9; Short—Tall
ChestW	Chest width	Ordinal	1, 2, … , 9; Narrow—Wide
RumpW	Rump width	Ordinal	1, 2, … , 9; Narrow—Wide
RLRV	Rear legs (rear view)	Ordinal	1, 2, … , 9; Hock in-Parallel
RLSV	Rear leg set (side view)	Ordinal	1, 2, … , 5 (Transformed); Strait/Sickled—Ideal
HockD	Hock development	Ordinal	1, 2, … , 9; Filled—Dry
Bone	Bone structure	Ordinal	1, 2, … , 9; Coarse—Fine and thin
FootA	Foot angle	Ordinal	1, 2, … , 5 (Transformed); Low/Steep—Ideal
FootD	Foot depth	Ordinal	1, 2, … , 9; Short—Tall
UdderW	Udder width	Ordinal	1, 2, … , 9; Narrow—Wide
Locom	Locomotion	Ordinal	1, 2, … , 9; Severe abduction—No abduction
Lameness	Lameness	Ordinal	1, 2, 3; Walks unevenly—Very lame
Farm	Farm number	Nominal	1, 2, 3, 4

External traits are described individually as ordinal variables. This scale complies with the standards of the ICAR [27]. The examined traits have two types of coding. The two traits (variables *RLSV* and *FootA*) are transformed, resulting in two opposite disadvantages in the ranking scale from 1 to 5 with ascending positive evaluation of the trait, in accordance with the evaluation instructions as per the type of ICAR. All other traits were measured linearly from one biological extreme to the other. The range of scores is from 1 to 9, and improvement of the characteristic corresponds to a higher value. The variable *Farm* is of categorical type, with 4 different values. The distribution by number of cows in the farms is 54, 32, 34, and 38.

It should be noted that in the general case, the relationships between the variables for exterior traits the productive and phenotypic characteristics of Holstein cattle are considered to be nonlinear (for example, [30]). Therefore, the machine learning approach has a better perspective to reveal the deep multidimensional dependencies between them.

Tables 1 and 2 list notations used in this paper.

Table 2. Nomenclature of the notations [1].

Notation	Description	Type
ARC	Arcing	method
CART	Classification and regression trees	method
CV	Cross-validation	out-of-sample testing
EBag	CART ensembles and bagging	method
PCA	Principal component analysis	method
IA, d	Index of agreement [31]	statistic
WSRT	Wilcoxon signed rank test	statistical test
RT	Reduced tree	list of trees
AR9, AR10	Arcing model (predicted values)	variable
EB, EB15, EB40	EBag model (predicted values)	variable
Hybr$_1$, Hybr$_2$	Stacked linear model (predicted values)	variable
PC1, PC2, . . .	Principal component, factor variable	variable
SSAR9	Simplified selective ARC model (predicted values)	variable
SSEB, SSEB11, SSEB25	Simplified selective EBag model (predicted values)	variable

[1] All variable names are in italic style.

2.2. Modeling Methods

Statistical analyses of the data were performed using principal component analysis (PCA), factor analysis, and ensemble methods EBag and ARC. We used EBag and ARC as ensemble methods based on bagging and boosting, respectively. The main types of ensemble methods, their characteristics, advantages, and disadvantages are discussed in [21,23,32].

2.2.1. Principal Component Analysis and Exploratory Factor Analysis

PCA is a statistical method for transforming a set of correlated variables into so-called principal components (PCs) [33]. The number of variables is equal to the number of extracted PCs. When the data include several strongly correlated variables, their linear combination can be replaced by a new common artificial variable through factor analysis. In this case, the number of initial variables is reduced at the cost of certain losses in the total variance explained by the new sample. Following the rotation procedure, the resulting rotated factor variables are non-correlated or correlate weakly with one another. These can be used in subsequent statistical analyses. PCA was used in [34,35].

2.2.2. CART Ensemble and Bagging (EBag)

An ensemble is a model that includes many single models (called components) of the same type. In our case, the components are decision trees constructed using the powerful ML and data-mining CART method [36]. CART is used for regression and classification of numerical, ordinal, and nominal datasets. For example, let an initial sample of n observations $\{Y, X\}$ be given, where $Y = \{y_1, y_2, \ldots, y_n\}$ is the target variable and $X = \{X_1, X_2, \ldots, X_p\}$, $p \geq 1$ are independent variables. The single CART model is a binary tree structure, T, obtained by recursively dividing the initial dataset into disjoint subsets called nodes of the tree. The predicted value for each case in the node, $\tau_\ell \in T$, is the mean value of Y of cases in τ_ℓ. The root of the tree contains all the initial observations, and its prediction is the mean value of the sample.

For each splitting of a given node, τ_ℓ, the algorithm of the method selects a predictor, X_k, and its threshold case, $X_{k,\theta}$, from all or from a pool of variables, X, and cases in τ_ℓ, to minimize some preselected type of model prediction error. The division of cases from τ_ℓ is performed according to the rule: if $X_{k,i} \leq X_{k,\theta}$, $X \in \tau_\ell$ then the observation with index i is assigned to the left child node of τ_ℓ—and in the case of $X_{k,i} > X_{k,\theta}$, to the right child node of τ_ℓ. The growth of the tree is limited and stopped by preset hyperparameters (depth of the tree, accuracy, etc.). Thus, all initial observations are classified into terminal nodes of the tree. If a training sample is specified, the CART model function can be written as [33]:

$$\hat{\mu}(X) = \sum_{\tau \in T} \hat{Y}(\tau) I_{[X \in \tau]} = \sum_{m}^{\ell=1} \hat{Y}(\tau_\ell) I_{[X \in \tau_\ell]} \tag{1}$$

where:

$$\hat{Y}(\tau_\ell) = \overline{Y}(\tau_\ell) = \frac{1}{n(\tau_\ell)} \sum_{X_i \in \tau_\ell} y_i, \quad I_{[X \in \tau_\ell]} = \begin{cases} 1, & X \in \tau_\ell \\ 0, & X \notin \tau_\ell \end{cases} \tag{2}$$

where m is the number of terminal nodes of the tree, and $n(\tau_\ell)$ is the number of observations in node τ_ℓ. For each case i, $\hat{y}_i = \hat{\mu}(X_i)$ is the predicted value for the observation, X_i.

An example of a CART model with 2 independent variables and 5 nodes is shown in Figure 1.

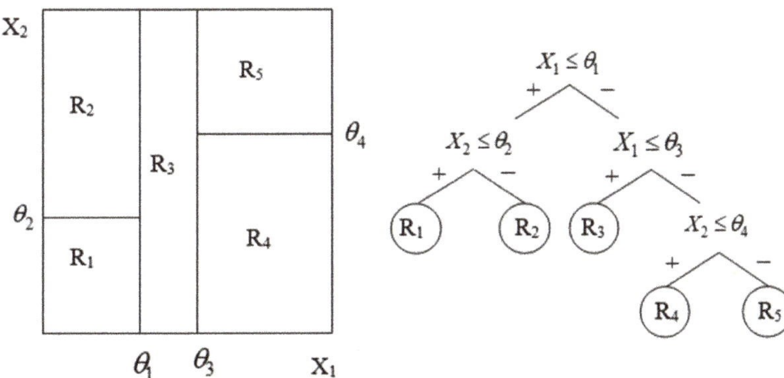

Figure 1. Example of a single-regression CART tree with two predictors and five terminal nodes.

CART ensembles and bagging is an ensemble method with ML for classification and regression proposed by Leo Breiman in [37]. For ensembles, the training set is perturbed repeatedly to generate multiple independent CART trees, and then the predictions are averaged by simple voting. In this study, we used the software engine CART ensembles and bagger included in the Salford Predictive Modeler [38].

In order to compile the ensemble, the researcher sets the number of trees, type of cross-validation, number of subsets of predictors for the splitting of each branch of each tree, limits for the minimum number of cases per parent and child node, and some other hyperparameters. The method's main advantage is that it leads to a dramatic decrease in test-set errors and a significant reduction in variance [39].

In terms of generating, the tree components of the ensemble are characterized by considerable differences in their performance and, individually, do not have high statistical indices. For this reason, in the literature, these are called "weak learners". However, after averaging, the statistics are adjusted, and the final ensemble model (for classification or regression) is more efficient. Component trees, which worsen the ensemble's statistics in any statistical measure, are called "negative" trees. Various heuristic algorithms have been developed to reduce the impact of these trees [19,26].

2.2.3. Adaptive Resampling and Combining Algorithm (Arcing)

Another approach that uses ensemble trees is based on the boosting technique first proposed in [40]. A variant of boosting is the Arcing algorithm developed and studied by Breiman in [39], also known as Arc-x4. The family of Arc-x(h) algorithms is differentiated from Adaboost [40] by the simpler weight updating rule in the form:

$$w_{t+1}(V_i) = \frac{1 + m\,(V_i)^h}{\sum\limits_i \left(1 + m\,(V_i)^h\right)}. \tag{3}$$

where $m\,(V_i)$ is the number of misclassifications of instance V_i by models generated in the previous iterations, and $1, 2, \ldots, t, h$ is an integer. In this way, the ensemble components are generated sequentially and penalize resampling in the cases that yield bad predictions up to the current step, t. Breiman showed that Arcing had error performance comparable to that of Adaboost.

Combining multiple models and applying any of the two methods—bagging or arcing—leads to a significant variance reduction, whereby arcing is more successful than bagging in test-set error reduction [39].

2.2.4. Proposed Simplified Selective Ensemble Algorithm

To improve predictive performance, we further developed the algorithm for building simplified selective ensembles that we recently proposed in [41] for time series analysis. In this study, used it in the case of a non-dynamic data type. We applied the algorithm separately for two types of ensembles from CART trees: with bagging and boosting. The simplified selective algorithm is presented for the case of EBag. It consists of the following steps:

- Step 1: Calculation of index of agreement (IA), d_E [31], for a selected initial EBag model, $EBtn$, with tn component trees;
- Step 2: Cycle with the application of a pruning criterion to live-out the j-th component tree T_j for $j = 1, 2, \ldots, tn \ldots$ and calculation of reduced tree RT_j;
- Step 3: Calculation of IA d_j for $j = 1, 2, \ldots, tn$ of all obtained reduced trees, RT_j. If $d_j > d_E$, then the tree, T_j, is considered "negative" and subject to possible removal from the ensemble. If the number of negative trees is s, we denote their set with $ss = \left\{T_1^-, T_2^-, \ldots, T_s^-\right\}$, where T_j^- is the negative tree.
- Step 4: Building s simplified selective models by removing cumulative sums from negative trees using the expression:

$$SSEB_{tn-k} = \frac{tn.\,EBtn - \sum\limits_{j=1}^{k} ss_j}{tn - k}, \quad k = 1, 2, \ldots, s. \tag{4}$$

In this way, removing the "negative" trees improves the IA of the initial EBag model and generates many new ensemble models for $k = 1, 2, \ldots, s$. The maximum simplified selective tree is obtained at $k = s$.

To implement the simplified selective algorithm, we used the generated EBag and ARC component trees using the ensembles and bagger engine of SPM software [38] and the authors' code in Wolfram Mathematica [42]. A detailed description of the simplified selective algorithm is given in Algorithm 1.

Algorithm 1: Simplified selective ensemble

Input: dataset E, T_j, tn // E is an ensemble model of weak learners T_j, $j = 1, 2, \ldots, tn$. E is an averaged sum of T_j.

Output: *SSE*, sn // *SSE* is a vector of indices of the resulting simplified selective ensembles, sn is the number of simplified selective models in *SSE*.

    $k \leftarrow 0$; // k is the number of the negative trees (learners).
    sind $\leftarrow \varnothing$; // sind is a list or array with the indices of negative trees or learners.
    $d_E \leftarrow$ IA(E); // Value of the Index of agreement (IA) of E ([31], see also Equation (5)).
    $j \leftarrow 1$;
    While $j <= tn$ do
        RT $\leftarrow$ (E $\setminus T_j$); // live-out the j-th component $T_j \in$ E and store in RT.
        $d_j \leftarrow$ IA(RT);
        If [$d_j > d_E$ then
            $k \leftarrow k + 1$;
            sind $\leftarrow$ Append [sind, j]; // List of indices of negative trees.
        ];
        $j \leftarrow j + 1$;
    end;
    $s \leftarrow k$;
    sn $\leftarrow$ tn-s;
    If [$s = 0$ then
        Break [Algorithm 1];
    ]; // in this case, there are not any simplified selective models.
    $j \leftarrow 1$;
    $SSE \leftarrow \varnothing$;
    While [$j <= (tn\text{-}s)$ do
        $SSEj \leftarrow$ T$_{\text{sind}[j]}$; // Calculation of the $SSEj$ model using Equation (4).
        $j \leftarrow j + 1$;
    end.

2.2.5. Methodology

In this study, regression models were constructed to determine the influence of the observed external characteristics of Holstein-Friesian cows and the farm on milk quantity and to predict the values of 305-day milk yield. First, EBag and arcing ensembles and corresponding simplified selective models were built, and their predictions were then combined linearly in stacked models according to the stacked generalization paradigm developed by Wolpert [43].

Our study was carried out under the following framework (see also Figure 2):

- Transformation of 12 independent variables for the external traits using the PCA method and factor analysis and obtaining 11 PCs (factor variables), denoted as *PC1*, *PC2*, ... , *PC11*;
- Random splitting of the sample for *Milk305* into learning and test datasets at a ratio of 75%:25%; the learning sample is denoted by the variable *Milk_miss40*, where 25% (40 cases) of the values for milk yield are considered as missing;
- Building and examination of rotation EBag, simplified selective EBag, and rotation ARC regression models with predictors *PC1*, ... , *PC11*, and *Farm* to predict *Milk_miss40*;

- Verification of the condition for diversity and selection of three base models using Wilcoxon signed-rank test (WSRT);
- Determination of the relative importance of predictors in the base models;
- Assessment of models against the initial full-sample *Milk*305.
- Combination of the selected base models using weights and assessment of the resulting stacked model.
- Assessment of model performance for the 25% holdout test sample.

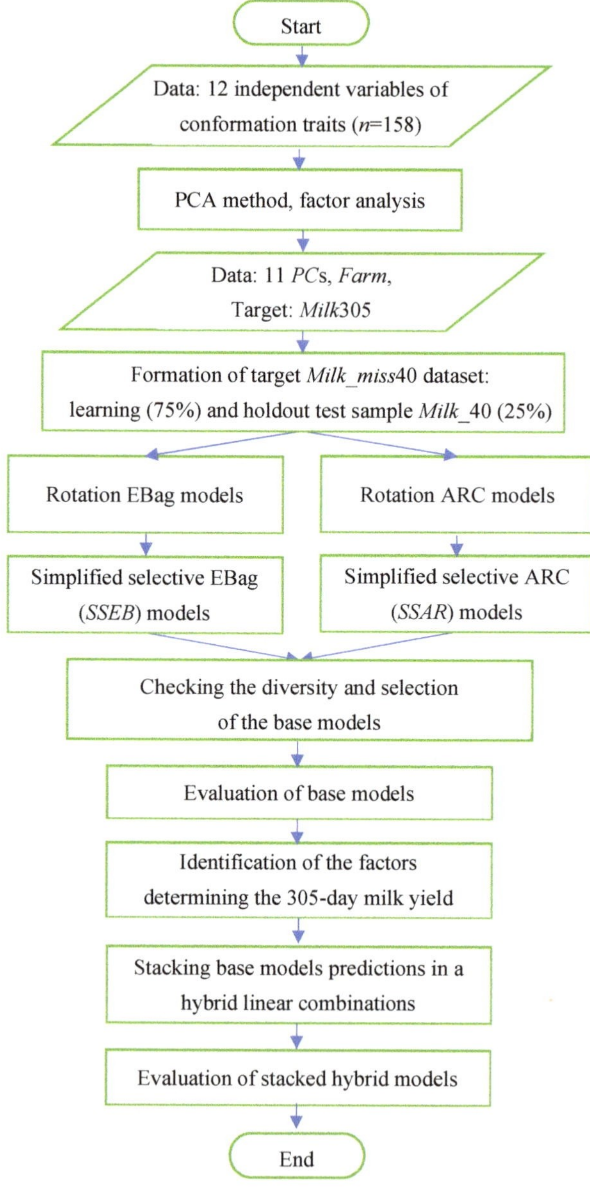

Figure 2. Framework of the study.

For application of the stacking paradigm in particular, the number of base models at the first stage has to be between 3 and 8. In addition, these models need to be differentiated from each other according to some diversity criteria [21–23].

2.2.6. Evaluation Measures

The quality of the built models was assessed and compared using standard measures of prediction accuracy: root mean squared error (RMSE), mean absolute percentage error (MAPE), goodness-of-fit measure (coefficient of determination R^2), and index of agreement (IA) d [31], defined as follows:

$$\text{RMSE} = \sqrt{\frac{1}{n}\sum_{k=1}^{n}(P_k - Y_k)^2}, \qquad \text{MAPE} = \frac{100}{n}\sum_{k=1}^{n}\left|\frac{P_k - Y_k}{Y_k}\right|,$$

$$R^2 = \frac{\left\{\sum_{k=1}^{n}(P_k-\overline{P})(Y_k-\overline{Y})\right\}^2}{\sum_{k=1}^{n}(P_k-\overline{P})^2 \cdot \sum_{k=1}^{n}(Y_k-\overline{Y})^2}, \qquad \text{IA} = d = 1 - \frac{\sum_{k=1}^{n}(P_k-Y_k)^2}{\sum_{k=1}^{n}\left(|P_k-\overline{Y}|+|Y_k-\overline{Y}|\right)^2}, \tag{5}$$

where Y_k and $\overline{Y}$ are the values and the mean of the dependent variable, Y, respectively; P_k and $\overline{P}$ are the predicted values and their mean, respectively; and n is the sample volume. Among these measures, a good predictive model should have a value close to 0 for RMSE and MAPE and a value close to 1 for R^2 and IA. IA is not a measure of correlation or association in the formal sense but a measure of the degree to which a model's predictions are error-free [31].

Furthermore, the nonparametric WSRT is used to compare diversity between the predictive models [44]. This test does not assume that the data follow the normal distribution.

3. Results and Discussion

3.1. Data Preprocessing

Table 3 shows the results of the descriptive statistics of the initial variables from Table 1. We see that the values of skewness and kurtosis for all variables are close to zero, and we can assume that the distribution of all variables is close to normal.

Table 3. Descriptive statistics of the measured data [1].

Variable	Mean	5% Lower Bound of Mean	5% Upper Bound of Mean	Median	Std. Dev.	Skewness	Kurtosis
Milk305, kg	6812.16	6451.67	7172.66	6784.25	2294.12	0.282	−0.866
Milk_miss40, kg	6789.32	6359.29	7226.36	6041.00	2397.14	0.310	−0.896
Milk_40, kg	6879.54	6244.59	7514.49	6743.19	1985.37	0.182	−0.960
Stature	4.68	4.39	4.96	5.00	1.83	−0.228	−0.558
ChestW	6.51	6.25	6.77	7.00	1.65	−0.358	−0.569
RumpW	6.09	5.91	6.28	6.00	1.18	0.241	−0.687
RLRV	4.91	4.68	5.14	5.00	1.45	0.054	0.291
RLSV	3.95	3.79	4.11	4.00	1.01	−0.577	−0.631
HockD	5.29	5.06	5.52	5.00	1.48	0.038	−0.170
Bone	6.13	5.89	6.37	6.00	1.53	−0.260	−0.477
FootA	4.51	4.42	4.61	5.00	0.59	−0.786	−0.349
FootD	6.42	6.24	6.59	7.00	1.10	−0.310	−1.434
UdderW	5.72	5.42	6.02	6.00	1.92	−0.368	−0.484
Locom	5.32	5.11	5.53	5.00	1.34	−0.092	−0.530
Lameness	1.65	1.55	1.76	2.00	0.67	0.535	−0.713

[1] Std. Err. Skewness is 0.193; for *Milk_miss40*, 0.223; for *Milk_40*, 0.374. Std. Err. Kurtosis is 0.384; for *Milk_miss40*, 0.442; for *Milk_40*, 0.733.

3.2. PCA Results

During the initial data processing, multicollinearity was found between the considered 12 independent variables for conformation traits from Table 1. In order to reduce the influence of multicollinearity and improve the accuracy of the regression models, these 12 initial variables were transformed into independent variables using exploratory factor analysis and PCA [33]. The goal is to retain information and preserve the total variance explained following this transformation as much as possible. The basic assumptions for procedural application are fulfilled, namely: close to a normal distribution of the 12 variables and small determinant of their correlation matrix, det $= 0.019 \approx 0$. In addition, the adequacy verification of factor analysis indicates that the Kaiser–Meyer–Olkin (KMO) measure of sampling adequacy is $0.658 > 0.5$, and the significance of the Bartlett's test of sphericity is Sig. $= 0.000$.

With the help of nonparametric Spearman's rho statistics R, the following correlation coefficients were found between the dependent variable, *Milk*305, and the 12 measured variables, respectively: with the variable *UdderW*, $R = 0.685$; with *Stature*, $R = 0.501$; with *ChestW*, $R = 0.492$; and with *Bone* $R = 0.343$. Other significantly correlated Spearman's rho coefficients are: $R(Stature, UdderW) = 0.558$, $R(Stature, RumpW) = 0.508$, $R(Stature, ChestW) = 0.466$, $R(Bone, Stature) = 0.466$, and $R(Laminess, Locom) = -0.929$. All correlation coefficients are significant at the 0.01 level (2-tailed). Research into this type of linear correlation is a known approach, including external traits [28,29]. This often leads to establishing both positive and negative linear correlations (e.g., $R(Laminess, Locom) = -0.929$), etc.). The latter can lead to an inaccurate interpretation of the influence of some external traits, the interactions of which are primarily nonlinear and difficult to determine [30].

The next step is to conduct factor analysis. In our case, 12 PCs were preset for extraction using the PCA method. Due to the strong negative correlation $R(Laminess, Locom) = -0.908$, these two variables were grouped in a common factor. This resulted in 11 factors extracted from the 12 independent variables. The factors were rotated using the Promax method. The resulting rotated matrix of factor loadings is shown in Table 4. The extracted 11 factor-score variables are very well differentiated. We denote them by *PC*1, *PC*2, ... , *PC*11. These 11 variables account for 99.278% of the total variance of the independent continuous variables. The residual variance is 0.722 and can be ignored. The correspondence between the initial 12 linear traits and the resulting 11 *PC*s is given in Table 4. The coefficients of the factor loadings are sorted by size, and coefficients with an absolute value below 0.1 are suppressed [33].

Table 4. Rotated pattern matrix with 11 PCs generated using Promax [1].

Initial Variable	Principal Components (Factor Variables)										
	*PC*1	*PC*2	*PC*3	*PC*4	*PC*5	*PC*6	*PC*7	*PC*8	*PC*9	*PC*10	*PC*11
Locom	0.978	−0.009	−0.001	0.007	0.000	0.016	0.028	0.011	0.025	0.002	−0.032
Lameness	−0.976	−0.009	−0.001	0.007	0.000	0.016	0.028	0.011	0.025	0.002	−0.032
RumpW	0.000	0.998	0.000	0.000	0.000	0.001	0.000	0.000	0.000	0.001	0.002
ChestW	0.000	0.000	0.998	0.001	0.000	0.000	0.000	0.000	0.000	0.001	0.001
UdderW	0.000	0.000	0.001	0.995	0.000	0.000	0.000	0.000	0.000	0.002	0.006
RLRV	0.000	0.000	0.000	0.000	1.000	0.000	0.000	0.000	0.000	0.000	0.000
FootD	0.000	.001	0.000	0.000	0.000	0.999	−0.001	0.000	−0.001	0.001	0.001
RLSV	0.000	0.000	0.000	0.000	0.000	−0.001	1.000	−0.001	−0.001	0.000	0.002
FootA	0.000	0.000	0.000	0.000	0.000	0.000	−0.001	1.000	−0.001	0.000	0.001
HockD	0.000	0.000	0.000	0.000	0.000	−0.001	−0.001	−0.001	1.000	0.000	0.002
Bone	0.000	0.002	0.002	0.002	0.001	0.001	0.000	0.000	0.000	0.995	0.003
Stature	0.000	0.006	0.003	0.011	0.000	0.001	0.002	0.001	0.002	0.004	0.986

[1] Extraction method: principal component analysis; Rotation method: Promax with Kaiser normalization; rotation converged in six iterations.

Considering that the coefficients along the main diagonal in the rotated pattern matrix of Table 4 are equal to 1 or almost 1, in subsequent analyses, we can interpret each generated factor as a direct match with the corresponding initial variable, except *PC*1, which groups *Locom* and *Lameness*.

3.3. Building and Evaluation of Base Models

To model and predict the milk yield dataset, *Milk_miss*40, we used the eleven *PCs* and *Farm* variables as predictors. The aim is to build between 3 and 8 base models that meet the diversity requirement, as recommended in the stacking paradigm [22,43,45]. In this study, we set the following four diversity criteria:

(C1) different learning datasets for each tree and ensemble derived from the algorithms;
(C2) different methods and hyperparameters to build the ensembles;
(C3) different number of trees in the ensemble models;
(C4) different types of testing or validation.

3.3.1. CART Ensembles and Bagging and Simplified Selective Bagged Ensembles

First, numerous CART-EBag models with different numbers of component trees $(tn = 10, 15, 20, \ldots, 60)$ were built. The hyperparameters were changed as follows: minimum cases in parent node to minimum cases in child node-14:7, 10:5, 8:4, 7:4. Cross-validation was varied from CV-5 fold, 10 fold, and 20-fold. Of these models, two ensemble models, *EB*15 and *EB*40, were selected, with $tn = 15$ and $tn = 40$ trees. The subsequent increase in the number of trees in the ensemble and the tuning of the hyperparameters led to a decrease in the statistical indices of the ensembles. These two models were used to generate selective ensembles according to the algorithm described in Section 2.2.4. Four negative trees were reduced from model *EB*15. The resulting simplified selective ensemble with 11 component trees is denoted as *SSEB*11. Accordingly, for the second model, *EB*40, 15 negative trees were identified, and after their removal, model *SSEB*25 with 25 component trees was obtained.

The analysis of the statistical indices of simplified selective ensembles revealed some special dependencies. We will demonstrate the main ones for the components of the *EB*40 model. Figure 3a illustrates the values of d_j, $j = 1, 2, \ldots, 40$, calculated for all component trees compared against the d_E of the initial ensemble. Values greater than d_E correspond to negative trees. Figure 3b–d show the change in the statistical indices for the generated selective models, $SSEB_{40-k}$, $k = 1, 2, \ldots, 15$, obtained from *EB*40 after the removal of the cumulative sums of negative trees in (4).

Figure 3b shows that the curves IA and R^2 of ensembles $SSEB_{40-k}$, $k = 1, 2, \ldots, s$ increase monotonically with the removal of each subsequent negative tree, T_j^-, as the values of R^2 increase faster. The behavior of the RMSE is inversely proportional and decreases monotonically with increased k. We found that with the removal of each subsequent negative tree, all statistics (5) improve, excluding MAPE. In our case, for the selected *SSEB*25 model and *Milk*305, IA increases by 0.5%, R^2 increases by 1.7%, RMSE is reduced by 12.8%, and MAPE is reduced by 6.6% compared to the initial ensemble, *EB*40 (see Section 3.3.4.

3.3.2. Arcing and Simplified Selective Arcing Models

Numerous ARC models with different hyperparameters were built by varying the number of component trees:$tn = 5, 10, \ldots, 30$. The hyperparameters were changed as follows: minimum cases in parent node to minimum cases in child node-14:7, 10:5, 8:4, 7:4, 6:3. Cross-validation was varied: CV-5-fold, 10-fold, and 20-fold. One model with 10 components was selected from the obtained ARC models, denoted as *AR*10, which satisfies the diversity criteria C1, $\ldots$, C4 with *EB*15 and *EB*40. This model was used to generate a selective ensemble with nine component trees denoted by *SSAR*9.

3.3.3. Diversity of the Selected Base Models and Their Hyperparameters

The diversity criteria between the base models were checked using a two-related-samples WSRT. The resulting statistics are given in Table 5. Because they are all significant at a level of $\alpha = 0.05$, we can assume that the selected base models are different [44].

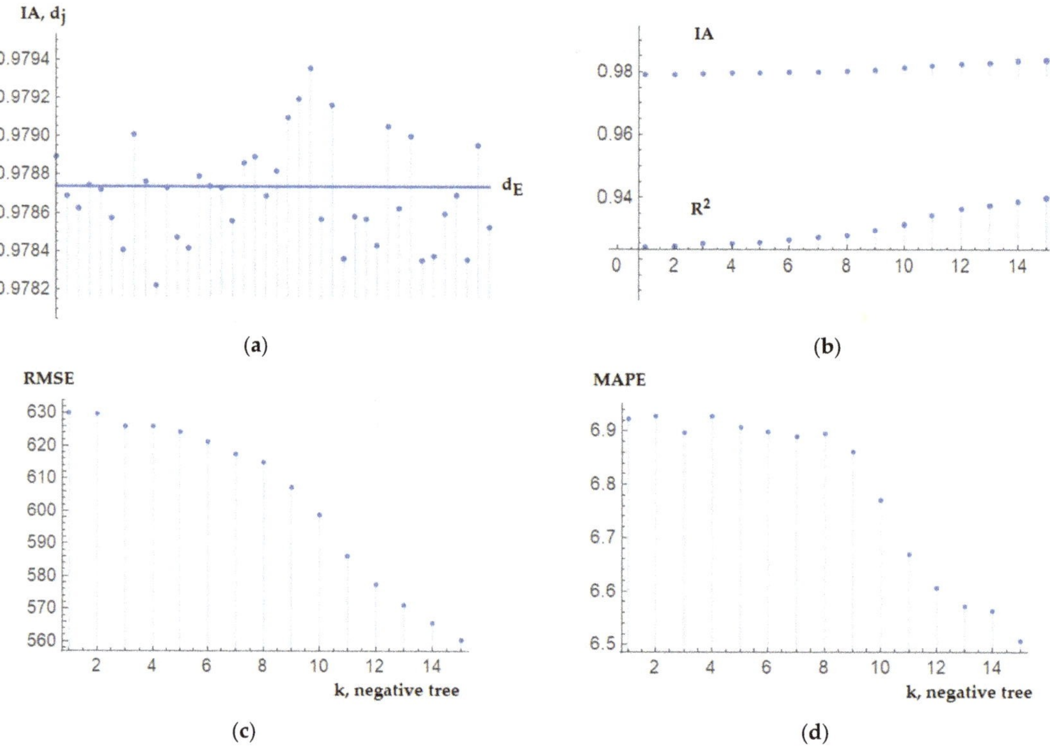

Figure 3. Statistics of the building selective models: (**a**) IA of all 40 component trees of the initial *EB*40 model; (**b**) comparison of IA and R^2 of the selective models, $SSEB_{40-k}$; (**c**) RMSE of $SSEB_{40-k}$; (**d**) MAPE of $SSEB_{40-k}$.

Table 5. Test statistics for diversity verification among the selected base models [a].

Statistics	Models					
	EB15-EB40	EB15-AR10	AR10-EB40	SSEB11-SSEB25	SSEB11-SSAR9	SSEB25-SSAR9
Z	−3.440 [b]	−3.475 [b]	−2.006 [b]	−2.360 [b]	−3.480 [b]	−2.332 [b]
Asymp. Sig. (2-tailed)	0.001	0.001	0.045	0.018	0.001	0.020

[a] Wilcoxon signed ranks test. [b] Based on negative ranks.

Table 6 shows the relevant hyperparameters of the base models in the following two groups:

- Group A: *EB*15, *EB*40, and *AR*10;
- Group B: *SSEB*11, *SSEB*25, and *SSAR*9.

The number of variables for splitting each node on each tree was set to 3. It should also be noted that the indicated value, k, of the cross-validation is applied to all trees in the respective ensemble model.

3.3.4. Evaluation Statistics of the Selected Base Models

First, let us estimate the reduction in the number of trees in the simplified selective ensembles. For the three base models, we have: from *EB*15 to *SSEB*11, 4 trees; from *EB*40 to *SSEB*25, 15 trees; and from *AR*10 to *SSAR*9, 1 tree. The relative reductions are 25%, 37.5%, and 10%, or an average of 30%.

Table 6. Hyperparameters of the selected base models.

Hyperparameter	Model		
	EB15, SSEB11	*EB40, SSEB25*	*AR10, SSAR9*
Number of trees in ensemble	15, 11	40, 25	10, 9
Minimum cases in parent node	8	8	10
Minimum cases in child node	4	4	1
Independent variables	*Farm, PC1, PC2, … , PC11*	*Farm, PC1, PC2, PC4, PC5, PC7, … , PC11*	*Farm, PC1, … , PC6, PC9, PC10, PC11*
Type of the k-fold cross-validation	10-fold	10-fold	20-fold

The performance statistics (5) of the selected two groups of base models for predicting the reduced dependent variable *Milk_miss*40 were evaluated and compared. In addition, the predicted values of these models were also compared against the initial sample, *Milk*305 with 158 cases; *Milk_miss*40 with 118 cases; and the holdout test sample, and *Milk_*40 with 40 cases, not used in the modeling procedure. The obtained basic statistics of predictive models are shown in the first six columns of Table 7. It can be seen that the performance results are similar, whereas all statistics from (5) of the selective ensembles are superior.

Table 7. Summary statistics of the predictions of obtained models against the measured values of the dependent variables.

Measure	Base Model Group A			Base Model Group B			Linear Combinations	
	EB15	*EB40*	*AR10*	*SSEB11*	*SSEB25*	*SSAR9*	*Hybr$_1$*	*Hybr$_2$*
Mean, 158	6739.11	6797.17	6872.41	6747.79	6790.98	6871.63	6787.81	6778.75
Mean, 118	6755.05	6810.56	6836.70	6758.16	6811.57	6844.17	6787.88	6779.66
Mean, 40	6692.06	6757.64	6977.76	6717.18	6730.25	6952.66	6787.61	6776.05
Std. Dev., 158	2086.27	2119.82	2029.76	2118.99	2143.82	2081.68	2062.66	2100.91
Std. Dev., 118	2163.54	2187.59	2077.31	2191.88	2225.50	2131.27	2132.25	2169.99
Std. Dev., 40	1864.37	1931.58	1903.79	1913.43	1907.36	1951.61	1867.60	1908.38
R^2, 158	0.933	0.925	0.929	0.938	0.941	0.930	0.941	0.944
R^2, 118	0.934	0.928	0.941	0.939	0.947	0.940	0.943	0.945
R^2, 40	0.931	0.919	0.891	0.942	0.926	0.895	0.935	0.945
RMSE, 158	611.791	632.277	632.855	580.404	560.473	620.607	579.461	556.051
RMSE, 118	631.401	651.280	632.878	605.778	562.188	612.666	601.317	581.328
RMSE, 40	549.885	572.555	656.169	498.077	555.382	643.463	509.555	473.690
MAPE, 158 (%)	6.63	6.94	8.36	6.40	6.51	7.68	6.45	6.23
MAPE, 118 (%)	6.87	7.03	8.59	6.65	6.42	7.66	6.75	6.51
MAPE, 40 (%)	5.93	6.68	7.68	5.65	6.76	7.33	5.55	5.44
d, 158	0.9801	9.9790	0.9777	0.9824	0.9837	0.9795	0.9820	0.9837
d, 118	0.9804	0.9794	0.9796	0.9822	0.9849	0.9813	0.9820	0.9835
d, 40	0.9788	0.9777	0.9703	0.9831	0.9788	0.9722	0.9818	0.9847

$R^2, 158 R^2, 118 R^2, 40$ In particular, the *SSEB*11 model demonstrates better performance than the *EB*15 model from which it is derived. For example, for the whole sample, the reduction in RMSE of *SSEB*11 compared to *EB*15 is 5.1%, whereas for the test sample, *Milk_*40, the error is reduced by 9.26%. Similarly, model *SSEB*25 outperforms the source model, *EB*40. In this case, the improvement in RMSE for the whole sample is 11.4%, and for the holdout sample, the error is reduced by 3.0% compared to that of *EB*40. For *SSAR*9, these indices are 2% and 1.9%, respectively. Overall, the indicators of model *AR*10 and its simplified selective model, *SSAR*9, are comparatively the weakest. This can be explained by the fact that they contain the smallest number of trees, and only one negative tree has been removed from the *AR*10 ensemble.

3.3.5. Relative Importance of the Factors Determining Milk305 Quantity

The regression models we built were used to predict 305-day milk yield, allowing us to determine, with high accuracy, how the considered factors explain the predicted values according to their weight in the models. For better interpretation, the initial names of the variables were recorded, along with the predictors, according to Table 4. The predictor with the most significant importance in the model has the highest weight (100 scores), and the other scores are relative to it.

The results in Table 8 show the relative variable importance of the predictors within the built base ensemble models. As expected, the main defining variable for 305-day milk yield with the greatest importance of 100 is *Farm*. The other significant conformation traits, in descending order, are *PC4* (*UdderW*), with relative weight between 60 and 68; *PC3* (*ChestW*), 45 to 58; *PC11* (*Stature*), 19 to 36; *PC10* (*Bone*), 19 to 27. The conformation trails with the weakest influence are *PC8* (*FootA*), with a relative weight of 8 to 14, and *PC7* (*RLSV*), with a relative weight of 7 to 11. Because all predictors have an average weight of more than five relative scores, we consider them all as essential traits on which milk depends.

Table 8. Relative averaged variable importance in base models.

Predictor Variable	Model					
	EB15	SSEB11	EB40	SSEB25	AR10	SSAR9
Farm	100.0	100.0	100.0	100.0	98.1	100.0
PC4 (*UdderW*)	67.6	67.7	64.5	66.3	64.2	60.2
PC3 (*ChestW*)	44.8	46.0	-	-	57.7	57.6
PC11 (*Stature*)	34.7	35.5	30.6	30.8	22.1	18.7
PC10 (*Bone*)	22.8	22.6	23.4	26.4	19.0	20.2
PC1 (*Locom & Lameness*)	13.5	14.5	17.1	19.8	28.5	30.0
PC9 (*HockD*)	6.6	6.7	12.4	14.4	36.2	38.0
PC5 (*RLRV*)	12.8	12.1	15.5	15.7	19.5	16.6
PC6 (*FootD*)	10.7	11.5	-	-	26.3	25.1
PC2 (*RumpW*)	9.7	10.3	11.0	11.9	30.4	30.8
PC8 (*FootA*)	7.8	8.0	12.3	14.0	-	-
PC7 (*RLSV*)	6.6	8.2	10.5	11.1	-	-

In an actual situation, the average values of the main conformation traits should be maintained within the limits of their lower and upper bounds of the means (5% confidence intervals). In our case, these limits are given in Table 3.

3.4. Building and Evaluation of the Linear Hybrid Models

The next stage of the proposed framework is combining the obtained predictions from the single base models. To illustrate the higher efficiency when using simplified selective ensembles, we compared the results obtained from the two groups of base models.

3.4.1. Results for Hybrid Models

Using the well-known approach of linear combinations of ensembles (see [45]), we sought to find a linear hybrid model, $\hat{y}$, of the type

$$\hat{y} = \alpha_1 E_1 + \alpha_2 E_2 + \alpha_3 E_3. \tag{6}$$

where E_i, $i = 1, 2, 3$ are ensemble models that satisfy the conditions for diversity, C1, ... , C4 (see Section 3.3), and the coefficients α_i are sought such that

$$\sum_{i=1}^{3} \alpha_i = 1, \quad \alpha_i \in [0, 1]. \tag{7}$$

When varying by step $h = 0.05$ in the interval $[0, 1]$ and all possible combinations for α_i, $i = 1, 2, 3$, the following two hybrid models with the least RMSE were obtained for the test sample *Milk_40*:

$$Hybr_1 = 0.55\ EB15 + 0.15\ EB40 + 0.3\ AR10. \tag{8}$$

$$Hybr_2 = 0.75\ SSEB11 + 0.25\ SSAR9. \tag{9}$$

The main statistics of these models are given in the last two columns of Table 7. Hybrid models improve all indicators of the base models. For the holdout test sample, *Milk_40*, the $Hybr_1$ model has an RMSE equal to 509.555 kg, which is less than the errors of Group A models by 7.9% for *EB15*, 12.4% for *EB40*, and 28.8% for *AR10*. Accordingly, model $Hybr_2$ improves the statistics of Group B models. In the case of the test sample, its RMSE = 473.690 kg, which is smaller than the *SSEB11*, *SSEB25*, and *SSAR9* models by 5.1%, 17.2%, and 35.8%, respectively. Furthermore, we obtained the desired result for the superiority of simplified selective models and $Hybr_2$ over the initial non-selective models and $Hybr_1$. In particular, the RMSE of $Hybr_2$ is smaller than that of $Hybr_1$ by 7% for the holdout test sample, *Milk_40*. MAPE coefficients of 5.5% were achieved.

A comparison of the values predicted by models (8) and (9) and the initial values for *Milk305* are illustrated in Figure 4.

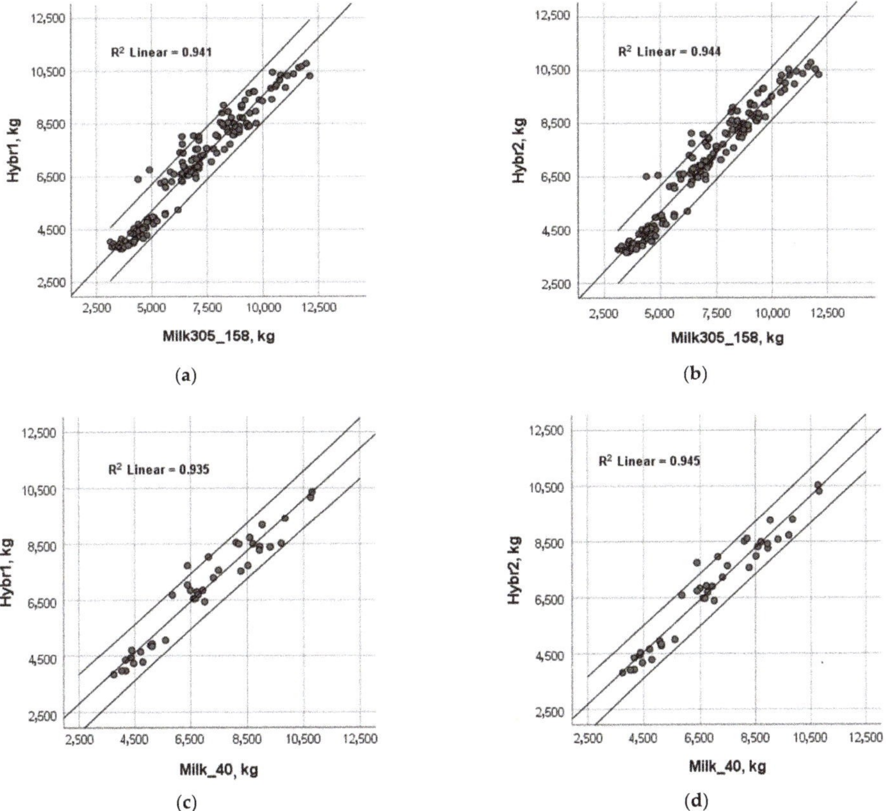

Figure 4. Quality of the coincidence of the measured values of milk yield and the predictions by the hybrid models with 5% confidence intervals: (**a**) model $Hybr_1$ against *Milk305*; (**b**) model $Hybr_2$ against *Milk305*; (**c**) model $Hybr_1$ against the holdout test sample, *Milk_40*; (**d**) model $Hybr_2$ against *Milk_40*.

3.4.2. Comparison of Statistics of All Models

A comparison of the performance statistics of all eight models constructed in this study for *Milk*305 and *Milk*_40 is illustrated in Figures 5 and 6. Figure 5 shows that the coefficients of determination for model *AR*10 and its simplified selective ensemble, *SSAR*9, are weaker than those of the other base models. However, despite their second largest coefficients in (8) and (9), respectively, the R^2 of the hybrid models is satisfactory for the small data samples studied. In the same context, Figure 6 illustrates the behavior of RMSE values, which do not deteriorate significantly in hybrid models due to their higher values in the *AR*10 and *SSAR*9 models.

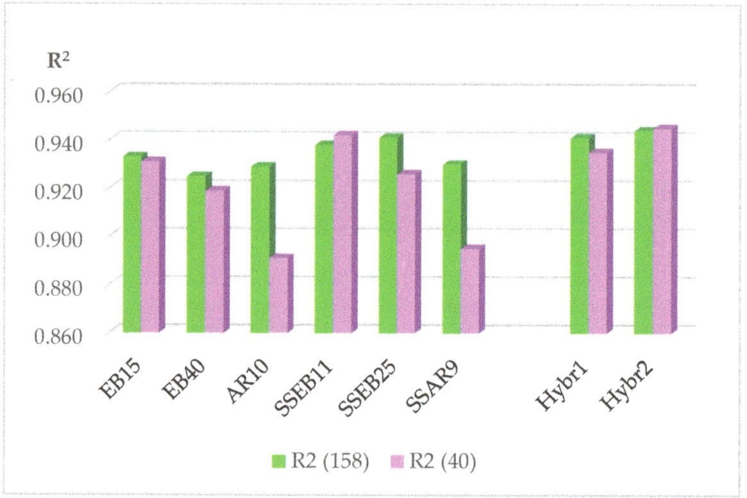

Figure 5. Comparison of coefficients of determination R^2 for all eight models for *Milk*305 and *Milk*_40 samples.

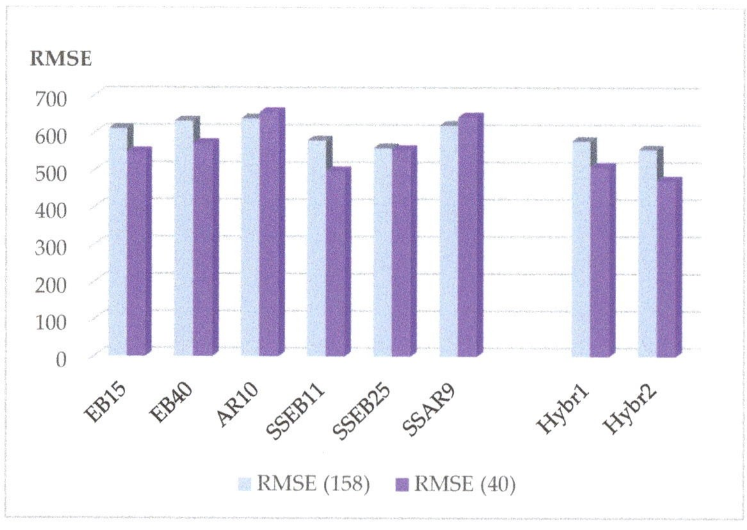

Figure 6. Comparison of coefficients of RMSE for all eight constructed models for *Milk*305 and *Milk*_40 samples.

Finally, we compared the RMSE and generalization error (mean squared error (MSE) = $RMSE^2$) of the built models for a randomly selected holdout test sample, *Milk_*40. The results are shown in Table 9. The $Hybr_2$ model produces RMSE 7% less than that produced by $Hybr_1$; compared to base models, the improvement varies from 5% to 26%. The comparison by generalization error shows 13.6% and 9.6% lower values for $Hybr_2$ than those for $Hybr_1$ and model $SSEB$11, respectively.

Table 9. Holdout test-set prediction errors.

Error, Improvement	Base Model Group A			Base Model Group B			Linear Combinations	
	EB15	**EB40**	**AR10**	**SSEB11**	**SSEB25**	**SSAR9**	**$Hybr_1$**	**$Hybr_2$**
RMSE, 40	549.885	572.555	656.169	498.077	555.382	643.463	509.555	473.690
Improvement by $Hybr_2$	7.3%	11.0%	22.3%	4.9%	14.7%	26.4%	7.0%	-
MSE, 40	302,373.5	327,819.2	430,557.8	248,080.7	308,449.2	414,044.6	259,646.3	224,382.22
Improvement by $Hybr_2$	14.1%	20.8%	39.7%	9.6%	27.3%	45.8%	13.6%	-

4. Discussion

We investigated the relationship between the 305-day milk yield of Holstein-Friesian cows and 12 external traits and the farm in a sample of 158 cows. To evaluate the constructed models, a random holdout test subsample was used, including 25% (40 entries) from the variable *Milk*305 for 305-day milk yield. In order to reveal the dependence and to predict milk yield, a new framework was developed based on ensemble methods using bagging and boosting algorithms and enhanced by a new proposed simplified selective ensemble approach.

We simultaneously applied the CART ensembles and bagging and Arcing methods for livestock data for the first time. To improve the predictive ability of the models, the initial ordinal variables were transformed using factor analysis to obtain rotation feature samples. Three initial base models (group A) were selected, satisfying four diversity criteria. Numerous simplified selective ensembles were built from each of these models. Using these, a second trio of base models (group B) was selected. Predictions for each group of base models were stacked into two linear hybrid models. The models successfully predict up to 94.5% of the data for the initial and holdout test samples. The obtained results for predicting 25% holdout values of daily milk showed that the two hybrid models have better predictive capabilities than the single base models. In particular, the RMSE of hybrid model $Hybr_2$ from the simplified selective ensembles is 7.0% lower than that of the other hybrid model based on non-selective ensembles. The number of trees in the three selective ensembles was decreased by 27%, 37.5%, and 10%, or an average of 30%.

Our proposed approach to build selective tree ensembles is characterized by a simple algorithm, reduces the dimensionality of the ensemble, improves basic statistical measures, and provides many new ensembles to be used to satisfy the diversity criteria. In addition, in the two-level stacking procedure, we used two different criteria: increasing the index of the agreement to build simplified selective ensembles and minimizing the RMSE for choosing the stacked model.

However, some shortcomings can be noted, including the selection of base models that meet the condition of diversity, which remains a challenging problem, known as "black art" [43]. Another disadvantage is determining the variable importance of the initial predictors in the stacked models. The method proposed in this study may have certain limitations when used in practical applications. It inherits all the main shortcomings of ensemble algorithms based on decision trees: it requires more computing resources compared to a single model, i.e., additional computational costs, training time and memory. Our method's more complex algorithm compared to standard ensemble methods would be an obstacle to its application to real-time problems unless greater accuracy and stability of predictions is sought. However, for parallel computer systems, these limitations are reduced by at least one order of magnitude. Another disadvantage is the more difficult interpretation of the obtained results.

Our results can be compared with those obtained by other authors. For example, selective ensembles were derived in [19,20] using genetic algorithms. In [19], a large empirical study was performed, including 10 datasets for regression generated from mathematical functions. Twenty neural network trees were used for each ensemble. The component neural networks were trained using 10-fold cross validation. As a result, the number of trees in selective ensembles was reduced to an average of 3.7 without sacrificing the generalization ability. In [20], selective C4.5 decision tree ensembles were constructed for 15 different empirical datasets. All ensembles initially consisted of 20 trees. A modified genetic algorithm with a 10-fold cross-validation procedure was applied. There were reductions in the number of trees in the range of 7 to 12, with an average of 8, and a reduction in the ensemble error by an average of 3%. Several methods for ensemble selection were proposed in [24], and a significant reduction (60–80%) in the number of trees in Adaboost ensembles was achieved without significantly deteriorating the generalization error. The authors of [26] developed a complex hierarchical selective ensemble classifier for multiclass problems using boosting, bagging, and RF algorithms and achieved accuracy of up to 94–96%.

The classical paper by Breiman [45] can be mentioned, wherein various linear combinations with stacked regressions, including decision trees ensembles, were studied. The stacking was applied for 10 CART subtrees of different sizes with 10-fold cross-validation for relatively small samples. Least squares under non-negativity constraints was used to determine the coefficients in the linear combination. A reduction in generalization error of 10% was obtained for 10% and 15% holdout test samples. These performance results are comparable with those achieved in the present empirical study. Here, under the constraints (5), we obtained a 9.6% to 13.6% reduction in the prediction generalization error of model $Hybr_2$ compared to $SSEB11$ and $Hybr_1$ models, respectively (see Table 9).

Furthermore, the proposed simplified selective algorithm easily adapts to other ensemble methods, including neural-network-type ensembles.

As a practical result of modeling, it was also found that 305-day milk yield depends on the following key factors (in descending order of importance): breeding farm, udder width, chest width, and the animals' stature. Furthermore, the farm as a breeding environment is found to be of crucial importance. In our case, numerous hard-to-measure factors were stochastically taken into account, such as state of the farm, comfort conditions for each animal, feeding method and diet, milking method, cleaning, animal healthcare, etc. With the obtained estimates, the indicators of the main external traits could be monitored within their mean values and confidence intervals to maintain and control a certain level of milk yield for each herd. The developed framework may also be used to forecast milk quantity in the case of measurements prior to the end of lactation.

This study shows a moderate to strong nonlinear dependence between conformation traits and 305-day milk yield, which presents an indirect opportunity to improve animal selection. However, to achieve real results in the management and selection of animals, it is recommended to accumulate data and perform statistical analyses periodically to monitor multiple dependencies between external, productive, and genetic traits and environmental factors.

Author Contributions: Conceptualization and methodology, S.G.-I.; software, S.G.-I. and A.Y.; validation, all authors; investigation, all authors; resources, A.Y.; data curation, A.Y. and H.K.; writing—original draft preparation, S.G.-I.; writing—review and editing, S.G.-I. and H.K.; funding acquisition, S.G.-I. and H.K. All authors have read and agreed to the published version of the manuscript.

Funding: The authors acknowledge the support of the Bulgarian National Science Fund, Grant KP-06-N52/9. The first author is partially supported by Grant No. BG05M2OP001-1.001-0003, financed by the Science and Education for Smart Growth Operational Program (2014–2020), co-financed by the European Union through the European Structural and Investment funds.

Institutional Review Board Statement: All measurements of the animals were performed in accordance with the official laws and regulations of the Republic of Bulgaria: Regulation No. 16 of 3 February 2006 on protection and humane treatment in the production and use of farm animals, the Regulation amending of the Regulation No. 16 (last updated 2017), and the Veterinary Law (Chapter 7: Protection and Human Treatment of Animals, Articles 149–169). The measurement procedures were carried out in compliance with Council Directive 98/58/EC concerning the protection of animals kept for farming purposes.

Conflicts of Interest: The authors declare no conflict of interest.

References

1. Berry, D.P.; Buckley, F.; Dillon, P.; Evans, R.D.; Veerkamp, R.F. Genetic Relationships among Linear Type Traits, Milk Yield, Bodyweight, Fertility and Somatic Cell Count in Primiparous Dairy Cows. *Irish J. Agric. Food Res.* **2004**, *43*, 161–176. Available online: https://www.jstor.org/stable/25562515 (accessed on 22 February 2022).
2. Almeida, T.P.; Kern, E.L.; Daltro, D.S.; Neto, J.B.; McManus, C.; Neto, A.T.; Cobuci, J.A. Genetic associations between reproductive and linear-type traits of Holstein cows in Brazil. *Rev. Bras. Zootecn.* **2017**, *46*, 91–98. [CrossRef]
3. Schneider, M.P.; Durr, J.W.; Cue, R.I.; Monardes, H.G. Impact of type traits on functional herd life of Quebec Holsteins assessed by survival analysis. *J. Dairy Sci.* **2003**, *86*, 4083–4089. [CrossRef]
4. Cockburn, M. Review: Application and prospective discussion of machine learning for the management of dairy farms. *Animals* **2020**, *10*, 1690. [CrossRef]
5. Dallago, G.M.; Figueiredo, D.M.D.; Andrade, P.C.D.R.; Santos, R.A.D.; Lacroix, R.; Santschi, D.E.; Lefebvre, D.M. Predicting first test day milk yield of dairy heifers. *Comput. Electron. Agric.* **2019**, *166*, 105032. [CrossRef]
6. Murphy, M.D.; O'Mahony, M.J.; Shalloo, L.; French, P.; Upton, J. Comparison of modelling techniques for milk-production forecasting. *J. Dairy Sci.* **2014**, *97*, 3352–3363. [CrossRef]
7. Cak, B.; Keskin, S.; Yilmaz, O. Regression tree analysis for determining of affecting factors to lactation milk yield in brown Swiss cattle. *Asian J. Anim. Vet. Adv.* **2013**, *8*, 677–682. [CrossRef]
8. Celik, S. Comparing predictive performances of tree-based data mining algorithms and MARS algorithm in the prediction of live body weight from body traits in Pakistan goats. *Pak. J. Zool.* **2019**, *51*, 1447–1456. [CrossRef]
9. Eyduran, E.; Yilmaz, I.; Tariq, M.M.; Kaygisiz, A. Estimation of 305-D Milk Yield Using Regression Tree Method in Brown Swiss Cattle. *J. Anim. Plant Sci.* **2013**, *23*, 731–735. Available online: https://thejaps.org.pk/docs/v-23-3/08.pdf (accessed on 27 February 2022).
10. Fenlon, C.; Dunnion, J.; O'Grady, L.; Doherty, M.; Shalloo, L.; Butler, S. Regression Techniques for Modelling Conception in Seasonally Calving Dairy Vows. In Proceedings of the 16th IEEE International Conference on Data Mining Workshops ICDMW, Barcelona, Spain, 12–15 December 2016; pp. 1191–1196. [CrossRef]
11. Van der Heide, E.M.M.; Kamphuis, C.; Veerkamp, R.F.; Athanasiadis, I.N.; Azzopardi, G.; van Pelt, M.L.; Ducro, B.J. Improving predictive performance on survival in dairy cattle using an ensemble learning approach. *Comput. Electron. Agric.* **2020**, *177*, 105675. [CrossRef]
12. Weber, V.A.M.; Weber, F.D.L.; Oliveira, A.D.S.; Astolfi, G.; Menezes, G.V.; Porto, J.V.D.A.; Rezende, F.P.C.; de Moraes, P.H.; Matsubara, E.T.; Mateus, R.G.; et al. Cattle weight estimation using active contour models and regression trees Bagging. *Comput. Electron. Agric.* **2020**, *179*, 105804. [CrossRef]
13. Grzesiak, W.; Błaszczyk, P.; Lacroix, R. Methods of predicting milk yield in dairy cows—Predictive capabilities of Wood's lactation curve and artificial neural networks (ANNs). *Comput. Electron. Agric.* **2006**, *54*, 69–83. [CrossRef]
14. Bhosale, M.D.; Singh, T.P. Comparative study of Feed-Forward Neuro-Computing with Multiple Linear Regression Model for Milk Yield Prediction in Dairy Cattle. *Cu. Sci. India* **2015**, *108*, 2257–2261. Available online: https://www.jstor.org/stable/24905663 (accessed on 22 February 2022).
15. Mathapo, M.C.; Tyasi, T.L. Prediction of body weight of yearling boer goats from morphometric traits using classification and regression tree. *Am. J. Anim. Vet. Sci.* **2021**, *16*, 130–135. [CrossRef]
16. Yordanova, A.P.; Kulina, H.N. Random forest models of 305-days milk yield for Holstein Cows in Bulgaria. *AIP Conf. Proc.* **2020**, *2302*, 060020. [CrossRef]
17. Balhara, S.; Singh, R.P.; Ruhil, A.P. Data mining and decision support systems for efficient dairy production. *Vet. World* **2021**, *14*, 1258–1262. [CrossRef]
18. Tamon, C.; Xiang, J. On the boosting pruning problem. In Proceedings of the 11th European Conference on Machine Learning, ECML 2000, Barcelona, Spain, 31 May–2 June 2000; Springer: Berlin/Heidelberg, Germany, 2000; pp. 404–412.
19. Zhou, Z.-H.; Wu, J.; Tang, W. Ensembling neural networks: Many could be better than all. *Artif. Intel.* **2002**, *137*, 239–263. [CrossRef]
20. Zhou, Z.-H.; Tang, W. Selective ensemble of decision trees. In Proceedings of the International Workshop on Rough Sets, Fuzzy Sets, Data Mining, and Granular-Soft Computing, RSFDGrC 2003, Lecture Notes in Computer Science, Chongqing, China, 26–29 May 2003; Springer: Berlin/Heidelberg, Germany, 2003; Volume 2639, pp. 476–483. [CrossRef]
21. Zhou, Z.H. *Ensemble Methods: Foundations and Algorithms*; CRC Press: Boca Raton, FL, USA, 2012.

22. Kuncheva, L. *Combining Pattern Classifiers: Methods and Algorithms*, 2nd ed.; Wiley and Sons: Hoboken, NJ, USA, 2014.
23. Mendes-Moreira, J.; Soares, C.; Jorge, A.M.; De Sousa, J.F. Ensemble approaches for regression: A survey. *ACM Comput. Surv.* **2012**, *45*, 10. [CrossRef]
24. Margineantu, D.D.; Dietterich, T.G. Pruning adaptive boosting. In Proceedings of the 14th International Conference on Machine Learning ICML'97, San Francisco, CA, USA, 8–12 July 1997; Morgan Kaufmann Publishers Inc.: San Francisco, CA, USA, 1997; pp. 211–218.
25. Zhu, X.; Ni, Z.; Cheng, M.; Jin, F.; Li, J.; Weckman, G. Selective ensemble based on extreme learning machine and improved discrete artificial fish swarm algorithm for haze forecast. *Appl. Intell.* **2017**, *48*, 1757–1775. [CrossRef]
26. Wei, L.; Wan, S.; Guo, J.; Wong, K.K. A novel hierarchical selective ensemble classifier with bioinformatics application. *Artif. Intel. Med.* **2017**, *83*, 82–90. [CrossRef]
27. ICAR. International Agreement of Recording Practices. *Conformation Recording of Dairy Cattle.* 2012. Available online: https://aberdeenangus.ro/wp-content/uploads/2014/03/ICAR.pdf (accessed on 22 February 2022).
28. Marinov, I. Linear Type Traits and Their Relationship with Productive, Reproductive and Health Traits in Black-and-White Cows. Ph.D. Thesis, Trakia University, Stara Zagora, Bulgaria, 2015. (In Bulgarian).
29. Penev, T.; Marinov, I.; Gergovska, Z.; Mitev, J.; Miteva, T.; Dimov, D.; Binev, R. Linear Type Traits for Feet and Legs, Their Relation to Health Traits Connected with Them, and with Productive and Reproductive Traits in Dairy Cows. *Bulg. J. Agric. Sci.* **2017**, *23*, 467–475. Available online: https://www.agrojournal.org/23/03-17.pdf (accessed on 22 February 2022).
30. Fuerst-Walt, B.; Sölkner, J.; Essl, A.; Hoeschele, I.; Fuerst, C. Non-linearity in the genetic relationship between milk yield and type traits in Holstein cattle. *Livest. Prod. Sci.* **1998**, *57*, 41–47. [CrossRef]
31. Willmott, C. On the validation of models. *Phys. Geogr.* **1981**, *2*, 184–194. [CrossRef]
32. Ren, Y.; Zhang, L.; Suganthan, P.N. Ensemble classification and regression-recent developments, applications and future directions. *IEEE Comput. Intell. Mag.* **2016**, *11*, 41–53. [CrossRef]
33. Izenman, A. *Modern Multivariate Statistical Techniques*; Springer: New York, NY, USA, 2008.
34. Török, E.; Komlósi, I.; Béri, B.; Füller, I.; Vágó, B.; Posta, J. Principal component analysis of conformation traits in Hungarian Simmental cows. *Czech J. Anim. Sci.* **2021**, *66*, 39–45. [CrossRef]
35. Mello, R.R.C.; Sinedino, L.D.-P.; Ferreira, J.E.; De Sousa, S.L.G.; De Mello, M.R.B. Principal component and cluster analyses of production and fertility traits in Red Sindhi dairy cattle breed in Brazil. *Trop. Anim. Health Prod.* **2020**, *52*, 273–281. [CrossRef]
36. Breiman, L.; Friedman, J.H.; Olshen, R.A.; Stone, C.J. *Classification and Regression Trees*; Wadsworth Advanced Books and Software: Belmont, CA, USA, 1984.
37. Breiman, L. Bagging predictors. *Mach. Learn.* **1996**, *24*, 123–140. [CrossRef]
38. SPM—Salford Predictive Modeler. 2021. Available online: https://www.minitab.com/enus/products/spm (accessed on 22 February 2022).
39. Breiman, L. Arcing Classifiers. *Ann. Stat.* **1998**, *26*, 801–824. Available online: https://www.jstor.org/stable/120055 (accessed on 22 February 2022).
40. Freund, Y.; Schapire, R.E. A decision-theoretic generalization of on-line learning and an application to boosting. *J. Comp. Syst. Sci.* **1997**, *55*, 119–139. [CrossRef]
41. Gocheva-Ilieva, S.; Ivanov, A.; Stoimenova-Minova, M. Prediction of daily mean PM10 concentrations using random forest, CART Ensemble and Bagging Stacked by MARS. *Sustainability* **2022**, *14*, 798. [CrossRef]
42. Wolfram Mathematica. Available online: https://www.wolfram.com/mathematica (accessed on 22 February 2022).
43. Wolpert, D.H. Stacked generalization. *Neural Netw.* **1992**, *5*, 241–260. [CrossRef]
44. Flores, B.E. The utilization of the wilcoxon test to compare forecasting methods: A note. *Int. J. Forecast.* **1989**, *5*, 529–535. [CrossRef]
45. Breiman, L. Stacked regressions. *Mach. Learn.* **1996**, *24*, 49–64. [CrossRef]

mathematics

MDPI

Article

Anomaly Detection in the Internet of Vehicular Networks Using Explainable Neural Networks (xNN)

Saddam Aziz [1,*], Muhammad Talib Faiz [1], Adegoke Muideen Adeniyi [1], Ka-Hong Loo [1,2,*], Kazi Nazmul Hasan [3], Linli Xu [2] and Muhammad Irshad [2]

[1] Centre for Advances in Reliability and Safety, New Territories, Hong Kong; talib.faiz@cairs.hk (M.T.F.); muideen.adegoke@cairs.hk (A.M.A.)

[2] Department of Electronic and Information Engineering, The Hong Kong Polytechnic University (PolyU), Hung Hom, Hong Kong; linli.xu@polyu.edu.hk (L.X.); mirsha@polyu.edu.hk (M.I.)

[3] School of Engineering, Royal Melbourne Institute of Technology (RMIT) University, Melbourne, VIC 3000, Australia; kazi.hasan@rmit.edu.au

* Correspondence: saddam.aziz@cairs.hk (S.A.); kh.loo@polyu.edu.hk (K.-H.L.)

Abstract: It is increasingly difficult to identify complex cyberattacks in a wide range of industries, such as the Internet of Vehicles (IoV). The IoV is a network of vehicles that consists of sensors, actuators, network layers, and communication systems between vehicles. Communication plays an important role as an essential part of the IoV. Vehicles in a network share and deliver information based on several protocols. Due to wireless communication between vehicles, the whole network can be sensitive towards cyber-attacks.In these attacks, sensitive information can be shared with a malicious network or a bogus user, resulting in malicious attacks on the IoV. For the last few years, detecting attacks in the IoV has been a challenging task. It is becoming increasingly difficult for traditional Intrusion Detection Systems (IDS) to detect these newer, more sophisticated attacks, which employ unusual patterns. Attackers disguise themselves as typical users to evade detection. These problems can be solved using deep learning. Many machine-learning and deep-learning (DL) models have been implemented to detect malicious attacks; however, feature selection remains a core issue. Through the use of training empirical data, DL independently defines intrusion features. We built a DL-based intrusion model that focuses on Denial of Service (DoS) assaults in particular. We used K-Means clustering for feature scoring and ranking. After extracting the best features for anomaly detection, we applied a novel model, i.e., an Explainable Neural Network (xNN), to classify attacks in the CICIDS2019 dataset and UNSW-NB15 dataset separately. The model performed well regarding the precision, recall, F1 score, and accuracy. Comparatively, it can be seen that our proposed model xNN performed well after the feature-scoring technique. In dataset 1 (UNSW-NB15), xNN performed well, with the highest accuracy of 99.7%, while CNN scored 87%, LSTM scored 90%, and the Deep Neural Network (DNN) scored 92%. xNN achieved the highest accuracy of 99.3% while classifying attacks in the second dataset (CICIDS2019); the Convolutional Neural Network (CNN) achieved 87%, Long Short-Term Memory (LSTM) achieved 89%, and the DNN achieved 82%. The suggested solution outperformed the existing systems in terms of the detection and classification accuracy.

Keywords: IoV; xNN; K-MEANS; anomaly detection

MSC: 62T07; 68T05

Citation: Aziz, S.; Faiz, M.T.; Adeniyi, A.M.; Loo, K.-H.; Hasan, K.N.; Xu, L.; Irshad, M. Anomaly Detection in the Internet of Vehicular Networks Using Explainable Neural Networks (xNN). *Mathematics* **2022**, *10*, 1267. https:// doi.org/10.3390/math10081267

Academic Editor: Snezhana Gocheva-Ilieva

Received: 5 March 2022
Accepted: 31 March 2022
Published: 11 April 2022

Publisher's Note: MDPI stays neutral with regard to jurisdictional claims in published maps and institutional affiliations.

1. Introduction

The IoV, is an open, convergent network system that encourages collaboration between people, vehicles, and the environment [1,2]. With the help of vehicular ad hoc networks (VANET), cloud computing, and multi-agent systems (MAS), this hybrid paradigm plays a crucial role in developing an intelligent transportation system that is both cooperative and effective [3]. The presence of an anomaly detection system in the IoV is essential in today's uncertain world for the sake of data validity and safety. When it comes to critical safety data analysis, the cost of real-time anomaly detection of all data in a data package must be considered [4].

IoV consists of three layers:

1. Experimental and control layers.
2. Computing layers.
3. Application layers.

In the experimental and control layers, the vehicle is controlled and monitored according to sensed data and information from its environment. In the computing layer, vehicles communicate with the help of WLAN, cellular (4G/5G), and short-range wireless networks [5]. In the application layer, closed and open service models, or IoVs, are present. Key components of an IoV system are shown in Figure 1.

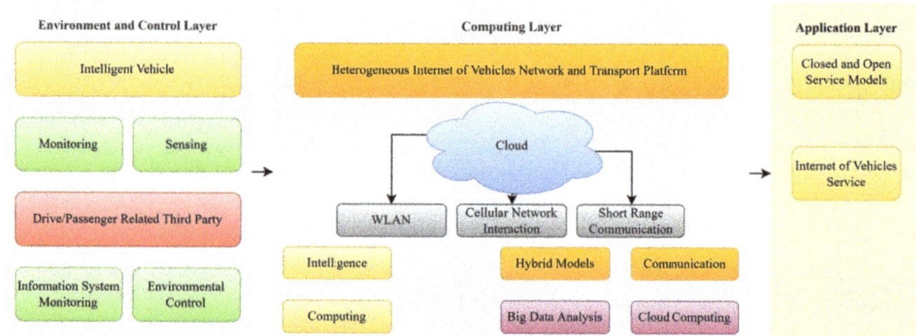

Figure 1. Key components and layers of an IoV system.

Unlike the internet's specific data security preventive techniques, the IoV data security issues start from internal and external factors [6,7]. The lack of a reliable data verification mechanism in automobiles, such as the Controller Area Network (CAN) protocol, is one way that vehicles' internal safety problems are reflected in existing internet communication protocols. The open architecture of IoV and widespread use make data breaches more difficult to defend against cyber-attacks [8]. An autonomous vehicle anomaly detection system is the subject of this paper. IoVs are unprecedented and vulnerable when backed by a dynamic and uncertain network [9].

Human safety and property can be jeopardized by malicious assaults and data tampering as well as system breakdowns [10]. Figure 2 shows the possible security risks in an IoV system. Vehicle-to-vehicle (V2V) communication is the first risk, where data can be attacked with an attacker and can cause harm to drivers. At the same time, a second security risk can be generated in the vehicle-to-infrastructure (V2I) communication scenario.

Numerous concerns have been raised about the privacy and security of intelligent vehicles and intelligent transportation networks due to multiple attack models for intelligent vehicles [10]. Cyber attackers might jam and spoof the signal of the VANET communication network, which raises serious security problems [11]. This could cause the entire V2X system to be impacted by misleading signaling and signal delays to ensure that the message conveyed is corrupted and does not fulfill its intended aims [12].

The internet or physical access to a linked vehicle's intelligence system is another security danger that intelligent automobiles encounter. In 2016, security professionals Charlie Miller and Chris Valasek, for example, wirelessly hacked the Jeep Cherokee's intelligence system [13], while the Jeep Cherokee's driver was still behind the wheel, researchers Miller and Valasek compromised the entertainment system, steering and brakes, and air conditioning system to show that the Jeep's intelligence system had security vulnerabilities. The Nissan Leaf's companion app was abused by cybercriminals utilizing the vehicle's unique identification number, which is generally displayed on the windows. Hackers were able to gain control of the HVAC system thanks to this flaw [14].

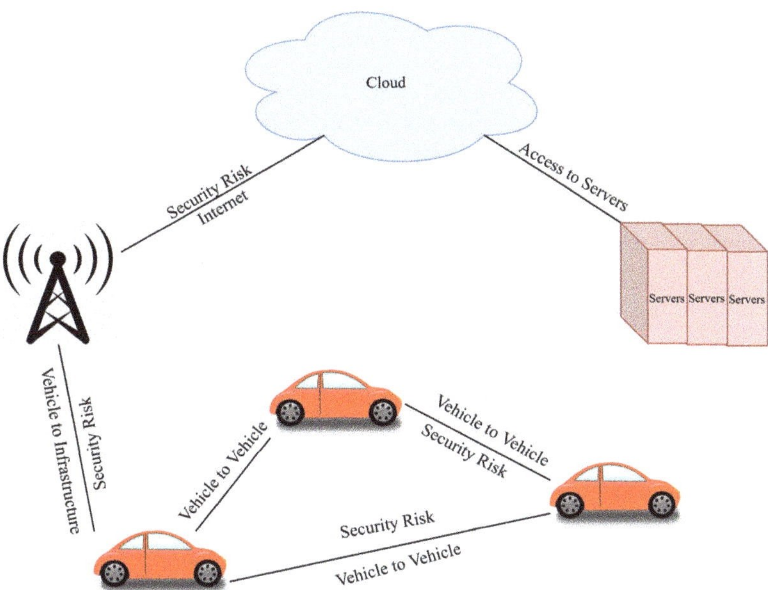

Figure 2. Key components and layers of an IoV system.

IoV's growth has been bolstered by embedded systems, hardware and software enhancements, and networking devices. However, there are still several dangers in the IoV, including security, accuracy, performance, networks, and privacy. Many security and privacy concerns have arisen due to the rising usage of intelligent services, remote access, and frequent network modifications. As a result, security vulnerabilities in IoV data transfer are a significant concern. Therefore, clustering [15,16] and deep-learning algorithms and approaches [17–19] can be used to handle network and security issues relating to the IoV. As part of this study, the security standards for IoV applications are outlined to improve network and user services efficiency. Denial of Service (DoS) assaults are detected using a novel model, xNN. The motivations of this study are:

- To propose a deep-learning model for detecting an anomaly in a vehicular network.
- To present a comprehensive framework to prepare network traffic data for IDS development.
- To propose an averaging feature selection method using K-Means clustering to improve the efficiency of the proposed IDS and to perform an analysis of network attributes and attacks for network monitoring uses.

2. Related Work

2.1. Anomaly Detection Systems

The safety of IoV's users is a significant concern. In the event of an infiltration attack on IoV system, hackers could gain direct control of vehicles, resulting in traffic accidents. Previously, many studies have been conducted on improving security for vehicular networks. To detect both known and unknown assaults on automotive networks, a multi-tiered hybrid IDS that integrates IDS with a signature and IDS with an anomaly was presented by Yang et al. [1]. The suggested system can detect several known assaults with 99.99% accuracy and 99.88% accuracy on the CICIDS2017 dataset, representing the CAN-intrusion-dataset's external vehicular network data.

The suggested system has strong F1 scores of 0.963 and 0.800 on both datasets above when it comes to zero-day attack detection. Intrusion detection networks, IDS design, and the limitations and characteristics of an IOV network were explored by Wu et al. [3]. The

IDS designs for IOV networks were discussed in detail, and a wide range of optimization targets were investigated and thoroughly analyzed in that study. Vehicular ad hoc networks (VANETs) provide wireless communication between cars and infrastructures. Connected vehicles may help intelligent cities and Intelligent Transportation Systems (ITS). VANET's primary goals are to reduce travel time and improve driver safety, comfort, and productivity. VANET is distinct from other ad hoc networks due to its extreme mobility. However, the lack of centralized infrastructure exposes it to several security flaws.

This poses a serious threat to road traffic safety. CAN is a protocol for reliable and efficient communication between in-vehicle parts. The CAN bus does not contain source or destination information; therefore, messages cannot be verified as they transit between nodes. An attacker can easily insert any message and cause system issues. Alshammari et al. [4] presented KNN and SVM techniques for grouping and categorizing VANET intrusions. The offset ratio and time gap between the CAN message request and answer were examined to detect intrusions.

2.2. Machine-Learning-Based Models

A data-driven IDS was designed by evaluating the link load behavior of the Roadside Unit (RSU) in the Internet of Things (IoT) against various assaults that cause traffic flow irregularities. An intrusion targeting RSUs can be detected using a deep-learning architecture based on a Convolutional Neural Network (CNN). The proposed architecture [5] uses a standard CNN and a basic error term based on the backpropagation algorithm's convergence. In the meantime, the suggested CNN-based deep architecture's probabilistic representation provides a theoretical analysis of convergence.

An IoV system must efficiently manage traffic, re-configure, and secure streaming data. Software-defined networks (SDN) provide network flexibility and control. However, these can attract hostile agents. The author's technique uses probabilistic data structures to detect aberrant IoV behaviour. Count-Min-Sketch is used to find suggestive nodes. Phase II uses Bloom filter-based control to check questionable nodes' signatures. Phase 3 uses a Quotient filter to store risky nodes quickly. To detect super points (malicious hosts connecting to several destinations), author counted the flows across each switch in phase 4. This was tested using a computer simulation. The proposed method of Garg et al. [7] outperformed the current standard in terms of detection ratios and false-positive rates.

In a generic threat model, an attacker can access the CAN bus utilising common access points. Xiao et al. [8] presented an in-vehicle network anomaly detection framework based on SIMATT and SECCU symmetry. To obtain state-of-the-art anomaly detection performance, SECCU and SIMATT are integrated. The authors want to reduce the computing overhead in training and detection stages. The SECCU and SIMATT models now have only one layer of 500 cells each, thus, reducing computing expenses. Numerous SIMATT-SECCU architectures evaluations have shown near-optimal accuracy and recall rates (with other traditional algorithms, such as LSTM, GRU, GIDS, RNN, or their derivatives) [20,21].

2.3. Anomaly Detection Based Driving Patterns

The Anomaly Detection Based on the Driver's Emotional State (EAD) algorithm was proposed by Ding et al. [9] to achieve the real-time detection of data related to safe driving in a cooperative vehicular network. A driver's emotional quantification model was defined in this research, which was used to characterize the driver's driving style in the first place. Second, the data anomaly detection technique was built using the Gaussian Mixed Model (GMM) based on the emotion quantization model and vehicle driving status information. Finally, the authors performed extensive experiments on a real data set (NGSIM) to demonstrate the EAD algorithm's high performance in combination with the application scenarios of cooperative vehicular networks.

With the IoV cloud providing a tiny amount of labelled data for a novel assault, Li et al. [10] suggested two model updating approaches. Cloud-assisted updates from the IoV can give a tiny quantity of data. Using the local update technique prevents the IoV cloud from sending labelled data promptly. This research shows that pre-labelled data can be leveraged to derive the pseudo label of unlabelled data in new assaults. A vehicle can update without obtaining labelled data from the IoV cloud. Schemes proposed by Li et al. improved the detection accuracy by 23% over conventional methods.

Connected vehicle cybersecurity and safety have been addressed using anomaly detection techniques. Prior research in this field is categorised according to Rajbahadur et al.'s [11] proposed taxonomy. There are nine main categories and 38 subcategories in the author's proposed taxonomy. Researchers found that real-world data is rarely used, and rather most results are derived from simulations; V2I and in-vehicle communication are not considered together; proposed techniques seldom compare to a baseline; and the safety of the vehicles is not given as much attention as cybersecurity.

Maintaining a safe and intelligent transportation system necessitates avoiding routes that are prone to accidents. With the help of crowd sourcing and historical accident data, intelligent navigation systems can help drivers avoid dangerous driving conditions (such as snowy roads and rain-slicked road areas). Using crowd-sourced data, such as images, sensor readings, and so on, a vehicle cloud can compute such safe routes and react faster than a centralised service. The security and privacy for each data owner must be ensured in the intelligent routing. Additionally, crowd sourced data needs to be verified in the vehicle cloud before being used. Joy et al. [12] investigated ways to ensure that vehicular clouds are secure, private, and protected against intrusion.

Over the past few years, the complexity and connectivity of today's automobiles has steadily increased. There has been a massive increase in the security risks for in-vehicle networks and the components in the context of this development. In addition to putting the driver and other road users at risk, these attacks can compromise the vehicle's critical safety systems. The detection of anomalies in automobile in-vehicle networks is discussed by Müter et al. [13]. A set of anomaly detection sensors was introduced based on the characteristics of typical vehicular networks, such as the CAN. These sensors allow the detection of attacks during vehicle operation without causing false positives. A vehicle attack detection system is also described and discussed in terms of its design and application criteria.

2.4. Distributed Anomaly Detection System

Negi et al. [14] proposed a framework for a distributed anomaly detection system that incorporates an online new data selection algorithm that directs retraining and modifies the model parameters as needed for self-driving and connected cars. Offline training of the LSTM model over many machines in a distributed manner using all available data is part of the framework's implementation. Anomaly detection occurs at the vehicle level using the trained parameters and is then sent to the individual vehicles. A more complex LSTM anomaly detection model is used, and the proposed distributed framework's accuracy in detecting anomalies is improved using the MXnet framework, which is used to test the framework's performance.

Sakiyama et al. [22] offered filter banks defined by a sum of sinusoidal waves in the graph spectral domain. These filter banks have low approximation errors even when using a lower-order shifted Chebyshev polynomial approximation. Their parameters can be efficiently obtained from any real-valued linear phase finite impulse response filter banks regularly. The author's proposed frequency-domain filter bank design has the same characteristics as a classical filter bank. The approximation precision determines the approximation orders. Many spectral graph wavelets and filter banks exist to test the author's techniques.

For autonomous and connected automobiles, securing vehicles is a top priority in light of the Jeep Cherokee incident of 2015, in which the vehicle was illegally controlled remotely by spoofing messages that were placed on the public mobile network. Security solutions for each unknown cyberattack involve the timely identification of attacks that occur throughout time in the vehicles' lifespan. Sporking communications at the central gateway can be detected using IDS as described by Hamada et al. [23]. Using communications from a real-world in-vehicle network, the author also reported on the system's detection performance.

2.5. Ad Hoc Vehicle Network Intrusion Detection System

Ad hoc vehicle networks are evolving into the Internet of Automobiles as the Internet of Things (IoT) takes hold of the IoV. The IoV can attract a large number of businesses and researchers due to the rapid advancement of computing and communication technologies. Using an abstract model of the IoTs, Yang et al. [24] provided an overview of the technologies needed to build the IoV, examined many IoV-related applications, and provided some open research challenges and descriptions of necessary future research in the IoV field.

Future Automated and Connected Vehicles (CAVs), or ITS, will form a highly interconnected network. City traffic flows can only be coordinated if vehicles are connected via the Internet of Vehicles (herein the Internet of CAVs). It will be possible to monitor and regulate CAVs using anonymized CAV mobility data. To ensure safe and secure operations, the early detection of anomalies is crucial. Wang et al. [25] proposed an unsupervised learning technique based on a deep autoencoder to detect CAV self-reported location abnormalities. Quantitative investigations on simulated datasets show that the proposed approach worked well in detecting self-reported location anomalies.

As real-time anomaly detection on complete data packages is expensive, Ding et al. [26] concentrated on crucial safety data analysis. The traffic cellular automata model was used for preprocessing to obtain optimal anomaly detection with minimal computer resources. An algorithm can discover irregularities in data related to safe driving in real time and online by modelling the driver's driving style. Starting with a driving style quantization model that describes a driver's driving style as a driving coefficient, then a Gaussian mixture model is used to detect data anomalies based on the driving style quantization and vehicle driving state (GMM). Finally, this study evaluated the suggested ADD algorithm's performance in IoV applications using real and simulated data.

In our study, authors summarized the research on anomaly detection. Authors categorised existing techniques into groups based on their core approach. Chandola et al. [27] created key assumptions for each category to distinguish normal from deviant behaviour. A few assumptions can be used to recommend testing a technique's efficacy in a specific domain. Using a basic anomaly detection technique, the authors showed how the existing techniques are all variations of the same technique. This template makes categorising and remembering techniques in each area easier. Each technique's pros and cons are listed separately. The authors also looked at the strategies' computing complexity, which is important in real-world applications. This study aims to better understand how strategies developed for one field can be applied to other fields. Authors hope the survey's results are useful.

The In-Vehicle Anomaly Detection Engine is a machine-learning-based intrusion detection technology developed by Araujo et al. [28]. The system monitors vehicle mobility data using Cooperative Awareness Messages (CAMs), which are delivered between cars and infrastructure via V2V and V2I networks (such as position, speed, and direction). The IVADE Lane Keeping Assistance system uses an ECU for signal measurement and control computations on a CAN bus (LKAS). To implement machine learning in IVADE, you need CAN message fields, automotive domain-specific knowledge about dynamic system behaviour, and decision trees. The simulation results suggest that IVADE may detect irregularities in in-vehicle applications, therefore, aiding safety functions.

2.6. In-Vehicle Network Intrusion Detection

A remote wireless attack on an in-vehicle network is possible with 5G and the Internet of Vehicles. Anomaly detection systems can be effective as a first line of defence against security threats. Wang et al. [29] proposed an anomaly detection system that leverages hierarchical temporal memory (HTM) to secure a vehicle controller area network bus. The HTM model may predict real-time flow data based on prior learning. The forecast evaluator's anomalous scoring algorithm was improved with manually created field modification and replay attacks. The results revealed that the distributed HTM anomaly detection system outperformed recurrent neural networks and hidden Markov model detection systems regarding the RCC score, precision, and recall.

Khalastchi et al. [30] described an online anomaly detection approach for robots that was light-weight and capable of considering a large number of sensors and internal measures with high precision. By selecting online correlated data, the authors presented a robot-specific version of the well-known Mahalanobis distance. The authors also illustrated how it may be applied to large dimensions. The authors tested these contributions using commercial Unmanned Aerial Vehicles (UAVs), a vacuum-cleaning robot, and a high-fidelity flight simulator. According to their findings, the Online Mahalanobis distance was superior to previous methods.

For example, autos are CPSs due to their unique sensors, ECUs, and actuators. External connectivity increases the attack surface, affecting those inside vehicles and those nearby. The attack surface has grown due to complex systems built on top of older, less secure common bus frameworks that lack basic authentication methods. In order to make such systems safer, authors treat this as a data analytic challenge. Narayanan et al. [31] employed a Hidden Markov Model to detect dangerous behaviour and send alerts when a vehicle is in motion. To demonstrate the techniques' ability to detect anomalies in vehicles, the authors tested them with single and dual parameters. Moreover, this technique worked on both new and old cars.

2.7. Feature Based Intrusion Detection System

Garg et al. [32] proposed an anomaly detection system with three stages: (a) feature selection, (b) SVM parameter optimization, and (c) traffic classification. The first two stages are expressed using the multi-objective optimization problem. The "C-ABC" coupling increases the optimizer's local search capabilities and speed. The final stage of data classification uses SVM with updated parameters. OMNET++ and SUMO were used to evaluate the proposed model extensively. The detection rate, accuracy, and false positive rate show the effectiveness.

Marchetti et al. [33] examined information-theoretic anomaly detection methods for current automotive networks. This study focused on entropy-based anomaly detectors. The authors simulated in-car network assaults by inserting bogus CAN messages into real data from a modern licenced vehicle. An experiment found that entropy anomaly detection applied to all CAN messages could detect a large number of false CAN signals. Forging CAN signals was only detectable via entropy-based anomaly detection, which requires many different anomaly detectors for each class of CAN message.

In order to accurately estimate a vehicle's location and speed, the AEKF must additionally take into account the situation of the traffic surrounding the vehicle. The car-following model takes into account a communication time delay factor to improve its suitability for real-world applications. Anomaly detection in [34] suggested that this method is superior to that of the AEKF with the typical 2-detector. Increasing the time delay had a negative effect on the overall detection performance.

2.8. Connected and Autonomous Vehicles

Connected and autonomous vehicles (CAV) are expected to revolutionise the automobile industry. Autonomous decision-making systems process data from external and on-board sensors. Signal sabotage, hardware degradation, software errors, power instability, and cyberattacks are all possible with CAV. Preventing these potentially fatal anomalies requires real-time detection [35] and identification. Oucheikh et al. [36] proposed a hierarchical model to reliably categorise each signal sequence in real-time using an LSTM auto-encoder.

The effect of model parameter modification on anomaly detection and the channel boosting benefits were examined in three cases. The model was 95.5% precise. The below Table 1 shows the comparative analysis of previous studies conducted to detect anomalies in the IoV. In the table below, it can be seen that multiple techniques have been used previously, i.e., Hybrid Models, Random Forests, Gaussian Mixture Models, MXNet, HTM Models, Support Vector Machines and various other machine and deep-learning models.

Table 1. Comparative analysis of previous studies.

Reference	Technique	Dataset	Accuracy
Yang et al. [1]	Hybrid Models	CICIDS2017	96.3%
Wu et al. [3]	Random Forests	CICIDS2017	95%
Ding et al. [9]	Gaussian Mixture Model	CICIDS2017	97%
Negi et al. [14]	MXNet	Offline Dataset	98.5%
Wang et al. [29]	HTM Model	UNSW-NB15	97.45%
Garg et al. [32]	Support Vector Machine	CICIDS2019	91%

2.9. Research Gap

The capacity of anomaly detection systems to detect unexpected assaults has garnered a great deal of interest, and this has led to its widespread use in fields, including artificial detection, pattern recognition, and machine learning. Traditional machine-learning techniques commonly employed in IDS rely on time-consuming feature extraction and feature selection processes. Additionally, the classification algorithm currently in use uses shallow machine learning. In a real-world network application, shallow machine-learning techniques can analyse high-dimensional inputs, resulting in a lower detection rate.

Last but not least, the data that IDS systems must deal with mostly consist of network traffic or host call sequences, and there are significant distinctions between the two. Host call sequences are more like a sequence problem than network traffic data. Although earlier methods are generally geared toward a specific case, the detection algorithms are not adaptive, especially to hybrid data source detection systems or advanced detection systems. Consequently, the previous detection algorithms are ineffective. For the purpose of feature selection, we used K-MEANS clustering to extract and select the best features. For classification of attack, we used an Explainable Neural Network (xNN).

The main research gaps are:

- For multi-class classification problems, to accurately identify or detect all the classes of data, classes may be imbalanced, and we tackle this problem.
- Sometimes, we deal with high dimensional data and features are sparse, and thus efficient feature selection is the point of concern.
- Detection and prediction are efficient in deep learning than traditional machine-learning techniques.

2.10. Contributions

In this article, a xNN model for anomaly detection in the IoV is proposed for the classification of attacks in two different data sets separately. Comparing with existing comparative literature, the commitments of this paper are bi-fold.

The contributions of this study are summarized as:

1. To the best of our knowledge, xNN has never been implemented in an IDS specially in the IoV.
2. K-Means-based feature scoring and ranking also contributed in this study to the best feature selection and ranking techniques based on weights.

The remainder of this paper is arranged as follows: Section 3 depicts the proposed xNN for anomaly detection in the IoV, in Section 4, the training method of xNN for IoV, and Sections 5 and 6 present our results and conclusions, respectively.

3. Proposed xNN for Anomaly Detection in the IoV

Data with sequential features is difficult for standard neural networks to deal with. The system call order is followed by host calls in the UNSWNB and CICIDS data [37,38]. An unusual behaviour may contain call sequence and sub sequences that are normal. As of this, the sequential properties of the system call must be taken into account while doing intrusion detection in the IoV. This means that the input data classification must take into account the current data as well as prior data and its shifted and scaled attributes. Thus, for the detection of intrusion designed to take the input instances with normal and abnormal sequences, we shift and scale the K-Means-clustered data features in order to meet the above requirements for the xNN. xNN works on the Additive Index Model as:

$$f(x) = g_1 \beta_1^T x + g_2 \beta_2^T x + [\ldots] + g_K \beta_K^T x \tag{1}$$

$f(x)$ is the function for classification of output variable, i.e., attacks. γ is the input feature. All of the features are arranged according to the K-based value from K-Means clustering, while x is the value of each instance from the feature. T is the scaling coefficient, which is directly related to β. From Equation (1), we added scaling parameters in the neural network, while in Equation (2), we added a shifting parameter of gamma with the coefficient of shifting, i.e., σ, and h is the hyper-parameter transfer function for over and under-fitting of the model. The alternative formulation for xNN is:

$$f(x) = \sigma + \gamma_1 h_1 \beta_1^T x + \gamma_2 h_2 \beta_2^T x + [\ldots] + \gamma_K h_K \beta_K^T x \tag{2}$$

When data is fed into the network, it is multiplied by the weights assigned to each number before being sent to the second layer of neurons as shown in Figure 3. The sigmoid activation function is constructed by summing the weighted sums of the activation functions of each of the neurons. Now, the weights of the connections between layers two and three are divided by these values. The process is then repeated until the final layer.

The architectural diagram of xNN can be seen below:

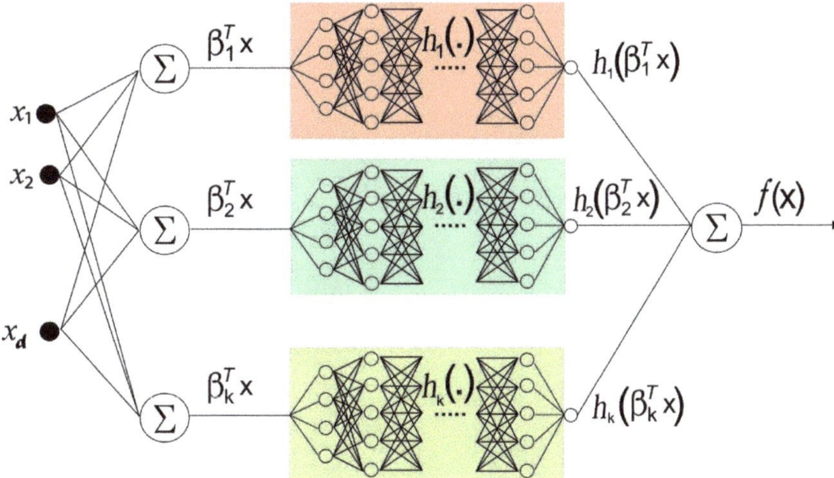

Figure 3. The proposed architecture of xNN.

If we let

- a_j^l denote the activation of the jth neuron in layer l;
- $w_{j,k}^l$ denote the value of the weight connecting the jth neuron in layer l and the kth neuron in layer $l - 1$;
- b_j^l denote the bias of the jth neuron in layer l; and
- n_l denote the number of neurons in layer l,

then, we can define a universal equation to find the activation of any neuron in an Explainable Neural Network (xNN)

$$a_j^l = \sigma\left(\left[\sum_{k=1}^{n_{l-1}} w_{j,k}^l a_k^{l-1}\right] + b_j^l\right) \tag{3}$$

A weighted directed graph can be used to conceptualise xNN, in which neurons are nodes and directed edges with weights connect the nodes. Information from the outside world is encoded as vectors and received by the neural network model. For d inputs, the notation $x(d)$ is used to designate these inputs.

The weights of each input are multiplied. The neural network relies on weights to help it solve a problem. Weight is typically used to represent the strength of the connections between neurons in a neural network.

The computing unit sums together all of the inputs that have been weighted (artificial neuron). In the event that the weighted total is zero, a bias is added to make the result non-zero or to increase the system's responsiveness. Weight and input are both equal to "1" in bias.

Any number from 0 to infinity can be added to the sum. The threshold value is used to limit the response to the desired value. An activation function f(x) is used to move the sum ahead.

To obtain the desired result, the activation function is set to the transfer function. The activation function might be linear or nonlinear.

4. Training Method of xNN for IoV

This section explains a detailed description of the dataset, methodology, and performance metrics. We used two recent datasets of autonomous vehicular networks, i.e., UNSW-NB15 and CICIDS2017, which contain a mix of common and modern attacks. The complete flow of the current methodology is shown in Figure 4 below.

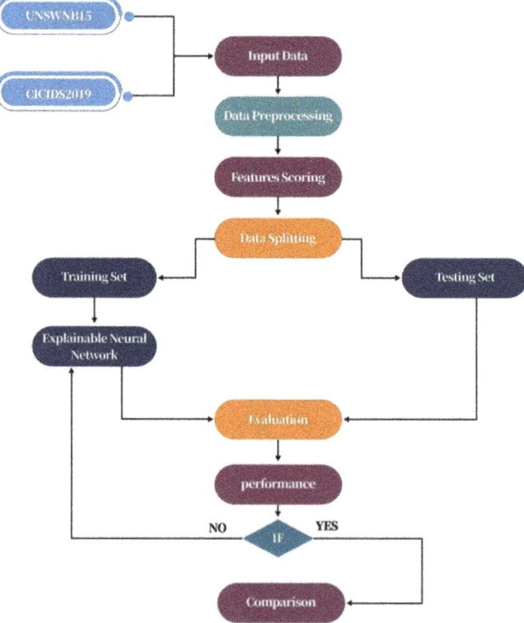

Figure 4. The proposed workflow.

4.1. Dataset Description

4.1.1. UNSW-NB15

Network intrusions are tracked in the UNSW-NB15 dataset. DoS, worms, Backdoors, and Fuzzers are only some of the nine various types of assaults included in this malicious software. Packets from the network are included in the dataset. There are 175,341 records in the training set and 82,332 records in the testing set of attack and normal records. The following table shows the dataset attributes, i.e., the ID, duration, protocols, state, flags, source and destination bytes, and packets. Attack is the output variable with multiple classes, i.e., DDoS, Backdoor attacks, Worms, and others. The description of UNSW-NB15 dataset is given below in Table 2:

The figure below shows the repartition and total counts of protocols, i.e., HTTP, FTP, FTP Data, SMTP, Pop3, DNS, SNMP, SSL, DHCP, IRC, Radius, and SSH.

Figure 5 shows the number of total categories of attacks present in the UNSW-NB15 dataset, i.e., Generic, Shell Code, DOS, Reconnaissance, Backdoor, Exploits, Analysis, Fuzzers, and Worms, while total 3500 instances were considered as Normal.

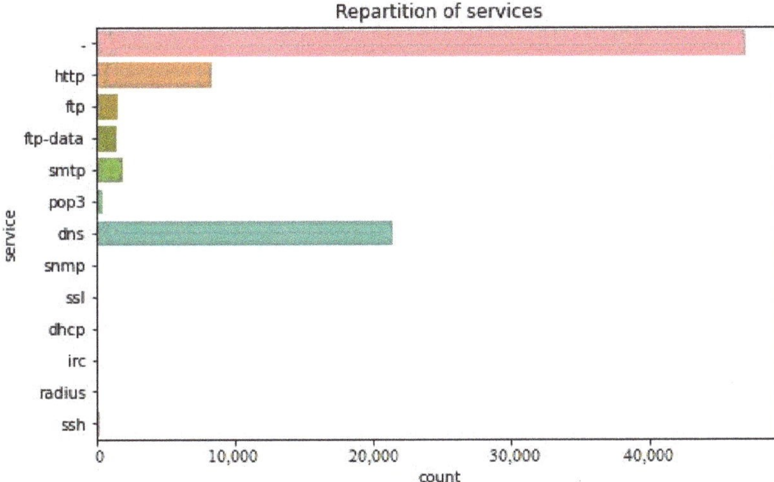

Figure 5. Repartition of services in UNSW-NB15.

4.1.2. CICIDS2019

The Table 3 shows the second dataset attributes used in this study from CICIDS2019. There are numbers of malicious attacks that can be found in vehicular networks in this dataset, which are related to real-world anomalies. A time stamp, source and destination IPs, source and destination ports, protocols, and attacks are included in the results of the network traffic analysis using Cyclometers. The extracted feature definition is also accessible. The data collection period lasted 5 days, from 9 a.m. on Monday, 3 July 2019, to 5 p.m. on Friday, 7 July 2019. Monday was a regular day with light traffic. Infiltration, Botnet and DDoS assaults were implemented Tuesday, Wednesday, Thursday, and Friday mornings and afternoons.

Figure 5 is showing repartition of services in UNSW-NB15 and Figure 6 is exhibting repartition of attack types. Figure 7 below shows the distribution of target variable, i.e., Attacks.

There has been a long-term interest in anomaly detection in several research communities. In some cases, advanced approaches are still needed to deal with complicated problems and obstacles. An important new path in anomaly detection has developed in recent years: deep-learning-enabled anomaly detection (sometimes known as "deep anomaly detection"). Using these two recent datasets, the suggested method is tested. The data sets are preprocessed so that deep-learning techniques may be applied to them. The homogeneity measure (k-means clustering) is a strategy for selecting relevant features from both sets of data in an unsupervised manner to improve the performance of classifiers. The performance of deep-learning models can be estimated and improved via five-fold cross validation. We used Explainable Neural Network (xNN) to classify attacks.

Table 2. UNSW-NB15 dataset description.

Feature/Attribute	Description	Value	Variable Type
ID	Vehicle ID	Any positive integer	Input Variable
Duration	Total time at which the vehicle is connected to network	Hours/minutes/seconds	Input Variable
Proto	Basic data-transmission mechanisms are included in communication protocols.	TCP/IP, HTTP	Input Variable
State	State of Vehicle (Connectivity)	0 (disconnected) or 1 (connected)	Input Variable
Spkts	Source Packets (Sent to destination)	Any positive integer	Input Variable
Dpkts	Destination Packets (Received at destination)	Any positive integer	Input Variable
Sbytes	Source Bytes (Sent from Source)	Any positive integer	Input Variable
Dbytes	Destination Bytes (Received from Source)	Any positive integer	Input Variable
$Attack_{Cat}$	Category of an Attack	There are a total of nine attacks in UNSW-NB15, i.e., DDoS, Backdoors, Worms, and others.	Output/Target Variable with Nine Classes

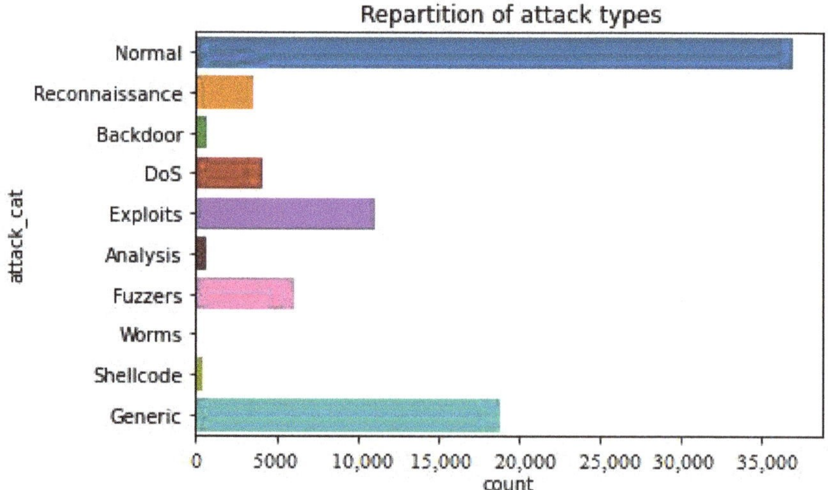

Figure 6. Repartition of attack types.

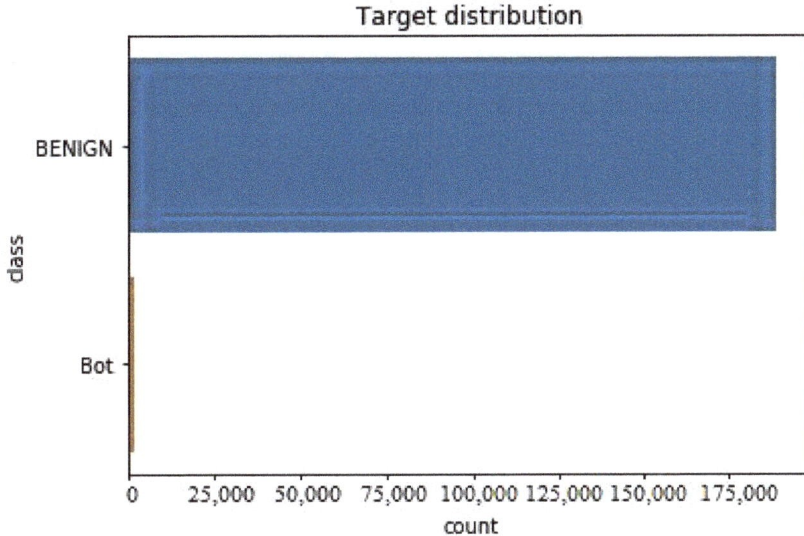

Figure 7. Target variable distribution in CICIDS2019.

Table 3. CICIDS2019 dataset description.

Feature/Attribute	Description	Value	Variable Type
ID	Vehicle ID	Any positive integer	Input Variable
Flow Duration	Total time at which the vehicle is connected to network	Hours/ minutes/ seconds	Input Variable
Destination Ports	Counts of data-transmission ports	2.0, 3.0	Input Variable
Total Forwarded Packets	Source Packets (Sent to destination)	0 (disconnected) or 1 (connected)	Input Variable
Total Backward Packets	Destination Packets (Received at destination)	Any positive integer	Input Variable
Length of Packets	Length of Forwarded and Backward Packets	Any positive integer	Input Variable
Sbytes	Source Bytes (Sent from Source)	Any positive integer	Input Variable
Dbytes	Destination Bytes (Received from Source)	Any positive integer	Input Variable
Attacks	Category of an Attack	There are two total anomalies, i.e., Benign and Botnet in the CICIDS2019 dataset	Output/Target Variable with 2 Classes

4.2. Data Preprocessing

The dataset is preprocessed to make it more appropriate for a neural network classifier.

4.2.1. Removal of Socket Information

For impartial identification, it is necessary to delete the IP address of the source and destination hosts in the network from the original dataset, since this information may result in overfitting training toward this socket information. Rather than relying on the socket information, the classifier should be taught by the packet's characteristics, so that any host with similar packet information will be excluded.

4.2.2. Remove White Spaces

When creating multi-class labels, white spaces may be included. As the actual value differs from the labels of other tuples in the same class, these white spaces result in separate classes.

4.2.3. Label Encoding

A string value is used to label the multi-class labels in the dataset, which include the names of attacks. In order to teach the classifier whose class each tuple belongs to, it is necessary to encode these values numerically. The multi-class labels are used for this operation, as the binary labels are already in the zero-one formation for this operation.

4.2.4. Data Normalization

The dataset contains a wide variety of numerical values, which presents a challenge to the classifier during training. This means that the minimum and maximum values for each characteristic should be set to zero and one, respectively. This gives the classifier more uniform values while still maintaining the relevancy of each attribute's values.

4.2.5. Removal of Null and Missing Values

The CICIDS2017 dataset contains 2867 tuples as missing and infinity values. This has been addressed in two ways, resulting in two datasets. In the second dataset, infinite values are replaced by maximum values, and missing values are replaced by averages. The proposed method was tested on both datasets. Only the attack information packets were used to evaluate the proposed approach with the data packets representing normal network traffic from both sets being ignored.

4.2.6. Feature Ranking

Preprocessed datasets are fed into the K-Means-clustering algorithm, which uses each attribute individually to rank them in terms of importance before applying it to cluster the entire dataset. For multi-class classification, k = the number of attacks in datasets, which means that the data point of feature is clustered into two groups: normal and anomalous. To rank the attributes, the clusters' homogeneity score is computed, with higher homogeneity denoting higher class similarity across the objects inside each cluster. Having a high score indicates that this attribute is important in the classification, while a low score indicates that this attribute is not important. For calculating the highest score similarity between the features, we first calculated the distance and then created an objective function

$$distance(C_j, p) = \sqrt{(\sum_{i}^{d} = 1[(C_{(j_i)} - p_i)]^2)} \tag{4}$$

From Equation (4), we computed the distance of the jth cluster from c centroid to check the jth feature's similarity at instance i with the data point p at instance i. After this, we created an objective function to minimize the distance between the cluster centroid and to check the homogeneity between selected features.

$$Obj(C_j) = \sum_{m}^{p}[distance(C_j, p)]^2 \tag{5}$$

For feature ranking, we derived the objective function for the jth features in Equation (5). This will calculate the minimal distance of Center C from p taking m as the starting point to rank the best features.

5. Results

This section shows the implementation and results of the xNN model on the selected datasets. We applied the xNN model on both datasets separately. Both datasets are publicly available on [37,38]. In experimental setup, we used python as a language source and a

GPU-based system consisting of Jupyter as a compiler with more than 3.2 GHz processor, which is the minimal simulation requirement for the experimental setup. In the first phase, we evaluated our model based on the accuracy, precision, recall, and F1 score for the classification of nine attacks in UNSW-NB15 dataset. Furthermore, in the second phase, the model was evaluated on the CICIDS2019 dataset.

5.1. Performance of xNN on UNSW-NB15

Figure 8 shows the performance of the xNN model on UNSW-NB15 after applying the K-Means-clustering-based feature scoring method. In the figure, the y axis shows the percentage of accuracy, and the x axis shows the accuracy, precision, recall, and F1 score of xNN. It shows that the model is 99.7% accurate in classifying the attacks in the IoV-based dataset.

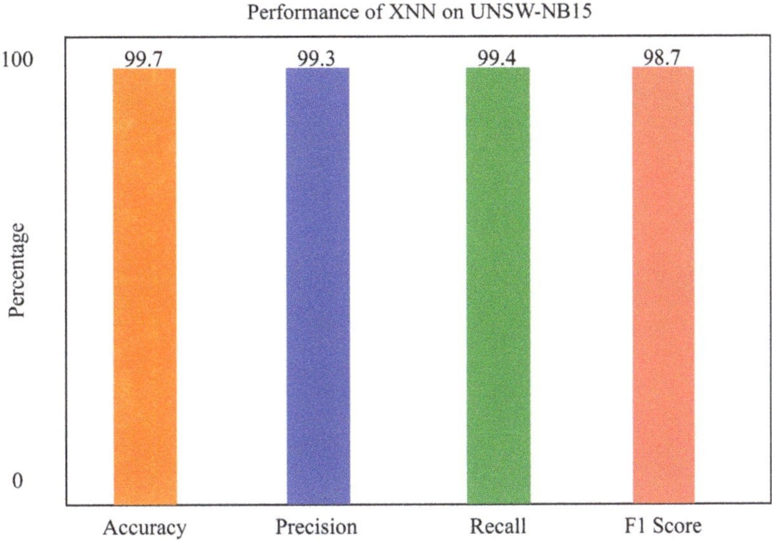

Figure 8. The performance of xNN on UNSW-NB15.

It can be seen from Figure 9 that, without feature scoring, the accuracy of xNN is 91.5%, which is less than the accuracy with feature scoring. In the figure, the y axis shows the percentage of accuracy, and the x axis shows the accuracy, precision, recall, and F1 score of xNN.

Figure 10 shows the confusion matrix with feature scoring, while Figure 11 shows the confusion matrix without feature scoring. It can be seen from Figure 10 that the true positive rate with feature scoring is much higher than without the feature scoring confusion matrix.

We also applied a Convolutional Neural Network and Long Short-Term Memory for the classification of attacks in order to compare our model with previous state-of-the-art models. xNN demonstrated promising accuracy and was the highest among the other deep-learning models. The comparison of deep-learning models for the classification of attacks in UNSW-NB15 is shown in Figure 12. In the figure, the y axis shows the percentage of accuracy, and the x axis shows the model's accuracy histogram.

5.2. Performance of xNN on CICIDS2019

Figure 13 shows the performance of the xNN model on CICIDS2019 after applying the K-Means-clustering-based feature scoring method. This shows that the model was 99.3% accurate in classifying the attacks in the IoV-based dataset. In the Figures 13 and 14, the y axis shows the percentage of accuracy, and x axis shows the model's accuracy histogram.

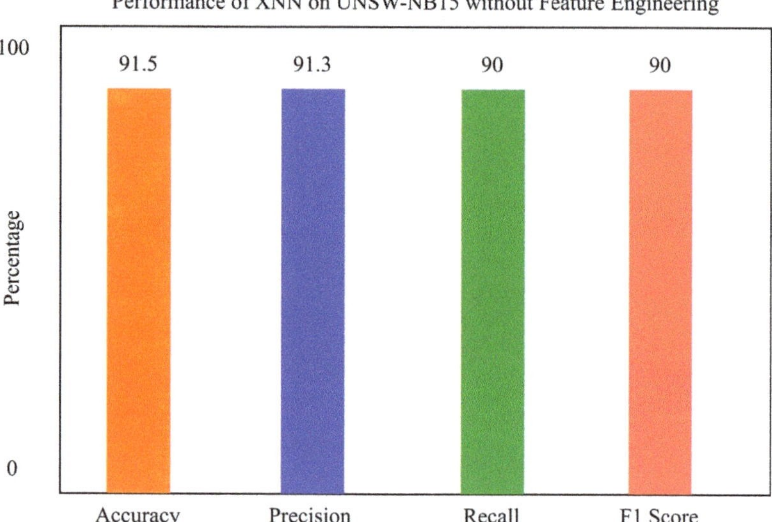

Figure 9. The performance of xNN on UNSW-NB15 without feature scoring.

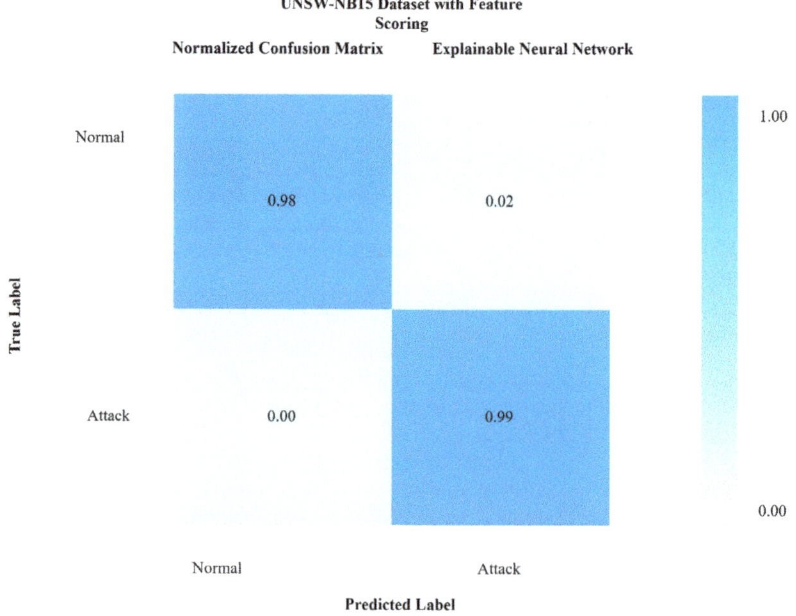

Figure 10. Confusion matrix of xNN for UNSW-NB15 with feature scoring.

It can be seen from Figure 13 that, without feature scoring, the accuracy of xNN is 87.3%, which is less than the accuracy with feature scoring. We also applied a Convolutional Neural Network and Long Short-Term Memory for the classification of attacks in order to compare our model with previous state-of-the-art models. xNN demonstrated promising accuracy and was the highest among the other deep-learning models. The comparison of deep-learning models for the classification of attacks in CICIDS2019 is shown in the figure below. In the figure, the y axis shows the percentage of accuracy, and the x axis shows the model's accuracy histogram.

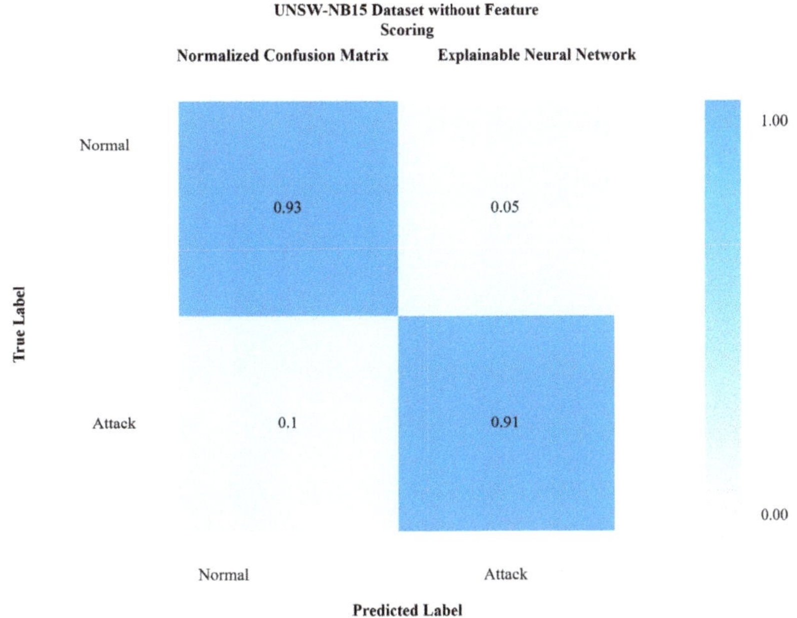

Figure 11. Confusion matrix of xNN for UNSW-NB15 without feature scoring.

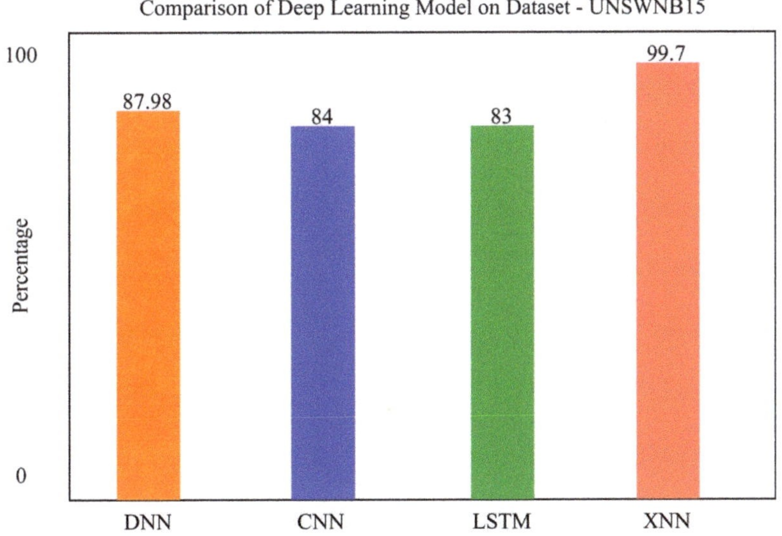

Figure 12. Comparison of deep-learning models for the classification of attacks in UNSW-NB15.

Comparatively, it can be seen that our proposed model xNN performed well after the feature-scoring technique. In Dataset 1 (UNSW-NB15), xNN performed well with the highest accuracy of 99.7%, while CNN scored 87%, LSTM scored 90%, and DNN scored

92%, while in the classification of attacks in the second dataset (CICIDS2019) xNN scored the highest accuracy of 99.3%, CNN scored 87%, LSTM scored 89%, and DNN scored 82%. Tables 4 and 5 shows the comparative analysis of deep-learning models proposed in this study to justify that xNN scored the highest accuracy and was a persistent model for the detection of intrusions on both datasets. Figures 15–17 show confusion matrix of xNN for CICIDS2019 with feature scoring, Confusion matrix of xNN for CICIDS2019 without feature scoring and comparison of the deep-learning model on the CICIDS2019 dataset, respectively.

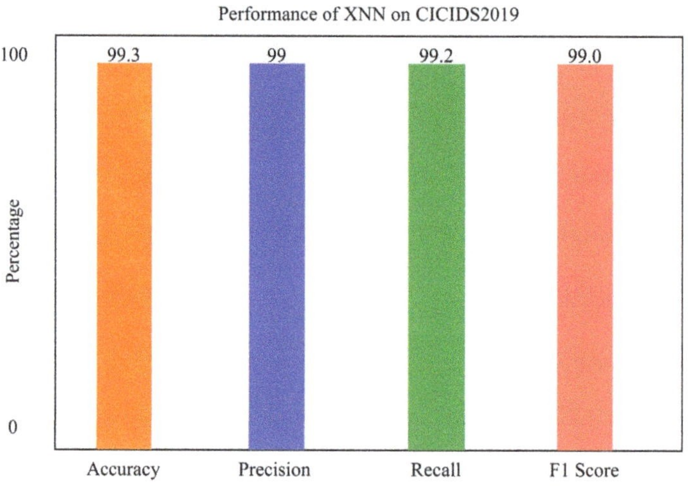

Figure 13. The performance of xNN on CICIDS2019.

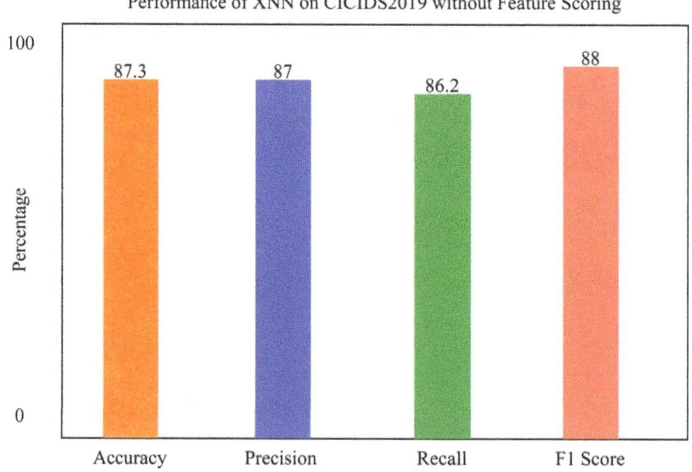

Figure 14. The performance of xNN on CICIDS2019 without feature scoring.

We compared our model with previous research. In a comparative analysis, we found that our proposed model scored the highest accuracy with respect to some of the recent previous research techniques.

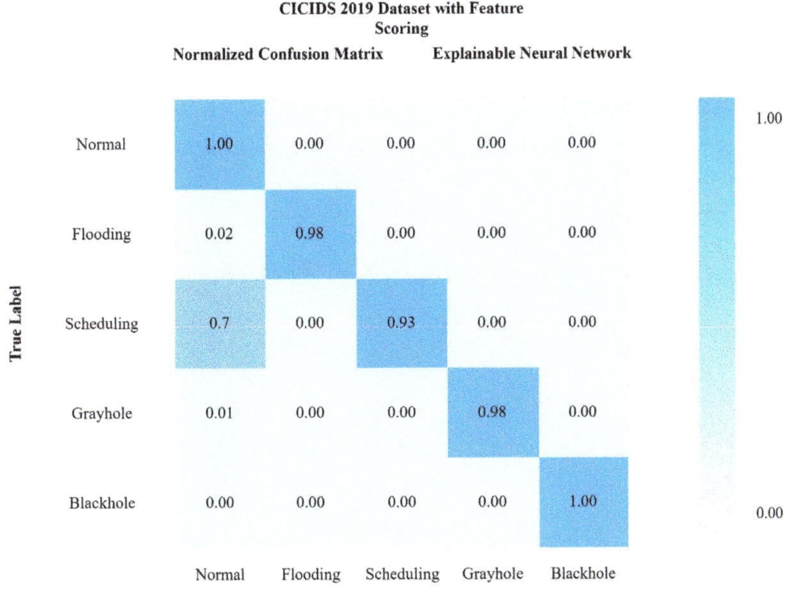

Figure 15. Confusion matrix of xNN for CICIDS2019 with feature scoring.

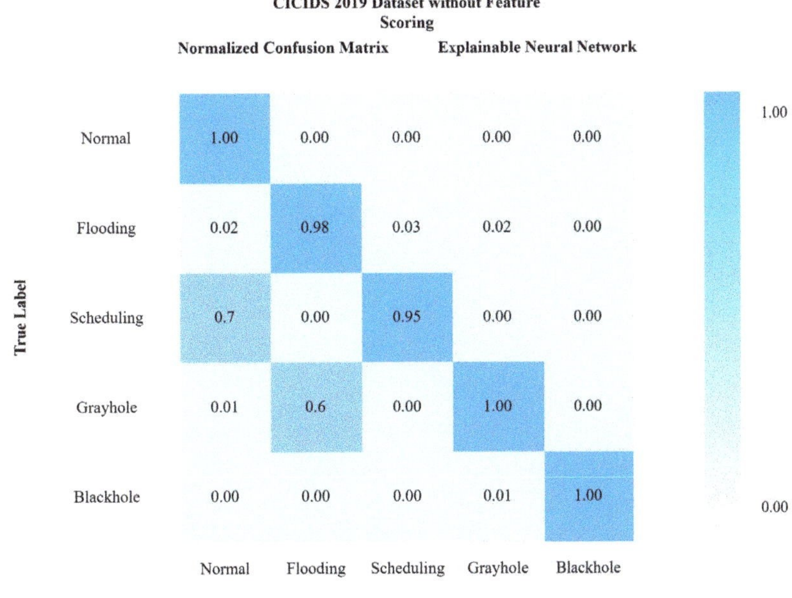

Figure 16. Confusion matrix of xNN for CICIDS2019 without feature scoring.

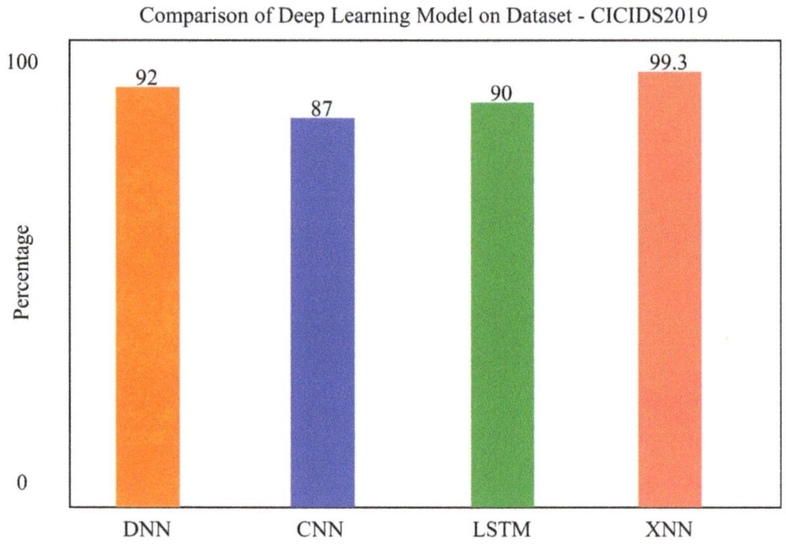

Comparison of Deep Learning Model on Dataset - CICIDS2019

Figure 17. Comparison of the deep-learning model on the CICIDS2019 dataset.

Table 4. Comparative analysis of the deep-learning models.

Model	Feature Scoring	Accuracy	Dataset
xNN	Default	87.3 %	CICIDS 2019
xNN	K-MEANS	**99.3%**	CICIDS 2019
xNN	Default	91.5%	UNSW-NB15
xNN	K-MEANS	**99.7%**	UNSW-NB15
LSTM	Default	89.7%	CICIDS 2019
LSTM	K-MEANS	90%	CICIDS 2019
LSTM	Default	78.65%	UNSW-NB15
LSTM	K-MEANS	83%	UNSW-NB15
CNN	Default	85.4%	CICIDS 2019
CNN	K-MEANS	87%	CICIDS 2019
CNN	Default	79.67%	UNSW-NB15
CNN	K-MEANS	84%	UNSW-NB15
DNN	Default	83.2%	CICIDS 2019
DNN	K-MEANS	92%	CICIDS 2019
DNN	Default	85%	UNSW-NB15
DNN	K-MEANS	87.89%	UNSW-NB15

Table 5. Comparative analysis of previous studies.

Reference	Technique	Dataset	Accuracy
Yang et al. [1]	Hybrid Models	CICIDS2017	96.3%
Wu et al. [3]	Random Forests	CICIDS2017	95%
Ding et al. [9]	Gaussian Mixture Model	CICIDS2017	97%
Negi et al. [14]	MXNet	Offline Dataset	98.5%
Wang et al. [29]	HTM Model	UNSW-NB15	97.45%
Garg et al. [32]	Support Vector Machine	CICIDS2019	91%
Our proposed	**Explainable Neural Network (xNN)**	**CICIDS2019** **UNSWNB15**	99.3% and 99.7%, respectively

6. Conclusions

One of the most difficult challenges is in developing systems that can detect CAN message attacks as early as possible. Vehicle networks can be protected from cyber threats through the use of artificial-intelligence-based technology. When an intruder attempts to enter the autonomous vehicle, deep learning safeguards it. The CICIDS2019 and UNSW-NB15 security systems were utilized to evaluate our proposed security system. Preprocessing is the process of converting category data into numerical data. K-Means clustering was used to determine which features were the most important.

Detecting attack types in this dataset was accomplished through the use of an Explainable Neural Network (xNN). The precision, recall, F1 score, and accuracy were all high for the model, which were encouraging results. Following the application of the feature-scoring technique, it can be seen that our suggested model xNN outperformed the competition. In Dataset 1 (UNSW-NB15), xNN outperformed the competition, scoring 99.7% accuracy, while CNN scored 87% accuracy, LSTM scored 90% accuracy, and DNN scored 92% accuracy. In the classification of attacks in the second dataset (CICIDS2019), xNN achieved the highest accuracy of 99.3%, followed by CNN with 87% accuracy, LSTM with 89% accuracy, and DNN with 82% accuracy.

With regard to accuracy in detection and classification, as well as real-time CAN bus security, the proposed approach outperformed the existing solutions in the study. Furthermore, this work can be extended to real-world scenarios and real-time controlled vehicles as well as on autonomous systems to protect against malicious attacks. The data package in the protocol analysed with the maximum values by applying the high-performance xNN model would be preferable for use in the future to reduce and eliminate security attacks, such as for the IoV.

Author Contributions: Data curation, S.A.; Funding acquisition, K.-H.L.; Investigation, S.A. and M.T.F.; Methodology, S.A.; Project administration, K.-H.L.; Resources, K.-H.L.; Software, A.M.A. and M.I.; Validation, K.N.H. and M.I.; Writing—original draft, S.A.; Writing—review & editing, A.M.A., K.-H.L., K.N.H. and L.X. All authors have read and agreed to the published version of the manuscript.

Funding: This research received no external funding.

Institutional Review Board Statement: Not applicable.

Informed Consent Statement: Not applicable.

Acknowledgments: The work presented in this article is supported by Centre for Advances in Reliability and Safety (CAiRS) admitted under AIR@InnoHK Research Cluster.

Conflicts of Interest: The authors declare no conflict of interest.

Abbreviations

The following abbreviations are used in this manuscript:

ANN	Artificial Neural Network
CICIDS	Canadian Institute for Obscurity Intrusion Detection System
CNN	Convolutional Neural Network
DT	Decision Trees
DFEL	Deep Feature Embedding Learning
DL	Deep Learning
DeeRaI	Deep Radial Intelligence
DoS	Denial of Service
DNS	Domain Name System
FTP	File Transfer Protocol
GNB	Gaussian Naive Bayes
GBT	Gradient Boosting Tree
HTTP	Hyper Text Transfer Protocol

IoT	Internet of Things
IP	Internet Protocol
IG	Information Gain
ID	Intrusion Detection
IDS	Intrusion Detection System
KNN	K-Nearest Neighbors
LR	Logistic Regression
LSTM	Long Short-Term Memory
ML	Machine Learning
MQTT	Message Queuing Telemetry Transport
MADAMID	Mining Audit Data for ID Automated Models
MLP	Multi-Layer Perceptron
NB	Naive Bayes
NIDS	Network Intrusion Detection System
NIMS	Network Information Management and Security Group
PCA	Principle Component Analysis
RBF	Radial Basis Function
RF	Random Forest
R2L	Remote to Local
RBM	Restricted Boltzmann Machine
RNN	Recurrent Neural Network
SOM	Self-Organizing Maps
SNN	Shared Nearest Neighbor
SVM	Support Vector Machine
TCP	Transmission Control Protocol
U2R	User to Root
UNSW	University of New South Wales
VANETS	Vehicular Ad hoc Networks
xNN	Explainable Neural Network

References

1. Yang, L.; Moubayed, A.; Shami, A. MTH-IDS: A Multitiered Hybrid Intrusion Detection System for Internet of Vehicles. *IEEE Internet Things J.* **2021**, *9*, 616–632. [CrossRef]
2. Irshad, M.; Liu, W.; Wang, L.; Khalil, M.U.R. Cogent Machine Learning Algorithm for Indoor and Underwater Localization Using Visible Light Spectrum. *Wirel. Pers. Commun.* **2021**, *116*, 993–1008. [CrossRef]
3. Wu, W.; Li, R.; Xie, G.; An, J.; Bai, Y.; Zhou, J.; Li, K. A Survey of Intrusion Detection for In-Vehicle Networks. *IEEE Trans. Intell. Transp. Syst.* **2020**, *21*, 919–933. [CrossRef]
4. Alshammari, A.; Zohdy, M.A.; Debnath, D.; Corser, G. Classification Approach for Intrusion Detection in Vehicle Systems. *Wirel. Eng. Technol.* **2018**, *9*, 79–94. [CrossRef]
5. Raziq, Y.; Sadiq, A.; Ali, H.; Asar, A.A. AI and Blockchain Integrated Billing Architecture for Charging the Roaming Electric Vehicles. *IoT* **2020**, *7*, 382–397. [CrossRef]
6. Li, Y.; Xue, W.; Wu, T.; Wang, H.; Zhou, B.; Aziz, S.; He, Y. Intrusion detection of cyber physical energy system based on multivariate ensemble classification. *Energy* **2021**, *218*, 119505. [CrossRef]
7. Garg, S.; Singh, A.; Aujla, G.S.; Kaur, S.; Batra, S.; Kumar, N. A Probabilistic Data Structures-Based Anomaly Detection Scheme for Software-Defined Internet of Vehicles. *IEEE Trans. Intell. Transp. Syst.* **2021**, *22*, 3557–3566. [CrossRef]
8. Xiao, J.; Wu, H.; Li, X. Internet of Things Meets Vehicles: Sheltering In-Vehicle Network through Lightweight Machine Learning. *Symmetry* **2019**, *11*, 1388. [CrossRef]
9. Ding, N.; Ma, H.; Zhao, C.; Ma, Y.; Ge, H. Driver's Emotional State-Based Data Anomaly Detection for Vehicular Ad Hoc Networks. In Proceedings of the 2019 IEEE International Conference on Smart Internet of Things (SmartIoT), Tianjin, China, 9–11 August 2019; pp. 121–126.
10. Li, X.; Hu, Z.; Xu, M.; Wang, Y.; Ma, J. Transfer learning based intrusion detection scheme for Internet of vehicles. *Inf. Sci.* **2021**, *547*, 119–135. [CrossRef]
11. Rajbahadur, G.K.; Malton, A.J.; Walenstein, A.; Hassan, A.E. A Survey of Anomaly Detection for Connected Vehicle Cybersecurity and Safety. In Proceedings of the 2018 IEEE Intelligent Vehicles Symposium (IV), Suzhou, China, 26–30 June 2018; pp. 421–426. [CrossRef]
12. Joy, J.; Rabsatt, V.; Gerla, M. Internet of Vehicles: Enabling safe, secure, and private vehicular crowdsourcing. *Internet Technol. Lett.* **2018**, *1*, e16. [CrossRef]

13. Muter, M.; Groll, A.; Freiling, F.C. A structured approach to anomaly detection for in-vehicle networks. In Proceedings of the 2010 Sixth International Conference on Information Assurance and Security, Atlanta, GA, USA, 23–25 August 2010; pp. 92–98. [CrossRef]
14. Negi, N.; Jelassi, O.; Chaouchi, H.; Clemencon, S. Distributed online Data Anomaly Detection for connected vehicles. In Proceedings of the 2020 International Conference on Artificial Intelligence in Information and Communication (ICAIIC), Fukuoka, Japan, 19–21 February 2020; pp. 494–500. [CrossRef]
15. Wang, W.; Xia, F.; Nie, H.; Chen, Z.; Gong, Z.; Kong, X.; Wei, W. Vehicle Trajectory Clustering Based on Dynamic Representation Learning of Internet of Vehicles. *IEEE Trans. Intell. Transp. Syst.* **2021**, *22*, 3567–3576. [CrossRef]
16. Jiang, Y.; Zhang, J. Interaction between company Manager's and Driver's decisions on expressway routes for truck transport. *Transp. Policy* **2019**, *76*, 1–12. [CrossRef]
17. Zhang, R.; Aziz, S.; Farooq, M.; Hasan, K.; Mohammed, N.; Ahmad, S.; Ibadah, N. A Wind Energy Supplier Bidding Strategy Using Combined EGA-Inspired HPSOIFA Optimizer and Deep Learning Predictor. *Energies* **2021**, *14*, 3059. [CrossRef]
18. Lydia, E.; Jovith, A.; Devaraj, A.; Seo, C.; Joshi, G. Green Energy Efficient Routing with Deep Learning Based Anomaly Detection for Internet of Things (IoT) Communications. *Mathematics* **2021**, *9*, 500. [CrossRef]
19. Nie, X.; Min, C.; Pan, Y.; Li, K.; Li, Z. Deep-Neural-Network-Based Modelling of Longitudinal-Lateral Dynamics to Predict the Vehicle States for Autonomous Driving. *Sensors* **2022**, *22*, 2013. [CrossRef]
20. Ma, Z.; Guo, S.; Xu, G.; Aziz, S. Meta Learning-Based Hybrid Ensemble Approach for Short-Term Wind Speed Forecasting. *IEEE Access* **2020**, *8*, 172859–172868. [CrossRef]
21. Irshad, M.; Liu, W.; Arshad, J.; Sohail, M.N.; Murthy, A.; Khokhar, M.; Uba, M.M. A Novel Localization Technique Using Luminous Flux. *Appl. Sci.* **2019**, *9*, 5027. [CrossRef]
22. Sakiyama, A.; Watanabe, K.; Tanaka, Y. Spectral Graph Wavelets and Filter Banks With Low Approximation Error. *IEEE Trans. Signal Inf. Process. Netw.* **2016**, *2*, 230–245. [CrossRef]
23. Hamada, Y.; Inoue, M.; Adachi, N.; Ueda, H.; Miyashita, Y.; Hata, Y. Intrusion detection system for in-vehicle networks. *SEI Tech. Rev.* **2019**, *88*, 76–81.
24. Yang, F.; Wang, S.; Li, J.; Liu, Z.; Sun, Q. An overview of Internet of Vehicles. *China Commun.* **2014**, *11*, 1–15. [CrossRef]
25. Wang, X.; Mavromatis, I.; Tassi, A.; Santos-Rodriguez, R.; Piechocki, R.J. Location Anomalies Detection for Connected and Autonomous Vehicles. In Proceedings of the 2019 IEEE 2nd Connected and Automated Vehicles Symposium (CAVS), Honolulu, HI, USA, 22–23 September 2019; pp. 1–5. [CrossRef]
26. Ding, N.; Ma, H.; Zhao, C.; Ma, Y.; Ge, H. Data Anomaly Detection for Internet of Vehicles Based on Traffic Cellular Automata and Driving Style. *Sensors* **2019**, *19*, 4926. [CrossRef] [PubMed]
27. Chandola, V.; Banerjee, A.; Kumar, V. Survey of Anomaly Detection. *ACM Comput. Surv.* **2009**, *41*, 1–72. [CrossRef]
28. Araujo. Innovative Approaches to Quality Assurance in Healthcare. *Bull. Roszdravnadzor* **2017**, *6*, 5–9.
29. Wang, C.; Zhao, Z.; Gong, L.; Zhu, L.; Liu, Z.; Cheng, X. A Distributed Anomaly Detection System for In-Vehicle Network Using HTM. *IEEE Access* **2018**, *6*, 9091–9098. [CrossRef]
30. Khalastchi, E.; Kaminka, G.A.; Kalech, M.; Lin, R. Online anomaly detection in unmanned vehicles. In Proceedings of the 10th International Conference on Advanced Agent Technology, Taipei, Taiwan, 2–6 May 2011; Volume 1, pp. 105–112.
31. Narayanan, S.N.; Mittal, S.; Joshi, A. OBD SecureAlert: An Anomaly Detection System for Vehicles. *IEEE Workshop Smart Serv. Syst.* **1993**. Available online: https://ebiquity.umbc.edu/_file_directory_/papers/792.pdf (accessed on 20 January 2022).
32. Garg, S.; Kaur, K.; Kaddoum, G.; Gagnon, F.; Kumar, N.; Han, Z. Sec-IoV. In Proceedings of the ACM MobiHoc Workshop on Pervasive Systems in the IoT Era-PERSIST-IoT '19, Catania, Italy, 2 July 2019; pp. 37–42. [CrossRef]
33. Aziz, H.S.; Wang, Y.; Liu, J.P.; Fu, X. An Approach to Kinetic Energy Recovery System for Electric Vehicle Considering SC and Bi-directional Converters. In Proceedings of the IEEE Innovative Smart Grid Technologies-Asia (ISGT Asia), Singapore, 22–25 May 2018; pp. 1273–1277. [CrossRef]
34. Yang, S.; Liu, Z.; Li, J.; Wang, S.; Yang, F. Anomaly Detection for Internet of Vehicles: A Trust Management Scheme with Affinity Propagation. *Mob. Inf. Syst.* **2016**, *2016*, 1–10. [CrossRef]
35. Oucheikh, R.; Fri, M.; Fedouaki, F.; Hain, M. Deep Real-Time Anomaly Detection for Connected Autonomous Vehicles. *Procedia Comput. Sci.* **2020**, *177*, 456–461. [CrossRef]
36. Wang, Y.; Masoud, N.; Khojandi, A. Real-Time Sensor Anomaly Detection and Recovery in Connected Automated Vehicle Sensors. *IEEE Trans. Intell. Transp. Syst.* **2021**, *22*, 1411–1421. [CrossRef]
37. IDS 2017 | Datasets | Research | Canadian Institute for Cybersecurity | UNB. Available online: https://www.unb.ca/cic/datasets/ids-2017.html (accessed on 29 January 2022).
38. Moustafa, N.; Slay, J. The evaluation of Network Anomaly Detection Systems: Statistical analysis of the UNSW-NB15 data set and the comparison with the KDD99 data set. *Inf. Secur. J. A Glob. Perspect.* **2016**, *25*, 18–31. [CrossRef]

Article

Robust Variable Selection Based on Penalized Composite Quantile Regression for High-Dimensional Single-Index Models

Yunquan Song *, Zitong Li and Minglu Fang

College of Science, China University of Petroleum, Qingdao 266580, China; slofzt_l@163.com (Z.L.);
pdmath@163.com (M.F.)
* Correspondence: syqfly1980@163.com

Abstract: The single-index model is an intuitive extension of the linear regression model. It has been increasingly popular due to its flexibility in modeling. In this work, we focus on the estimators of the parameters and the unknown link function for the single-index model in a high-dimensional situation. The SCAD and Laplace error penalty (LEP)-based penalized composite quantile regression estimators, which could realize variable selection and estimation simultaneously, are proposed; a practical iterative algorithm is introduced to obtain the efficient and robust estimators. The choices of the tuning parameters, the bandwidth, and the initial values are also discussed. Furthermore, under some mild conditions, we show the large sample properties and oracle property of the SCAD and Laplace penalized composite quantile regression estimators. Finally, we evaluated the performances of the proposed estimators by two numerical simulations and a real data application.

Keywords: single-index models; composite quantile regression; SCAD; Laplace error penalty (LEP)

MSC: 62F12; 62G08; 62G20; 62J07T07

Citation: Song, Y.; Li, Z.; Fang, M. Robust Variable Selection Based on Penalized Composite Quantile Regression for High-Dimensional Single-Index Models. *Mathematics* **2022**, *10*, 2000. https://doi.org/10.3390/math10122000

Academic Editors: Snezhana Gocheva-Ilieva, Atanas Ivanov and Hristina Kulina

Received: 23 March 2022
Accepted: 23 May 2022
Published: 10 June 2022

Publisher's Note: MDPI stays neutral with regard to jurisdictional claims in published maps and institutional affiliations.

1. Introduction

As a generalized regression model, the single-index regression model has a wide range of applications in the fields of finance, economics, biomedicine, etc. The single-index regression model not only avoids the so-called "curse of dimensionality" in the nonparametric models, but also significantly improves the efficiency of model estimation and reveals the relationship between the response variables and the high-dimensional covariates, to keep good interpretability of the parametric models and flexibility of the nonparametric models simultaneously [1–5]. However, the single-index regression model also inherits the shortcomings of the classical regression models. For example, in practical applications, especially in heavy-tailed error distribution scenarios, it is difficult to satisfy the bounded error variance, which a single-index regression model requires. Moreover, in the mean regression scenario, the estimation results of a single-index regression model are very sensitive to extreme values. To overcome these drawbacks, robust regression methods are necessary for the single-index regression model when fitting the real data.

Compared with the mean regression, the quantile regression proposed by [6] can measure the effect of the explanatory variable, not only on the distribution center but also on the upper and lower tails of the response variable. The quantile regression (QR) estimation, which is not restricted by the error distribution and can effectively avoid the impact of outliers, is more robust than the least squares estimation. Furthermore, in order to utilize the information on different quantiles adequately, composite quantile regression (CQR) was proposed by [7]. [8] added the SCAD-L2 penalty to the loss function and proposed a robust variable selection method based on the weighted composite quantile regression (WCQR), which made variable selection insensitive to high-leverage points and outliers. In this article, we studied the estimation and variable selection of the single-index quantile regression model. The single-index quantile regression model is specified in the following form

$$Y = g(\boldsymbol{X}^{\top}\boldsymbol{\gamma}) + \varepsilon, \tag{1}$$

where Y is the response variable, $\boldsymbol{X}$ is a d-dimensional covariate vector, $\boldsymbol{\gamma}$ is an unknown parameter vector, $g(\cdot)$ is an unknown link function, ε is the random error, and the τth conditional quantile is zero, i.e., $P(\varepsilon \leq 0|\boldsymbol{X}) = \tau$. In order to identify it more easily, we assume that $\parallel \boldsymbol{\gamma} \parallel = 1$ and the first component of $\boldsymbol{\gamma}$ is positive, where $\parallel \cdot \parallel$ denotes the Euclidean norm.

There are two estimation problems for the single-index quantile regression model. One is the estimation of parameters and the other is the estimation of the link function. The study of estimation for single-index quantile regression models began with [9], which generalized the average derivative method. Meanwhile, [10] proposed a simple algorithm to achieve the quantile regression for single-index models and proved the asymptotic properties of estimators. [3] proposed D-Vine Copula-based quantile regression, which is a new algorithm that does not require accurately assuming the shape of conditional quantiles and avoids the typical defects of linear models, such as multicollinearity. [11] proposed a non-iterative coincidence quantile regression (NICQR) estimation algorithm for the single-index quantile regression model, which has high computational efficiency and is suitable for analyzing massive data sets.

In real data, the model is often sparse. The variables inevitably contain a few irrelevant and unnecessary variables while modeling the real data, which can degrade the efficiency of the resulting estimation procedure and increase the complexity of models. In the case of linear models, many authors have considered variable selection via penalized least squares, which allows for a simultaneous selection of variables and estimation of regression parameters. Several penalty functions, including the SCAD [12], the adaptive LASSO [13], and the adaptive elastic net [14] have been shown to possess favorable theoretical properties: unbiased, sparsity, and continuity; it is regarded as the basic properties that a good estimator should enjoy [15]. It enjoys the oracle property. [5] combined the SCAD penalty variable selection method with LM-ANN for modeling, making good use of the advantages of SCAD in dimension reduction and the efficiency of LM-ANN in nonlinear relationship modeling.

Similar to the linear regression model, the set of predictors for the single-index quantile regression model can contain a large number of irrelevant variables. Therefore, it is important to select the relevant variables when fitting the single-index quantile regression model. However, the problem of variable selection for the high-dimensional single-index quantile regression model is not well settled in the literature. In recent years, many significant research results have emerged on the variable selection problem of the single-index quantile regression model. [16] proposed a non-iterative estimation and variable selection method for the single-index quantile regression model. The initial value and the weight of the penalty function were obtained via the inverse regression technique, which is the key to this method. [17] combined least absolute deviations (LAD) and SCAD for single-index models. However, we note that SCAD is a piecewise continuous spline function. Because of this structure, different splines need different derivative formulas; it is necessary to select different derivative formulas to match different splines when we carry out penalty optimization. This certainly adds to the programming complexity. So, [18] proposed a continuous bounded smooth penalty function–Laplace error penalty (LEP) that does not have a piecewise spline structure and proved its oracle property. LEP is infinitely differentiable everywhere except at the origin and, therefore, is much smoother than SCAD. Furthermore, LEP can approach the L_0 penalty as close as possible, which is viewed as the optimal penalty. Moreover, LEP can yield a convex objective function for optimization under mild conditions, such that it is easier to calculate and obtain the only optimal solution with desired properties.

In this paper, we combined (composite) the quantile regression method with the SCAD penalty and Laplace error penalty to construct two sparse estimators for the single-index quantile regression model. Our method realizes variable selection and parameter estimation simultaneously. In addition, we prove that the proposed estimator has large sample properties, including N-consistency and oracle properties. A simulation study showed that our method has some resistance to heavy tail errors and outliers, and the accuracy of parameter estimation is higher.

The rest of this paper is organized as follows. In Section 2, the SCAD penalized composite quantile regression and the Laplace penalized composite quantile regression for single-index models are introduced. Furthermore, an iterative algorithm for the single-index model is analyzed and the selections of bandwidth, tuning parameters, and initial values are discussed. In Section 3, we state the large sample properties of SCAD and Laplace penalized composite quantile estimators for single-index models. In Section 4, we show our method and algorithm by two numerical simulations and real data. Section 5 includes some concluding remarks. Technical proofs and the algorithm based on LEP are relegated to Appendix A and Appendix B, respectively.

2. Problem Setting and Methodology

2.1. Composite Quantile-SCAD Method for Single-Index Models

We assume $\{X_i, Y_i, i = 1, 2, \ldots, n\}$ are n independent samples from the single-index model (1). Note that there are two estimation problems, which are the estimation of the parameter vector γ and the estimation of the link function $g(\cdot)$. Given an accurate estimate of γ, the link function $g(\cdot)$ can be locally approximated by a linear function

$$g(\mathbf{X}^\top \gamma) \approx g(u) + g'(u)(\mathbf{X}^\top \gamma - u) = a + b(\mathbf{X}^\top \gamma - u), \tag{2}$$

for $\mathbf{X}^\top \gamma$ in the neighborhood of u, where $a = g(u)$ and $b = g'(u)$ are local constants. Namely, we can obtain a good local linear estimation of $g(u)$ and $g'(u)$, which are $\widehat{g}(u) = \widehat{a}$ and $\widehat{g'}(u) = \widehat{b}$, respectively, based on an accurate estimate of γ. So our main interest is to estimate the parameter vector. Following [19], we adopt the MAVE estimate of γ, which is obtained by solving the minimization problem

$$\min_{a,b,\|\gamma\|=1} \sum_{j=1}^{n} \sum_{i=1}^{n} [Y_i - a_j - b_j(\mathbf{X}_i^\top \gamma - \mathbf{X}_j^\top \gamma)]^2 w_{ij}, \tag{3}$$

where $w_{ij} = k_h(\mathbf{X}_i^\top \gamma - \mathbf{X}_j^\top \gamma) / \sum_{l=1}^{n} k_h(\mathbf{X}_l^\top \gamma - \mathbf{X}_j^\top \gamma)$, $a = (a_1, a_2, \ldots, a_n)^\top$, $b = (b_1, b_2, \ldots, b_n)^\top$, $k_h(\cdot) = k(\cdot/h)/h$ and $k(\cdot)$ is a symmetric kernel function, h is the bandwidth. [20] combined the MAVE and LASSO to obtain the sparse estimate (sim-lasso) of γ by solving the following minimization problem

$$\min_{a,b,\|\gamma\|=1} \sum_{j=1}^{n} \sum_{i=1}^{n} [Y_i - a_j - b_j(\mathbf{X}_i^\top \gamma - \mathbf{X}_j^\top \gamma)]^2 w_{ij} + \lambda \sum_{j=1}^{n} |b_j| \sum_{k=1}^{d} |\gamma_k|, \tag{4}$$

where λ is a nonnegative penalty parameter. Note that the above target loss function is the square loss function based on the least squares method and, naturally, the LAD is extended to a single-index model as an alternative to the LS method. [17] combined LAD with SCAD to construct a sparse estimator of γ by solving the following minimization problem

$$\min_{a,b,\|\gamma\|=1} \sum_{j=1}^{n} \sum_{i=1}^{n} |Y_i - a_j - b_j(\mathbf{X}_i^\top \gamma - \mathbf{X}_j^\top \gamma)| w_{ij} + \sum_{j=1}^{n} |b_j| \sum_{k=1}^{d} p_\lambda(|\gamma_k|), \tag{5}$$

where $p_\lambda(\cdot)$ is the SCAD penalty function proposed by [3]; it is defined in terms of its first order derivative. For $\theta > 0$

$$p'_\lambda(\theta) = \lambda\{I(\theta \le \lambda) + \frac{(a\lambda - \theta)_+}{(a-1)\lambda}I(\theta > \lambda)\}, \tag{6}$$

where $a > 2$ and λ is a nonnegative penalty parameter, the notation Z_+ stands for the positive part of Z. The LAD is a special case of the quantile regression, which only indicates the case when the quantile is $1/2$. Thus, this motives us to generalize composite quantile regression for single-index models. Combining the SCAD penalty function with the compound quantile regression, we can obtain a sparse estimation $\hat{\gamma}^{qr.sim.scad}$ of the parameter γ, which is the solution to the following minimization problem

$$\min_{a,b,\|\gamma\|=1} \sum_{j=1}^{n}\sum_{q=1}^{Q}\sum_{i=1}^{n} \rho_{\tau_q}[Y_i - a_j - b_j(\mathbf{X}_i^\top\gamma - \mathbf{X}_j^\top\gamma)]w_{ij} + \sum_{j=1}^{n}|b_j|\sum_{k=1}^{d}p_\lambda(|\gamma_k|) \tag{7}$$

where $\tau_q = \frac{q}{q+1} \in (0,1)$ stands for τ_q-quantile and $q = 1,2,\ldots,Q$ with the number of quantile Q, and $\rho_{\tau_q}(z) = \tau_q z \cdot I_{[0,\infty]}(z) - (1-\tau_q)z \cdot I_{(-\infty,0)}(z)$ is the τ_q-quantile loss function. In addition, we assume that the τ_q-quantile of the random error ε is 0. Thus, $g(\mathbf{X}^\top\gamma)$ is the conditional τ_q-quantile of the response variable Y. We denote the target function in (7) by $Q_\lambda^S(a,b,\gamma)$.

2.2. Composite Quantile–LEP Method for Single-Index Models

The Laplace error penalty function with two tuning parameters is proposed by [18]. Unlike other penalty functions, this new penalty function is naturally constructed as a bounded smooth function rather than a piecewise spline. The figure of LEP is similar to SCAD, but is much smoother than SCAD, which prompts us to apply it to the composite quantile regression for single-index models. Combining LEP with composite quantile regression, we can obtain a sparse estimation $\hat{\gamma}^{qr.sim.lep}$ of the parameter γ, which is the solution to the following minimization problem

$$\min_{a,b,\|\gamma\|=1} \sum_{j=1}^{n}\sum_{q=1}^{Q}\sum_{i=1}^{n} \rho_{\tau_q}[Y_i - a_j - b_j(\mathbf{X}_i^\top\gamma - \mathbf{X}_j^\top\gamma)]w_{ij} + \sum_{j=1}^{n}|b_j|\sum_{k=1}^{d}p_{\lambda,\kappa}(|\gamma_k|) \tag{8}$$

where $P_{\lambda,\kappa}(\cdot)$ is LEP. For $\theta > 0$,

$$P_{\lambda,\kappa}(\theta) = \lambda(1 - e^{-\frac{\theta}{\kappa}}), \tag{9}$$

where λ and κ are two nonnegative tuning parameters regularizing the magnitude of penalty and controlling the degree of approximation to the L_0 penalty, respectively. This penalty function is called Laplace penalty function because function $e^{-\frac{\theta}{\kappa}}$ has the form of the Laplace density. We denote the target function in (8) by $Q_{\lambda,\kappa}^S(a,b,\gamma)$.

2.3. Computation

Given the initial estimate $\hat{\gamma}$, the SCAD penalty function can be locally linear, approximated as follows [21]. For $\hat{\gamma}_j \ne 0$,

$$p_\lambda(|\gamma_j|) \approx p_\lambda(|\hat{\gamma}_j|) + p'_\lambda(|\hat{\gamma}_j|)(|\gamma_j| - |\hat{\gamma}_j|), \tag{10}$$

where $\gamma_j \approx \hat{\gamma}_j$. Remove a few irrelevant terms, (7) can be rewritten as

$$\min_{a,b,\|\gamma\|=1} \sum_{j=1}^{n}\sum_{q=1}^{Q}\sum_{i=1}^{n} \rho_{\tau_q}[Y_i - a_j - b_j(\mathbf{X}_i^\top\gamma - \mathbf{X}_j^\top\gamma)]w_{ij} + \sum_{j=1}^{n}|b_j|\sum_{k=1}^{d}p'_\lambda(|\hat{\gamma}_k|)|\gamma_k|. \tag{11}$$

We denote the target function in (11) by $Q_\lambda^{S*}(\boldsymbol{a}, \boldsymbol{b}, \gamma)$. We can easily discover that Q_λ^{S*} is invariant, so when minimizing Q_λ^{S*}, we restrict $\| \gamma \| = 1$ to be the unit length $\| \gamma \| = 1$ through normalization γ.

In order to obtain an accurate estimate of γ and $g(\cdot)$, we introduce a new iterative algorithm. Then our estimation procedure is described in detail as follows:

Step 0. Obtain an initial estimate of γ. Standardize the initial estimate $\hat{\gamma}$, such that $\| \gamma \| = 1$ and $\hat{\gamma}_1 > 0$.

Step 1. Given an estimate $\hat{\gamma}$, we obtain $\{\hat{a}_j, \hat{b}_j, j = 1, 2, \ldots, n\}$ by solving

$$
\min_{(a_j, b_j)} \sum_{i=1}^{n} \sum_{q=1}^{Q} \rho_{\tau_q}[Y_i - a_j - b_j(\boldsymbol{X}_i^\top \hat{\gamma} - \boldsymbol{X}_j^\top \hat{\gamma})]w_{ij} + | b_j | \sum_{k=1}^{d} p_\lambda'(| \hat{\gamma}_k |) | \hat{\gamma}_k |
$$
$$
= \min_{(a_j, b_j)} \sum_{i=1}^{n+1} \sum_{q=1}^{Q} \rho[Y_i^* - (A, B)\begin{pmatrix} a_j \\ b_j \end{pmatrix}]w_{ij}^*, \tag{12}
$$

where h is the optimal bandwidth, $(\rho, Y_i^*, A, B, w_{ij}^*) = (\rho_{\tau_q}, Y_i, 1, \boldsymbol{X}_i^\top \hat{\gamma} - \boldsymbol{X}_j^\top \hat{\gamma}, w_{ij})$ for $i = 1, 2, \ldots, n$, and $(\rho, Y_i^*, A, B, w_{ij}^*) = (1/Q, 0, 0, \sum_{k=1}^{d} p_\lambda'(| \hat{\gamma}_k |) | \hat{\gamma}_k |, 1)$ for $i = n + 1$. The $rq(\cdot)$ function in R package "quantreg" is helpful to obtain $\{\hat{a}_j, \hat{b}_j, j = 1, 2, \ldots, n\}$. Moreover, for the SCAD penalty, we can apply a difference-of-convex algorithm [22] to the simple computation.

Step 2. Given $\{\hat{a}_j, \hat{b}_j, j = 1, 2, \ldots, n\}$, update $\hat{\gamma}$ by solving

$$
\min_{\gamma} \sum_{j=1}^{n} \sum_{q=1}^{Q} \sum_{i=1}^{n} \rho_{\tau_q}[Y_i - \hat{a}_j - \hat{b}_j(\boldsymbol{X}_i^\top \gamma - \boldsymbol{X}_j^\top \gamma)]w_{ij} + \sum_{j=1}^{n} | \hat{b}_j | \sum_{k=1}^{d} p_\lambda'(| \hat{\gamma}_k |) | \gamma_k |. \tag{13}
$$

We can apply a fast and efficient coordinate descent algorithm [23] if d is very large, or combine the MM algorithm [24] to reduce the calculation.

Step 3. Scale $\hat{\boldsymbol{b}} \leftarrow \text{sgn}(\hat{\gamma}_1) \cdot \| \hat{\gamma} \| \hat{\boldsymbol{b}}$, and $\hat{\gamma} \leftarrow \text{sgn}(\hat{\gamma}_1) \cdot \hat{\gamma} / \| \hat{\gamma} \|$.

Step 4. Continue Step 1–Step 3 until convergence.

Step 5. Given the final estimate $\hat{\gamma}$ from Step 4, we estimate $g(\cdot)$ at any u by $\hat{g}(\cdot, h, \hat{\gamma}) = \hat{a}$, where

$$
(\hat{a}, \hat{b}) = \min_{(a,b)} \sum_{q=1}^{Q} \sum_{i=1}^{n} \rho_{\tau_q}[Y_i - a - b(\boldsymbol{X}_i^\top \hat{\gamma} - u)]k_h(\boldsymbol{X}_i^\top \hat{\gamma} - u). \tag{14}
$$

Remark 1. *The above algorithm is aimed at the SCAD penalty function. Moreover, similarly, we can obtain the other algorithm for the Laplace penalty function, replacing SCAD with LEP.*

2.4. The Selections of Bandwidth, Tuning Parameters, and Initial Value

The selection of the bandwidth plays a crucially important role in local polynomial smoothing because it controls the curvature of the fitted function. The cross-validation (CV) and the generalized cross-validation (GCV) can be utilized to choose a proper bandwidth, but these methods are not computationally practical due to the large calculation amounts. For the local linear quantile regression, [25] obtained an approximate optimal bandwidth under some suitable assumptions and found the rule-of-thumb bandwidth: $h_\tau = h_m\{\tau(1 - \tau)/\psi^2(\Phi^{-1}(\tau))\}^{1/5}$, where $\psi(\cdot)$ and $\Phi(\cdot)$ are the probability density function and the cumulative distribution function of the normal distribution, respectively; h_m is the optimal bandwidth of the least squares regression. There are many algorithms for the selection of h_m. [26] found that the rule-of-thumb bandwidth: $h_m = \{4/(d+2)\}^{1/(4+d)}n^{-1/(4+d)}$ in the single-index models acts fairly well, where d is the dimension of the kernel function. We combined a multiplier only consisting of τ with the optimal bandwidth h_m of the LS regression to obtain a h_τ with good characters.

There are several kinds of selection methods for SCAD's nonnegative tuning parameter λ, such as CV, GCV, AIC, BIC, and so on. Following [27], we utilized the BIC criterion to choose a proper tuning parameter of SCAD in this paper

$$\text{BIC}(\lambda) = \frac{1}{\widetilde{\sigma}} \sum_{i=1}^{n} \sum_{q=1}^{Q} \rho_{\tau_q}[Y_i - g(\boldsymbol{X}_i^\top \widehat{\gamma}(\lambda))] + log(n) \cdot df/2, \tag{15}$$

where $\widetilde{\sigma} = (1/n) \sum_{i=1}^{n} \sum_{q=1}^{Q} \rho_{\tau_q}[Y_i - g(\boldsymbol{X}_i^\top \widetilde{\gamma})]$ with $\widetilde{\gamma}$ being the composite quantile estimator without penalty and df is the number of non-zero coefficients of $\widehat{\gamma}(\lambda)$. Then, we chose the optimal tuning parameter by minimizing the above criteria. Moreover, for LEP, we utilized the extended Bayesian information criterion (EBIC) [28]to choose proper tuning parameters λ and κ.

$$\text{EBIC}(\lambda, \kappa) = log(\widehat{\sigma}^2) + \frac{log(n) + loglog(d)}{n} df \tag{16}$$

where $\widehat{\sigma}^2 = 1/(n-1) \sum_{i=1}^{n} \sum_{q=1}^{Q} \rho_{\tau_q}[Y_i - g(\boldsymbol{X}_i^\top \widehat{\gamma})]$ and df is the number of non-zero coefficients of $\widehat{\gamma}(\lambda, \kappa)$. Similarly, in order to select the best tuning parameters, we minimized the above criteria in the arrangement of λ values.

The initial value of the unknown parameter is required at the beginning of the iteration of our algorithm. A convenient choice is $\widehat{\gamma}/\parallel \widehat{\gamma} \parallel$ where $\widehat{\gamma}$ is the composite quantile estimator without penalty.

3. Theoretical Properties

A good estimate is supposed to satisfy unbiasedness, continuity, and the so-called oracle property. Thus, in this section, we discuss the large sample properties of the SCAD penalized composite quantile regression and the Laplace penalized composite quantile regression for single-index models. We consider the data $\{(\boldsymbol{X}_i, Y_i), i = 1, 2, \ldots, n\}$ including n observations from model (1), such as Section 2. Moreover, let $\boldsymbol{X}_i = (\boldsymbol{X}_{i1}^\top, \boldsymbol{X}_{i2}^\top)^\top$, $\gamma = (\gamma_1^\top, \gamma_2^\top)^\top$, $\boldsymbol{X}_{i1} \in \Re^s$, $\boldsymbol{X}_{i2} \in \Re^{d-s}$. In addition, $\gamma_0 = (\gamma_{10}^\top, \gamma_{20}^\top)^\top$ stands for the true regression parameters of model (1) and $\parallel \gamma_0 \parallel = 1$, where the s components in γ_{10} are not zero. We suppose the following regularity conditions to hold:

(i)   The density function of $\boldsymbol{X}^\top \gamma$ is positive and uniformly continuous for γ in a neighborhood of γ_0. Further, the density of $\boldsymbol{X}^\top \gamma_0$ is continuous and bounded away from 0 and ∞ on its support D.

(ii) The function $g(\cdot)$ has a continuous and bounded second derivative in D.

(iii) The kernel function $k(\cdot)$ is a symmetric density function with bounded support and a bounded first derivative.

(iv) The density function $f_Y(\cdot)$ of Y is continuous and has a bounded derivative; it is bounded away from 0 and ∞ on compact support.

(v)   The following expectations exist:

$$C_0 = E\{g'(\boldsymbol{X}^\top \gamma_0)^2 [\boldsymbol{X} - E(\boldsymbol{X}|\boldsymbol{X}^\top \gamma_0)][\boldsymbol{X} - E(\boldsymbol{X}|\boldsymbol{X}^\top \gamma_0)]^\top\}$$
$$C_1 = E\{f_Y(g(\boldsymbol{X}^\top \gamma_0))g'(\boldsymbol{X}^\top \gamma_0)^2 [\boldsymbol{X} - E(\boldsymbol{X}|\boldsymbol{X}^\top \gamma_0)][\boldsymbol{X} - E(\boldsymbol{X}|\boldsymbol{X}^\top \gamma_0)]^\top\}$$

(vi) $h \to 0$ and $nh \to \infty$.

Given $(\widehat{a}_j, \widehat{b}_j)$, let $H = \sum_{j=1}^{n} | \widehat{b}_j |$, $a_n = \max\{P_\lambda'(\gamma_{0j}) : \gamma_{0j} \neq 0\}$ and $\widehat{\gamma}^{qr.sim.scad}$ be the solution of (7). We should note that under condition (ii), the first derivative is bounded. Thus, $H = O(n)$.

Theorem 1. *Under the conditions (i)–(v). If* $\max\{P_\lambda''(| \gamma_{0k} |) : \gamma_{0k} \neq 0\} \to 0$ *and* $a_n = O(n^{-1/2})$, *then there exists a local minimizer in (7) such that* $\parallel \widehat{\gamma}^{qr.sim.scad} - \gamma_0 \parallel = O_P(n^{-1/2} + a_n)$ *with* $\parallel \widehat{\gamma}^{qr.sim.scad} \parallel = \parallel \gamma_0 \parallel = 1$.

According to Theorem 1, we show that there exists a $\sqrt{n}$-consistent SCAD penalized composite quantile regression estimate for γ if a proper tuning parameter λ is selected. Let $c_n = \{p'_\lambda(|\gamma_{01}|)\,\mathrm{sgn}(\gamma_{01}),\ldots,p'_\lambda(|\gamma_{0s}|)\,\mathrm{sgn}(\gamma_{0s})\}^\top$, and $\Sigma_\lambda = \mathrm{diag}(p''_\lambda(|\gamma_{01}|),\ldots,p''_\lambda(|\gamma_{0s}|))$.

Lemma 1. *Under the same conditions as in Theorem 1. Assume that*

$$\liminf_{n\to+\infty}\liminf_{\theta\to 0^+} p'_{\lambda_n}(\theta/\lambda_n) > 0. \tag{17}$$

If $\lambda \to 0$ and $\sqrt{H}\lambda \to \infty$ as $n \to \partial$, then with probability tending to 1, for any given $\widehat{\gamma}_1$ satisfying $\|\widehat{\gamma}_1 - \gamma_{10}\| = O_P(n^{-1/2})$, and any constant C, we have

$$Q^S_\lambda((\gamma_1^\top, \mathbf{0}^\top)^\top) = \min_{\|\gamma_2\| \le Cn^{-1/2}} Q^S_\lambda((\gamma_1^\top, \gamma_2^\top)^\top). \tag{18}$$

Theorem 2. *Under the same conditions as in Theorem 1—assume that the penalty function $p_\lambda(|\theta|)$ satisfies condition (17). If $\lambda \to 0$ and $\sqrt{H}\lambda \to \infty$, then with the probability tending to 1, the $\sqrt{n}$-consistent local minimizer $\widehat{\gamma}^{qr.sim.scad} = ((\widehat{\gamma}_1^{qr.sim.scad})^\top, (\widehat{\gamma}_2^{qr.sim.scad})^\top)^\top$ in Theorem 1 must satisfy:*
(i) Sparsity: $\widehat{\gamma}_2^{qr.sim.scad} = 0$.
(ii) Asymptotic normality:

$$\sqrt{n}\{(QC_{11} + H\textstyle\sum_\lambda /n)(\widehat{\gamma}_1^{qr.sim.scad} - \gamma_{10}) + Hc_n/n\} \xrightarrow{D} N(0, 0.2C_{01}),$$

where C_{11} is the top-left s-by-s sub-matrix of C_1 and C_{01} is the top-left s-by-s sub-matrix of C_0.

Theorem 2 shows that the SCAD penalized composite quantile regression estimator has the so-called oracle property when $\lambda \to 0$ and $\sqrt{H}\lambda \to \infty$.

Remark 2. *In this section, we discuss the large sample properties of the SCAD penalized composite quantile estimator ($\widehat{\gamma}^{qr.sim.scad}$) in detail. Similarly, we can also show the large sample properties of the Laplace penalized composite quantile estimator ($\widehat{\gamma}^{qr.sim.lep}$).*

4. Numerical Studies

4.1. Simulation Studies

In this section, we evaluate the proposed estimator by simulation studies. We compare the performances of different penalized estimators with the oracle estimator. Specially, in order to reduce the burden of computation and simplify the calculation, we take the Gaussian kernel as the kernel function in our simulations. Moreover, we do not tune the value of the parameter a and set $a = 3.7$, which is suggested by [12] for the SCAD penalty. Moreover, we set the quantile number: $Q = 5$. Next, we compare the performances of the following four estimates for the single-index model:

- lad.sim.scad: the LAD estimators with the SCAD penalty;
- cqr.sim.scad: the composite quantile estimators with the SCAD penalty;
- cqr.sim.lep: the composite quantile estimators with the SCAD penalty;
- Oracle: the oracle estimators (composite quantile regression without penalty under the true model).

In order to evaluate the performances of the above estimators, we consider the following criteria:

- MAD (the mean absolute deviation) of $\widehat{\gamma}$: $\mathrm{MAD} = \frac{1}{n}\sum_{i=1}^{n} |X_i^\top \widehat{\gamma} - X_i^\top \gamma_0|$.
- NC: the average number of non-zero coefficients that are correctly estimated to be non-zero.
- NIC: the average number of zero coefficients that are incorrectly estimated to be non-zero, respectively.

Additionally, an estimated coefficient is viewed as 0 if its absolute value is smaller than 10^{-6}.

Scenario 1. We assume that the single-index model has the following form:

$$Y = 2\boldsymbol{X}^\top \gamma_0 + 10 \exp(-(\boldsymbol{X}^\top \gamma_0)^2 / 5) + \epsilon,$$

where $\gamma_0 = \gamma / \parallel \gamma \parallel$ with $\gamma = (1, -1, 2, -0.5, 0, \ldots, 0)^\top$ being a 15-dimensional vector with only four non-zero values (the true coefficients). The X-variables are generated from the multivariate normal distribution and set the correlation between X_i and X_j to be $0.5^{|i-j|}$ and the Y-variable is generated from the above model. Then, to eliminate the impacts of different error distributions, we consider the following five error distributions:

- $N(0,1)$: the standard normal distribution (N);
- $t(3)$: the t-distribution with 3 degrees of freedom;
- DE: the double exponential distribution with media 0 and scale parameter $1/\sqrt{2}$;
- CN: the polluted normal distribution $0.9N(0,1) + 0.1N(0,25)$ (CN);
- *Outlier*: an outlier case is considered, in which 10% of the responses are shifted with a constant $c = 5$.

In order to perform the simulations, we generated 200 replicates with moderate sample sizes, $n = 100, 200$. Then, the corresponding results are reported in Table 1.

Table 1. Simulation results for Scenario 1 based on 200 replications.

Error Distribution	Method	$n = 100$			$n = 200$		
		MAD (%)	NC	NIC	MAD (%)	NC	NIC
$N(0,1)$	lad.sim.scad	11.65	3.96	3.53	7.63	4.00	1.57
	cqr.sim.scad	11.61	3.93	3.45	7.60	4.00	1.54
	cqr.sim.lep	11.59	3.91	3.44	7.58	4.00	1.53
	Oracle	11.57	3.90	3.42	7.56	4.00	1.51
$t(3)$	lad.sim.scad	13.72	3.90	3.73	9.25	3.99	1.99
	cqr.sim.scad	13.70	3.95	3.70	9.21	4.00	1.94
	cqr.sim.lep	13.68	3.96	3.68	9.18	4.00	1.93
	Oracle	13.67	3.98	3.67	9.15	4.00	1.91
DE	lad.sim.scad	8.79	3.97	3.20	5.69	4.00	1.76
	cqr.sim.scad	8.76	3.97	3.08	5.65	4.00	1.76
	cqr.sim.lep	8.74	3.98	3.05	5.63	4.00	1.76
	Oracle	8.72	3.99	3.00	5.61	4.00	1.76
CN	lad.sim.scad	16.65	3.82	2.83	10.78	3.94	1.55
	cqr.sim.scad	16.63	3.85	2.80	10.75	3.95	1.53
	cqr.sim.lep	16.62	3.87	2.78	10.74	3.97	1.52
	Oracle	16.61	3.89	2.77	10.71	3.98	1.50
Outlier	lad.sim.scad	13.76	3.95	2.84	10.24	3.97	1.84
	cqr.sim.scad	13.74	3.96	2.83	10.23	3.97	1.81
	cqr.sim.lep	13.73	3.97	2.82	10.22	3.98	1.80
	Oracle	13.72	3.98	2.81	10.20	3.99	1.78

MAD (the mean absolute deviation) of $\widehat{\gamma}$: MAD $= \frac{1}{n} \sum_{i=1}^{n} | X_i^\top \widehat{\gamma} - X_i^\top \gamma_0 |$; NC: the average number of non-zero coefficients that are correctly estimated to be non-zero; NIC: the average number of zero coefficients that are incorrectly estimated to be non-zero, respectively.

Scenario 2. The model set-up is similar to Example 1, except the link function is $\boldsymbol{X}^\top \gamma_0 + 4\sqrt{| \boldsymbol{X}^\top \gamma_0 + 1 |}$. These link functions are also analyzed by [20]. Then, Table 2 summarizes the corresponding results.

Table 2. Simulation results for Scenario 2 based on 200 replications.

Error Distribution	Method	$n = 100$			$n = 200$		
		MAD (%)	NC	NIC	MAD (%)	NC	NIC
$N(0,1)$	lad.sim.scad	9.90	3.98	3.27	8.26	4.00	1.41
	cqr.sim.scad	9.84	3.98	3.24	8.19	4.00	1.35
	cqr.sim.lep	9.81	3.99	3.23	8.16	4.00	1.34
	Oracle	9.79	3.90	3.21	8.14	4.00	1.32
$t(3)$	lad.sim.scad	12.15	3.97	3.41	8.57	4.00	1.72
	cqr.sim.scad	12.08	3.98	3.36	8.51	4.00	1.68
	cqr.sim.lep	12.05	3.99	3.34	8.50	4.00	1.67
	Oracle	12.03	3.88	3.32	8.47	4.00	1.64
DE	lad.sim.scad	7.63	4.00	3.16	4.97	4.00	2.18
	cqr.sim.scad	7.56	4.00	3.13	4.94	4.00	2.11
	cqr.sim.lep	7.54	4.00	3.11	4.92	4.00	2.08
	Oracle	7.51	4.00	3.09	4.89	4.00	2.06
CN	lad.sim.scad	12.02	3.95	3.06	11.31	3.97	1.24
	cqr.sim.scad	11.97	3.96	3.03	11.26	3.97	1.21
	cqr.sim.lep	11.96	3.98	3.02	11.25	3.98	1.18
	Oracle	11.93	3.86	2.97	11.23	3.88	1.15
$Outlier$	lad.sim.scad	11.95	3.95	3.18	9.47	4.00	1.62
	cqr.sim.scad	11.92	3.96	3.15	9.42	4.00	1.59
	cqr.sim.lep	11.89	3.98	3.13	9.41	4.00	1.58
	Oracle	11.86	3.87	3.10	9.39	4.00	1.55

MAD (the mean absolute deviation) of $\hat{\gamma}$: MAD $= \frac{1}{n} \sum_{i=1}^{n} | X_i^{\top} \hat{\gamma} - X_i^{\top} \gamma_0 |$; NC: the average number of non-zero coefficients that are correctly estimated to be non-zero; NIC: the average number of zero coefficients that are incorrectly estimated to be non-zero, respectively.

From Tables 1 and 2, we can note that the performance of cqr.sim.lep is best, cqr.sim.scad is second, and lad.sim.scad is the worst for five different error distributions. This is consistent with our theoretical findings. Furthermore, with the sample size increasing, all estimators become better.

4.2. Real Data Application: Boston Housing Data

In this section, the methods are illustrated through an analysis of Boston housing data. The data (506 observations and 14 variables) are available in the package ('MASS') in R, and the definitions of the dependent variable (MEDV) and explanatory variables are described in Table 3. We checked whether there were missing values in the data through the violin diagram of each variable. Figures 1 and 2 show the violins between the first and last seven variables, respectively. It is obvious from Figures 1 and 2 that there are obvious outliers in CRIM and Black columns. In order to test the linear relationship among variables, the heat map between the variables is given in Figure 3. It can be seen from the heat map that variables RM, Ptratio, lstat, and MEDV have certain correlations. The correlation coefficients between Indus and nox, CRIM and RAD, RAD and tax, and Indus and tax were 0.7, 0.8, 0.9, and 0.7, respectively. Therefore, there was a high correlation between variables, so the single-index regression model could be considered.

Boston housing data have been utilized by many regression studies; the potential relationship between MEDV and X-variables was also founded [10,17]. For the single-index quantile regression, [10] introduced a practical algorithm where the unknown link function $g(\cdot)$ is estimated by local linear quantile regression and the parametric index was estimated through linear quantile regression. However, the authors did not consider the variable selection. For the single-index regression models, [17] considered the penalized LAD regression, which dealt with variable selection and estimation simultaneously. However, the LAD estimator is only the special case of the quantile estimator in which the quantile τ

is equal to 0.5. Moreover, the two literature studies mentioned above only used the case of a single quantile. In this article, we constructed new sparse estimators for single-index quantile regression models based on the composite quantile regression method combined with the SCAD penalty and Laplace error penalty.

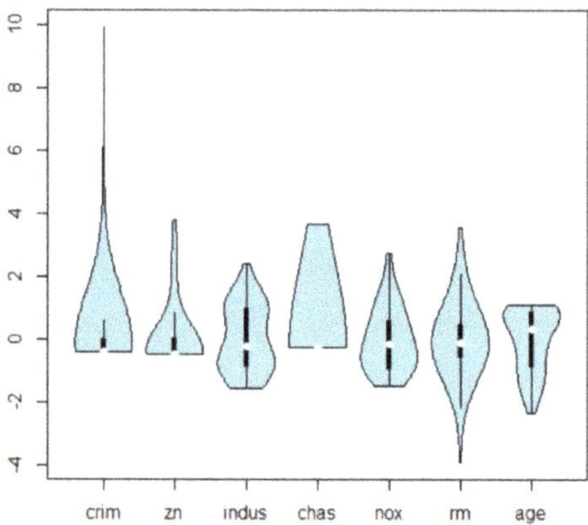

Figure 1. Violin diagram of the first seven variables.

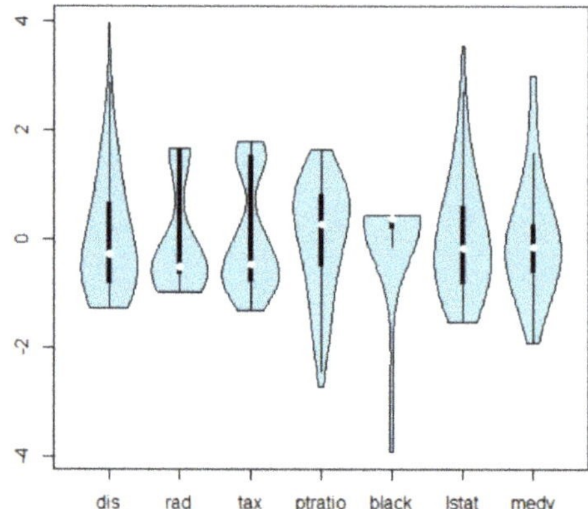

Figure 2. Violin diagram of the last seven variables.

Due to the sparsity of data in the region concerned, possible quantile curves cross at both tails similar to [14]. The results of the real data example and simulation studies confirm the reasonableness and effectiveness of our method in practice.

In order to better numerical performance, we need to standardize the response variable MEDV and the predictor variables except CHAS before applying our method. The estimated coefficient is treated as 0 if its absolute value is smaller than 10^{-12}. Then, the corresponding results are reported in Table 4.

From Table 4, we see that all methods can achieve the variable selection and parameter estimation simultaneously in the real problem. Moreover, all methods choose the sparse model including RM, DIS, PTRATIO, LSTAT, the same as the one using all predictors without penalty (cqr.sim). Moreover, the estimation of cqr.sim.lep is the closest to cqr.sim. These results indicate that only four explanatory variables are significant and the rest are irrelevant.

Table 3. Description of variables for Boston housing data.

Variables	Description
MEDV	Median value of owner-occupied homes in USD thousands
CRIM	Per capita crime rate by town
ZN	Proportion of residential land zoned for lots over 25,000 sq.ft.
INDUS	Proportion of non-retail business acres per town
CHAS	Charles River dummy variable (=1 if tract bounds river, 0 otherwise)
NOX	Nitric oxide concentrations (parts per 10 million)
RM	Average number of rooms per dwelling
AGE	Proportion of owner-occupied units built prior to 1940
DIS	Weighted distances to five Boston employment centers
RAD	Index of accessibility to radial highways
TAX	Full-value property-tax rate per USD 10,000
PTRATIO	Pupil–teacher ratio by town
B	$1000(Bk - 0.63)^2$ which Bk is the black proportion of the population
LSTAT	% lower status of the population

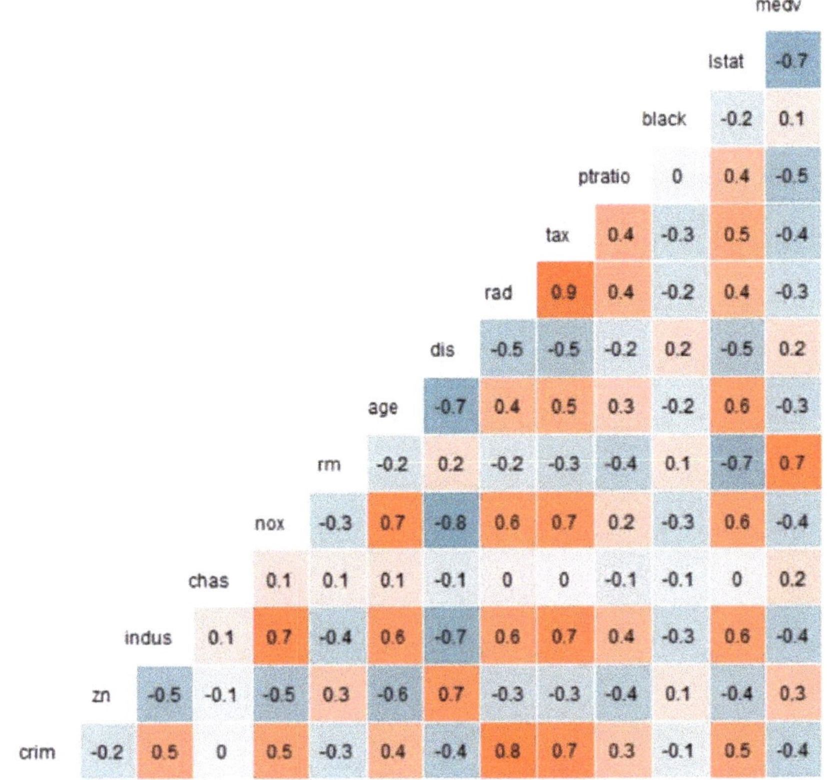

Figure 3. Heat map between the variables.

Table 4. Coefficient estimates for Boston housing data.

Variables	Methods							
	cqr.sim.scad		cqr.sim.lep		lad.sim.scad	ls.sim.lasso	cqr.sim	
	$\tau = 0.25$	$\tau = 0.75$	$\tau = 0.25$	$\tau = 0.75$	$\tau = 0.5$		$\tau = 0.25$	$\tau = 0.75$
CRIM	0.3092	0.3089	0.3082	0.3081	0.3083	0	0.3076	0.3075
ZN	0	0	0	0	0	−0.069	0	0
INDUS	0	0	0	0	0	0	0	0
CHAS	0	0	0	0	0	0	0	0
NOX	0	0	0	0	0	0	0	0
RM	−0.1884	−0.1883	−0.1871	−0.1870	−0.1872	−0.5300	−0.1866	−0.1864
AGE	0	0	0	0	0	0	0	0
DIS	0.1453	0.1451	0.1443	0.1442	0.1444	0.1163	0.1439	0.1437
RAD	0	0	0	0	0	−0.0460	0	0
TAX	0	0	0	0	0	0	0	0
PTRATIO	0.1877	0.1876	0.1870	0.1868	0.1871	0.1069	0.1865	0.1863
B	0	0	0	0	0	0	0	0
LSTAT	0.9042	0.9040	0.9031	0.9029	0.9032	0.8319	0.9024	0.9023

5. Conclusions

In this article, we propose SCAD and Laplace penalized composite quantile regression estimators for single-index models in a high-dimensional case. Compared with the least squares method, composite quantile regression can obtain the robust estimator with respect to heavy-tailed error distributions and outliers. Then, a practical iterative algorithm was introduced. It is based on composite quantile regression and uses local linear smoothing to estimate the unknown link function. This method realizes parameter selection and estimation simultaneously by combining two kinds of penalty functions with the composite quantile regression. In addition, we proved that the proposed estimator has large sample properties, including $\sqrt{n}$-consistence and the oracle property. Furthermore, the estimator was evaluated and illustrated by numerical studies. Moreover, we can draw the conclusion from Boston housing data: the sparse model with the same significant variables was selected by all three estimation methods; however, the estimators of cqr.sim.lep were the closest to that of cqr.sim. This reveals that using—or not using—the LEP penalty essentially acts the same when we estimate the link function.

Author Contributions: Formal analysis, Z.L.; Methodology, Y.S.; Software, M.F. All authors have read and agreed to the published version of the manuscript.

Funding: This research was supported by the NNSF project (61503412) of China and the NSF project (ZR2019MA016) of the Shandong Province of China.

Institutional Review Board Statement: Not applicable.

Informed Consent Statement: Not applicable.

Data Availability Statement: Not applicable.

Conflicts of Interest: The authors declare no conflict of interest.

Appendix A. Proof of Theorems

Proof of Theorem 1. Given $(\widehat{a}_j, \widehat{b}_j)$, we need to definite other symbols before proving. Let $\alpha_n = n^{-1/2} + a_n$, $Y_{ij} = Y_i - \widehat{a}_j - \widehat{b}_j X_{ij}^\top \gamma_0$, $X_{ij} = X_i - X_j$, $\gamma = \alpha_n u + \gamma_0$ where u is a d-dimensional vector, $S(u) = \sum_{i,j,q} \rho_{\tau_q} [Y_{ij} - \alpha_n \widehat{b}_j X_{ij}^\top u] w_{ij} - \sum_{i,j,q} \rho_{\tau_q} (Y_{ij}) w_{ij}$ and set $\| u \| = C$ where C is a large enough constant.

Our purpose is to prove that $\widehat{\gamma}^{qr.sim.scad}$ is $\sqrt{n}$-consistent; that is, to show that for any given $\epsilon > 0$ and large n, there is a large enough constant C, such that

$$P\{\inf_{\|u\|=C} Q_\lambda^S(\gamma_0 + \alpha_n u) > Q_\lambda^S(\gamma_0)\} \geq 1 - \epsilon, \tag{A1}$$

which implies that there exists a local minimum $\widehat{\gamma}$ in the ball $\{\alpha_n u + \gamma_0 : \| u \| \leq C\}$, such that $\| \widehat{\gamma} - \gamma_0 \| = O_p(\alpha_n)$ with probability of at least $1 - \epsilon$.
Let

$$D_n(u) = Q_\lambda^S(\alpha_n u + \gamma_0) - Q_\lambda^S(\gamma_0)$$

$$\geq S(u) + H \sum_{k=1}^s [p_\lambda(| \alpha_n u_k + \gamma_{0k} |) - p_\lambda(| \gamma_{0k} |)] \tag{A2}$$

$$=: I + \mathrm{II}$$

First, we consider I and partition it into I_1 and I_2. We have

$$I = \sum_{i,j,q} \rho_{\tau_q}[Y_{ij} - \widehat{b}_j X_{ij}^\top \alpha_n u]w_{ij} - \sum_{i,j,q} \rho_{\tau_q}(Y_{ij})w_{ij}$$

$$= \sum_{i,j,q} w_{ij}\{\widehat{b}_j X_{ij}^\top \alpha_n u [I(Y_{ij} < \widehat{b}_j X_{ij}^\top \alpha_n u) - \tau_q]\} + \sum_{i,j} Qw_{ij}Y_{ij}I(\widehat{b}_j X_{ij}^\top \alpha_n u < Y_{ij} < 0) \tag{A3}$$

$$= I_1 + I_2$$

Obviously,

$$\| I_1 \| \leq \| \sum_{i,j} Qw_{ij}\widehat{b}_j X_{ij}^\top \alpha_n u \|$$

$$= \sqrt{n}\alpha_n \| u \| \| \sum_{i,j} Qw_{ij}\widehat{b}_j X_{ij}^\top / \sqrt{n} \| \tag{A4}$$

Note that $\| \sum_{i,j} Qw_{ij}\widehat{b}_j X_{ij}^\top / \sqrt{n} \| = O_P(1)$, which can refer to the proof of Theorem 2 of [10]. Therefore, we can obtain that $\| I_1 \| = O_P(\sqrt{n}\alpha_n) \| u \| = O_P(n\alpha_n^2) \| u \|$. Then, we can obtain the mean and variance of I_2 by direct computation.

$$EI_2 = \sum_{i,j} Qw_{ij} \int_{-\infty}^{+\infty} Y_{ij} \cdot I(\widehat{b}_j X_{ij}^\top \alpha_n u < Y_{ij} < 0) \cdot f_{Y_{ij}}(y)dy$$

$$= \sum_{i,j} Qw_{ij} \int_{\widehat{b}_j X_{ij}^\top \alpha_n u}^{0} Y_{ij} \cdot f_{Y_{ij}}(y)dy$$

$$= \sum_{i,j} Qw_{ij} \cdot P(\widehat{b}_j X_{ij}^\top \alpha_n u < Y_{ij} < 0) \tag{A5}$$

$$= \sum_{ij} Qw_{ij}P_{ij}$$

where $f_{Y_{ij}}(\cdot)$ is the probability density function of Y_{ij}, P_{ij} stands for $P(\widehat{b}_j X_{ij}^\top \alpha_n u < Y_{ij} < 0)$. Note that $EI_2 > 0$, furthermore, $EI_2 \to 0$. Moreover,

$$Var(I_2) = \sum_{i,j} Qw_{ij} \cdot E[Y_{ij} \cdot I(\widehat{b}_j X_{ij}^\top \alpha_n u < Y_{ij} < 0) - P_{ij}]^2$$

$$\leq \sum_{i,j} Qw_{ij} \max_{i,j} | Y_{ij} | P_{ij} - P_{ij}^2 \tag{A6}$$

$$= \sum_{i,j} Qw_{ij}P_{ij}[\max_{i,j} | Y_{ij} | - P_{ij}] \to 0$$

In addition, by taking Taylor's expansion for $P_\lambda(|\gamma_k|)$ and the basic inequality, we obtain that,

$$\mathrm{II} = H \sum_{k=1}^{s} [P_\lambda(|\gamma_{0k} + \alpha_n u_k|) - P_\lambda(|\gamma_{0k}|)]$$

$$= H \sum_{k=1}^{s} [\alpha_n P'_\lambda(|\gamma_{0k}|)\mathrm{sgn}(\mathrm{fl}_{0k})u_k + 0.5\mathrm{ff}_n^2 P''_\lambda(|\mathrm{fl}_{0k}|)u_k^2] \tag{A7}$$

$$\leq \sqrt{s}H\alpha_n a_n \| u \| + H \max_{1 \leq k \leq s} P''_\lambda(|\gamma_{0k}|)\alpha_n^2 \| u \|^2$$

According to the condition $H = O_P(n)$, $\max\{P''_\lambda(|\gamma_{0k}|) : \gamma_{0k} \neq 0\} \to 0$, and $\| u \| = C$, $D_n(u)$ in (A2) is mainly determined by I_2, which is positive. Thus, we prove (A1). $\square$

Proof of Lemma 1. Due to $\gamma = \alpha_n u + \gamma_0$, let $u_1 = \alpha_n^{-1}(\gamma_1 - \gamma_{01}), u_2 = \alpha_n^{-1}(\gamma_2 - \gamma_{02})$, $u = (u_1^\top, u_2^\top)^\top$. After the computation, we obtain

$$Q_\lambda^S((\gamma_1^\top, 0^\top)^\top) - Q_\lambda^S((\gamma_1^\top, \gamma_2^\top)^\top)$$

$$= S((u_1^\top, 0^\top)^\top) - S((u_1^\top, u_2^\top)^\top) - H \sum_{k=s+1}^{d} P_\lambda(|\gamma_k|) \tag{A8}$$

According to the proof of Theorem 1 and $\| u \| = O(1)$, we have $\| I_1 \| = O_P(n\alpha_n^2)$ and $I_2 = O_P(1)$; thus, we prove that $\| S((u_1^\top, u_2^\top)^\top) \| = \| I \| = O_P(1)$. Similarly, $\| S((u_1^\top, 0^\top)^\top) \| = O_P(1)$. By the mean value theorem and $P_\lambda(0) = 0$, we can obtain the following inequality

$$H \sum_{k=s+1}^{d} P_\lambda(|\gamma_k|) = H \sum_{k=s+1}^{d} P'_\lambda(|\gamma_k^*|)|\gamma_k|$$

$$\geq H\lambda(\liminf_{\lambda \to 0} \liminf_{\theta \to 0^+}(P'_\lambda(\theta/\lambda))) \sum_{k=s+1}^{d} |\gamma_k| \tag{A9}$$

where $0 < |\gamma_k^*| < |\gamma_k|$ $(k = s+1, \ldots, d)$. We can obtain that $H\lambda = \sqrt{H}(\sqrt{H}\lambda)$ is of higher order than $O(\sqrt{H})$ because of the condition $\sqrt{H}\lambda \to \infty$, which implies that the last term of (A8) dominates in magnitude. As a result, $Q_\lambda^S((\gamma_1^\top, 0^\top)^\top) - Q_\lambda^S((\gamma_1^\top, \gamma_2^\top)^\top) < 0$ for large n. This proves **Lemma 1.** $\square$

Proof of Theorem 2.
(i) Follows from Lemma 1.
(ii) By partitioning the vectors $u = (u_1^\top, u_2^\top)^\top$, $P_\lambda(0) = 0$ and (A2), we have

$$D_n((u_1^\top, 0^\top)^\top) = S((u_1^\top, 0^\top)^\top) + H \sum_{k=1}^{s} [P_\lambda(|\gamma_{0k} + \alpha_n u_k|) - P_\lambda(|\gamma_{0k}|)]$$

$$= S((u_1^\top, 0^\top)^\top) + P_\lambda(u_1) \tag{A10}$$

where $P_\lambda(u_1) = H \sum_{k=1}^{s}[P_\lambda(|\gamma_{0k} + \alpha_n u_k|) - P_\lambda(|\gamma_{0k}|)]$. Moreover, by Taylor's expansion and calculation, $P_\lambda(u_1)$ can be rewritten as

$$P_\lambda(u_1) = H\alpha_n c_n^\top u_1 + \frac{1}{2}H\alpha_n^2 u_1^\top \sum\nolimits_\lambda u_1 \tag{A11}$$

Let

$$\delta^* = \widehat{a}_j + \widehat{b}_j X_{1ij}^\top(\gamma_{01} + \alpha_n \widehat{u}_1)$$

$$\delta_1^* = \widehat{a}_j + \widehat{b}_j X_{1ij}^\top \gamma_{01}$$

In order to find the minimized $\widehat{u}_1$ of $D_n((u_1^\top, 0^\top)^\top)$, we compute the derivation of it and set $D_n'((u_1^\top, 0^\top)^\top) = 0$. Thus, we obtain the following equation.

$$-\sum_{i,j,q} w_{ij}\widehat{b}_j X_{1ij}\alpha_n[\tau_q - I(Y_i - \widehat{a}_j - \widehat{b}_j X_{1ij}^\top(\gamma_{01} + \alpha_n\widehat{u}_1) < 0)] + H\alpha_n c_n + H\alpha_n^2 \sum_\lambda \widehat{u}_1 = 0 \tag{A12}$$

That is,

$$-\frac{1}{n}\sum_{i,j,q}\widehat{b}_j X_{1ij}w_{ij}[I(Y_i < \delta^*) - \tau_q] = \frac{1}{n}[Hc_n + H\alpha_n \sum_\lambda \widehat{u}_1] \tag{A13}$$

Let

$$Z_1 = n^{-1/2}\sum_{i,j,q}\widehat{b}_j X_{1ij}w_{ij}[I(Y_i < \delta_1^*) - \tau_q]$$

$$B_1 = n^{-1}\sum_{i,j,q}\widehat{b}_j X_{1ij}w_{ij}[F_Y(\delta_1^*) - F_Y(\delta^*)]$$

$$B_2 = n^{-1}\sum_{i,j,q}\widehat{b}_j X_{1ij}w_{ij}\{[I(Y_i < \delta_1^*) - I(Y_i < \delta^*)] - [F_Y(\delta_1^*) - F_Y(\delta^*)]\}$$

where $F_Y(\cdot)$ is the cumulative distribution function of Y. Therefore, we have

$$-\frac{1}{n}\sum_{i,j,q}\widehat{b}_j X_{1ij}w_{ij}[I(Y_i < \delta^*) - \tau_q] = -\frac{1}{\sqrt{n}}Z_1 + B_1 + B_2 \tag{A14}$$

By taking the Taylor's expansion for $F_Y(\cdot)$, we can obtain that

$$B_1 = -Q\alpha_n n^{-1}\sum_{i,j}\widehat{b}_j^2 f_Y(\delta_1^*)w_{ij}X_{1ij}X_{1ij}^\top\widehat{u}_1$$
$$\to -Q\alpha_n C_{11}\widehat{u}_1 \tag{A15}$$

where $f_Y(\cdot)$ is the probability density function of Y. According to the direct calculation of the mean and variance in [15], we have $B_2 = o_P(\frac{Q}{\sqrt{n}}) = o_P(\frac{1}{\sqrt{n}})$. Moreover, combing (A14), (A15) and $\widehat{u}_1 = \alpha_n^{-1}(\widehat{\gamma}_1 - \gamma_{01})$, (A13) can be rewritten in the following form:

$$\sqrt{n}\{(QC_{11} + \frac{H}{n}\sum_\lambda)(\widehat{\gamma}_1 - \gamma_{01}) + \frac{H}{n}c_n\} = -Z_1 + o_P(\frac{1}{\sqrt{n}}) \tag{A16}$$

Note that $Z_1 \xrightarrow{D} QN(0, 0.25C_{01})$. We can obtain that

$$\sqrt{n}\{(QC_{11} + \frac{H}{n}\sum_\lambda)(\widehat{\gamma}_1 - \gamma_{01}) + \frac{H}{n}c_n\} \xrightarrow{D} N(0, Q^2 0.25C_{01}) \tag{A17}$$

Thus, we prove Theorem 2. $\square$

Remark A1. *Above all, we prove the $\sqrt{n}$-consistency and oracle property for the SCAD penalized composite quantile estimator $\widehat{\gamma}^{qr.sim.scad}$. Similarly, we can also show the same properties for the Laplace penalized composite quantile estimator $\widehat{\gamma}^{qr.sim.lep}$*

Appendix B. The Algorithm Based on LEP

Similar to the SCAD penalty function, by the local linear approximation of LEP and removal of a few irrelevant terms, (8) can be rewritten as

$$\min_{a,b,\|\gamma\|=1}\sum_{j=1}^{n}\sum_{q=1}^{Q}\sum_{i=1}^{n}\rho_{\tau_q}[Y_i - a_j - b_j(X_i^\top\gamma - X_j^\top\gamma)w_{ij} + \sum_{j=1}^{n}|b_j|\sum_{k=1}^{d}p_{\lambda,\kappa}'(|\widehat{\gamma}_k|)|\gamma_k|. \tag{A18}$$

We denote the target function in (A18) by $Q^{S*}_{\lambda,\kappa}(a, b, \gamma)$. Moreover, the iterative algorithm based on LEP is as follows.

Step 0. We obtain an initial estimate of γ. We standardize the initial estimate $\widehat{\gamma}$ such that $\|\gamma\| = 1$ and $\widehat{\gamma}_1 > 0$.

Step 1. Given an estimate $\widehat{\gamma}$, we obtain $\{\widehat{a}_j, \widehat{b}_j, j = 1, 2, \ldots, n\}$ by solving

$$\min_{(a_j, b_j)} \sum_{i=1}^{n} \sum_{q=1}^{Q} \rho_{\tau_q}[Y_i - a_j - b_j(X_i^\top \widehat{\gamma} - X_j^\top \widehat{\gamma})]w_{ij} + |b_j| \sum_{k=1}^{d} p'_{\lambda,\kappa}(|\widehat{\gamma}_k|) |\widehat{\gamma}_k|$$

$$= \min_{(a_j, b_j)} \sum_{i=1}^{n+1} \sum_{q=1}^{Q} \rho[Y_i^* - (A, B)\begin{pmatrix} a_j \\ b_j \end{pmatrix}]w_{ij}^*, \tag{A19}$$

where h is the optimal bandwidth, $(\rho, Y_i^*, A, B, w_{ij}^*) = (\rho_{\tau_q}, Y_i, 1, X_i^\top \widehat{\gamma} - X_j^\top \widehat{\gamma}, w_{ij})$ for $i = 1, 2, \ldots, n$, and $(\rho, Y_i^*, A, B, w_{ij}^*) = (1/Q, 0, 0, \sum_{k=1}^{d} p'_{\lambda,\kappa}(|\widehat{\gamma}_k|) |\widehat{\gamma}_k|, 1)$ for $i = n + 1$.

Step 2. Given $\{\widehat{a}_j, \widehat{b}_j, j = 1, 2, \ldots, n\}$, update $\widehat{\gamma}$ by solving

$$\min_{\gamma} \sum_{j=1}^{n} \sum_{q=1}^{Q} \sum_{i=1}^{n} \rho_{\tau_q}[Y_i - \widehat{a}_j - \widehat{b}_j(X_i^\top \gamma - X_j^\top \gamma)]w_{ij} + \sum_{j=1}^{n} |\widehat{b}_j| \sum_{k=1}^{d} p'_{\lambda,\kappa}(|\widehat{\gamma}_k|) |\gamma_k|. \tag{A20}$$

Step 3. Scale $\widehat{b} \leftarrow \text{sgn}(\widehat{\gamma}_1)\cdot \|\widehat{\gamma}\| \widehat{b}$, and $\widehat{\gamma} \leftarrow \text{sgn}(\widehat{\gamma}_1) \cdot \widehat{\gamma}/\|\widehat{\gamma}\|$.

Step 4. Continue Step 1–Step 3 until convergence.

Step 5. Given the final estimate $\widehat{\gamma}$ from Step 4, we estimate $g(\cdot)$ at any u by $\widehat{g}(\cdot, h, \widehat{\gamma}) = \widehat{a}$, where

$$(\widehat{a}, \widehat{b}) = \min_{(a,b)} \sum_{q=1}^{Q} \sum_{i=1}^{n} \rho_{\tau_q}[Y_i - a - b(X_i^\top \widehat{\gamma} - u)]k_h(X_i^\top \widehat{\gamma} - u). \tag{A21}$$

References

1. Kuruwita, C.N. Variable selection in the single-index quantile regression model with high dimensional covariates. *Commun. Stat.-Simul. Comput.* **2021**, 1–13. [CrossRef]
2. Sara, M.; Amena, U.; Faridoon, K.; Mohammed, N.A.; Mohammed, A.; Sanaa, A. Comparison of weighted lag adaptive LASSO with Autometrics for Covariate Selection and forecasting using time-series data. *Complexity* **2022**, *2022*, 2649205.
3. Kraus, D.; Czado, C. D-vine copula based quantile regression. *Comput. Stat. Data Anal.* **2017**, *110*, 1–18. [CrossRef]
4. Imtiaz, S.; Abdul, G.; Abdollah, A.M. The COVID-19 pandemic and speculation in energy, precious metals, and agricultural futures. *J. Behav. Exp. Financ.* **2021**, *30*, 100498.
5. Mozafari, Z.; Arab Chamjangali, M.; Arashi, M.; Goudarzi, N. Performance of smoothly clipped absolute deviation as a variable selection method in the artificial neural network based QSAR studies. *J. Chemom.* **2021**, *35*, e3338. [CrossRef]
6. Koenker, R.; Basset, G. Regression quanties. *Econometrica* **1978**, *46*, 33–50. [CrossRef]
7. Zou, H.; Yuan, M. Composite quantile regression and the oracle model selection Theory. *Ann. Stat.* **2008**, *36*, 1108–1126. [CrossRef]
8. Cao, Z.; Kang, X.; Wang, M. Doubly robust weighted composite quantile regression based on SCAD-L2. *Can. J. Stat.* **2021**. [CrossRef]
9. Chaudhuri, P.; Doksum, K.; Samarov, A. On average derivative quantile regression. *Ann. Stat.* **1997**, *25*, 715–744. [CrossRef]
10. Wu, T.Z.; Yu, K.; Yu, Y. Single-index quantile regression. *J. Multivar. Anal.* **2010**, *101*, 1607–1621. [CrossRef]
11. Jiang, R.; Yu, K. Single-index composite quantile regression for massive data. *J. Multivar. Anal.* **2020**, *180*, 104669. [CrossRef]
12. Fan, J.; Li, R. Variable selection via nonconcave penalized likelihood and its oracle properties. *J. Am. Stat. Assoc.* **2001**, *96*, 1348–1360. [CrossRef]
13. Zou, H. The adaptive lasso and its oracle properties. *J. Am. Stat. Assoc.* **2006**, *101*, 1418–1429. [CrossRef]
14. Zou, H.; Hastie, T. Regularization and variable selection via the elastic net. *J. R. Stat. Soc.* **2005**, *67*, 301–320. [CrossRef]
15. Fan, J.; Lv, J. A selection overview of variable selection in high dimensional feature space. *Stat. Sin.* **2010**, *20*, 101–148.
16. Kuruwita, C.N. Non-iterative estimation and variable selection in the single-index quantile regression model. *Commun. Stat.-Simul. Comput.* **2016**, *45*, 3615–3628. [CrossRef]
17. Yang, H.; Lv, J.; Guo, C. Penalized LAD regression for single-index models. *Commun. Stat.-Simul. Comput.* **2016**, *45*, 2392–2408. [CrossRef]

18. Wen, C.; Wang, X.; Wang, S. Laplace error penalty-based variable selection in high dimension. *Scand. J. Stat.* **2015**, *42*, 685–700. [CrossRef]
19. Xia, Y.; Tong, H.; Li, W.K. An adaptive estimation of dimension reduction space (with discussion). *J. R. Stat. Soc. Ser. B* **2002**, *64*, 363–410. [CrossRef]
20. Zeng, P.; He, T.; Zhu, Y. A Lasso-type approach for estimation and variable selection in single index moedls. *J. Comput. Graph. Stat.* **2012**, *21*, 92–109. [CrossRef]
21. Zou, H.; Li, R. One-step sparse estimates in nonconcave penalized likelihood models. *Ann. Stat.* **2008**, *36*, 1509–1533. [PubMed]
22. An, L.T.H.; Tao, P.D. Solving a class of linearly constrained indefinite quadratic problems by d.c. algorithms. *J. Glob. Optim.* **1997**, *11*, 253–285.
23. Wu, T.T.; Lange, K. Coordinate descent algorithms for lasso penalized regression. *Ann. Appl. Stat.* **2008**, *2*, 224–244. [CrossRef]
24. Hunter, D.R.; Lange, K. Quantile regression via an MM algorithm. *J. Comput. Graph. Stat.* **2000**, *9*, 60–77.
25. Yu, K.; Jones, M. Local linear quantile regression. *J. Am. Stat. Assoc.* **1998**, *93*, 228–237. [CrossRef]
26. Wang, Q.; Yin, X. A nonlinear multi-dimensional variable selection method for high dimensional data: Sparse MAVE. *Comput. Stat. Data Anal.* **2008**, *52*, 4512–4520. [CrossRef]
27. Shows, H.S.; Lu, W.; Zhang, H.H. Sparse estimation and inference for censored median regression. *J. Stat. Plan. Inference* **2010**, *140*, 1903–1917. [CrossRef]
28. Chen, J.; Chen, Z. Extended Bayesian information for model selection with large model spaces. *Biometrika* **2008**, *95*, 759–771. [CrossRef]

 *mathematics*

Article

The FEDHC Bayesian Network Learning Algorithm

Michail Tsagris

Department of Economics, University of Crete, Gallos Campus, 74100 Rethymnon, Greece; mtsagris@uoc.gr

Abstract: The paper proposes a new hybrid Bayesian network learning algorithm, termed Forward Early Dropping Hill Climbing (FEDHC), devised to work with either continuous or categorical variables. Further, the paper manifests that the only implementation of MMHC in the statistical software R is prohibitively expensive, and a new implementation is offered. Further, specifically for the case of continuous data, a robust to outliers version of FEDHC, which can be adopted by other BN learning algorithms, is proposed. The FEDHC is tested via Monte Carlo simulations that distinctly show that it is computationally efficient, and that it produces Bayesian networks of similar to, or of higher accuracy than MMHC and PCHC. Finally, an application of FEDHC, PCHC and MMHC algorithms to real data, from the field of economics, is demonstrated using the statistical software R.

Keywords: causality; Bayesian networks; scalability

MSC: 62H22

Citation: Tsagris, M. The FEDHC Bayesian Network Learning Algorithm. *Mathematics* **2022**, *10*, 2604. https://doi.org/10.3390/math10152604

Academic Editors: Snezhana Gocheva-Ilieva, Atanas Ivanov and Hristina Kulina

Received: 23 May 2022
Accepted: 20 July 2022
Published: 26 July 2022

Publisher's Note: MDPI stays neutral with regard to jurisdictional claims in published maps and institutional affiliations.

1. Introduction

Learning the causal relationships among variables using non-experimental data is of high importance in many scientific fields, such as economics and econometrics (for a general definition of causality specifically in economics and econometrics, see [1]). When the aim is particularly to recreate the causal mechanism that generated the data, graphical models, such as causal networks and Bayesian Networks (BNs) (also known as Bayes networks, belief networks, decision networks, Bayes(ian) models or probabilistic directed acyclic graphical models) are frequently employed. The advantages of BNs include simultaneous variable selection among all variables, and hence, the detection of conditional associations between variables. On a different route, BNs form the scheme for synthetic population generation [2], and have been used synergetically with agent-based models [3,4].

BNs enjoy applications to numerous fields, but the focus of the current paper is on fields related to economics applications, such as production economics [5], macroeconomics [6] and environmental resource economics [7]. Applications of BNs can also be found in financial econometrics [8], banking and finance [9], credit scoring [10], insurance [11] and customer service [12], to name a few. Despite the plethora of applications of BNs, not many BN algorithms exist, and most importantly, fewer are publicly available in free software environments, such as the statistical software R. The Max-Min Hill Climbing (MMHC) [13] is an example of a widely used BN learning algorithm (The relevant paper is one of the classic papers in the Artificial Intelligence field, and has received more than 1870 citations according to scholar.google.com as of July 2022.) that is publicly available, in the R package *bnlearn* [14]. PC Hill Climbing (PCHC) [15] is a recently suggested hybrid algorithm that is also publicly available, in the R package *pchc* [16].

Ref. [15] showed that when the sample size is in the order of hundreds of thousands, MMHC's implementation in the R package *bnlearn* requires more than a day with continuous data, even with 50 variables. On the contrary, PCHC is a computationally efficient and scalable BN learning algorithm [15]. With modern technology and vast data generation, the computational cost is a considerable parameter. Every novel algorithm must be computationally efficient and scalable to large sample sizes. Seen from the green economy point of view, this cost also has an economic and environmental impact; a faster algorithm will produce results in a more timely manner, facilitating faster decision making, consuming less energy and hence reducing its carbon footprint.

Moving along those lines, this paper proposes a new computationally highly efficient algorithm termed Forward with Early Dropping Hill Climbing (FEDHC), which is publicly available in the *R* package *pchc*. FEDHC shares common ideas with PCHC and MMHC. It applies the Forward Backward with Early Dropping (FBED) variable selection algorithm [17] to each variable as a means of skeleton identification, followed by a Hill Climbing (HC) scoring phase. FEDHC can handle millions of observations in just a few minutes, and retains similar or better accuracy levels than PCHC and MMHC. With continuous data, FEDHC performs fewer errors than PCHC, but the converse is true with categorical data. FEDHC further enjoys the same scalability property as PCHC, and its computational cost is proportional to the sample size of the data. Increasing the sample size by a factor increases the execution time by the same factor. Finally, a new, computationally efficient implementation of MMHC is offered that is also publicly available in the *R* package *pchc*.

The choice of the BN learning algorithm is not only computational cost-dependent, but also quality-dependant. Regardless of the algorithm used, the quality of the learned BN can be significantly affected by outliers. Robustness to outliers is an important aspect that, surprisingly enough, has not attracted substantial research attention in the field of BN learning. Ref. [18] were the first to propose a robustified version of the PC algorithm, by replacing the empirical standard deviations with robust scale estimates. Ref. [19] on the other hand, removed the outliers, but their algorithm is only applicable to BNs with a known topology. Robustification of the proposed FEDHC algorithm takes place by adopting techniques from the robust statistics literature. The key concept is to identify and remove the outliers prior to applying FEDHC.

The rest of the paper is structured as follows. Preliminaries regarding BNs that will assist in making the paper comprehensible, and a brief presentation of the PCHC and MMHC algorithms are unveiled in Section 2. The FEDHC is introduced in Section 3, along with its robustified version (the robustified versions are applicable to PCHC and MMHC as well), which will be shown to be remarkable and utterly insensitive to outliers. The theoretical properties and computational details of FEDHC, and the conditional independence tests utilised for continuous and categorical data are delineated in the same section. Section 4 contains Monte Carlo simulation studies comparing FEDHC to PCHC and MMHC in terms of accuracy, computational efficiency and number of tests performed. Section 5 illustrates the FEDHC, PCHC and MMHC on two real cross-sectional datasets using the *R* package *pchc*. The first dataset contains continuous data on the credit history for a sample of applicants for a type of credit card [20]. The second dataset contains categorical data on the household income plus some more demographic variables. Ultimately, Section 6 contains the conclusions drawn from this paper.

2. Preliminaries

Graphical models or probabilistic graphical models express visually the conditional (in)dependencies between random variables (V_i, $i = 1, \ldots, D$). Nodes (or vertices) are used to represent the variables V_i and edges between the nodes; for example, $V_i - V_j$ indicates the relationship between the variables V_i and V_j. Directed graphs are graphical models that contain arrows instead of edges, indicating the direction of the relationship; for example, $V_i \rightarrow V_j$. The parents of a node V_i are the nodes whose direction (arrows) points towards V_i. Consequently, node V_i is termed the child of those nodes and the common parents of those nodes are called spouses. Directed acyclic graphs (DAG) are stricter in the sense that they impose no cycles on these directions. For any path between V_i and V_j, $V_i \rightarrow V_k \rightarrow \ldots \rightarrow V_j$, no path from V_j to V_i ($V_j \rightarrow \ldots \rightarrow V_i$) exists. In other words, the natural sequence or relationship between parents and children or ancestors and descendants is mandated.

2.1. Bayesian Networks

Assume there is a collection **V** of D variables whose joint distribution P is known. The BN (BN is a special case of a DAG) [21,22] $B = \langle G, \mathbf{V} \rangle$ arises from linking P to G through the Markov condition (or Markov property), which states that each variable is conditionally independent of its non-descendants, given its parents. By using this condition, the joint distribution P can be factorised as:

$$P(V_1, \ldots, V_D) = \prod_{i=1}^{D} P(V_i | Pa(V_i)), \tag{1}$$

where $Pa(V_i)$ denotes the parents set of V_i in G.

If G entails only conditional independencies in P and all conditional independencies in P are entailed by G, based on the Markov condition, then G, P and G are faithful to each other, and G is a perfect map of P [22].

The BN whose edges can be interpreted causally is called causal BN; an edge $V_i \rightarrow V_j$ exists if V_i is a direct cause of V_j. A necessary assumption made by the algorithms under study is causal sufficiency; there are no latent (hidden, non-observed) variables among the observed variables **V**.

The triplet (V_i, V_k, V_j), where $V_i \rightarrow V_k \leftarrow V_j$ is called V-structure. If there is no edge between V_i and V_j, the node V_k is called an unshielded collider. In Figure 1, the triplet (V_1, V_3, V_2) is a V-structure as there is no edge between V_1 and V_2, and hence, node V_3 is an unshielded collider. The unshielded collider V_k implies that V_i and V_j are independent conditioning on V_k, provided that the faithfulness property holds true [22]. Conversely, the triplet of nodes (V_i, V_k, V_j) such that $V_k \rightarrow V_i$ and $V_k \rightarrow V_j$ is termed Λ-structure (nodes V_3, V_4 and V_5 in Figure 1 is such an example). The Λ-structure implies that V_i and V_j are conditionally independent, given V_k.

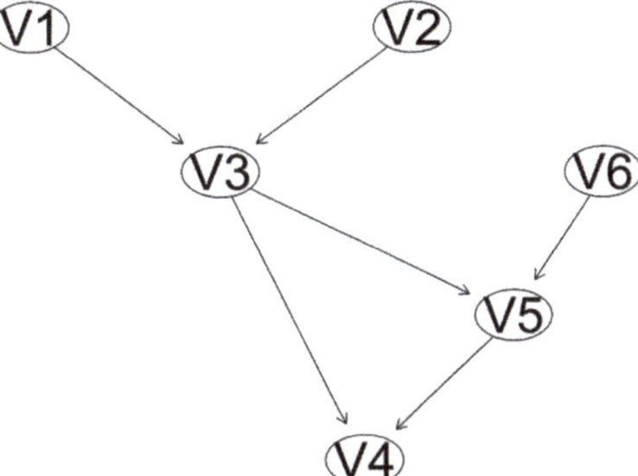

Figure 1. An example of a DAG. Nodes V1 and V2 are the parents of V3, whose children are nodes V4 and V5. V2 is the spouse of V1 (and vice versa, V1 is the spouse of V2).

Two or more BNs are called Markov equivalent, if and only if they have the same skeleton and the same V-structures [23]. The set of all Markov equivalent BNs forms the Markov equivalence class that can be represented by a complete partially DAG, which in addition to directed edges, contains undirected edges. (Undirected edges may be oriented either way in BNs of the Markov equivalence class (in the set of all valid combinations), while directed and missing edges are shared among all equivalent BNs.)

2.2. Classes of BN Learning Algorithms

BN learning algorithms are typically constraint-based, score-based or hybrid. Constraint-based learning algorithms, such as PC (PC stands for Peter and Clark, named after Peter Spirtes and Clark Glymour, the names of the two researchers who invented it) [24] and

FCI [22] employ conditional independence (CI) tests to discover the structure of the network (skeleton), and then orient the edges by repetitively applying orientation rules. On the contrary, score-based methods [25–27] assign a score on the whole network and perform a search in the space of BNs to identify a high-scoring network. Hybrid algorithms, such as MMHC [13] and PCHC [15], combine both aforementioned methods; they first perform CI tests to discover the skeleton of the BN, and then employ a scoring method to direct the edges in the space of BNs. For a series of CI tests for continuous and categorical data, please see Appendix A.

2.3. PCHC and MMHC Algorithms

The PCHC's skeleton identification phase is the same as that of the PC algorithm [15]. The phase commences with all pairwise unconditional associations and removes the edge between ordered pairs that are not statistically significantly associated. Subsequently, CI tests are performed with the cardinality of the conditioning set (denoted by k) increasing by 1 at a time. At every step, the conditioning set consists of subsets of the neighbours, adjacent to each variable V_i $(adj(G, V_i))$. This process is repeated until no edge can be removed.

Ref. [22] suggested three heuristics to select the pairs of variables, and the order is crucial, as it can yield erroneous results. The optimal process, for a given variable V_i, is to first test those variables **V** that are least probabilistically dependent on V_i, conditional on those subsets of variables that are most probabilistically dependent on V_i. Note that the pairs are first ordered according to the third heuristic of [22], and so, the order of selection of the pairs is deterministic. Hence, the skeleton identification phase is independent of the order at which the variables are located in the dataset [28].

MMHC's skeleton identification phase performs a variable selection process for each variable (call it target variable, V_i), described as follows. A search for its statistically significantly associated variable V_s is performed via unconditional statistical tests. The associations are stored, and the variable with the highest association (V_j) is chosen; an edge is added between this V_i and V_j, and all non-statistically significant variables are excluded from further consideration. In the second step, all CI tests between the target variable and previously identified variables, conditional on the previously selected variable, are performed $(V_i \perp\!\!\!\perp V_m | V_j, \; m \neq i, j)$, and the non-statistically significant variables are neglected. The previously stored associations are updated; for each variable, the minimum between the old and the new variables is stored. The variable with the highest association (Max-Min heuristic) is next selected. In subsequent steps, while the set of the selected variables increases, the conditioning set does not, as its cardinality is at most equal to k. (This algorithm resembles the classical forward variable selection in statistics with two distinct differences. At each step, non-significant variables are excluded from future searches, instead of conditioning on all selected variables. Secondly, the CI tests for the next variable conditions upon all possible subsets, up to a pre-specified cardinality, of the already selected variables.) Upon completion, a backward phase, in the same spirit as the forward, applies to remove falsely detected variables.

This variable selection process is repeated for all variables. The edges detected remain only if they were identified by all variables. If, for example, V_j was found to be associated with V_i, but V_i was not found to be associated with V_j, then no edge between V_i and V_j will be added.

A slightly modified version of MMHC's skeleton identification phase is implemented in the *R* package *pchc*. The backward phase is not performed, in order to make the algorithm faster. To distinguish between them, *bnlearn*'s implementation will be denoted by MMHC-1, and *pchc*'s implementation will be denoted by MMHC-2, hereafter.

The orientation of the discovered edges takes place in the second, Hill Climbing (HC) scoring, phase of PCHC and MMHC, and is the same phase employed by FEDHC as well.

3. The FEDHC BN Learning Algorithm

Similarly to PCHC and MMHC, the skeleton identification phase of FEDHC relies on a variable selection algorithm. Thus, prior to introducing the FEDHC algorithm, the Forward Backward with Early Dropping (FBED) variable selection algorithm [17] is briefly presented.

3.1. The FBED Variable Selection Algorithm

In the classical forward selection algorithm, all available predictor variables are constantly used, and their statistical significance is tested at each step. Assuming that out of $10,000$ predictor variables, only 10 are selected. This implies that almost $10,000 \times 10$ regression models must be fitted, and the same amount of statistical tests must be executed. The computational cost is tremendous, rendering this computationally expensive algorithm impractical, and hence, prohibitive. The authors of [17] introduced the FBED algorithm as a speed-up modification of the traditional forward selection algorithm coupled with the backward selection algorithm [29]. FBED relies on the Early Dropping heuristic to speed up the forward selection. The heuristic drops the statistically non-significant predictor variables at each step, thus removing them from further consideration, resulting in a computationally dramatically cheaper algorithm that is presented in Algorithm 1. Especially for the case of continuous data this phase can be completed computationally efficient using only the correlation matrix (see Appendix B for more details).

Algorithm 1 The FBED variable selection algorithm.

1: **Input**: A response variable y and a set of D predictor variables **V**.
2: Let $\mathbf{S} = \emptyset$ denote the set of selected variables.
3: Perform all regression models of y on each V_i, $i = 1, \ldots, D$, $y \sim f(V_i)$, where f denotes a function of V_i; e.g., a linear model $y = a + bV_i + e$, and retain only the statistically significant predictor variables $\mathbf{V}_{sig}$.
4: Choose V_j from $\mathbf{V}_{sig}$ that has the highest association, add it in **S** and use that to perform all regression models of y on the V_j and each V_ℓ, $y \sim f(V_j, V_\ell)$, where $\ell \in \mathbf{V}$, with $\ell \neq j$ and again retain only the statistically significant predictor variables, thus reducing $|\mathbf{V}_{sig}|$ and increasing $|\mathbf{S}|$.
5: Repeat until no predictor variable is left, i.e., $\mathbf{V}_{sig} = \emptyset$.
6: This process can be repeated k times, using all neglected predictor variables, where k is a pre-defined number, until $|\mathbf{S}|$ cannot further increase.
7: Perform a backward selection phase attempting to remove the non statistically significant predictor variables.
8: **Return S**.

3.2. Skeleton Identification Phase of the FEDHC Algorithm

The skeleton identification phase of the FEDHC algorithm is the one presented in Algorithm 2, but it must be stressed that the backward phase of FBED is not performed, so as to reduce the computational cost. The FBED algorithm (Algorithm 1) is used for each variable (call it target variable, V_i). This variable selection process is repeated for all variables. The edges detected remain only if they were identified by all variables. If, for example, V_j was found to associated with V_i, but V_i was not found to be associated with V_j, then no edge between V_i and V_j will be added.

Algorithm 2 Skeleton identification phase of the FEDHC algorithm.

1: **Input:** Data set on a set of D variables **V**.
2: Let the adjacency matrix G be full of zeros.
3: **Repeat** for all variables $V_i, i = 1, \ldots, D$
4: Perform the FBED algorithm in Algorithm 1, excluding the backward phase, and return $\mathbf{S}_i$.
5: Set $G_{ij} = 1$ for all $j \in \mathbf{S}_i$.
6: **If** $G_{ij} \neq G_{ji}$ set $G_{ij} = G_{ji} = 0$.
7: **Return** G.

3.3. Hill Climbing Phase of the FEDHC Algorithm

The first phase of FEDHC, MMHC and of PCHC is to discover any possible edges between the nodes, using CI tests. In the second phase, a search for the optimal DAG is performed, where the edges turn to arrows or are deleted towards the maximisation of a score metric. This scoring phase performs a greedy HC search in the space of BNs, commencing with an empty graph [13]. The edge deletion or direction reversal that leads to the largest increase in score, in the space of BNs (This implies that every time an edge removal or arrow direction is implemented, a check for cycles is performed. If cycles are created, the operation is canceled regardless of whether it increases the score), is applied, and the search continues recursively. The fundamental difference from standard greedy search is that the search is constrained to the orientation of the edges discovered by the skeleton identification phase (For more information, see [13]).

Tabu search is an iterative local searching procedure adopted by [13] for this purpose. Its performance is enhanced by using a list where the last 100 structures explored are stored, while searching in the neighborhood of each solution. The search is also capable of escaping from a local optima, in which the normal local search techniques often become stuck. Instead of applying the best local change, the best local change that results in a structure not on the list is performed, in an attempt to escape the local maxima [13]. This change may actually reduce the score. When a number of changes (10–15) occur without an increase in the maximum score ever encountered during a search, the algorithm terminates. The overall best scoring structure is then returned.

The Bayesian Information Criterion (BIC) [30] is a frequent score used for continuous data, while other options include the multivariate normal log-likelihood, the Akaike Information Criterion (AIC) and the Bayesian Gaussian equivalent [31] score. (The term *"equivalent"* refers to their attractive property of giving the same score to equivalent structures (Markov equivalent BNs), i.e., structures that are statistically indistinguishable [13]) The Bayesian Dirichlet equivalent (BDE) [32], the BDe uniform score (BDeu) [27], the multinomial log-likelihood score [33] and the MDL score [34,35] are four scoring options for discrete data.

The combination of the FBED algorithm during the skeleton identification phase with the HC scoring method forms the FEDHC algorithm. Interestingly enough, the skeleton identification phase of FEDHC performs substantially fewer statistical tests than PCHC and MMHC.

3.4. Prior Knowledge

All BN learning algorithms are agnostic of true relationships among the input data. It is customary though, for practitioners and researchers to have prior knowledge of the necessary directions (forbidden or not) of some of the relationships among the variables. For instance, variables such as sex or age cannot be caused by any economic or demographic variables. Economic theory (or theory from any other field) can further assist in improving the quality of the fitted BN by imposing or forbidding directions among some variables. All of the prior information can be inserted into the scoring phase of the aforementioned BN learning algorithms, leading to less errors and more realistic BNs.

3.5. Theoretical Properties of FEDHC

The theoretical properties and guarantees of MMHC and PCHC can be found in [13,15], respectively. As for the FEDHC, while there is no theoretical guarantee of the skeleton identification phase of FEDHC, Ref. [17] showed that running FBED with two repeats recovers the MB of the response variable if the joint distribution of the response and the predictor variables can be faithfully represented by a BN. When used for BN learning though, FBED need not be run more than once for each variable. In this case, FBED, similarly to MMHC, will identify the children and parents of a variable V_i, but not the spouses of the children [17], as this is not necessary during the skeleton identification phase. When FBED is run on the children of the variable V_i, it will again identify the children's parents who are the spouses of the variable V_i. Hence, upon completion, the FEDHC algorithm will have identified the MB of each variable.

Additionally, the early dropping heuristic does not only reduce the computational time, but also reduces the problem of multiple testing, in some sense [17]. When FBED is run only once (as in the current situation), in the worst-case scenario, it is expected to select about $\alpha \cdot D$ variables (where α is the significance level), since all other variables will be dropped in the first (filtering) phase. However, simulation studies have shown that FBED selects fewer false positives than expected and the authors' recommendation is to reduce the number of runs to further limit the number of falsely selected variables, a strategy that FEDHC follows by default.

Similar to MMHC, the FEDHC is a local learning algorithm, and hence during the HC phase, the overall score is decomposed [13], exploiting the Markov property of BNs (1). The local learning has several advantages (see [13]) and the scores (BDe, BIC., etc.) are locally consistent [25].

3.6. Robustification of the FEDHC Algorithm for Continuous Data

It is not uncommon for economic datasets to contain outliers, observations with values that are far from the rest of the data. Income is such an example that contains outliers, but if outliers appear only in that variable, their effect will be minor. The effect of outliers is propagated when they exist in more variables, and in order to mitigate their effect, they must be identified in the multivariate space. If these outliers are not detected or not treated properly, BN learning algorithms will yield erroneous results. FEDHC will employ the Reweighted Minimum Covariance Determinant (RMCD) [36,37] as a means to identify outliers and remove them. (The reason for why one cannot use the robust correlation matrix directly is because the independence property between two variables no longer holds true. The robust correlation between any two variables depends on the other variables, and so adding or removing a variable modifies the correlation structure [38].)

The RMCD estimator is computed in two stages. In the first stage, a subset of observations h $(n/2 \leq h < n)$ is selected, such that the covariance matrix has the smallest determinant, and a robust mean vector is also computed. The second stage is a re-weighting scheme that increases the efficiency of the estimator, while preserving its high-breakdown properties. A weight $w_i = 0$ is given to observations whose first-stage robust distance exceeds a threshold value, otherwise the weight of $w_i = 1$ $(i = 1, \ldots, n)$ is given. Using the re-weighted robust covariance matrix and mean vector, robust Mahalanobis distances are computed $d^2_{i(RMCD)} = \left(\mathbf{x}_i - \tilde{\boldsymbol{\mu}}_{(RMCD)} \right)^T \tilde{\boldsymbol{\Sigma}}^{-1}_{(RMCD)} \left(\mathbf{x}_i - \tilde{\boldsymbol{\mu}}_{(RMCD)} \right)$ and proper cut-off values are required to detect the outliers. Those cut-off values are based on the following accurate approximations [39,40]:

$$d^2_{i(RMCD)} \begin{array}{l} \sim \dfrac{(w-1)^2}{w} Be\left(\dfrac{D}{2}, \dfrac{w-D-1}{2}\right) \quad \text{if } w_i = 1 \\[2ex] \sim \dfrac{w+1}{w} \dfrac{(w-1)D}{w-D} F_{D,w-D} \quad \text{if } w_i = 0, \end{array}$$

where $w = \sum_{i=1}^{n} w_i$, and Be and F denote the Beta and F distributions, respectively.

The observations whose Mahalananobis distance $d^2_{i(RMCD)}$ exceeds the 97.5% quantile of either distribution (Be or F) are considered to be outliers, and are hence removed from the dataset. The remainder of the dataset, assumed to be outlier-free, will be used by FEDHC to learn the BN.

The default value for h is $[(n + p + 1)/2]$, where $[.]$ denotes the largest integer. This value was proven to have the highest breakdown point [41], but a low efficiency, on the other hand. Changing h yields an estimator with lower robustness properties and increases the computational cost of the RMCD estimator. For these reasons, this is the default value used inside the robustification process of the FEDHC algorithm.

The case of $n < p$ and $n \ll p$ (a very high-dimensional case) in general can be treated in a similar way, by replacing the RMCD estimator with the high-dimensional MCD approach of [42].

4. Monte Carlo Simulation Studies

Extensive experiments were conducted on simulated data to investigate the quality of the estimation of FEDHC compared to PCHC and MMHC-2. MMHC-1 participated in the simulation studies only with categorical data and not with continuous data, because it is prohibitively expensive. The continuous data were generated by synthetic BNs that contained a various number of nodes, $p = (20, 30, 50)$, with an average of three and five neighbours (edges) for each variable. For each case 50 random BNs were generated with Gaussian data and various sample sizes. Categorical data were generated, utilising two famous (in the BN learning community) realistic BNs, and the sample sizes were left varying. The R packages *MXM* [43] and *bnlearn* were used for the BN generation, and the R packages *pchc* and *bnlearn* were utilised to apply the FEDHC, PCHC, MMHC-2 and the MMHC-1 algorithms, respectively. All simulations were implemented in a desktop computer with an Intel Core i5-9500 CPU at 3.00 GHz with 48 GB RAM and an SSD installed. The R codes for the simulation studies are available in the Supplementary Material.

The metrics of quality of the learned BNs were the structural Hamming distance (SHD) [13] of the estimated DAG from the true DAG (This is defined as the number of operations required to make the estimated graph equal to the true graph. Instead of the true DAG, the Markov equivalence graph of the true BN is used; that is, some edges have been un-oriented as their direction cannot be statistically decided. The transformation from the DAG to the Markov equivalence graph was carried out using Chickering's algorithm [44]), the computational cost and the number of tests performed during the skeleton identification phase and the total duration of the algorithm. PCHC and the MMHC-1 algorithms have been implemented in C++; henceforth the comparison of the execution times is not really fair at the programming language level. FEDHC and MMHC-2 have been implemented in R (skeleton identification phase) and C++ (scoring phase).

4.1. Synthetic BNs with Continuous Data

The procedure used to generate the data for X is summarised in the steps below. Let X be a variable in G, and let $Pa(X)$ be the parents of X in G.

1. Sample the coefficients β of $f(Pa(X))$ uniformly at random from $[-1, -0.1] \cup [0.1, 1]$.
2. In case $Pa(X)$ is empty, X is sampled from the standard normal distribution. Otherwise, $X = f(Pa(X)) = \beta_0 + \sum_i \beta_i Pa_i(X) + \epsilon_X$, a linear function (in general, this can represent any (non-linear) function) depending on X, where ϵ_X is generated from a standard normal distribution.

The average number of connecting edges (neighbours) was set to 3 and 5. The higher the number of edges is, the denser the network is and the harder the inference becomes. The sample sizes considered were $n = (100, 500, 1000, 5000, 1 \times 10^4, 3 \times 10^4, 5 \times 10^4, 1 \times 10^5, 3 \times 10^5, 5 \times 10^5, 1 \times 10^6, 3 \times 10^6, 5 \times 10^6)$.

Figures 2–5 present the SHD and the number of CI tests performed of each algorithm for a range of sample sizes (in log-scale). With three neighbours on average per node, the differences in the SHD are noticeably rather small, yet FEDHC achieves lower numbers.

With five neighbours on average though, the differences are more significant and increasing with increasing sample sizes. As for the number of CI tests executed during the skeleton identification phase, FEDHC is the evident winner, as it executes up to six times less tests, regardless of the average neighbours. Moreover, the SHD of the FEDHC is lower than the SHD of its competitors for all cases, and the difference is magnified when the sample size is in the order of millions.

The common observation for all algorithms is that as the dimensionality increases, the SHD requires a greater sample size to achieve low levels. With 20 and 30 variables, the SHD may reach single-digit figures (with three neighbours on average), but with 50 and 100 variables, it never goes below 10. A similar conclusion is drawn when there are five neighbours on average.

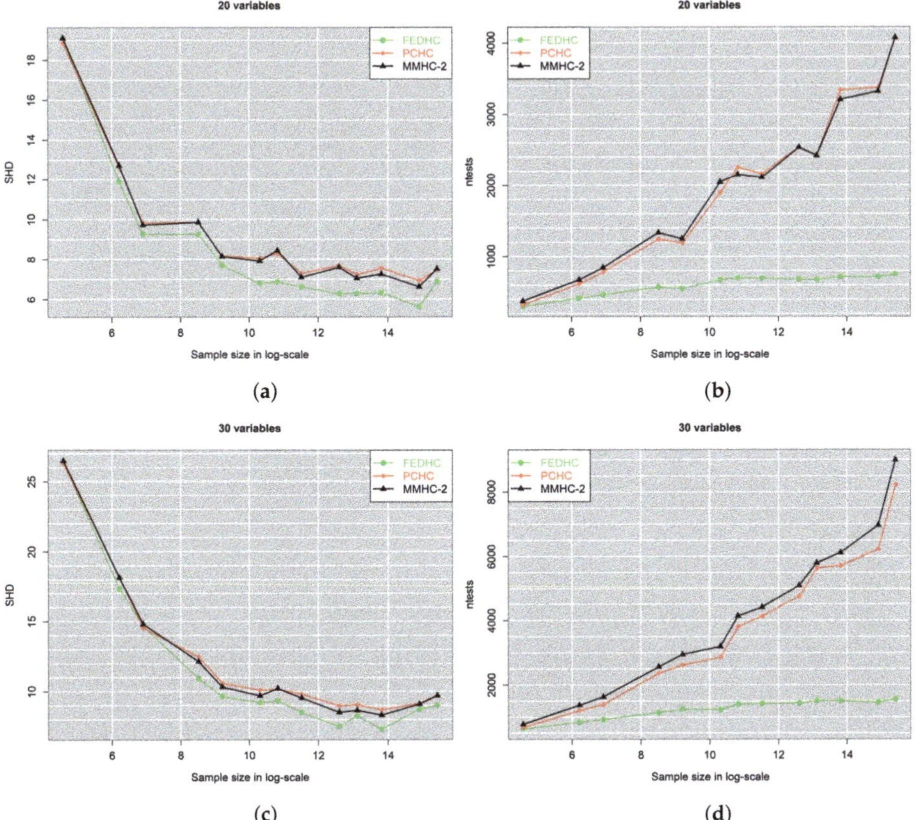

Figure 2. SHD and number of CI tests against log of sample size for 20 and 30 dimensions, with **3 neighbours** on average. (**a**) SHD vs. log of sample size. (**b**) Number of CI tests vs. log of sample size. (**c**) SHD vs. log of sample size. (**d**) Number of CI tests vs. log of sample size.

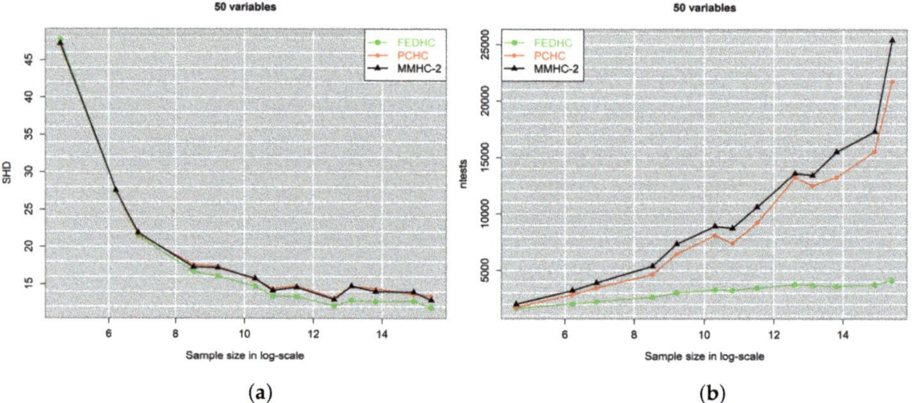

(**a**)

(**b**)

Figure 3. *Cont.*

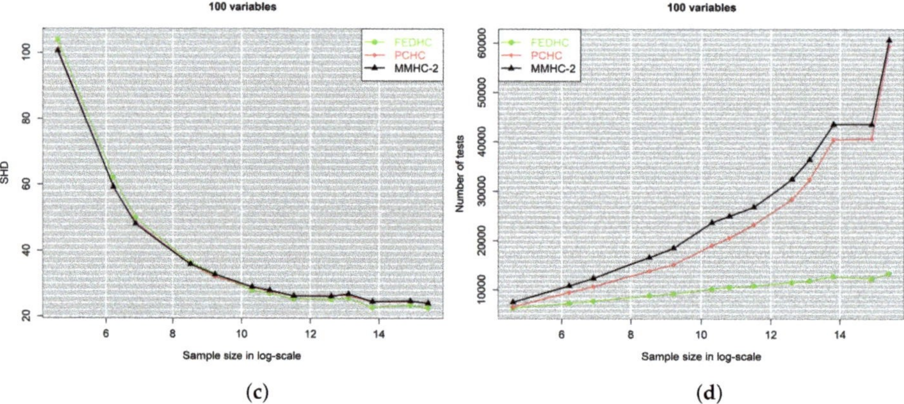

(**c**)

(**d**)

Figure 3. SHD and number of CI tests against log of sample size for 50 and 100 dimensions, with **3 neighbours** on average. (**a**) SHD vs. log of sample size. (**b**) Number of CI tests vs. log of sample size. (**c**) SHD vs. log of sample size. (**d**) Number of CI tests vs. log of sample size.

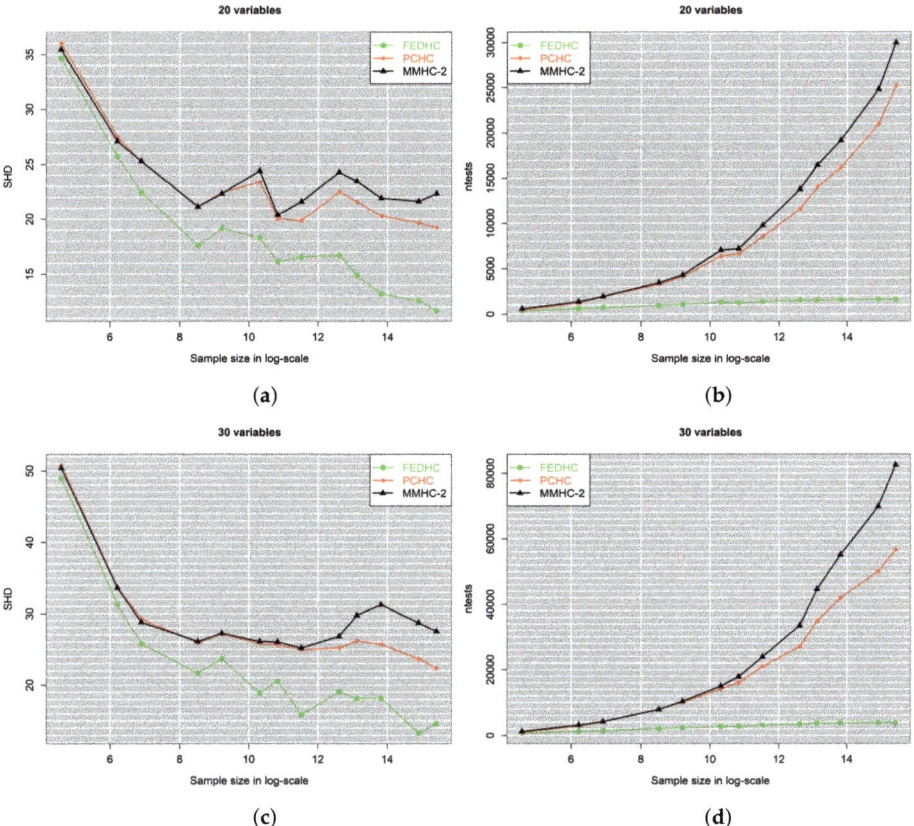

(**a**)

(**b**)

(**c**)

(**d**)

Figure 4. SHD and number of CI tests against log of sample size for 20 and 30 dimensions, with **5 neighbours** on average. (**a**) SHD vs. log of sample size. (**b**) Number of CI tests vs. log of sample size. (**c**) SHD vs. log of sample size. (**d**) Number of CI tests vs. log of sample size.

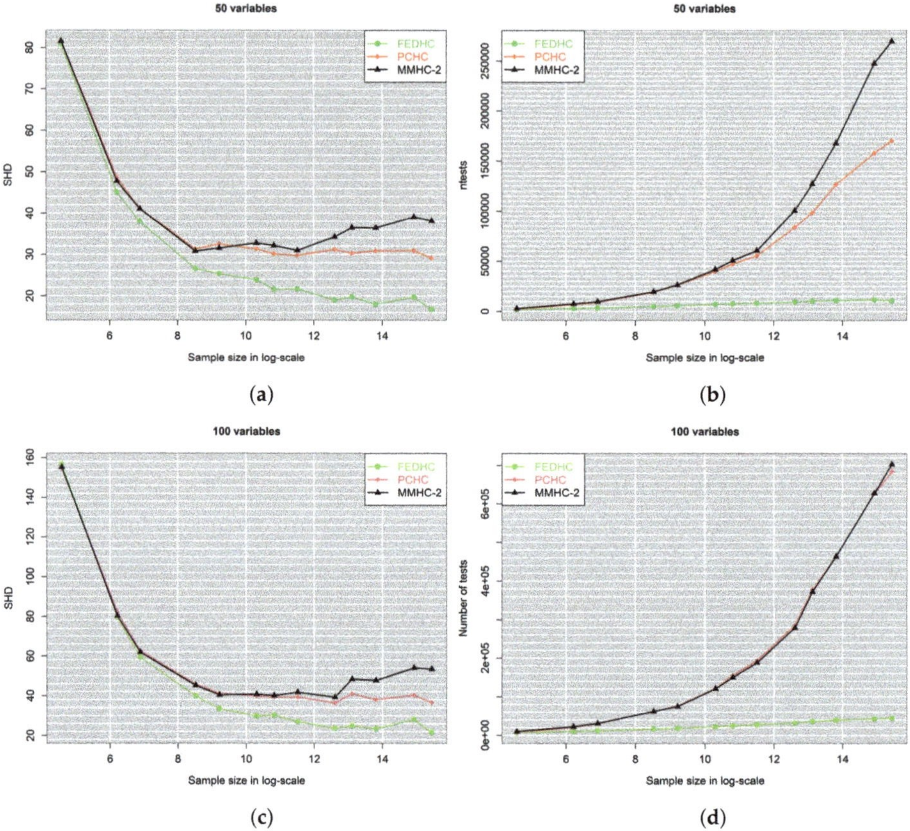

Figure 5. SHD and number of CI tests against log of sample size for various dimensions, with **5 neighbours** on average. (**a**) SHD vs. log of sample size. (**b**) Number of CI tests vs. log of sample size. (**c**) SHD vs. log of sample size. (**d**) Number of CI tests vs. log of sample size.

4.2. Robustified FEDHC for Continuous Data

An examination of the robustified FEDHC contains two axes of comparison; the outlier-free and the outliers present cases. At first, the performances of the raw and the robustified FEDHC in the outlier-free case are evaluated.

Figures 6 and 7 signify that there is no loss in the accuracy when using the robustified FEDHC over the raw FEDHC. Computationally speaking though, the raw FEDHC is significantly faster than the robustified FEDHC. For small sample sizes, the robustified FEDHC can be 10 times higher, while for large sample sizes, its cost can be double or only 5% higher than that of the raw FEDHC.

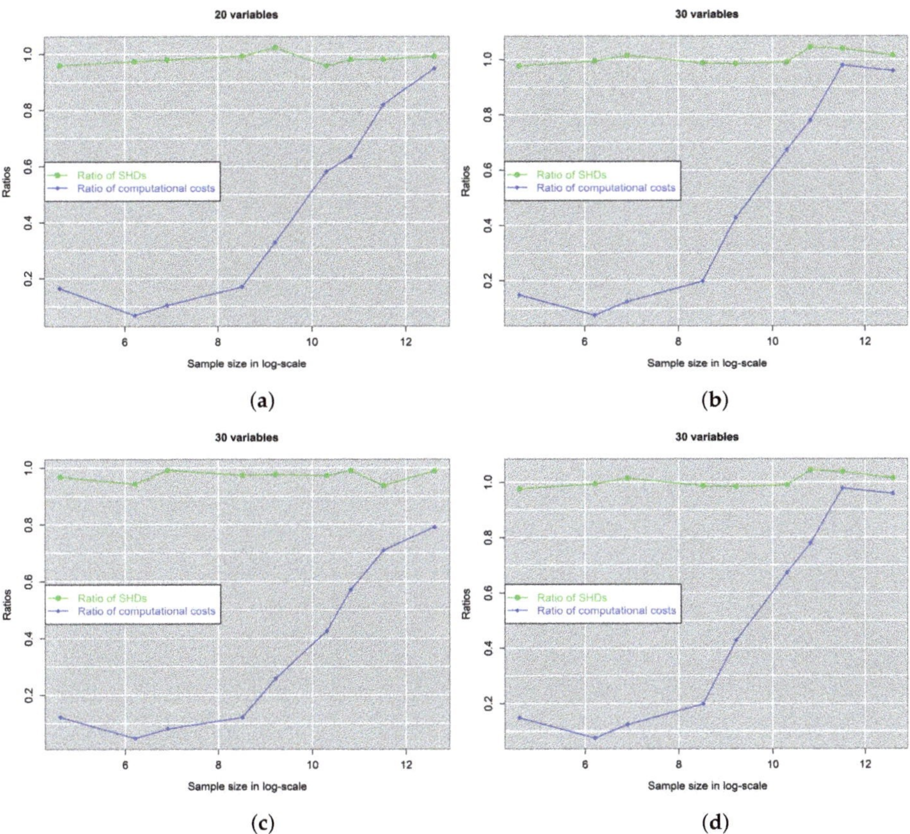

Figure 6. Ratios of SHD and computational cost against log of sample size for various dimensions, with **3 neighbours** and **5 neighbours** on average. The ratios depict the errors and computational cost of the raw FEDHC relative to the robustified FEDHC with NO outliers. (**a**,**c**) 3 neighbours. (**b**,**d**) 5 neighbours.

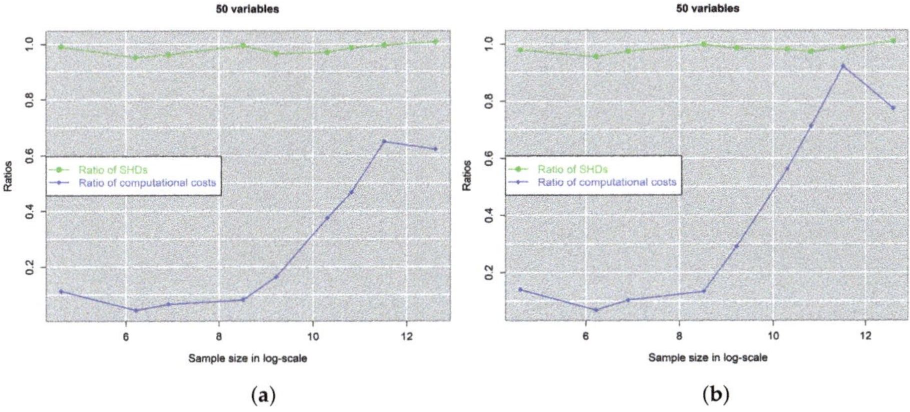

Figure 7. *Cont.*

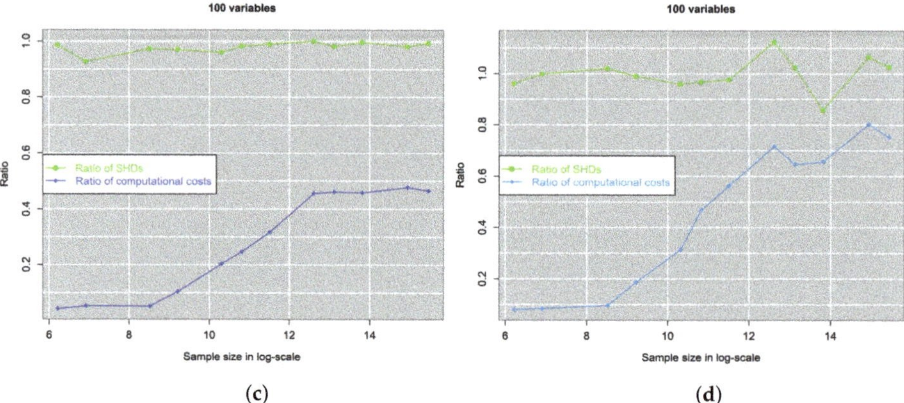

(c) (d)

Figure 7. Ratios of SHD and computational cost against log of sample size for various dimensions, with **3 neighbours** and **5 neighbours** on average. The ratios depict the errors and computational cost of the raw FEDHC relative to the robustified FEDHC with NO outliers. (**a,c**) 3 neighbours. (**b,d**) 5 neighbours.

The performances of the raw FEDHC and of the robustified FEDHC in the presence of extreme outliers are evaluated next. The BN generation scheme is the one described in Section 4.1, with the exception of having added a 5% of outlying observations. The considered sample sizes are smaller, as although FEDHC is computationally efficient, it becomes really slow in the presence of outliers.

The results presented in Figures 8 and 9 evidently show the gain when using the robustified FEDHC over the raw FEDHC. The SHD of the raw FEDHC increases by as little as 100%, and up to 700% with 3 neighbours on average and 50 variables. The duration of the raw FEDHC increases substantially. (Similar patterns were observed for the duration of the skeleton learning phase and for the number of CI tests.) The raw FEDHC becomes up to more than 200 times slower than the robustified version, with hundreds of thousands of observations, and 50 variables. This is attributed to the HC phase of the raw FEDHC, which consumes a tremendous amount of time. The outliers produce noise that escalates the labour of the HC phase.

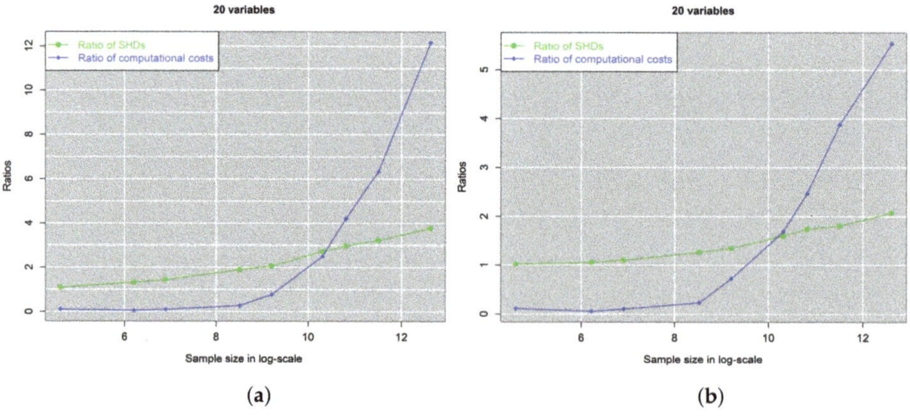

(a) (b)

Figure 8. *Cont.*

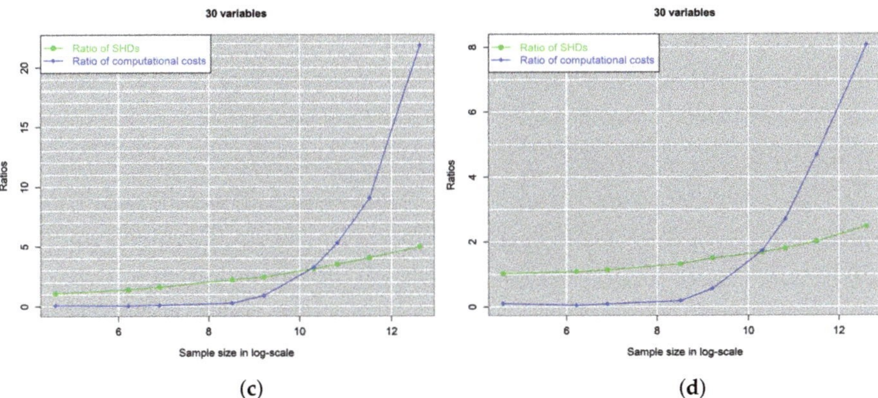

(c)

(d)

Figure 8. Ratios of SHD and computational cost against log of sample size for 20 and 30 dimensions with **3 neighbours** and **5 neighbours** on average. The ratios depict the errors and computational cost of the raw FEDHC relatively to the robustified FEDHC with 5% outliers. (**a**,**c**) 3 neighbours. (**b**,**d**) 5 neighbours.

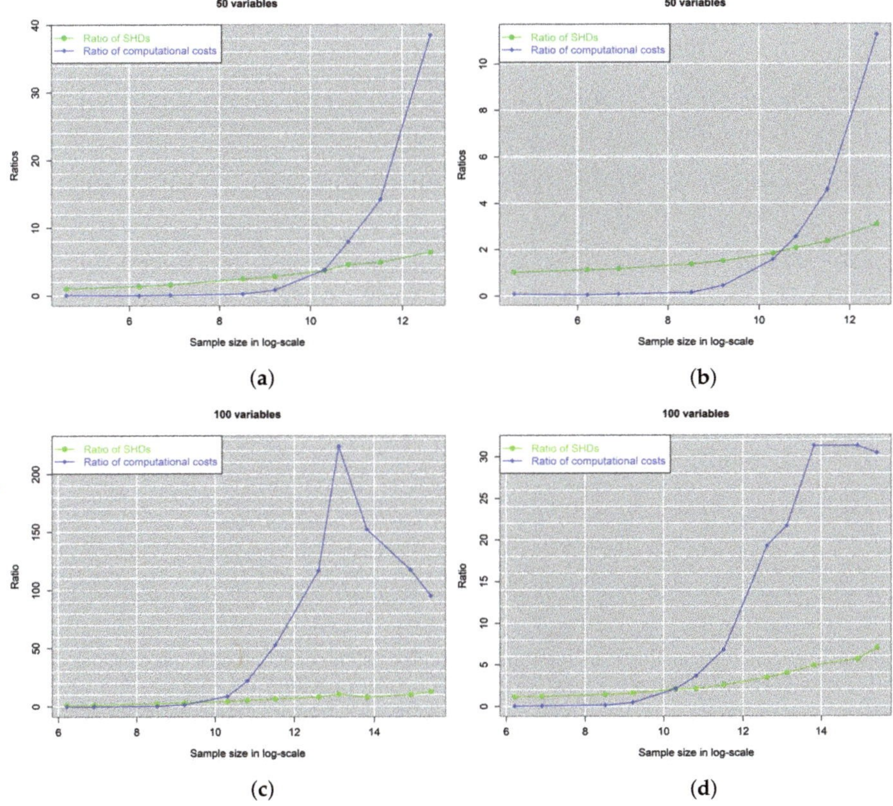

(a)

(b)

(c)

(d)

Figure 9. Ratios of SHD and computational cost against log of sample size for 50 and 100 dimensions with **3 neighbours** and **5 neighbours** on average. The ratios depict the errors and computational cost of the raw FEDHC relatively to the robustified FEDHC with 5% outliers. (**a**,**c**) 3 neighbours. (**b**,**d**) 5 neighbours.

4.3. Realistic BNs with Categorical Data

The $f(Pa(X))$ function utilised in the continuous data case relies on the β coefficients. The larger the magnitude of their values, the stronger the association between the edges becomes, and hence, it becomes easier to identify them. For BNs with categorical data, one could apply the same generation technique and then discretise the simulated data. To avoid biased or optimistic estimates favoring one or the other method, two real BNs with categorical data were utilised to simulate data. These are (a) the *Insurance* BN, used for evaluating car insurance risks [45], which consists of 27 variable (nodes) and 52 (directed) edges and (b) the *Alarm* BN, designed to provide an alarm message system for patient monitoring, and consists of 37 variables and 45 (directed) edges. The *R* package *bnlearn* contains a few thousand categorical instantiations from these BNs, but for the purpose of the simulation studies more instantiations were generated using the same package. The sample sizes considered were $n = (1 \times 10^4, 2 \times 10^4, 5 \times 10^4, 1 \times 10^5, 2 \times 10^5, 5 \times 10^5, 1 \times 10^6, 2 \times 10^6, 5 \times 10^6)$.

Figure 10 shows the SHD and the number of CI tests executed by each algorithm against the sample size. The MMHC-1 evidently has the poorest performance in both axes of comparison. Our implementation (MMHC-2) performs substantially better, but the overall winner is the PCHC. FEDHC, on the other hand, performs better than MMHC-1, yet is the second-best option.

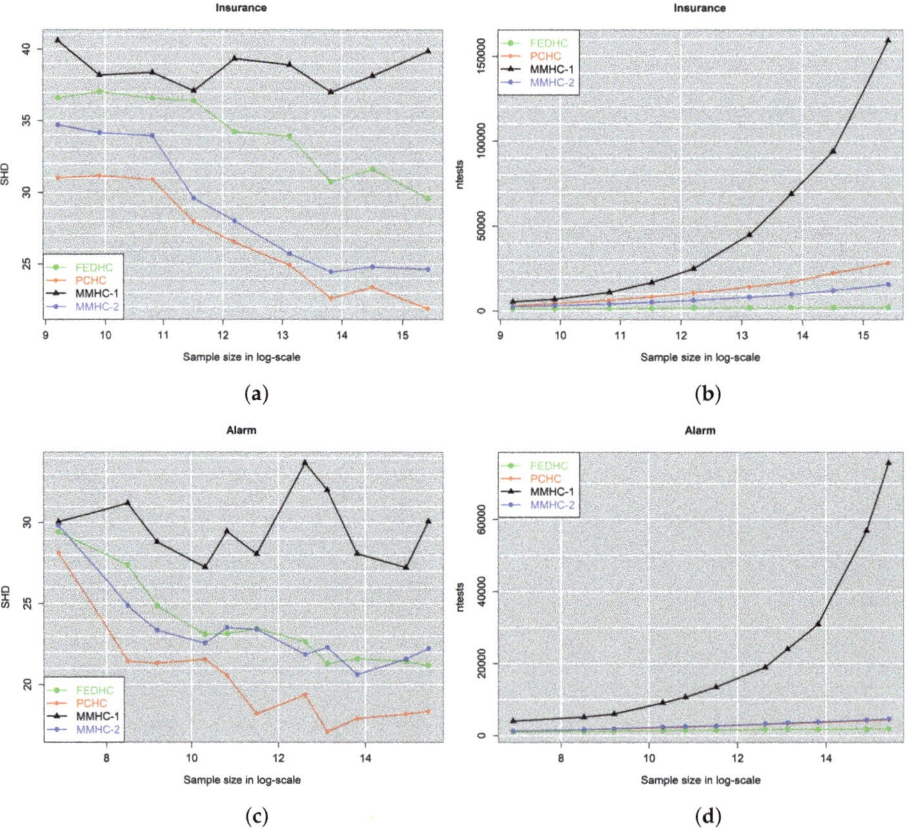

Figure 10. SHD and number of CI tests against log of sample size with **categorical** data. (**a,c**) SHD vs. log of sample size. (**b,d**) Number of CI tests vs. log of sample size.

4.4. Scalability of FEDHC

The computational cost of each algorithm was also measured, appearing in Figure 11 as a function of the sample size. The empirical slopes of all lines in Figure 11 are nearly equal to 1, indicating that the scalability of FEDHC, PCHC, and MMHC-2 is linear in the sample size. Hence, the computational cost of all algorithms increases linearly with respect to the sample size. For any percentage-wise increase in the sample size, the time increases by the same percentage. Surprisingly enough, the computational cost of MMHC-1 was not evaluated for the categorical data case, because similarly to the continuous data case, it was too high to evaluate.

It is surprising though that the computational cost of FEDHC is similar to that of PCHC and MMHC-2. In fact the skeleton identification phase requires about the same amount of time, and it requires only 8 seconds with 5 million observations. The scoring phase is the most expensive phase of the algorithms, absorbing 73–99% of the total computation time. Regarding FEDHC and MMHC-2, since the initial phase of both has been implemented in R, this can be attributed to the fact that the calculations of the partial correlation in FEDHC are heavier than those in MMHC-2, because the conditioning set in the former can grow larger than the conditioning set in MMHC-2, which is always bounded by a pre-specified value k. Thus, MMHC-2 performs more but computationally lighter calculations than FEDHC.

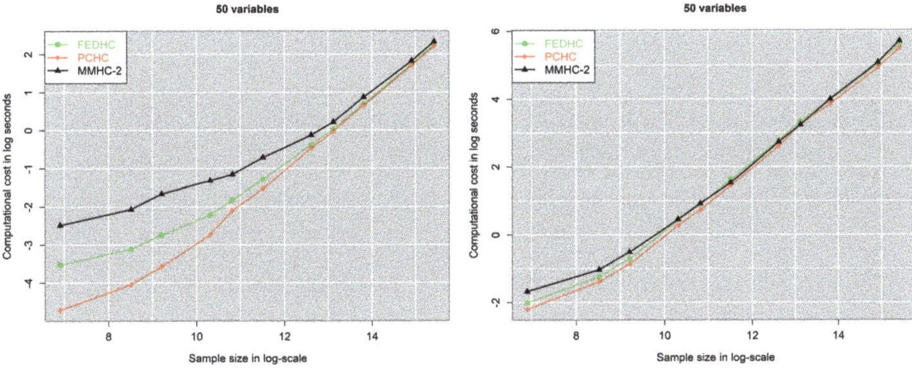

Continuous data with 3 neighbours on average.

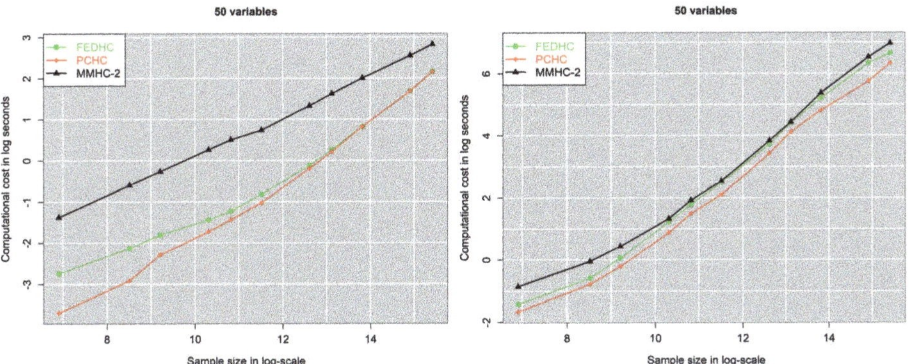

Continuous data with 5 neighbours on average.

Figure 11. *Cont.*

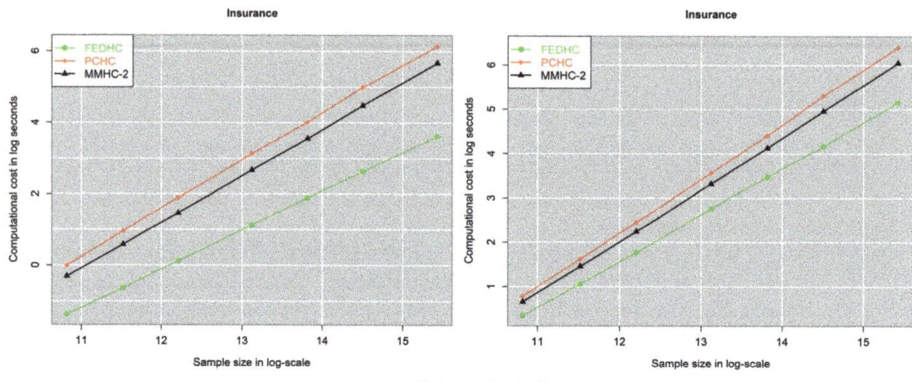

Categorical data.

Figure 11. Scalability of the algorithms with respect to the sample size for some selected cases. The results for the other cases convey the same message and are thus not presented. The left column refers to the skeleton identification phase, whereas the right column refers to both phases.

5. Illustration of the Algorithms on Real Economics Data Using the *R* Package *pchc*

The *R* package *pchc* is used with two examples with the datasets used in [15] to illustrate the performance of FEDHC against its competitors, PCHC, MMHC-1 and MMHC-2. More details about the package can be found in Appendix C. The advantages of BNs have already been discussed in [15], and hence the examples focus on the comparison of FEDHC to PCHC, MMHC-1 and MMHC-2.

5.1. Expenditure Data

The first example concerns a dataset with continuous variables containing information on the monthly credit card expenditure of individuals. This is the **Expenditure** dataset [20] and is publicly accessible via the *R* package *AER* [46]. The dataset contains information about 1319 observations (10% of the original data set) on the following 12 variables. Whether the application for a credit card was accepted or not (**Card**), the number of major derogatory reports, (**Reports**), the age in years plus twelfths of a year (**Age**), the yearly income in \$10,000s (**Income**), the ratio of monthly credit card expenditure to yearly income (**Share**), the average monthly credit card expenditure (**Expenditure**), whether the person owns their home or they rent (**Owner**), whether the person is self employed or not (**Selfemp**), the number of dependents + 1 (**Dependents**), the number of months living at current address (**Months**), the number of major credit cards held (**Majorcards**) and the number of active credit accounts (**Active**).

The *R* package *AER* contains the data and must be loaded and processed for the algorithms to run.

```
> library(AER)   ## CreditCard are available
> library(bnlearn)  ## To run MMHC-1
> data(CreditCard)  ## load the data
> x <- CreditCard
> colnames(x) <- c( ''Card'', ''Reports'', ''Age'', ''Income'', ''Share'', ''Expenditure'',
+            ''Owner'', ''Selfemp'', ''Dependents'', ''Months'',  ''Majorcards'', ''Active'')
## Prepare the data
> for (i in 1:12)  x[, i] <- as.numeric(x[, i])
> x <- as.matrix(x)
> x[, c(1, 7, 8)] <- x[, c(1, 7, 8)] - 1
## Run all 4 algorithms
> a1 <- bnlearn::mmhc( as.data.frame(x), restrict.args =
```

```
+                            list(alpha = 0.05, test = ''zf'') )
> a2 <- pchc::mmhc(x, alpha = 0.05)
> a3 <- pchc::pchc(x, alpha = 0.05)
> a4 <- pchc::fedhc(x, alpha = 0.05)
```

In order to plot the fitted BNs of each algorithm, the following commands were used.

```
> pchc::bnplot(a1)
> pchc::bnplot(a2$dag)
> pchc::bnplot(a3$dag)
> pchc::bnplot(a4\$dag)
```

This example shows the practical usefulness of the BNs. Evidently, this small scale experiment shows that companies can customise their products according to the key factors that determine the consumers' behaviours. Instead of selecting one variable only, a researcher/practitioner can identify the relationships among all of the variables by estimating the causal mechanistic system that generated the data. The BN can further reveal information about the variables that are statistically significantly related.

According to FEDHC (Figure 12a), the age of the individual affects their income, the number of months they have been living at their current address, whether they own their home or not, and the ratio of their monthly credit card expenditure to their yearly income. The only variables associated with the number of major derogatory reports (Reports) are whether the consumer's application for a credit card was accepted or not (Card) and the number of active credit accounts (Active). In fact, these two variables are parents of Reports, as the arrows are directed towards it. A third advantage of BNs is that they provide a solution to the variable selection problem. The parents of the variable Majorcards (number of major credit cards held) are Card (whether the application for credit card was accepted or not) and Income (yearly income in $10,000), its only child is Active (number of active credit accounts) and its only spouse (parent of Active) is Owner (whether the consumer owns their home). The collection of those parents, children and spouses form the Majorcards' MB. That is, any other variable does not increase the information on the number of major credit cards held by the consumer. For any given variable, one can straightforwardly obtain (and visualise) its MB, which can be used for the construction of the appropriate linear regression model.

Figure 12 contains the BNs using both implementations of MMHC, the PCHC and the FEDHC algorithms fitted to the expenditure data, with the variables sorted in a topological order [44], a tree-like structure. The BIC of the BN learned by MMHC-1 and MMHC-2 are equal to $-32,171.75$ and $-32,171.22$, and for the PCHC and FEDHC, they are both equal to $-32,171.75$. This is an indication that all four algorithms produced BNs of nearly the same quality. On a closer examination of the graphs, one can detect some differences between the algorithms. For instance, **Age** is directly related to **Active**, according to PCHC and MMHC-2, but not according to FEDHC and MMHC-1. Further, all algorithms have identified the **Owner** as the parent of **Income**, and not vice-versa. This is related to the prior knowledge discussed in Section 3.4, and will be examined in the next categorical example dataset.

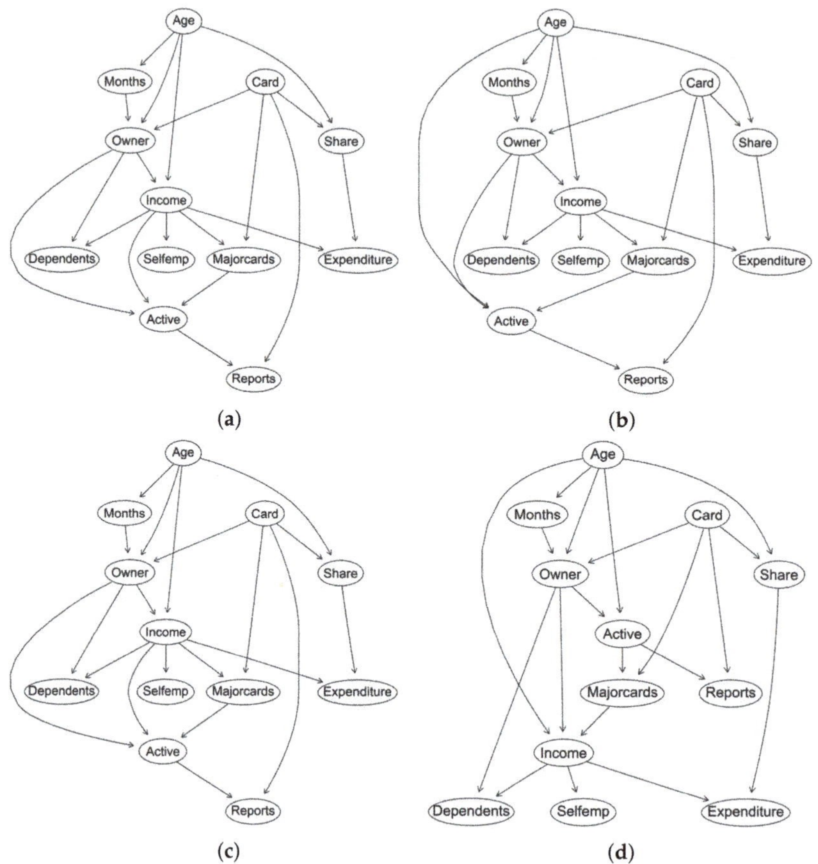

Figure 12. Expenditure data. Estimated BNs using (**a**) FEDHC, (**b**) PCHC, (**c**) MMHC-1 and (**d**) MMHC-2.

5.2. Income Data

The second example dataset contains categorical variables and originates from an example in the book "The Elements of Statistical Learning" [47], and is publicly available from the *R* package *arules* [48]. It consists of 6876 instances (obtained from the original dataset with 9409 instances, by removing observations with a missing annual income) and a mixture of 13 categorical and continuous demographic variables. The continuous variables were discretised, as suggested by the authors of the package. The continuous variables (age, education, income, years in bay area, number in household and number of children) were discretised based on their median values. **Income**: "$0–$40,000" or "$40,000+", **Sex**: "male" or "female", **Marriage**: "married", "cohabitation", "divorced", "widowed" or "single", **Age**: "14–34" or "35+", **Education**: "college graduate" or "no college graduate", **Occupation**, "professional/managerial", "sales", "laborer", "clerical/service", "homemaker", "student", "military", "retired" or "unemployed", **Bay** (number of years in bay area): "1–9" or "10+", **No of people** (number of of people living in the house): "1" or "2+", **Children**: "0" or "1+", **Rent**: "own", "rent" or "live with parents/family", **Type**: "house", "condominium", "apartment", "mobile home" or "other", **Ethnicity**: "American Indian", "Asian", "black", "east Indian", "hispanic", "white", "pacific islander" or "other" and **Language** (language spoken at home): "english", "spanish" or "other".

The dataset is at first accessed via the *R* package *arules* and is prepossessed, as suggested in *arules*.

```
> library(arules)
> data(IncomeESL)
## remove incomplete cases
> IncomeESL <- IncomeESL[complete.cases(IncomeESL), ]
## preparing the data set
> IncomeESL[[``income``]] <- factor((as.numeric(IncomeESL[[``income``]]) > 6) + 1,
+ levels = 1 : 2 , labels = c(``0-40,000``, ``40,000+``))
> IncomeESL[[``age``]] <- factor((as.numeric(IncomeESL[[``age``]]) > 3) + 1,
+ levels = 1 : 2 , labels = c(``14-34``, ``35+``))
> IncomeESL[[``education``]] <- factor((as.numeric(IncomeESL[[``education``]]) > 4) +
+ 1, levels = 1 : 2 , labels = c(``no college graduate``, ``college graduate``))
> IncomeESL[[``years in bay area``]] <- factor(
+ (as.numeric(IncomeESL[[``years in bay area``]]) > 4) + 1,
+ levels = 1 : 2 , labels = c(``1-9``, ``10+``))
> IncomeESL[[``number in household``]] <- factor(
+ (as.numeric(IncomeESL[[``number in household``]]) > 3) + 1,
+ levels = 1 : 2 , labels = c(``1``, ``2+``))
> IncomeESL[[``number of children``]] <- factor(
+ (as.numeric(IncomeESL[[``number of children``]]) > 1) + 0,
+ levels = 0 : 1 , labels = c(``0``, ``1+``))
```

Some more steps are required prior to running the BN algorithms.

```
> x <- IncomeESL
> x <- x[, -8]
> colnames(x) <- c( "Income", "Sex", "Marriage", "Age", "Education", "Occupation",
+     "Bay", "No of people", "Children", "Rent", "Type", "Ethnicity", "Language" )
> nam <- colnames(x)
```

The importance of prior knowledge incorporation discussed in Section 3.4 becomes evident in this example. Prior knowledge can be added in the **blacklist** argument denoting the forbidden directions (arrows).

```
> black <- matrix(nrow = 26, ncol = 2)
> black <- as.data.frame(black)
> for (i in 1:13)  black[i, ] <- c(nam[i], nam[2])
> for (i in 1:13)  black[13 + i, ] <- c(nam[i], nam[4])
> black <- black[-c(2, 17), ]
> black <- rbind( black, c(nam[9], nam[3]) )
> black <- rbind( black, c(nam[3], nam[6]) )
> black <- rbind( black, c(nam[9], nam[6]) )
> black <- rbind( black, c(nam[6], nam[5]) )
> black <- rbind( black, c(nam[3], nam[1]) )
> black <- rbind( black, c(nam[1], nam[5]) )
> black <- rbind( black, c(nam[10], nam[1]) )
> black <- rbind( black, c(nam[10], nam[5]) )
> black <- rbind( black, c(nam[10], nam[6]) )
> black <- rbind( black, c(nam[13], nam[12]) )
> colnames(black) <- c(``from``, ``to``)
```

Finally, the four BN algorithms are applied to the Income data.

```
> b1 <- bnlearn::mmhc( x, blacklist = black, restrict.args =
+                        list(alpha = 0.05, test = ``mi``) )
> b2 <- pchc::mmhc(x, method = ``cat``, alpha = 0.05, blacklist = black,
+ score = ``bic``)
```

```
> b3 <- pchc::pchc(x, method = ''cat'', alpha = 0.05, blacklist = black,
+ score = ''bic'')
> b4 <- pchc::fedhc(x, method = ''cat'', alpha = 0.05, blacklist = black,
+ score = ''bic'')
```

Figure 13 presents the fitted BNs of the MMHC-1, MMHC-2, PCHC and FEDHC algorithms. There are some distinct differences between the algorithms. For instance, PCHC is the only algorithm that has not identified **Education** as the parent of **Bay**. Additionally, the BN learned by MMHC-2 is the densest one (contains more arrows), whereas PCHC learned the BN with the fewest arrows.

This example further demonstrates the necessity of prior knowledge. BN learning algorithms fit a model to the data, ignoring the underlying truthfulness and ignoring the relevant economic theory. Economic theory can be used as prior knowledge to help mitigate the errors and lead to more truthful BNs. The exclusion of the blacklist argument (forbidden directions) would yield some irrational directions; for instance, that occupation or age might affect sex, or that marriage affects age, simply because these directions could increase the score. Finally, BNs are related to synthetic population generation, where the data are usually categorical. This task requires the specification of the joint distribution of the data, and BNs accomplish this [2]. Based on the Markov condition (1), the joint distribution can be written down explicitly, allowing for synthetic population generation in a sequential order. One commences by generating values for education and sex. Using these two variables, values for occupation are generated. These values, along with income and age, can be used to generate for the marital status, and so on.

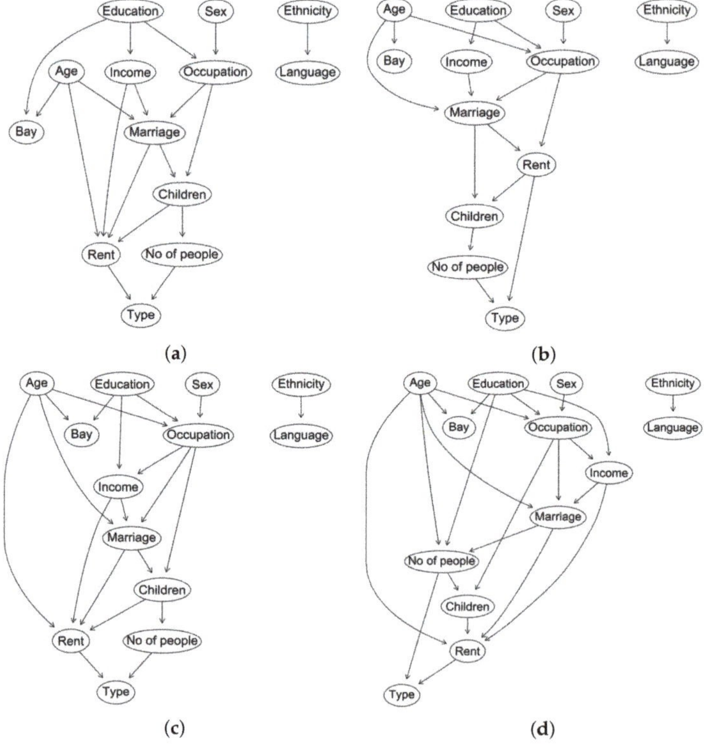

Figure 13. Income data. Estimated BNs using (**a**) FEDHC, (**b**) PCHC, (**c**) MMHC-1 and (**d**) MMHC-2.

6. Conclusions

This paper proposed to combine the first phase of the FBED variable selection algorithm with the HC scoring phase, leading to a new hybrid algorithm, termed FEDHC. Additionally, a new implementation of the MMHC algorithm was provided. Finally, the paper presented robustified (against outliers) versions of FEDHC, PCHC and MMHC. The robustified version of FEDHC was shown to be nearly 40 times faster than the raw version, and yielded BNs of higher quality, when outliers were present. Simulation studies manifested that in terms of computational efficiency, FEDHC is comparable to PHCHC, and along with MMHC-2, FEDHC was able to fit BNs to continuous data, with sample sizes in the order of hundreds of thousands in a few seconds and in the order of millions in a few minutes. It must be highlighted though that the skeleton identification phase of FEDHC and MMHC-1 have been implemented in R and not in C++. Additionally, FEDHC always executed significantly fewer CI tests than its competitors. Ultimately, in terms of accuracy, FEDHC outperformed is competitors with continuous data, and it was more accurate than or on par with MMHC-1 and MMHC-2 with categorical data, but less accurate than PCHC.

The rationale of MMHC and PCHC is to perform variable selection to each node, and then to apply a HC to the resulting network. In the same spirit, Ref. [49] used LASSO for variable selection with the scopus of constructing an un-directed network. The HC phase could be incorporated in the graphical LASSO to learn the underlying BN. Broadly speaking, the combination of a network learning phase with a scoring phase can yield hybrid algorithms. Other modern hybrid methods for BN learning include [50] on hybrid structure learning and sampling. They combine constraint-based pruning with MCMC inference schemes (also to improve the overall search space) and find a combination that is relatively efficient, with relatively good performance. The constraint-based part is interchangeable, and could connect well with MMHC, PCHC or FEDHC.

FEDHC is not the first algorithm that has outperformed MMHC. Recent algorithms include PCHC [15], the SP algorithm for Gaussian DAGs [51] and the NOTEARS [52]. The algorithms of [53,54] were also shown to outperform MMHC in the presence of latent confounders, not examined here. The advantage of the latter two is that they employ non-parametric tests such as the kernel CI test, thus allowing for non-linear relationships. BNs that detect non-linear relationships among the variables, such as the algorithms proposed by [53,54] is what this paper did not cover. Further, our comparative analysis was only with MMHC [13] and PCHC [15], due to their close relationship with FEDHC.

Future research includes a comparison of all algorithms in terms of more directions. For instance, (a) the effect of the Pearson and Spearman CI tests and the effect of X^2 and G^2 CI tests, (b) the effect of the outliers, (c) the effect of the scoring methods (Tabu search and HC), (d) the effect of the average neighbours (network density), and (e) the effect of the number of variables on the quality of the BN learned by either algorithm. These directions can be used to numerically evaluate the asymptotic properties of the BN learning algorithms with tens of millions of observations. Another interesting direction is the incorporation of fast non-linear CI tests, such as the distance correlation [55–58]. The distance correlation could be utilised during the skeleton identification of the FEDHC, mainly because it performs fewer CI tests than its competitors.

Supplementary Materials: The following supporting information can be downloaded at: https://www.mdpi.com/article/10.3390/math10152604/s1, R codes for simulation studies.

Funding: This research received no external funding.

Informed Consent Statement: Not applicable.

Data Availability Statement: Data is contained within the article.

Conflicts of Interest: The authors declare no conflict of interest.

Appendix A. Conditional Independence Tests

The type of CI tests executed during the skeleton identification phase depends upon the nature of the data, and they are used to test the following. Let X and Y be two random variables, and $\mathbf{Z}$ be a (possibly empty) set of random variables. Statistically speaking, X and Y are conditionally independent, given $\mathbf{Z}$ ($X \perp\!\!\!\perp Y|\mathbf{Z}$), if $P(X, Y|\mathbf{Z}) = P(X|\mathbf{Z}) \cdot P(Y|\mathbf{Z})$, and this holds for all values of X, Y and $\mathbf{Z}$. Equivalently, the conditional independence of X and Y, given $\mathbf{Z}$ implies $P(X|Y, \mathbf{Z}) = P(X|\mathbf{Z})$ and $P(Y|X, \mathbf{Z}) = P(Y|\mathbf{Z})$.

Appendix A.1. Pearson Correlation for Continuous Data

A frequently employed CI test for two continuous variables X and Y conditional on a set of variables $\mathbf{Z}$ is the partial correlation test [59] that assumes linear relationships among the variables. The test statistic for the partial Pearson correlation is given by:

$$T_p = \frac{1}{2} \left| \log \frac{1 + r_{X,Y|\mathbf{Z}}}{1 - r_{X,Y|\mathbf{Z}}} \right| \sqrt{n - |\mathbf{Z}| - 3}, \tag{A1}$$

where n is the sample size, $|\mathbf{Z}|$ denotes the number of conditioning variables and $r_{X,Y|\mathbf{z}}$ is the partial Pearson correlation (The partial correlation is efficiently computed using the correlation matrix of X, Y and $\mathbf{Z}$ [59]) of X and Y conditioning on $\mathbf{Z}$ (In the R package *Rfast*, its implementation of the PC algorithm compares T_p (A1) against a t distribution with $n - |\mathbf{Z}| - 3$ degrees of freedom, whereas the MMHC algorithm in the R package *bnlearn* compares T against the standard normal distribution. The differences are evident in small sample sizes, but become negligible when the sample sizes are in the order of a few tens). When $\mathbf{Z}$ is empty ($|\mathbf{Z}| = 0$), the partial correlation drops to the usual Pearson correlation coefficient.

Appendix A.2. Spearman Correlation for Continuous Data

The non-parametric alternative that is assumed to be more robust to outliers is the Spearman correlation coefficient. The Spearman correlation is equivalent to the Pearson correlation applied to the ranks of the variables. Its test statistic, however, is given by $T_s = T_p \times 1.029563$ [60,61].

Appendix A.3. G^2 Test of Independence for Categorical Data

The G^2 test of independence of two categorical variables X and Y, conditional on a set of variables $\mathbf{Z}$, is defined as [62]:

$$G^2 = 2 \sum_l \sum_{i,j} O_{ij|l} \log \frac{O_{ij|l}}{E_{ij|l}}, \tag{A2}$$

where O_{ij} are the observed frequencies of the i-th and j-th values of X and Y, respectively, for the l-th value of $\mathbf{Z}$. The E_{ij} are their corresponding expected frequencies computed by $E_{ij} = \frac{O_{i+|l} O_{+j|l}}{O_{++|l}}$, where $O_{i+|l} = \sum_{j=1}^{n} O_{ij|l}$, $O_{+j|l} = \sum_{i=1}^{n} O_{ij|l}$ and $O_{++|l} = n_l$. Under the conditional independence assumption, the G^2 test statistic follows the χ^2 distribution with $(|X| - 1)(|X| - 1)(|\mathbf{Z}| - 1)$ degrees of freedom, where $|\mathbf{Z}|$ refers to the cardinality of $\mathbf{Z}$ and the total number of values of $\mathbf{Z}$.

Appendix A.3.1. X^2 Test of Independence for Categorical Data

Alternatively, one could use the Pearson X^2 test statistic $X^2 = \sum_l \sum_{i,j} \frac{\left(O_{ij|l} - E_{ij|l}\right)^2}{E_{ij|l}^2}$ that has the same properties as the G^2 test statistic (A2). The drawback of X^2 is that it cannot be computed when $E_{ij|l} = 0$. On the contrary, G^2 is computed in such cases, since $\lim_{x \to 0} x \log x = 0$. For either aforementioned test, when $|\mathbf{Z}|$ is the empty set, both tests examine the unconditional association between variables X and Y. (For a practical comparison between the two tests based on extensive simulation studies, see [63].)

Appendix A.3.2. Permutation-Based p-Values

The aforementioned test statistics produce asymptotic p-values. In the case of small sample sizes, computationally intensive methods such as permutations might be preferable. With continuous variables for instance, when testing for unconditional independence, the idea is to distort the pairs multiple times, and each time, calculate the relevant test statistic. For the conditional independence of X and Y conditional on $\mathbf{Z}$, the partial correlation is computed from the residuals of two linear regression models, $X \sim \mathbf{Z}$ and $Y \sim \mathbf{Z}$. In this instance, the pairs of the residual vectors are distorted multiple times. With categorical variables, this approach is more complicated, and care must be taken so as to retain the row and column totals of the resulting contingency tables. For either case, the p-value is then computed as the proportion of times that the permuted test statistics exceed the observed test statistic that is computed using the original data. Permutation-based techniques have shown to improve the quality of BNs [64] in small sample sized cases. On the contrary, the FEDHC algorithm aims at making inferences on datasets with large sample sizes, for which asymptotic statistical tests are valid and reliable enough to produce the correct decisions.

Appendix B. Computational Details of FEDHC

With continuous data, the correlation matrix is computed once and utilised throughout the skeleton identification phase. FEDHC returns the correlation matrix and the matrix of the p-values of all pairwise associations that are useful in a second run of the algorithm with a different significance level. This is a significant advantage when BNs have to fit to large scale datasets and the correlation matrix can be given as an input to FEDHC to further reduce FEDHC's computational cost.

The partial correlation coefficient is given by:

$$
r_{X,Y|\mathbf{Z}} = \left\{
\begin{array}{ll}
\dfrac{R_{X,Y} - R_{X,z} R_{Y,z}}{\sqrt{\left(1 - R_{X,z}^2\right)^T \left(1 - R_{Y,z}^2\right)}} & \text{if } |\mathbf{Z}| = 1 \\[2ex]
-\dfrac{\mathbf{A}_{1,2}}{\sqrt{\mathbf{A}_{1,1} \mathbf{A}_{2,2}}} & \text{if } |\mathbf{Z}| > 1
\end{array}
\right\},
$$

where $R_{X,Y}$ is the correlation between the variables X and Y; $R_{X,Z}$ and $R_{Y,Z}$ denote the correlations between X & Z and Y & Z. $\mathbf{A} = R_{X,Y,\mathbf{Z}}^{-1}$, with $\mathbf{A}$ denoting the sub-correlation matrix of variables $X, Y, \mathbf{Z}$ and $A_{i,j}$ symbolises the element in the i-row and j-th column of matrix A.

The CI tests executed during the initial phase compute the logarithm of the p-value, instead of the p-value itself, to avoid numerical overflows observed with a large test statistic that produces a p-value that is equal to 0. Additionally, the computational cost of FEDHC's first phase can be further reduced via parallel programming.

It is also possible to store the p-values of each CI test for future reference. When a different significance level must be used, this will further decrease the associated computational cost of the skeleton identification phase in a second run. However, as will be exposed in Section 4.4, the cost of this phase is very small (a few seconds), even for millions of observations. The largest portion of this phase's computational cost is attributed to the calculation of the correlation matrix, which can be passed into subsequent runs of the algorithm.

Finally, Ref. [15] disregarded the potential of applying the PC-orientation rules [22,24] prior to the scoring phase as a means of improving the performance of FEDHC and MMHC, and this is not pursued any further.

Appendix C. The *R* Package *pchc*

The package *pchc* was first launched in *R* in July 2020 and initially contained the PCHC algorithm. It now includes the FEDHC and MMHC-2 algorithms, functions for testing (un)conditional independence with continuous and categorical data, data generation, BN visualisation and utility functions. It imports the *R* packages *bnlearn* and *Rfast*, and the built-in package *stats*. *pchc* is distributed as part of the CRAN R package repository and is compatible with MacOS-X, Windows, Solaris and Linux operating systems. Once the package is installed and loaded,

```
> install.packages (''pchc'')
> library(pchc)
```

it is ready to use without internet connection. The signature of the function **fedhc**, along with a short explanation of its arguments, is displayed below.

```
> fedhc(x, method = ''pearson", alpha = 0.05, robust = FALSE, ini.stat = NULL,
+  R = NULL, restart = 10, score = ''bic-g", blacklist = NULL, whitelist = NULL)
```

- x: A numerical matrix with the variables. If you have a data.frame (i.e. categorical data) turn them into a matrix using. Note, that for the categorical case data, the numbers must start from 0. No missing data are allowed.
- method: If you have continuous data, this must be "pearson" (default value) or ""cat" if you have categorical data . With categorical data, one has to make sure that the minimum value of each variable is zero. The function *g2test* from the package *Rfast* and the relevant functions work that way.
- alpha: The significance level for assessing the p-values. The default value is 0.05.
- robust: If outliers are be removed prior to applying the FEDHC algorithm, this must be set to TRUE.
- ini.stat: If the initial test statistics (univariate associations) are available, they can passed to this argument.
- R: If the correlation matrix is available, pass it here.
- restart: An integer, the number of random restarts. The default value is 10.
- score: A character string, the label of the network score to be used in the algorithm. If none is specified, the default score is the Bayesian Information Criterion for continuous data sets. The available score for continuous variables are: "bic-g" (default value), "loglik-g", "aic-g", "bic-g" or "bge". The available score of categorical variables are: "bde", "loglik" or "bic".
- blacklist: A data frame with two columns (optionally labeled "from" and "to"), containing a set of forbidden directions.
- whitelist: A data frame with two columns (optionally labeled "from" and "to"), containing a set of must-add directions.

The output of the **fedhc** function is a list including:

- ini: A list including the output of the *fedhc.skel* function.
- dag: A "bn" class output, a list including the outcome of the Hill-Climbing phase. See the package *bnlearn* for more details.
- scoring: The highest score value observed during the scoring phase.
- runtime: The duration of the algorithm.

References

1. Hoover, K.D. *Causality in Economics and Econometrics*; Palgrave: Macmillan UK, 2017; pp. 1–13.
2. Sun, L.; Erath, A. A Bayesian network approach for population synthesis. *Transp. Res. Part Emerg. Technol.* **2015**, *61*, 49–62. [CrossRef]
3. Kocabas, V.; Dragicevic, S. Agent-based model validation using Bayesian networks and vector spatial data. *Environ. Plan. Plan. Des.* **2009**, *36*, 787–801. [CrossRef]
4. Kocabas, V.; Dragicevic, S. Bayesian networks and agent-based modeling approach for urban land-use and population density change: A BNAS model. *J. Geogr. Syst.* **2013**, *15*, 403–426. [CrossRef]

5. Hosseini, S.; Barker, K. A Bayesian network model for resilience-based supplier selection. *Int. J. Prod. Econ.* **2016**, *180*, 68–87. [CrossRef]

6. Spiegler, R. Bayesian networks and boundedly rational expectations. *Q. J. Econ.* **2016**, *131*, 1243–1290. [CrossRef]

7. Xue, J.; Gui, D.; Lei, J.; Sun, H.; Zeng, F.; Feng, X. A hybrid Bayesian network approach for trade-offs between environmental flows and agricultural water using dynamic discretization. *Adv. Water Resour.* **2017**, *110*, 445–458. [CrossRef]

8. Mele, A. A structural model of dense network formation. *Econometrica* **2017**, *85*, 825–850. [CrossRef]

9. Chong, C; Kluppelberg, C. Contagion in financial systems: A Bayesian network approach. *SIAM J. Financ. Math.* **2018**, *9*, 28–53. [CrossRef]

10. Leong, C.K. Credit risk scoring with Bayesian network models. *Comput. Econ.* **2016**, *47*, 423–446. [CrossRef]

11. Sheehan, B.; Murphy, F.; Ryan, C.; Mullins, M.; Liu, H.Y. Semi-autonomous vehicle motor insurance: A Bayesian Network risk transfer approach. *Transp. Res. Part Emerg. Technol.* **2017**, *82*, 124–137. [CrossRef]

12. Cugnata, F.; Kenett, R.; Salini, S. Bayesian network applications to customer surveys and InfoQ. *Procedia Econ. Financ.* **2014**, *17*, 3–9. [CrossRef]

13. Tsamardinos, I.; Brown, L.E.; Aliferis, C.F. The max-min hill-climbing Bayesian network structure learning algorithm. *Mach. Learn.* **2006**, *65*, 31–78. [CrossRef]

14. Scutari, M. Learning Bayesian Networks with the bnlearn R Package. *J. Stat. Softw.* **2010**, *35*, 1–22. [CrossRef]

15. Tsagris, M. A new scalable Bayesian network learning algorithm with application to economics. *Comput. Econ.* **2021**, *57*, 341–367. [CrossRef]

16. Tsagris, M. pchc: Bayesian Network Learning with the PCHC and Related Algorithms. R package version 0.5. 2021. Available online: https://cran.r-project.org/web/packages/pchc/index.html (accessed on 22 May 2022).

17. Borboudakis, G; Tsamardinos, I. Forward-Backward selection with Early Dropping. *J. Mach. Learn. Res.* **2019**, *20*, 276–314.

18. Kalisch, M.; Bühlmann, P. Robustification of the PC-algorithm for directed acyclic graphs. *J. Comput. Graph. Stat.* **2008**, *17*, 773–789. [CrossRef]

19. Cheng, Y.; Diakonikolas, I.; Kane, D.; Stewart, A. Robust learning of fixed-structure Bayesian networks. *Adv. Neural Inf. Process. Syst.* **2018**, *31*, 10283–10295.

20. Greene, W.H. *Econometric Analysis*; Pearson Education India: Noida, India, 2003.

21. Pearl, J. *Probabilistic Reasoning in iNtelligent Systems: Networks of Plausible Reasoning*; Morgan Kaufmann Publishers: Los Altos, CA, USA, 1988.

22. Spirtes, P.; Glymour, C.N.; Scheines, R. *Causation, Prediction, and Search*; MIT Press: Cambridge, MA, USA, 2000.

23. Verma, T.; Pearl, J. Equivalence and synthesis of causal models. In Proceedings of the Sixth Conference on Uncertainty in Artificial Intelligence, Cambridge, MA, USA, 27–29 July 1991; pp. 220–227.

24. Spirtes, P.; Glymour, C. An algorithm for fast recovery of sparse causal graphs. *Soc. Sci. Comput. Rev.* **1991**, *9*, 62–72. [CrossRef]

25. Chickering, D.M. Optimal structure identification with greedy search. *J. Mach. Learn. Res.* **2002**, *3*, 507–554.

26. Cooper, F.G.; Herskovits, E. A Bayesian method for the induction of probabilistic networks from data. *Mach. Learn.* **1992**, *9*, 309–347. [CrossRef]

27. Heckerman, D.; Geiger, D.; Chickering, D.M. Learning Bayesian networks: The combination of knowledge and statistical data. *Mach. Learn.* **1995**, *20*, 197–243. [CrossRef]

28. Tsagris, M. Bayesian network learning with the PC algorithm: An improved and correct variation. *Appl. Artif. Intell.* **2019**, *33*, 101–123. [CrossRef]

29. Draper; R, N.; Smith, H. *Applied Regression Analysis*; John Wiley & Sons: Hoboken, NJ, USA, 1998.

30. Schwarz, G. Estimating the dimension of a model. *Ann. Stat.* **1978**, *6*, 461–464. [CrossRef]

31. Geiger, D; Heckerman, D. Learning Gaussian networks. In Proceedings of the 10th International Conference on Uncertainty in Artificial Intelligence, Seattle, WA, USA, 29–31 July 1994; pp. 235–243.

32. Buntine, W. Theory refinement on Bayesian networks. In *Uncertainty Proceedings*; Elsevier: Amsterdam, The Netherlands, 1991; pp. 52–60.

33. Bouckaert, R.R. *Bayesian Belief Networks: From Construction to Inference*. Ph.D. Thesis, University of Utrecht, Utrecht, The Netherlands, 1995.

34. Lam, W.; Bacchus, F. Learning Bayesian belief networks: An approach based on the MDL principle. *Comput. Intell.* **1994**, *10*, 269–293. [CrossRef]

35. Suzuki, J. A construction of Bayesian networks from databases based on an MDL principle. In *Uncertainty in Artificial Intelligence*; Morgan Kaufmann: Burlington, MA, USA, 1993; pp. 266–273.

36. Rousseeuw, P.J. Multivariate estimation with high breakdown point. *Math. Stat. Appl.* **1985**, *8*, 283–297.

37. Rousseeuw, P.J.; Driessen, K.V. A fast algorithm for the minimum covariance determinant estimator. *Technometrics* **1999**, *41*, 212–223. [CrossRef]

38. Raymaekers, J.; Rousseeuw, P.J. Fast robust correlation for high-dimensional data. *Technometrics* **2021**, *63*, 184–198. [CrossRef]

39. Cerchiello, P; Giudici, P. Big data analysis for financial risk management. *J. Big Data* **2016**, *3*, 18. [CrossRef]

40. Cerioli, A. Multivariate outlier detection with high-breakdown estimators. *J. Am. Stat. Assoc.* **2010**, *105*, 147–156. [CrossRef]

41. Hubert, M.; Debruyne, M. Minimum covariance determinant. *Comput. Stat.* **2010**, *2*, 36–43. [CrossRef]

42. Ro, K.; Zou, C.; Wang, Z.; Yin, G. Outlier detection for high-dimensional data. *Biometrika* **2015**, *102*, 589–599. [CrossRef]

43. Tsagris, M.; Tsamardinos, I. Feature selection with the R package MXM. *F1000Research* **2019**, *7*, 1505. [CrossRef] [PubMed]
44. Chickering, D.M. A transformational characterization of equivalent Bayesian network structures. In Proceedings of the Eleventh conference on Uncertainty in Artificial Intelligence, Montreal, QC, Canada, 18–20 August 1995; pp. 87–98.
45. Beinlich, I.A.; Suermondt, H.J.; Chavez, R.M.; Cooper, G.F. The ALARM monitoring system: A case study with two probabilistic inference techniques for belief networks. In *AIME 89*; Springer: Berlin/Heidelberg, Germany, 1989; pp. 247–256.
46. Kleiber, C.; Zeileis, A. *Applied Econometrics with R*; Springer: New York, NY, USA, 2008.
47. Friedman, J.; Hastie, T.; Tibshirani, R. *The Elements of Statistical Learning*; Springer: New York, NY, USA, 2001.
48. Hahsler, M.S.; Chelluboina; Hornik, K.; Buchta, C. The arules R-Package Ecosystem: Analyzing Interesting Patterns from Large Transaction Datasets. *J. Mach. Learn. Res.* **2011**, *12*, 1977–1981.
49. Meinshausen, N.; Bühlmann, P. High-dimensional graphs and variable selection with the Lasso. *Ann. Stat.* **2006**, *34*, 1436–1462. [CrossRef]
50. Kuipers, J.; Suter, P.; Moffa, G. Efficient sampling and structure learning of Bayesian networks. *arXiv* **2020**, arXiv:1803.07859.
51. Raskutti, G.; Uhler; C Learning directed acyclic graph models based on sparsest permutations. *Stat* **2018**, *7*, e183. [CrossRef]
52. Zheng, X.; Aragam, B.; Ravikumar, P.K.; Xing, E.P. Dags with no tears: Continuous optimization for structure learning. *Adv. Neural Inf. Process. Syst.* **2018**, *31*, 9492–9503.
53. Zhang; Peters, K.; Janzing, J.; D; Schölkopf, B. Kernel-based conditional independence test and application in causal discovery. In Proceedings of the 27th conference on Uncertainty in Artificial Intelligence, Quebec City, QC, Canada, 270030 July 2012; pp. 804–813.
54. Chalupka, K.; Perona, P.; Eberhardt, F. Fast conditional independence test for vector variables with large sample sizes. *arXiv* **2018**, arXiv:1804.02747.
55. Huo, X.; Székely, G.J. Fast computing for distance covariance. *Technometrics* **2016**, *58*, 435–447. [CrossRef]
56. Shen, C.; Panda, S.; Vogelstein, J.T. The chi-square test of distance correlation. *J. Comput. Graph. Stat.* **2022**, *31*, 254–262. [CrossRef]
57. Székely, G.J.; Rizzo, M.L. Partial distance correlation with methods for dissimilarities. *Ann. Stat.* **2014**, *42*, 2382–2412. [CrossRef]
58. Székely, G.J.; Rizzo, M.L.; Bakirov, N.K. Measuring and testing dependence by correlation of distances. *Ann. Stat.* **2007**, *35*, 2769–2794. [CrossRef]
59. Baba, K.; Shibata, R.; Sibuya, M. Partial correlation and conditional correlation as measures of conditional independence. *Aust. N. Z. J. Stat.* **2004**, *46*, 657–664. [CrossRef]
60. Fieller, E.C.; Hartley, H.O.; Pearson, E.S. Tests for rank correlation coefficients. I. *Biometrika* **1957**, *44*, 470–481. [CrossRef]
61. Fieller, C.E.; Pearson, E.S. Tests for rank correlation coefficients: II. *Biometrika* **1961**, *48*, 29–40.
62. Agresti, A. *Categorical Data Analysis*, 2nd ed.; Wiley Series in Probability and Statistics: Hoboken, NJ, USA, 2002.
63. Alenazi, A. A Monte Carlo comparison of categorical tests of independence. *arXiv* **2020**, arXiv:2004.00973.
64. Tsamardinos, I.; Borboudakis, G. Permutation testing improves Bayesian network learning. In Proceedings of the Joint European Conference on Machine Learning and Knowledge Discovery in Databases, Barcelona, Spain, 20–24 September 2010; pp. 322–337.

mathematics

Article

Jewel 2.0: An Improved Joint Estimation Method for Multiple Gaussian Graphical Models

Claudia Angelini [1,†], Daniela De Canditiis [2,†] and Anna Plaksienko [1,*,†]

1   Istituto per le Applicazioni del Calcolo "Mauro Picone", CNR-Napoli, 80131 Naples, Italy
2   Istituto per le Applicazioni del Calcolo "Mauro Picone", CNR-Roma, 00185 Rome, Italy
*   Correspondence: a.plaksienko@na.iac.cnr.it
†   These authors contributed equally to this work.

Abstract: In this paper, we consider the problem of estimating the graphs of conditional dependencies between variables (i.e., graphical models) from multiple datasets under Gaussian settings. We present *jewel 2.0*, which improves our previous method *jewel 1.0* by modeling commonality and class-specific differences in the graph structures and better estimating graphs with hubs, making this new approach more appealing for biological data applications. We introduce these two improvements by modifying the regression-based problem formulation and the corresponding minimization algorithm. We also present, for the first time in the multiple graphs setting, a stability selection procedure to reduce the number of false positives in the estimated graphs. Finally, we illustrate the performance of *jewel 2.0* through simulated and real data examples. The method is implemented in the new version of the R package `jewel`.

Keywords: group lasso penalty; data integration; network estimation; stability selection

MSC: 62A09; 62J07; 92-08

Citation: Angelini, C. ; De Canditiis, D.; Plaksienko, A. *Jewel 2.0*: An Improved Joint Estimation Method for Multiple Gaussian Graphical Models. *Mathematics* **2022**, *10*, 3983. https://doi.org/10.3390/math 10213983

Academic Editors: Snezhana Gocheva-Ilieva, Atanas Ivanov and Hristina Kulina

Received: 5 September 2022
Accepted: 22 October 2022
Published: 26 October 2022

Publisher's Note: MDPI stays neutral with regard to jurisdictional claims in published maps and institutional affiliations.

1. Introduction

Gaussian graphical models (GGMs) are becoming essential tools for studying the relationships between Gaussian variables. They are pervasive in many fields, especially biology and medicine, where the variables are usually genes or proteins, and the edges represent their interactions. In addition, researchers now often have several datasets measuring the same set of variables, i.e., data collected under slightly different conditions, on varying types of equipment, in different labs, or even for sub-types of disease. In this case, we expect most connections between variables to be the same or similar across the datasets; hence, GGM joint estimation is desirable to improve the estimation accuracy.

In [1], we proposed *jewel*, a technique for the joint estimation of a GGM in the multiple dataset framework under the hypothesis that the graph structure is the same across the classes. The *jewel* technique uses a node-wise regression approach (based on [2]) with a group lasso penalty and has the advantage of providing a symmetric estimate of the adjacency matrix, which encodes the graph's structure. In this paper, we present *jewel 2.0*, which attempts to extend *jewel* by addressing several aspects and enlarging its range of applications.

Firstly, we modified the problem formulation to allow the simultaneous modeling of commonalities and differences between datasets. In particular, we estimated a graph for each class or dataset, assuming that all graphs share considerable amount of information (denoted as the common part in the text, representing the edges present in all graphs) but can exhibit some class-specific differences (representing the edges present only in some graphs). Such an assumption significantly extends the range of applications since the estimation of class-specific differences is of interest in several contexts, for example, when we want to estimate gene regulatory networks associated with different disease sub-types.

In such cases, the common part captures the main mechanisms associated with the disease, while the class-specific model captures the differences related to a particular sub-type. Although other joint estimation methods (see Section 3.3) have previously allowed this extension, *jewel 2.0* is the first method that both provides symmetric estimates of the graphs (as with our previous *jewel 1.0*) and accounts for differences between graphs.

Secondly, we improved the method's performance when applied to graphs with hubs, which often describe biological networks. In the numerical studies presented in [1], we noticed that the performance of *jewel*, as well as of the other joint estimation methods, deteriorates when the underlying graphs have prominent hubs (i.e., a few nodes with high degrees). We argued that this phenomenon was due to the type of "democratic" penalty used in the problem formulation that does not allow some vertices to get the power to become a hub/leader. Therefore, in *jewel 2.0*, we introduced specific weights into the penalty function to enable hubs to emerge. The weights reduce the penalization of edges incident to the potential hub node, allowing even more edges to "join" that vertex. This modification considerably improves the performance of *jewel 2.0*, as shown by numerical simulations carried out on synthetic graphs.

Finally, in this paper, we also incorporate a stability selection procedure to reduce the number of false positives (i.e., estimated edges that are not truly present in the underlying graph). In the high-dimensional context (i.e., when $p >> n$), methods often suffer from increasing false positives or lack of power, depending on the choice of the regularization parameter. Although simulations show that the overall performance is competitive, estimated graphs must be sparse to be interpretable, but the presence of false positive edges decreases the interpretability of the estimated network. We observed a significant presence of incorrectly estimated edges in all methods we compared (under high dimensional settings), although ROC curves are not dramatically impacted. Stability selection procedures can alleviate the problem of false positives at the price of a slight loss of statistical power. Our stability procedure extends the ideas of [3] to the multiple graph context, suggesting the choice of only edges that persistently appear in the several runs of the method on subsampled data; see Section 2.4 for details. To the best of our knowledge, *jewel 2.0* is the first method that employs a stability selection procedure to refine the estimated networks in the context of joint inference.

The rest of the paper is organized as follows. In Section 2, we provide the necessary background and introduce the *jewel 2.0* method as well as the numerical algorithm for its evaluation. In Section 3, we use synthetic data to demonstrate the performance of *jewel 2.0* in several scenarios and present a comparison with other existing methods. Then, in Section 4, we demonstrate the application of *jewel 2.0* to breast cancer gene expression datasets. Finally, in Section 5, we discuss our study's advantages and limitations and provide directions for future work.

2. Materials and Methods

This section introduces the mathematical notations and the assumptions made in this paper. Then, we describe the penalization model that allows the approach both to incorporate differences among classes and to handle the presence of hubs. After that, we propose the *jewel 2.0* algorithm for the joint estimation of Gaussian graphical models. Finally, the section also describes the choice of the regularization parameters and the stability selection procedure and highlights the differences from our previous method, *jewel 1.0*.

2.1. Problem Set-Up

Let $\mathbf{X}^{(1)}, \mathbf{X}^{(2)}, \ldots, \mathbf{X}^{(K)}$ be $K \geq 2$ datasets containing measurements of (almost) the same variables under K different but similar conditions (e.g., sub-types of disease) or collected in distinct classes (e.g., different equipment or laboratories). Each dataset $\mathbf{X}^{(k)}$ is an $n_k \times p_k$ data matrix with n_k observations of p_k variables. We assume that observations

$(x_1^{(k)}, \ldots, x_{n_k}^{(k)})^\top$ are independent and identically distributed samples from a p_k-variate Gaussian distribution with zero mean and covariance matrix $\Sigma^{(k)}$.

Every distribution $\mathcal{N}(0, \Sigma^{(k)})$ is associated with a graphical model $G^{(k)} = (V_k, E_k)$, where vertices correspond to random variables, i.e., $V_k = \{X_1^{(k)}, \ldots, X_{p_k}^{(k)}\}$, and the absence of edges (where $E_k \subseteq V_k \times V_k$) implies the conditional independence of the corresponding variables, i.e., $(i,j) \notin E_k \Leftrightarrow X_i^{(k)} \perp\!\!\!\perp X_j^{(k)} | X_{\{l, l \neq i, j\}}^{(k)}$. It is well known that the support of the precision matrix encodes the graph structure, i.e., $(i,j) \in E_k \iff \Omega_{ij}^{(k)} \neq 0$, where $\Omega^{(k)} = (\Sigma^{(k)})^{-1}$ is the true precision matrix for the k-th class. Therefore, for each dataset, the problem of graph estimation becomes equivalent to estimating the support of the precision matrix, as illustrated in Figure 1. However, when the K datasets share some dependency structure (as occurs when we consider similar datasets), a joint inference can be more powerful and accurate, as already shown in [1] and referenced therein. The joint inference requires modeling how the information about the graphs $G^{(k)}$ is shared across different datasets.

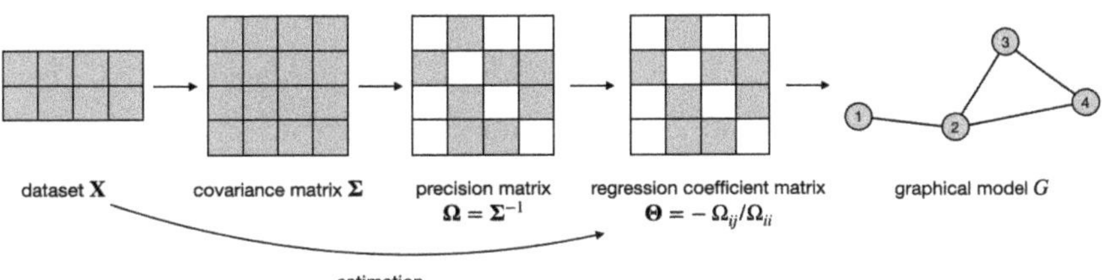

Figure 1. Idea of regression-based graphical model estimation for a single dataset **X**: estimate the regression coefficient matrix Θ from the data and use its support as an adjacency matrix of the graph G. See text for details.

In [1], we proposed the following joint estimation approach. We started with an assumption that although the covariance matrices $\Sigma^{(k)}$, $k = 1 \ldots K$, might be different, the structures of K graphs coincide, i.e., the graph G is the same across all datasets. Therefore, we needed to estimate the same support from K precision matrices. However, instead of doing that directly, we estimated the support of K regression coefficient matrices. We defined them as $\Theta^{(k)} \in R^{p_k \times p_k}$ with entries $\Theta_{ij}^{(k)} = -\Omega_{ij}^{(k)}/\Omega_{ii}^{(k)}$ and $\Theta_{ii}^{(k)} = 0$. By construction, the support of the extra-diagonal entries of $\Theta^{(k)}$ also encodes the graph structure, i.e., $(i,j) \in E_k \iff \Theta_{ij}^{(k)} \neq 0$. Hence, in *jewel 1.0*, we simultaneously estimated $\hat{\Theta}^{(1)}, \ldots, \hat{\Theta}^{(K)}$ by solving the following minimization problem:

$$(\hat{\Theta}^{(1)}, \ldots, \hat{\Theta}^{(K)}) = \underset{\substack{\Theta^{(1)} \in \mathbb{R}^{p_1 \times p_1} \\ \vdots \\ \Theta^{(K)} \in \mathbb{R}^{p_K \times p_K}, \\ \text{diag} = 0}}{\arg\min} \left\{ \frac{1}{2} \sum_{k=1}^{K} \frac{1}{n_k} ||\mathbf{X}^{(k)} - \mathbf{X}^{(k)}\Theta^{(k)}||_F^2 + \lambda \sum_{i<j=1}^{p} \sqrt{g_{ij}} \sqrt{\sum_{k:\{X_i, X_j\} \subset V_k} \left(\Theta_{ij}^{(k)}\right)^2 + \left(\Theta_{ji}^{(k)}\right)^2} \right\}, \tag{1}$$

where g_{ij} denotes the cardinality of the group of symmetric variables $(\Theta_{ij}^{(1)}, \Theta_{ji}^{(1)}, \ldots\ldots, \Theta_{ij}^{(K)}, \Theta_{ji}^{(K)})$ across all the datasets that contain the couple of variables (i,j). As a result, we obtained K matrices $(\hat{\Theta}^{(1)}, \ldots, \hat{\Theta}^{(K)})$ with the same symmetric support, which represents the adjacency matrix of the common estimated graph $\hat{G}$.

However, while the symmetry of the solution of Equation (1) is one of the main advantages of our original formulation, forcing the datasets to have exactly the same underlying graph might be a limitation in some cases. For example, the assumption that the datasets $\mathbf{X}^{(k)}, k = 1\ldots K$, share the same graph G might be reasonable when they represent the gene expression of the same type of cells, measured in different laboratories or with different instruments. In such cases, we expect the actual underlying regulatory mechanisms to remain the same despite the technology. However, the assumption becomes limited when the datasets represent the gene expression in cells isolated from different sub-types or stages of some disease. In such a context, we expect a common underlying mechanism that can be associated with that disease, but there could be sub-type-specific differences that are not shared across all the datasets but characterize only one (or some, but not all) condition. To overcome this limitation, in this paper, we modify the formulation of the minimization problem in Equation (1) to allow the modeling of both commonalities and differences between the graphs $G^{(k)}, k = 1\ldots K$. Therefore, by relaxing the assumptions, we increase the range of applications of our approach.

Additionally, in [1] we demonstrated that *jewel 1.0* performs comparably well or even better than other joint approaches for GGM (i.e., JGL [4] and the proposal of Guo et al. [5]). However, we also showed that all methods' performances significantly decreased when the true graph contained hubs. Scale-free graphs with a power of preferential attachment bigger than 1 constitute typical examples of graphs with hubs. In general, many real-life graphs such as gene regulatory networks or protein–protein interaction networks are estimated to have a power law between 2 and 3. Therefore, we introduced some weights into the penalization problem to allow for a better estimation of hubs. The key idea is that small weights must be assigned to the edges linked to potential hubs so that hubs can emerge (in other words, we allow the preferential attachment of an edge to a hub). We will show that this modification leads to a considerable improvement in performance when some preliminary information on the hubs is available. We note that although other graph estimation methods with weighted penalties exist for one dataset, e.g., DW-lasso [6], *jewel 2.0* is the first joint method for several datasets with a weighted penalty.

To incorporate both changes, we reformulate the minimization problem as follows. We define the set $V = V_1 \cup \cdots \cup V_K$ with p being its cardinality. We define matrices of weights for each graph, $\mathbf{W}^{(k)}$, with entries $W_{ij}^{(k)} \in (0, 1]$. These matrices incorporate information about hubs when available (smaller weights should be assigned to edges incident to hubs, larger weights to the others); otherwise, we set $\mathbf{W}^{(k)} = \mathbf{1}$. For each class $k = 1\ldots K$ we set $\mathbf{\Theta}^{(k)} = \mathbf{\Xi}^{(k)} + \mathbf{\Gamma}^{(k)}$, where matrices $\mathbf{\Xi}^{(k)}$ share the same support structure among the K classes (i.e., they represent the common information shared across different graphs) while $\mathbf{\Gamma}^{(k)}$ are class-specific (hence they allow to model differences among the classes). We emphasize that $\mathbf{\Xi}^{(k)}$ and $\mathbf{\Gamma}^{(k)}, k = 1\ldots K$, act as auxiliary (or dummy) variables and do not exactly represent common and specific parts of the graphs $G^{(k)}$. For example, non-zero elements in position i, j of all $\mathbf{\Gamma}^{(k)}$ are an indication of the common edge, despite the fact of being present in class-specific $\mathbf{\Gamma}^{(k)}$s. In our procedure, we estimate $\hat{G}^{(k)}$ through the support of $\mathbf{\Theta}^{(k)} = \mathbf{\Xi}^{(k)} + \mathbf{\Gamma}^{(k)}$. Once we have estimated $\hat{G}^{(k)}, k = 1\ldots K$, we can later identify their common part as the intersection of the estimated graphs and the specific parts as the difference between the common part and the individual estimates. With this notation, we estimate $\hat{\mathbf{\Theta}}^{(1)}, \ldots, \hat{\mathbf{\Theta}}^{(K)}$ by solving the following problem:

$$
(\hat{\Xi}^{(1)}, \hat{\Gamma}^{(1)}, \ldots, \hat{\Xi}^{(K)}, \hat{\Gamma}^{(K)}) = \underset{\substack{\Xi^{(1)}, \Gamma^{(1)} \in \mathbb{R}^{p_1 \times p_1} \\ \vdots \\ \Xi^{(K)}, \Gamma^{(K)} \in \mathbb{R}^{p_K \times p_K}, \\ \text{diag} = 0}}{\arg\min} \left\{ \frac{1}{2} \sum_{k=1}^{K} \frac{1}{n_k} ||\mathbf{X}^{(k)} - \mathbf{X}^{(k)}\Xi^{(k)} - \mathbf{X}^{(k)}\Gamma^{(k)}||_F^2 + \right.
$$

$$
+\lambda_1 \sum_{i<j=1}^{p} \sqrt{g_{ij}}\,\overline{W}_{ij} \sqrt{\sum_{k:\{X_i, X_j\} \subset V_k} \left(\Xi_{ij}^{(k)}\right)^2 + \left(\Xi_{ji}^{(k)}\right)^2}
$$

$$
\left. +\lambda_2 \sum_{i<j=1}^{p} \sqrt{2} \sum_{k:\{X_i, X_j\} \subset V_k} W_{ij}^{(k)} \sqrt{\left(\Gamma_{ij}^{(k)}\right)^2 + \left(\Gamma_{ji}^{(k)}\right)^2} \right\},
$$

$$(2)$$

where $\overline{W}_{ij} = 1/K \sum_k W_{ij}^{(k)}$ and λ_1, λ_2 are two regularization parameters.

Note that the minimization problem in Equation (2) has two penalty terms. The first penalty is applied to the entire group $(\Xi_{ij}^{(1)}, \Xi_{ji}^{(1)}, \ldots, \Xi_{ij}^{(K)}, \Xi_{ji}^{(K)})$ and enforces the presence/absence of an edge across all classes containing that edge (to capture common dependencies). The second penalty is applied independently to each group $(\Gamma_{ij}^{(k)}, \Gamma_{ji}^{(k)}), k = 1 \ldots K$. This enforces the symmetry of the relation between two nodes in each class, allowing class-specific differences to emerge. Figure 2 provides an illustration of the idea.

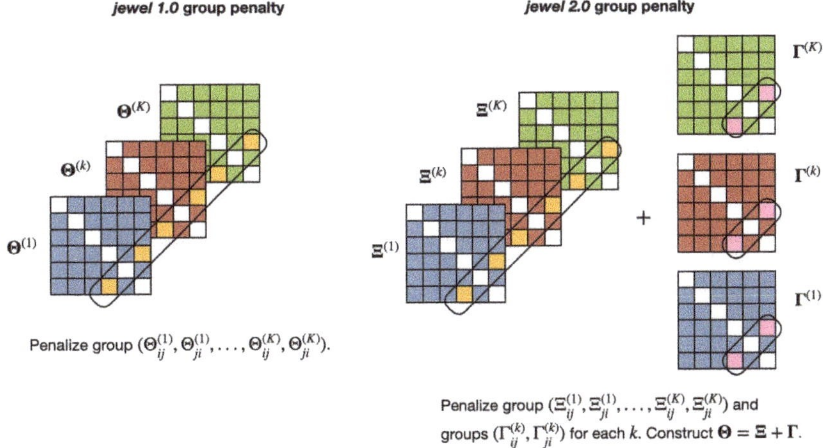

Figure 2. Illustration of the group penalties applied in *jewel 1.0* (**left panel**) and *jewel 2.0* (**right panel**). In *jewel 1.0*, the penalty forces the datasets to share the same graph by either setting to zero or retaining the coefficients associated with the entire group $(\Theta_{ij}^{(1)}, \Theta_{ji}^{(1)}, \ldots, \Theta_{ij}^{(K)}, \Theta_{ji}^{(K)})$. In *jewel 2.0*, the first penalty is similar to the one in *jewel 1.0*, applied to the entire group $(\Xi_{ij}^{(1)}, \Xi_{ji}^{(1)}, \ldots, \Xi_{ij}^{(K)}, \Xi_{ji}^{(K)})$. However, the second penalty is applied to each group $(\Gamma_{ij}^{(k)}, \Gamma_{ji}^{(k)}), k = 1 \ldots K$, independently, allowing the approach to set to zero or retain edges in specific classes.

Moreover, the weights $W_{ij}^{(k)}$ in the penalties allow hubs to emerge. By assigning lower weights to edges linked to potential hubs, we reduce the penalty on those edges and allow hubs to emerge. Instead, by choosing $W_{ij}^{(k)} = 1$, we have a more democratic approach that is equivalent to an unweighted formulation. Weights could be estimated from the data or provided by the user from prior knowledge, literature, and databases. Currently, using information already available in the literature (from previous experiments) or knowledge stored in databases is becoming widespread, particularly in omics science, where international projects and consortiums have released an enormous amount of data in open form. For example, in [7], the authors suggested using gene networks retrieved from databases to improve survival prediction. Here, we propose the use of information concerning potential highly influential genes to estimate networks with hubs better. Section 3.2.2 discusses weight choice in detail.

Finally, we note that the minimization problem in Equation (2) is not identifiable in terms of $\Xi^{(k)}$ and $\Gamma^{(k)}$ but is identifiable in terms of the support of $\Theta^{(k)}$, provided that we estimate it using $\Xi^{(k)} + \Gamma^{(k)}$. Furthermore, as a result of the minimization problem in Equation (2), we obtain K graphs $\hat{G}^{(k)}$ with largely the same structure G but also allow some class-specific edges. See Figure 3 for an illustration of the idea.

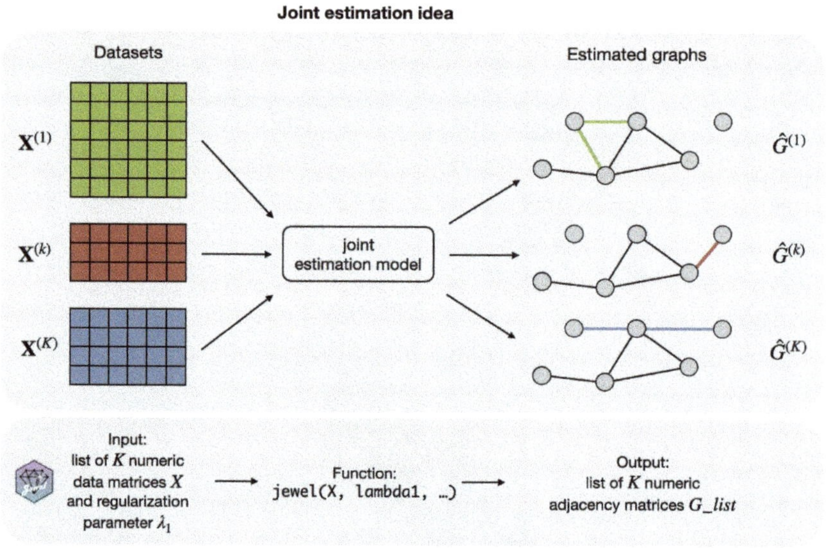

Figure 3. Illustration of how *jewel 2.0* estimates the graphs with largely the same support (i.e., the black part of the graphs $\hat{G}^{(k)}$) but also allows for some class-specific edges (colored part of the graphs $\hat{G}^{(k)}$). The lower part of the figure demonstrates how the idea translates to the R package `jewel` described in Section 2.5.

2.2. Jewel 2.0 Algorithm

To solve the minimization problem in Equation (2), we apply the group descent algorithm presented in [8]. To better describe this algorithm, we rewrite the problem in Equation (2) using an equivalent formulation. To this end, we define the following matrices and vectors (note that for the ease of notation without loss of generality, we suppose $p_1 = \cdots = p_K = p$):

- $X_{.i}^{(k)}$ the i-th column of matrix $\mathbf{X}^{(k)}$ and $\mathbf{X}_{.-i}^{(k)}$ the submatrix of $\mathbf{X}^{(k)}$ without the i-th column;

- $y = \left(X_{.1}^{(1)\top}, \ldots, X_{.p}^{(1)\top}, \ldots, X_{.1}^{(K)\top}, \ldots, X_{.p}^{(K)\top} \right)^{\top}$ denotes the vector concatenating the columns of all data matrices, $\dim(y) = Np \times 1$, $N = \sum_{k=1}^{K} n_k$;

- $\xi = \left(\Xi_{21}^{(1)}, \ldots, \Xi_{p1}^{(1)}, \ldots, \Xi_{1p}^{(K)}, \ldots, \Xi_{(p-1)p}^{(K)} \right)$, $\dim(\xi) = 1 \times p(p-1)K$, and
$\gamma = \left(\Gamma_{21}^{(1)}, \ldots, \Gamma_{p1}^{(1)}, \ldots, \Gamma_{1p}^{(K)}, \ldots, \Gamma_{(p-1)p}^{(K)} \right)$, $\dim(\gamma) = 1 \times p(p-1)K$,
are obtained by concatenating the vectorized matrices over the K classes;

$$X = \begin{pmatrix} \begin{pmatrix} \mathbf{X}^{(1)}_{.-1} & 0 & \cdots & 0 \\ 0 & \mathbf{X}^{(1)}_{.-2} & \cdots & 0 \\ \vdots & & \ddots & \\ 0 & \cdots & & \mathbf{X}^{(1)}_{.-p} \end{pmatrix} & & & \\ & \ddots & & \\ & & \begin{pmatrix} \mathbf{X}^{(K)}_{.-1} & 0 & \cdots & 0 \\ 0 & \mathbf{X}^{(K)}_{.-2} & \cdots & 0 \\ \vdots & & \ddots & \\ 0 & \cdots & & \mathbf{X}^{(K)}_{.-p} \end{pmatrix} \end{pmatrix}$$

denotes the block-diagonal matrix made up of the block-diagonal matrices $\mathbf{X}^{(k)}_{.-j}$, $k = 1\ldots K, j = 1\ldots p, \dim(\mathbf{X}) = Np \times p(p-1)K$;

- augmented matrix $\tilde{\mathbf{X}} = [\mathbf{X}\,\mathbf{X}]$;
- diagonal matrix $\mathbf{D} = \mathrm{blkdiag}\big((1/\sqrt{n_k})\,I_{n_k p}\big)_{k=1\ldots K}$, $\dim(\mathbf{D}) = Np \times Np$.

With these notations, the problem in Equation (2) is equivalent to the following linear regression model with non-overlapping weighted group lasso penalties:

$$(\hat{\xi}, \hat{\gamma}) = \underset{\xi,\gamma \in \mathbb{R}^{p(p-1)K}}{\arg\min} \underbrace{\frac{1}{2}\Big|\Big|y - \tilde{\mathbf{X}}[\xi\,\gamma]^\top\Big|\Big|_{D^2} + \lambda_1 \sum_{i<j=1}^{p} \sqrt{g_{ij}\overline{W}_{ij}}||\xi_{[ij]}|| + \lambda_2 \sum_{i<j=1}^{p} \sqrt{2}\sum_k W^{(k)}_{ij}||\gamma_{[ijk]}||}_{F(\xi,\gamma)}. \tag{3}$$

Function $F(\xi, \gamma)$ in Equation (3) is jointly convex in ξ and γ, and the two penalties involve ξ or γ independently. Hence, we can apply an alternating optimization algorithm as follows:

- initialize vector γ;
- given γ, estimate ξ by

$$\hat{\xi} = \underset{\xi \in \mathbb{R}^{p(p-1)K}}{\arg\min} \frac{1}{2}\Big|\Big|\tilde{y} - \mathbf{X}\xi^\top\Big|\Big|_{D^2} + \lambda_1 \sum_{i<j=1}^{p} \sqrt{g_{ij}\overline{W}_{ij}}||\xi_{[ij]}||, \text{ with } \tilde{y} = y - \mathbf{X}\gamma^\top;$$

- given ξ, estimate γ by

$$\hat{\gamma} = \underset{\gamma \in \mathbb{R}^{p(p-1)K}}{\arg\min} \frac{1}{2}\Big|\Big|\tilde{y} - \mathbf{X}\gamma^\top\Big|\Big|_{D^2} + \lambda_2 \sum_{i<j=1}^{p} \sqrt{2}\sum_k W^{(k)}_{ij}||\gamma_{[ijk]}||, \text{ with } \tilde{y} = y - \mathbf{X}\xi^\top.$$

The two steps are alternated and repeated until convergence.

Since the groups are non-overlapping and orthogonal by construction, each minimization step can be solved using the group descent algorithm of [8]. Algorithm 1 illustrates the steps of the proposed *jewel 2.0* algorithm in details.

Note that Algorithm 1 generalizes the one presented in [1] to the double penalties (which are alternately updated) in the minimization problem in Equation (2). However, it still uses the idea of the *Active* matrices discussed in [1], where only non-zero entries are updated. The algorithm provided here also has a minor difference compared to the *jewel 1.0* version: now, the order of variables is randomized instead of being $1 \to p$. Although the algorithm converges regardless of the order [8], we decided to use the random order of updates because we have empirically seen that it provides an advantage in the running time without loss in performance. Finally, we note that the matrices and vectors defined in this subsection to describe the algorithm do not need to be explicitly constructed to implement the algorithm, as discussed in [1].

Algorithm 1 The *jewel 2.0* algorithm.

INPUT: data $\mathbf{X}^{(1)}, ..., \mathbf{X}^{(K)}$, weights $\mathbf{W}^{(1)}, ..., \mathbf{W}^{(K)}$
parameters $\lambda_1, \lambda_2, tol$ and $t_{\max}$

INITIALIZE:
Common part: $\Xi^{(1,0)}, ..., \Xi^{(K,0)}$
Specific part: $\Gamma^{(1,0)}, ..., \Gamma^{(K,0)}$
Residuals (common and specific): $RC^{(k)} = RS^{(k)} = \mathbf{X}^{(k)} - \mathbf{X}^{(k)}\Gamma^{(k,0)} - \mathbf{X}^{(k)}\Xi^{(k,0)}$

Matrices of active pairs $\mathbf{Active} = \mathbf{Active}^{(k)} = \begin{pmatrix} 0 & 1 & \cdots & 1 \\ 0 & 0 & & 1 \\ \vdots & & \ddots & \vdots \\ 0 & 0 & \cdots & 0 \end{pmatrix} \ \forall k$

REPEAT UNTIL CONVERGENCE
Fix the specific part $\Gamma^{(1,t)}, ..., \Gamma^{(K,t)}$, *update the COMMON part.*
Generate $order_\Xi$ by resampling from 1 to p.
for $j \in order_\Xi$ **do**
   for $i = j+1 \ldots p$ **do**
     if $Active_{ij} \neq 0$ **then**
       evaluate $\mathbf{z} = \left(z_{ij}^{(1)}, z_{ji}^{(1)}, \ldots, z_{ij}^{(K)}, z_{ji}^{(K)} \right)$ by

$$z_{ij}^{(k)} = \frac{1}{n_k} X_{.i}^{(k)\top} RC_{.j}^{(k)} + \Xi_{ij}^{(k,t)}$$
$$z_{ji}^{(k)} = \frac{1}{n_k} X_{.j}^{(k)\top} RC_{.i}^{(k)} + \Xi_{ji}^{(k,t)}$$

       compute $\overline{W}_{ij} = \sum_k W_{ij}^{(k)} / K$
       evaluate $threshold = 1 - \lambda_1 \sqrt{g_{ij}} \overline{W}_{ij} / \|z\|$
       if $threshold < 0$ **then**
         $Active_{ij} \leftarrow 0$ and $z \leftarrow 0$
       else
         $z \leftarrow z \cdot threshold$
       end if
       update residuals

$$RC_{.j}^{(k)} = RC_{.j}^{(k)} + X_{.i}^{(k)} \left(\Xi_{ij}^{(k,t)} - z_{ij}^{(k)} \right)$$
$$RC_{.i}^{(k)} = RC_{.i}^{(k)} + X_{.j}^{(k)} \left(\Xi_{ji}^{(k,t)} - z_{ji}^{(k)} \right)$$

       update coefficients $\left(\Xi_{ij}^{(1,t+1)}, \Xi_{ji}^{(1,t+1)}, ..., \Xi_{ij}^{(K,t+1)}, \Xi_{ij}^{(K,t+1)} \right) \leftarrow z$
     end if
   end for
end for

Update residuals $RS^{(k)} = \mathbf{X}^{(k)} - \mathbf{X}^{(k)}\Gamma^{(k,t)} - \mathbf{X}^{(k)}\Xi^{(k,t+1)}$.

Algorithm 1 *Cont.*

Fix the common part $\Xi^{(1,t+1)}, ..., \Xi^{(K,t+1)}$, *update the SPECIFIC part.*
Generate *order*$_\Gamma$ by resampling from 1 to p.
for $k = 1 \ldots K$ **do**
  for $j \in order_\Gamma$ **do**
    for $i = j+1 \ldots p$ **do**
      if $Active_{ij}^{(k)} \neq 0$ **then**
        evaluate $z = \left(z_{ij}^{(k)}, z_{ji}^{(k)} \right)$ by

$$z_{ij}^{(k)} = \frac{1}{n_k} {X_{.i}^{(k)}}^\top RS_{.j}^{(k)} + \Gamma_{ij}^{(k,t)}$$

$$z_{ji}^{(k)} = \frac{1}{n_k} {X_{.j}^{(k)}}^\top RS_{.i}^{(k)} + \Gamma_{ji}^{(k,t)}$$

        evaluate $threshold = 1 - \lambda_2 \sqrt{2} W_{ij}^{(k)} / \|z\|$
        if $threshold < 0$ **then**
          $Active_{ij}^{(k)} \leftarrow 0$ and $z \leftarrow 0$
        else
          $z \leftarrow z \cdot threshold$
        end if
        update residuals

$$RS_{.j}^{(k)} = RS_{.j}^{(k)} + X_{.i}^{(k)} \left(\Gamma_{ij}^{(k,t)} - z_{ij}^{(k)} \right)$$

$$RS_{.i}^{(k)} = RS_{.i}^{(k)} + X_{.j}^{(k)} \left(\Gamma_{ji}^{(k,t)} - z_{ji}^{(k)} \right)$$

        update coefficients $(\Gamma_{ij}^{(k,t+1)}, \Gamma_{ji}^{(k,t+1)}) \leftarrow z$
      end if
    end for
  end for
end for
Update residuals $RC^{(k)} = \mathbf{X}^{(k)} - \mathbf{X}^{(k)} \Gamma^{(k,t+1)} - \mathbf{X}^{(k)} \Xi^{(k,t+1)}$.

Combine common and specific parts $\Xi^{(k,t+1)} + \Gamma^{(k,t+1)} = \Theta^{(k,t+1)}$.
Check convergence: stop if $\dfrac{\sum_k \left| \Theta^{(k,t+1)} - \Theta^{(k,t)} \right|}{\sum_k \left| \Theta^{(k,t)} \right|} < tol$ or $t > t_{\max}$.

OUTPUT:
$\hat{G}^{(k)} = \mathrm{supp}\, \hat{\Theta}^{(k,t^*)}$, where t^* is the last iteration to achieve the convergence.
$\hat{G} = \cap_k \hat{G}^{(k)}$

2.3. Selection of Regularization Parameter

The minimization problem of Equation (2) contains two regularization parameters: λ_1 which penalizes the common part of the graphs, $\Xi^{(k)}$, $k = 1 \ldots K$, and λ_2 which penalizes the class-specific part of the graphs, $\Gamma^{(k)}$, $k = 1 \ldots K$. In general, larger values of the parameters provide a more sparse estimator, which can lead to many false negatives. In contrast, small values of regularization parameters result in dense graphs with more false positives and less interpretability. Therefore, the choice of such parameters is crucial for the success of any regularization method. In this context, the two parameters are not independent since edges set to zero in the common part might be included in the class-specific part and vice-versa.

To better explain the interplay relation between λ_1 and λ_2, we first consider the reparametrization proposed in JGL [4], which connects the regularization parameters to two physical parameters ω_1 and ω_2 representing the sparsity of the graphs and the similarity across graphs in different classes

$$\text{sparsity}: \omega_1 = \frac{\lambda_1}{\sqrt{2K}} + \frac{\lambda_2}{\sqrt{2}}$$

$$\text{similarity}: \omega_2 = \frac{\lambda_2/\sqrt{2}}{\omega_1}.$$

With this reparametrization, we have $\lambda_1 = \sqrt{2K}\omega_1(1 - \omega_2)$ and $\lambda_2 = \sqrt{2}\omega_1\omega_2$. The motivation behind this reparameterization is that it is easier to elicit prior information on ω_1 and ω_2 than on λ_1 and λ_2.

In a more data-driven spirit, Chapter 9.7 of [9] suggests the use of a proportional relation between the two regularization parameters, namely $\lambda_2 = \phi\lambda_1$. In the specific setting of matrix decomposition in the multivariate regression, the author proposes the following estimate (see Equation (9.7) of [9]):

$$\phi = \frac{\sqrt{\text{maximum size over all groups}} + \sqrt{\log(\#\text{groups})}}{\sqrt{\log(\#\text{parameters to estimate})}}.$$

In our case, we still use the relation $\lambda_2 = \phi\lambda_1$. However, to avoid a computationally intensive data-driven search over ϕ, we chose the value ϕ empirically after extensive numerical experimentation under different settings, where we evaluated ROC curves and edges for a range of values $\phi = 1, 1.1, 1.2, 1.3, 1.4, 1.5$. We set $\phi = 1.4$ (the value that provided the best performance on average among the tested values) and used it in all the subsequent analyses on synthetic and real datasets.

With the established relation $\lambda_2 = \phi\lambda_1$ and having fixed the value of ϕ, the complexity of the parameter space reduces to a choice of only the regularization parameter λ_1. In principle, one can extend the Bayesian information criterion (BIC) as done in [1]. However, there is a long ongoing debate on using BIC in high-dimensional settings. For example, [10] reported poor performance. In general, BIC might be too liberal in the high-dimensional regime. Therefore, the BIC estimate might represent only an empirical rough estimate of the optimal regularization parameter. Its usage beyond empirical evidence would require studying the conditions to guarantee the recovery of the true structure. Since this paper introduces the stability selection procedure (described in the next section), we suggest that the user chooses a value for λ_1 within a plausible range and then applies the stability selection to mitigate the impact on the final estimate of non-optimal choices. We used this suggestion in Section 4. We further discuss the choice of the regularization parameter in Section 5.

2.4. Stability Selection

Graph estimation can be regarded as a binary classification problem: for each pair of vertices $\{i, j\}$, we decide whether an edge (i, j) exists or not. As with any binary classification method, it is essential to estimate as many true edges as possible and avoid false positives for better interpretability, which becomes especially valuable in high dimensions.

In this respect, another important novelty of *jewel 2.0* compared to *jewel 1.0* is the implementation of a stable variable selection procedure that decreases the number of false positives. The idea is that actual positive edges should be more stable than false positive edges because the former result from true numerical significance while the latter are merely the result of a chance. With this in mind, one expects that by repeating the calculation several times (on different realizations with a fixed regularization parameter), the true positive edges are more frequent (i.e., appear more stable) than the false positive edges. Motivated by this argument, we extended the idea presented in [3] for the first time to the multiple graphs estimation problem.

The variable stability selection procedure implemented in *jewel 2.0* works as follows. Fix *#subsets*, representing the number of times we re-run the method on random subsets of the data, and fix *chosen fraction*, representing the fraction of times that an edge must appear in the results produced on random subsets to be considered stable. Then,

- Repeat for $s = 1 \ldots$ *#subsets*

    - randomly subsample the data matrices $\mathbf{X}^{(1,s)}, \mathbf{X}^{(2,s)}, \ldots, \mathbf{X}^{(K,s)}$ of the size $n_k/2 \times p_k$ from $\mathbf{X}^{(1)}, \mathbf{X}^{(2)}, \ldots, \mathbf{X}^{(K)}$;
    - obtain $\hat{G}^{(k)}(s)$, $k = 1 \ldots K$, by applying *jewel 2.0* to the subsampled data.

- Select an edge $\{i, j\}$ in the graph k if $1/\textit{\#subsets} \sum_{s=1}^{\textit{\#subsets}} Adj(\hat{G}_{ij}^{(k)}(s) \neq 0) \geq$ *chosen fraction*.

In our approach, the regularization parameter λ_1 is the same throughout the entire stability selection procedure. One might choose, for example, λ_1 obtained with a model selection estimator such as BIC or select a user-defined value (as performed in Section 4) within a reasonable range. The main advantage of the stability selection procedure is that the final estimate of the graphs $\hat{G}^{(k)}$ is not only sparser but also does not critically depend on the specific choice of the regularization parameter. As we show in the numerical experiment, the stability selection procedure effectively refines the graphs (providing sparser solutions) and reduces the number of false positive edges.

2.5. Code Availability

The *jewel 2.0* approach is implemented as an R package `jewel`, which is freely available at https://github.com/annaplaksienko/jewel (accessed on 15 October 2022). As illustrated in Figure 3, the main function `jewel` performs the entire algorithm and is relatively simple to use: the user must provide only the list of K numeric data matrices and a numeric value of λ_1, as all other parameters are optional. See package documentation and READ.ME file for the details. All the code to reproduce the simulation studies is provided at https://github.com/annaplaksienko/jewel_simulation_studies (accessed on 15 October 2022).

3. Results on Synthetic Data

This section presents simulation results to demonstrate the specific advantages of *jewel 2.0* in handling differences among classes, dealing with network hubs, and refining the networks to reduce false positives and improve interpretability. Moreover, we also compare *jewel 2.0* to similar methods for joint Gaussian graphical model estimation. Before presenting the results, in Section 3.1, we briefly describe the data generation procedure for our experimental settings.

3.1. Experimental Settings

To demonstrate the capability of our approach, we used scale-free graphs since they can describe many social and biological processes. Using the following procedure, we generated K scale-free graphs $G^{(k)}$ with similar supports. We first generated a scale-free graph $G^{(1)}$ with p vertices with the Barabasi–Albert algorithm [11] (`barabasi.game` function from the `igraph` package [12]). We tuned graph sparsity with the m parameter, which describes the number of edges added at each iteration of the Barabasi–Albert algorithm. The resulting graph $G^{(1)}$ has $mp - (2m - 1)$ edges. We monitored the hub structure with the *power* parameter, which tunes the preferential attachment. With increased power, vertices with more edges are more likely to have new edges to be added to them at each step of the Barabasi–Albert algorithm. Hence, by modifying the *power* parameter, we can generate networks with different hub/not-hub structures.

Then, given the graph $G^{(1)}$, we modified it $K - 1$ times (to obtain K graphs total) with `igraph`'s function `rewire(..., with = keeping_degseq)`, which moves the edges of a given graph, preserving its order and the degree distribution. We tuned the number of differences introduced in each modified graph using the *niter* parameter, i.e., the number of iterations of the algorithm (unless stated otherwise, parameter *niter* $= 0.08 * p$, making the graphs have about 26% of edges not in common, i.e., not in the intersection).

We used the resulting graphs $G^{(k)}$, $k = 1 \ldots K$, as the support to construct the precision matrices $\mathbf{\Omega}^{(k)}$. We considered the adjacency matrices of the graphs and replaced all 1s with realizations from the uniform distribution on $[-0.8, -0.2] \cup [0.2, 0.8]$. To ensure positive definiteness of $\mathbf{\Omega}^{(k)}$, we set its diagonal elements equal to $|\mu_{min}(\mathbf{\Omega}^{(k)})| + 0.1$, with μ_{min} being the minimum eigenvalue of the matrix. Then, we constructed covariance matrices $\mathbf{\Sigma}^{(k)}$ as $\Sigma_{ij}^{(k)} = \left(\Omega^{(k)}\right)_{ij}^{-1} / \sqrt{\left(\Omega^{(k)}\right)_{ii}^{-1} \left(\Omega^{(k)}\right)_{jj}^{-1}}$. Finally, we generated data matrices $\mathbf{X}^{(k)}$ as $n_k = n$ independent identically distributed observations from $\mathcal{N}(0, \mathbf{\Sigma}^{(k)})$.

In our experimental setting, we chose $K = 3$, $p = 500$, and $n = 100$, and we repeated the above procedure 20 times. We evaluated the performance using the true positive rate $TPR = TP/(TP + FN)$ and false positive rate $FPR = TN/(TN + FP)$, where FP is the number of false positives, TP the number of true positives, FN the number of false negatives, and TN the number of true negatives. *jewel 2.0* returns as an output K graphs $\hat{G}^{(k)}$, instead of the single graph $\hat{G}$ obtained from *jewel 1.0*. Therefore, we first calculated $TPR^{(k)}$ and $FPR^{(k)}$ for each graph and then calculated TPR and FPR by averaging over $K = 3$ graphs. Finally, we averaged the results over 20 independent runs.

Simulations were carried out on an 8-core 4.2 GHz processor and 32 GB RAM computer.

3.2. Performance of Jewel 2.0

This section aims to illustrate the three main novelties we have introduced with this work. First, we demonstrate the performance of *jewel 2.0* when graphs $G^{(k)}$ have varying amount of differences. Then, we deal with graphs with a non-uniform edge distribution (i.e., graphs with hubs). Finally, we demonstrate how stability selection can reduce the number of false positives and lead to more interpretable graphs.

3.2.1. Performance on Graphs with Varying Differences

We motivated the minimization problem in Equation (2) by the need to estimate graphs $G^{(k)}$ that share a common part but can have class-specific differences. Therefore, here, we evaluated the performance of *jewel 2.0* when applied to datasets with varying differences between their underlying graphs $G^{(k)}$.

We set the parameter *niter* in the `rewire(..., with = keeping_degseq(niter))` function to $2, 4, 8, 10\%$ of number of vertices p, resulting in graphs with 7, 13, 26, and 32% of difference (on average over 20 independent runs). Here, by "difference" we mean " #edges not in the intersection of $K = 3$ graphs".

ROC curves obtained with the *jewel 2.0* method applied to $K = 3$ datasets of the size $p = 500$, $n_k = 100$ and varying underlying graphs are reported in Figure 4. We set the parameter *power* $= 1$, and we compare two different sparsity scenarios: with parameter $m = 1$, i.e., 499 edges, and $m = 2$, i.e., 997 edges. Here, we set weights $W_{ij}^{(k)} = 1$ regardless of the graph structure.

As we can observe from Figure 4, *jewel 2.0* demonstrates good performances in all scenarios of varying amounts of differences between K graphs. Unsurprisingly, the performance decreases as the graphs become increasingly different, but even for 32% of difference, the method still performs well.

3.2.2. Performance on Graphs with Hubs

In [1], we have noticed that the performance of our previous method *jewel 1.0* and similar joint estimation methods deteriorates with the increase in the power decay of the degree distribution (i.e., for graphs that contain a few nodes with a significant number of connections and most of the nodes with limited connections). The problem was already noticeable in our simulations for *power* $= 1.5$. To face this problem, in this work, we introduced weights $W_{ij}^{(k)}$ into the model formulation of Equation (2), whose idea is to adjust the penalty on edge (i, j) according to the degree of its incident nodes i and j. When i and/or j have a high degree, the penalty on the groups involving $\{i, j\}$ is decreased to favor the edge (i, j) to emerge, whereas when i and j have a low degree, the penalty is increased to favor the removal of the edge (i, j).

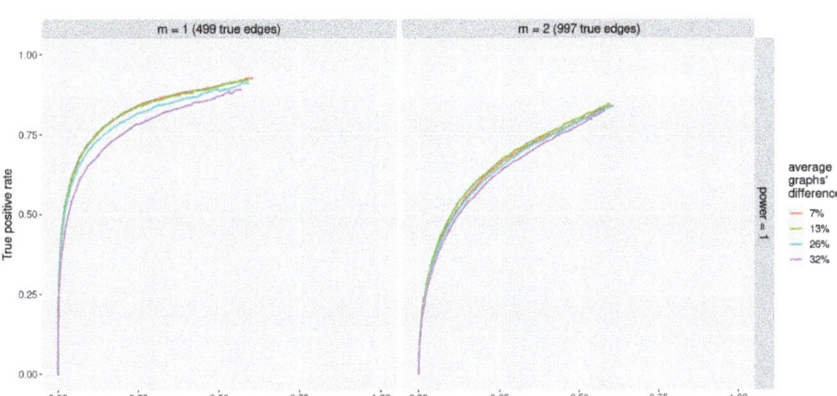

Figure 4. ROC curves for *jewel 2.0* method applied to $K = 3$ datasets of the size $p = 500$, $n_k = 100$ with various differences between their underlying graphs (denoted by different colors). Parameter $power = 1$, all weights are set $W_{ij}^{(k)} = 1$. **Left panel**: performance for $m = 1$, i.e., 499 edges. **Right panel**: performance for $m = 2$, i.e., 997 edges.

We first describe an ideal procedure to demonstrate the advantages of our weighted approach by using oracle weights obtained from the true degrees of the nodes, which, of course, are not available in real data applications.

Suppose an oracle provides a vector of true degrees for each class $k = 1 \dots K$ and denote it $\boldsymbol{d}^{(k)} \in \mathrm{N}^p$, with $\mathrm{N} = \{0, 1, 2, 3 \dots\}$. We then define the oracle weights matrix $\mathbf{W}^{(k)}$ for the class $k = 1 \dots K$ by the following formulae:

$$\mathbf{W}^{(k)} = \mathbf{W}^{(k)} / \max(\mathbf{W}^{(k)}), \quad \text{with} \quad W_{ij}^{(k)} = \frac{1}{\sqrt{d_i^{(k)} \cdot d_j^{(k)}}}. \tag{4}$$

Note that the re-scaling by $\max(\mathbf{W}^{(k)})$ assures that weights are in the interval $(0, 1]$ and are not dependent on the number of nodes p. Figure 5 (upper black lines) demonstrates that with the oracle choice of weights *jewel 2.0* provides excellent performance. In particular, the oracle weights provide a great improvement compared to the no-weight approach (i.e., $\mathbf{W}^{(k)} = \mathbf{1}$, lower black lines in Figure 5).

According to the results of the oracle estimator, we might suggest the use of a two-step procedure where one first applies *jewel 2.0* with $\mathbf{W}^{(k)} = \mathbf{1}$ and then estimates the degree vectors $\hat{\boldsymbol{d}}^{(k)}$, $k = 1 \dots K$, and reapplies *jewel 2.0* using $\hat{\boldsymbol{d}}^{(k)}$ as an oracle. However, such a procedure becomes time consuming (since it requires running *jewel 2.0* twice) and does not show the same excellent performance as the oracle estimator.

In the spirit of proposing a practical procedure, we noticed that to retain good performance, it is not necessary to know precisely the weights $W_{ij}^{(k)}$ as given in Equation (4), but it is sufficient to distinguish potential hubs from other nodes. Furthermore, in many applications, it is reasonable to assume that we have prior information on whether or not specific nodes are hubs (but it is less feasible to have prior information on the node degrees). For example, in protein–protein interaction networks, the key players are known from the literature, so we can assume that these nodes are hubs without knowing the exact degree. To evaluate whether a simple procedure is effective, we performed the following simulation:

- for each k, we considered the vector of true nodes' degrees $\boldsymbol{d}^{(k)}$;
- for each k, we fixed a threshold $cut^{(k)}$ as to choose only a top % of all degrees;

-     if $d_i^{(k)} >= cut^{(k)}$, then replace it with 10 (to identify it as a "hub"); else, replace it with 1 (to identify it as "not hub");
-     finalize weights construction as in Equation (4).

We have evaluated this procedure for choosing weights by setting $cut^{(k)}$ to select $1, 3, 5\%$ of the highest degree vertices as "hubs" for each k. Results are reported in Figure 5 with different colors, as well as the results obtained using $\mathbf{W}^{(k)} = \mathbf{1}$ and the oracle weights.

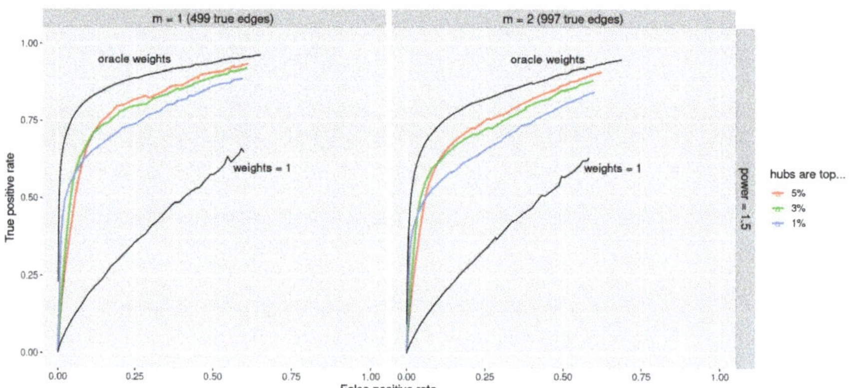

Figure 5. ROC curves for *jewel 2.0* method applied to $K = 3$ datasets of the size $p = 500, n_k = 100$. Parameter *power* $= 1.5$. The upper black lines demonstrate the excellent performance obtained with the oracle weights compared to the lower black lines that correspond to $\mathbf{W}^{(k)} = \mathbf{1}$ (i.e., the standard unweighted approach). Performance with the simple procedure that assigns weights as hub/non-hub using prior information is given in different colors depending on the percentages of nodes declared hubs. **Left panel**: performance for $m = 1$, i.e., 499 edges. **Right panel**: performance for $m = 2$, i.e., 997 edges.

Figure 5 shows the performance for the power of preferential attachment *power* $= 1.5$. We can see that although the simple procedure is unable to reach the performance of the oracle weights, it outperforms the standard unweighted approach (i.e., $\mathbf{W}^{(k)} = \mathbf{1}$). Moreover, results are quite robust to the percentage of nodes identified as hubs. Results are also robust to the specific value assigned to the hubs (data not shown). Indeed, we applied the same simple procedure assigning 3 or 5 to the hubs instead of 10 and obtained a similar conclusion. Therefore, although an optimal choice of the weights is still needed, the weighted approach proposed in Equation (2) can face the problem of graphs with hubs representing the Achilles' heel of most of the available methods.

3.2.3. Stability Selection Reduces the Number of False Positives

In this section, we compare the results obtained by running *jewel 2.0* on the same dataset without the stability procedure and with the stability procedure described in Section 2.4 where we fixed *#subsets* $= 25, 50, 100$ and *chosen fraction* $= 0.6, 0.7, 0.8$. The results are shown in Figure 6 with different colors and line types. In particular, in the left panel of Figure 6, we show the average (over $K = 3$) order of the estimated graphs $\hat{G}^{(k)}$ (i.e., $\log_2$ of the average number of estimated edges) as a measure of graph's "sparseness"; in the middle panel of Figure 6, we show the average precision to measure the proportion of true positive edges, while in the right panel of Figure 6, we show the average F1-score, defined as $F1 = 2TP/(2TP + FP + FN)$, to measure the overall accuracy. As we can observe from the inspection of Figure 6, the "sparseness" of the estimated graphs decreases with the stability procedure, as expected. More importantly, the stability selection procedure reduces the number of false positives at a much higher rate than the loss of true positives. Overall, it increases the precision (middle panel), maintaining a good accuracy (right panel).

We also note that the gain in performance is obtained even with #*subsets* = 25, meaning that stability selection can be used even when a high number of re-sampled sets is not computationally feasible.

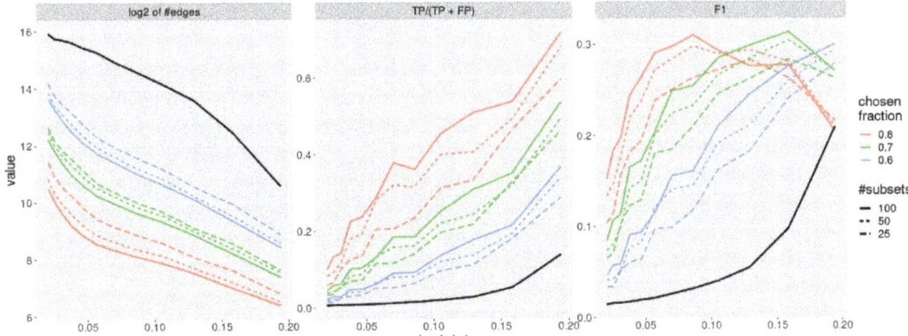

Figure 6. Performance of the *jewel 2.0* method applied to $K = 3$ datasets of the size $p = 500, n_k = 100$, $m = 1, power = 1$, all weights are set $W_{ij}^{(k)} = 1$. The solid black line denotes performance without stability procedure. Colour denotes a varying threshold of % of subsets in which edge needs to be present to be chosen. Line-type denotes a varying number of subsets. **Left panel**: log_2 of the order of the graphs. **Middle panel**: precision. **Right panel**: F1-score.

To highlight the advantage of having more precise estimates with the same accuracy, i.e., estimated graphs with greater "sparseness", in Figure 7, we compared results with and without stability selection for the same graph. It is evident that the stability selection estimates sparser graphs than those obtained without stability selection. Comparison is provided for #*subsets* = 25 and *chosen fraction* = 0.8. Figure 7 is a part of a more extensive comparison on a finer grid of λ_1. When considering the entire study, we also observed that stability makes the final graph estimates less influenced by the specific choice of λ_1. To conclude this subsection, we note that although the idea of the stability selection procedure is not novel, to our knowledge, *jewel 2.0* is the first joint estimation method to adopt it in the context of multiple graphs.

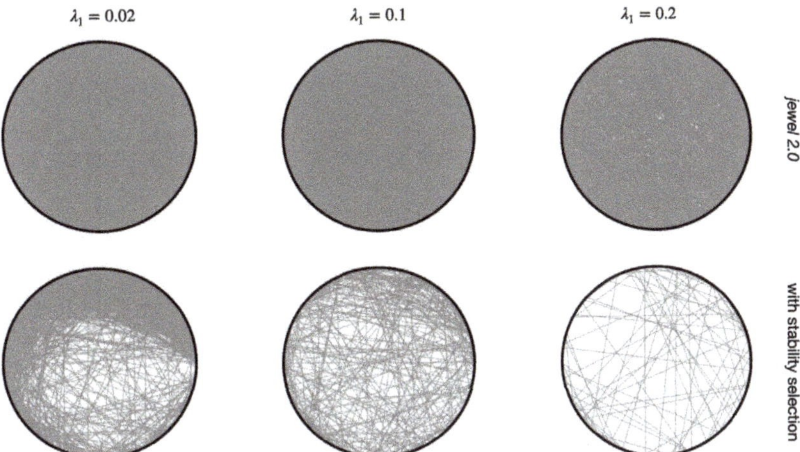

Figure 7. Estimated graph $\hat{G}^{(1)}$ of one of the independent runs. Rows demonstrate results with *jewel 2.0* and results with an additional stability selection procedure (#*subsets* = 25, choose edges present in 80% of results), columns correspond to different values of regularization parameter λ_1.

3.3. Comparison of Jewel 2.0 with Other Joint Estimation Methods

In this subsection, we compare the performance of *jewel 2.0* with other methods for joint estimation: joint graphical lasso (JGL) with group penalty [4], and the proposal of Guo et al. [5]. JGL requires two tuning parameters λ_1 and λ_2, where the first controls for differences between the graphs and the second for graph sparsity. The authors suggested the use of the relation $\lambda_1 = (1 - \omega_2)/(\sqrt{2}\omega_2) \cdot \lambda_2$. We set parameter $\omega_2 = 0.7$ since it provides better performances in the original paper. Hence, here, we vary only their parameter λ_2.

We also compared *jewel 2.0* with another joint estimation method, *simone* [13] (which, as discussed in [1], is the most similar to *jewel 2.0*), but we did not include the results in the full comparisons for the following technical reasons. When we provided the range of λ parameters from 1 to 0.01 to the simone function, the estimation produced "out of convergence" results for $\lambda \approx 0.15$ or lower (depending on the dataset realization). Using the default function parameters, the simone function went out of convergence even faster. This behavior did not allow us to produce a meaningful ROC curve for [13]. We should note that our simulation settings are different from the ones considered in [13], where the number of variables p was lower, and the authors explored only the $n > p$ setting.

We considered four different $m - power$ scenarios, with parameter $m = 1, 2$ (resulting in 499 edges with 0.4% sparsity and 997 edges with 0.8% sparsity, respectively, the same settings as we had in all previous experiments) and parameter $power = 1, 1.5$. In the case of $power = 1.5$, we also added *jewel 2.0* with a priori weights to the comparison to demonstrate its advantage. In that case, we estimated the weights using the simple approach where we chose 1% of vertices as hubs—even though the performance with this setting was slightly worse than with 3% or 5%, we deemed this one more realistic. Figure 8 illustrates the results of the comparison study.

As we can see in Figure 8, *jewel 2.0* and JGL demonstrate similar performance in the case of $power = 1$, both superior to the performance of the proposal of Guo et al. As already observed, in the case $power = 1.5$, the performance of all three methods drops drastically; however, once we use *jewel 2.0* with a simple choice of weights, we see a significant gain in performance. Note that neither *JGL* nor Guo et al. include methods for dealing with hubs. Therefore, while *jewel 2.0* can adapt its penalization to allow hubs to emerge, the other methods remain democratic in their penalization and do not perform well when graphs have hubs.

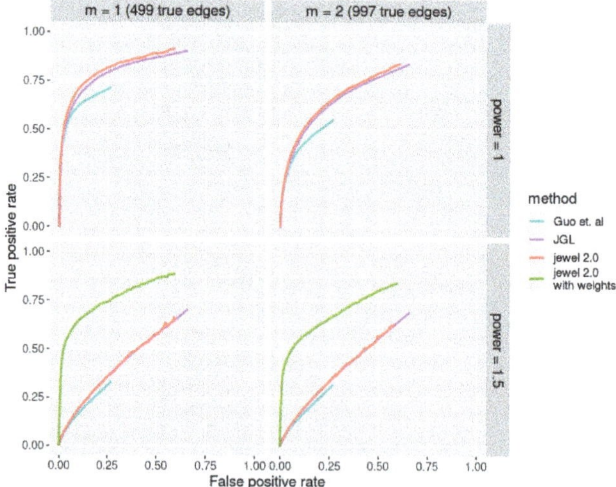

Figure 8. ROC curves corresponding to different joint estimation methods are denoted by different colors. Each panel demonstrates performance in different $m - power$ settings [5].

4. Results on Real Data

The estimation of multiple GGMs could be useful in various contexts. For instance, GGMs allow connections to be found between stocks' prices (considering different markets as K classes) or social relations (considering different social media as K classes), and so on. In the context of estimating gene networks from gene expression, we can consider gene expression data obtained from different equipment or laboratories (as we did, for example, for *jewel 1.0* [1]), or we can consider different sub-types of disease. Identifying the gene regulatory networks and differences associated with a particular sub-disease can help to tailor treatments. Since this paper discusses the advantages of our algorithm from a methodological point of view, in the following, we provide only a small example of an application to real data without investigating the biological implications of our findings.

We apply *jewel 2.0* to the gene expression datasets of the patients with breast cancer, which is the most common type of cancer among women. We consider four molecular breast cancer sub-types: luminal A, luminal B, basal-like, and HER2-enriched. Each sub-type can have specific regulatory mechanisms. However, most of the regulatory mechanisms are shared across all sub-types.

We used the gene expression microarray data available in The Cancer Genome Atlas and described in [14]. Gene expressions were measured using Agilent G450 microarrays. The dataset contains 522 primary tumor samples among which there are $n_1 = 231$ samples of luminal A cancers, $n_2 = 127$ of luminal B cancers, $n_3 = 98$ of basal-like cancers, and $n_4 = 58$ of HER2-enriched cancers. These $K = 4$ sub-types were identified in the original paper of [14]. We used the data with $K = 4$ datasets to reveal sub-type-specific gene regulatory networks.

For the sake of simplicity, we limited our attention to the genes belonging to the following 10 pathways from the Kyoto Encyclopedia of Genes and Genomes database [15]: breast cancer pathway (hsa05224), estrogen signaling pathway (hsa04915), p53 signaling pathway (hsa04115), PI3K-Akt signaling pathway (hsa04151), GnRH signaling pathway (hsa04912), PPAR signaling pathway (hsa03320), Wnt signaling pathway (hsa04310), NF-kappa B signaling pathway (hsa04064), notch signaling pathway (hsa04330), and hedgehog signaling pathway (hsa04340). According to the literature, these pathways are associated with breast cancer. These pathways involve 945 genes; out of them, 901 were measured in our datasets (with $p = 900$ also annotated in the STRING database [16], see below). Therefore, we applied *jewel 2.0* (with weights for hub detection and with stability selection) to the $K = 4$ submatrices with this subset of genes.

We retrieved prior weights information by building a broad network using the STRING database [16] with $p = 900$ genes. STRING is a database of known and predicted protein–protein interactions that can be physical and functional and derived from lab experiments, known co-expression, and genomic context predictions and knowledge in the text mining of the databases. We limited the query to connections from "experiments" and "databases" as active interaction sources and set the minimum required interaction score to the highest value of 0.9. As a result, the STRING network had 775 out of 900 vertices connected to any other node (i.e., 125 nodes were isolated) and 7514 edges.

From the STRING network, we chose the 27 vertices (3% of $p = 900$) with the highest true degrees as "hubs". Therefore, in *jewel 2.0*, we set their degree to 10 while the degree of all the other vertices was set to 1. We then computed edges' weights with the Equation (4) formula. We chose regularization parameter empirically as $\lambda_1 = 0.35$. We then ran *jewel 2.0* with this parameter, estimated weights, and performed a stability selection procedure with 25 subsets, choosing edges that appeared in at least 80% of the results. The resulting networks are presented in Figure 9.

The resulting networks $\hat{G}^{(k)}$, $k = 1 \ldots 4$, had 3336, 3297, 3318, and 3313 edges, respectively. There were 3171 edges in their intersection (gray edges in Figure 9, i.e., about 4–6% of edges in each graph were class-specific). For each estimated network, we measured the number of edges in common with the STRING database network and observed 418, 417, 408, and 412 edges in common, respectively. The p-values of the hypergeometric test to assess the significance of the edge overlaps were strictly less than 10^{-10} for all four networks. Therefore, the estimated graphs showed a significant overlap with the STRING networks compared to random graphs of the same size. This result encourages the quality of the connection, although we also note that connections in the STRING database are not tissue or disease-specific and are not necessarily of the same nature as the ones estimated with *jewel 2.0* (conditional dependence). Thus, we did not regard a considerable overlap as the main quality criteria.

We observe that for each of the K estimated graphs, the nodes with the highest degree include the 27 vertices we initially provided as potential hubs. Some of them are key genes in breast cancer, such as LCK, which was shown to influence cell motility in breast cancer, or TRAF6, which promotes tumorigenesis.

Finally, to investigate the impact of the choice of the regularization parameter, we repeated the analysis with a different value (e.g., $\lambda_1 = 0.3$), reporting similar results in terms of estimated networks.

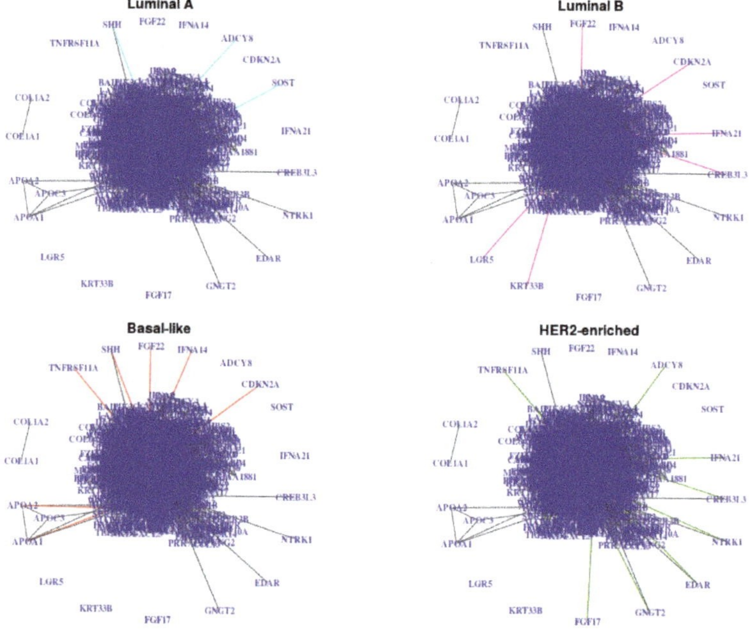

Figure 9. Networks estimated with *jewel 2.0* with $\lambda_1 = 0.35$, with weights derived from the prior information (27 (3% of $p = 900$) vertices with the highest degree in the STRING networks are identified as "hubs" with degree 10, all other vertices have degree 1) and with stability procedure (*#subsets* = 25, *chosen fraction* = 0.8). Edges common to all $K = 4$ graphs are in grey, and class-specific edges are colored. Note that vertices that are isolated in the union of these graphs are not plotted for simplicity.

5. Discussion

The proposed method represents a significant advancement of our original method *jewel*, presented in [1]. *jewel 2.0* extends the range of applications by relaxing the assumptions and also provides several other improvements. Namely, by reformulating the minimization problem as in Equation (2), i) *jewel 2.0* allows us to jointly estimate both common and class-specific parts of GGMs from multiple datasets, and ii) it allows the user to specify weights to capture the graph topologies that present hubs better. Moreover, with *jewel 2.0*, we introduced a stability selection procedure to the multiple joint graphical model context. This procedure extends the idea of [3]. It reduces the number of false positives, providing sparser and more explicative graphs, and reduces the influence of the specific choice of the regularization parameter on the estimated graphs. Finally, we demonstrated the performance of *jewel 2.0* in simulation and with real data applications.

Although we showed that *jewel 2.0* performs well, we believe there is still room for further improvement. Therefore, in the following, we emphasize our study's limitations and the directions of future work. Furthermore, we stress that limits are not specific to our approach but represent common challenges to all methods available in this context.

The *jewel 2.0* minimization problem requires two regularization parameters: λ_1 and λ_2. The choice of the regularization parameters is known to impact the estimator's performance. In general, under high-dimensional settings, the problem of finding suitable estimates of the regularization parameters is still open, with limited theoretical results available for guaranteeing the recovery of the true structure given the chosen parameter. In this paper, we chose to reduce the complexity of the space by setting $\lambda_2 = \phi\lambda_1$, fixing ϕ to a default value (selected to produce good performance under different settings). The value of λ_1 can be either estimated from the data (e.g., using BIC or similar data-driven criteria) or chosen by the user in a plausible range of values. In simulations, we investigated the performance of *jewel 2.0* when using the ROC curve over a wide range of λ_1. In the real data example, we chose λ_1 empirically and then used the stability selection to reduce the impact of the choice on the final estimate. However, a data-driven estimation of λ_1 or both ϕ and λ_1 would better adapt to the specific data structure. The work of [17] provides an interesting suggestion in this direction.

Another direction of future work consists of improving the stability selection procedure. Inspired by [3], we were the first to introduce a stability selection approach to reduce false positives in the context of multiple graphical model estimation. However, in this context, one can consider further adapting the idea of [3] for setting the bound on the number of false positives or extending the idea of [10]. Both methods used the graphical lasso on a single dataset. Hence, their adaptation to regression-based approaches and multiple datasets might not be straightforward. In general, the study of convergence properties of the resulting estimator would be advisable.

With the weighted approach, we have demonstrated the great improvement that *jewel 2.0* can bring when dealing with graphs containing hubs. In several applications, such as gene networks, knowledge available from the literature might give an indication of which genes can act as hubs. The incorporation of this information in the weights improves the estimate. However, the choice of optimal weights remains an open challenge to be addressed in future works.

Finally, the computational cost of GGMs methods on big data remains challenging. Both *jewel 1.0* and *jewel 2.0* perform well for a number of variables p of the order of several hundreds. Both become unfeasible when applied to tens or hundreds of thousands of variables that might arise from big data analysis. In [1], we showed that other similar methods suffer from the same problem (some more than others), with our approach being the fastest. Although we have introduced some speed-ups (such as the active shooting approach, for example), we believe there is still much room for improvement.

Author Contributions: Conceptualization, C.A., D.D.C. and A.P.; methodology, C.A., D.D.C. and A.P.; software, A.P.; formal analysis, A.P.; investigation, C.A., D.D.C. and A.P.; resources, C.A.; data curation, A.P.; writing—original draft preparation, C.A., D.D.C. and A.P.; writing and editing, C.A., D.D.C. and A.P.; supervision, C.A. and D.D.C. All authors have read and agreed to the published version of the manuscript.

Funding: This work was supported by the "Antitumor Drugs and Vaccines from the Sea (ADViSE)" project (CUP B43D18000240007–SURF 17061BP000000011) funded by POR Campania FESR 2014-2020 "Technology Platform for Therapeutic Strategies against Cancer"—Action 1.2.1 and 1.2.2.

Data Availability Statement: TCGA breast cancer gene expression dataset can be downloaded from https://gdc.cancer.gov/about-data/publications/brca_2012, (accessed on 8 June 2022) as *BRCA.exp.547.med.txt* file with sub-types information in *BRCA.547.PAM50.SigClust.Subtypes.txt* file.

Conflicts of Interest: The authors declare no conflict of interest.

References

1. Angelini, C.; De Canditiis, D.; Plaksienko, A. Jewel: A Novel Method for Joint Estimation of Gaussian Graphical Models. *Mathematics* **2021**, *9*, 2105 . [CrossRef]
2. Meinshausen, N.; Bühlmann, P. High-dimensional graphs and variables selection with lasso. *Ann. Stat.* **2006**, *34*, 1436–1462. [CrossRef]
3. Meinshausen, N.; Bühlmann, P. Stability selection. *J. R. Stat. Soc. B* **2010**, *72*, 417–473. [CrossRef]
4. Danaher, P.; Wang, P.; Witten, D. The joint graphical lasso for inverse covariance across multiple classes. *J. R. Stat. Soc. B* **2014**, *76*, 373–397. [CrossRef] [PubMed]
5. Guo, G.; Levina, E.; Michailidis, G.; Zhu, J. Joint estimation of multiple graphical models. *Biometrika* **2011**, *98*, 1–15. [CrossRef] [PubMed]
6. Sulaimanov, N.; Kumar, S.; Burdet, F.; Ibberson, M.; Pagni, M.; Koeppl, H. Inferring gene expression networks with hubs using a degree weighted Lasso approach. *Bioinformatics* **2019**, *35*, 987–994. [CrossRef] [PubMed]
7. Iuliano, A.; Occhipinti, A.; Angelini, C.; De Feis, I.; Liò, P. COSMONET: An R Package for Survival Analysis Using Screening-Network Methods. *Mathematics* **2021**, *9*, 3262 . [CrossRef]
8. Breheny, P.; Huang, J. Group descent algorithms for nonconvex penalized linear and logistic regression models with grouped predictors. *Stat Comput.* **2015**, *25*, 173–187. [CrossRef] [PubMed]
9. Wainwright, M.J. *High Dimensional Statistics: A Non-Asymptotic Viewpoint*; Cambridge University Press: Cambridge, UK, 2019. [CrossRef]
10. Liu, H.; Roeder, K.; Wasserman, L. Stability Approach to Regularization Selection (StARS) for High Dimensional Graphical Models. In *Advances in Neural Information Processing Systems*; Lafferty, J., Williams, C., Shawe-Taylor, J., Zemel, R., Culotta, A., Eds.; Curran Associates, Inc.: Red Hook, NY, USA, 2010; Volume 23.
11. Barabasi, A.; Albert, R. Emergence of Scaling in Random Networks. *Science* **1999**, *286*, 509–512. [CrossRef] [PubMed]
12. Csardi, G.; Nepusz, T. The igraph software package for complex network research. *InterJournal Complex Syst.* **2006**, *1695*, 1–9.
13. Chiquet, J.; Grandvalet, Y.; Ambroise, C. Inferring multiple graphical structures. *Stat. Comput.* **2011**, *21*, 537–553. [CrossRef]
14. Koboldt, D.C.; Fulton, R.S.; McLellan, M.D.; Schmidt, H.; Kalicki-Veizer, J.; McMichael, J.F.; Fulton, L.L.; Dooling, D.J.; Ding, L.; Mardis, E.R.; et al. Comprehensive molecular portraits of human breast tumours. *Nature* **2012**, *490*, 61–70. [CrossRef]
15. Kanehisa, M.; Furumichi, M.; Sato, Y.; Ishiguro-Watanabe, M.; Tanabe, M. KEGG: Integrating viruses and cellular organisms. *Nucleic Acids Res.* **2021**, *49*, D545–D551. [CrossRef] [PubMed]
16. Jensen, L.J.; Kuhn, M.; Stark, M.; Chaffron, S.; Creevey, C.; Muller, J.; Doerks, T.; Julien, P.; Roth, A.; Simonovic, M.; et al. STRING 8—A global view on proteins and their functional interactions in 630 organisms. *Nucleic Acids Res.* **2009**, *37*, D412–D416. [CrossRef] [PubMed]
17. Boulesteix, A.L.; Bin, R.D.; Jiang, X.; Fuchs1, M. IPF-LASSO: Integrative -Penalized Regression with Penalty Factors for Prediction Based on Multi-Omics Data. *Bioinformatics* **2017**, *2017*, 7691937. [CrossRef] [PubMed]

Article

Approximation and Analysis of Natural Data Based on NARX Neural Networks Involving Wavelet Filtering

Oksana Mandrikova [1,*], Yuryi Polozov [1], Nataly Zhukova [2] and Yulia Shichkina [3]

[1] Institute of Cosmophysical Research and Radio Wave Propagation, Far Eastern Branch of the Russian Academy of Sciences, Mirnaya St., 7, Kamchatskiy Kray, 684034 Paratunka, Russia
[2] Laboratory of Big Data Technologies in Socio-Cyberphysical Systems, Saint-Petersburg Federal Research Centre of the Russian Academy of Sciences, 199178 St. Petersburg, Russia
[3] Department of Technologies of Artificial Intelligence in Physiology and Medicine, Alexander Popov International Innovation Institute for Artificial Intelligence, Cybersecurity and Communications, St. Petersburg State Electrotechnical University "LETI", 197022 St. Petersburg, Russia
*   Correspondence: oksanam1@mail.ru

Citation: Mandrikova, O.; Polozov, Y.; Zhukova, N.; Shichkina, Y. Approximation and Analysis of Natural Data Based on NARX Neural Networks Involving Wavelet Filtering. *Mathematics* **2022**, *10*, 4345. https://doi.org/10.3390/math10224345

Academic Editors: Snezhana Gocheva-Ilieva, Atanas Ivanov and Hristina Kulina

Received: 12 October 2022
Accepted: 17 November 2022
Published: 19 November 2022

Publisher's Note: MDPI stays neutral with regard to jurisdictional claims in published maps and institutional affiliations.

Abstract: Recurrent neural network (RNN) models continue the theory of the autoregression integrated moving average (ARIMA) model class. In this paper, we consider the architecture of the RNN with embedded memory—«Process of Nonlinear Autoregressive Exogenous Model» (NARX). Though it is known that NN is a universal approximator, certain difficulties and restrictions in different NN applications are still topical and call for new approaches and methods. In particular, it is difficult for an NN to model noisy and significantly nonstationary time series. The paper suggests optimizing the modeling process for a complicated-structure time series by NARX networks involving wavelet filtering. The developed procedure of wavelet filtering includes the application of the construction of wavelet packets and stochastic thresholds. A method to estimate the thresholds to obtain a solution with a defined confidence level is also developed. We introduce the algorithm of wavelet filtering. It is shown that the proposed wavelet filtering makes it possible to obtain a more accurate NARX model and improves the efficiency of the forecasting process for a natural time series of a complicated structure. Compared to ARIMA, the suggested method allows us to obtain a more adequate model of a nonstationary time series of complex nonlinear structure. The advantage of the method, compared to RNN, is the higher quality of data approximation for smaller computation efforts at the stages of network training and functioning that provides the solution to the problem of long-term dependencies. Moreover, we develop a scheme of approach realization for the task of data modeling based on NARX and anomaly detection. The necessity of anomaly detection arises in different application areas. Anomaly detection is of particular relevance in the problems of geophysical monitoring and requires method accuracy and efficiency. The effectiveness of the suggested method is illustrated in the example of processing of ionospheric parameter time series. We also present the results for the problem of ionospheric anomaly detection. The approach can be applied in space weather forecasting to predict ionospheric parameters and to detect ionospheric anomalies.

Keywords: time series model; wavelet transform; neural network NARX; ionospheric parameters

MSC: 62C12; 62C20; 62L20; 68T05; 68T07

1. Introduction

Time series modeling and analysis form an important fundamental basis for the investigation of processes and phenomena of different nature. This theory can be applied in different spheres of human activities (physics, biology, medicine, economy, etc.). A separate class of problems of time series analysis is directed on the diagnostics of object states and anomaly detection. Such problems have special relevance in the area of geophysical monitoring, they are: anomaly detection in geological medium [1]; in the near-earth space [2–4]; the prediction of tsunamis [5,6], earthquakes [7], and other catastrophic natural phenomena. Anomaly detection and identification are also very topical in medicine [8]. The most important requirements for such methods are accuracy, promptness of answer reception, as well as the adaptability to have the possibility to record fast nonstationary changes of the system or object state.

Natural data time series have a complex structure that complicates the process of construction of analysis models and methods. Classical methods of time series analysis (AR, ARMA models [9,10], stochastic approximation [11,12], etc.) do not allow us to describe data complex structures adequately, and do not satisfy the adaptation requirement [3,13]. In applications, hybrid approaches are increasingly frequently used. They are based on the combination of deterministic and stochastic methods involving elements of machine learning [3,13–19]. They allow us to improve the procedure of complex data analysis. For example, in the paper [15], simplified selection ensembles based on trees were used to model and predict the data on milk yield. Preliminary data processing included their reduction into rotating main components. The authors [15] developed a simplified selective algorithm on the index of concordance that allowed them to optimize the method's performance. In the paper [15], two linear hybrid models were constructed and investigated. Another hybrid approach is considered in the paper [13] to analyze hydrological data. The authors of the paper [13] showed the efficiency of the joint application of wavelet transform [20–22] with neural networks (NN): wavelet neural network models. A flexible apparatus of the wavelet transform made it possible to apply it successfully in data analysis application [2]. A set of wavelet decomposition schemes and a wide library of basic wavelets allow us to adapt this method for the data of different-structure and according to the investigation's aim. The authors of the papers [23,24] illustrated the efficiency of application of wavelet transform with ARIMA models to model ionospheric parameter time variations and to detect anomalies. This paper continues that work. Here, we use the combination of wavelet packets with recurrent neural networks (RNN) [25], which continue the theory of the autoregression integrated moving average (ARIMA) model class [9,10].

Neural network methods are widely applied now in different areas of experience [3,4,7,13,26,27]. However, we should note that NN efficiency depends on the properties of training data and their representativity. Though the NN apparatus includes a wide set of paradigms and allows us to approximate complicated dependencies, some difficulties and restrictions in different applications are still topical and require the development of new approaches and methods [28–31]. In particular, NN efficiency decreases significantly for very noisy and nonstationary data. For example, it is difficult for an NN to model the nonstationary not associated with seasonal regularities, especially when it has long time delays [28]. Thus, the application of an NN requires data pre-processing (suppression of noise, elimination of trends, seasonality, etc.) in most cases to obtain an optimal result [28,32–35]. In this case, the combination with different methods makes it possible to overcome the problems in NN applications. For example, it was suggested in the paper [17], to apply the LSTM neural network together with discrete wavelet decomposition and ARIMA models. A combination of discrete wavelet decomposition with neural network and ARIMA was also suggested in the paper [36] to forecast the hydrological time series.

This paper considers RNN network architecture with embedded memory—«Process of Nonlinear Autoregressive Exogenous Model» (NARX) [25,27,28,30,33]. The evident advantages of regression models are their mathematical validity, formalized method of model identification, and the test for adequacy. Moreover, the advantage of the NARX network with the training gradient algorithm is their rapid convergence and good capacity for generalization [29,30].

However, we should note that one of RNN's problems is the problem of long-term dependencies [37]. Many researchers tried to solve it. The authors of [38] showed that in certain cases, RNN are capable of reflecting time delays of not less than 100 time steps. A complex approach to the solution of the problem of long-term dependencies was proposed by [39]. The authors [39] applied the architecture of the segmented-memory recurrent neural network (SMRNN) together with extended real-time recurrent learning (eRTRL). However, the eRTRL had a high computational complexity; thus, the authors [39] introduced an auxiliary condition in the form of extended back propagation through time (eBPTT) for SMRNN together with a layer-local unsupervised pre-training procedure. The theoretical solution of the question of vanishing gradient is represented in the paper [40]. The authors [40] used a regularization term, which prevents the error signal from vanishing during its motion back in time. It was also shown in the paper [40] that the proposed solutions improved RNN performance on the considered synthetic data sets. The authors [41] suggested a Fourier Recurrent Unit (FRU), which stabilizes gradients arising during network training. The FRU summarizes hidden states in the temporal dimension by Fourier basic functions. The experimental part of the paper [41] showed for the smaller number of parameters, the suggested architecture exceeded other RNN for many problems. One more approach to the solution of the problem of vanishing gradients and the problem of long-term dependences associated with it, was suggested in [42]. The authors [42] introduced a new recurrent unit with a residual error on the stage of training (Res-RNN network). It was shown in the paper [42] that the proposed Res-RNN was effective in standard RNN modifications.

One of the effective solutions of the problem of long-term dependencies for RNN is the long short-term memory (LSTM) architecture [43,44]. Multiple investigations caused the development of the architecture and its application in different fields. For example, in the paper [45], the authors showed the LSTM application for the graph of pump operation in drinking water production. The system, obtained by the authors [45], made it possible to take into account such information as day of a week, and holidays when solving the problem of long-term dependencies. The development of LSTM architecture was presented by the authors [46], who used the model of improved seasonal-trend decomposition LSTM (ISTL-LSTM) to forecast bus passenger traffic during COVID-19. The model [46], based on STL, several functions, and three neural LSTM networks made it possible to forecast the daily bus passenger traffic in Beijing during the pandemic. As the authors [47] showed, the application of LSTM is possible in hybrid format. In the paper [47], the combination of two types of NN was applied. That was determined by a different dimension of input data. The convolution neural network (CNN) was used to process two-dimensional precipitation maps and LSTM to process one-dimensional output CNN data and to calculate the downstream flux. The results [47] showed that the CNN-LSTM model was useful to estimate water supply and to make flood warning. The paper [48] demonstrated the results of the comparison of the architectures RNN, LSTM, and GRU. It was shown that LSTM and GRU are often better than RNN in the accuracy of approximation and data forecast, but their convergence takes more time.

At the same time, despite the illustrated examples of successful application of LSTM networks, this architecture has significant complexity compared to standard RNN. The disadvantage of LSTM is the long time for training and, as a consequence, it requires a long machine time [49]. At the same time, LSTM does not guarantee the complete solution of the problems of gradient explode or their vanishing. They occur rarely and quite slowly (during a large number of time steps) [40,49,50]. In spite of the great diversity of the current modification of LSTM, they do not give a significant benefit compared to the initial LSTM [49].

In the paper, we suggest optimizing the process of data modeling by NARX network involving wavelet filtering. The proposed procedure of wavelet filtering allows us to decrease the noise level and to improve NARX network efficiency. Compared to LSTM, the suggested method does not require long-term time series recorded into memory for a retrospective analysis. That makes it possible to use standard RNN without serious risks to obtain the problem of long-term dependencies [37,40], which are reduced by the simplification of input vectors by wavelet filtering. Wavelet filtering is based on wavelet packet construction with the use of stochastic thresholds. In the paper, we introduce the algorithm of wavelet filtering and propose the technique for estimating stochastic thresholds to obtain solutions with defined confidence coefficient. Moreover, we consider a scheme of implementation of the approach for the problem of anomaly detection in natural data.

The paper considers the ionospheric parameter time series (ionospheric layer F2 critical frequency, foF2). The ionospheric time series have regular variation and anomalies of different forms and time durations. The anomalies are observed during increased solar and geomagnetic activities [3,51]. In seismically active regions, ionospheric anomalies may also occur during earthquakes [51]. The detection of ionospheric anomalies is important in different aspects of life such as space craft operation, radio communication, navigation system operation, etc. The applied traditional methods of time series analysis (median method, moving average, ARIMA models) are not efficient enough to detect ionospheric anomalies [3,52,53]. In the paper, we show that the application of the wavelet filtering procedure makes it possible to obtain a more accurate NARX model of ionospheric parameter time variation. We compare the method with a direct application of NARX networks that also confirms its efficiency. On the example of the analysis of the data during a magnetic storm, the possibility of application of the method to detect anomalies in the space weather problem is illustrated.

2. Method Description

2.1. Wavelet Filtering with Stochastic Thresholds

There is a discrete noisy signal $y(t_n)$ ($n \in \mathbb{N}$, $\mathbb{N}$ are natural numbers including zero)

$$y(t_n) = f(t_n) + e(t_n), \tag{1}$$

where $y(t_n)$ is the recorded data, $f(t_n)$ is a useful signal, and $e(t_n)$ is noise.

To detect the signal structure, according to the paper [20], we apply packet wavelet decompositions [21,22]:

$\mathcal{B}_j^p = \left\{ \phi_j^p \left(t - 2^j k \right) \right\}_{k \in \mathbb{N}}$, where $\mathcal{B}_j^p$ is the basis of the space V_j^p of the wavelet packet tree (Figure 1) generated by the scaling function $\phi_j^p(t) = 2^{-j/2} \phi^p \left(2^{-j} t \right)$;

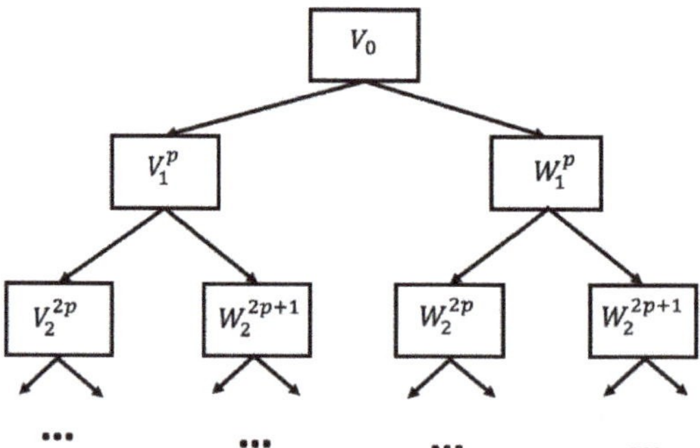

Figure 1. Wavelet packet tree.

$\mathcal{B}_j^p = \left\{ \Psi_j^p \left(t - 2^j k \right) \right\}_{k \in \mathbb{N}}$, where $\mathcal{B}_j^p$ is the basis of the space W_j^p of the wavelet packet tree (Figure 1) generated by the wavelet $\Psi_j^p(t) = 2^{-j/2} \Psi^p \left(2^{-j} t \right)$. When moving downwards along the tree of the space V_j^p, W_j^p are divided into orthogonal subspaces

$$V_j^p = V_{j+1}^{2p} \oplus W_{j+1}^{2p+1}; \; W_j^p = W_{j+1}^{2p} \oplus W_{j+1}^{2p+1}. \tag{2}$$

Signal $y(t_n)$ in the wavelet packet space at the decomposition level m has the form

$$y(t_n) = y_m^p(t_n) + \sum_j g_j^p(t_n),\tag{3}$$

where $y_m^p(t_n) = \sum_k c_{m,k}^p \phi_{m,k}^p(t_n)$ is the smoothed component; the coefficients $c_{m,k}^p = \left\langle y, \phi_{m,k}^p \right\rangle$; $\phi_{m,k}^p(t_n) = 2^{-\frac{m}{2}} \phi_m^p(t_n - 2^m k)$, $g_j^p(t_n) = \sum_k d_{j,k}^p \Psi_{j,k}^p(t_n)$ are detailing components; the coefficients $d_{j,k}^p = \left\langle y, \Psi_{j,k}^p \right\rangle$, $\Psi_{j,k}^p(t_n) = 2^{-j/2} \Psi_j^p(t_n - 2^j k)$ are the wavelet.

To determine the decomposition level m, we apply the NAS algorithm suggested in the paper [54]. The NAS algorithm allows us to construct a wavelet packet tree by suppressing noises and detecting signal coherent structures (the algorithm is in Appendix A).

To estimate the signal $\widetilde{f}$, according to the paper [54], we apply the following hard threshold to the absolute values of the coefficients $d_{j,k}^p$ of the components $g_j^p(t_n)$ in each tree node

$$P_{T_j^p}\left(d_{j,k}^p\right) = \begin{cases} d_{j,k}^p, & if \ \left|d_{j,k}^p\right| > T_j^p, \\ 0, & if \ \left|d_{j,k}^p\right| \le T_j^p. \end{cases}\tag{4}$$

The estimate $\widetilde{f}$, based on (4), is

$$\widetilde{f}(t_n) = y_m^p(t_n) + \sum_{j,k} T_j^p\left(d_{j,k}^p\right) \Psi_{j,k}^p(t_n).\tag{5}$$

The risk of such an estimate for $\widetilde{f} \in L^2(\mathbb{R})$ $(L^2(\mathbb{R})$, Lebesgue space [55]), is [56]

$$r\left(\widetilde{f}, f\right) = E\left\{\|\widetilde{f} - f\|^2\right\},\tag{6}$$

where E is the mathematical expectation; $\|\cdot\|$ is the norm.

It is obvious that to minimize the risk r, the threshold T_j^p should be likely higher than the noise coefficient maximum level. As it was shown in the papers [21,22], outside the neighborhoods containing signal local features, absolute values of the coefficients $\left|d_{j,k}^p\right|$ with respect to the argument k are close to zero. Local features in a signal are observed during anomalies and are rare events; thus, based on the thee-sigma rule [57], we can state with high confidence ($\alpha \approx 0.99$) that the values $d_{j,k}^p$ with respect to the argument k are within the interval $(\mu_j - 3\sigma_j; \ \mu_j + 3\sigma_j)$, where $\mu_j \approx 0$ is the mathematical expectance of the value $d_{j,k}^p$, and σ_j is the standard deviation $d_{j,k}^p$.

Then, in the case of normal distribution of the value $d_{j,k}^p$, according to the paper [34], we can estimate the thresholds T_j^p for each level j with the defined confidence coefficient as

$$T_j^p = t_{1-\frac{\alpha}{2}, N-1} \hat{\sigma}_j,\tag{7}$$

where $t_{\alpha, N}$ are α-quantiles Student's distribution [57]; $\hat{\sigma}_j$ is the sample standard diviation of the value $d_{j,k}^p$ which is estimated during the periods without anomalies in the data.

We should note that the risk of estimate (5) is also associated with the error of the approximation f in the basis $\mathfrak{B}$ that should also be taken into account. We can determine the basis for the approximation f as, for example, it was suggested in the paper [20] using the Schur's function [58] and the concordant fitting algorithm [59].

Based on the described operations, we obtain the following algorithm of wavelet filtering:

1. Decomposition of signal y into wavelet packets

$$y(t_n) = y_m^p(t_n) + \sum_j g_j^p(t_n),\tag{8}$$

where $y_m^p(t_n) = \sum_k c^p{}_{m,k} \phi^p_{m,k}(t_n)$, $c^p{}_{m,k} = \left\langle y, \phi^p_{m,k} \right\rangle$, $\phi^p_{m,k}(t_n) = 2^{-\frac{m}{2}} \phi^p_m(t_n - 2^m k)$;

$g_j^p(t_n) = \sum_k d^p{}_{j,k} \Psi^p_{j,k}(t_n)$, $d^p{}_{j,k} = \left\langle y, \Psi^p_{j,k} \right\rangle$, $\Psi^p_{j,k}(t_n) = 2^{-j/2} \Psi^p_j(t_n - 2^j k)$.

2. Application of the threshold function to the coefficients $d^p{}_{j,k}$ of the components g_j^p:

$$P_{T_j^p}\left(d^p{}_{j,k}\right) = \begin{cases} d^p{}_{j,k}, \ if \ \left| d^p{}_{j,k} \right| \geq T_j^p \\ 0, \ if \ \left| d^p{}_{j,k} \right| < T_j^p \end{cases}, \tag{9}$$

where $T_j^p = t_{1-\frac{\alpha}{2},N-1}\hat{\sigma}_j$, $t_{\alpha,N}$ are the α-quantiles Student's distribution; $\hat{\sigma}_j$ is the sample standard deviation of the value $d^p{}_{j,k}$.

3. Wavelet reconstruction of the signal

$$\widetilde{f}(t_n) = y_m^p(t_n) + \sum_{j,k} P_{T_j^p}\left(d^p{}_{j,k}\right) \Psi^p_{j,k}(t_n). \tag{10}$$

2.2. Application of NARX Network

After the wavelet filtering, the signal $\widetilde{f}$ is approximated by the neural NARX network [4,25,27,28]. The architecture of the recurrent NARX PA network [28] is illustrated in Figure 2.

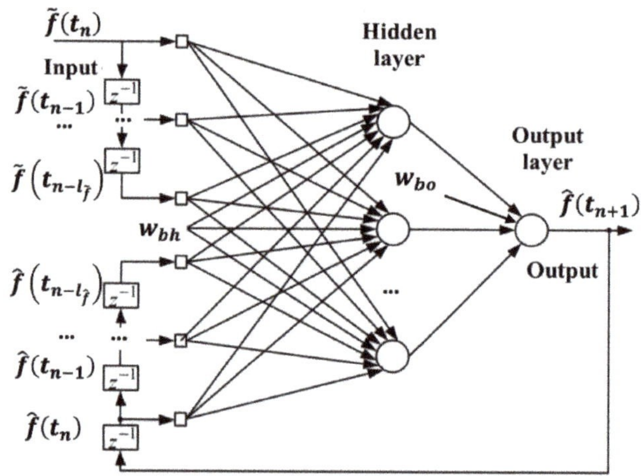

Figure 2. Architecture of the recurrent NARX PA network.

According to the NARX PA network architecture, the network input is $\widetilde{f}(t_n)$, and the network output is $\hat{f}(t_n + 1)$, i.e., the network predicts the data by one step ahead.

The vector, sent to the network hidden layer neurons, consists of the following components:

- current $\widetilde{f}(t_n)$ and preliminary values $\widetilde{f}(t_{n-1}), \ldots, \widetilde{f}\left(t_{n-l_{\widetilde{f}}}\right)$;
- output values $\hat{f}(t_n), \hat{f}(t_{n-1}), \ldots, \hat{f}\left(t_{n-l_{\widehat{f}}}\right)$.

The analytical representation of the signal model based on NARX PA has the form

$$\hat{f}(t_{n+1}) = F_o\left(w_{bo} + \sum_{h=1}^{D} w_{ho} \cdot F_h\left(w_{bh} + \sum_{i=0}^{l_{\widetilde{f}}} w_{ih}\widetilde{f}(t_{n-i}) + \sum_{z=0}^{l_{\widehat{f}}} w_{zh}\hat{f}(t_{n-z}) \right) \right), \tag{11}$$

where $\widetilde{f}(t_n)$ и $\hat{f}(t_n)$ is the NN input signal and its approximation by the network, respectively; $l_{\widetilde{f}}, l_{\hat{f}}$ is the number of delay lines; w_{zh} are weight coefficients of the values arriving from NN output to the hidden layer neurons; w_{ih} are weight coefficients of input values arriving to the hidden layer neurons; w_{bh} and w_{bo} are constant terms for the hidden and output layers, respectively; F_h and F_o are activation functions for the neurons of the hidden and output layers, respectively; w_{ho} are weight coefficients for the values arriving on output layer neurons; D is the number of hidden layer neurons.

It is known that network architecture affects forecast efficiency. NARX model architecture depends on the size of the embedded memory of input ($l_{\widetilde{f}}$), of output ($l_{\hat{f}}$) and the neuron number in the hidden layer. It is not a trivial task to determine these parameters. The number of the delay lines of input $l_{\widetilde{f}}$ and output $l_{\hat{f}}$ can be determined by minimizing the network error [28]. The technique to determine these parameters and the obtained results are represented below in this paper.

The Bayesian regularization algorithm is used for network training. This algorithm updates the weights and the shifts leading to the network neurons according to the Levenberg–Marquardt optimization [25]. The Bayesian regularization technique allows one to form a combination of neuron and weight number of the hidden layer in such a way that the network has the highest degree of generalization [28]. The regularization function minimizes the linear combination of squared errors and weight coefficients of the network at the stage of training. That makes it possible to optimize the neuron number of the hidden layer and to avoid the overtraining effect.

2.3. Scheme of Method Realization

The scheme of method realization is illustrated in Figure 3. Disorder in the system evidently indicates an anomaly in the data. A disorder can be detected based on the analysis of the vector of neural network summary errors estimated in the time window of the length $\mathcal{L} = 2l + 1$

$$\varepsilon_i = \sum_{i=i-l}^{i+l} \left| \hat{f}(i) - \widetilde{f}(i) \right|. \tag{12}$$

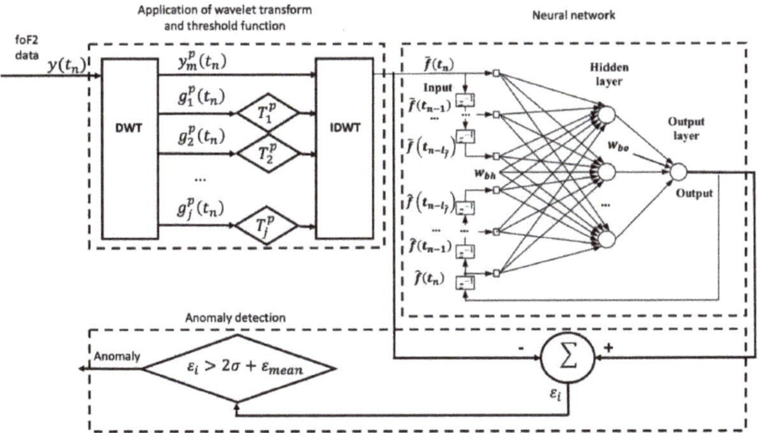

Figure 3. Scheme of method realization.

In this case, we can consider that there is an anomaly in the data if

$$\varepsilon_i > 2\sigma + \varepsilon_{mean}, \tag{13}$$

where σ is the standard deviation of network summary errors, it is estimated during the periods without anomalies; ε_{mean} is the average of network summary errors during the periods without anomalies.

3. Results of Method Application for Ionospheric Data

In the paper, we used the ionospheric layer F2 critical frequency (foF2) data for the period 1969–2015. The data were recorded at IKIR FEB RAS (Paratunka site, Kamchatskiy kray, Russia) from 1968 up to the present time. According to the suggested method, the input and reference values of NN were obtained after the wavelet filtering procedure. In the operations of wavelet filtering, we used orthonormal third-order Daubechies [21], which were determined by minimizing foF2 data approximation errors [60]. To evaluate the method, NN were also trained using the foF2 initial data without wavelet filtering.

When forming training and control NN samples, we took into account the dependence of foF2 data time variation on the season and solar activity level. Thus, NN were constructed for different seasons and different levels of solar activity separately. Two periods of solar activity were considered, the period of high solar activity and the period of low solar activity (the level of solar activity was estimated by mean monthly values of radio emission at the wavelength of f10.7 [61]). To obtain NARX models describing foF2 data regular time variation, data for the periods of calm ionosphere were used in the training process. For each NN, training samples contained one vector of the length from 2000 to 4000 counts. We constructed 24 networks.

When constructing NN, input and output delay lines $l_{\tilde{f}} = l_{\hat{f}} = 2$, $l_{\tilde{f}} = l_{\hat{f}} = 3$, $l_{\tilde{f}} = l_{\hat{f}} = 5$ were used. The parameters $l_{\tilde{f}}$ and $l_{\hat{f}}$ were determined according to the investigation results of [24]. In the paper [24], an autocorrelation function (ACF) and partial autocorrelation function (PACF) were studied to determine the order of ARIMA models of the foF2 series. It was shown [24] that after wavelet filtering and obtaining the first differences, AR models of foF2 series had the orders 2 and 3 depending on the season and solar activity level. However, we should note that in the general case, the question of the determination of $l_{\tilde{f}}$ and $l_{\hat{f}}$ is important and requires additional study. As was shown in the paper [28], the NARX model quality significantly depends on the size of input and output embedded memory.

The selection of NN inner architecture was based on NN error estimates. The standard deviations of errors (STD) for the networks were determined as

$$\text{STD} = \sqrt{\frac{1}{N-1} \sum_{i=1}^{N} \left(e_i - \bar{e} \right)^2},\qquad(14)$$

where $e = \frac{1}{N} \sum_{i=1}^{N} e_i$, $e_i = \hat{f}_0(i) - \tilde{f}_0(i)$.

As an example, Table 1 shows NN error estimates for wintertime depending on the neuron number of the hidden layer. An analysis of Table 1 shows that the STD error decreased when the number of neurons was 20 in the hidden layer. Then, the network error remained unchanged. Based on these results, we determined the wintertime network architecture with the number of neurons of the hidden layer equal to 20. Making similar investigations, we determined the number of neurons of the hidden layer were also equal to 20 for the summertime.

Table 1. Construction of network architecture for the data during winter season and high solar activity.

Neuron Number	4	8	12	16	20	24	28
STD	0.54	0.48	0.42	0.42	0.40	0.40	0.41

Table 2 shows the STD errors of NN for different delay lines. An analysis of the results shows that the number of NN approximations increased insignificantly as the number of delay lines grew for the NN trained without wavelet filtering. The application of wavelet filtering made it possible to increase significantly the NN approximation quality especially during low solar activity. That confirmed the efficiency of the proposed method.

Table 2. Standard deviations of neural network errors.

Season	Delay 2	Delay 2 Wavelet Filtering	Delay 3	Delay 3 Wavelet Filtering	Delay 5	Delay 5 Wavelet Filtering
Winter (low solar activity)	0.71	0.49	0.69	0.5	0.69	0.49
Summer (low solar activity)	0.6	0.33	0.54	0.32	0.46	0.27
Winter (high solar activity)	1.3	0.87	1.31	0.85	1.3	0.87
Summer (high solar activity)	0.54	0.5	0.52	0.51	0.49	0.49

The results of NN quality estimates, based on the control set data during the periods without anomalies, are illustrated in Table 3. The analysis shows significant improvement of NN approximation quality when using the wavelet filtering procedure. The application of wavelet filtering made it possible to decrease significantly the average error (ε_{mean}) and STD (σ) for different delay lines. We should also note that the application of wavelet filtering allowed us to use the low number of input and output delay lines when the network performance quality was good.

Table 3. Results of NN performance (summer and winter, low solar activity).

Delay Lines $l_{\bar{f}} = l_{\hat{f}}$	Season	ε^{y}_{mean} without Wavelet Filtering	σ^{y} without Wavelet Filtering	$\tilde{\varepsilon}^{f}_{mean}$ with Wavelet Filtering	$\sigma^{\tilde{f}}$ with Wavelet Filtering
2	Sum	1.3	0.6	0.48	0.33
3	Sum	1.42	0.54	0.47	0.32
5	Sum	1.27	0.46	0.46	0.27
2	Win	1.39	0.71	0.65	0.49
3	Win	1.24	0.69	0.67	0.50
5	Win	1.21	0.69	0.64	0.49

The test for the adequacy of the obtained NARX models was based on the Ljung-Box test [62]:

$$Q = M(M+2) \sum_{s=1}^{L} \frac{\rho_s^2}{M - s},\tag{15}$$

where M is the observations number, ρ_s is the autocorrelation of the s-th order, and L is the number of lags under the check. If $Q > \chi^2_{1-\alpha,\,L}$, where $\chi^2_{1-\alpha,\,L}$ is the quantile of chi-square distribution with L degrees of freedom, then the presence of autocorrelation of the L-th order in the time series is admitted.

The results of the Ljung-Box test are presented in Table 4. The analysis of the results shows that for the networks constructed without wavelet filtering, Ljung-Box test values exceeded significantly the corresponding critical value $\chi^2_{1-\alpha,\,L}$. That indicates the correlation of network errors and, as a sequence, the not-quite-good-enough quality of foF2 data approximation. We should note that the error correlation grew significantly for large lags L that were evidently associated with the presence of long time dependencies (foF2 diurnal variation) in foF2 data. As was mentioned in the paper [28], in the systems with large time dependencies for the training algorithms based on gradient, information on step gradient m in the past vanished at large m (the problem of vanishing gradients). Thus, the application of RNN faces problems when modeling data with long time dependencies, especially when forecasting nonlinear nonstationary signals [28]. It was also shown in the paper [25] that the problem of vanishing gradients made the investigation of long-term dependencies in training algorithms, based on gradient, difficult and in some cases almost impossible. When the delay lines grew, the data approximation quality increased (Table 4). However, the adequacy was confirmed only for NARX models obtained with wavelet filtering. For the network delay lines $l_{\tilde{f}} = l_{\hat{f}} = 3$, $l_{\tilde{f}} = l_{\hat{f}} = 5$, according to the Ljung-Box test, network errors were uncorrelated. That confirms their adequacy to foF2 data and shows the efficiency of the suggested method.

Table 4. Ljung-Box test values (summer, low solar activity).

Delay Lines $l_x=l_y$	Lag Number L	Q_y without Wavelet Filtering	$Q_{\tilde{f}}$ with Wavelet Filtering	$\chi^2_{1-\alpha,\, L}$
2	1	0.04	1.47	3.84
2	4	30.4	16.3	9.48
2	8	69.1	28.1	15.5
2	12	128	41.7	21
3	1	0.02	0.04	3.84
3	4	0.9	1.9	9.48
3	8	12.6	9.6	15.5
3	12	64.9	18.2	21
5	1	0.5	0.05	3.84
5	4	1.4	3.8	9.48
5	8	15.6	15.2	15.5
5	12	44.6	19.9	21

Figure 4 shows the results of NN performance during a moderate magnetic storm on 16–17 July 2017. A red dashed line in Figure 4 indicates the time of the magnetic storm beginning. To analyze the geomagnetic activity index, DST index values are illustrated in Figure 4e [63]. During the strongest geomagnetic disturbances on 16 July 2017, the DST index reached the minimum of -72 nT (Figure 4e). An analysis of foF2 data (Figure 4a) shows insignificant changes in fluctuation amplitude during the magnetic storm that was determined by ionospheric disturbance occurrences. Median value data (dashed lines in Figure 4a) also confirmed the presence of an anomaly in the ionosphere during the magnetic storm. The processing results (Figure 4b–d,f–h) illustrated a significant increase in NN errors during the strongest geomagnetic disturbances that indicated anomalous changes in the data. The comparison of the results of the NN trained on the initial data (Figure 4b–d) with the results of the NN obtained after wavelet filtering (Figure 4f–h) confirmed the significant improvement of NN quality when using wavelet filtering. Errors of the NN trained after the wavelet filtering procedure were close to zero. In the error vector of the NN trained on the initial data, an oscillation process was observed which was likely to be associated with foF2 diurnal variation. The result confirms the assumption mentioned above that the application of RNN faced problems when modeling the data with long time dependencies (problem of vanishing gradients). The result also confirms the efficiency of the suggested wavelet filtering procedure to improve the NARX performance quality when modeling nonstationary and noisy data.

Comparing the results of NN with a different number of delay lines, we have learned that for the delay lines $l_{\tilde{f}} = l_{\hat{f}} = 5$ (Figure 4h), anomalous changes were detected on a longer interval that agreed well with the obtained median values of foF2 (dashed line in Figure 4a). A comparison of the NARX results with the median method shows a higher efficiency of the NN. Due to the significant nonstationarity of foF2 data time variation during the magnetic storm, there were errors in median values during the period after the storm on 18 July 2017. There were no errors in the NN model.

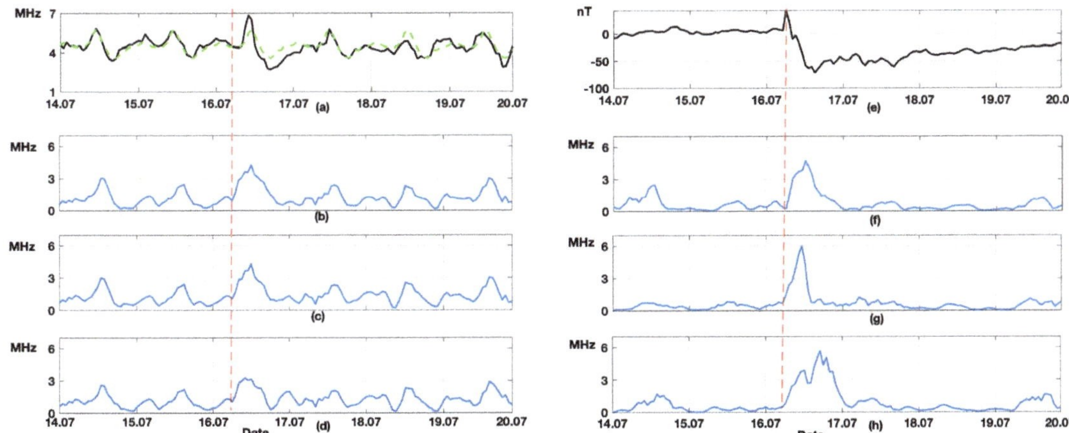

Figure 4. Results of data processing for the period 14–19 July 2017. (**a**) foF2 initial data (black) and foF2 median (green); (**b**–**d**) NN errors with delays 2, 3, and 5, respectively, obtained without wavelet filtering; (**e**) DST; (**f**–**h**) errors with delays 2, 3, and 5, respectively, obtained with wavelet filtering. Red dashed line is the magnetic storm beginning.

Figure 5 shows the results of data processing during a weak magnetic storm on 5–6 August 2019. The red vertical line indicates the magnetic storm beginning (Figure 5). Results in Figure 5 are similar to those illustrated above for the event on 16–17 July 2017. The estimated median values (Figure 5a) show long changes in foF2 data time variation during the magnetic storm. An analysis of NN errors also shows their increase during the event that indicates anomaly occurrence in the ionosphere. The comparison of the results of NN performance without wavelet filtering (Figure 5b–d) and with wavelet filtering (Figure 5f–h) shows a significant decrease in NN errors based on the suggested approach. That is similar to the results of the event on 16–17 July 2017. The NN with the delay lines $l_{\tilde{f}} = l_{\hat{f}} = 5$ (Figure 5h) shows the best results. It has the least errors and the anomalous period in ionospheric data is clearly detectable.

Table 5 shows quantitative estimates of the NN performance during the events described above. The estimates were carried out separately during calm and disturbed periods. An analysis of the results from Table 5 shows that wavelet filtering allows one to decrease significantly the average values of network errors and their STD during calm periods. A decrease in the NN error level by more than 3 times is observed after the wavelet filtering procedure. During the anomalous period, the STD of the network trained after the wavelet filtering may increase by 17 times. That makes it possible to detect anomalous changes in the ionosphere accurately. We should also note that as the number of delay lines increase, the quality of anomaly detection by this network improves. The results confirm the efficiency of the suggested method.

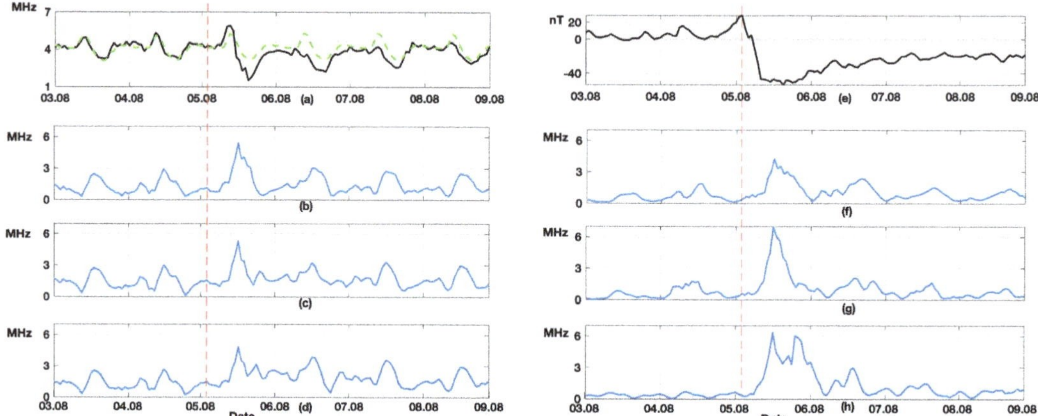

Figure 5. Results of data processing for the period 3–8 August 2019. (**a**) foF2 initial data (black) and foF2 median (green); (**b–d**) NN errors with delays 2, 3, and 5, respectively, obtained without wavelet filtering; (**e**) DST; (**f–h**) errors with delays 2, 3, and 5, respectively, obtained with wavelet filtering. Red dashed line is the magnetic storm beginning.

Table 5. Results of NN performance.

Delay Lines $l_{\tilde{f}}=l_{\tilde{f}}$	Year	ε^y_{mean} without Wavelet Filtering	σ^y without Wavelet Filtering	$\tilde{\varepsilon}^{\tilde{f}}_{mean}$ with Wavelet Filtering	$\tilde{\sigma}^{\tilde{f}}$ with Wavelet Filtering
		calm period			
2	2017	1.02	0.63	0.39	0.27
3	2017	1.05	0.57	0.37	0.24
5	2017	0.98	0.53	0.24	0.15
2	2019	1.17	0.61	0.42	0.29
3	2019	1.42	0.64	0.31	0.24
5	2019	1.31	0.58	0.33	0.12
		anomaly period			
2	2017	1.86	1.19	1.81	1.4
3	2017	1.83	1.11	1.6	1.64
5	2017	1.65	0.94	2.58	1.7
2	2019	1.83	1.41	1.68	1.2
3	2019	2.02	1.06	2.18	1.96
5	2019	2.16	0.97	2.88	2.05

4. Conclusions

The application of the method showed its efficiency in the problem of ionospheric data modeling and analysis. The suggested procedure of wavelet filtering allows us to improve the NARX neural network performance quality and gives the possibility to obtain an adequate model for noisy and nonstationary data.

As was mentioned in the papers [25,28], data modeling based on NARX has some difficulties associated with the presence of long time dependences caused by the "vanishing gradient". It was shown on the example of ionospheric data that the wavelet filtering procedure makes it possible to solve this problem if there is a long period. The Ljung-Box test confirmed the adequacy of the obtained neural network models.

On the example of the magnetic storms that occurred on 16–17 July 2017 and on 5–6 August 2019, we confirmed the possibility to apply the method for the detection of ionospheric anomalies based on foF2 data during magnetospheric disturbances. A comparison of the NARX network with the median method, traditionally used for ionospheric data analysis, showed the NN efficiency. The ionospheric data time variation change during the magnetic storms under analysis entailed error occurrences in the estimates of median values, which were absent in the NN model. The method can be used to monitor the ionosphere state during space weather forecasting.

We plan to continue the investigation in this direction involving ionospheric data from other regions. We also plan to apply the developed method for a more detailed study of ionospheric parameters during increased solar activity and magnetic storms.

Author Contributions: Conceptualization, O.M.; methodology, O.M. and Y.P.; software, Y.P.; validation, Y.P. and N.Z.; formal analysis, O.M. and Y.S.; investigation, O.M. and Y.P.; resources, N.Z. and Y.S.; data curation, Y.P.; writing—original draft preparation, Y.P.; writing—review and editing, O.M.; project administration, O.M.; funding acquisition, Y.S. All authors have read and agreed to the published version of the manuscript.

Funding: This work was supported by the Ministry of Science and Higher Education of the Russian Federation by the Agreement № 075-15-2022-291 on the provision of a grant in the form of subsidies from the federal budget for the implementation of state support for the establishment and development of the world-class scientific center «Pavlov center «Integrative physiology for medicine, high-tech healthcare, and stress-resilience technologies».

Institutional Review Board Statement: Not applicable.

Informed Consent Statement: Not applicable.

Data Availability Statement: Not applicable.

Acknowledgments: The work was carried out according to the Subject AAAA-A21-121011290003-0 "Physical processes in the system of near space and geospheres under solar and lithospheric influences" IKIR FEB RAS. The work was realized by the means of the Common Use Center "North-Eastern Heliogeophysical Center" CKP_558279, USU 351757. The authors are grateful to the World Data Center for Geomagnetism, Kyoto (http://wdc.kugi.kyoto-u.ac.jp/dstae/index.html (accessed on 20 June 2022)).

Conflicts of Interest: The authors declare no conflict of interest.

Appendix A

NAS algorithm [54]:

(1) signal X is decomposed into wavelet packets

$W_j^0 : W_j^0 = \oplus_{i=0}^{I} W_{j_i}^{p_i}$, $\left\{ \Psi_{j_i}^{p_i}(2^{j_i}t - m) \right\}_{m \in \mathbb{N}}$ is the basis of the space $W_{j_i}^{p_i}$;

(2) based on the estimate of normalized energies, we determine the tree branches corresponding to signal structural components: basis $B_{j_i}^{p_i}$ of the space $W_{j_i}^{p_i}$ is the basis

$$B_{j_i}^{p_i} = \begin{cases} \left\{ \Psi_{j_i}^{p_i}(2^{j_i}t - m) \right\}_{m \in \mathbb{N}}, & \text{if } \sum_{m \in I^{p_i}} \left| \left\langle X, \Psi_{j_i,m}^{p_i} \right\rangle \right|^2 \geq \sum_{m \in I^{2p_i}} \left| \left\langle X, \Psi_{j_i+1,m}^{2p_i} \right\rangle \right|^2 + \sum_{m \in I^{2p_i+1}} \left| \left\langle X, \Psi_{j_i+1,m}^{2p_i+1} \right\rangle \right|^2 \\[2ex] \left\{ \Psi_{j_i+1}^{2p_i} \right\}_{m \in \mathbb{N}} \cup \left\{ \Psi_{j_i+1}^{2p_i+1} \right\}_{m \in \mathbb{N}}, & \text{if } \sum_{m \in I^{p_i}} \left| \left\langle X, \Psi_{j_i,m}^{p_i} \right\rangle \right|^2 < \sum_{m \in I^{2p_i}} \left| \left\langle X, \Psi_{j_i+1,m}^{2p_i} \right\rangle \right|^2 + \sum_{m \in I^{2p_i+1}} \left| \left\langle X, \Psi_{j_i+1,m}^{2p_i+1} \right\rangle \right|^2 \end{cases} \quad \text{(A1)}$$

where the index set I^l, $l = p_i,\ 2p_i,\ 2p_i + 1$ is determined as follows: index $m \in I^l$, if $\left| \left\langle X, \Psi_{j_i,m}^{l} \right\rangle \right| \geq T_{j_i}$, threshold $T_{j_i} = K * \sigma_{j_i}^l$, $\sigma_{j_i}^l = \sqrt{\frac{1}{L} \sum_{m=1}^{L} \left(\left\langle X, \Psi_{j_i,m}^{l} \right\rangle - \overline{\left\langle X, \Psi_{j_i,m}^{l} \right\rangle} \right)^2}$, where the coefficient of the threshold K is determined by estimating a posteriori risk, $\overline{\left\langle X, \Psi_{j_i,m}^{l} \right\rangle}$ is the average of the set $\left\{ \left| \left\langle X, \Psi_{j_i,m}^{l} \right\rangle \right| \right\}_{0 \leq m < L}$, L is the element number.

References

1. Alperovich, L.; Eppelbaum, L.; Zheludev, V.; Dumoulin, J.; Soldovieri, F.; Proto, M.; Bavusi, M.; Loperte, A. A New Combined Wavelet Methodology: Implementation to GPR and ERT Data Obtained in the Montagnole Experiment. *J. Geophys. Eng.* **2013**, *10*, 025017. [CrossRef]
2. Bailey, R.L.; Leonhardt, R. Automated Detection of Geomagnetic Storms with Heightened Risk of GIC. *Earth Planets Space* **2016**, *68*, 99. [CrossRef]
3. Tang, R.; Zeng, F.; Chen, Z.; Wang, J.-S.; Huang, C.-M.; Wu, Z. The Comparison of Predicting Storm-Time Ionospheric TEC by Three Methods: ARIMA, LSTM, and Seq2Seq. *Atmosphere* **2020**, *11*, 316. [CrossRef]
4. Boussaada, Z.; Curea, O.; Remaci, A.; Camblong, H.; Mrabet Bellaaj, N. A Nonlinear Autoregressive Exogenous (NARX) Neural Network Model for the Prediction of the Daily Direct Solar Radiation. *Energies* **2018**, *11*, 620. [CrossRef]
5. Chierici, F.; Embriaco, D.; Pignagnoli, L. A New Real-Time Tsunami Detection Algorithm: Tsunami detection algorithm. *J. Geophys. Res. Oceans* **2017**, *122*, 636–652. [CrossRef]
6. Kim, S.-K.; Lee, E.; Park, J.; Shin, S. Feasibility Analysis of GNSS-Reflectometry for Monitoring Coastal Hazards. *Remote Sens.* **2021**, *13*, 976. [CrossRef]
7. Perol, T.; Gharbi, M.; Denolle, M. Convolutional Neural Network for Earthquake Detection and Location. *Sci. Adv.* **2018**, *4*, e1700578. [CrossRef] [PubMed]
8. Amigó, J.M.; Small, M. Mathematical Methods in Medicine: Neuroscience, Cardiology and Pathology. *Philos. Trans. R. Soc. A* **2017**, *375*, 20170016. [CrossRef] [PubMed]
9. Marple, S.L. *Digital Spectral Analysis: With Applications*; Prentice-Hall signal processing series; Prentice-Hall: Englewood Cliffs, NJ, USA, 1987; ISBN 978-0-13-214149-9.
10. Box, G.E.P.; Jenkins, G.M. *Time Series Analysis: Forecasting and Control, Revised Edition*; Holden-Day series in time series analysis and digital processing; Holden-Day: San Francisco, CA, USA, 1976; ISBN 978-0-8162-1104-3.
11. Liu, J.; Kumar, S.; Palomar, D.P. Parameter Estimation of Heavy-Tailed AR Model With Missing Data Via Stochastic EM. *IEEE Trans. Signal Process.* **2019**, *67*, 2159–2172. [CrossRef]
12. Robbins, H.; Monro, S. A Stochastic Approximation Method. *Ann. Math. Stat.* **1951**, *22*, 400–407. [CrossRef]
13. Estévez, J.; Bellido-Jiménez, J.A.; Liu, X.; García-Marín, A.P. Monthly Precipitation Forecasts Using Wavelet Neural Networks Models in a Semiarid Environment. *Water* **2020**, *12*, 1909. [CrossRef]
14. Pavlicko, M.; Vojteková, M.; Blažeková, O. Forecasting of Electrical Energy Consumption in Slovakia. *Mathematics* **2022**, *10*, 577. [CrossRef]
15. Gocheva-Ilieva, S.; Yordanova, A.; Kulina, H. Predicting the 305-Day Milk Yield of Holstein-Friesian Cows Depending on the Conformation Traits and Farm Using Simplified Selective Ensembles. *Mathematics* **2022**, *10*, 1254. [CrossRef]
16. Li, S.; Wang, Q. India's Dependence on Foreign Oil Will Exceed 90% around 2025—The Forecasting Results Based on Two Hybridized NMGM-ARIMA and NMGM-BP Models. *J. Clean. Prod.* **2019**, *232*, 137–153. [CrossRef]
17. Wu, X.; Zhou, J.; Yu, H.; Liu, D.; Xie, K.; Chen, Y.; Hu, J.; Sun, H.; Xing, F. The Development of a Hybrid Wavelet-ARIMA-LSTM Model for Precipitation Amounts and Drought Analysis. *Atmosphere* **2021**, *12*, 74. [CrossRef]
18. Mbatha, N.; Bencherif, H. Time Series Analysis and Forecasting Using a Novel Hybrid LSTM Data-Driven Model Based on Empirical Wavelet Transform Applied to Total Column of Ozone at Buenos Aires, Argentina (1966–2017). *Atmosphere* **2020**, *11*, 457. [CrossRef]
19. Mehdizadeh, S.; Fathian, F.; Adamowski, J.F. Hybrid Artificial Intelligence-Time Series Models for Monthly Streamflow Modeling. *Appl. Soft Comput.* **2019**, *80*, 873–887. [CrossRef]
20. Mallat, S.G. *A Wavelet Tour of Signal Processing*; Academic Press: San Diego, CA, USA, 1999; ISBN 978-0-12-466606-1.
21. Daubechies, I. *Ten Lectures on Wavelets*; Society for Industrial and Applied Mathematics: Philadelphia, PA, USA, 1992; ISBN 978-0-89871-274-2.
22. Chui, C.K. *An Introduction to Wavelets*; Wavelet analysis and its applications; Academic Press: Boston, MA, USA, 1992; ISBN 978-0-12-174584-4.
23. Mandrikova, O.; Polozov, Y.; Fetisova, N.; Zalyaev, T. Analysis of the Dynamics of Ionospheric Parameters during Periods of Increased Solar Activity and Magnetic Storms. *J. Atmos. Sol.-Terr. Phys.* **2018**, *181*, 116–126. [CrossRef]
24. Mandrikova, O.; Fetisova, N.; Polozov, Y. Hybrid Model for Time Series of Complex Structure with ARIMA Components. *Mathematics* **2021**, *9*, 1122. [CrossRef]
25. Haykin, S.S. *Neural Networks: A Comprehensive Foundation*, 2nd ed.; Prentice Hall: Upper Saddle River, NJ, USA, 1999; ISBN 978-0-13-273350-2.
26. Singh, J.; Barabanov, N. Stability of Discrete Time Recurrent Neural Networks and Nonlinear Optimization Problems. *Neural Netw.* **2016**, *74*, 58–72. [CrossRef]
27. Ma, Q.; Liu, S.; Fan, X.; Chai, C.; Wang, Y.; Yang, K. A Time Series Prediction Model of Foundation Pit Deformation Based on Empirical Wavelet Transform and NARX Network. *Mathematics* **2020**, *8*, 1535. [CrossRef]
28. Diaconescu, E. The use of NARX neural networks to predict chaotic time series. *WSEAS Trans. Comp. Res.* **2008**, *3*, 182–191.
29. Lin, T.; Horne, B.G.; Tino, P.; Giles, C.L. Learning Long-Term Dependencies in NARX Recurrent Neural Networks. *IEEE Trans. Neural Netw.* **1996**, *7*, 1329–1338. [CrossRef] [PubMed]

30. Gao, Y.; Er, M.J. NARMAX Time Series Model Prediction: Feedforward and Recurrent Fuzzy Neural Network Approaches. *Fuzzy Sets Syst.* **2005**, *150*, 331–350. [CrossRef]
31. Tsungnan, L.; Giles, C.L.; Horne, B.G.; Kung, S.Y. A Delay Damage Model Selection Algorithm for NARX Neural Networks. *IEEE Trans. Signal Process.* **1997**, *45*, 2719–2730. [CrossRef]
32. Dorffner, G. Neural Networks for Time Series Processing. *Neural Netw. World* **1996**, *6*, 447–468.
33. Mandic, D.P.; Chambers, J.A. *Recurrent Neural Networks for Prediction: Learning Algorithms, Architectures, and Stability*; Wiley series in adaptive and learning systems for signal processing, communications, and control; John Wiley: Chichester, UK; New York, NY, USA, 2001; ISBN 978-0-471-49517-8.
34. Mandrikova, O.; Mandrikova, B. Hybrid Method for Detecting Anomalies in Cosmic ray Variations Using Neural Networks Autoencoder. *Symmetry* **2022**, *14*, 744. [CrossRef]
35. Mandrikova, O.; Mandrikova, B. Method of Wavelet-Decomposition to Research Cosmic Ray Variations: Application in Space Weather. *Symmetry* **2021**, *13*, 2313. [CrossRef]
36. Phan, T.-T.-H.; Nguyen, X.H. Combining Statistical Machine Learning Models with ARIMA for Water Level Forecasting: The Case of the Red River. *Adv. Water Resour.* **2020**, *142*, 103656. [CrossRef]
37. Bengio, Y.; Simard, P.; Frasconi, P. Learning Long-Term Dependencies with Gradient Descent Is Difficult. *IEEE Trans. Neural Netw.* **1994**, *5*, 157–166. [CrossRef]
38. Schaefer, A.M.; Udluft, S.; Zimmermann, H.-G. Learning Long-Term Dependencies with Recurrent Neural Networks. *Neurocomputing* **2008**, *71*, 2481–2488. [CrossRef]
39. Glüge, S.; Böck, R.; Palm, G.; Wendemuth, A. Learning Long-Term Dependencies in Segmented-Memory Recurrent Neural Networks with Backpropagation of Error. *Neurocomputing* **2014**, *141*, 54–64. [CrossRef]
40. Pascanu, R.; Mikolov, T.; Bengio, Y. On the difficulty of training Recurrent Neural Networks. In Proceedings of the 30th International Conference on Machine Learning, Atlanta, GA, USA, 17–19 June 2013.
41. Zhang, J.; Lin, Y.; Song, Z.; Dhillon, I.S. Learning Long Term Dependencies via Fourier Recurrent Units. *Int. Conf. Mach. Learn.* **2018**, *80*, 5815–5823. [CrossRef]
42. Yue, B.; Fu, J.; Liang, J. Residual Recurrent Neural Networks for Learning Sequential Representations. *Information* **2018**, *9*, 56. [CrossRef]
43. Gers, F.A.; Schmidhuber, J.; Cummins, F. Learning to Forget: Continual Prediction with LSTM. *Neural Comput.* **2000**, *12*, 2451–2471. [CrossRef]
44. Hochreiter, S.; Schmidhuber, J. Long Short-Term Memory. *Neural Comput.* **1997**, *9*, 1735–1780. [CrossRef]
45. Kühnert, C.; Gonuguntla, N.M.; Krieg, H.; Nowak, D.; Thomas, J.A. Application of LSTM Networks for Water Demand Prediction in Optimal Pump Control. *Water* **2021**, *13*, 644. [CrossRef]
46. Jiao, F.; Huang, L.; Song, R.; Huang, H. An Improved STL-LSTM Model for Daily Bus Passenger Flow Prediction during the COVID-19 Pandemic. *Sensors* **2021**, *21*, 5950. [CrossRef]
47. Li, P.; Zhang, J.; Krebs, P. Prediction of Flow Based on a CNN-LSTM Combined Deep Learning Approach. *Water* **2022**, *14*, 993. [CrossRef]
48. Noh, S.-H. Analysis of Gradient Vanishing of RNNs and Performance Comparison. *Information* **2021**, *12*, 442. [CrossRef]
49. Greff, K.; Srivastava, R.K.; Koutnik, J.; Steunebrink, B.R.; Schmidhuber, J. LSTM: A Search Space Odyssey. *IEEE Trans. Neural Netw. Learn. Syst.* **2017**, *28*, 2222–2232. [CrossRef] [PubMed]
50. Gers, F. *Long Short-Term Memory in Recurrent Neural Networks*; EPFL: Lausanne, Switzerland, 2001. [CrossRef]
51. Danilov, A.D. Ionospheric F-Region Response to Geomagnetic Disturbances. *Adv. Space Res.* **2013**, *52*, 343–366. [CrossRef]
52. Tebabal, A.; Radicella, S.M.; Nigussie, M.; Damtie, B.; Nava, B.; Yizengaw, E. Local TEC Modelling and Forecasting Using Neural Networks. *J. Atmos. Sol.-Terr. Phys.* **2018**, *172*, 143–151. [CrossRef]
53. Dmitriev, A.V.; Suvorova, A.V.; Klimenko, M.V.; Klimenko, V.V.; Ratovsky, K.G.; Rakhmatulin, R.A.; Parkhomov, V.A. Predictable and Unpredictable Ionospheric Disturbances during St. Patrick's Day Magnetic Storms of 2013 and 2015 and on 8–9 March 2008. *J. Geophys. Res. Space Phys.* **2017**, *122*, 2398–2423. [CrossRef]
54. Mandrikova, O.; Mandrikova, B.; Rodomanskay, A. Method of Constructing a Nonlinear Approximating Scheme of a Complex Signal: Application Pattern Recognition. *Mathematics* **2021**, *9*, 737. [CrossRef]
55. Rudin, W. Functional Analysis. In *International Series in Pure and Applied Mathematics*, 2nd ed.; McGraw-Hill: New York, NY, USA, 1991; ISBN 978-0-07-054236-5.
56. Korostelev, A.P.; Korosteleva, O. *Mathematical Statistics: Asymptotic Minimax Theory*; Graduate studies in mathematics; American Mathematical Society: Providence, RI, USA, 2011; ISBN 978-0-8218-5283-5.
57. Berger, J.O. *Statistical Decision Theory and Bayesian Analysis*, 2nd ed.; Springer series in statistics; Springer: New York, NY, USA, 1993; ISBN 978-0-387-96098-2.
58. Zhang, X.-M. Schur-Convex Functions and Isoperimetric Inequalities. *Proc. Am. Math. Soc.* **1998**, *126*, 461–470. [CrossRef]
59. Priestley, M.B.; Priestley, M.B. *Spectral Analysis and Time Series*; Probability and mathematical statistics; Repr.; Elsevier: Amsterdam, The Netherlands; Heidelberg, Germany, 2004; ISBN 978-0-12-564922-3.
60. Mandrikova, O.; Polozov, Y.; Geppener, V. Method of Ionospheric Data Analysis Based on a Combination of Wavelet Transform and Neural Networks. *Procedia Eng.* **2017**, *201*, 756–766. [CrossRef]
61. Tapping, K.F. The 10.7 Cm Solar Radio Flux ($F_{10.7}$): F10.7. *Space Weather* **2013**, *11*, 394–406. [CrossRef]

62. Ljung, G.M.; Box, G.E. On a measure of lack of fit in time series models. *Biometrika* **1978**, *65*, 297–303. [CrossRef]
63. Sugiura, M. Hourly values of equatorial Dst for the IGY. *Ann. Int. Geophys. Year* **1964**, *35*, 7–45.

Article

Efficient Monte Carlo Methods for Multidimensional Modeling of Slot Machines Jackpot

Slavi Georgiev [1,2] **and Venelin Todorov** [1,3,*]

[1] Department of Informational Modeling, Institute of Mathematics and Informatics, Bulgarian Academy of Sciences, Acad. G. Bonchev Str. Bl. 8, 1113 Sofia, Bulgaria

[2] Department of Applied Mathematics and Statistics, Faculty of Natural Sciences and Education, University of Ruse, POB 7004 Ruse, Bulgaria

[3] Department of Parallel Algorithms, Institute of Information and Communication Technologies, Bulgarian Academy of Sciences, Acad. G. Bonchev Str. Bl. 25A, 1113 Sofia, Bulgaria

* Correspondence: vtodorov@math.bas.bg or venelin@parallel.bas.bg

Abstract: Nowadays, entertainment is one of the biggest industries, which continues to expand. In this study, the problem of estimating the consolation prize as a fraction of the jackpot is dealt with, which is an important issue for each casino and gambling club. Solving the problem leads to the computation of multidimensional integrals. For that purpose, modifications of the most powerful stochastic quasi-Monte Carlo approaches are employed, in particular lattice and digital sequences, Halton and Sobol sequences, and Latin hypercube sampling. They show significant improvements to the classical Monte Carlo methods. After accurate computation of the arisen integrals, it is shown how to calculate the expectation of the real consolation prize, taking into account the distribution of time, when different numbers of players are betting. Moreover, a solution to the problem with higher dimensions is also proposed. All the suggestions are verified by computational experiments with real data. Besides gambling, the results obtained in this study have various applications in numerous areas, including finance, ecology and many others.

Keywords: gambling; jackpot; multidimensional integrals; Monte Carlo methods; lattice sequences; digital sequences

MSC: 62P30; 65C05; 68W20; 91A60

Citation: Georgiev, S.; Todorov, V. Efficient Monte Carlo Methods for Multidimensional Modeling of Slot Machines Jackpot. *Mathematics* **2023**, *11*, 266. https://doi.org/10.3390/math11020266

Academic Editors: Snezhana Gocheva-Ilieva, Atanas Ivanov and Hristina Kulina

Received: 7 December 2022
Revised: 28 December 2022
Accepted: 31 December 2022
Published: 4 January 2023

1. Introduction

The gambling industry plays a significant role in modern life [1,2]. It is one of the most profitable businesses worldwide with prognosed value more than USD 640 billion by 2027 [3]. In the recent years, there are more and more opportunities for everyone seeking such kind of joy. The most popular game machines are the slot machines [4], also called "fruit machines" or even "one-armed bandits" [5]. However, due to the competition, the payback rate (Return-to-Player, RTP) is as high, as it reaches 98% [6]. For every casino and gambling club, it is vital to plan its expenditures in a precise way in order to be both competitive and profitable.

1.1. General Framework

In this paper, we consider the gambling club systems with slot machines [7]. The revenues are formed entirely by the player's bets. The greatest deal of the expenditures is composed by the direct 'payline' wins. Here, the bonuses and the standalone jackpots are also included. Then, it comes the linked progressive jackpot (hereinafter called jackpot). Its size is based on the size of the bets, so it constitutes a deterministic part of the expenses. This is not the case, though, for the consolation prize. Its upper limit is equal to the jackpot or a predefined part of it. However, its particular size depends on the player who won the jackpot and their bet, so its size is a stochastic variable. The aim of this paper is to propose a robust method to compute its expectation. For the sake of completeness, the other part of the costs concerns the drink and food in the casino as well as the staff salary, equipment and housing.

The consolation prize is divided between all the players except the one who won the jackpot. Everyone gets a share, proportional to their bet. So, basically, if $\mathbb{E}[X]$ is the expected bet share of the winner, $1 - \mathbb{E}[X]$ is the expected size (in percentage) of the consolation prize. How the bet is placed is explained in the following subsection.

1.2. Bet Collection

Firstly, a player should deposit a cash amount in the machine. This is done directly via the bill validator or by the dealer with the «attendant» electronic key. Then, before choosing a game, the player selects how many credits he/she bets on every spin and sets the credit denomination, or the prize of one credit. After, the player can choose a particular game. From the game settings, the number of lines can be selected. Roughly speaking, 30 lines with bet of 30 credits means playing simultaneously 30 games, each of them with a bet of 1 credit.

The first slot machines had real mechanical reels, while the recent have screens with virtual reels. The player pushes a button, which activates the spinning of the reels. When they stop, the player wins a payline prize if there are the same symbols on an active line (which is in general a pattern rather than a straight line). Regardless of the outcome, the bet is collected for every spin.

Every game is characterized with volatility [8,9]. It is measured in a discrete scale between 1 and 5. An exact formula does not exist—it should be interpreted just as the higher the number, the more volatile the win size. A game has different settings for the RTP level [3,10–12], which often varies between 88% and 96%, but usually is higher than 91–92%. Every RTP level is associated with a different set of reels. It is preset by the owner of the machine and cannot be altered on the go.

1.3. Jackpot Winning

So, for every bet, a predefined amount is dedicated to compose the jackpot prize. When the event for hitting the jackpot comes, it is won by a single player. As we discussed earlier, the jackpot win probability of each player is proportional to their bet. The process of hitting is visualized as follows. On the screen, a tube following its perimeter appears (which, obviously, has a rectangular shape). The tube is partitioned such that each player is assigned a segment of the tube with proportional length. Then, a ball starts circulating over the tube with decreasing velocity. The segment it stops determines the jackpot winner. The others receive the consolation prize.

The main novelty of the study is the reformulation of the problem of finding the expectation of the consolation price into a multidimensional integral evaluation problem, and the design of an algorithm to obtain this value by employing advanced stochastic approaches and numerical techniques. The paper itself is organized as follows. The next Section 2 introduces the models of integral representations, the algorithms for point transformations and the stochastic methods used in the integral computation. Section 3 is devoted to the detailed presentation of the obtained results and their thorough explanation. In Section 4, a particular case study is considered with real data, where it is demonstrated how to derive the real consolation prize expected value. The paper is concluded with Section 5.

2. Algorithms and Methods

Before presenting the model, we reveal one more constraint which has to be taken care of. No matter how small a single bet is, the associated probability cannot be less than 0.5%. This automatically suggests that the upper limit of a single player's probability is $(100 - 0.5(N - 1))\%$, where N is the number of players participating in the play. Henceforward, we define $L := 0.005$ and $U := 0.995$. Obviously, this setting is valid for, at most, $N \leq 200$ players.

Let the probability for i^{th} player $(i = 1, \ldots, N)$ to win the jackpot be defined with x_i. By the aforementioned arguments, it is obvious that

$$\sum_{i=1}^{N} x_i = 1 \tag{1}$$

and

$$L \leq x_i \leq U - L \cdot N \quad \text{for} \quad i = 1, \ldots, N. \tag{2}$$

Equality (1) suggests that the points should be drawn from the N-dimensional simplex. Inequalities (2), though, are more complicated to satisfy. In order to cope with it, we will present two approaches. However, to explain them better, firstly we present the expectation operator.

2.1. Integral Representation

Let us restate our aim to find the expected size of the consolation prize. If the first player wins the jackpot, the (relative) size of the consolation prize is $1 - x_1$. However, the probability of the first player to win the jackpot is exactly x_1. Of course, this is true for all players. So, the size of the consolation prize (CP), given in a percentage, in the case of N players is

$$\mathbb{E}[CP] = \mathbb{P}[\text{first player wins}] * \text{Size}[CP|\text{first player wins}]+$$
$$+ \mathbb{P}[\text{second player wins}] * \text{Size}[CP|\text{second player wins}]+$$
$$+ \ldots +$$
$$+ \mathbb{P}[\text{last player wins}] * \text{Size}[CP|\text{last player wins}]$$
$$= \sum_{i=1}^{N} x_i(1 - x_i). \tag{3}$$

In this case, the expectation would look like

$$\mathbb{E}[CP] = \int\int \cdots \int_{\mathbf{x} \in \Delta^{N-1}} \sum_{i=1}^{N} x_i(1 - x_i) \mathrm{d}x_N \mathrm{d}x_{N-1} \cdots \mathrm{d}x_1, \tag{4}$$

where Δ^{N-1} is the standard $(N-1)$-simplex, transformed according to (2).

However, we can reduce the dimension of the integral (4) with one using $x_N = 1 - x_1 - x_2 - \ldots - x_{N-1}$ (1):

$$\mathbb{E}[CP] = \sum_{i=1}^{N-1} x_i(1 - x_i) + \left(1 - \sum_{i=1}^{N-1} x_i\right) \sum_{i=1}^{N-1} x_i. \tag{5}$$

Setting $D := N - 1$, then the integral would be

$$\mathbb{E}[CP] = \int\int \cdots \int_{\mathbf{x} \in \overline{V}^D} \sum_{i=1}^{D} x_i(1 - x_i) + \left(1 - \sum_{i=1}^{D} x_i\right) \sum_{i=1}^{D} x_i \mathrm{d}x_D \cdots \mathrm{d}x_1, \tag{6}$$

where $\overline{V}^D$ is the *space* between standard $(D-1)$-simplex and the coordinate hyperplanes in $\mathbb{R}^D$, again transformed according to (2).

For clarity purposes, we write the integrals with their respective limits for the first values of D:

- For $D = 1$:

$$\int_L^U x_1(1 - x_1) + (1 - x_1)x_1 \mathrm{d}x_1,$$

- For $D = 2$:

$$\int_L^{(U-L)} \int_L^{(U-x_1)} x_1(1 - x_1) + x_2(1 - x_2) + (1 - x_1 - x_2)(x_1 + x_2)\mathrm{d}x_2\mathrm{d}x_1,$$

- For $D = 3$:

$$\int_L^{(U-2L)} \int_L^{(U-L-x_1)} \int_L^{(U-x_1-x_2)} x_1(1 - x_1) + x_2(1 - x_2) + x_3(1 - x_3) + (1 - x_1 - x_2 - x_3)(x_1 + x_2 + x_3)\mathrm{d}x_3\mathrm{d}x_2\mathrm{d}x_1,$$

- For $D = k$:

$$\int_L^{\left(U-(k-1)L\right)} \int_L^{\left(U-(k-2)L-x_1\right)} \cdots \int_L^{\left(U-\sum_{i=1}^{k-1} x_i\right)} \sum_{i=1}^{k} x_i(1 - x_i) + \left(1 - \sum_{i=1}^{k} x_i\right) \sum_{i=1}^{k} x_i \, \mathrm{d}x_k \cdots \mathrm{d}x_2\mathrm{d}x_1.$$

For $D = 1$ and $D = 2$, the integrands are plotted on Figure 1.

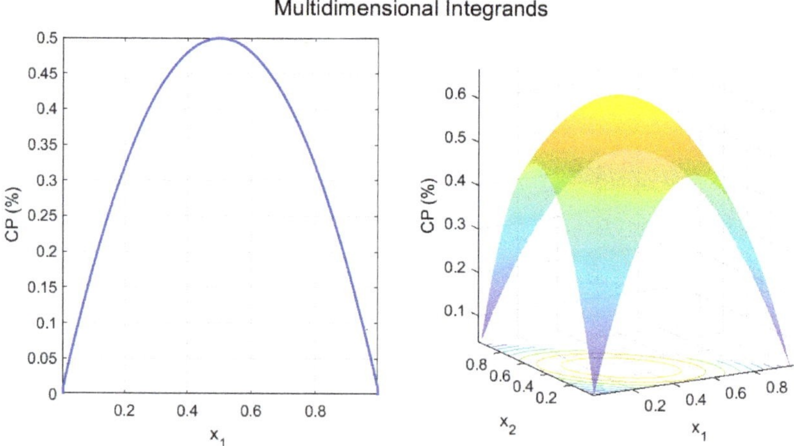

Figure 1. Integrands for $D = 1$ and $D = 2$.

In the next subsections, we will describe the algorithm for drawing points for both (4) and (6). Henceforward, let $C \gg 1$ be the total number of points.

2.2. Algorithm for Drawing Point for (4)

This approach is rather simple. Firstly, we draw C D-dimensional points $\hat{\mathbf{x}}^D$, uniformly distributed in the D-dimensional hypercube. Then, we sort the coordinates of every point, independently from the other points, and name the new points $\tilde{\mathbf{x}}^D$. Subsequently, we map $\tilde{\mathbf{x}}^D$ to the points $\tilde{\mathbf{x}}^{D+2}$ from the $(D+2)$-dimensional hypercube as

$$\tilde{\mathbf{x}}^{D+2}(i) := \tilde{\mathbf{x}}^D(i-1) \quad \text{for} \quad i = 2,\ldots,D+1$$

and set

$$\tilde{\mathbf{x}}^{D+2}(1) := 0, \qquad \tilde{\mathbf{x}}^{D+2}(D+2) := 1.$$

Now, we are sure that the coordinates of each point in $\tilde{\mathbf{x}}^{D+2}$ are sorted and lie on the line $[0,1]$, including the boundaries 0 and 1. If we take the difference between every two adjacent coordinates and in such a way define a new coordinate, we arrive at points $\hat{\mathbf{x}}^N$ in the $(D+1)$-dimensional hypercube, which

$$\hat{\mathbf{x}}^N(i) := \tilde{\mathbf{x}}^{D+2}(i+1) - \tilde{\mathbf{x}}^{D+2}(i).$$

The points $\hat{\mathbf{x}}^N$ indeed belong to the standard D-simplex.

In that way, we fulfilled (1). In order to satisfy (2), we apply a *linear* transformation on $\hat{\mathbf{x}}^N$:

$$\mathbf{x}^N := \hat{\mathbf{x}}^N(1 - N \cdot L) + L, \tag{7}$$

where the operations should be applied element-wisely.

Thus, the points $\mathbf{x}^N$ (7) satisfy both (1) and (2) and belong to Δ^D.

2.3. Algorithm for Drawing Point for (6)

This algorithm is also not complicated. To begin with, we again draw C D-dimensional points $\hat{\mathbf{x}}^D$, uniformly distributed in the D-dimensional hypercube. Now, it is enough to *linearly* scale the point coordinates as follows:

$$\mathbf{x}^D(i) := \hat{\mathbf{x}}^D(i) \cdot \left(U - (D - i + 1)L - \sum_{j=1}^{i-1} \hat{\mathbf{x}}^D(j) \right) + L, \tag{8}$$

where, of course, the sum is equal to 0 for $i = 1$.

The points $\mathbf{x}^D$ (8) satisfy

$$\sum_{i=1}^{D} x_i \leq U \quad \text{and} \quad x_i \geq L \text{ for } i = 1,\ldots,D.$$

Thus, they truly belong to $\overline{V}^D$ and satisfy the requirements to be used for the evaluation of (6).

Of course, for that purpose, we could use the former algorithm and truncate the last coordinate of $\mathbf{x}^N$ (7). This operation is actually a projection of $\mathbf{x}^N$ onto the D-dimensional hyperplane $Ox_1x_2\ldots x_D$.

It is worth saying that we indeed use the first algorithm with the truncation of the last coordinate since the second one does not distribute the points in an optimal way.

2.4. Monte Carlo Algorithms

The Monte Carlo methods [13] come in handy when the deterministic methods fail [14–16]. They have tremendous applications in many areas, including financial derivatives evaluation [17] and even slot machines play [18] and reels reconstruction [19]. Now we mention some of the fundamental Monte Carlo approaches.

Plain (crude) Monte Carlo is the earliest and probably the most used Monte Carlo (MC) method to solve multidimensional integrals [14]. The MC quadrature formula lies on the probabilistic interpretation of the integral

$$I[f] = \int_{\Omega} f(x)p(x)\mathrm{d}x.$$

Let the random variable $\theta = f(\xi)$ be such that

$$\mathbf{E}\theta = \int_{\Omega} f(x)p(x)\mathrm{d}x,$$

where the random points $\xi_1, \xi_2, \ldots, \xi_N$ are independent realizations of the random point ξ with probability density function $p(x)$ and $\theta_1 = f(\xi_1), \ldots, \theta_N = f(\xi_N)$. Then the plain MC approach for the integral I is defined as [14]

$$\bar{\theta}_N = \frac{1}{N} \sum_{i=1}^{N} \theta_i.$$

Latin hypercube sampling (LHS) is a type of stratified sampling (SS) [14]. In the case of SS, one must divide $[0,1]^d$ into M^d disjoint subdomains, each of volume $\frac{1}{M^d}$, and to sample one point at each subdomain. It is proved in [15] that the variance of a SS could never exceed the variance of a plain random sampling. LHS is a highly researched topic [20–23].

By definition, *quasi-Monte Carlo (QMC) methods* are based on quasi-random sequences that are built in such a way as to minimize a measure of their deviation from uniformity, called discrepancy [24,25].

Let $x_i = (x_i^{(1)}, x_i^{(2)}, \ldots, x_i^{(s)})$, $i = 1, 2, \ldots$ The representation of n in base b is presented by the following formula [26]: $n = \ldots a_3(n), a_2(n), a_1(n),\ n > 0, n \in \mathbb{Z}$.

The radical inverse sequence is defined as [27]: $n = \sum_{i=0}^{\infty} a_{i+1}(n)b^i$, $\phi_b(n) = \sum_{i=0}^{\infty} a_{i+1}(n)b^{-(i+1)}$ and its discrepancy satisfies: $D_N^* = \mathcal{O}\left(\frac{\log N}{N}\right)$. The Van der Corput sequence [28] is obtained when $b = 2$.

Halton sequence [29,30] is defined as

$$s_n^{(k)} = \sum_{i=0}^{\infty} \sigma_{i+1}^{(k)} a_{i+1}^{(k)}(n) b_k^{-(i+1)},$$

where $(b_1, b_2, \ldots, b_s) \equiv (2, 3, 5, \ldots, p_s)$, and p_i denotes the ith prime, and $\sigma_i^{(k)}$, $i \geq 1$: set of permutations on $(0, 1, 2, \ldots, p_k - 1)$.

Sobol sequence [17,31–34] is defined by

$$x_k \in \bar{\sigma}_i^{(k)}, k = 0, 1, 2, \ldots$$

where $\bar{\sigma}_i^{(k)}$, $i \geq 1$: set of permutations on every $2^k, k = 0, 1, 2, \ldots$ subsequent points of the Van der Corput sequence. In binary, we have that: $x_n^{(k)} = \bigoplus_{i\geq 0} a_{i+1}(n)v_i$, where v_i, $i = 1, \ldots, s$ is a set of direction numbers [34].

To scramble the *Halton sequence*, we used a permutation of the radical inverse coefficients derived by applying a reverse-radix operation to all of the possible coefficient values. The algorithm is proposed in [35]. To scramble the *Sobol sequence*, we used a random linear scramble combined with a random digital shift. The algorithm is suggested in [36].

When the integrand is sufficiently regular, the *lattice sequences*, using special types of sequences with low discrepancy, generally outperform the basic MC methods. Sloan and Kachoyan [37], Niederreiter [38], Hua and Wang [39], Wang and Hickernell [40] and Sloan and Joe [41] provide comprehensive expositions on the theory of lattice sequences.

We constructed our lattice sequence with the optimal generating vector by using a special algorithmic [42–45] construction of rank-1 lattice rules with prime number of points and with product weights with 2^{30} points.

Niederreiter [27,46] introduced a special family of digital (t, m, s)-nets over F_b. Those nets are obtained from rational functions over finite fields [47–49]. We will use a special type of digital sequences, namely *interlaced digital sequences* [50–53], a special class of digital nets, a concept analogous to lattice sequences, but based on linear algebra over finite fields [54].

We will use the generating matrices for an implementation of the Sobol' sequence from [55] with 21201 dimensions for the *digital sequence*, as well as the generating matrices for interlaced Sobol' sequences with interlacing factor $d = 2$ for the *interlaced digital sequence*.

3. Results and Discussion

In this section, we make an overview of the results, obtained by the aforementioned methods. We recall that C denotes the total number of points used in the integration.

For the 10-dimensional integral (Table 1), the best approach is the lattice sequence. It achieves the smallest error in 7 of 21 cases. The other suitable method is the interlaced digital sequence, producing the five smallest errors, but they are obtained for large values of C, and they are of one order better than the errors produced by the other methods.

Table 1. The 10-dimensional integral absolute errors.

# of pts	Crude	Lattice Sequence	Halton (Scrambled)	Sobol (Scrambled)	LHS	Digital Sequence	Dig. Seq. (Interlaced)
2^{10}	1.6125e-04	5.9472e-03	**1.2844e-04**	7.2665e-04	1.0475e-03	5.9037e-04	1.0728e-03
2^{11}	1.9346e-04	1.8509e-03	1.8755e-04	**4.0143e-06**	5.2541e-04	6.6748e-04	8.3025e-04
2^{12}	3.4622e-05	5.8246e-04	2.4591e-04	**1.5847e-05**	9.0208e-04	1.0248e-04	4.4663e-04
2^{13}	2.7674e-04	1.9345e-04	2.9789e-04	8.5159e-05	1.8386e-04	8.4683e-05	**2.8420e-05**
2^{14}	7.8357e-05	**2.0888e-06**	2.3893e-04	2.6495e-05	2.7664e-04	1.5048e-05	1.3011e-04
2^{15}	6.8036e-05	**6.2652e-06**	6.4250e-05	5.9894e-05	4.2919e-05	7.1324e-06	8.6867e-05
2^{16}	6.7842e-05	**5.6128e-06**	2.7236e-05	2.0672e-05	4.6293e-05	4.2045e-05	4.2164e-05
2^{17}	3.4242e-05	2.2065e-05	6.4611e-06	**2.7191e-06**	3.2974e-05	3.7721e-06	2.9521e-05
2^{18}	1.3859e-05	1.4018e-05	4.3472e-06	5.2437e-06	3.4679e-05	5.4494e-06	**1.9901e-06**
2^{19}	1.0718e-05	6.3245e-06	**1.2579e-06**	4.8620e-06	4.3226e-05	2.5429e-06	9.4656e-06
2^{20}	3.5234e-05	**2.6706e-06**	2.8323e-06	3.3937e-06	8.7798e-06	5.1221e-06	8.2347e-06
2^{21}	1.0182e-05	1.6646e-06	1.9961e-06	5.3631e-06	1.6481e-05	1.8632e-06	**5.9903e-07**
2^{22}	2.2655e-05	**3.2259e-07**	1.6827e-06	2.4378e-06	2.4166e-06	4.2597e-07	7.2949e-07
2^{23}	1.7509e-05	**3.3866e-07**	1.1103e-06	2.1528e-06	2.1024e-05	1.3517e-06	8.3793e-07
2^{24}	1.6180e-05	**1.3048e-07**	2.9587e-07	6.1431e-07	9.9364e-06	2.1059e-07	3.7635e-07
2^{25}	2.1837e-06	1.4345e-07	**4.7869e-08**	6.7600e-08	4.8745e-06	1.2202e-07	3.5241e-07
2^{26}	9.3048e-07	8.9044e-08	1.9305e-07	**2.4566e-08**	8.1265e-07	2.4635e-07	1.3593e-07
2^{27}	1.9097e-06	1.5722e-07	1.6952e-07	7.3093e-08	3.6900e-06	1.9022e-07	**7.1400e-08**
2^{28}	3.1659e-06	2.5281e-07	2.0586e-07	1.3335e-07	4.5442e-06	1.3973e-07	**8.8798e-08**
2^{29}	1.7997e-06	2.5890e-07	**9.7798e-08**	1.3165e-07	3.3598e-06	1.0323e-07	1.3916e-07
2^{30}	7.0793e-07	2.1939e-07	1.2303e-07	1.1717e-07	1.9125e-06	**8.8701e-08**	1.5022e-07

Regarding the 20-dimensional integral (Table 2), the best approach is the digital sequence with the five smallest errors. The other suitable approaches for large C are the scrambled versions of Halton and Sobol sequences, but the best errors are mostly of the same magnitude with the other errors.

Table 2. The 20-dimensional integral absolute errors.

# of pts	Crude	Lattice Sequence	Halton (Scrambled)	Sobol (Scrambled)	LHS	Digital Sequence	Dig. Seq. (Interlaced)
2^{10}	4.2424e-04	2.2186e-03	9.2765e-04	**1.2899e-04**	3.6004e-04	5.2874e-04	1.3937e-04
2^{11}	4.6117e-04	7.0176e-04	1.4455e-04	8.9927e-05	2.3571e-04	2.1758e-04	**3.0062e-05**
2^{12}	2.0007e-04	1.5822e-04	7.4068e-05	1.6044e-04	1.0083e-04	1.0073e-04	**5.3337e-05**
2^{13}	2.0158e-04	7.0237e-05	1.4219e-04	1.9860e-05	2.8870e-05	**1.4031e-05**	8.7705e-05
2^{14}	5.2760e-05	6.2024e-05	9.3461e-05	1.2797e-05	**7.3244e-06**	1.7751e-04	8.2802e-05
2^{15}	8.2842e-05	4.4449e-05	5.5727e-05	1.9360e-05	**4.9510e-07**	1.0716e-04	1.3102e-04
2^{16}	1.8965e-05	2.9679e-05	2.2945e-05	1.1282e-05	5.0190e-05	2.4556e-05	**6.0506e-06**
2^{17}	**1.0528e-06**	6.9826e-06	2.1535e-05	1.4995e-05	3.0443e-06	1.5096e-05	5.2518e-05
2^{18}	1.1727e-05	9.7206e-06	1.3592e-05	1.7442e-06	4.8608e-05	**1.4890e-06**	8.4102e-06
2^{19}	**1.1050e-06**	8.7650e-06	3.6968e-06	2.0281e-06	2.1769e-05	2.1187e-06	7.0668e-06
2^{20}	4.6550e-06	1.0659e-05	**9.6641e-07**	3.2260e-06	1.2835e-05	5.0257e-06	7.7813e-06
2^{21}	9.9240e-06	3.3764e-06	**1.9763e-07**	1.0475e-06	9.2554e-07	8.3166e-07	8.3535e-06
2^{22}	7.8955e-06	3.6975e-06	**5.6247e-07**	5.9110e-07	6.2199e-06	1.1169e-06	5.9651e-06
2^{23}	4.3561e-06	4.1806e-06	9.6957e-07	6.9539e-07	1.2914e-06	**5.4250e-07**	4.6332e-06
2^{24}	2.9360e-06	3.1509e-06	1.5560e-06	7.1811e-07	1.4429e-06	**3.9447e-07**	3.0476e-06
2^{25}	1.1241e-06	2.6445e-06	4.2063e-07	3.8353e-07	2.2397e-06	**3.1203e-07**	2.1824e-06
2^{26}	8.7692e-07	2.1141e-06	3.5672e-08	**1.5187e-08**	1.6691e-06	4.5273e-07	5.2714e-07
2^{27}	4.3518e-07	**1.0892e-07**	1.4269e-07	1.4882e-07	2.9563e-06	3.6523e-07	2.6921e-07
2^{28}	6.8053e-07	**1.9842e-08**	1.4691e-07	1.2274e-07	1.4889e-06	3.5155e-08	2.9726e-07
2^{29}	4.9385e-07	2.8625e-07	**2.4991e-08**	5.3652e-08	7.4508e-07	7.1262e-08	1.2514e-07
2^{30}	4.5742e-08	2.0564e-07	7.8722e-08	**1.9992e-08**	5.4737e-08	3.6093e-08	3.1281e-08

The results for the 10- and 20-dimensional integrals are visualized on Figure 2.

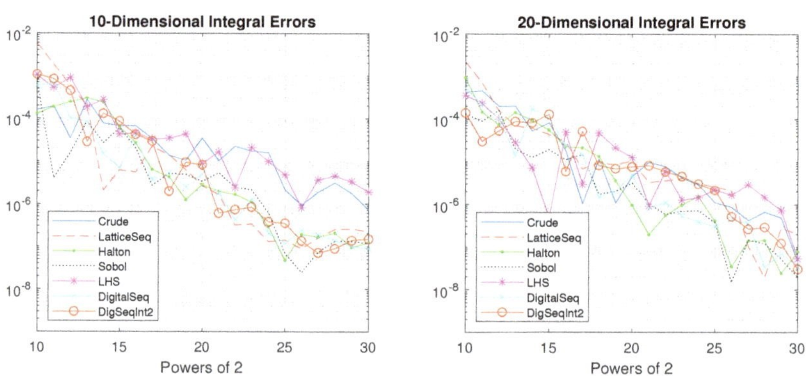

Figure 2. The 10- (**left**) and 20-dimensional (**right**) integral absolute errors.

Considering the 30-dimensional integral (Table 3), the scrambled Halton sequence stands out with the 10 smallest errors. For large C, only the interlaced digital sequence produces comparable results.

Table 3. The 30-dimensional integral absolute errors.

# of pts	Crude	Lattice Sequence	Halton (Scrambled)	Sobol (Scrambled)	LHS	Digital Sequence	Dig. Seq. (Interlaced)
2^{10}	5.6739e-04	1.0656e-03	8.0536e-04	2.4543e-04	3.6416e-04	1.9768e-03	**2.4082e-04**
2^{11}	5.0974e-04	1.3895e-04	3.1916e-04	9.8819e-05	2.2928e-04	7.7937e-04	**1.8871e-05**
2^{12}	2.3304e-04	1.3790e-04	1.6958e-04	9.5142e-05	**1.9455e-05**	3.3060e-04	3.4341e-05
2^{13}	1.1975e-04	5.3935e-05	2.3725e-05	**1.8203e-05**	2.0798e-05	8.4316e-05	9.2937e-05
2^{14}	5.5627e-05	3.5630e-05	3.4593e-05	2.6009e-05	**1.4971e-05**	1.5621e-04	1.0520e-04
2^{15}	2.1237e-05	**1.8310e-06**	8.2029e-06	2.9298e-05	2.4766e-06	8.9506e-05	9.4057e-05
2^{16}	1.9101e-05	2.3731e-05	**1.5520e-05**	1.7346e-05	2.7570e-05	5.9149e-05	3.1495e-05
2^{17}	4.3098e-06	1.1266e-05	**1.2141e-06**	1.4796e-05	2.0351e-05	3.5717e-05	7.5926e-06
2^{18}	1.3111e-05	1.7714e-05	**1.0349e-06**	1.4350e-06	1.2427e-05	1.9233e-05	1.0986e-05
2^{19}	9.3056e-06	9.2828e-06	**1.2580e-06**	3.1220e-06	1.3078e-06	4.6659e-06	2.1766e-06
2^{20}	**1.6502e-07**	1.2191e-05	1.1799e-06	2.1905e-06	7.9287e-06	7.8017e-07	5.9582e-07
2^{21}	7.7765e-06	1.5628e-06	**9.5832e-07**	1.9508e-06	2.1812e-06	4.3073e-06	1.2697e-06
2^{22}	2.7534e-06	1.3731e-06	**2.6880e-07**	2.6999e-06	3.1743e-06	3.3863e-06	3.9830e-06
2^{23}	2.7670e-06	1.6556e-06	**6.9770e-07**	1.5534e-06	2.9464e-06	3.5417e-06	2.7309e-06
2^{24}	1.6428e-06	2.4656e-06	**1.8664e-07**	5.4349e-07	2.4260e-06	1.7892e-06	5.0548e-07
2^{25}	1.2102e-06	2.0020e-06	7.5073e-07	**3.9239e-08**	1.0994e-06	4.6812e-07	4.4462e-07
2^{26}	8.7894e-07	1.1624e-06	1.3480e-07	2.1915e-07	5.9294e-07	**1.2355e-07**	1.7329e-07
2^{27}	4.1233e-07	2.6590e-07	1.4617e-07	2.3914e-07	1.0625e-06	4.3637e-07	**7.5010e-08**
2^{28}	5.0533e-07	1.3181e-07	**3.6327e-08**	1.0879e-07	1.7287e-07	2.7534e-07	2.0400e-07
2^{29}	7.8876e-08	7.3116e-08	**9.0219e-09**	3.5619e-08	8.0690e-08	2.2416e-07	5.2949e-08
2^{30}	3.6846e-08	3.7030e-08	3.0655e-08	3.1748e-08	2.0135e-07	9.2595e-08	**2.3311e-08**

Similar is the situation with the 40-dimensional integral (Table 4), where the best methods are the scrambled versions of Halton and Sobol sequences with seven respective best errors. It makes an impression that the scrambled Halton sequences achieves order of error 1e-9 for both integrals.

Table 4. The 40-dimensional integral absolute errors.

# of pts	Crude	Lattice Sequence	Halton (Scrambled)	Sobol (Scrambled)	LHS	Digital Sequence	Dig. Seq. (Interlaced)
2^{10}	2.7181e-04	1.4648e-03	1.5098e-04	**4.3883e-06**	2.9901e-04	1.5932e-03	2.4472e-04
2^{11}	1.1533e-04	3.7009e-04	1.9943e-04	5.6922e-05	2.2411e-04	6.5545e-04	**5.3065e-05**
2^{12}	5.8559e-05	2.4444e-05	2.2240e-04	**1.1855e-06**	1.1090e-04	2.5692e-04	9.3302e-05
2^{13}	3.0213e-05	7.7243e-05	**1.3250e-05**	5.0104e-05	6.3212e-05	1.0417e-04	8.1908e-05
2^{14}	2.6176e-05	8.8000e-05	**1.0513e-05**	3.0773e-05	4.3708e-05	3.5951e-05	3.7869e-05
2^{15}	2.5704e-05	2.2879e-05	**6.0667e-06**	1.5847e-05	3.1172e-05	2.4964e-05	5.4438e-05
2^{16}	1.6400e-05	6.4601e-06	2.6509e-05	1.6833e-05	**3.9807e-06**	2.5353e-05	1.6738e-05
2^{17}	2.5723e-05	2.3011e-06	9.4629e-06	3.7741e-06	**1.4830e-06**	2.0617e-05	3.5685e-06
2^{18}	3.6339e-06	7.9537e-07	3.5313e-06	**2.7030e-07**	4.2998e-06	1.7559e-05	1.9698e-06
2^{19}	2.4027e-06	3.4205e-06	2.1489e-06	**9.8305e-07**	1.3022e-06	7.8761e-06	2.7688e-06
2^{20}	1.0616e-06	**2.6758e-07**	6.7986e-07	5.3424e-07	6.5435e-06	4.0980e-06	5.9513e-06
2^{21}	1.2396e-06	**3.5144e-08**	2.5375e-07	1.5510e-06	3.7089e-07	7.6012e-07	6.1507e-06
2^{22}	2.9497e-06	1.3839e-06	2.4879e-07	3.8104e-07	2.6274e-07	**1.7574e-07**	3.0190e-06
2^{23}	6.3118e-07	1.3022e-06	5.4231e-07	**7.0660e-08**	5.0872e-07	4.6938e-07	1.1428e-06
2^{24}	3.9910e-07	5.6549e-07	**4.2073e-08**	8.2035e-08	1.0986e-06	9.7703e-07	1.0759e-06
2^{25}	1.3857e-07	3.5614e-07	2.6281e-07	**7.8423e-08**	3.0330e-07	6.5340e-07	5.5114e-07
2^{26}	1.2456e-07	3.1465e-07	1.4513e-07	**5.6594e-08**	5.2112e-07	6.7542e-07	1.6924e-07
2^{27}	3.8877e-08	4.5444e-07	**7.6692e-09**	1.2056e-07	4.2312e-07	2.6774e-08	8.5632e-08
2^{28}	4.9357e-08	3.1409e-07	**3.2753e-09**	5.7784e-08	3.3662e-07	3.2027e-07	8.3400e-08
2^{29}	5.8756e-08	1.5696e-07	4.0094e-08	7.5299e-08	**1.5620e-08**	1.1288e-07	2.2737e-08
2^{30}	4.7747e-08	1.3307e-07	**1.7172e-09**	1.8884e-08	5.4771e-08	5.3675e-08	3.3688e-08

The results for them are displayed on Figure 3.

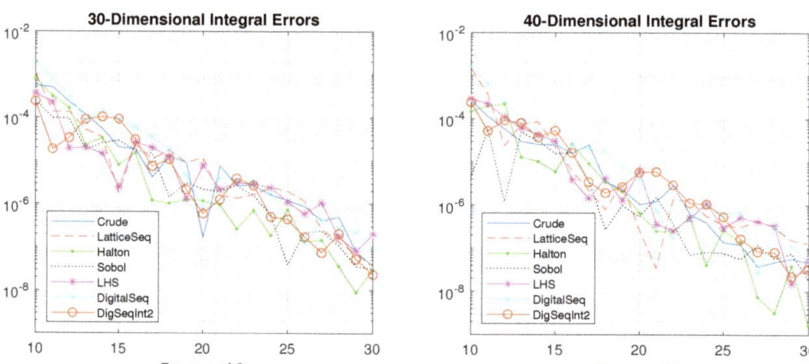

Figure 3. The 30- (**left**) and 40-dimensional (**right**) integral absolute errors.

Going to higher dimensions, the best approach for the 50-dimensional integral (Table 5) is again the scrambled Halton sequences with five smallest errors. For the largest values of C, the Digital Sequence produces the best results. It is also noticeable that the former achieves an order of error 1e-9.

Table 5. The 50-dimensional integral absolute errors.

# of pts	Crude	Lattice Sequence	Halton (Scrambled)	Sobol (Scrambled)	LHS	Digital Sequence	Dig. Seq. (Interlaced)
2^{10}	1.3467e-04	8.6149e-04	2.5185e-05	**1.2217e-05**	2.2807e-05	1.5673e-03	4.0934e-04
2^{11}	9.8530e-05	2.1244e-04	1.2350e-04	**2.8501e-05**	1.0423e-04	6.8519e-04	1.5751e-04
2^{12}	6.4999e-05	**1.4588e-05**	1.4909e-04	8.1798e-05	4.0251e-05	3.1762e-04	1.1229e-04
2^{13}	2.9633e-05	**1.0840e-05**	3.3027e-05	1.5929e-05	2.6352e-05	9.4241e-05	7.3354e-05
2^{14}	2.2212e-05	4.6066e-05	2.2826e-05	1.1102e-05	**7.2073e-06**	2.6834e-05	5.0587e-05
2^{15}	1.2054e-05	1.8725e-05	**1.7282e-06**	3.8114e-06	1.2671e-05	9.1230e-06	5.5251e-05
2^{16}	1.2823e-05	3.0327e-06	1.1558e-05	3.7256e-06	**1.1825e-06**	2.3945e-05	1.7108e-05
2^{17}	1.3401e-05	1.6111e-06	6.4843e-06	2.9136e-06	**9.6110e-07**	1.7040e-05	9.7979e-06
2^{18}	6.8943e-06	6.7873e-06	**3.5997e-07**	1.4022e-06	1.4739e-06	1.7244e-05	9.7943e-07
2^{19}	9.5558e-07	5.2841e-06	1.2372e-07	5.5378e-07	7.9296e-07	1.1623e-05	**4.0592e-08**
2^{20}	2.5459e-06	3.9763e-06	**2.3143e-07**	6.7444e-07	3.3572e-06	4.4196e-06	6.9266e-07
2^{21}	5.4562e-07	2.4796e-06	5.2787e-07	**3.3814e-07**	9.0660e-07	1.7345e-06	1.2081e-06
2^{22}	1.2542e-06	4.9482e-07	2.2211e-07	2.8405e-07	9.3243e-07	**9.0756e-09**	1.6494e-07
2^{23}	1.3561e-06	4.6829e-07	3.4447e-07	**2.1075e-07**	2.2970e-07	1.0215e-06	7.3312e-07
2^{24}	4.1329e-07	4.0596e-07	3.7870e-07	1.9101e-07	**1.0655e-07**	9.1786e-07	1.1180e-07
2^{25}	**2.1102e-08**	4.0582e-08	2.3473e-07	1.5027e-07	2.6465e-07	6.2692e-07	2.8602e-07
2^{26}	1.6030e-07	1.0501e-07	**7.5193e-08**	2.5815e-07	4.3020e-07	3.1049e-07	3.1752e-07
2^{27}	1.5580e-07	**1.7071e-08**	1.3795e-07	1.1045e-07	2.8985e-07	2.8060e-07	6.7037e-08
2^{28}	9.5970e-08	3.6384e-08	5.3992e-08	1.1026e-07	1.2426e-07	**1.6109e-08**	4.2623e-08
2^{29}	1.2839e-07	7.4896e-08	**2.9562e-09**	3.9335e-08	1.9903e-07	1.2624e-08	1.4648e-07
2^{30}	5.5678e-08	6.7599e-08	1.8549e-08	3.0563e-08	7.2682e-08	**1.4640e-08**	8.7382e-08

For the last integral tested, the 60-dimensional one (Table 6), the most accurate approaches are the scrambled Sobol sequence and the Latin hypercube sampling, producing six respective best errors. The LHS is suitable for lower values of C, while the scrambled Sobol sequence and the lattice sequence perform well for larger values of C. Most of the methods achieve 1e-9 order of error, but staring at the order of convergence, it is obvious that this phenomenon is pure luck in the crude Monte Carlo approach.

Table 6. The 60-dimensional integral absolute errors.

# of pts	Crude	Lattice Sequence	Halton (Scrambled)	Sobol (Scrambled)	LHS	Digital Sequence	Dig. Seq. (Interlaced)
2^{10}	1.5710e-04	8.9419e-04	1.8618e-04	**6.5101e-06**	1.8320e-05	1.4589e-03	3.1380e-04
2^{11}	9.2361e-05	4.4859e-04	2.8858e-05	3.8786e-05	**2.8711e-05**	6.6735e-04	1.2787e-04
2^{12}	5.8379e-05	1.5565e-04	6.6255e-05	1.8726e-05	**1.0374e-05**	2.9109e-04	6.8179e-05
2^{13}	3.3845e-05	8.1592e-05	2.4342e-05	**7.1920e-07**	1.3416e-05	9.8755e-05	5.6511e-05
2^{14}	5.2370e-06	2.0600e-05	1.4788e-05	7.0306e-06	**3.9418e-06**	3.6814e-05	3.0916e-05
2^{15}	**2.7906e-07**	7.7793e-06	9.4128e-06	1.3473e-06	1.1746e-05	1.7796e-05	4.0068e-05
2^{16}	6.2211e-06	6.0242e-07	6.3586e-07	5.5014e-06	**1.9997e-07**	2.6316e-05	6.6292e-06
2^{17}	6.4514e-06	3.7087e-06	5.8152e-06	7.0639e-06	**1.7552e-06**	1.6112e-05	3.7249e-06
2^{18}	4.6898e-06	4.5985e-06	2.3757e-06	2.6404e-06	**6.7808e-07**	1.1124e-05	1.8802e-06
2^{19}	1.6862e-06	1.7638e-06	4.1548e-06	1.3125e-06	3.1274e-06	7.7935e-06	**8.1426e-07**
2^{20}	1.2556e-06	1.7011e-06	2.6991e-06	**3.4837e-07**	1.9031e-06	2.1677e-06	3.8992e-07
2^{21}	1.1742e-07	2.4503e-06	7.1783e-07	**5.2443e-08**	8.0455e-07	9.4538e-07	3.3688e-07
2^{22}	2.8181e-07	1.7158e-06	5.3859e-07	**7.4264e-08**	1.8953e-07	1.0210e-07	1.7921e-07
2^{23}	2.6950e-07	**8.0970e-08**	1.6078e-07	2.3135e-07	5.4508e-07	4.9568e-07	9.5768e-07
2^{24}	1.7559e-07	**1.6269e-07**	2.6148e-07	3.1655e-07	2.4941e-07	3.2188e-07	3.4249e-07
2^{25}	**7.1632e-09**	1.5228e-07	2.8353e-07	8.7367e-08	2.1903e-07	5.2079e-07	1.4805e-07
2^{26}	**9.2080e-09**	3.7241e-07	6.8674e-08	6.0311e-08	2.5069e-07	2.9650e-07	3.2618e-07
2^{27}	1.1020e-07	1.7140e-07	**3.9169e-08**	9.4363e-08	2.0381e-07	2.2828e-07	9.1299e-08
2^{28}	1.0817e-07	**5.9808e-09**	1.3801e-08	7.1774e-09	5.3067e-08	5.3760e-08	1.1753e-07
2^{29}	5.3383e-08	3.8234e-08	5.0781e-09	**1.1354e-09**	8.3442e-08	2.6882e-08	5.3939e-08
2^{30}	7.4783e-08	3.5218e-08	1.7194e-08	2.6418e-08	1.6789e-08	1.3200e-08	**1.2365e-08**

The result for the 50- and 60-dimensional integrals are plotted on Figure 4.

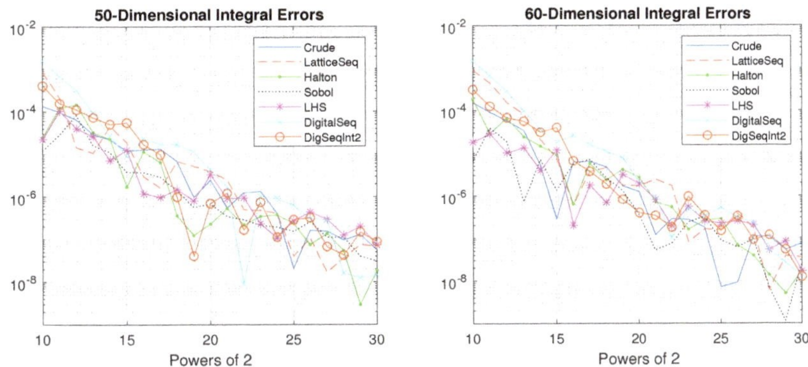

Figure 4. The 50- (**left**) and 60-dimensional (**right**) integral absolute errors.

A number of conclusions could be drawn. Firstly, the achieved absolute errors are very small, even for the large-scale problems. Secondly, the lattice and digital sequences perform well for a lower number of dimensions, while the scrambled Halton and Sobol sequences are suitable for a larger number of dimensions. It is difficult to say in general, though, which method performs superior to the others.

There is a reason for this outcome. The integrand functions are smooth multivariate polynomials. Some of the adaptive methods, for example, Latin hypercube sampling, have advantages over irregular and non-smooth functions, which is not the case here. Therefore, the scrambled Halton sequence and the lattice sequence with a good generation vector are recommended for accurate evaluation of the studied integrals.

It is worth mentioning a couple of notes about the implementation of the stochastic algorithms. First of all, the two digital sequence (interlaced or not) are implemented in

C++, mainly to gain performance, while the other methods and the rest of the operations are implemented in MATLAB®. Secondly, it is difficult to maintain in the RAM 2^{30} multidimensional points which coordinates are stored in the 8-byte 'double' type. Even for the 10-dimensional points, the required storage amounts to 80 GiB (gibibytes). However, after all, it is not needed. We have manually implemented a simple variant of a MapReduce model, where we evaluate the integrals over chunks of 2^{10} points, save the results, and eventually average again all the approximations. Some of the stochastic methods are suitable for parallel implementation, but the elements of other quasi-sequences depend on the previous elements in the sequence, which makes an effective parallelization impossible.

4. A Real Case Study

In this section, we apply the described algorithm for assessment of the consolation prize expectation to real data from gambling clubs in Bulgaria.

Let us also recall that D-dimensional integral $f(D)$ denotes the consolation prize (CP) expectation in a game with $N = D + 1$ players. In a game with one player, (s)he gets the jackpot and $CP = 0$. Now, we plot the results for $D = 1, \ldots, 63$ on Figure 5, showing the mathematical expectation and the standard deviation of the CP.

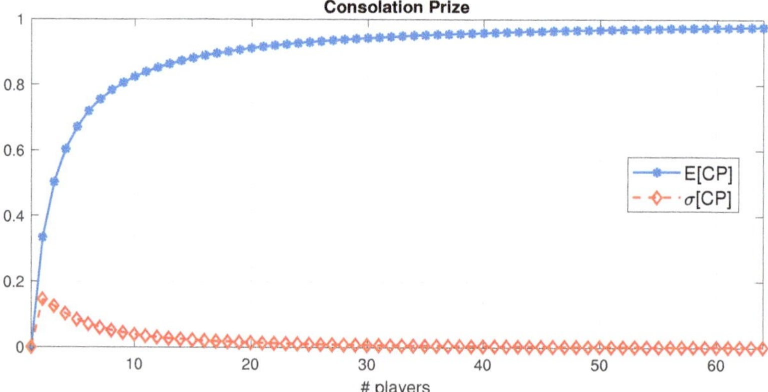

Figure 5. Consolation prize statistics.

The value of $f(D)$ represents the share of the jackpot that the casino expects to pay as a consolation prize if $D + 1$ players play all the time. Of course, this is not the case. In particular, in the small gambling clubs, most of the time, low numbers of players are found. Furthermore, there is a day-and-night cyclicity in the attendance. The distribution could be even bimodal or multimodal. It is given for two gambling clubs in mid-sized city in Bulgaria for 2017 on Figure 6. In each club, there are 32 slot machines, but it appeared that never more than 25 attendants in the first club and 16 attendants in the second one were playing simultaneously.

The x-axis denotes the number of attendants playing, while the y-axis shows the relative portion of time. Now, we calculate the *real consolation prize* $f'(D)$, which is defined as the CP expectation in the case of at least 1, and at most $D + 1$ attendants played considering a predefined distribution. To compute the confidence intervals (CIs), we need to compute the standard deviation, using the standard formulae (9), assuming independence between the different numbers of attendants, playing simultaneously.

$$\mathbb{E}[f'(D)] = \sum_{i=1}^{D} w_i \mathbb{E}[f(i)] \text{ and } \sigma[f'(D)] = \sqrt{w_i^2 \sum_{i=1}^{D} \sigma^2[f(i)]} \text{ for } D = 1, \ldots, 24, \quad (9)$$

where $w_i, i = 1, \ldots, D$ are the relative weights and $\sum_{i=1}^{D} w_i = 1$ must hold for every D.

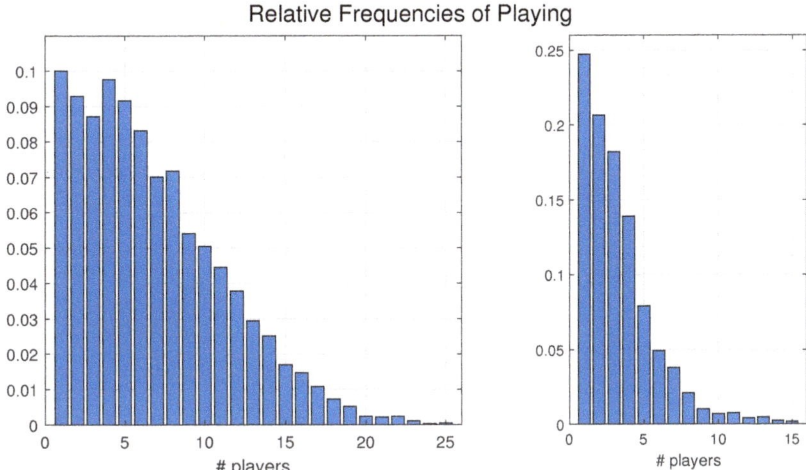

Figure 6. Distribution of simultaneous play.

Finally, assuming the normality of the real CP $f'(D)$ for $D = 1, \ldots, 24$, its expectation and CIs are plotted for both distributions on Figures 7 and 8, where n denotes the number of jackpot hits.

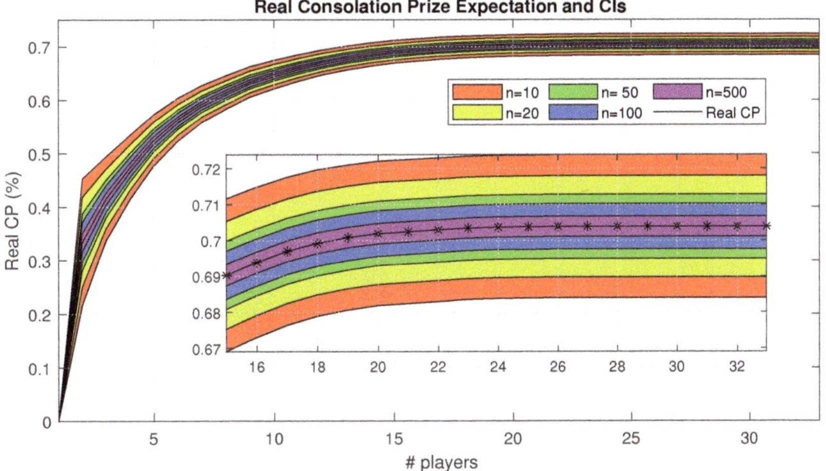

Figure 7. Real consolation prize expectation and CIs (first gaming club/distribution).

The real CP of the second gambling club has higher standard deviation and thus broader CIs because low numbers of attendants play for relatively more time; see Figure 6. The lower the number of players, the higher the deviation; see Figure 5. On the other hand, the usually low number of players has a lower expectation of the real CP.

The overall conclusion is that with 99% confidence ($z^* \approx 2.57$), the realized real consolation prize would not be farther than 1% from its expectation, in absolute units. This is true if the jackpot is hit on a daily basis, for less than two years ($n = 500$ days).

We conclude this section with a brief discussion about the bigger casinos. In the case of more machines and a time distribution of simultaneous play with low or even negative skew, the expectation of the real CP would be higher and closer to one. Of course, in this case, the jackpot would be hit more frequently, but also the absolute sizes of the jackpot and CP would be much greater compared to their counterparts of the small gambling clubs. So, the accurate computation of the CP expectation is also of a paramount importance for the big casinos.

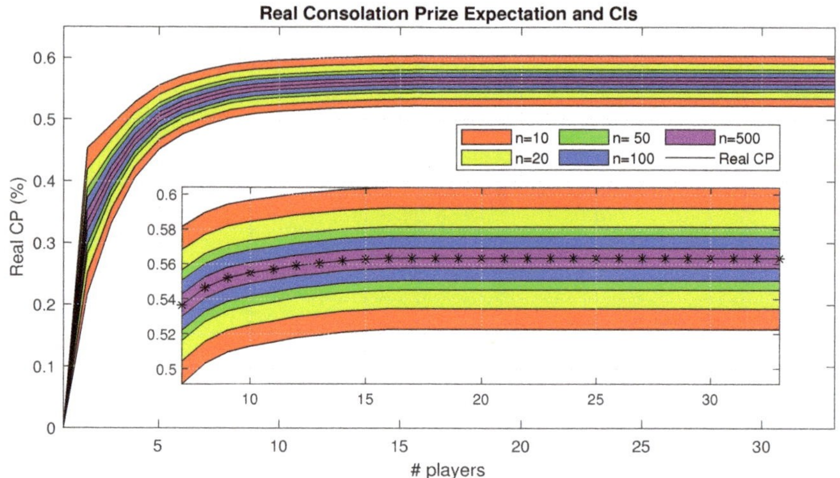

Figure 8. Real consolation prize expectation and CIs (second gaming club/distribution).

Here arises the question for the calculation of integrals with hundreds of dimensions. The approaches, described in the paper, are robust and capable of dealing with large-scale problems, but when the number of dimensions gets huge, all methods become slow. A reasonable question is whether the CP values $f(D)$ for large D could be extrapolated from CP values for lower D, which are already computed.

Our investigation shows that $f(D)$, see Figure 5, could be approximated by the functional form of the Michaelis–Menten saturation curve (10):

$$g(D; \mathbf{p}) = \frac{aD}{b+D} + c, \tag{10}$$

where the parameters are $\mathbf{p} = \{a, b, c\}$.

We fit the model (10) to only the first ten values for $f(D)$, $D = 0, \ldots, 9$, recalling $f(0) = 0$. The fitted values of $\mathbf{p}$ are called a nonlinear least-squares estimator and it is denoted with $\check{\mathbf{p}}$. Let us also define the least-squared error functional as $\Phi(\mathbf{p}) = \sum_{D=0}^{9} \left(f(D) - g(D; \mathbf{p}) \right)^2$.

The fit is indeed good since the norm of the step $\delta\mathbf{p}_k = 8.24163e - 5$, the first-order optimality measure is $\|\nabla\Phi(\check{\mathbf{p}})\|_\infty = 2.35e - 9$ and the error functional $\Phi(\check{\mathbf{p}}) = 4.24941e - 8$ are very small. What is more, the variance of the residuals $\tilde{\sigma}^2 = 2.0614e - 5$ and the root mean squared error $\hat{\sigma} = 7.7914e - 5$ are very small and the coefficient of determination is practically $R^2 = 1.0000$.

All the parameters $\mathbf{p}$ are statistically significant, and their fitted values are $\check{\mathbf{p}} = \{a, b, c\} = \{2.006, 1.014, -0.9962\}$. Finally, we evaluate $g(\check{\mathbf{p}}; D)$ for $D = 0, \ldots, 63$ and plot the absolute error $\epsilon(D) = f(D) - g(D; \check{\mathbf{p}})$ on Figure 9.

The errors are of magnitude 1e-4, but the fit was performed only on the first ten values. If all known values are fitted, the errors will be negligible. This shows that one could use (10) to extrapolate the real consolation prize for higher values of D at low computational cost with acceptable error.

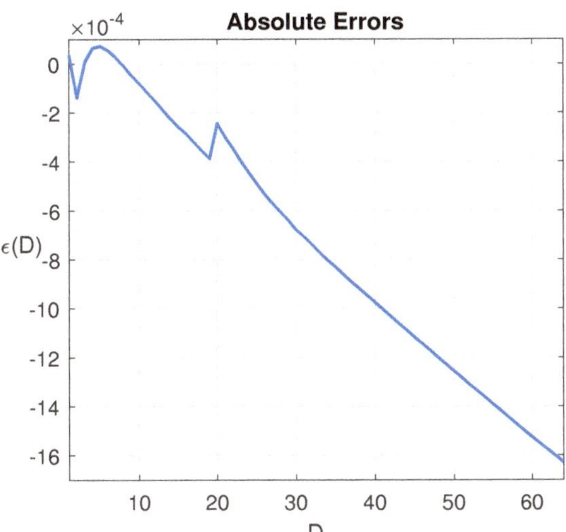

Figure 9. Absolute error between the actual and extrapolated CP values.

5. Conclusions

In this novel experimental study, for the first time, it is solved the problem of determining the expected value of the consolation prize as a fraction of the jackpot. This is extremely vital for each casino and gambling club, regardless of their size, due to the tight budget planning. This problem is formulated as multidimensional integral evaluations. Some of the most advanced quasi-Monte Carlo methods are used, in particular Sobol and Halton sequences with scrambling, lattice and digital sequences with interlacing, and Latin hypercube sampling. All of them are demonstrated to have superior performance compared to the basic Monte Carlo approaches.

The other novel element in the paper is the formulation of the expectation of the real consolation prize, taking into account the temporal distribution of the different number of playing attendants. Eventually, it is suggested an approach to cope with very high dimensions through extrapolation of the already calculated results.

The proposed algorithm is able to calculate the consolation prize not only for linked in-house jackpots, but also for wide area jackpots (which run across machines from multiple casinos). Another possible way to further develop this investigation is to optimize the stochastic approaches with respect to execution time, accuracy and largeness of number of dimensions.

The results, obtained in this investigation, could be used in many areas of life. They could play a significant role in the estimation of Sobol sensitivity indices for large-scale pollution models. Furthermore, such findings are heavily used in quantitative finance to evaluate and calibrate multidimensional financial derivatives. Finally, the results would help other scientists to perform demanding computations in diverse fields of knowledge. **Disclaimer**: This paper must not be understood as advice to play slot games or not to do so. Its aim is to propose an algorithm for practical and applied scientific purposes.

Author Contributions: All authors contributed equally. Conceptualization, S.G.; Methodology, V.T.; Software, S.G.; Validation, V.T.; Formal analysis, S.G.; Investigation, S.G.; Resources, V.T.; Writing—review & editing, V.T.; Supervision, V.T.; Funding acquisition, V.T. All authors have read and agreed to the published version of the manuscript.

Funding: Venelin Todorov is supported by the Bulgarian National Science Fund under the Bilateral Project KP-06-Russia/17 "New Highly Efficient Stochastic Simulation Methods and Applications" and by the Bulgarian National Science Fund under Project KP-06-N52/5 "Efficient methods for modeling, optimization and decision making". Slavi Georgiev is supported by the Bulgarian National Science Fund under Project KP-06-M32/2—17.12.2019 "Advanced Stochastic and Deterministic Approaches for Large-Scale Problems of Computational Mathematics" and by the National Program "Young Scientists and Postdoctoral Researchers—2"—Bulgarian Academy of Sciences and by the Scientific Research Fund of University of Ruse under FNSE-03.

Data Availability Statement: Restrictions apply to the availability of these data.

Conflicts of Interest: The authors declare no conflict of interest. The funders had no role in the design of the study; in the collection, analyses, or interpretation of data; in the writing of the manuscript; or in the decision to publish the results.

Abbreviations

The following abbreviations are used in this manuscript:

RTP	Return-To-Player
CP	Consolation prize
LHS	Latin hypercube sampling
SS	Stratified sampling
(Q)MC	(Quasi-) Monte Carlo
(F)CBC	(Fast) component-by-component
CI	Confidence interval(s)

References

1. Fitch, R.A.; Mueller, J.M.; Ruiz, R.; Rousse, W. Recreation matters: Estimating millennials' preferences for native American cultural tourism. *Sustainability* **2022**, *14*, 11513. [CrossRef]
2. Cooper, M. Sit and spin; How slot machines give gamblers the business. *The Atlantic* **2005**. Available online: https://www.theatlantic.com/magazine/archive/2005/12/sit-and-spin/304392/ (accessed on 28 December 2022).
3. Kamanas, P.-A.; Sifaleras, A.; Samaras, N. Slot machine RTP optimization using variable neighborhood search. *Math. Probl. Eng.* **2021**, *2021*, 8784065. [CrossRef]
4. Turner, N.; Horbay R. How do slot machines and other electronic gamblingmachines actually work? *J. Gambl. Issues* **2004**, *11*, 11.
5. Oses, N. Markov chain applications in the slot machine industry. *Insight* **2008**, *21*, 9–21. [CrossRef]
6. Bărboianu, C. *The Mathematics of Slots: Configurations, Combinations, Probabilities*; INFAROM Publishing: Craiova, Romania, 2013.
7. Epstein, R.A. *The Theory of Gambling and Statistical Logic*, 2nd ed.; Academic Press: Oxford, UK, 2012.
8. Balabanov, T. Estimation of volatility based on the estimation of segmentation. *Probl. Eng. Cybern. Robot.* **2021**, *77*, 3–10.
9. Balabanov, T. Volatility index estimation by reverse engineering. *Proc. Int. Sci. Conf. UniTech* **2021**, *1*, 229–234.
10. Keremedchiev, D.; Tomov, P.; Barova, M. Slot machine base game evolutionary RTP optimization. In Proceedings of the International Conference on Numerical Analysis and Its Applications, Lozenetz, Bulgaria, 15–22 June 2016; Dimov, I., Faragó, I., Vulkov, L., Eds.; Springer: Cham, Switzerland, 2017; Volume 10187, pp. 406—413.
11. Balabanov, T.; Zankinski, I.; Shumanov, B. Slot machine RTP optimization and symbols wins equalization with discrete differential evolution. In *Large-Scale Scientific Computing (LSSC 2015)*; Lirkov, I., Margenov, S.D., Waśniewski, J., Eds.; Springer: Berlin, Germany, 2015; Volume 9374, pp. 210–217.
12. Balabanov, T.; Zankinski, I.; Shumanov, B. Slot machines RTP optimization with genetic algorithms. In *Numerical Methods and Applications (NMA 2014)*; Dimov, I., Fidanova, S., Lirkov, I., Eds.; Springer: Berlin, Germany, 2015; Volume 8962, pp. 55–61.
13. Metropolis, N.; Ulam, S. The Monte Carlo Method. *J. Amer. Stat. Assoc.* **1949**, *44*, 335–341. [CrossRef]
14. Dimov, I.T. *Monte Carlo Methods For Applied Scientists*; World Scientific: Singapore, 2007.
15. Sobol, I.M. *Monte Carlo Numerical Methods*; Nauka: Moscow, Russia, 1973. (In Russian)
16. Kalos, M.A.; Whitlock, P.A. *Monte Carlo Methods, Volume 1: Basics*; Wiley: New York, NY, USA, 1986.
17. Paskov, S.H. *Computing High Dimensional Integrals with Applications to Finance*; Technical Report CUCS-023-94; Columbia University: New York, NY, USA, 1994.
18. Barr, G.D.I.; Durbach, I.N. A Monte Carlo analysis of hypothetical multi-line slot machine play. *Int. Gambl. Stud.* **2008**, *8*, 265–280. [CrossRef]
19. Tomov, P.; Zankinski, I.; Balabanov, T. Slot machine reels reconstruction with Monte-Carlo search. *Proc. Int. Sci. Conf. UniTech* **2017**, *2*, 384–387.
20. McKay, M.D.; Beckman, R.J.; Conover, W.J. A comparison of three methods for selecting values of input variables in the analysis of output from a computer code. *Technometrics* **1979**, *21*, 239–245.

21. Eglajs, V.; Audze, P. New approach to the design of multifactor experiments. *Probl. Dyn. Strengths* **1977**, *35*, 104–107. (In Russian)
22. Minasny, B.; McBratney, B. A conditioned Latin hypercube method for sampling in the presence of ancillary information. *J. Comput. Geosci. Arch.* **2006**, *32*, 1378–1388. [CrossRef]
23. Minasny, B.; McBratney, B. Conditioned Latin Hypercube Sampling for Calibrating Soil Sensor Data to Soil Properties. In *Proximal Soil Sensing*; Progress in Soil Science; Springer: Dordrecht, The Netherlands, 2010; pp. 111–119.
24. Karaivanova, A.; Dimov, I.; Ivanovska, S. A quasi-monte carlo method for integration with improved convergence. In *Large-Scale Scientific Computing (LSSC 2001)*; Lirkov, I., Margenov, S.D., Waśniewski, J., Eds.; Springer: Berlin, Germany, 2001; Volume 2179, pp. 158–165.
25. Sobol, I.M. Distribution of points in a cube and approximate evaluation of integrals. *USSR Comput. Math. Math. Phys.* **1967**, *7*, 86–112. [CrossRef]
26. Niederreiter, H. Existence of good lattice points in the sense of Hlawka. *Monat. Math.* **1978**, *86*, 203–219. [CrossRef]
27. Niederreiter, H. *Random Number Generation and Quasi-Monte Carlo Methods*; CBMS-NSF Regional Conference Series in Applied Mathematics 63; SIAM: Philadelphia, PA, USA, 1992.
28. van der Corput, J. Verteilungsfunktionen I & II. *Nederl. Akad. Wetensch. Proc.* **1935**, *38*, 813–820 & 1058–1066.
29. Halton, J. On the efficiency of certain quasi-random sequences of points in evaluating multi-dimensional integrals. *Numer. Math.* **1960**, *2*, 84–90. [CrossRef]
30. Halton, J.; Smith, G.B. Algorithm 247: Radical-inverse quasi-random point sequence. *Commun. ACM* **1964**, *7*, 701–702. [CrossRef]
31. Antonov, I.; Saleev, V. An economic method of computing LP_τ-sequences. *USSR Comput. Math. Math. Phys.* **1979**, *19*, 252–256. [CrossRef]
32. Bratley, P.; Fox, B. Algorithm 659: Implementing Sobol's Quasirandom Sequence Generator. *ACM Trans. Math. Softw.* **1988**, *14*, 88–100. [CrossRef]
33. Fox, B. Algorithm 647: Implementation and relative effciency of quasirandom sequence generators. *ACM Trans. Math. Softw.* **1986**, *12*, 362–376. [CrossRef]
34. Joe, S.; Kuo, F. Remark on Algorithm 659: Implementing Sobol's quasirandom sequence generator. *ACM Trans. Math. Softw.* **2003**, *29*, 49–57. [CrossRef]
35. Kocis, L.; Whiten, W.J. Computational investigations of low-discrepancy sequences. *ACM Trans. Math. Softw.* **1997**, *23*, 266–294. [CrossRef]
36. Matousek, J. On the L2-discrepancy for anchored boxes. *J. Complex.* **1998**, *14*, 527–556. [CrossRef]
37. Sloan, I.H.; Kachoyan, P.J. Lattice methods for multiple integration: Theory, error analysis and examples. *SIAM J. Numer. Anal.* **1987**, *24*, 116–128. [CrossRef]
38. Niederreiter, H. *Monte Carlo and Quasi-Monte Carlo Methods*; Springer: Berlin/Heidelberg, Germany, 2002.
39. Hua, L.K.; Wang, Y. *Applications of Number Theory to Numerical Analysis*; Springer: Beijing, China, 1981.
40. Wang, Y.; Hickernell, F. J. An historical overview of lattice point sets. In *Monte Carlo and Quasi-Monte Carlo Methods*; Fang, K.-T., Hickernell, F.J., Niederreiter, H., Eds.; Springer: Berlin/Heidelberg, Germany, 2002; pp. 158–167.
41. Sloan, I.H.; Joe, S. *Lattice Methods for Multiple Integration*; Oxford University Press: Oxford, UK, 1994.
42. Kuo, F.Y.; Nuyens, D. Application of quasi-Monte Carlo methods to elliptic PDEs with random diffusion coefficients—A survey of analysis and implementation. *Found. Comput. Math.* **2016**, *16*, 1631–1696. [CrossRef]
43. Nuyens, D.; Cools, R. Fast algorithms for component-by-component construction of rank-1 lattice rules in shift-invariant reproducing kernel Hilbert spaces. *Math. Comp.* **2006**, *75*, 903–920. [CrossRef]
44. Nuyens, D.; Cools, R. Fast component-by-component construction of rank-1 lattice rules with a non-prime number of points. *J. Complex.* **2006**, *22*, 4–28. [CrossRef]
45. Sloan, I.H.; Reztsov, A.V. Component-by-component construction of good lattice rules. *Math. Comp.* **2002**, *71*, 263–273. [CrossRef]
46. Niederreiter, H. Finite fields, pseudorandom numbers, and quasirandom points. In *Finite Fields, Coding Theory, and Advances in Communications and Computing*; Mullen, G.L., Shiue, P.J.-S., Eds.; Marcel Dekker: New York, NY, USA, 1993; pp. 375–394.
47. Lemieux, C.; L' Ecuyer, P. Randomized polynomial lattice rules for multivariate integration and simulation. *SIAM J. Sci. Comput.* **2003**, *24*, 1768–1789. [CrossRef]
48. Lidl, R.; Niederreiter, H. *Introduction to Finite Fields and Their Applications*, 1st ed.; Cambridge University Press: Cambridge, UK, 1994.
49. Dick, J.; Pillichshammer, F. *Digital Nets and Sequences: Discrepancy Theory and Quasi–Monte Carlo Integration*; Cambridge University Press: Cambridge, UK, 2010.
50. Goda, T. Good interlaced polynomial lattice rules for numerical integration in weighted Walsh spaces. *J. Comput. Appl. Math.* **2015**, *285*, 279–294. [CrossRef]
51. Baldeaux, J.; Dick, J.; Greslehner, J.; Pillichshammer, F. Construction algorithms for higher order polynomial lattice rules. *J. Complex.* **2011**, *27*, 281–299. [CrossRef]
52. Baldeaux, J.; Dick, J.; Leobacher, G.; Nuyens, D.; Pillichshammer, F. Efficient calculation of the worst-case error and (fast) component-by-component construction of higher order polynomial lattice rules. *Numer. Algor.* **2012**, *59*, 403–431. [CrossRef]
53. Dick, J.; Pillichshammer, F. Strong tractability of multivariate integration of arbitrary high order using digitally shifted polynomial lattice rules. *J. Complex.* **2007**, *23*, 436–453. [CrossRef]

54. Dick, J.; Kuo, F.Y.; Sloan, I.H. High dimensional integration: The quasi-Monte Carlo way. *Acta Numer.* **2013**, *22*, 133288. [CrossRef]
55. Joe, S.; Kuo, F.Y. Constructing Sobol' sequences with better two-dimensional projections. *SIAM J. Sci. Comput.* **2008**, *30*, 2635–2654. [CrossRef]

Article

Surface Approximation by Means of Gaussian Process Latent Variable Models and Line Element Geometry

Ivan De Boi [1,*], Carl Henrik Ek [2] and Rudi Penne [1]

[1] Research Group InViLab, Department Electromechanics, Faculty of Applied Engineering,
     University of Antwerp, B 2020 Antwerp, Belgium
[2] Department of Computer Science and Technology University of Cambridge, Cambridge CB3 0FD, UK
*   Correspondence: ivan.deboi@uantwerpen.be

Abstract: The close relation between spatial kinematics and line geometry has been proven to be fruitful in surface detection and reconstruction. However, methods based on this approach are limited to simple geometric shapes that can be formulated as a linear subspace of line or line element space. The core of this approach is a principal component formulation to find a best-fit approximant to a possibly noisy or impartial surface given as an unordered set of points or point cloud. We expand on this by introducing the Gaussian process latent variable model, a probabilistic non-linear non-parametric dimensionality reduction approach following the Bayesian paradigm. This allows us to find structure in a lower dimensional latent space for the surfaces of interest. We show how this can be applied in surface approximation and unsupervised segmentation to the surfaces mentioned above and demonstrate its benefits on surfaces that deviate from these. Experiments are conducted on synthetic and real-world objects.

Keywords: surface approximation; surface segmentation; surface denoising; gaussian process latent variable model; line geometry; line elements

MSC: 60G15

Citation: De Boi, I.; Ek, C.H.; Penne, R. Surface Approximation by Means of Gaussian Process Latent Variable Models and Line Element Geometry. *Mathematics* 2023, 11, 380. https://doi.org/10.3390/math11020380

Academic Editors: Snezhana Gocheva-Ilieva, Atanas Ivanov and Hristina Kulina

Received: 14 December 2022
Revised: 4 January 2023
Accepted: 6 January 2023
Published: 11 January 2023

1. Introduction

Extracting structural information as shapes or surfaces from an unordered set of 3D coordinates (point cloud) has been an important topic in computer vision [1]. It is a crucial part of many applications such as autonomous driving [2], scene understanding [3], reverse engineering of geometric models [4], quality control [5], simultaneous localization and mapping (SLAM) [6] and matching point clouds to CAD models [7]. Over the last decade, hardware developments have made the acquisition of those point clouds more affordable. As the availability, ease of use and hence the popularity of various 3D sensors increases so does the need for methods to interpret the data they generate.

However, in this work, we mainly focus on detecting simple geometrical surfaces such as planes, spheres, cylinders, cones, spiral and helical surfaces, surfaces of revolution, etc. as described in [8]. Examples of these surfaces can be found in Figure 1. In [8], the close relation between these shapes, spatial kinematics and line geometry are formulated. A point cloud, as a set of noisy points on a surface, is transformed into a set of normals (also referred to as normal lines or normal vectors) that show exploitable properties for that surface. For instance, the normals of a sphere intersect in a single point, the normals of a surface of revolution intersect in an axis of rotation, and the normals of a helical surface can be seen as path normals of a helical motion. These insights led to applications in surface reconstruction and robotics [8,9]. Later, their method was refined in [10,11] to address pipe surfaces, profile surfaces and developable surfaces in general. In [12], the authors introduced principal component analysis (PCA) to approximate the set of normals. This laid the groundwork for a more general approach in [13] using so-called *line elements*.

These are constructed for every point of the point cloud. They are formed by the (Plücker) coordinates of the normal line and the surface point which lies on that line. The key insight of their work is that the line elements of simple geometric surfaces lie on a linear subspace in $\mathbb{R}^7$, which can be found by solving an ordinary eigenvalue problem. We elaborate more on this approach in Section 2.2.

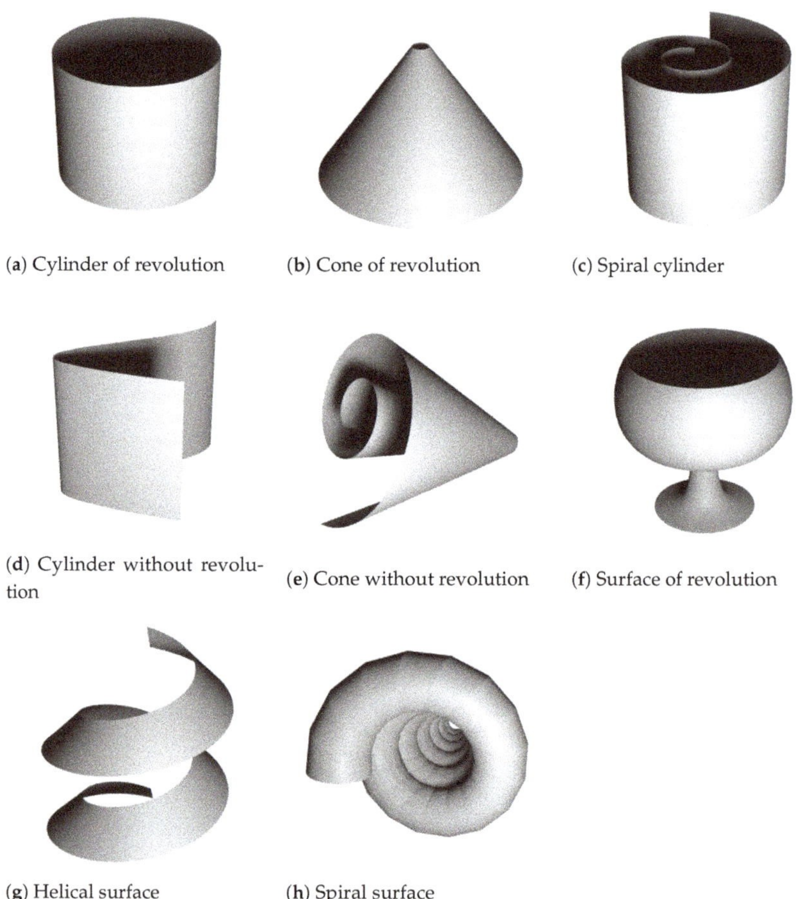

(**a**) Cylinder of revolution   (**b**) Cone of revolution   (**c**) Spiral cylinder

(**d**) Cylinder without revolution   (**e**) Cone without revolution   (**f**) Surface of revolution

(**g**) Helical surface   (**h**) Spiral surface

Figure 1. Examples of equiform kinematic surfaces.

Although a mathematically very elegant way to describe 3D surfaces, this approach does have several drawbacks. First, the surface classification is strict. This means that only very primitive shapes can be treated. Real-world objects do not always fall neatly into one of these categories. For example, imperfect shapes like a slight bend plane, a sphere with a dent or shapes found in nature or human anatomy. Blindly following this method, results in a misrepresentation of the data. Second, because PCA minimises an L2-norm, it is very sensitive to outliers. This can be mitigated by iterative RANSAC or by downweighting the outliers. However, this comes at the cost of increased computation time. Third, real-world point clouds show various other imperfections like non-uniform sampling, noise, missing regions, etc. This highly affects the quality of the representation. Fourth, the authors of [10–13] propose to look for *small* eigenvalues. The obvious question arises: when is an eigenvalue small? Even though some guidelines are provided, these threshold values remain domain specific and are challenging to set.

Most of these drawbacks can be attributed to the eigenvalue problem (or its PCA formulation) used to find an appropriate linear subspace in $\mathbb{R}^7$. In essence, this is a linear dimensionality reduction from the seven-dimensional space of line elements to a lower-dimensional latent space. In this work, we build on that method by introducing the Gaussian process latent variable model (GPLVM) [14] as an alternative. This allows for a non-linear relationship between a latent space and a higher dimensional data space, where observations are made. We implement a multi-output Gaussian process (seven outputs in this case) and try to find a mapping from a lower dimensional latent space to the line elements. Several variants on this theme exist, which we explain in more depth in Section 2.5. No longer confined by the linearity of PCA, our models can handle a wider range of shapes. Moreover, Gaussian processes handle noise very well, even in low data regimes [15]. The GPLVM places a Gaussian process prior to the mapping from the latent to the observed space. By exploiting strong priors, we can significantly reduce the amount of data needed for equally accurate predictions.

In our approach, we can handle shapes (or surfaces) that fall in the categories described in [8–13] but also shapes that significantly deviate from these. For instance, a surface of revolution whose central axis is not a straight line or an imperfect plane with one of the corners slightly bent. In fact, we drop the strict classification and allow for shapes that can be seen as somewhere in between the categories. This makes our methods more appropriate for handling surfaces that can be found in nature or when modelling the human body. Moreover, our formulation can handle multiple types of subsurfaces at once. This means we can perform segmentation in the latent space.

For completeness, we mention that in recent years various deep learning techniques have been successfully introduced to discover objects in point clouds. A thorough overview can be found in [16] and more recently in [1,17]. These techniques vary from ordinary multilayer perception models (MLP) to convolutional- and graph-based models. Numerous datasets have been made public to encourage the field further to develop new models (e.g., ScanObjectNN [18], ShapeNet [19], ScanNet [20], KITTI Vision Benchmark Suite [21], ModelNet40 [22,23], . . .). Generally, these data-driven models are trained on more complex shapes: vehicles, urban objects, and furniture, . . . These models are specifically designed for detecting obstacles, such as vehicles in autonomous driving, but not so for accurate object reconstruction from detailed 3D scanning. In this work, we focus on the latter. Moreover, whenever a new shape has to be learned, the underlying model has to be trained again.

To summarise, for every point on a given point cloud, we can formulate a so-called line element. Dimensionality reduction on the set of line elements reveals the characteristics of the surface captured by that point cloud. Existing methods rely on PCA, which is a linear mapping. In contrast, our model is built on the Gaussian process latent variable model, which allows for non-linear mapping. This results in a more nuanced way of representing the surface. The main contributions of this work are the following:

- We expand existing methods based on kinematic surfaces and line element geometry by introducing GPLVM to describe surfaces in a non-linear way.
- We apply our method to surface approximation.
- We test our method to perform unsupervised surface segmentation.
- We demonstrate our method to perform surface denoising.

All of our 3D models, sets of line elements, trained GPLVM, notebooks with code and many more experiments and plots can be found on our GitHub repository (https://github.com/IvanDeBoi/Surface-Approximation-GPLVM-Line-Geometry, accessed on 10 January 2023).

The rest of this paper is structured as follows. In the next section, we give some theoretical background on line element geometry, kinematic surfaces, approximating the data, Gaussian processes and Gaussian process latent variable models in particular. The third section describes the results of our method applied to surface approximation, surface segmentation and surface denoising. Section four presents a discussion of our findings.

2. Materials and Methods

2.1. Line Element Geometry

In projective 3-space $\mathbb{P}^3$, a straight line $\mathbf{L}$ can be represented by a direction vector $\mathbf{l}$ and an arbitrary point x on that line. The so-called moment vector $\bar{\mathbf{l}}$ for that line with respect to the origin, can be written as

$$\bar{\mathbf{l}} = \mathbf{x} \times \mathbf{l}, \tag{1}$$

where $\mathbf{x}$ are the coordinates of x in $\mathbb{R}^3$. The *Plücker coordinates* for a line are defined as $(\mathbf{l}, \bar{\mathbf{l}}) = (l_1 : l_2 : l_3 : l_4 : l_5 : l_6)$ [24]. These are homogeneous coordinates, meaning they are scale invariant. Notice that the scale factor is determined by the norm of the direction vector. Moreover, they are independent of the choice of x. Since we are not concerned about the orientation, $(\mathbf{l}, \bar{\mathbf{l}})$ and $(-\mathbf{l}, -\bar{\mathbf{l}})$ describe the same line, which also follows from the homogeneity.

For example, a line $\mathbf{L}$ is spanned by two given points x and y, possibly at infinity. By following the notation in [24], we write the homogenous coordinates for x and y as $(x_0, \mathbf{x})$ and $(y_0, \mathbf{y})$ respectively. Then, the homogenous Plücker coordinates for $\mathbf{L}$ are found as

$$\mathbf{L} := (\mathbf{l}, \bar{\mathbf{l}}) = (x_0 \mathbf{y} - y_0 \mathbf{x}, \mathbf{x} \times \mathbf{y}) \in \mathbb{R}^6. \tag{2}$$

Not every combination of six numbers yields a straight line. To do so, the following condition is necessary and sufficient:

$$\mathbf{l} \cdot \bar{\mathbf{l}} = 0. \tag{3}$$

This is called the *Grassmann–Plücker relation*. Plücker coordinates can also be regarded as homogeneous points coordinates in projective 5-space $\mathbb{P}^5$, where straight lines are points lying on a quadric given by the equation

$$l_1 l_4 + l_2 l_5 + l_3 l_6 = 0. \tag{4}$$

This quadric is called the *Klein quadric* and is denoted as M_2^4. The interpretation of points in projective 5-space has proved useful in a variety of line geometry applications [24].

Plücker coordinates of a line in $\mathbb{R}^3$ can be extended to *line elements* by adding a specific point x on that line [13]. To do so, we start by choosing an orientation for the unit direction vector $\mathbf{l}$ of the line. A seventh coordinate λ is needed to locate x on that line, which can be defined as

$$\lambda = \mathbf{x} \cdot \mathbf{l}. \tag{5}$$

Notice that the norm of $\mathbf{l}$ matters, which is why we work with the (normalised) unit direction vector. This yields the seven-tuple $(\mathbf{l}, \bar{\mathbf{l}}, \lambda)$ of coordinates for a line element based on a line and a point, in which $\|\mathbf{l}\| = 1$ and $\mathbf{l} \cdot \bar{\mathbf{l}} = 0$.

Each point on a smooth surface Φ of a 3D volume has an outward unit normal vector $\mathbf{n}$. For every point x on that surface, a line element can be defined as $(\mathbf{n}, \mathbf{x} \times \mathbf{n}, \mathbf{x} \cdot \mathbf{n})$. These line elements constitute an associated surface $\Gamma(\Phi)$ in $\mathbb{R}^7$. An important property of many simple geometrical shapes in $\mathbb{R}^3$ (planes, spheres, cones, ...), is that their $\Gamma(\Phi)$ is contained in a linear subspace of $\mathbb{R}^7$. We will see in Section 2.2 that this aspect can be exploited in surface approximation, surface segmentation and surface denoising.

2.2. Kinematic Surfaces

Rigid body motions can be seen as a superposition of rotations and translations. These can be extended by adding a scaling, making them the family of *equiform motions*, also known as *similarities* [10]. Such a one-parameter motion $M(t)$ is either a rotation, translation, a central similarity, a spiral motion or a combination of any of them. The velocity vector field of $M(t)$ is constant (time-independent) and can be written as

$$\mathbf{v}(\mathbf{x}) = \bar{\mathbf{c}} + \gamma \mathbf{x} + \mathbf{c} \times \mathbf{x}, \tag{6}$$

where $\bar{\mathbf{c}}$, $\gamma\mathbf{x}$ and $\mathbf{c}\times\mathbf{x}$ are the translation, scale and rotation component of the velocity vector $\mathbf{v}$ at a point x. A curve undergoing an equiform motion forms an *equiform kinematic surface*.

As defined in [13], a *linear complex of line elements* is the set of line elements whose coordinates $(\mathbf{l},\bar{\mathbf{l}},\lambda)$ satisfy the linear equation

$$\bar{\mathbf{c}}\cdot\mathbf{l}+\mathbf{c}\cdot\bar{\mathbf{l}}+\gamma\lambda=0, \tag{7}$$

where $(\mathbf{c},\bar{\mathbf{c}},\gamma)$ is de coordinate vector of the complex. The following theorem from [25] shows the relation between linear complexes of lines and equiform kinematics:

Theorem 1. *The surface normal elements of a regular C^1 surface in $\mathbb{R}^3$ are contained in a linear line element complex with coordinates $(\mathbf{c},\bar{\mathbf{c}},\gamma)$ if and only if the surface is part of an equiform kinematic surface. In that case, the uniform equiform motion has the velocity vector field as given in Equation (6).*

Here, we will give an overview of such motions $M(t)$ and their corresponding surfaces Φ. For a thorough explanation of these (and multiple applications), we refer the reader to the works [8,10–13,25,26].

- $\gamma=0$:
  - $\mathbf{c}=0,\bar{\mathbf{c}}=0$: $M(t)$ is the identical motion (no motion at all).
  - $\mathbf{c}=0,\bar{\mathbf{c}}\neq0$: $M(t)$ is a translation along $\bar{\mathbf{c}}$ and Φ is a cylinder (not necessarily of revolution).
  - $\mathbf{c}\neq0,\mathbf{c}\cdot\bar{\mathbf{c}}=0$: $M(t)$ is a rotation about an axis parallel to $\mathbf{c}$ and Φ is a surface of revolution.
  - $\mathbf{c}\neq0,\mathbf{c}\cdot\bar{\mathbf{c}}\neq0$: $M(t)$ is a helical motion about an axis parallel to $\mathbf{c}$ and Φ is a helical surface.
- $\gamma\neq0$:
  - $\mathbf{c}\neq0$: $M(t)$ is a spiral motion and Φ is a spiral surface.
  - $\mathbf{c}=0$: $M(t)$ is a central similarity, and Φ is a conical surface (not necessarily of revolution).

Examples of these surfaces can be found in Figure 1.

This alternative way of describing surfaces as linear complexes of line elements opens up a new way of studying them, as explained below.

2.3. Approximating the Complex

Suppose a scanning process results in a set of points X (a point cloud), i.e., the results of the scanning process. The aim is to determine the type of surface Φ on which these points lie. This knowledge would allow us to reconstruct the surface using its underlying geometrical properties. For instance, if we know our points result from the scan of a surface of revolution, we could determine the central axis etc. So, we are interested in the (linear) complex (of line elements) that best describes the given points. Its coordinates $(\mathbf{c},\bar{\mathbf{c}},\gamma)$ determine the type of surface [13].

First, we calculate the unit normal vectors from the point cloud at every point. This topic has been very well documented in the literature. We refer the reader to [27] for a more in-depth discussion. For each x_i in X with $i=1,2,\ldots,N$ we obtain a unit normal vector $\mathbf{n_i}$. From these normal vectors and corresponding points, we calculate their line elements $(\mathbf{n_i},\mathbf{x_i}\times\mathbf{n_i},\mathbf{x_i}\cdot\mathbf{n_i})$.

Second, according to Equation (7), a complex with coordinates $(\mathbf{c},\bar{\mathbf{c}},\gamma)$ that best fits these line elements minimises

$$F(\mathbf{c},\bar{\mathbf{c}},\gamma)=\sum_{i=1}^{N}(\bar{\mathbf{c}}\cdot\mathbf{l_i}+\mathbf{c}\cdot\bar{\mathbf{l}}_i+\gamma\lambda_i)^2, \tag{8}$$

under the condition $\mathbf{c}^2 + \bar{\mathbf{c}}^2 + \gamma^2 = 1$. We follow the notation used in [12], in which $\mathbf{a}^2 = \mathbf{a} \cdot \mathbf{a}$. For this condition to make sense, we normalise our point cloud such that $\max\|x_i\| \approx 1$. We also centre it around the origin. We can rewrite this as

$$F(\mathbf{c}, \bar{\mathbf{c}}, \gamma) = (\mathbf{c}, \bar{\mathbf{c}}, \gamma) M (\mathbf{c}, \bar{\mathbf{c}}, \gamma)^T, \tag{9}$$

where $M = \sum_{i=1}^{N} (\bar{\mathbf{l}}_\mathbf{i}, \mathbf{l}_\mathbf{i}, \lambda_i)^T (\bar{\mathbf{l}}_\mathbf{i}, \mathbf{l}_\mathbf{i}, \lambda_i)$. This is an ordinary eigenvalue problem. The smallest eigenvalue of M corresponds to an eigenvector $(\hat{\mathbf{c}}, \hat{\bar{\mathbf{c}}}, \hat{\gamma})$ which best approximates Equation (7) for the given $(\mathbf{l}_\mathbf{i}, \bar{\mathbf{l}}_\mathbf{i}, \lambda_i)$.

Some surfaces are invariant under more than one one-parameter transformation [8,10–13,25,26]. In that case, k small eigenvalues appear as solutions to Equation (8). The corresponding eigenvectors can be seen as a basis for a subspace in $\mathbb{R}^7$. We list the possibilities below:

- $k = 4$: Only a plane is invariant to four independent uniform motions.
- $k = 3$: A sphere is invariant to three independent uniform motions (all rotations).
- $k = 2$: The surface is either a cylinder of revolution, a cone of revolution or a spiral cylinder.
- $k = 1$: The surface is either a cylinder without revolution (pure translation), a cone without revolution (central similarity), a surface of revolution, a helical surface or a spiral surface.

Further examination of the coordinate $(\mathbf{c}, \bar{\mathbf{c}}, \gamma)$ determines the exact type of surface, as described in Section 2.2. Multiple examples, applications and variations on this theme can be found in above mentioned references.

Although this is a very elegant and powerful approach, some issues are discussed in the works listed above. First, this method is very sensitive to outliers. A solution proposed by the authors is to apply a RANSAC variant or to downweigh the outliers by iteratively

$$M = \frac{1}{\sum \sigma_i} \sum_{i=1}^{N} \sigma_i (\bar{\mathbf{l}}_\mathbf{i}, \mathbf{l}_\mathbf{i}, \lambda_i)^T (\bar{\mathbf{l}}_\mathbf{i}, \mathbf{l}_\mathbf{i}, \lambda_i). \tag{10}$$

This obviously results in longer computation times. Second, numerical issues can arise calculating the eigenvalues (especially for planes and spheres). Third, some shapes do not fall into the classification of these simple geometric forms. This is certainly the case for organic surfaces that can be found in nature or when modelling the human body. Reconstructing a surface based on a simple geometric shape is obviously only valid if the surface resembles the shape well. Fourth, some shapes are either a combination or a composition of the elementary simple shapes (e.g., pipe constructions). In this case, the question arises of what constitutes as a small eigenvalue and where to draw the line between steadily increasing values. Even though some guidance is given in the literature, these thresholds are often application-specific parameters.

Our approach provides a solution for these issues, by finding a representative lower dimensional latent space for the line elements in a more flexible non-linear way. This is no longer a linear subspace in $\mathbb{R}^7$.

2.4. Gaussian Processes

By definition, a Gaussian process (GP) is a stochastic process (a collection of random variables), with the property that any finite subset of its variables is distributed as a multivariate Gaussian distribution. It is a generalization of the multivariate Gaussian distribution to infinitely many variables. Here, we only give an overview of the main aspects. We refer the reader to the book [15] for a more detailed treatise.

Let a dataset $\mathcal{D} = \{X, \mathbf{y}\}$ consist of n observations, where $X = [\mathbf{x}_1, \mathbf{x}_2, \dots, \mathbf{x}_n]^T$ is an $n \times d$ matrix of n input vectors of dimension d and $\mathbf{y} = [y_1, y_2, \dots, y_n]^T$ is a vector of continuous-valued scalar outputs. These data points are also called training points. In regression, the aim is to find a mapping $f : \mathbb{R}^d \to \mathbb{R}$,

$$y = f(\mathbf{x}) + \epsilon, \quad \epsilon \sim \mathcal{N}(0, \sigma_\epsilon^2), \tag{11}$$

with ϵ being identically distributed observation noise. In this work, this mapping is implemented by a Gaussian process. As stated above, a Gaussian process generalises the multivariate Gaussian distribution to infinitely many variables. Just like the multivariate Gaussian distribution is fully defined by its mean vector and covariance matrix, a Gaussian process is fully defined by its mean as a function $m(\mathbf{x})$ and *covariance function* $k(\mathbf{x}, \mathbf{x}')$. It is generally denoted as $f(\mathbf{x}) \sim \mathcal{GP}(m(\mathbf{x}), k(\mathbf{x}, \mathbf{x}'))$. The covariance function is parametrised by a vector of hyperparameters $\boldsymbol{\theta}$. By definition, a GP yields a distribution over a collection of functions that have a joint normal distribution [15],

$$\begin{bmatrix} \mathbf{f} \\ \mathbf{f}_* \end{bmatrix} \sim \mathcal{N}\left(\begin{bmatrix} \boldsymbol{m}_X \\ \boldsymbol{m}_{X_*} \end{bmatrix}, \begin{bmatrix} \mathbf{K}_{X,X} & \mathbf{K}_{X,X_*} \\ \mathbf{K}_{X_*,X} & \mathbf{K}_{X_*,X_*} \end{bmatrix} \right), \tag{12}$$

where X are the input vectors of the n observed training points and X_* are the n_* input vectors of the unobserved test points. The mean value for $\mathbf{X}$ is given by $\boldsymbol{m}_X$. Likewise, the mean value for X_* is given by $\boldsymbol{m}_{X_*}$. The covariance matrices $\mathbf{K}_{X,X}$, $\mathbf{K}_{X_*,X_*}$, $\mathbf{K}_{X_*,X}$ and $\mathbf{K}_{X,X_*}$ are constructed by evaluating the covariance function k at their respective pairs of points. In real-world applications, we do not have access to the latent function values. We are depending on noisy observations $\mathbf{y}$.

The conditional predictive posterior distribution of the GP can be written as:

$$\mathbf{f}_* | X, X_*, \mathbf{y}, \boldsymbol{\theta}, \sigma_\epsilon^2 \sim \mathcal{N}(\mathbb{E}(\mathbf{f}_*), \mathbb{V}(\mathbf{f}_*)), \tag{13}$$

$$\mathbb{E}(\mathbf{f}_*) = \boldsymbol{m}_{X_*} + \mathbf{K}_{X_*,X}\left[\mathbf{K}_{X,X} + \sigma_\epsilon^2 I\right]^{-1}\mathbf{f}, \tag{14}$$

$$\mathbb{V}(\mathbf{f}_*) = \mathbf{K}_{X_*,X_*} - \mathbf{K}_{X_*,X}\left[\mathbf{K}_{X,X} + \sigma_\epsilon^2 I\right]^{-1}\mathbf{K}_{X,X_*}. \tag{15}$$

The hyperparameters $\boldsymbol{\theta}$ are usually learned by using a gradient-based optimisation algorithm to maximise the log marginal likelihood,

$$\log p(\mathbf{y}|\theta, X) \propto -\frac{1}{2}\left[\mathbf{y}^T\left[\mathbf{K}_{X,X} + \sigma_\epsilon^2 I\right]\mathbf{y} + \log|\mathbf{K}_{X,X} + \sigma_\epsilon^2 I)|\right], \tag{16}$$

which is a combination of a data fit term and complexity penalty and, thus, automatically incorporates Occam's Razor [15]. This guards the Gaussian process model against overfitting. In our experiments, we use BFGS, a quasi-Newton method described in [28]. The linear system $\left[\mathbf{K}_{X,X} + \sigma_\epsilon^2 I\right]\mathbf{y}$ is often calculated by first calculating the Cholesky decomposition factor L of $\left[\mathbf{K}_{X,X} + \sigma_\epsilon^2 I\right]$ and then solving

$$\left[\mathbf{K}_{X,X} + \sigma_\epsilon^2 I\right]\mathbf{y} = L^T \setminus (L \setminus \mathbf{y}). \tag{17}$$

In the literature, many kernel functions have been extensively studied and reviewed. An overview can be found in [29]. A very popular kernel is the squared exponential kernel. It is suited for a wide range of applications because it is infinitely differentiable and, thus, yields smooth functions. Moreover, it only has two tunable hyperparameters. It has the form:

$$k_{SE}(\mathbf{x}, \mathbf{x}') = \sigma_f^2 \exp\left(-\frac{|\mathbf{x} - \mathbf{x}'|^2}{2l^2}\right), \tag{18}$$

in which σ_f^2 is a scale factor and l is the length-scale that controls the decline of the influence of the training points with distance. For the squared exponential kernel the hyperparameters θ_{SE} are $\left\{\sigma_f^2, l\right\}$. For the function $k : X \times X \to \mathbb{R}$ to be a valid kernel, it must be positive semi-definite (PSD), which means that for any vector $\mathbf{x} \in X^d$, the kernel matrix K is positive semi-definite. This implies that $\mathbf{x}^T K \mathbf{x} \geq 0$ for all $\mathbf{x} \in \mathbb{R}^d$.

In this work, we do implement a different length-scale parameter for every input dimension. This technique is called automatic relevance determination (ARD) and allows for functions that vary differently in each input dimension [29]. The kernel has the form:

$$k_{SEARD}(\mathbf{x}, \mathbf{x}') = \sigma_f^2 \exp\left(-\frac{1}{2} \sum_{j=1}^{d} \left(\frac{\left| \mathbf{x}_j - \mathbf{x}_j' \right|}{l_j} \right)^2 \right),$$ (19)

in which l_j is a separate length-scale parameter for each of the d input dimensions.

2.5. Gaussian Process Latent Variable Models

Principal component analysis (PCA) transforms a set of data points to a new coordinate system, in which the greatest variance is explained by the first coordinate (called the first principal component), the second greatest variance by the second coordinate, etc. This reprojection of the data can be exploited in dimensionality reduction by dropping the components with the smallest variance associated. The result will still contain most of the information of the original data. This method can also be explained as a statistical model known as probabilistic PCA (PPCA) [30], which implies that the principal components associated with the largest variance also maximise the likelihood of the data.

In dimensionality-reduction, the representation of the original data by its retained principal components can be interpreted as a latent variable model, in which the n latent variables $\mathbf{X} = \left[\mathbf{x}_1, \mathbf{x}_2, \dots, \mathbf{x}_n\right]^T$ are of a dimension k that is lower than the dimension d of the original data. PPCA requires a marginalisation of those latent variables and an optimisation of the mapping from the latent space to the data (observation) space. For n d-dimensional observations $\mathbf{Y} = \left[\mathbf{y}_1, \mathbf{y}_2, \dots, \mathbf{y}_n\right]^T$ we can write

$$\mathbf{y}_i = \mathbf{W}\mathbf{x}_i + \epsilon, \quad \epsilon \sim \mathcal{N}(0, \sigma_\epsilon^2),$$ (20)

in which $\mathbf{x}_i$ is a k-dimensional latent variable with $k < d$, $\mathbf{W}$ is a $d \times k$ matrix representing the mapping and ϵ is observation noise.

In [14,31], a dual approach is proposed by marginalising the mapping $\mathbf{W}$ and optimising the latent variables $\mathbf{X}$. This approach is called the Gaussian process latent variable model (GPLVM) and is achieved by maximising the Gaussian process likelihood $\mathcal{L}$ with respect to the latent variables. We optimise

$$\mathcal{L}(\mathbf{X}) = -\frac{dn}{2} \log 2\pi - \frac{d}{2} \log |\mathbf{K}| - \frac{1}{2} \mathrm{tr}(\mathbf{K}^{-1}\mathbf{Y}\mathbf{Y}^\top),$$ (21)

with respect to $\mathbf{X}$. It is proved in [14] that this approach is equivalent to PCA when using a linear kernel to compose $\mathbf{K}$, which can be written as

$$k_{linear}(\mathbf{x}, \mathbf{x}') = \mathbf{x}^T \mathbf{x}'.$$ (22)

However, by choosing a nonlinear kernel, we can establish a nonlinear relationship between the latent variables $\mathbf{X}$ and the observations $\mathbf{Y}$. This relationship can also be seen as placing a Gaussian process prior on each column of the $n \times d$ matrix $\mathbf{Y}$ and allows for a more flexible mapping between latent and data space.

In the original GPLVM, the unobserved inputs are treated as latent variables which are optimised. Another approach is to variationally integrate them and compute a lower bound on the exact marginal likelihood of the non-linear variable model. This is known as the Bayesian Gaussian process latent variable model (BGPLVM) [32]. It is more robust to overfitting and can automatically detect the relevant dimensions in the latent space. These dimensions are characterised by a larger Automatic Relevance Determination (ARD) contribution, which is the inverse of the length-scales l_j in Equation (19). Every component in data space is a vector whose components are formed by as many Gaussian processes as there are input dimensions. These ARD contributions determine the weight of the outcomes of each of the Gaussian processes and, thus, its corresponding input dimension. Less relevant dimensions result in longer length scales and are pruned out. In this work, we exploit this by performing this Bayesian non-linear dimensionality reduction on the seven-dimensional line elements. For most shapes in 3D, a lower-dimensional representation in a latent space can be found, as we show below.

The GPLVM is a map from latent to data space. As such, it preserves local distances between points in the latent space. However, this does not imply that points close by in the data space are also close by in the latent space. To incorporate this extra feature, one can equip the GPLVM with a so-called back constraint [33]. This constraint is accomplished by introducing a second distance-preserving map from the data to the latent space. We refer to this model as the back-constrained Gaussian process latent variable model (BCGPLVM). A thorough review of GPLVM and its variants, including more than the ones mentioned here, can also be found in [34,35] and more recently in [36,37].

2.6. Our Approach

In this section, we explain how all of the above-mentioned concepts come together in our approach. To recap, we can represent a straight line in 3D space by Plücker coordinates, which are six-tuples. By adding a seventh component, we can specify a point on that line. We can do this for every n point in a given point cloud. The line we choose through each point is the normal line to the surface that is captured by that point cloud. We, thus, obtain a set of seven-dimensional line elements, that captures the information about the surface we want to examine.

The theory of kinematic surfaces links the line elements that are contained in a linear line element complex to an equiform kinematic surface. Finding this complex comes down to solving an ordinary eigenvalue problem. The dimensionality of the linear subspace, in which the line elements live, and the resulting eigenvalues determine the type of surface. In essence, this is dimensionality reduction on the seven-dimensional line elements via PCA.

However, PCA is a linear mapping. In contrast, our model is built on the Gaussian process latent variable model (GPLVM), which allows for non-linear mapping. This results in a more nuanced way of representing the surface. Our model is only given the seven-dimensional line elements and finds the mapping from a latent (unobserved) space to these line elements. Each of the seven dimensions of the line elements is assigned to a Gaussian process (GP). The outputs (predictions) of those GPs are the components of the line elements. The inputs (training data) are the latent points, which are treated as variables of the overall model and are optimised (or integrated out in the Bayesian formulation).

In the next section, we will describe in more detail how we compose the datasets and elaborate on our experiments.

3. Results

All 3D models, datasets, plots and trained GP models described below can be found in our GitHub repository. These include supplementary experiments and plots we omitted here, so we do not overload the text.

To assess the latent representation of various 3D shapes, we composed a collection of both synthetically generated point clouds and real-world scanned objects. An overview can be found in Table 1. The synthetically generated point clouds are based on objects drawn in the free and open source Blender 3.3 LTS (https://www.blender.org/, accessed on 10 January 2023). Point clouds resulting from real-world scans were created on an Android mobile phone using the photogrammetry KIRI engine (https://www.kiriengine.com/, accessed on 10 January 2023) and imported in Blender, where they are cleaned up by dissolving disconnected points, removing the background and subsampling using standard Blender tools. However, they still contain some overlapping triangles and other mesh irregularities. Synthetic models were made noisy by first subdividing the mesh several times and then applying the Blender Randomize tool on the vertices. This breaks the lattice structure of the vertices. Moreover, this makes them resemble a real-world scan, where imperfections are inevitable. In this paper, we restrict ourselves to one noise level and leave the effect of the amount of noise on our point clouds as future work. The noiseless and noisy bend torus are the same as their ordinary torus variant with a Simple Deform modifier of 45° applied to it. All models are exported in the Polygon File Format format (.ply), resulting in files consisting of points and unit normals for those points.

The line elements are calculated in Matlab R2020b and exported as comma-separated values (.csv). These serve as the data space for the GPLVM models, which are implemented using the python GPy library (http://sheffieldml.github.io/GPy/, accessed on 10 January 2023). Some point clouds were subsampled uniformly for performance reasons. All GPLVM models were initialised with the results from a PCA. The BCGPLVM models were implemented with an MLP mapping with five hidden layers. The details are in Table 1. All code for training the models, as well as the trained models themselves, are available via notebooks in the GitHub repository.

Table 1. An overview of the surfaces and their corresponding GPLVM and properties. Larger point clouds are subsampled uniformly to a smaller set. The number of points retained for training is given in # Train. Noise is the Gaussian noise variance hyperparameter for the GPLVM model, which is either a fixed value or a value that has to be learned along with the other hyperparameters. The number of inducing points for the Bayesian GPLVM is shown in # Ind. To make sure we do not end up in local minima, we restarted the training of the model a number of times given in # Restarts.

	Model	# Vertices	# Train	Noise	# Ind	# Restarts
Cylinder of revolution	BGPLVM	2176	2176	1×10^{-4}	15	10
Cone of revolution	BGPLVM	2176	2176	free	50	10
Spiral cylinder	BGPLVM	2210	2210	free	25	10
Cylinder w/o revolution	BGPLVM	1717	1717	free	50	10
Cone w/o revolution	BGPLVM	2210	2210	free	50	10
Surface of revolution	BGPLVM	2816	2500	free	50	10
Helical surface	BGPLVM	2582	2500	free	25	10
Spiral surface	BGPLVM	1842	1842	free	50	10
Torus	BGPLVM	2048	2048	free	50	10
Torus bend	BGPLVM	2048	2048	free	25	10
Pear	BGPLVM	6356	5000	free	50	5
Mixture 1	BCGPLVM	10,653	1000	1×10^{-6}	NA	3
Mixture 2	BCGPLVM	6555	1000	1×10^{-6}	NA	3
Mixture 3	BCGPLVM	15,681	1000	1×10^{-4}	NA	3
Hinge	BGPLVM	22,282	5000	free	50	3
Torus bend noisy	BGPLVM	8192	8192	free	50	3

3.1. Surface Approximation

We trained a Bayesian Gaussian process latent variable model for all examples of the equiform kinematic surfaces listed in Section 2.2. As can be seen by the ARD contributions in Figure 2, these surfaces can be represented by a lower dimensional representation. These dimensions are characterised by the largest ARD contribution and, thus, the smallest length scales. A 2D plot of the surface points in their latent space is given by Figure 3. The Supplementary Material also includes plots in 3D latent space and provides PCA bar charts for comparison. They are omitted here not to overload this text with too many plots. These experiments were repeated for the noisy variants of the surfaces as well. The same underlying structure can be observed. Again, we refer to the Supplementary Material.

All surfaces show a clear structure in their latent space. Note that the number of small eigenvalues does not necessarily correspond with the number of relevant dimensions in latent space. The latter is the result of an optimization algorithm in which both the latent points and the kernel hyperparameters are found. This can be seen in the ARD contribution plot for the helical surface. The plot for the cylinder of revolution even has a significant value for all seven dimensions. This effect can be thought of as overfitting [37], as the model attributes importance to more latent dimensions than needed. In our experiments, we tried to lower this effect by making the model less flexible. We added a fixed noise term to the hyperparameters and lowered the number of inducing points. For details per surface, we refer to Table 1. All trained models are available in the Supplementary Material on the GitHub repository.

Another important remark is that the mapping from latent to data space is non-linear. Care must be taken when interpreting the 2D latent space plots. For instance, the spiral surface clearly has a one-dimensional subspace. However, the 2D plot shows a scattered cloud of points. This is an artefact of the visualization. The ARD plot indicates that only dimension 1 has a significant contribution. Another example is given by the cylinder without revolution. Its subspace in $\mathbb{R}^7$ is one-dimensional, which manifests itself as a curve-like trail of points in the 2D latent space.

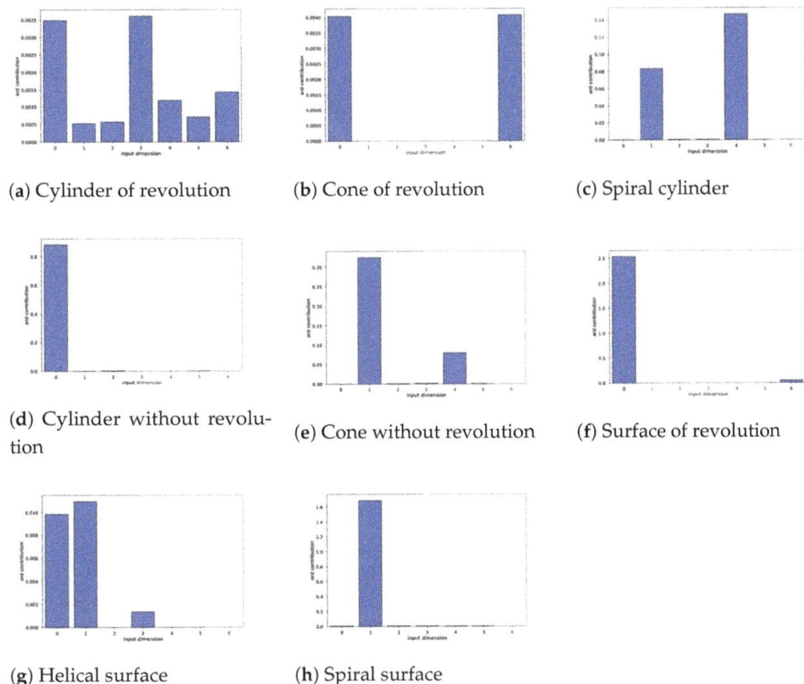

(**a**) Cylinder of revolution   (**b**) Cone of revolution   (**c**) Spiral cylinder

(**d**) Cylinder without revolution   (**e**) Cone without revolution   (**f**) Surface of revolution

(**g**) Helical surface   (**h**) Spiral surface

Figure 2. ARD contributions for the dimensions of the latent space for the examples of equiform kinematic surfaces.

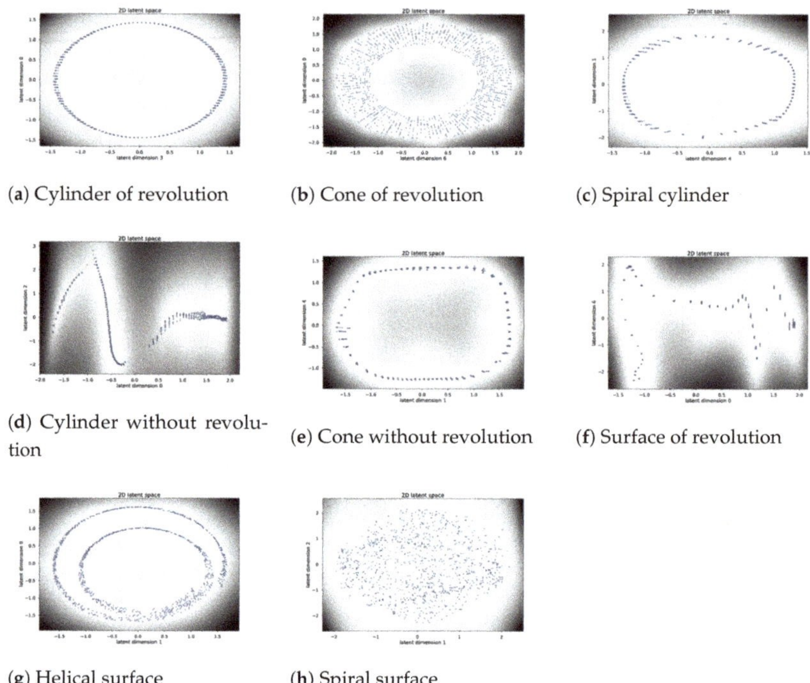

(**a**) Cylinder of revolution

(**b**) Cone of revolution

(**c**) Spiral cylinder

(**d**) Cylinder without revolution

(**e**) Cone without revolution

(**f**) Surface of revolution

(**g**) Helical surface

(**h**) Spiral surface

Figure 3. A 2D representation of the points of the kinematic surfaces in their latent space. The amount of black in the background indicates the posterior uncertainty of the BGPLVM.

So far, nothing has been gained by this new Bayesian GPLVM way of representing surfaces. The difference with the approach described in Section 2.2, is that we are no longer restricted to the simple geometric surfaces of Figure 1 and their linear subspaces of $\mathbb{R}^7$. We can now also describe surfaces that do not fall into the categories listed above. We investigate two cases.

First, we apply our method to a bend torus. This is a surface of revolution, which we altered using the Simple Deform modifier in Blender to bend it 45° around an axis perpendicular to the axis of rotational symmetry of the original torus. This removes the rotational symmetry altogether. The results can be seen in Figure 4. We notice that the BGPLVM only deemed one dimension as significant. The 2D plot reveals the latent structure.

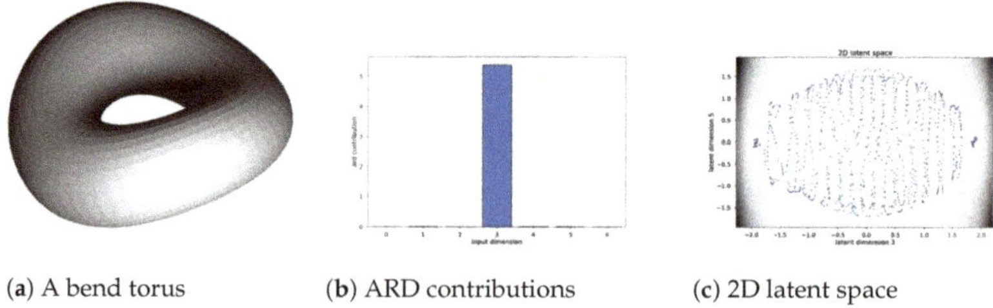

(**a**) A bend torus

(**b**) ARD contributions

(**c**) 2D latent space

Figure 4. Results for a bend torus. One latent dimension is found to be dominant.

Second, we look at the surface of the point cloud obtained by scanning a pear as described above. This is an organic shape, so it possesses the same challenges as working with shapes that can be found in other items from nature or when modelling the anatomy of humans and animals. We are only interested in the shape of the body, so we removed the stalk and the bottom part when cleaning up the 3D model. In this case, the 3D shape resembles a surface of revolution, but the axis is bent irregularly and the rotational symmetry is broken (not all normals intersect the axis of rotation). The results can be seen in Figure 5. The darker region in the 2D latent plot indicates more posterior uncertainty. In the latent space, we observe a set of points similar to what we saw for a cylinder of revolution with an additional distortion in a third latent dimension.

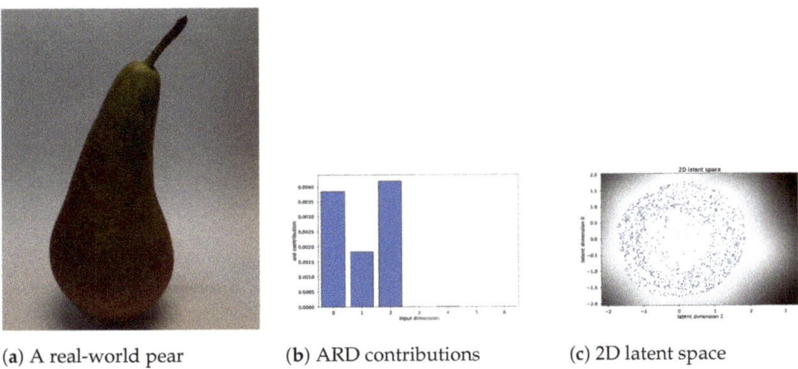

(**a**) A real-world pear   (**b**) ARD contributions   (**c**) 2D latent space

Figure 5. Results for a real world pear scanned with a mobile phone app.

Both the bend torus and the pear can not be described by an equiform kinematic surface. Applying the methods of Section 2.2 (i.e., approximating by a linear complex of line elements) for classification is numerically still possible. A small set of eigenvalues can be found. However, their interpretation would be faulty. The bend torus shows one small eigenvalue, $\mathbf{c} \neq (0,0,0)$, $\gamma = 0$ and $\mathbf{c} \cdot \bar{\mathbf{c}} \approx 0$. Unsurprisingly, these values fit a surface of revolution. They resemble the values for the torus or the torus with noise. However, blindly using the methods from [10] would result in a perfect surface of revolution. The same reasoning can be applied to the scanned pear's point cloud. Below, we show how to exploit our newfound GPLVM representation in surface approximation, surface segmentation and surface denoising.

3.2. Surface Segmentation

A major challenge in point cloud classification is the segmentation of sub-regions within that cloud. Once points are grouped together in simpler shapes, the underlying structure can be found via either our method or the methods described in [8,10–13,25,26]. In these works, several approaches are described for discovering the sub-regions. Mostly, they are based on time-consuming trial and error RANSAC. Here, we show that working in a latent space can be beneficial. The challenge is to group points together, whose line elements show similar behaviour.

As we want to separate coherent groups of points in latent space, we care about their local distances. Points close by in the latent space should be close by in the data space as well. Therefore, we expand our GPLVM with a back constraint as described in Section 2.5. We implement both an RBF kernel with ARD and a multi-layer perceptron (MLP) mapping to capture the back constraint [33,37]. The details for the different 3D models can be found in Table 1. As before, all code is available in the GitHub repository. The notebooks also include 3D plots made with the python open source graphing library Plotly (https://plotly.com/python/, accessed on 10 January 2023), that allow user interaction such as 3D rotations. By rotating the viewpoint, we can clearly see how separable the latent points are.

To demonstrate our approach, we first designed three objects composed of different simpler geometric shapes. They can be found in Figure 6. The parts of these three models fall under the different categories described in Section 2.2. The aim of surface segmentation is to find those parts in an unsupervised manner.

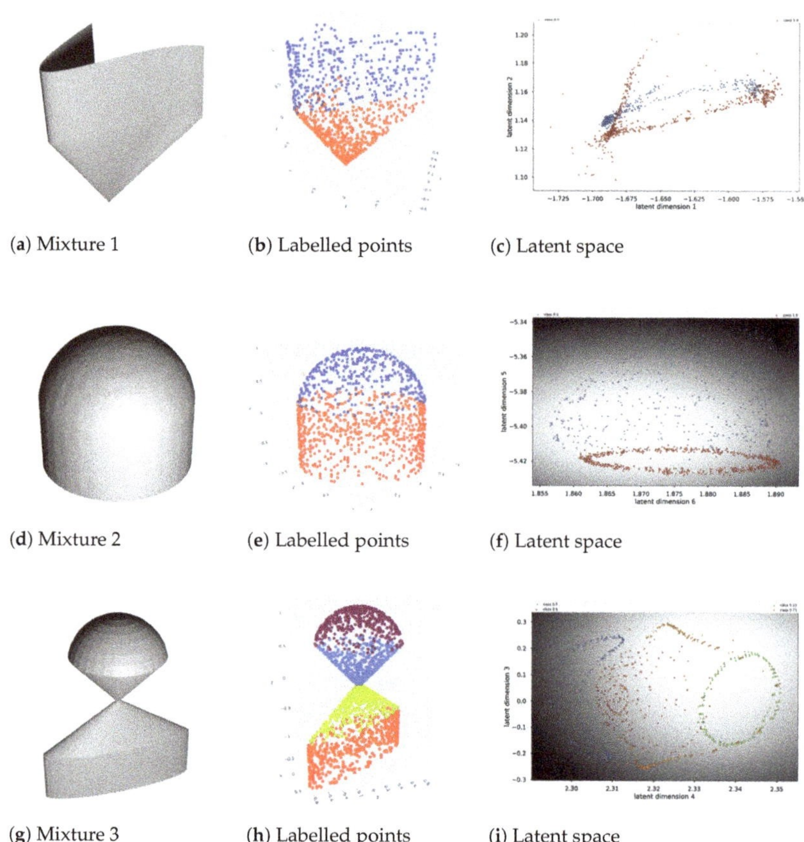

(**a**) Mixture 1   (**b**) Labelled points   (**c**) Latent space

(**d**) Mixture 2   (**e**) Labelled points   (**f**) Latent space

(**g**) Mixture 3   (**h**) Labelled points   (**i**) Latent space

Figure 6. Three synthetically generated 3D models by combining primitive surfaces. The BCGPLVM is able to show distinguishable structures for points in latent space.

First, we created a 3D model called Mixture 1, which consists of a cylinder and cone, neither without rotational symmetry. Both of those shapes individually show one small eigenvalue and a clearly distinguishable curve in their 2D latent space, as can be seen in Figure 3. Combined, their latent space looks like two curves, shown in Figure 6. Notice that the 3D points that lie both on the cylinder and the cone, fall into both categories. Moreover, their normal is inconsistent with either of the two shapes. For this cylinder, all normals are horizontal. For the cone, normals for points on a line connecting the cone's apex and its generating curve, are parallel. For points on the intersection of the cylinder and the cone, the normals are weighted with their neighbouring points. This results in a latent space that is not easily separable by clustering.

Second, the 3D model named Mixture 2 consists of a noisy cylinder of revolution where one end is closed by a demi-sphere. The former is characterised by two small eigenvalues and the latter by three. Again, this behaviour can be clearly observed in the latent space. Notice how the BCGPLVM formulates latent shapes for each part that are consistent with the kinematic surface described in Section 2.2. For the sphere, we observe a 2D shape. For the cylinder of revolution, an annulus can be seen. The supplementary material includes an interactively rotatable 3D plot where this cloud of latent points can be observed in more detail. We also see that the region for the tip of the demi-sphere has a darker background in the 2D latent plot, indicating more uncertainty in this region of the posterior. This can be explained by the fact that the normals of a sphere all intersect at the centre of the sphere. As such, no normals are parallel. This results in line elements whose vector components vary more. Points with normals that lie in parallel planes, as is the case for a cylinder, have more similarity in the direction components of their line elements. Moreover, the hyperparameters in the mapping from latent to data space are optimised globally. This means for all latent points simultaneously. The strong structure in the cylinder part renders the large variations in the tip of the demi-sphere part as less likely. Hence the larger posterior variance.

Finally, in the 3D model Mixture 3, we grouped together the upper half of a sphere, a cone of revolution, a cone without revolution and a cylinder without revolution. These parts have three, two, one and one small eigenvalues, respectively. As this model consists of four different parts, the segmentation is more complex. Nonetheless, the BCGLVM is able to find distinct substructures in the latent space, even in just two dimensions.

For a real-world and more challenging example, we scanned a metal hinge, as described above. It can be found in Figure 7. The original 3D model and the cleaned-up one can be found in the supplementary material. The 3D model is a collection of a cylinder of revolution, two planes and a cone-like aperture. It is important to notice that the scan itself is of poor quality, mainly due to the shininess of the metal and the lack of distinct features. There are holes and bumps in the surface, even after cleaning up the model in Blender. Moreover, the cone-like aperture does not have a lot of vertices (the region around the apex is completely missing). The latent space still shows the formation of clusters, especially when three dimensions are taken into account.

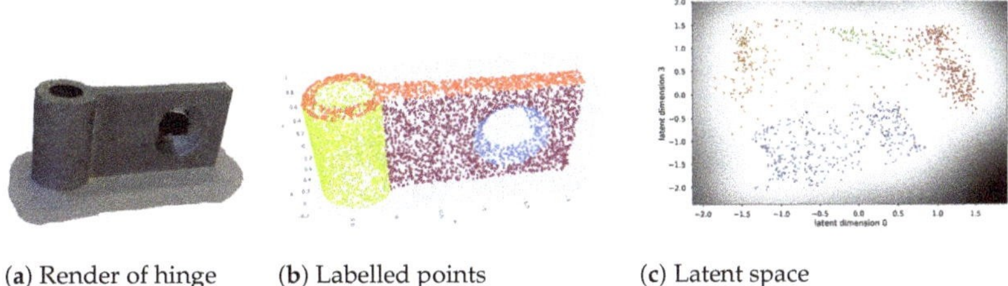

(**a**) Render of hinge   (**b**) Labelled points   (**c**) Latent space

Figure 7. The results for a real-world scanned metal hinge. Again, the BGPLVM is able to separate the points in latent space.

Once a latent space is found, the segmentation can be done via either a manual selection of the latent points or a form of unsupervised learning. In the case of separable clusters, we can perform the well-studied k-means clustering algorithm or draw (hyper)planes determined by support vector machines (SVM). The details of these are outside the scope of this work. The reader is referred to [38] and [39], respectively. This segmentation can then be the basis for fitting simple geometric surfaces to each cluster of points. As we can observe from the plots, some of the latent points do not belong to any of the found substructures. In practice, these can be ignored or filtered out. We are left with enough points to perform the best fit. Afterwards, we can determine whether or not such a rogue point belongs to the best-fit subsurface or not.

3.3. Surface Denoising

In general, a Gaussian process can handle noise very well, even in low data regimes [15]. This means our technique is beneficial to denoise point clouds. Once a mapping is found from a latent space to a data space, it can be queried to predict new points in the data space. This can be used to handle missing data [36,37]. Here, we take advantage of this feature by correcting noisy points in the lower dimensional latent space and predicting their counterparts in the data space. The smooth mapping allows re-predict the line elements for every latent point.

From a predicted line element $(1, \bar{1}, \lambda)$, with $\|1\| = 1$, we can calculate a corresponding 3D coordinate $\mathbf{x}$ for a point x using

$$\mathbf{x} = 1 \times \bar{1} + \lambda 1. \tag{23}$$

To demonstrate this, we again work on the bend torus model. We introduce random noise with the Blender Randomize tool and select a hundred vertices at random, which we translate to simulate shot noise. The results can be seen in Figure 8. The 3D model, the .ply file with the point coordinates and unit normal vectors, the .csv file with the line elements and the notebook with the executed code for the BGPLVM can be found in the supplementary material. Once the BGPLVM is trained on the noisy point cloud, we use it to predict line elements for the latent point. From these line elements, we extract 3D coordinates for points via Equation (23). We observe that the BGPLVM is able to smooth out the translated vertices. This approach can also be used to detect and remove outliers.

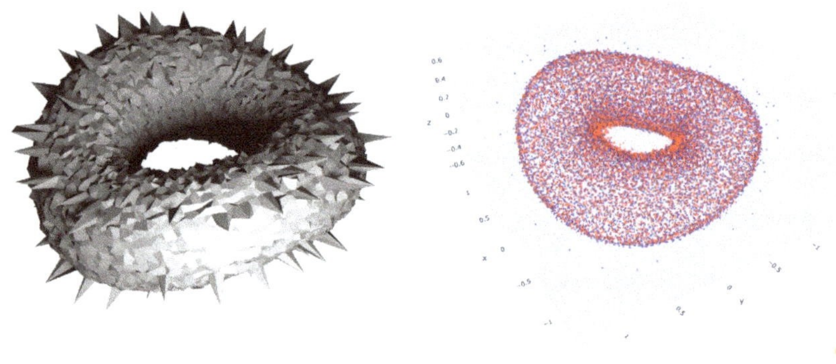

(a) Deformed bend torus   (b) Denoised bend torus

Figure 8. A bend torus. Noise is added to the entire surface. Moreover, A hundred vertices were translated. (**b**) The BGPLVM is able to smooth out the surface. Blue are the noisy points. Red are the denoised points.

4. Discussion

This work presented the first findings for this new GPLVM approach to describe 3D surfaces. In this manuscript, we wanted to focus on the theoretical principles themselves and not overload the paper with additional research questions that determine the limits of this idea. Even though these are both interesting and important in real-world applications, we leave them for future work.

We have shown surface segmentation for surfaces that are the combination of a few different simpler geometrical shapes. The question remains how many sub-regions can be detected and what the complexity of those regions can be?

We presented the Bayesian GPLVM and the GPLVM with back constraints. There are more variations on this topic investigated in the literature. A recent paper describes a generalised GPLVM with stochastic variational inference [37]. They also present models for applying these techniques on a larger dataset. This would be most applicable to larger point clouds, which are often obtained in real-world applications.

A line element is formed by a line and a point on that line. By working with normal lines for points on a surface, we effectively introduced a second so-called *view* for those points, where we follow the terminology used in [34,36]. Those works present a multi-view unsupervised learning technique called manifold relevance determination (MRD), which offers another worthwhile approach.

The prediction as seven-tuples made by the model does not automatically follow the Grassmann–Plücker relationship in Equation (3) for their direction and moment vector. This leads to faulty line elements. In other words, the first six components of a line element vector are the Plücker coordinates of the line where the point of the line element lies on. Not all six-tuples represent a straight line in $\mathbb{P}^3$. In general, a *screw centre* C can be written as $(\mathbf{c}, \bar{\mathbf{c}})$. The pitch of C is defined as

$$\rho = \frac{\mathbf{c} \cdot \bar{\mathbf{c}}}{\|\mathbf{c}\|^2}. \tag{24}$$

This only holds for $\mathbf{c}$ not being the zero vector, in which case C would be a line at infinity. The pitch can be thought of as the deviation of the screw to a perfectly straight line. We can always write C as

$$C = (\mathbf{c}, \bar{\mathbf{c}} - \rho\mathbf{c}) + (\mathbf{0}, \rho\mathbf{c}) = A + (\mathbf{0}, \rho\mathbf{c}), \tag{25}$$

in which A is called the *Poinsot* or *central axis* of the screw centre C. The term $(\mathbf{0}, \rho\mathbf{c})$ represents the line at infinity where the planes perpendicular on A meet. Since A does satisfy the Grassmann–Plücker relation, it is a straight line in $\mathbb{P}^3$. This allows us to correct the predicted six tuples (by six distinct Gaussian processes) into straight lines via

$$A = C - (\mathbf{0}, \rho\mathbf{c}). \tag{26}$$

This approach is taken in [40]. Another way to ensure the Grassmann–Plücker relation is given in [41], where constraints are built in the kernel functions of the Gaussian process themselves, although at a considerable extra computational cost. A representation that does not suffer from this hurdle is the stereographic projection of a line [24]. In this approach, the line is made to intersect two arbitrary parallel planes. Only the 2D coordinates on those planes are kept as data points. Predictions on those planes, a point on each, are then used to calculate the Plücker coordinates of the predicted line. By doing so, the Grassmann–Plücker relation is always ensured. The problem herein is that the line parallel to the two planes can not be captured. Numerically, a line close to being parallel to the two planes also causes issues. As 3D surfaces can have normals in any direction, this latter approach is not recommended in a general setting.

5. Conclusions

We provided a theoretical introduction to kinematic surfaces and showed how they could be used to perform surface detection. Many simple geometric shapes manifest themselves as linear subspaces of line or line element space. This approach is limited by the linearity of the underlying eigenvalue problem. We expanded on this by reformulating this as a probabilistic non-linear non-parametric dimensionality reduction technique known as the Gaussian process latent variable model. We showed how this could be applied to many simple geometric surfaces, as well as surfaces that do not fall into any of these categories. Moreover, we showed the benefits of unsupervised surface segmentation and surface denoising. We presented findings on synthetically generated surfaces and scanned real-world objects.

The main goal of the current study was to determine the feasibility of applying the Gaussian process latent variable model to line element geometry. Even though several experiments are explained, and several more are included in the supplementary material, considerably more work will need to be done to determine the limits of this method. For instance, it remains an open question how noise affects the overall representation in the latent space. Moreover, we did not implement any optimizations on the training part of the underlying models, which is paramount for real-world settings. We leave this as future work.

Another natural progression of this work is to exploit further the found latent space in the case of missing data. Point clouds sometimes have missing regions, caused by bad lighting conditions, occluded areas or areas that simply can not be reached by the scanning device. Finding the 3D coordinates for the missing points is a classic example of the missing data problem. In our case, it manifests itself as a region in the latent space that is missing values. If the found structure in the latent space is enough to reconstruct those missing latent points, then according to data space points can also be inferred by the Gaussian process latent variable model.

More broadly, we plan to study the benefits of working on latent spaces not just for line elements, but for the lines themselves (in which case, we drop the point on the line and only keep the description of the line). This technique could be used in the calibration of various devices that are built on the usage of straight lines. Cameras, for instance, produce images in which a pixel is the result of a single incoming ray of light. Another example is galvanometric laser scanners, which guide a laser beam by means of two rotating mirrors. Calibrating such a device means finding the relationship between the two angles of the mirrors and the outgoing beam. So, in this case, a 2D latent space must exist. This would be a fruitful area for further work.

Supplementary Materials: All of our 3D models, sets of line elements, trained GPLVM, notebooks with code and many more experiments and plots can be found on our GitHub repository https://github.com/IvanDeBoi/Surface-Approximation-GPLVM-Line-Geometry (accessed on 10 January 2023).

Author Contributions: Conceptualisation, I.D.B., C.H.E. and R.P.; methodology, I.D.B., C.H.E. and R.P.; software, I.D.B.; validation, I.D.B.; formal analysis, I.D.B. and R.P.; investigation, I.D.B.; resources, I.D.B.; data curation, I.D.B.; writing—original draft preparation, I.D.B.; writing—review and editing, I.D.B., C.H.E. and R.P.; visualisation, I.D.B.; supervision, R.P.; project administration, I.D.B.; funding acquisition, R.P. All authors have read and agreed to the published version of the manuscript.

Funding: This research has been funded by the University of Antwerp (BOF FFB200259, Antigoon ID 42339).

Institutional Review Board Statement: Not applicable.

Informed Consent Statement: Not applicable.

Data Availability Statement: All of our 3D models, sets of line elements, trained GPLVM, notebooks with code and many more experiments and plots can be found on Supplementary Materials.

Acknowledgments: We thank the anonymous reviewers whose comments helped improve the quality of this paper.

Conflicts of Interest: The authors declare no conflict of interest.

References

1. Guo, Y.; Wang, H.; Hu, Q.; Liu, H.; Liu, L.; Bennamoun, M. Deep Learning for 3D Point Clouds: A Survey. *IEEE Trans. Pattern Anal. Mach. Intell.* **2021**, *43*, 4338–4364. [CrossRef]
2. Chen, S.; Liu, B.; Feng, C.; Vallespi-Gonzalez, C.; Wellington, C. 3d point cloud processing and learning for autonomous driving: Impacting map creation, localization, and perception. *IEEE Signal Process. Mag.* **2020**, *38*, 68–86. [CrossRef]
3. Behley, J.; Garbade, M.; Milioto, A.; Quenzel, J.; Behnke, S.; Gall, J.; Stachniss, C. Towards 3D LiDAR-based semantic scene understanding of 3D point cloud sequences: The SemanticKITTI Dataset. *Int. J. Robot. Res.* **2021**, *40*, 959–967. [CrossRef]
4. Várady, T.; Martin, R.R.; Cox, J. Reverse engineering of geometric models—An introduction. *Comput.-Aided Des.* **1997**, *29*, 255–268. [CrossRef]
5. Almamou, A.A.; Gebhardt, T.; Bock, S.; Hildebrand, J.; Schwarz, W. Quality control of constructed models using 3d point cloud. In Proceedings of the 20th International Conference on the Application of Computer Science and Mathematics in Architecture and Civil Engineering, Weimar, Germany, 20–22 July 2015.
6. Łukasz Sobczak.; Filus, K.; Domański, A.; Domańska, J. LiDAR point cloud generation for SLAM algorithm evaluation. *Sensors* **2021**, *21*, 3313.
7. Naeini, A.A.; Ahmad, A.; Sheikholeslami, M.M.; Claudio, P.; Sohn, G. An Unsupervised Registration of 3D Point Clouds to 2D CAD Model: a Case Study of Floor Plan. *ISPRS Ann. Photogramm. Remote Sens. Spat. Inf. Sci.* **2020**, *V-2-2020*, 9–13. [CrossRef]

8. Pottmann, H.; Lee, I.K.; Randrup, T. Reconstruction of kinematic surfaces from scattered data. In Proceedings of Symposium on Geodesy for Geotechnical and Structural Engineering, Eisenstadt, Austria, 20–24 April 1998; pp. 483–488.

9. Pottmann, H.; Peternell, M.; Ravani, B. Approximation in Line Space—Applications in Robot Kinematics and Surface Reconstruction. *Adv. Robot. Kinematics Anal. Control.* **1998**, 403–412. [CrossRef]

10. Lee, I.K.; Wallner, J.; Pottmann, H. Scattered data approximation with kinematic surfaces. *SAMPTA* **1999**, *99*, 72–77.

11. Pottmann, H.; Wallner, J.; Leopoldseder, S. *Kinematical Methods for the Classification, Reconstruction, and Inspection of Surfaces*; University of Vienna: Vienna, Austria, 2001.

12. Pottmann, H.; Hofer, M.; Odehnal, B.; Wallner, J. *Line Geometry for 3D Shape Understanding and Reconstruction*; Springer: Berlin/Heidelberg, Germany, 2004; pp. 297–309.

13. Hofer, M.; Odehnal, B.; Pottmann, H.; Steiner, T.; Wallner, J. *3D Shape Recognition and Reconstruction Based on Line Element Geometry*; University of Vienna: Vienna, Austria, 2005, Volume. 2, pp. 1532–1538. [CrossRef]

14. Lawrence, N.D. *Gaussian Process Latent Variable Models for Visualisation of High Dimensional Data*; MIT Press: Cambridge, UK, 2003; pp. 329–336.

15. Rasmussen, C.E.; Williams, C.K.I. *Gaussian Processes for Machine Learning*; The MIT Press: Cambridge, UK, 2006.

16. Berger, M.; Tagliasacchi, A.; Seversky, L.M.; Alliez, P.; Levine, J.A.; Sharf, A.; Silva, C.T. *State of the Art in Surface Reconstruction from Point Clouds*; The Eurographics Association: Saarbrucken, Germany, 2014. [CrossRef]

17. Goyal, A.; Law, H.; Liu, B.; Newell, A.; Deng, J. Revisiting point cloud shape classification with a simple and effective baseline. *arXiv* **2021**, arXiv:2106.05304v1.

18. Uy, M.A.; Pham, Q.H.; Hua, B.S.; Nguyen, T.; Yeung, S.K. Revisiting point cloud classification: A new benchmark dataset and classification model on real-world data. *arXiv* **2019**, arXiv:1908.04616v2.

19. Chang, A.X.; Funkhouser, T.; Guibas, L.; Hanrahan, P.; Huang, Q.; Li, Z.; Savarese, S.; Savva, M.; Song, S.; Su, H.; et al. Shapenet: An information-rich 3d model repository. *arXiv* **2015**, arXiv:1512.03012.

20. Dai, A.; Chang, A.X.; Savva, M.; Halber, M.; Funkhouser, T.; Nießner, M. Scannet: Richly-annotated 3d reconstructions of indoor scenes. *arXiv* **2017**, arXiv:1702.04405v2.

21. Geiger, A.; Lenz, P.; Stiller, C.; Urtasun, R. The KITTI Vision Benchmark Suite. 2015, 2. Available online: http://www.cvlibs.net/datasets/kitti (accessed on 10 January 2023).

22. Sun, J.; Zhang, Q.; Kailkhura, B.; Yu, Z.; Xiao, C.; Mao, Z.M. Benchmarking robustness of 3d point cloud recognition against common corruptions. *arXiv* **2022**, arXiv:2201.12296.

23. Romanengo, C.; Raffo, A.; Qie, Y.; Anwer, N.; Falcidieno, B. Fit4CAD: A point cloud benchmark for fitting simple geometric primitives in CAD objects. *Comput. Graph.* **2022**, *102*, 133–143. [CrossRef]

24. Pottmann, H.; Wallner, J. *Computational Line Geometry*; Springer Science and Business Media: Berlin/Heidelberg, Germany, 2009. [CrossRef]

25. Odehnal, B.; Pottmann, H.; Wallner, J. Equiform kinematics and the geometry of line elements. *Beitr. Algebra Geom.* **2006**, *47*, 567–582.

26. Pottmann, H.; Randrup, T. Rotational and helical surface approximation for reverse engineering. *Computing* **1998**, *60*, 307–322. [CrossRef]

27. Mitra, N.J.; Nguyen, A. *Estimating Surface Normals in Noisy Point Cloud Data*; Association for Computing Machinery: New York, NY, USA, 2003; pp. 322–328. [CrossRef]

28. Liu, D.C.; Nocedal, J. On the limited memory BFGS method for large scale optimization. *Math. Program.* **1989**, *45*, 503–528. [CrossRef]

29. Duvenaud, D.K.; College, P. *Automatic Model Construction with Gaussian Processes Declaration*; University of Cambridge: Cambridge, UK, 2014.

30. Tipping, M.E.; Bishop, C.M. Probabilistic principal component analysis. *J. R. Stat. Soc. Ser. Stat. Methodol.* **1999**, *61*, 611–622. . [CrossRef]

31. Lawrence, N. Probabilistic Non-linear Principal Component Analysis with Gaussian Process Latent Variable Models. *J. Mach. Learn. Res.* **2005**, *6*, 1783–1816.

32. Titsias, M.; Lawrence, N.D. Bayesian Gaussian Process Latent Variable Model. *Proc. Mach. Learn. Res.* **2010**, *9*, 844–851.

33. Lawrence, N.D.; Quiñonero-Candela, J. *Local Distance Preservation in the GP-LVM through Back Constraints*; Association for Computing Machinery: New York, NY, USA, 2006; pp. 513–520. [CrossRef]

34. Damianou, A.C.; Ek, C.H.; Titsias, M.K.; Lawrence, N.D. *Manifold Relevance Determination*; Omnipress: Madison, WI, USA, 2012; pp. 531–538.

35. Li, P.; Chen, S. A review on Gaussian Process Latent Variable Models. *CAAI Trans. Intell. Technol.* **2016**, *1*, 366–376.. [CrossRef]

36. Damianou, A.C.; Lawrence, N.D.; Ek, C.H. Multi-view Learning as a Nonparametric Nonlinear Inter-Battery Factor Analysis. *J. Mach. Learn. Res.* **2021**, *22*, 86:1–86:51.

37. Lalchand, V.; Ravuri, A.; Lawrence, N.D. Generalised GPLVM with Stochastic Variational Inference. *Proc. Mach. Learn. Res.* **2022**, *151*, 7841–7864.

38. Ahmed, M.; Seraj, R.; Islam, S.M.S. The k-means Algorithm: A Comprehensive Survey and Performance Evaluation. *Electronics* **2020**, *9*, 1295.. [CrossRef]

39. Cervantes, J.; Garcia-Lamont, F.; Rodríguez-Mazahua, L.; Lopez, A. A comprehensive survey on support vector machine classification: Applications, challenges and trends. *Neurocomputing* **2020**, *408*, 189–215. [CrossRef]
40. Boi, I.D.; Sels, S.; Penne, R. Semidata-Driven Calibration of Galvanometric Setups Using Gaussian Processes. *IEEE Trans. Instrum. Meas.* **2022**, *71*, 1–8. [CrossRef]
41. Boi, I.D.; Sels, S.; Moor, O.D.; Vanlanduit, S.; Penne, R. Input and Output Manifold Constrained Gaussian Process Regression for Galvanometric Setup Calibration. *IEEE Trans. Instrum. Meas.* **2022**, *71*, 1–8. [CrossRef]

Article

Using Machine Learning in Predicting the Impact of Meteorological Parameters on Traffic Incidents

Aleksandar Aleksić, Milan Ranđelović and Dragan Ranđelović *

Faculty of Diplomacy and Security, University Union-Nikola Tesla Belgrade, Travnicka 2, 11000 Belgrade, Serbia
* Correspondence: dragan.randjelovic@fdb.edu.rs

Abstract: The opportunity for large amounts of open-for-public and available data is one of the main drivers of the development of an information society at the beginning of the 21st century. In this sense, acquiring knowledge from these data using different methods of machine learning is a prerequisite for solving complex problems in many spheres of human activity, starting from medicine to education and the economy, including traffic as today's important economic branch. Having this in mind, this paper deals with the prediction of the risk of traffic incidents using both historical and real-time data for different atmospheric factors. The main goal is to construct an ensemble model based on the use of several machine learning algorithms which has better characteristics of prediction than any of those installed when individually applied. In global, a case-proposed model could be a multi-agent system, but in a considered case study, a two-agent system is used so that one agent solves the prediction task by learning from the historical data, and the other agent uses the real time data. The authors evaluated the obtained model based on a case study and data for the city of Niš from the Republic of Serbia and also described its implementation as a practical web citizen application.

Keywords: machine learning; regression; classification; prediction; meteorological parameters; traffic incidents; multi-agent architecture

MSC: 68T05; 68T42

Citation: Aleksić, A.; Ranđelović, M.; Ranđelović, D. Using Machine Learning in Predicting the Impact of Meteorological Parameters on Traffic Incidents. *Mathematics* **2023**, *11*, 479. https://doi.org/10.3390/math11020479

Academic Editors: Snezhana Gocheva-Ilieva, Atanas Ivanov and Hristina Kulina

Received: 16 December 2022
Revised: 5 January 2023
Accepted: 7 January 2023
Published: 16 January 2023

1. Introduction

The parameters affecting the occurrence of traffic incidents (TI) comprise three main groups, and they are as follows: human factors, vehicle and environment [1]. However, in [2], the authors divide the main factors into five groups, i.e., in addition to the listed three groups, they add roadway as well as occupants and other road users, and in [3], the authors consider more types of parameters without any groups; therefore, it could be concluded that there is no single taxonomy. In this paper, the authors consider the influence of the mentioned third group, environmental factors, and in it, just the meteorological subgroup which belongs to a wider subgroup of atmospheric parameters from the environment factors group (Dastoorpoor et al. [4]). The prediction of the impact of atmospheric parameters on TI is an important task for solving one global, serious problem because they cause not only human losses but also economic damages. By 2030, TIs are predicted to become the sixth leading cause of death, overtaking cancer [5], i.e., the seventh leading cause of death, and overtaking HIV/AIDS [6] worldwide. TIs also have an economic importance because they cause 3% of the gross domestic product yearly loss globally and roughly double that in lower-middle-income countries [6].

Having in mind the above-mentioned data on the significantly expressed negative consequences of the occurrence of TI on human lives and the economy, it is obvious that the previously mentioned prediction of the influence of various (including meteorological), factors is one important task in preventing their occurrences. This process of predicting the impact of different factors on the occurrence of a traffic accident has two main tasks: firstly, to help citizens themselves reduce the possibility that they will have any incidents in traffic, and, secondly, to help traffic police increase their control over known locations in specific weather conditions and, in this way, reduce the number of incidents. In this way, with the realization of those two main tasks, using the mentioned prediction, consequently, can reduce human casualties as well as economic damage. As we already mentioned, the subject of this paper is the prediction of the impact of meteorological factors as a subgroup of the group of atmospheric parameters and the wider group of environmental parameters. All those parameters included and others, such as sociological, geographical and so on, are of a different type and can be viewed in different ways. Therefore, for example, Chan et al. in [7] observe those parameters in groups of meteorological variables (temperature, pressure, humidity, wind speed, etc.), pollutant variables (PM, CO, O_3, SO_2, etc.), auxiliary variables (geographical, time, sociological, economic, relation to the type of road, etc.). Jalilian et al. in [8] consider each factor individually without their grouping. It is very important to remark that many of these groups of factors are considered as variables with different values through time historically which enables later learning of knowledge from them. The authors deal, in this paper, only with the first group of meteorological factors, from all the mentioned groups, and their impact on traffic accidents in a day. Therefore, the authors suggest that, in addition to the available data in real life from competent institutions, there are also large amounts of historical data collected in those institutions for the purpose of gaining knowledge using machine learning (ML) to predict the impact of the meteorological factors on the occurrence of TI.

Furthermore, in the paper, the authors propose an ensemble method of aggregation to solve the task of prediction. For this purpose, they used one aggregation of the mentioned two approaches of using historical and real-time data into a methodology that can be effectively implemented in a multi-agent system using modern intelligent technology.

For the evaluation of the impact of these factors on TI, we can find in the literature several classic statistical methods, and the most used among these is regression analysis, followed by factor and discriminant analysis and, on the other hand, some algorithms of data mining and artificial intelligence—between which, the most used are artificial neural networks and different algorithms of classification. Practically, this process means that the choice of the subset from the set of parameters must lead to the problem of the feature selection before creating a prediction [9]. Having in mind these facts, the authors set out to provide the report on one research method as the main objective of this manuscript, and the advantage of aggregation in the prediction model for determining the impact of the meteorological factors on TI in two methods will be discussed. These two methods that the authors proposed are the most used methods from the previously mentioned two groups, both in one ensemble ML prediction model: from the group of statistical methods, binary regression and from the group of ML methods, classification with feature selection. Moreover, as an obligatory part of this research was considering the realization of a developed ensemble model as one multi-agent system (MAS) in a global case, concrete in this paper is a two-agent system in which agent 1 draws knowledge through ML from historically available data, and then agent 2 deals with those same parameters, but in real time. Such two-agent architecture enables decision making using the algorithm which could be a decision matrix from the group of decision makers, and this will be proposed in the paper in the section which deals with the technical solution of the implementation of the proposed MAS including one emergent intelligence technique which enables the integration of MAS into a collaborative whole precisely based on that algorithm. Having in mind the complexity of the considered problem and the already-mentioned fact that the impact of meteorological factors on TI is only one small part of all the groups of factors—such as the presence of human factors, vehicle factors, other environmental parameters from different particles in the atmosphere including air pollution, road factors, geographical factors as well as factors of economic development and so on—it is an obvious need that this model implementation with one MAS must enable its permanent, continuous upgrading. Such a solution, based on the approach of using MAS in the proposed form, the authors could not find in the literature.

In this paper, for the purpose of evaluating the proposed model, the authors used one case study which observes daily TI data for the city of Niš in the Republic of Serbia in the period from 1999–2009 and data for different meteorological factors for this period for the same city. This study determines individual influence of each of considered meteorological factor on a happening of TIs using for that the model of aggregation different classification algorithms. It is based on an algorithm which was previously pre-processed using different methods of feature selection from ML and binary regression analysis from the group of traditional statistics methodologies in one ensemble method of ML. In this way, the conditions for implementation are ensured in the already-described two-agent system for early warning of interested parties, before everyone else, all ordinary citizens and traffic police, including and using today's most popular social media platforms as can be found in the paper of Lu et al. [10]

Description of influence of different meteorological conditions on TI can be found in papers that use the application of different forms of regression models, from linear and binary regression, than general linearized model to the combination of artificial intelligence and regression and different autoregressive methods for that purpose. This type of statistical models is also often used for the predicting and impact of different mentioned groups as, for example, from an environmental group that could be a location, type of road, date and time and so on, and some individual factors from these groups and their combinations. The global review of possibilities and characteristics of different types of regression methods could be found in Trencevski et al. [11] and Gupta et al. [12]. Too many studies address the impacts of different meteorological parameters on traffic safety [13]. In one of them, a meta-analysis of 34 studies which deal with the effect of precipitation is given and, as a result, gave an average increase in traffic accidents of 71% and 84%, in case of rain and snowfall, respectively [14]. However, in [15], authors considered terms of crash severity and concluded that there is a significant reduction under rainy conditions compared to fine weather. Additionally, the effect of precipitation on traffic accidents is considered on Finnish motorways and it is concluded it could be different for different types of accidents, so that the relative risk for single accidents in relation with multiple accidents in case of snow is 3.37/1.98 [16]. In the paper [17] we find one investigation on the influence of 17 meteorological factors on the number of crashes in the Netherlands during 2002. The impact of a combination of the meteorological factors of temperature and precipitation is given in [18]. Study [19] investigates the impact of weather elements and extreme snow or rain weather changes on seven crash types using five years of data collected for the City of Edmonton in Canada. In [20], authors deal with different vehicle types, from high-sided trucks and buses to vans that are the most affected by strong wind; also, we can find in literature that in general, greater wind speeds increase the severity of traffic accidents caused by single trucks [21].

The effect of the sun glare on traffic accidents is the subject of a small number of studies, but authors of the paper [22] deal with this problem using data from signalized crossroads in the city of Tucson, USA.

They concluded that traffic accidents occur more frequently during glares from the rear-end and sideways and that a sun glare has no effect on the crash severity. However, in paper [23] we can find that traffic accidents in Japan indicate that the sun glare has a strong impact on pedestrian traffic accidents, crashes at crossroads, and bicycle crashes, while there is no indication that the impact of sun glare increases with vehicle speed [23].

In [24], authors deal with determining the impact of snowfall on TI. The different studies mentioned are focused on the impacts of individual or a group of meteorological factors on specific traffic accident types, but these studies could differ with relation to region, time period and methodology, and because of that, they are difficult for comparing the results.

In [25], the study in which correlation and linear regression analysis were conducted to estimate the influence of meteorological factors on road traffic injuries stratified by severity is presented. The study Khan et al. [26] shows that the occurrence of traffic accidents in hazardous weather conditions of wind, rainfall, snowfall and fog broadly follows the patterns for those weather parameters. A paper which deals with weather impacts on various types of road crashes: a quantitative analysis using Generalized Additive Model (GAM) method we can find in [27], but the paper [28] considers the same problem using the combined backward propagation-artificial neural network model (BP–ANN) regression model. In [29] one integer autoregressive model for prediction with four traffic safety categories: vehicle accidents, vehicle fatalities, pedestrian accidents and pedestrian fatalities in Athens was proposed. In [30], we can find the application of one autoregressive integrated moving average (ARIMA) model for determining the impact of weather factors on TI in France and comparing the general linearized model and ARIMA in [31] in the case of considering this problem in France, Greece, and the Netherlands. In [10], we can find the use of the regression model in one modern, conceptualized, complex system for prediction of influence of different whether factors on TI in China with help of data obtained from modern social media, combining these with physically sensed data and also with the help of regression methodology.

On the other hand, using ML algorithms for determining the importance of the individual impact of each of the many meteorological factors on traffic accidents as well as in determining suitable prediction models to solve this problem is today the other frequently used methodology. We can find more and more papers in the existing literature that use these two groups of methods to solve the posed problem discussed in this paper. These methods belong to different individual types of ML: classification, clustering, neural networks, and other standard ML methods; to the aggregations of these standard ML methods mutually or with classic statistical methods as for example regression, and in the end, the newest different ensemble methods is where the solution proposed by the authors belongs.

Thus, in [32], Zheng et al. consider different groups of atmospheric factors: meteorological variables (temperature, pressure, humidity, wind speed, etc.), pollutant variables (PM, CO, O3, SO2, etc.), auxiliary variables (geographical, time, sociological, related to the type of road, etc.), and we could practically find one comprehensive review and taxonomy of different types of ML methods which could be applied in atmospheric environment studies on TI for what is compatible with content presented in the already-cited reference [11], which particularly processed regression models. A similar problem from the standpoint of sensor using in this purpose is presented in [33], but in [34], a review of urban traffic flow prediction techniques with special focus on the literature review is presented. In [35–38], we can also find a similar comprehensive review of different artificial neural network (ANN) methods used for the same purpose. Using ML models based on ANN is a highly effective way to simulate the atmospheric environment, which is very important in the case of time-limited applications [39], and in this group, deep learning has received special research attention [40–42]. Different models of ANN are available, for example, recurrent ANN [43]. Additionally, the ANN predictions of meteorological impact factors on traffic accidents are available for geographically diverse areas across the globe: Switzerland [44], Bangladesh [45], Jordan [46], Iran [47], the USA [48], Australia [49], and are generally considered for developing countries [50].

Moreover, in the literature, we can find an aggregation of the most applicable ML ANN method with other ML methods: for example, with genetic algorithms in [51], with cluster algorithms in [52], using a logit model and factor analysis [53], with the random forest [54,55], and with the second most used ML the decision tree from a classification group of methods in the case study for data from Nigeria in [56]. Additionally, it is used in the case study of Nord England using the UK stats19 data set [57], and in the case study for data from the USA [58]. We can find the application of aggregated different classification methods in papers such as J48,ID3, classification and regression tree (CART), decision tree and Naive Bayes in [59]; and CHAID, J48 decision tree and Naive Bayes in [60].

In the already-cited reference [32], it is remarked that increasing the model type of ML models for prediction of the impact of atmospheric parameters on different fields of human life were ensemble models; this is the case in the field of traffic accident prediction as well. In [61], one systematic review of ML methods is given where ensemble methods, as most modern types, are considered in separate sections and in [62–65] we could find descriptions of different ensemble methods which deal with ensemble learning for predicting traffic accidents affected by meteorological parameters. Having in mind the model which authors will propose in this paper, it is especially important to remark that the ensemble methods based on aggregation classification and regression tree in one ensemble algorithm for the purpose to solve the considered problem of prediction as an impact of meteorological factors on traffic accidents are very rarely in the literature, but they could be found, as, for example, in [66].

Particularly, there is a trend of developing forecast models to predict future states in all types of traffic at the beginning of the 21st century. Different taxonomies of those models can be found, for example the division into parametric and non-parametric models depending on the distribution of input values [67], then a division into deterministic models in which the model outputs are fully determined by the input factors values, and probabilistic, i.e., stochastic models [68]. ARIMA is one of the most-used parametric methodologies with its different subtypes: for example, multivariate spatial-temporal autoregressive (MSTAR) model [69], which at the same time belongs into probabilistic methods according to the second mentioned division while time-series analysis and trends belong to deterministic methodology, for example [70].

Bayesian deep learning approach and convolutional neural networks are increasingly present in recently published literature to predict the influence of uncertain environmental parameters, including the meteorological factors considered in the paper on the TI [71]. It is especially expressed in the subfield of so-called short-term predictions of trajectories in different types of public traffic, for example, in aircraft trajectory predicting [71,72] as well as in the prediction of road traffic in general and autonomous driving [73]. Because the authors set as the main goal of this paper that it should give an answer to the two research questions:

(1) Is it possible to construct one ML ensemble method which aggregates ML classification methods and methods of future selection for attribute selection with the binary regression method and which demonstrated better characteristics of prediction than each individually of included in ensemble method?

(2) Can this new ensemble method be implemented in one multi-agent supported technological system?

To give an answer on these two research questions and confirm those two hypotheses, the authors used evaluation of the proposed ensemble model on the case study for the city of Niš, Republic of Serbia, using its meteorological and data for TI for ten years in the beginning of 21 century.

In order to realize the set goal and present that the proposed ensemble model is an effective solution for the considered problem of predicting traffic accidents, the authors realized the rest of this manuscript in the following way: after this first section, the Introduction, the second section follows: Materials and Methods, where the authors gave a description of the material used and a comprehensive review of applied methodologies; then comes the third section—Results and Findings, in which the results of applying the proposed model in the case study are described; in the next section—Technological Implementation of Proposed Ensemble Model, the authors described the implementation of the proposed model as one technical solution and at the end there is a fifth section—Conclusions, in which contributions of this research are given and future work on efficiently solving the problem discussed in this paper is proposed.

2. Materials and Methods

Having in mind the present development of improved solutions for the prediction of the impact of atmospheric parameters on the occurrence of traffic accidents which are computer based and often using the ML techniques existing today, it could be said that its group of mentioned ensemble methods is a trend in solving such a complex problem. Implementation of such solutions using multi-agent solutions follows this trend directly. However, in the literature, there is still not a large enough number of references which integrate more methods of ML, different or of the same type in the ensemble models of prediction, so additional research of such methods is needed; that was the motivation for the authors to develop one such novel method.

In this paper, the authors described not only the new proposed model but also its implementation as one of agents in one multi-agent system of emergent intelligence technique (EIT) for the purpose of one citizens warning system. For the evaluation of the model proposed as such, the authors conduct the material from case study for the City of Niš in the Republic of Serbia which is presented in this paper. In it, the analyzed material is classified so that all data in the period considered is divided into two classes: positive when the daily number of traffic accidents is bigger than the average value for this period, and negative in all other cases. This way, it could be said that the positive class includes the instances when conditions significant enough for the occurrence of traffic accidents on that day are present in the atmosphere.

2.1. Methods

The problem of predicting the impact of meteorological parameters on TI that is the subject of consideration in this paper belongs to the group of classification problems for whose solving two main groups of methods are available: the classic statistical methods of logical regression and ML based classification.

With the logistic regression model, we describe the relationship between predictors that can be continuous, binary, categorical and categorically dependent variables. For example, the dependent variable can be binary-based on some predictors; we predict whether something will happen or not. We actually estimate the probabilities of belonging to each category for a given set of predictors. Depending on the type of dependent variable, we have:

Binary logistic regression—the dependent variable is binary (for example: answer true or false on the questions);

Nominal logistic regression—the dependent variable has three or more categories that cannot be compared in value (for example, colors (white, black, red, green, blue, etc.);

Ordinal logistic regression—the dependent variable has three or more categories that can naturally be compared, but the ranking does not necessarily mean that the "distances" between them are equal (for example: health status (stable, serious or critical).

Logistic regression is used when the dependent variable takes only a finite set of values.

We wonder if we can still use linear regression in classification problems. In the case of binary logistic regression, we consider the dependent variable to be a Bernoulli random variable in notation Y as it is shown in Equation (1). Then, we have two categories that we code with: 0 for failure and 1 for success.

$$Y = \begin{matrix} 0 - \text{failure} \\ 1 - \text{success} \end{matrix} \tag{1}$$

Therefore, the dependent variable is a Bernoulli and not some continuous random variable, meaning that errors cannot be normal. Additionally, if we did run a linear regression, we would get some meaningless fitted values—values outside the set {0,1}. In the case of a binary dependent variable, one way to use linear regression for a classification problem can be as follows: for a given set of predictors, if the fitted value by linear regression is greater than 0.5, then we classify that observation as a success, and if not, a failure. This method is then equivalent to the linear discriminant analysis, which we will discuss later.

With this method, we only get a classification for some observation: "success" or "failure". If the fitted values by linear regression are close to 0.5, then we are less confident in our decision. We will also say that, if the dependent variable takes more than two values, then linear regression cannot be used as we described a moment ago, but the linear discriminant analysis must be used instead.

ML is one comprehensive discipline based on statistical analysis and artificial intelligence and it is used for learning of knowledge, i.e., concrete learning of rules, concepts, models, etc. which should be understood and accepted by the people. In the ML process, it is obligatory to have some kind of evaluation of the validity of the knowledge learned in this process, i.e., some kind evaluation of obtained rules, concepts, or models. For this purpose, two evaluation methods are available based on the process in which the available set is divided in different ways into a learning set and a test set:

(1)   Evaluation using the test suite-holdout method, whose technique divides the original data set into two disjoint subsets, for training and for classifier testing (e.g., in a ratio of 70:30). Then, the model of classification is obtained on the basis of training data, after which the performance model on test data is evaluated. Thus, the accuracy of the classification can be assessed based on the test data;

(2)   K-fold cross-validation is a classification model evaluation technique that is a better choice compared to evaluation using a test set. In general, it is performed by dividing the original data set into k equal subsets (layers). One subset is used for testing and all others for training. The resulting model makes predictions on the current layer. This procedure is repeated for k iterations using each subset exactly once for testing.

One of the most important measures of success of learned knowledge is named predictive accuracy. It is the ratio of the total number of successful classifications to the total number of classifications. For measuring a success of learned knowledge are also often used and precision, recall, F1 measure and receiver operating characteristic curve which will be described in the continuation of this chapter. The basic goal of any predicting process is to obtain one model based on the exact numerically determined combination of independent variables for the dependent variable. It is important to remark that in this process, the choice of variables that will be included in this process from a given data set affects the accuracy and other measures of the obtained prediction model, so because of that, it is necessary to use different techniques for a selection of variables in the data preparation phase, i.e., to apply some method of the so-called feature selection procedure.

One ensemble model of ML is proposed in this paper for predicting the potential risk of traffic accidents caused from meteorological, i.e., atmospheric parameters. As we already mentioned, the proposed method is one aggregation that optimizes more different classification algorithms using attribute reduction and binary regression. Implementation of this algorithm could represent one agent in considered and described two-agent system in this paper in which other agent realizes alarm calculations accordingly to value of meteorological parameters in real time. This two-agent system could be proposed in general as a wider and more complex multi-agent system which could be included and other types of environment parameters beside meteorological and which could be based on different possible forms of emergent intelligence for collective decision making. Such an implementation of an EIT solution as an emergency software tool could be realized as a web application accessible to all stakeholders of human society, starting with citizens and other interested parties.

The subchapters which follow in this paper are devoted for a brief description of these methodologies because the proposed ensemble method aggregates the method of logical regression with ML methods of classification methods and feature selection.

2.1.1. Classification Methodology

Classification algorithms belong to the supervised ML technique and can be used for the task of predictive modelling. Using the classification methodology for this purpose implies the existence of labeled instances in each of more than one class (attribute) of objects so that it predicts the value of obligatory categorical type of class (attribute) using the values of the remaining predicting attributes [74].

The selection of the appropriate classification algorithm for the concrete considered application is not only the beginning but is also the most important place in the process of ML from big data. For solving the problem which is considered in this paper, in their proposed ensemble model, the authors use a classification which makes the classification into two classes, positive and negative that correspond to true or false in both of them. All possible outcomes of prediction are presented in the confusion matrix shown in Table 1.

Table 1. The confusion matrix for the two-class classifier.

		Predicted Label	
		Positive	**Negative**
Actual label	Positive	TP(true positive)	FN(false negative)
	Negative	FP(false positive)	TN(true negative)

The number of members in the considered set shown in Table 1 is the sum of positive and negative cases and will be classified in notation N, i.e., TP + FN + FP + TN = N. All results that are presented in Table 1, for a considered case of two-class classifier, can be given for the most important measures of classification accuracy, precision, recall and F1 measure with the following formulas:

$$\text{Accuracy} = (TP + TN)/N \tag{2}$$

$$\text{Precision} = TP/(TP + FP) \tag{3}$$

$$\text{Recall} = TP/(TP + FN) \tag{4}$$

$$\text{F1measure} = 2 \cdot \frac{\text{precision} \cdot \text{recall}}{\text{precision} + \text{recall}} \tag{5}$$

In the evaluation of the prediction performance of any classifier, the Receiver Operating Characteristic (ROC) curve is also often used; it represents the value of false positive on the OX axis, and on the OY axis, the value of true positive cases [75,76], so that, for example, point (0, 1) represents perfect prediction, where all the samples are classified correctly, and point (1, 0) represents a classification that classifies all samples incorrectly. Therefore, it is important to known that the output in ROC space produced from naive neural networks or Bayes classifier is a probability which is a score-numeric value and discrete classifiers produce only a single point, but in both cases they represent the degree to which a particular instance belongs to a certain class [77]. The area under the curve (AUC) is the most-used measure of diagnostic accuracy of the model and AUC values greater than 70% have good classification processes.

Practically, classification is the task of ML, but can also be the task of data mining, which performs separation of instances of a considered data set based on the value of the input variables into one of pre-determined ones class of the output variable [78].

The literature review shows that the most commonly applied classifiers include Neural networks, Bayes networks, Decision Trees, K–nearest neighbor, etc. [79].

For the proposed model, the authors used some of the most-used classification algorithms which belong to five different groups of types as it is grouped in one of the most used software for this purpose, Weka [80], i.e., Bayes, meta, trees, rules and functions. Because of that, below this subchapter is a short description of one selected algorithm from each of the mentioned Weka classifiers groups.

The Naive Bayes classifier [81,82] from the Bayes group of Weka belonging to the group of oldest classification algorithms and generates a prediction model using Bayes' theorem. It is called "naive", because of that simplifies the problem of classification by two important assumptions, first that the attributes used in the prediction procedure are conditionally independent and with a known classification, and second, that there are no hidden attributes that could affect the prediction. In this way, these assumptions allow an efficient classification ML algorithm. For conditionally independent attributes $A_1, \ldots, A_k$ probability for class attribute A is calculated using the following rule:

$$P(A_1, \ldots, A_k | A) = \prod_{i=1}^{k} (A_i | A) \qquad (6)$$

The main advantages of the Naive Bayes classifier in relation to other classifiers are primarily efficiency, simplicty, and convenience for small data sets of data.

The LogitBoost classifier from the meta group of Weka is widely applied in practice because it has very good characteristics, primarily thanks to the boosting algorithm [83]. This classifier uses the principle that finding multiple simple rules could be more efficient than finding a single precise rule, and because of that, usually complex prediction rules. It represents, essentially, one general method for improving the accuracy of ML algorithms.

Decision trees [84] from the trees group of Weka is the most used classification technique, because it includes more possible ways of its construction that are very convenient for interpretation. The trees can be used with all kinds of classification attributes (categorical or numerical). ID3 [85] and C4.5 [86] are the most-used algorithms from this group of classifiers and from the trees in the Weka tool, one of the most known is tree J48.

The PART classifier from the rules group of Weka builds a partial decision tree so that it uses the C4.5 decision tree classifier in each of its iterations and constructs the best sheet and a suitable rule in the tree. This classifier does not belong to the group of oft-used classifiers, but it is useful in binary classification, as applied in this paper.

SMO from the functions group of Weka refers to the specific efficient optimization algorithm used inside the support vector machines (SVM) algorithm implementation. Practically, it solves the quadratic programming problem, which arises during the training of SVM on classification tasks defined on sparse sets of data. Additionally, it is not one of the oft-used classifiers, but it is used in this paper because it is appropriate for binary classification with numerical and binary types of attributes, which is the case in this paper.

2.1.2. Logistic Regression

In ML, in many cases, probabilistic classifiers that return not only the label for the most likely class, but also the probability of that class, are needed. Such a so-called probabilistic classifier is well-calibrated if the predicted probability matches the true probability of the event which is of interest and can be checked using a calibration plot, which demonstrates how good a classifier is in a given set of data with known outcomes that is valid for the binary classifiers considered in this paper (in the case of multi-class classifiers, a separate calibration plot is needed for each of classes).

The authors used the idea of calibration, like many other authors did, as, for example, in [87], and as seen in [83], the univariate calibration using logistic regression for transforming classifier scores into probabilities of class membership for the two-class case.

The main goal of logistic regression is to obtain the best-fitting model for describing the relationship between the dichotomous characteristic of interest, which is a dependent variable (response or outcome variable) with a set of independent variables (predictor or explanatory variables).

Logistic regression generates the coefficients of a formula to predict a logit transformation of the characteristic of interest presence probability which can be notated as p (with determined standard error and significance level):

$$\text{logit}(p) = b_0 + b_1 X_1 + b_2 X_2 + \ldots + b_k X_k \qquad (7)$$

The logit transformation is defined as the logged odds:

$$\text{odds} = \frac{p}{1-p} = \frac{\text{probability of characteristics presence}}{\text{probability of characteristics absence}} \qquad (8)$$

and

$$\text{logit}(p) = \ln\left(\frac{p}{1-p}\right) \tag{9}$$

In ordinary regression, the choosing of parameters that minimize the sum of squared errors is present, while in logistic regression it chooses parameters that maximize the likelihood of observed sample values. The regression equation coefficients are the coefficients $b_0, b_1, b_2, \ldots b_k$. The logistic regression coefficients show increasing (when $b_i > 0$), and decreasing (when $b_i < 0$) in the predicted logged odds for the independent variables. In the case the independent variables X_a and X_b are dichotomous, then the impact of these on the dependent variable is simply determined by comparing their coefficients of regression b_a and b_b. By taking the exponent for both sides in the regression equation as it is shown above, the equation can be given as one of form of logistic regression:

$$\text{odds} = \frac{p}{1-p} = e^{b_0} \cdot e^{b_1 X_1} \cdot e^{b_2 X_2} \cdot e^{b_s X_s} \cdot \ldots \cdot e^{b_k X_k} \tag{10}$$

From the given formula, it is evident that when a variable Xi increases by 1 unit, and all other parameters remain unchanged, then the odds will increase by a parameter e^{b_i}.

$$e^{b_t(1+X_t)} - e^{b_t X_t} = e^{b_t X_t} = e^{b_t(1+X_t) - b_t X_t} = e^{b_t + b_t X_t - b_t X_t} = e^{b_t} \tag{11}$$

This factor e^{b_i} is the odds ratio (O.R.) for the independent variable X_i, and it gives the relative amount by which the odds of the outcome increase (O.R. greater than 1) or decrease (O.R. less than 1) when the value of the independent variable is increased by one unit.

Implementation of several methods for performing logistic regression can be found in statistical programs, of which IBM SPSS [88] is the most famous. This tool realizes three basic methods of binary regression and that is the enter method, stepwise method and hierarchical method. The enter method includes all the independent variables in the regression model together, stepwise methods include two categories of regression procedures-forward selection and backward elimination, and in the hierarchical method, the researcher themself determines the order of inclusion of independent variables in the model. Otherwise, all of the three methods are used to remove independent variables that are weakly correlated with the dependent variable. The authors use the standard enter method for the model proposed in this paper.

2.1.3. Future Selection Techniques

Classification methods of ML are sensitive from data dimensionality and it is showed evidently that application of dimensionality reduction enables them giving better results. Selecting a suitable subset before the application of these methods finds a set of attributes which together achieve the best result.

Algorithms for feature subset extraction perform a space search based on candidate evaluation [89]. The optimal subset is selected when the search is complete. Some of the existing evaluation measures that have been shown to be effective in removing irrelevant and redundant features include the consistency measure [90] and the correlation measure [91]. The consistency measure seeks to find the minimum number of features that consistently separate the class labels into a complete set. An inconsistency is defined for two instances that have different class labels for the same feature values.

- Future selection methods can be realized using three groups of methods [92]:
- Filter, where the most known are Relief, Infogain, Gainratio, and so on.
- Wrapper, among which the most well-known are BestFirst, RankSearch, GeneticSerch, and so on.

Embedded, which combine the qualities of the filter and wrapper methods and where, among others, ridge regression (as one technique for analyzing multiple regression data that suffer from multicollinearity) and different types of decision tree based algorithms as BoostedTrees, RandomForest, NBTree, and so on, belong.

One of the free-to-use software that has an option that performs feature selection, reducing the amount of included attributes by applying different type algorithms, is the already-mentioned software tool Weka [80]. Because of that, this software was used to evaluate the proposed model on a selected case study. Practically, this evaluation results in determining the importance of factors that influence the risk of a traffic accident as well as for determining one prediction model using techniques such as regression and/or classification for this tasks.

Because the first two groups of methods are used in model which authors proposed in this paper these are described in short hereinafter.

Filter-Ranker Methods

Filter models rely on the general characteristics of the data to estimate the exclusion features of the learning algorithm. For some data set D, the filter algorithm starts the search by initializing a subset S1 (the empty set, the full set, or a randomly selected subset) and searches the feature value space using a specific search strategy. Each generated subset S is evaluated against an independent measure and compared to the previous best. If it is found to be better than the previous best, it is considered the current best subset. The search continues until a previously defined stopping criterion is met. The output of the algorithm is the last best subset and that is the final result. By changing the search strategy and evaluation measure, different algorithms can be implemented within the filter model. The feature selection process often uses the entropy measure as one characterization of the purity of an arbitrary collection of examples, and considers a measure of the system's unpredictability.

The entropy of Y is:

$$H(Y) = -\sum_{y \subset Y} p(y) \cdot \log_2(p(y)) \tag{12}$$

At the same time, feature selection methods differ in how they treat the problems of irrelevant as well as redundant attributes [93].

For the proposed model, authors used the following five shortly described filter algorithms.

Having in mind that the entropy could be a criterion of impurity in a training set S, it is possible to define a measure reflecting additional information about each Attribute which is generated by Class, and that is the amount by which the entropy of Attribute decreases [94]. This measure is named the information gain and, in abbreviation, is notated as InfoGain and favors variables with more values.

InfoGain evaluates the worth of an Attribute according to Class using the following formula:

$$\text{InfoGain}(\text{Class}, \text{Attribute}) = H(\text{Class}) - H(\text{Class}|\text{Attribute}) \tag{13}$$

where H is the entropy of information. The information gained about an attribute after observing class is equal to the information gained using observation in the reverse direction.

The information gain ratio, noted as GainRatio, is one so-called non-symmetrical measure that was introduced in the theory of feature selection to compensate for the bias of the already-described measure InfoGain [95]. GainRatio is one modification of the InfoGain that reduces its bias on different attributes and it is given with the following formula:

$$\text{GainRatio} = \frac{\text{InfoGain}}{H(\text{Class})} \tag{14}$$

As it is given in Formula (13), when it is needed to predict some variable-Attribute, the InfoGain is normalized so that it is divided by the entropy of Class, and in vice versa. This normalization enables that the GainRatio values must be ever in the range [0, 1]. GainRatio = 1 means that the knowledge of Class completely predicts variable-Attribute, but GainRatio = 0 indicates that there is no relation between variable-Attribute and Class.

The GainRatio favors variables with fewer values. Thus, for example, the decision tree classification algorithms C4.5 [96] and ID3 [97] use the GainRatio criterion to select the attributes that should be at every node of the tree.

FilteredAttributeEval is a classifier class for running an arbitrary evaluator on data that has been passed through an arbitrary filter which are structured based exclusively on training data. This classifier executes nominal and binary classifications with nominal, string, relational, binary, unary, as well as missing attributes.

SymmetricalUncertAttributeEval is a classifier which evaluates the worth of an attribute by measuring the symmetrical uncertainty with respect to the class.

$$\mathrm{SymmU(Class, Attribute)} = 2 * (\mathrm{H(Class)} - \mathrm{H(Class|Attribute)})/\mathrm{H(Class)} + \mathrm{H(Attribute)} \quad (15)$$

This classifier executes nominal, binary, and classification of missing classes with nominal, binary, unary, as well as attributes.

ChiSquaredAttributeEaval is a classifier based on the chi-square test used to test the independence of two events so that, for the given data of two variables, we can obtain the observed count O and the expected count E and, using the Chi-Square measure, how expected count E and observed count O deviate from each other, which is shown in Equation (16):

$$\chi_c^2 = \sum_i \frac{(O_i - E_i)^2}{E_i} \quad (16)$$

In Equation (16) c is degrees of freedom, O_i is observed value and E_i is expected value whereby degrees of freedom refer to the total number of observations reduced by the number of independent constraints which are imposed with the observations, and having in mind definitions that the random variable follows chi-square distribution only if it can be written in the form of the sum of squared standard normal variables like it is given in Equation (17):

$$\chi^2 = \sum_i Z_i{}^2 \quad (17)$$

where Z_i are standard normal variables.

Degrees of freedom refer to the maximum number of logically independent values, which have the freedom to vary. In simple words, it can be defined as the total number of observations minus the number of independent constraints imposed on the observations.

Wrapper Methods

In the case of these learning methods, certain modeling algorithms are used in order to evaluate subsets of attributes in relation to their classification or predictive power. It is a computationally very demanding procedure due to the frequent execution of the ML algorithm. It is practically necessary to evaluate the performance of the corresponding model for each subset of attributes, and the total number of subsets grows exponentially when the number of attributes increases. For these reasons, different search techniques are used from the group of greedy techniques, which represent an approach to solving the problem based on the best selected option available at that moment [98].

According to some of the classification frameworks [99], wrapper methods can be broadly classified according to the method of searching a set of attributes into deterministic and randomized wrapper methods. The first subgroup of wrapper methods—deterministic wrapper methods, use a complete strategy of attribute space search in one sub-subgroup and certainly give the best results with a very demanding time and sequential strategies or heuristic search in the second subgroup of deterministic wrapper methods. Another subgroup of wrapper methods consists of randomized methods, which in turn rely on stochastic search approaches. The authors chose and used five methods from this wrapper group of methods for the proposed model in this paper which are implemented in the Weka software, and those are: from the deterministic subgroup and sub-subgroup of complete strategy search the ExhaustiveSearch and sub-subgroup sequential strategies or heuristic search—three of them—Best First, LinearForvardSelection, and GreediStepvise, and from another subgroup of wrapper methods named stohastic-GeneticSearch, and all of them with CfsSubsetEval classifier.

I.   Algorithms from the group of deterministic search wrapper methods

    I.1   The first subgroup are those with full search, and these algorithms usually showed the good results.

ExhaustiveSearch is the most well-known algorithm from this subgroup; it conducts an exhaustive search through the complete space of attribute subsets starting from the empty set of attributes. On end reports the best subset found.

    I.2   The second subgroup of deterministic search wrapper methods is the group of algorithms with sequential search techniques which are the most-used wrapper algorithms, and because of that, the authors use primarily different algorithms from this subgroup in the proposed algorithm.

The BestFirst algorithm as a basic algorithm from this subgroup searches the space of attribute subsets by greedy hill climbing augmented with a backtracking facility. This algorithm may start with the empty set of attributes and search forward, or start with the full set, i.e., all attributes and search backward, or start at any point between those, and search in both directions.

The LinearForwardSelection algorithm is one Extension of the BestFirst algorithm. Takes a restricted number of k attributes into account. Fixed-set selects a fixed number k of attributes, whereas k is increased in each step when fixed-width is selected. The search uses the initial ordering to select the top k attributes, but can also use the ranking. The search direction is forward or floating forward selection with using optional backward search steps.

The Subset Size Forward Selection algorithm is one Extension of the LinearForwardSelection algorithm.

GreedyStepwise performs a greedy search in both directions, forward or backward, through the space of attribute subsets. It may start with no or all attributes, or from an arbitrary point in the space. It stops in the moment when the addition, i.e., deletion of any remaining attributes results in a decrease in evaluation. It can also produce a ranked list of attributes by traversing the space from one side to the other and recording the order that attributes are selected in.

II.   Algorithms from the group of stochastic search of wrapper methods

The most-known from this group is the genetic algorithm which the authors use in the proposed algorithm as representative of that subgroup of methods. This algorithm belongs to a wider class of so-called population methods, i.e., evolutionary algorithms that use stochastic optimization. Genetic algorithms only select the initial population at random; in later steps, the selection procedure is strictly defined. The steps of the genetic algorithm are iteratively repeated until the desired target is reached value, i.e., the stopping criterion of the algorithm.

As we already mentioned, all of the wrapper methods used are applied in the proposed model with using the CfsSubsetEval classifiers (Correlation-based feature selection).This method ranks and selects the attribute sets with biases towards to subsets containing features that are highly correlated with the class, and at the same time, they are uncorrelated with each other. Measuring the significance of attributes in this method is on the basis of predictive ability of attributes and their redundancy degree.

2.1.4. Ensemble Method for Prediction of Meteorological Impact on Occurrence of TI

It is known that, in ML, methods that use several individual aggregated algorithms to achieve better results than those that would be achieved with any of the algorithms individually aggregated into it are called ensemble ML methods. To solve the predictive problem which is considered in this paper, the authors proposed an ensemble algorithm showen with the procedure, which is given in Algorithm 1 and showed as the block schema in Figure 1.

Algorithm 1: Obtaining significant predictors of TI caused by atmospheric factors

---

1. Perform a logistic-binary regression Enter method for a model in which n atmospheric factors are predictors and the dependent variable is the number of TI logically determined by a threshold, which could be a value greater than 150% of the average value of daily TI for considered case study, and has a nominal value 1 in that case and 0 in all others. We start the algorithm in first cycle i = 1 with referent value which represents the number of attributes which is in start step number noted as n1–in concrete case study n1 = 27. In the Enter method of binary regression used, all of the predictors will be included in the prediction; only in the possible presence of impermissible collinearity of certain predictors, they will be excluded from the model. After that, using the Cox and Snell R Square and Nagelkerke R Square test, the algorithm will determine the value of the percentage of the variance that is explained, i.e., the connection between the tested factors and the dependent variable, and using the Hosmer and Lemeshow tests, the algorithm will determine its goodness-of-fit, i.e., the adaptation of the model to the given data, i.e., calibration which will evaluate the goodness of the proposed ensemble model in this and in the later steps, including the most important last step of the proposed algorithm in order to use the AUC to determine the quality measure of the classification binary regression analysis model.
2. Apply a set of at least five methods of classification which belong to different types of classification (for example, how it is already mentioned in Weka software, so any five, each from different types—Decision trees, Bayes, Meta, Rules, Functions, MI, etc.) and find two classification algorithms from this set that has the highest value of AUC among other algorithms used (also other parameters such as precision, recall, and F-measure which are with good values). That classification algorithm will be used in the step that follows in which attribute selection is carried out to select the best of several used attribute selection algorithms from two different types of groups.
The values of Hosmer and Lemeshow test and even more significant AUC values that determine the threshold of whether the desired level of goodness of the model has been reached—take the values determined in steps 1, i.e., step 2 of this algorithm, respectively.
3. Using five algorithms from each of both groups of feature selection methods is with the basic aim to use in this ensemble classification algorithms that are good and eliminate bad characteristics:
3.1. Using at least five of the mentioned attribute selection algorithms from both the wrapper and the filter groups more broadly explained in Section 2.1.3. of this paper, perform attribute classification in one class of the two possible classes of instances which are defined in step 1 of this algorithm and according to the criterion of whether the value of this attribute exceeds or does not exceed the daily TI threshold.
3.1.1. Classifiers for filter attribute selection could be any five different algorithms: for example Information-Gain Attribute evaluation, Gain-Ratio Attribute evaluation, Symmetrical Uncertainty Attribute evaluation, Chi-Square Attribute evaluation, Filtered Attribute Eval, Relief Attribute, Principal Components, etc. The authors used the first five of these in this paper. Those chosen algorithms are used to determine the feature subset of attribute $A' = \{\ldots, a_{i-1}, ai\}$ and their ranks from the starting set $A = \{a_1, a_2, \ldots, a_n\}, i \leq n$. It is necessary to remark that n is the starting number of attributes in such a way that the decision to exclude a particular attribute is made by the majority of exclusion decisions made individually by each of the algorithms.
3.1.2. Classifiers for wrapper attribute selection can be any five from this group of algorithms: for example Best First, Linear Forward Selection, Genetic Search, Greedy Stepwise, Subset Size Forward Selection, etc. The authors used the first five of these in this paper. Those chosen algorithms are used to compute a subset $A'' = \{\ldots, a_{j-1}, a_j\}$ from the starting set $A = \{a_1, a_2, \ldots, a_n\}, j \leq n$. It is necessary to remark that n is the starting number of attributes in such a way that the decision to exclude a particular attribute is made by the majority of exclusion decisions made individually by each of the algorithms.
3.2. Determine a subset $A''' = A' \cap A'' = \{\ldots, a_{m-1}, a_m\}$ from the starting set $A = \{a_1, a_2, \ldots, a_n\}$, $m \leq i, j, n$, where n is the starting number of attributes and i and j values determined in the previous steps of the algorithm 3.1.1 and 3.1.2

Algorithm 1: *Cont.*

We could have, at the end of this step, not only a different number of selected attributes using both groups of attribute selection algorithms considered as it is given in 3.1.1. and 3.1.2., possibly different notated attributes as well, and that is why we use the intersection operation for these obtained subsets A′ and A″, which determines only common attributes as those that will be removed from the initial, i.e., in later cycles from the observed set A.

3.3. If m < n exists, which is determined in the previous step 3.2., and Hosmer and Lemeshow test determined the goodness of the algorithm as positive, the algorithm continues with the next step 4 using set A‴ = { . . . , a_{m-1}, a_m} attributes; otherwise, finish with the prediction which determined the existing number of parameters which was in the observed set.

4. Choose one from five filter classifiers with the smallest number of attributes l_i which has the highest AUC value using for that already determined two classification algorithms in step 2 of this algorithm.

5. Perform the binary regression Enter method again now with a smaller number of attributes li selected in step 4 of this algorithm, and if the values of Hosmer and Lemeshow tests are worse than those obtained in the previous test executed in step 3 of this algorithm or the obtained number of attributes satisfied value preset in advance, the procedure is finished; otherwise the procedure continues cyclically with step 3 of this algorithm with new set referent value. Preset value of the number of selected attributes on the specific need for each case separately and for the case study in this paper, the authors chose it at less than 15% from the starting number of attributes.

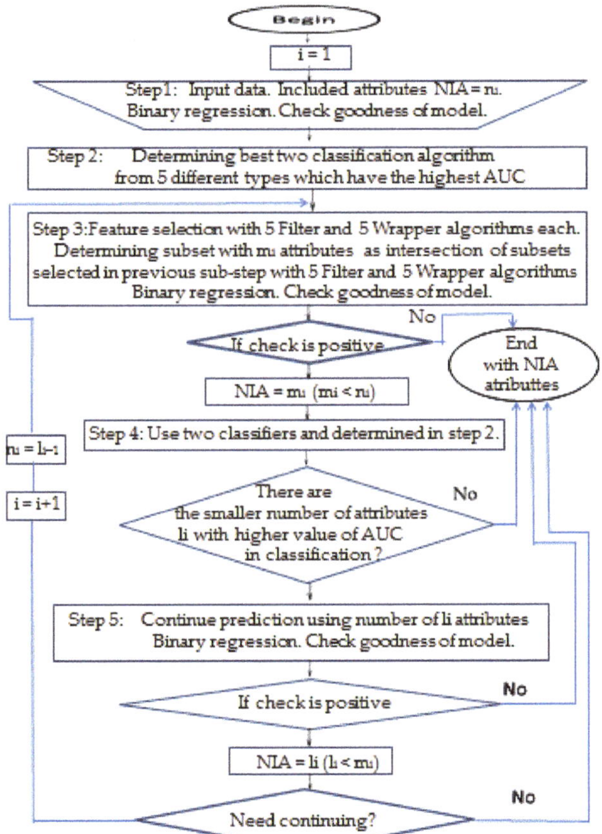

Figure 1. Block schema for the procedure which is described with Algorithm 1.

2.2. Materials

The weight coefficients determination applied in this study used the data covering the period from 1992 up to 2009 of atmospheric factors and daily traffic accidents related to the City of Niš, Republic of Serbia. The atmospheric data used in this case study is for twenty-seven variables. Data used in this study was derived from several sources. Atmospheric data was obtained from the Republic Hydro-meteorological Institute for 1992–2009, and the database of the number of daily traffic accidents for the same period was supplied by the Ministry of Interior of the Republic of Serbia. All of this data is given as a Supplementary File in which the dependent variable is given in the excel table as twenty eighths, which is shown in the table—Table 2. In order to conduct the case study more efficiently, the dates were organized on daily level in the period of eighteen years which the authors consider in the case study of this paper.

Table 2. Atmospheric parameters used in case study.

Variable	Parameter
1-V1	Air pressure at 7 o'clock (mbar)
2-V2	Air pressure at 14 o'clock (mbar)
3-V3	Air pressure at 21 o'clock (mbar)
4-V4	Mean daily air pressure (mbar)
5-V5	Maximum daily temperature (°C)
6-V6	Minimum daily temperature (°C)
7-V7	Daily temperature amplitude (°C)
8-V8	Temperature at 7 o'clock (°C)
9-V9	Temperature at 14 o'clock (°C)
10-V10	Temperature at 21 o'clock (°C)
11-V11	Mean daily temperature (°C)
12-V12	Relative humidity at 7 o'clock -percent
13-V13	Relative humidity at 14 o'clock -percent
14-V14	Relative humidity at 21 o'clock -percent
15-V15	Mean daily relative humidity-percent
16-V16	Water vapour saturation at 7 o'clock (mbar)
17-V17	Water vapour saturation at 14 o'clock (mbar)
18-V18	Water vapour saturation at 21 o'clock (mbar)
19-V19	Mean daily water vapour saturation (mbar)
20-V20	Mean daily wind speed (m/sec)
21-V21	Insolation (h)
22-V22	Cloudiness at 7 o'clock (in tenths of the sky)
23-V23	Cloudiness at 14 o'clock (in tenths of the sky)
24-V24	Cloudiness at 21 o'clock (in tenths of the sky)
25-V25	Mean daily cloudiness (in tenths of the sky)
26-V26	Snowfall (cm)
27-V27	Rainfall (mm)
28-V28	Number of daily traffic accidents

3. Results and Findings

Prediction of the impact of the meteorological factors on the appearance of traffic accidents is realized in this paper using the meteorological and the traffic factor data related to the City of Niš, Republic of Serbia. The data is for the period from 1992 up to 2009 from which twenty-seven variables are used for meteorological and one variable was available which represents the number of daily traffic accidents. Meteorological data used in this study was derived from the Republic Hydro-meteorological Institute and the database of daily traffic accidents was supplied by the Ministry of Interior of the Republic of Serbia. All variables are given in Table 2 and the case study is realized with the data attached in the excel table Mathematics-NovoTrafficAccidentsNaj1.

The authors had in mind that the basic aim of each prediction process is to create a model that, using a suitable combination of independent variables, draws conclusions for the dependent variable. Bearing in mind the task set in the research which is the subject of this paper, we prepare the data for daily traffic accidents in binary form. As it is mentioned in this paper, the value of the dependent variable take value logic-exactly, i.e., binary-1 in the case that the number of daily traffic accidents is greater than 10, which is about 150% of the mean value for the considered period.

3.1. Application of Proposed Algorithm of Ensemble Learning

In the first step according to the steps from algorithm 1, a binary regression procedure using SPSS 17 tool [88] was carried out on the available data. All 27 meteorological parameters are used as predictors and the dichotomous variable of daily traffic accidents is used as dependable variable.

The results of applied binary regression obtained are shown in Table 3.

Table 3. Results of applied binary regression—all 27 parameters.

	B	**S.E.**	**Wald**	**Df**	**Sig.**	**Exp (B)**
			Binary Regression			
1-V1	−0.076	0.061	1.583	1	0.208	0.927
2-V2	−0.057	0.073	0.610	1	0.435	0.945
3-V3	−0.129	0.061	4.508	1	0.034	0.879
4-V4	0.265	0.148	3.199	1	0.074	1.303
5-V5	0.078	0.095	0.661	1	0.416	1.081
6-V6	−0.045	0.097	0.215	1	0.643	0.956
7-V7	−0.020	0.092	0.050	1	0.824	0.980
8-V8	−0.018	0.067	0.077	1	0.782	0.982
9-V9	−0.094	0.065	2.088	1	0.148	0.910
10-V10	−0.137	0.085	2.572	1	0.109	0.872
11-V11	0.229	0.143	2.557	1	0.110	1.257
12-V12	0.083	0.057	2.072	1	0.150	1.086
13-V13	0.092	0.058	2.527	1	0.112	1.096
14=V14	0.068	0.058	1.368	1	0.242	1.070
15-V15	−0.220	0.170	1.672	1	0.196	0.802
16-V16	0.018	0.078	0.053	1	0.817	1.018
17-V17	−0.069	0.069	1.005	1	0.316	0.933
18-V18	0.072	0.082	0.759	1	0.384	1.074
19-V19	−0.031	0.149	0.045	1	0.832	0.969
20-V20	−0.162	0.075	4.640	1	0.031	0.850
21-V21	−0.020	0.031	0.402	1	0.526	0.981
22-V22	−0.023	0.064	0.132	1	0.716	0.977
23-V23	−0.050	0.065	0.584	1	0.445	0.951
24-V24	0.028	0.063	0.194	1	0.660	1.028
25-V25	−0.004	0.182	0.000	1	0.984	0.996
Constant	0.057	0.033	3.098	1	0.078	1.059

Classification Table [a,b]

	Observed		Predicted Number of daily traffic accidents > 10		Percentage Correct
			0	1	
Step 0	Number of daily traffic accidents > 10	0	3522	0	100.0
		1	468	0	0.0
	Overall Percentage				88.3

a. Constant is included in the model. b. The cut value is 0.500.

Model Summary

	−2 Log likelihood	Cox–Snell R Square	Nagelkerke R Square
Step 1	2833.054 [c]	0.013	0.025

c. Estimation terminated at iteration 5 because parameter estimates changed by less than 0.001.

Hosmer and Lemeshow Test.

	Chi-square	Df	Sig.
Step 1	12.187	8	0.143

Sig > 0.05 indicates that the data fit the model.

The result shows that the model of logistic regression using all the 27 meteorological factors monitored explains the considered problem with the 1.3 percent of variance by Cox and Snell and 2.5 by Nagelkerke, which indicates its insignificant connection with the data (bigger than 0 and less than 0.3) [100], the Hosmer and Lemeshow test value

0.143 indicates that the data fit with the model (because Sig. > 0,05); what this means is that the model is well calibrated [101] and also that the model is without excluding any of these 27 parameters because of correlation. Given that 468 instances that cause an increased number of TI and 3522 that did not are identified in the examined sample, the accuracy of the classification by random selection is (468/3990)2 + (3522/3990)2 = 0.7929, which is 79.29%, so it can be seen that the model of binary logistic regression analysis with 88.3% has a higher classification accuracy than random selection models [102]. As the quality of the model significantly determines the value of the AUC [103], the value of that measure is determined in a separate following step of the proposed model.

In the second step of the proposed Algorithm 1, five classification algorithms applied each from different types that were chosen by the authors for this purpose in this paper are Naive Bayes, J48 Decision Trees, SMO, LogitBoost, and PART algorithms. The method of 10 folds cross-validation test was applied in the model estimation. The performance indicators of five classification algorithms are given in Table 4, which shows that the LoogitBoost and classifiers achieved the most accurate prediction results especially having in mind that the most important measure is AUC value.

Table 4. Performance indicators—classification using all 27 parameters.

	Accuracy	Recall	F1 Measure	ROC
J48	0.794	0.881	0.828	0.496
Naive Bayes	0.809	0.827	0.817	0.541
Logit Boost	0.779	0.881	0.827	0.547
PART	0.815	0.882	0.829	0.524
SMO	0.779	0.883	0.828	0.500

As presented in Table 4, the LogitBoost and Naive Bayes classifiers achieved the two highest values for AUC at 0.547 and 0.541, respectively, and also the next similar values for other measures of classification, i.e., accuracy of 77.9 and 80.9%, recall 88.1 and 82.7% and F1 measure of 82.7%, and 81.7%, respectively, which implies that between these two classification algorithms, there will be one which will order predictors with highest value of AUC for the smaller number of attribute subset.

In step 3 of the proposed algorithm, the process of attribute selection by searching the attribute subsets using evaluation with two types of this method and that filter and wrapper type is realized.

3.1.1. Filter

Filter feature subset evaluation methods were conducted with a rank searching to determine the best attribute subset, and they are listed as follows:

(1)   Information-Gain Attribute evaluation(IG),
(2)   Gain-Ratio Attribute evaluation (GR),
(3)   SymmetricalUncertAttributeEval (SU),
(4)   Chi-Square Attribute evaluation (CS),
(5)   Filtered Attribute Eval (FA).

The ranks of considered parameters obtained by the above three methods on the training data are given in Table 5 where the four attributes that are selected are presented: V7, V13,V-15 and V-20.

Table 5. Feature selection using five filter ranker classifiers (smaller serial number represents bigger rank of factor).

	SU	GR	IG	CS	FA
13-V13	1/0.0063	1/0.0054	1/0.0038	1/23.13	1/0.0038
7-V7	2/0.0055	2/0.0051	2/0.0031	2/19.29	2/0.0031

Table 5. *Cont.*

	SU	**GR**	**IG**	**CS**	**FA**
20-V20	3/0.0039	3/0.0034	4/0.0023	4/11.89	4/0.0023
15-V15	4/0.0038	4/0.0029	3/0.0029	3/16.32	3/0.0029
4-V4	5/0	5/0	5/0	5/0	5/0
10-V10	6/0	6/0	9/0	9/0	9/0
3-V3	7/0	7/0	14/0	14/0	14/0
11-V11	8/0	8/0	7/0	7/0	7/0
9-V9	9/0	9/0	8/0	8/0	8/0
8-V8	10/0	10/0	10/0	10/0	10/0
2-V2	11/0	11/0	6/0	6/0	6/0
5-V5	12/0	12/0	11/0	11/0	11/0
6-V6	13/0	13/0	12/0	12/0	12/0
12-V12	14/0	14/0	13/0	13/0	13/0
27-V27	15/0	15/0	15/0	15/0	15/0
14-V14	16/0	16/0	16/0	16/0	16/0
26-V26	17/0	17/0	17/0	17/0	17/0
24-V24	18/0	18/0	18/0	18/0	18/0
25-V25	19/0	19/0	19/0	19/0	19/0
22-V22	20/0	20/0	20/0	20/0	20/0
23-V23	21/0	21/0	21/0	21/0	21/0
21-V21	22/0	22/0	22/0	22/0	22/0
16-V16	23/0	23/0	23/0	23/0	23/0
17-V17	24/0	24/0	24/0	24/0	24/0
18-V18	25/0	25/0	25/0	25/0	25/0
19-V19	26/0	26/0	26/0	26/0	26/0
1-V1	27/0	27/0	27/0	27/0	27/0

3.1.2. Wrapper

Wrapper feature subset evaluation methods were conducted without rank searching to determine the best attribute subset, and they are listed as follows:

(1) Best First (BF),
(2) Linear Forward Selection (LF),
(3) Genetic Search (GS),
(4) Greedy Stepwise (GST),
(5) Subset Size Forward Selection (SSFS).

The obtained results presented in Table 6 shown that the same four attributes, V7,V13, V-15 and V-20, were selected using five wrapper algorithms as it was the case with five filter classifiers.

Table 6. Results of feature selection using five wrapper classifiers (symbol $\sqrt{}$ notates selection of attribute).

	BF	**LF**	**GS**	**GST**	**SSFS**
7-V7	✓	✓	✓	✓	✓
13-V13	✓	✓	✓	✓	✓
20-V20	✓	✓	✓	✓	✓
15-V15	✓	✓	✓	✓	✓

In substep 3.2. of the proposed algorithm, we determine the selected attributes as a set operation, the intersection of a subset of the selected attributes using the filter and wrapper methodology, and based on the obtained results, we notice that in our case study, we are talking about the same four attributes: V7, V13,V-15 and V-20, i.e., m = 4.

We examine the next subset 3.3 and determine that there are four selected which is less than the initial 27 attributes in the model and at the end of this substep, we check the goodness of the model used, whose results are given in Table 7.

Table 7. Results of the binary regression Enter method using the 4 selected attributes.

Binary Regression Enter Method						
	B	**S.E.**	**Wald**	**Df**	**Sig.**	**Exp (B)**
V7	0.025	0.017	2.039	1	0.153	1.025
V13	0.013	0.008	3.002	1	0.083	1.013
V15	0.003	0.010	0.068	1	0.794	1.003
V20	−0.184	0.078	5.601	1	0.018	0.832
Constant	0.003	0.010	0.068	1	0.794	1.003

Classification Table [a,b]				
		Predicted		
Observed		Number of daily traffic accidents > 10		Percentage Correct
		0	1	
Step 0	Number of daily 0	3522	0	100.0
	traffic accidents > 10 1	468	0	0.0
	Overall Percentage			88.3

a. Constant is included in the model. b. The cut value is 0.500.

Model Summary			
Step	−2 Log likelihood	Cox–Snell R Square	Nagelkerke R Square
1	2860.403 [c]	0.006	0.012

c. Estimation terminated at iteration number 4 because parameter estimates changed by less than 0.001.

Hosmer and Lemeshow Test			
Step	Chi-square	Df	Sig.
1	11.234	8	0.189

Sig > 0.05 indicates that the data fit the model.

The result shows that the model of logistic regression is taking into consideration feature of the selected 4 meteorological parameters to explain the considered problem with the same accuracy of classification value of 88.3%, with the 0.6 percent of variance by Cox and Snell The result shows that the model of logistic regression taking into consideration selected 4 meteorological parameters explain considering problem with same accuracy of classification value of 88.3% as when uses all 27 parameters, i.e., 1.2 by Nagelkerke without excluding any of this parameters because of correlation and with Hosmer and Lemeshow test value 0.189, which is evidently better than the results obtained in step 1 when it was used for all 27 attributes in regression model.

Additionally, we can see in Table 8 that the classification measure values for determined two best classification algorithms have better characteristics than results obtained in step 2 of this algorithm presented in Table 4.

Table 8. Performance indicators obtained by the classification algorithms using 4 parameters.

	Accuracy	**Recall**	**F1 Measure**	**ROC**
Naive Bayes	0.809/0.779	0.827/0.883	0.817/0.828	0.541/0.565
Logit Boost	0.779/0.897	0.881/0.883	0.827/0.828	0.547/0.610

Results given in Tables 7 and 8 clearly show that the applied two groups of filter and wrapper methodologies with five specific algorithms each with reduced dimension from 27 parameters to only four attributes, i.e., variables show good results of correctness of such a reduced model, and because of that, we can continue with step 4 of the proposed algorithm 1; otherwise, that would be the end and exit from the procedure with undone dimensionality reduction.

In step 4 of proposed algorithm 1, we generate a diagram with AUC values depending on the number of attributes used, for the best classification algorithm Loogitboost which is determined on the basis of the results given in Tables 4 and 8 and on the basis of results for each from the chosen five filter classifiers given in Table 5. The x-axis shows the number of attributes, and the y-axis shows the AUC value of feature subset generated for each of the five filter classifiers. In this way, we determine if the best results for the AUC measure we can obtain with a decreasing number of attributes, in our case the number of four attributes determined in step 3 and that using the ranking of the subset of attributes obtained with SymmetricalUncertAttributeEval classifier where it should be noted that the GainRatio classifier gives the same ranking of attributes. The rank of each of the 27 attributes which is obtained with SU and GR classifier determines the order of elimination of each one individually starting attribute and begins with the one with the lowest 27th rank and a suitable value of AUC determined using the LogitBoost classification algorithm. At the end in the diagram shown in Figure 2., it is clearly presented that three is the minimal number of used attributes with the maximal value of AUC for the number of attributes smaller than the four determined in the previous third step of the algorithm, also taking into account other classification measures, and in this way, determines the definitively chosen feature subset.

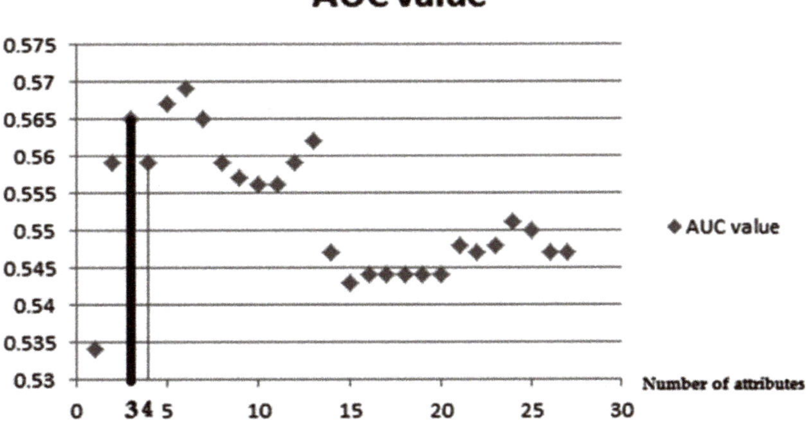

Figure 2. Diagram for determining maximum AUC value of classification for minimum number of attributes.

As we can conclude using results from the Diagram presented in Figure 2 and results determined with the best filter classifiers SU, i.e., GR given in Table 5, in this step of the algorithm, we obtain an added decrease of the selected attributes which will be included in the prediction formula in the following three: V13-Relative humidity at 14 o'clock in percent, V7-Daily temperature amplitude in °C and V20-Mean daily wind speed in m/sec.

The LogitBoost algorithm of classification shows, evidently, the best results in each of the measures including the AUC value for a reduced number of the three attributes mentioned as it is given in Table 9.

Table 9. Result evaluation of LogitBoost classification using all 27, 4 and 3 parameters.

	Accuracy	Recall	F1 Measure	ROC
27 parameters	0.779	0.881	0.827	0.547
4 parameters	0.897	0.883	0.828	0.610
3 parameters	0.897	0.883	0.828	0.613

In the last step 5 of Algorithm 1, a logistic regression is carried out, as in steps 1 and 3, to check the goodness of the model with 3 parameters selected in the previous step 4, and the results are given in Table 10.

Table 10. Results of applied logic regression with the selected subset of 3 parameters.

Binary Regression						
	B	S.E.	Wald	Df	Sig.	Exp (B)
V7	0.025	0.017	2.120	1	0.145	1.025
V13	0.015	0.004	11.002	1	0.001	1.015
V20	−0.191	0.073	6.877	1	0.009	0.826
Constant	−2.896	0.457	40.170	1	0.000	0.055

Classification Table [a,b]

	Observed		Predicted		Percentage Correct	
			Number of daily traffic accidents > 10			
			0	1		
Step 0	Number of daily traffic accidents > 10	0	3522		0	100.0
		1	468		0	0.0
	Overall Percentage					88.3

a. Constant is included in the model. b. The cut value is 0.500.

Model Summary

Step 1	−2 Log likelihood	Cox–Snell R Square	Nagelkerke R Square
	2860.472 [c]	0.006	0.012

c. Estimation terminated at iteration number 4 because parameter estimates changed by less than 0.001.

Hosmer and Lemeshow Test

Step 1	Chi-square	Df	Sig.
	10.469	8	0.234

Sig > 0.05 indicates that the data fit the model.

The result shows that the model of logistic regression taking in consideration the three selected meteorological parameters explain the considered problem with the 0.6 percent of variance by Cox and Snell, i.e., 1.2 percent of variance by Nagelkerke without excluding any of these parameters because of correlation and with Hosmer and Lemeshow test value 0.234 which is evidently better than the results obtained in step 3 when it was used with four attributes in the regression model. Because of that, we can continue with step 3 of the proposed algorithm 1 to check eventual further decreasing of attributes; otherwise, it would be the end and exit from the procedure with dimensionality reduction done to this moment. However, in the end of this last step of the proposed algorithm, before continuing the algorithm with step 3, it is obligatory to check the case that it is obtained value preset in advance. This is the case in our paper, because the reduced number on three important attributes is smaller than the preset threshold value which is four attributes, so this fact implies the exit from the procedure in our case study.

For the concrete considered case study in this paper, the predictive formula is as follows:

$$-2.896 + 0.025V7 + 0.015V13 - 0.191V20 > 10 \tag{18}$$

3.2. The Model of Emergent Intelligence as One Implementation of the Proposed Ensemble Method

As the authors had already mentioned in the introduction of Section 2. Materials and methods, in this paper they described not only the new proposed model but also its implementation as one of the agents in one multi-agent system of the emergent intelligence technique (EIT) for the purpose of one citizens warning system—Figure 3. In this respect, let us mark the task of giving a warning to those from one region or big city interested in the meteorological parameters that has reached the existence of conditions which affect the increased possibility of traffic accidents in this concrete place with T. The task is performed on the basis of measuring the values of all parameters included in the proposed model in this paper with real time and obtaining historical data of those values from specialized electronic data sources. In carrying out the set task, it is obligatory to use suitable prediction models as well as the proposed model in Section 2.1.4 of this paper and the data in real time.

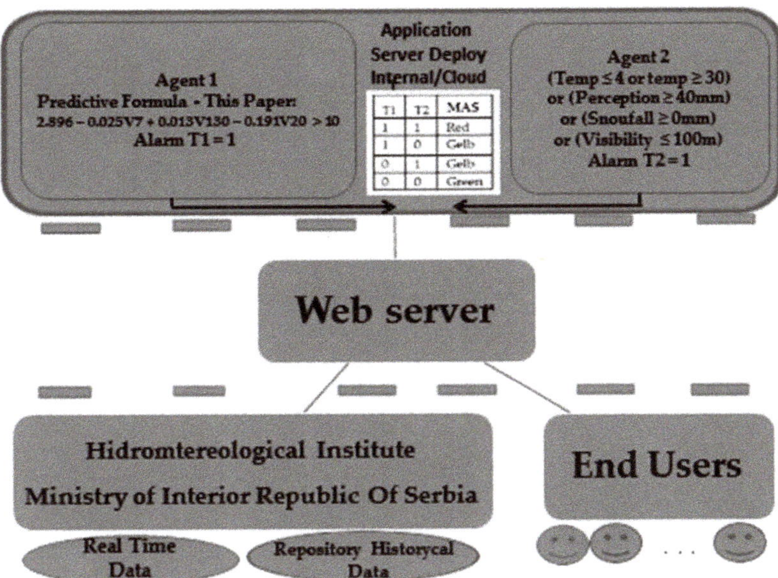

Figure 3. EIT two-agent system for generating a warning of the possibility of traffic accidents.

That is why we divide the set task T into 2 subtasks for the model of the two-agent EIT system, and these would be the tasks: T1, which determines the warning of the existence and possibilities of increased traffic accidents based on a prediction from historical data, already described in Section 2.1.4 using the proposed ensemble model of ML and prediction formula given with Equation (18), and subtask T2, which determines the existence of that possibility based on the given exceeding or undershooting pre-set values for some of the most important meteorological parameters in real time like Temperature ($\leq$4 or $\geq$30), Precipitation ($\geq$40 mm), Snowfall ($\geq$0 mm), and Visibility ($\leq$100 m). In the proposed EIT, the two-agent system in Figure 3, the decision matrix realizes one warning alarm which is in the node of EIT where the main task T is solving, using the already-solved agents tasks T1 and T2, and this matrix is given in Table 11 on a way to generate the red alarm in the case that both agents T1 and T2 give a warning; the yellow alarm is generated if only one of them gives a warning, while there is no warning if neither of them gives a warning.

Table 11. Decision matrix of EIT for generating a warning of the possibility of traffic accidents.

T1	T2	EITalarm
1	1	Red
1	0	Gelb
0	1	Gelb
0	0	Green

4. Technological Implementation of the Proposed Ensemble Model

The technical implementation of the proposed solution implies the implementation of the considered two-agent system EIT with additional indication of the possibility in the future for different implementations in a more complex and multidimensional agent system, and some specific types of parameters that could and should be included in such a system are listed. The proposed technical solution is considered through two subsections in this paper—architecture and implementation.

4.1. The Architecture of the Proposed Technical Solution

The proposed technical solution is client server architecture which uses Firebase as the cloud messenger service in the proposed solution, and can also be used as a real-time database in the Backend-as-a-Service application development platform. In this architecture, Firebase connects user applications from client side with the server application on the server side consisting of four modules noted as Agent 1, Agent 2, EIT and notification module.

The user application works on the client side in this solution. The user application, which is the client application, works with different mobile operating platforms such as IOS and android, android auto, Google assistant driving mode; the same story with Apple devices and car-play systems, and the authors realized it in the proposed solution on IOS. During the installation, the application requests permission from the user to track the location in the background. Then, the server application, specifically the notification module, requests a list of hydro-meteorological stations with their geo locations, as well as data on topic names for the defined alarms. Since the topic, among other mentioned parameters, is made up of the name of the hydro-meteorological station, the nearest station is determined based on the current geolocation of the user and the geolocation of the hydro-meteorological stations. After selecting a hydro-meteorological station, the user fills in information about the type of alarm he is interested in, and more precisely, what type of vehicle they drive and whether they wear glasses. Based on this data, a topic is created to which the user application logs on to Firebase. Furthermore, the application monitors the change of location, and with each change, determines whether there is a station that is closer than the currently selected one; when this happens, the application logs out of the previous topic and logs in to the new one. Additionally, in the case when the notification module sends a notification for a topic for which the client has registered, that notification is displayed to the user.

The notification module serves to provide the client application with data about hydro-meteorological stations and their locations, as well as other options for determining the topic. Additionally, when the EIT module from the server determines this, this module addresses Firebase and forwards a notification to all users logged in to the topic defined.

Agents 1 has a database of historical data that it uses to generate an alarm according to the prediction formula that is generated by the proposed prediction model from this paper that takes meteorological conditions into account. In this way, it decides whether to raise an alarm notated T1. Thereby, the historical data is updated by the Hydro-meteorological Institute of the Republic of Serbia and from the Ministry of Interior of Serbia, the number and place of the accident-city, i.e., the number of roads. The data is given to clients and official members of the MUP, in which case the EIT generates a report that includes cases of binoculars and not both truck and car and gives such a report to an official person—that is, in all four variants.

Agents 2 decides whether to raise the alarm based on the defined rules and the current situation. Agent 2 generates an alarm T2 in the logical function of meeting the meteorological conditions of the given conditions in the image for temperature, rain, snow, wind, and fog, as well as the type of vehicle (truck or car) and visibility.

The EIT module addresses the agents at a defined time and takes answers from them. Based on the answers received, it forwards an alarm to the notification module for groups that need it, which then forwards notifications to Firebase.

4.2. The Implementation of Proposed Technical Solution

The implementation of the proposed technical solution, which is based on the diagram given in Figure 4, is realized with attached program codes for each part included in the proposed EIT system separately with server-TrafficIncidents-master and clients application-TrafficAccidentPrevention. Software implementation of the proposed technical solution is realized using Python as a widespread software platform (see Algorithm 2).

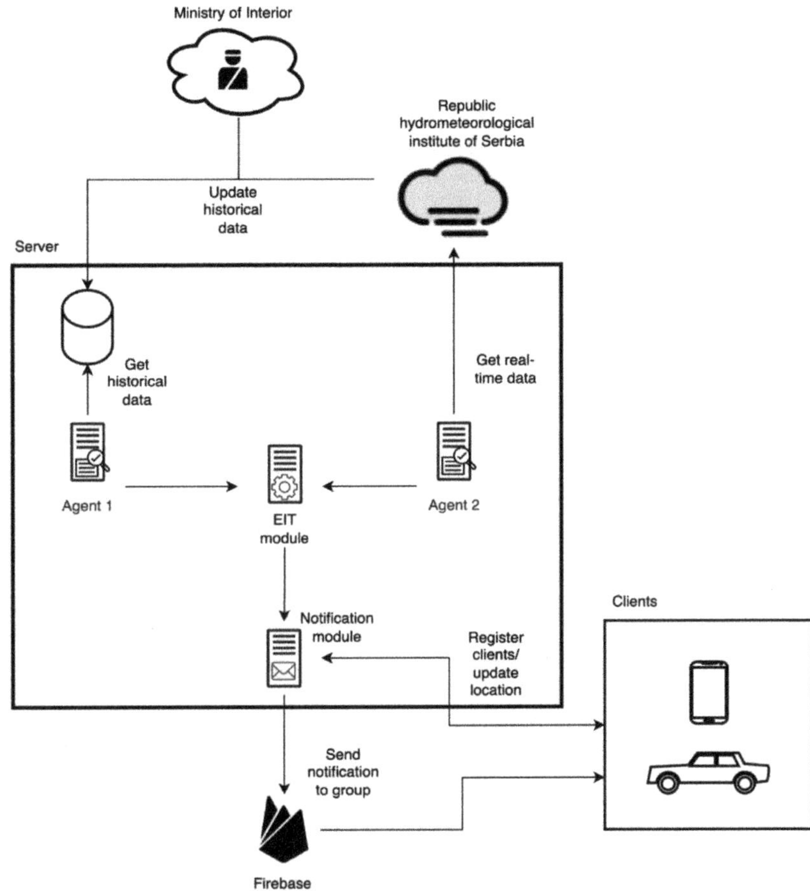

Figure 4. EIT two-agent system implementation—generating a warning of the possibility of traffic accidents.

Implementation of the Agent 1 that generates alarm T1

    Data:

    V7 is the daily temperature amplitude in degrees Celsius

    V13 Relative humidity at 14 o'clock in percent

    V20 is Mean daily wind speed m/sec

    if $(-2.896 - 0.025v7 + 0.013v13 - 1.191v20 > 10)$

    Alarm T1 = 1

    else

    Alarm T1 = 0

Implementation of the Agent 2 algorithm that generates alarm T2

    Data on the current hydro-meteorological situation:

    temp-current temperature INT

    fog-presence of fog BOOLEAN

    wind-wind speed in m/s INT

    snowfall-is it snowing BOOLEAN

    rain-is it raining BOOLEAN

    cloudiness-is it cloudy BOOLEAN

    User data:

    tracks-whether they drive a truck or a bus BOOLEAN

cars-do they drive a car BOOLEAN
farsightedness-whether they wear glasses while driving BOOLEAN
if (
(temp $\leq$ 4)
or (temp $\geq$ 30)
or (fog and farsightedness)
or (rain)
or (wind $\geq$ 50 and tracks)
or (wind $\geq$ 65 and cars)
or (snowfall)
or (cloudiness and farsightedness)
)
Alarm T2 = 1
else
Alarm T2 = 0

Algorithm 2: Implementation of the EIT algorithm that generates alarm EITalarm

---

T1 and T 2 agent alarms
f (T1 = 1 and T2 = 1)
Red alarm
else
if (T1 = 1 or T2 = 1)
Yellow alarm
else
Green alarm-no alarm

---

5. Conclusions

The authors had two main aims in this paper which was directly connected with proving two set hypotheses. The results of the research with the proposed ensemble method of aggregation of five methods from different classification groups of algorithms and binary regression algorithm confirmed the first set hypothesis. It could be concluded that it is possible to aggregate several classification methods and include several feature selection methods into one ensemble method with better characteristics than each individually installed method when it is applied alone to solve the same task. Thereby, each used classification methods of ML belongs to a different type of classification algorithms, and also, each algorithm of attribute reduction belongs to different types of feature selection algorithms. The authors also gave an answer on the second hypothesis set and the question: Is it possible for such potential obtained ensemble method to be implemented in one multi agent system? They did it in a way that they proposed one technological system supported with emergence intelligence as one good framework for the implementation of the proposed model defined with the algorithm described.

The authors confirmed those two hypotheses using the results obtained in the case study conducted for the data for the City of Niš in the Republic of Serbia and these were evaluated using a 10-fold cross validation for each of the applied algorithms in Weka software.

The authors have claimed that the proposed model has not demonstrated significant limitations. The authors will deal with it by examining the inclusion of a greater number of types of classification groups and feature selection algorithms and the inclusion of n-modular redundancy into the construction of the proposed ensemble algorithm in their future work related to this topic. Moreover, the authors will also consider the implementation of the proposed model in multi agent systems with more than two included agents based on the emergence of intelligence technology and for obtaining better prediction models for TI for solving similar prediction problems in different fields of human life.

Supplementary Materials: The following supplementary materials which are mentioned and used in this paper are available online at http://www.diplomatija.com/nastavni-kadar/prof-dr-dragan-randelovic/mathematics-work-in-progress/ (accessed on 15 December 2022).

Author Contributions: A.A.: resources, data curation, funding acquisition, software, validation; M.R.: investigation, writing—original draft, formal analysis, project administration; D.R.: conceptualization, methodology, writing—review and editing, visualization, supervision. All authors have read and agreed to the published version of the manuscript.

Funding: This research received no external funding.

Data Availability Statement: Not applicable.

Acknowledgments: The authors thank the Faculty of Diplomacy and Security, University Union Nikola Tesla, Belgrade, Republic of Serbia for their support in the publishing of this paper.

Conflicts of Interest: The authors declare no conflict of interest.

References

1. Gao, J.; Chen, X.; Woodward, A.; Liu, X.; Wu, H.; Lu, Y.; Li, L.; Liu, Q. The association between meteorological factors and road traffic injuries: A case analysis from Shantou city, China. *Sci. Rep.* **2016**, *6*, 37300. [CrossRef]
2. Verster, T.; Fourie, E. The good, the bad and the ugly of South African fatal road accidents. *S. Afr. J. Sci.* **2018**, *114*. [CrossRef] [PubMed]
3. Lankarani, K.B.; Heydari, S.T.; Aghabeigi, M.R.; Moafian, G.; Hoseinzadeh, A.; Vossoughi, M.J. The impact of environmental factors on traffic accidents in Iran. *Inj Violence Res.* **2014**, *6*, 64–71. [CrossRef]
4. Dastoorpoor, M.; Idani, E.; Khanjani, N.; Goudarzi, G.; Bahrampour, A. Relationship Between Air Pollution, Weather, Traffic, and Traffic-Related Mortality. *Trauma Mon.* **2016**, *21*, e37585. [CrossRef]
5. Chekijian, S.; Paul, M.; Kohl, V.P.; Walker, D.M.; Tomassoni, A.J.; Cone, D.C.; Vaca, F.E. The global burden of road injury: Its relevance to the emergency physician. *Emerg. Med. Int.* **2014**, *2014*, 139219. [CrossRef] [PubMed]
6. Xie, S.H.; Wu, Y.S.; Liu, X.J.; Fu, Y.B.; Li, S.S.; Ma, H.W.; Zou, F.; Cheng, J.Q. Mortality from road traffic accidents in a rapidly urbanizing Chinese city: A 20-year analysis in Shenzhen, 1994–2013. *Traffic Inj. Prev.* **2016**, *17*, 3943. [CrossRef]
7. Chan, C.T.; Pai, C.W.; Wu, C.C.; Hsu, J.C.; Chen, R.J.; Chiu, W.T.; Lam, C. Association of Air Pollution and Wheather Factors with Traffic Injuri Severity: A Study in Taiwan. *Int. J. Environ. Res. Public Health* **2022**, *19*, 7442. [CrossRef] [PubMed]
8. Jalilian, M.M.; Safarpour, H.; Bazyar, J.; Keykaleh, M.S.; Malekyan, L.; Khorshidi, A. Environmental Related Risk Factors to Road Traffic Accidents in Ilam, Iran. *Med. Arch.* **2019**, *73*, 169–172. [CrossRef]
9. Guyon, I.; Elisseeff, A. An Introduction to Variable and Feature Selection. *J. Mach. Learn. Res.* **2003**, *3*, 1157–1182.
10. Lu, H.; Zhu, Y.; Shi, K.; Yisheng, L.; Shi, P.; Niu, Z. Using Adverse Weather Data in Social Media to Assist with City-Level Traffic Situation Awareness and Alerting. *Appl. Sci.* **2018**, *8*, 1193. [CrossRef]
11. Trenchevski, A.; Kalendar, M.; Gjoreski, H.; Efnusheva, D. Prediction of Air Pollution Concentration Using Weather Data and Regression Models. In Proceedings of the 8th International Conference on Applied Innovations in IT, (ICAIIT), Koethen (Anhalt), Germany, 9 March 2020; pp. 55–61.
12. Gupta, A.; Sharma, A.; Goel, A. Review of Regression Analysis Models. *Int. J. Eng. Res. Technol.* **2017**, *6*, 58–61.
13. Theofilatos, A.; Yannis, G. A review of the effect of traffic and weather characteristics on road safety. *Accid. Anal. Prev.* **2014**, *72*, 244–256. [CrossRef]
14. Qiu, L.; Nixon, W.A. Effects of adverse weather on traffic crashes: Systematic review and meta-analysis. *Transp. Res. Rec.* **2008**, *2055*, 139–146. [CrossRef]
15. Edwards, J.B. The relationship between road accident severity and recorded weather. *J. Saf. Res.* **1998**, *29*, 249–262. [CrossRef]
16. Malin, F.; Norros, I.; Innamaa, S. Accident risk of road and weather conditions on different road types. *Accid. Anal. Prev.* **2019**, *122*, 181–188. [CrossRef] [PubMed]
17. Brijs, T.; Offermans, C.; Hermans, E.; Stiers, T. The Impact of Weather Conditions on Road Safety Investigated on an HourlyBasis. In Proceedings of the Transportation Research Board 85th Annual Meeting, Washington, DC, USA, 22–26 January 2006.
18. Antoniou, C.; Yannis, G.; Katsochis, D. Impact of meteorological factors on the number of injury accidents. In Proceedings of the 13th World Conference on Transport Research (WCTR 2013), Rio de Janeiro, Brazylia, 15–18 July 2013; Volume 15.
19. El-Basyouny, K.; Barua, S.; Islam, M.T. Investigation of time and weather effects on crash types using full Bayesian multivariate Poisson lognormal models. *Accid. Anal. Prev.* **2014**, *73*, 91–99. [CrossRef]
20. Baker, C.; Reynolds, S. Wind-induced accidents of road vehicles. *Accid. Anal. Prev.* **1992**, *24*, 559–575. [CrossRef]
21. Naik, B.; Tung, L.W.; Zhao, S.; Khattak, A.J. Weather impacts on single-vehicle truck crash injury severity. *J. Saf. Res.* **2016**, *58*, 57–65. [CrossRef] [PubMed]
22. Mitra, S. Sun glare and road safety: An empirical investigation of intersection crashes. *Saf. Sci.* **2014**, *70*, 246–254. [CrossRef]
23. Hagita, K.; Mori, K. The effect of sun glare on traffic accidents in Chiba prefecture, Japan. *Asian Transp. Stud.* **2014**, *3*, 205–219. [CrossRef]

24. Buisán, S.T.; Earle, M.E.; Collado, J.L.; Kochendorfer, J.; Alastrué, J.; Wolff, M.; Smith, C.D.; López-Moreno, J.I. Assessment of snowfall accumulation underestimation by tipping bucket gauges in the Spanish operational network. *Atmos. Meas. Tech.* **2017**, *10*, 1079–1091. [CrossRef]

25. Lio, C.F.; Cheong, H.H.; Un, C.H.; Lo, I.L.; Tsai, S.Y. The association between meteorological variables and road traffic injuries: A study from Macao. *PeerJ* **2019**, *7*, e6438. [CrossRef] [PubMed]

26. Khan, G.; Qin, X.; Noyce, D. Spatial Analysis of Weather Crash Patterns. *J. Transp. Eng.* **2008**, *134*, 191–202. [CrossRef]

27. Becker, N.; Rust, H.W.; Ulbrich, U. Predictive modeling of hourly probabilities for weather-related road accidents. *Nat. Hazards Earth Syst. Sci.* **2020**, *20*, 2857–2871. [CrossRef]

28. Song, X.; Zhao, X.; Zhang, Y.; Li, Y.; Yin, C.; Chen, J. The effect of meteorological factors on road traffic injuries in Beijing. *Appl. Ecol. Environ. Res.* **2019**, *17*, 9505–9514. [CrossRef]

29. Matthew, G.K.; Yannis, G. Weather Effects on Daily Traffic Accidents and Fatalities: Time Series Count Data Approach. In Proceedings of the Transportation Research Board 89th Annual Meeting, Washington, DC, USA, 10–14 January 2010; p. 17.

30. Bergel-Hayat, R.; Depire, A. Climate, road traffic and road risk—An aggregate approach. In Proceedings of the 10th WCTR (World Conference on Transport Research Society), Istanbul, Turkey, 4–8 July 2004.

31. Bergel-Hayat, R.; Debbarh, M.; Antoniou, C.; Yannis, G. Explaining the road accident risk: Weather effects. *Accid. Anal. Prev.* **2013**, *60*, 456–465. [CrossRef]

32. Zheng, L.; Lin, R.; Wang, X.; Chen, W. The Development and Application of Machine Learning in Atmospheric Environment Studies. *Remote Sens.* **2021**, *13*, 4839. [CrossRef]

33. Yuan, Q.; Shen, H.; Li, T.; Li, Z.; Li, S.; Jiang, Y.; Xu, H.; Tan, W.; Yang, Q.; Wang, J. Deep learning in environmental remote sensing: Achievements and challenges. *Remote Sens. Environ.* **2020**, *241*, 111716. [CrossRef]

34. Medina-Salgado, B.; Sánchez-DelaCruz, E.; Pozos-Parra, P.; Sierra, J.E. Urban traffic flow prediction techniques: A review. *Sustain. Comput. Inform. Syst.* **2022**, *35*, 100739. [CrossRef]

35. Shaik, M.E.; Islam, M.M.; Hossain, Q.S. A review on neural network techniques for the prediction of road traffic accident severity. *Asian Transp. Stud.* **2021**, *7*, 100040. [CrossRef]

36. Moghaddam, F.R.; Afandizadeh, S.; Ziyadi, M. Prediction of accident severity using artificial neural networks. *Int. J. Civ. Eng.* **2011**, *9*, 41–49.

37. Pradhan, B.; Sameen, M.I. Review of traffic accident predictions with neural networks. In *Laser Scanning Systems in Highway and Safety Assessment, Technology & Innovation (IEREK Interdisciplinary Series for Sustainable Development)*; Springer: Cham, Switzerland, 2020; pp. 97–109.

38. Profillidis, V.A.; Botzoris, G.N. Chapter 8—Artificial intelligence—Neural network methods. In *Modeling of Transport Demand Analyzing, Calculating, and Forecasting Transport Demand*; Elsevier: St. Louis, MO, USA, 2019; pp. 353–382. [CrossRef]

39. Yuan, J.; Abdel-Aty, M.; Gong, Y.; Cai, Q. Real-time crash risk prediction using long short-term memory recurrent neural network. *Transport. Res. Rec. J. Transport. Res. Board* **2019**, *2673*, 1–13. [CrossRef]

40. Rezapour, M.; Nazneen, S.; Ksaibati, K. Application of deep learning techniques in predicting motorcycle crash severity. *Eng. Rep.* **2020**, *2*, e12175. [CrossRef]

41. Sameen, M.I.; Pradhan, B.; Shafri, H.Z.M.; Hamid, H.B. Applications of deep learning in severity prediction of traffic accidents. In *Global Civil Engineering Conference*; Springer: Singapore, 2019; pp. 793–808.

42. Zheng, M.; Li, T.; Zhu, R.; Chen, J.; Ma, Z.; Tang, M.; Cui, Z.; Wang, A.Z. Traffic accident's severity prediction: A deep-learning approach-based CNN network. *IEEE Access* **2019**, *7*, 39897–39910. [CrossRef]

43. Sameen, M.I.; Pradhan, B. Severity prediction of traffic accidents with recurrent neural networks. *Appl. Sci.* **2017**, *7*, 476. [CrossRef]

44. Soto, B.G.; Bumbacher, A.; Deublein, M.; Adey, B.T. Predicting road traffic accidents using artificial neural network models. *Infrastruct. Asset Manag.* **2018**, *5*, 132–144. [CrossRef]

45. Ebrahim, S.; Hossain, Q.S. An Artificial Neural Network Model for Road Accident Prediction: A Case Study of Khulna Metropolitan City, Bangladesh. In Proceedings of the Fourth International Conference on Civil Engineering for Sustainable Development (ICCESD 2018), Khulna, Bangladesh, 9–11 February 2018; KUET: Khulna, Bangladesh, 2018.

46. Jadaan, K.S.; Al-Fayyad, M.; Gammoh, H.F. Prediction of road traffic accidents in Jordan using artificial neural network (ANN). *J. Traffic Log. Eng.* **2014**, *2*, 92–94. [CrossRef]

47. Moslehi, S.; Gholami, A.; Haghdoust, Z.; Abed, H.; Mohammadpour, S.; Moslehi, M.A. Predictions of traffic accidents based on wheather coditions in Gilan provice using artificial neuran network. *J. Health Adm.* **2021**, *24*, 67–78.

48. Liu, Y. Weather Impact on Road Accident Severity in Maryland. Ph.D. Thesis, Faculty of Graduate School, Maryland University, College Park, MD, USA, 2013.

49. Zou, X. Bayesian network approach to causation analysis of road accidents using Netica. *J. Adv. Transp.* **2017**, *2017*, 2525481. [CrossRef]

50. Ogwueleka, F.N.; Misra, S.; Ogwueleka, T.C.; Fernandez-Sanz, L. An artificial neural network model for road accident prediction: A case study of a developing country. *Acta Polytech. Hung.* **2014**, *11*, 177–197.

51. Kunt, M.M.; Aghayan, I.; Noii, N. Prediction for traffic accident severity: Comparing the artificial neural network, genetic algorithm, combined genetic algorithm and pattern search methods. *Transport* **2011**, *26*, 353–366. [CrossRef]

52. Taamneh, M.; Taamneh, S.; Alkheder, S. Clustering-based classification of road traffic accidents using hierarchical clustering and artificial neural networks. *Int. J. Inj. Control Saf. Promot.* **2017**, *24*, 388–395. [CrossRef]

53. Ghasedi, M.; Sarfjoo, M.; Bargegol, I. Prediction and Analysis of the Severity and Number of Suburban Accidents Using Logit Model, Factor Analysis and Machine Learning: A case study in a developing country. *SN Appl. Sci.* **2021**, *3*, 13. [CrossRef]

54. Mondal, A.R.; Bhuiyan, M.A.; Yang, F. Advancement of weather-related crash prediction model using nonparametric machine learning algorithms. *SN Appl. Sci.* **2020**, *2*, 1372. [CrossRef]

55. Liang, M.; Zhang, Y.; Yao, Z.; Qu, G.; Shi, T.; Min, M.; Ye, P.; Duan, L.; Bi, P.; Sun, Y. Meteorological Variables and Prediction of Road Traffic Accident Severity in Suzhou city of Anhui Province of China. 2020. Available online: https://www.researchgate.net/publication/340197416MeteorologicalVariables_and_Prediction____Road_Traffic_Accident_Severity_in_Suzhou_city_of_Anhui_Province_of_China (accessed on 20 November 2022). [CrossRef]

56. Olutayo, V.A.; Eludire, A.A. Traffic accident analysis using decision trees and neural networks. *Int. J. Inf. Technol. Comput. Sci.* **2014**, *6*, 22–28.

57. Silva, H.C.E.; Saraee, M.H. Predicting road traffic accident severity using decision trees and time-series calendar heat maps. In Proceedings of the 6th IEEE Conference on Sustainbility Utilization and Development in Engineering and Technology, Penang, Malaysia, 7–9 November 2019.

58. Chong, M.; Abraham, A.; Paprzycki, M. Traffic Accident Analysis Using Decision Trees and Neural Networks. *arXiv* **2004**, arXiv:cs/0405050.

59. Bahiru, T.K.; Kumar Singh, D.; Tessfaw, E.A. Comparative study on Data Mining Classification Algorithms for Predicting Road Traffic Accident Severity. In Proceedings of the 2018 Second Inernational Conference on Inventive Communication and Computational Technologies ICICCT, Coimbatore, India, 20–21 April 2018; pp. 1655–1660. [CrossRef]

60. Al-Turaiki, I.; Aloumi, M.; Aloumi, N.; Alghamdi, K. Modeling traffic accidents in Saudi Arabia using classification techniques. In Proceedings of the 2016 4th Saudi International Conference on Information Technology (Big data aNALYSIS) KACSTIT, Ryadh, Saudi Arabia, 6–9 November 2016; pp. 1–5. [CrossRef]

61. Lepperod, A.J. Air Quality Prediction with Machine Learning. Master's Thesis, Norwegian University of Science and Technology, Oslo, Norway, 2019.

62. Dong, S.; Khattak, A.; Ullah, I.; Zhou, J.; Hussain, A. Predicting and Analyzing Road Traffic Injury Severity Using Boosting-Based Ensemble Learning Models with SHAPley Additive exPlanations. *Int. J. Environ. Res. Public Health* **2022**, *19*, 2925. [CrossRef] [PubMed]

63. Kim, J.H.; Kim, J.; Lee, G.; Park, J. Machine Learning-Based Models for Accident Prediction at a Korean Container Port. *Sustainability* **2021**, *13*, 9137. [CrossRef]

64. Gutierrez-Osorio, C.; González, F.A.; Pedraza, C.A. Deep Learning Ensemble Model for the Prediction of Traffic Accidents Using Social Media Data. *Computers* **2022**, *11*, 126. [CrossRef]

65. Yuexu, Z.; Wei, D. Prediction in Traffic Accident Duration Based on Heterogeneous Ensemble Learning. *Appl. Artif. Intell.* **2022**, *36*, 2018643. [CrossRef]

66. Chang, L.Y.; Wang, H.W. Analysis of traffic injury severity: An application of non-parametric classification tree techniques. *Accid. Anal. Prev.* **2006**, *38*, 1019–1027. [CrossRef] [PubMed]

67. Yang, G.; Wang, Y.; Yu, H.; Ren, Y.; Xie, J. Short-Term Traffic State Prediction Based on the Spatiotemporal Features of Critical Road Sections. *Sensors* **2018**, *18*, 2287. [CrossRef]

68. Li, G.; Knoop, V.L.; Van Lint, H. Estimate the limit of predictability in short-term traffic forecasting: An entropy-based approach. *Transp. Res. Part C Emerg. Technol.* **2022**, *138*, 103607. [CrossRef]

69. Min, W.; Wynter, L. Real-time road traffic prediction with spatio-temporal correlations. *Transp. Res. Part C Emerg. Technol.* **2011**, *19*, 606–616. [CrossRef]

70. Paz, A.; Veeramisti, N.; De la Fuente-Mella, H. Forecasting Performance Measures for Traffic Safety Using Deterministic and Stochastic Models. In Proceedings of the IEEE 18th International Conference on Intelligent Transportation Systems, Gran Canaria, Spain, 15–18 September 2015; pp. 2965–2970. [CrossRef]

71. Pang, Y.; Zhao, X.; Yan, H.; Liu, Y. Data-driven trajectory prediction with weather uncertainties: A bayesian deep learning approach. *Transp. Res. Part C Emerg. Technol.* **2021**, *130*, 103326. [CrossRef]

72. Pang, Y.; Zhao, X.; Hu, J.; Yan, H.; Liu, Y. Bayesian spatio-temporal graph transformer network(b-star) for multi-aircraft trajectory prediction. *Knowl. Based Syst.* **2022**, *249*, 108998. [CrossRef]

73. Pang, Y.; Guo, Z.; Zhuang, B. Prospectnet: Weighted conditional attention for future interaction modeling in behavior prediction. *arXiv* **2022**, arXiv:2208.13848.

74. Romero, C.; Ventura, S.; Espejo, P.; Hervas, C. Data mining algorithms to classify students. Proceedings for the 1st IC on Educational Data Mining (EDM08), Montreal, QC, Canada, 20–21 June 2008; pp. 20–21.

75. Fawcett, T. *ROC Graphs: Notes and Practical Considerations for Data Mining Researchers*; Technical Report HP Laboratories: Palo Alto, CA, USA, 2003.

76. Vuk, M.; Curk, T. ROC curve, lift chart and calibration plot. *Metod. Zv.* **2006**, *3*, 89–108. [CrossRef]

77. Dimić, G.; Prokin, D.; Kuk, K.; Micalović, M. Primena Decision Trees i Naive Bayes klasifikatora na skup podataka izdvojen iz Moodle kursa. In Proceedings of the Conference INFOTEH, Jahorina, Bosnia and Herzegovina, 21–23 March 2012; Volume 11, pp. 877–882.

78. Witten, H.; Eibe, F. *Data Mining: Practical Machine Learning Tools and Techniques*, 2nd ed.; Morgan Kaufmann Series in Data Management Systems; Elsevier: Cambridge, MA, USA, 2005.

79. Benoit, G. Data Mining. *Annu. Rev. Inf. Sci. Technol.* **2002**, *36*, 265–310. [CrossRef]
80. Weka (University of Waikato: New Zealand). Available online: http://www.cs.waikato.ac.nz/ml/weka (accessed on 20 November 2022).
81. Berrar, D. Bayes' Theorem and Naive Bayes Classifier. *Encycl. Bioinform. Comput. Biol.* **2018**, *1*, 403–412. [CrossRef]
82. Zhang, H. *The Optimality of Naive Bayes, FLAIRS Conference*; AAAI Press: Miami Beach, FL, USA, 2004.
83. Friedman, J.; Hastie, T.; Tibshirani, R. Additive Logistic Regression: A Statistical View of Boosting. *Ann. Stat.* **2000**, *28*, 337–407. [CrossRef]
84. Rokach, L.; Maimon, O. *Decision Trees. In The Data Mining and Knowledge Discovery Handbook*; Springer: Boston, MA, USA, 2005; pp. 165–192. [CrossRef]
85. Xiaohu, W.; Lele, W.; Nianfeng, L. An Application of Decision Tree Based on ID3. *Phys. Procedia* **2012**, *25*, 1017–1021. [CrossRef]
86. Quinlan, J.R. *C4.5: Programs for Machine Learning*; Morgan Kaufmann: San Mateo, CA, USA, 1993.
87. Bella, A.; Ferri, C.; Hernández-Orallo, J.; Ramírez-Quintana, M.J. Calibration of machine learning models. In *Handbook of Research on Machine Learning Applications*; IGI Global: Hershey, PA, USA, 2009.
88. SPSS Statistics 17.0 Brief Guide. Available online: http://www.sussex.ac.uk/its/pdfs/SPSS_Statistics_Brief_Guide_17.0.pdf (accessed on 20 November 2022).
89. Liu, H.; Motoda, H. *Feature Selection for Knowledge Discovery and Data Mining*; Kluwer Academic: Boston, MA, USA, 1998.
90. Dash, M.; Liu, H.; Motoda, H. Consistency based feature selection. In Proceedings of the Fourth Pacific Asia Conference on Knowledge Discovery and Data Mining, Kyoto, Japan, 18–20 April 2000; pp. 98–109.
91. Hall, M.A. Correlation-Based Feature Selection for Discrete and Numeric Class Machine Learning. In Proceedings of the 17th IEEE Int'l Conf. Machine Learning, Orlando, FL, USA, 17–20 December 2000; pp. 359–366.
92. Novaković, J. Rešavanje klasifikacionih problema mašinskog učenja. In *Bussines Process Reeingineering*; Faculty of Technical sciences Čačak, University of Kragujevac: Kragujevac, Serbia, 2013; Volume 4.
93. Daelemans, W.; Hoste, V.; Meulder, F.D.; Naudts, B. Combined Optimization of Feature Selection and Algorithm Parameter Interaction in Machine Learning of Language. In Proceedings of the 14th European Conference on Machine Learning (ECML-2003), Lecture Notes in Computer Science 2837, Cavtat-Dubrovnik, Croatia, 22–26 September 2003; pp. 84–95.
94. Hall, M.A.; Smith, L.A. Practical feature subset selection for machine learning. In Proceedings of the 21st Australian Computer Science Conference, Perth, Australia, 4–6 February 1998; pp. 181–191.
95. Moriwal, R.; Prakash, V. An efficient info-gain algorithm for finding frequent sequential traversal patterns from web logs based on dynamic weight constraint. In Proceedings of the CUBE International Information Technology Conference (CUBE '12), Pune, India, 3– 6September 2012; ACM: New York, NY, USA, 2012; pp. 718–723.
96. Salzberg, L.S. Book Review: C4.5: By J. Ross Quinlan. Inc., 1993. Programs for Machine Learning Morgan Kaufmann Publishers. *Mach. Learn.* **1994**, *16*, 235–240. [CrossRef]
97. Thakur, D.; Markandaiah, N.; Raj, D.S. Re optimization of ID3 and C4.5 decision tree. In Proceedings of the 2010 International Conference on Computer and Communication Technology (ICCCT 2010), Allahabad, Uttar Pradesh, India, 17–19 September 2010; pp. 448–450.
98. Available online: https://www.programiz.com/dsa/greedy-algorithm (accessed on 15 November 2022).
99. Girish, S.; Chandrashekar, F. A survey on feature selection methods. *Comput. Electr. Eng.* **2014**, *40*, 16–28.
100. Moore, S.; Notz, I.; Flinger, A. *The Basic Practice of Statistics*; W.H. Freeman: New York, NY, USA, 2013.
101. Ilin, V. The Models for Identification and Quantification of the Determinants of ICT Adoption in Logistics Enterprises. Ph.D. Thesis, Faculty of Technical Sciences University Novi Sad, Novi Sad, Serbia, 2018.
102. Hair, J.F.; Anderson, R.E.; Tatham, R.L.; Black, W.C. *Multivariate Data Analysis*; Prentice-Hall, Inc.: New York, NY, USA, 1998.
103. Yang, T.; Ying, Y. AUC Maximization in the Era of Big Data and AI: A Survey. *ACM Comput. Surv.* **2022**, *37*. [CrossRef]

 *mathematics*

Article

Multi-Step Ahead Ex-Ante Forecasting of Air Pollutants Using Machine Learning

Snezhana Gocheva-Ilieva *, Atanas Ivanov, Hristina Kulina and Maya Stoimenova-Minova

Faculty of Mathematics and Informatics, Paisii Hilendarski University of Plovdiv, 24 Tzar Asen St, 4000 Plovdiv, Bulgaria
* Correspondence: snow@uni-plovdiv.bg

Abstract: In this study, a novel general multi-step ahead strategy is developed for forecasting time series of air pollutants. The values of the predictors at future moments are gathered from official weather forecast sites as independent ex-ante data. They are updated with new forecasted values every day. Each new sample is used to build- a separate single model that simultaneously predicts future pollution levels. The sought forecasts were estimated by averaging the actual predictions of the single models. The strategy was applied to three pollutants—PM_{10}, SO_2, and NO_2—in the city of Pernik, Bulgaria. Random forest (RF) and arcing (Arc-x4) machine learning algorithms were applied to the modeling. Although there are many highly changing day-to-day predictors, the proposed averaging strategy shows a promising alternative to single models. In most cases, the root mean squared errors (RMSE) of the averaging models (aRF and aAR) for the last 10 horizons are lower than those of the single models. In particular, for PM_{10}, the aRF's RMSE is 13.1 vs. 13.8 micrograms per cubic meter for the single model; for the NO_2 model, the aRF exhibits 21.5 vs. 23.8; for SO_2, the aAR has 17.3 vs. 17.4; for NO_2, the aAR's RMSE is 22.7 vs. 27.5, respectively. Fractional bias is within the same limits of $(-0.65, 0.7)$ for all constructed models.

Keywords: air pollution; machine learning; random forest; arcing; ARIMA errors; MIMO averaging strategy; multi-step ahead prediction; unmeasured forecast

MSC: 62-07; 62P12

Citation: Gocheva-Ilieva, S.; Ivanov, A.; Kulina, H.; Stoimenova-Minova, M. Multi-Step Ahead Ex-Ante Forecasting of Air Pollutants Using Machine Learning. *Mathematics* **2023**, *11*, 1566. https://doi.org/10.3390/math11071566

Academic Editor: Ioannis G. Tsoulos

Received: 14 February 2023
Revised: 6 March 2023
Accepted: 21 March 2023
Published: 23 March 2023

1. Introduction

Air pollution is a major and worsening environmental problem in many countries worldwide. The systematic accumulation of harmful aerosols in the air in populated areas is the cause of many diseases among their inhabitants. It leads to undesirable changes in the climate, forest, land, and all vital ecological systems [1,2]. Particulate matter, in particular, is dangerous for human health, examples include PM_{10} (with a diameter of less than 10 microns), $PM_{2.5}$ (with a diameter of less than 2.5 microns), nitrogen dioxide (NO_2), sulfur dioxide (SO_2), ground-level ozone (O_3), and others. Numerous studies have established the harmful influence of elevated concentrations of pollutants in ambient air, leading to heart disease, acute respiratory infection, chronic obstructive pulmonary disease, allergic dysfunction, lung cancer, and more [3,4]. Even at low concentrations, the presence of a constant background of polluted air is dangerous, primarily for small children and the elderly, as well as for the chronically ill [5]. The leading causes of poor quality air in populated areas can be conditionally divided into two large groups. On the one hand, low-quality air is a product of the anthropogenic sources of increased concentrations of pollutants due to human activity, such as production facilities, power plants, car traffic, household combustion, and others [1,6]. This type of air pollution source has a relatively constant character. Weather and atmospheric conditions are the other major factors affecting air quality. With the adverse trend of climate change, they are becoming increasingly chaotic and unsustainable.

Air pollution forecasting is a non-trivial task in which the atmospheric pollution concentrations for a given location and time are expected to be predicted based on existing data measurements of various factors. For research purposes, they are divided into global, regional, and local. From the point of view of the individual in the society, what is of practical value is the impact of local factors, more specifically, a given settlement, and taking into account the local climatic, geographical, industrial and other types of characteristics and factors affecting the degree of pollution and the consequences related to human health [7]. Standard solutions for this task produce computer numerical models for simulating atmospheric chemical composition and atmospheric dispersion modeling systems based on mathematical and chemical equations describing pollutant transport and diffusion chemical processes [8–11]. The practical implementation of this type of numerical model presupposes the presence of detailed input information on current air quality, monitored by local stations, remote sensing, forecasted weather conditions, data on the geographical terrain, and others. These models are complex, and their creation requires significant computing resources.

A promising alternative to numerical modeling is a large group of methods for environmental pollution modeling inspired by machine learning (ML). ML allows the construction of effective predictive models that can be easily implemented into mobile applications. Popular classical statistical methods for linear type time series include multiple linear regression (MLR), nonlinear regression, parametric type stochastic methods, Auto-Regressive Moving Average (ARIMA), GARCH, and many of their variants [12–20]. A recent large-scale, extensive study using spatial interpolation and MLR found close air pollutant-meteorological interactions in China [12]. Another study also focused on the importance of meteorological conditions on air pollution [13]. In one study [14], univariate SARIMA models were built with intervention variables to reflect the outliers for $PM_{2.5}$ and PM_{10}. The MLR is implemented in [15] for PM_{10}, depending on temperature changes. In another study [16], the MLR, Loess seasonal and trend decomposition with ARIMA, and SARIMA models are built and compared in the forecast of PM_{10}. Other studies have incorporated the influence of atmospheric factors and pollutant modeling with MLR, ARIMA, and integrated ARFIMA [17,18]. The hybrid ARIMA-GARCH models of PM_{10} concentrations were used in another study [19]. It should be noted that in the presence of the linear nature of the studied time series, linear methods can provide adequate and sufficiently good prediction without yielding to advanced ML algorithms.

In recent years, more and more studies have used high-performance ML techniques capable of extracting the hidden relationship between the input data and the regression prediction target as well as predicting with great accuracy empirical data of any kind. The main methods of this class are Neural Network (NN) regression, Recurrent Neural Network (RNN), Multilayer Perception (MLP), Deep Learning, Random Forest (RF), Classification and Regression Trees (CART), Multivariate Adaptive Regression Splines (MARS), Support Vector Machine (SVM), Genetic algorithm (GA), and more, including hybrid ones. The complex relationships among air pollutants and meteorology are quantitatively revealed in [21] using RF analysis. Additionally, RNN-based accurate forecasts of pollutants, including SO_2, NO_2, CO, $PM_{2.5}$, PM_{10}, and O_3, were obtained. An ensemble approach is applied in [22] for predicting fine particulate matter ($PM_{2.5}$) in the greater London area. Many models, including ensemble RF, bagging, and additive regression, were built and compared to single models with SVM, MLP, linear regression, and regression trees [23] to predict NO_2 concentration levels. It has been shown that ensemble models statistically outperform other models. Four ANN ensemble models and an innovative Fuzzy Inference Ensemble (FIE) model were proposed in [24] and are capable of estimating the concentration levels of O_3, CO, NO, NO_2, SO_2, PM_{10}, and $PM_{2.5}$. In [25], a stacked ensemble model is developed for forecasting the daily average concentrations of $PM_{2.5}$ in Beijing, China, based on levels of other pollutants and meteorological data. The base models in the stacking strategy are built with LASSO, AdaBoost, XgBoost, and GA-MLP. Their predictions are stacked using SVM. It has been shown that the resulting stacked model outperforms all base models.

In [26], a hybrid forecasting model was developed by incorporating the Taylor expansion to correct the residuals of traditional ANN and SVM models based only on the local meteorological data used as input variables. The experimental results of forecasting the average daily concentrations of PM_{10} and SO_2 have shown that the forecasting accuracy of the proposed model is very satisfactory. Other studies in the class of ML methods considered are [27–30]. There are other approaches to improving regression models' accuracy, particularly residual correction using ARIMA, as described in [31]. This approach is also suitable for ML predictive models, as demonstrated in [32,33]. Additional information on ML approaches and algorithms in the field can be found in review papers [34,35].

The primary purpose and application of regression models is to use them to forecast for a period of time called forecasting horizon. That is, the forecasting horizon is the length of time into the future for which forecasts are to be determined. They compare the preponderance of research extracts from known historical data outside of the working samples. The criteria for the accuracy and other qualities of the forecast for the selected horizon are different—here, there are no generally accepted established standards or theoretical results. In short-term prediction, the tested and selected model is usually used once to predict the level of concentrations for a fixed short horizon. Multi-step ahead forecasting (long-term) strategies are much less often applied. In this case, forecasting is done in successive steps, with the forecasting horizon shifted forward in time, either step by step or all at once with several steps.

However, in an actual situation, the researcher usually does not have the necessary information and the exact values of the independent factors (predictors) for the regression models since they will be measured in the future. When forecast data is used for the predictors, we talk about ex-ante ahead forecasting. It is natural to expect that the model's predictions will be affected by the corresponding uncertainty of these data. Evaluating the capabilities of ex-ante forecasting models is an open research problem, particularly for advanced ML approaches, to which this paper is devoted.

This study aims to develop a new multi-step ex-ante forecasting strategy for multivariate time series based on ML methods. The goal is to build and analyze models for predicting future pollution based on historical data and standard weather forecasts for h-days horizons. Moreover, for each subsequent day of a given horizon, the values of the pollutants and meteorological time series are replaced with the actually measured ones. Also, the weather forecasts are updated for the entire next horizon. Another main objective is to statistically investigate and compare the predictive abilities of two powerful ensemble tree machine learning methods—RF and Arcing (Arc-x4). The proposed real-type prediction approach can be classified as a generalization of the multi-input multi-output (MIMO) strategy, extending it in several aspects. This includes a new formula for calculating the final forecasts by averaging the forecasted values from the current single MIMO model and actual previous single models, the use of independent external forecasts for the predictors and lagged variables, and the implementation of five different statistical measures for evaluating and comparing the obtained results and the accuracy of models.

The main advantage of the developed strategy is the averaging of already obtained forecasts, which, to some extent, models directly existing relationships between the members of the forecasted time series. This refers to lagged variable-type relationships and internal dependencies that characterize each real-world time series. Another advantage is the minimal computation costs after the ML models are built. A drawback of the proposed approach is the possible accumulation of errors when summing the predictions of single MIMO models from the current and previous horizons. Besides, in our case, the great randomness of the predictors compensates for such types of errors, which are intended for real-world settings and do not significantly affect the good final results. Also, the bias is stable. Another difference with the standard MIMO strategy is that it uses all historical time series data, not just some fixed sliding data window.

The rest of the paper is organized as follows: Section 2 briefly introduces the concepts and reviews the literature on multi-step ahead forecasting strategies. Section 3 describes the framework of the proposed multi-step ahead forecasting approach, the model assumptions, and brief information on the methods and statistical measures used. The next section presents the study area, experiment data, the results of the application of the approach for three real-world air pollutants, data preprocessing, construction, investigation, and comparison of models. The last section discusses the study's main findings and draws conclusions.

This research is a part of the cloud Internet of Things (IoT) platform EMULSION [36].

2. Concepts of Multi-Step Ahead Strategies and Literature Review

The purpose of multi-step-ahead prediction is to forecast h values $\{\hat{y}_{N+1}, \ldots, \hat{y}_{N+h}\}$, where h is a forecast horizon ($h > 1$), based on known historical data $\{y_1, y_2, \ldots, y_N\}$ of the target time series Y. According to [37], three types of multi-step ahead strategies can be classified: multi-stage or recursive prediction, direct or independent value prediction, and parameter prediction. However, in more recent publications, this classification has been updated to five types [38–40]. All these strategies use a fixed number of historical data D, where D is called the embedding size. These strategies are Recursive, Direct, direct Recursive (DirRec), multi-input multi-output (MIMO), and direct MIMO (DIRMO) [38–40]. Some generalizations of these strategies are also discussed in [38], including lazy earning and some averaging algorithms for models built with these five strategies for the same horizon. The latter can be considered stacking models.

- Recursive Strategy

One of the most common approaches is recursive prediction (Rec). In the Rec strategy, the constructed time series model is applied h times sequentially as a one-step-ahead forecast procedure. Initially, the time series Y data used are $\{y_{N+1-D}, \ldots, y_N\}$ to predict $\hat{y}_{N+1}$. To predict the next value $\hat{y}_{N+2}$, data $\{y_{N+2-D}, \ldots, y_N, \hat{y}_{N+1}\}$ are used, etc. It is known that this strategy can produce accumulated errors and is therefore appropriate for relatively short forecasts (3–7 steps ahead). This is because the bias and variance from previous time steps are propagated into future prediction, as established in [37] for ARIMA-type models. However, the recursive strategy has been successfully applied to real-world time series with different ML algorithms (see [38]).

- Direct Strategy

In the direct prediction strategy, a separate model is built for each subsequent prediction $\hat{y}_{N+i}$, $i = 1, 2, \ldots, h$ using the identical observations $\{y_{N+1-D}, \ldots, y_N\}$. So the number of models equals the number of prediction steps on the horizon. The Rec and Dir strategies are applied and compared for MLR, RNN, and hybrid HMM/MLR models in [37] for many different datasets. The authors concluded that the most accurate results were obtained using the direct prediction strategy.

- DirRec Strategy

DirRec is a combination of the Dir and Rec approaches. A separate model based on $\{y_{N+1-D}, \ldots, y_N, \hat{y}_{N+1}, \ldots, y_{N+i-1}\}$ data is generated to predict each new $\hat{y}_{N+i}$, $i = 1, 2, \ldots, h$ value from horizon h. Note that the size D is different from other strategies.

- MIMO Strategy

The multi-input multi-output (MIMO) strategy involves building a single model with data $\{y_{N+1-D}, \ldots, y_N\}$ to predict $\{\hat{y}_{N+1}, \ldots, \hat{y}_{N+h}\}$ at a time. Thus, the forecasts are obtained with only one step for the entire horizon.

- DIRMO Strategy

Direct-MIMO (DIRMO) is a combination of the Dir and MIMO approaches. For this purpose, the horizon h is decomposed into several parts (blocks), and a MIMO strategy is applied to each block. The same $\{y_{N+1-D}, \ldots, y_N\}$ data is used.

The five strategies described above have diverse applications with many ML methods. Various US economic time series were modeled in [41] using the Rec and Dir strategies. A hybrid system to generate multi-step deterministic and probabilistic forecasting is proposed in [42]. A complex of five different ML algorithms is utilized: wavelet packet decomposition (WPD), gradient-boosted regression tree (GBRT), linear programming boosting (LPBoost), MLP, and the Dirichlet process mixture model. The models were used to predict $PM_{2.5}$ concentrations from 1 to h interval data. The Dir strategy used for 1-, 2-, and 3-steps ahead is applied based on historical type test values. Similar results were obtained in [30], where, in addition, the 1 to h interval results were aggregated to a lower resolution of 1 day, which naturally improved the predictive ability of the models. In one study, the Rec versus Dir prediction strategy with RF models is compared for a period of 1 to 6 hours ahead in the case of wind speed [43]. The Dir approach is employed in [44] for predicting Spanish electricity consumption data for 10 years measured with a 10-minute frequency. The forecasts have been obtained using decision trees, GBRT, and RF algorithms with subsequent stacking.

The five commonly used methods described above, along with ARIMA and MLP for preliminary forecasting of the independent time series, have been applied and compared for daily $PM_{2.5}$ forecasts for the next 10 days [39]. A recent study [40] developed a complex ensemble multi-step ahead forecasting system based on the same five methods. Least Square Support Vector Regression (LSSVR) and Long Short-Term Memory neural network (LSTM) are employed as the prediction tools. These are combined separately and compared with the Ensemble Empirical Mode Decomposition (EEMD) technique, boosting and stacking to obtain forecasts from 1-day-ahead to 10-day-ahead. In [38,45], more results and a literature review on multi-step ahead forecasting are presented.

3. Materials and Methods

3.1. Proposed Approach

3.1.1. Single Models

The objective of time series analysis and forecasting is to identify dependencies in its values and build a model able to predict the next values. A time series is an ordered, finite sequence of time-dependent data of the type

$$Z = \{z_1, z_2, \ldots z_t, \ldots, z_n\}, \quad z_t \in \mathbb{R}. \tag{1}$$

where t is the temporal index and n is the number of observations. Usually, the data are equidistant, with a different resolution scale (high-level—hourly and daily, or low-level—monthly, annual, or other types). The time series can be univariate or multivariate when it depends on other series determined in the same time period. In general, many time series are characterized by a complex structure and contain trends, seasonality, jumps, outliers, and other nonlinearities that complicate the task of building an adequate model.

This paper uses the following time series representation of the dependent variable to be predicted:

$$Y = \{y_1, y_2, \ldots, y_t, \ldots, y_{N_0}, y_{N_0+1}, \ldots, y_{N_0+s}\}, \quad s = 1, 2, \ldots. \tag{2}$$

where $y_t \in \mathbb{R}$, N_0 is the number of observations at some starting moment, and s stands for period step ahead in a multi-step procedure, which values are updated with the measured values at each increase of $t = s$ by 1. That is, a successive updating horizon is applied. In a real situation, for forecasting with a regression model with a horizon h, future values of r independent variables $\mathbf{X}_t = (X_{1,t}, X_{2,t}, \ldots, X_{r,t})$ should be available. To reflect this, in the multi-step modeling, we assume that each of these is given as a dynamically changing time series:

$$X_j^{(s)} = \left\{ x_{j,1}, x_{j,2}, \ldots, x_{j,N}, \widetilde{x}_{j,N+1}, \widetilde{x}_{j,N+2}, \ldots, \widetilde{x}_{j,N+h} \right\},$$
$$N = N_0 + s - 1, \quad j = 1, 2, \ldots, r; \quad s = 1, 2, \ldots, S \tag{3}$$

where N is a calibration data end of known target values, $x_{j,k}$ are measured values, and $\widetilde{x}_{j,k}$ are unmeasured forecasted future values, which are updated with the new measured values at each increase of s by 1.

We will consider the simultaneous prediction of h future values of Y at prediction step s by assuming the following general type of dependence:

$$\mathbf{Y}_t^{(s)} = (Y_{N+1}, Y_{N+2}, \ldots, Y_{N+h}) =$$
$$F_t\left(Y_{t-p'}, Y_{t+1-p'}, \ldots, Y_{t-1}, Y_t; \mathbf{X}_{t-q'}, \mathbf{X}_{t+1-q'}, \ldots, \mathbf{X}_{t-1}, \mathbf{X}_t; \widetilde{\mathbf{X}}_{N+1}, \ldots, \widetilde{\mathbf{X}}_{N+h}\right) + \varepsilon_t, \qquad (4)$$
$$t = 1, 2, \ldots, N+h$$

where F_t is a non-linear real-valued function dependent on the values of the dependent variable Y in some previous moments $t - p', \ldots, t - 1, t$, $\mathbf{X}_t = (X_{1,t}, X_{2,t}, \ldots, X_{r,t})$ are the predictors in the previous and/or current time $t - q', \ldots, t$, the terms $\widetilde{\mathbf{X}}_{N+1}, \ldots, \widetilde{\mathbf{X}}_{N+h}$ denote the h forecasted ahead predictor values, and $\varepsilon_t \in N(0, \sigma^2)$ is supposed to be a white noise process. The forecasted values are denoted by

$$\hat{\mathbf{Y}}_t^{(s)} = \left(\hat{Y}_{N+1}, \hat{Y}_{N+2}, \ldots, \hat{Y}_{N+h}\right) = \hat{F}_t \qquad (5)$$

To determine them for every step $s = 1, 2, \ldots$ a single predictive model $\hat{G}_t^{(s)}$ of type (5) with forecasts is first built:

$$\left(\hat{g}_{N+1}^{(s)}, \hat{g}_{N+2}^{(s)}, \ldots, \hat{g}_{N+h}^{(s)}\right), \quad N = N_0 + s - 1 \qquad (6)$$

Our study will consider that these single models are constructed with the same method as the successive rolling procedure. However, they could be generated using different methods and algorithms since they are independent.

3.1.2. Averaging Models

To extend the multi-step ahead forecasting strategies known in the literature, we propose the following approach. We will define the sought predictions (5) for each horizon step s by averaging the already calculated and actual predictions of the single models $\hat{g}_t^{(i)}$ up to step i by the expressions

$$\left(\hat{Y}_{t+1}, \hat{Y}_{t+2}, \ldots, \hat{Y}_{t+h}\right)^{(s)} = \begin{cases} \left(\hat{g}_{t+1}^{(1)}, \hat{g}_{t+2}^{(1)}, \hat{g}_{t+h}^{(1)}\right) & s = 1 \\[2mm] \left(\frac{1}{2}\sum_{i=1}^{2}\hat{g}_{t+2}^{(i)}, \frac{1}{2}\sum_{i=1}^{2}\hat{g}_{t+3}^{(i)}, \ldots, \frac{1}{2}\sum_{i=1}^{2}\hat{g}_{t+h}^{(i)}, \hat{g}_{t+h+1}^{(2)}\right) & s = 2 \\[2mm] \cdots & \cdots \\[2mm] \left(\frac{1}{s}\sum_{i=1}^{s}\hat{g}_{t+s}^{(i)}, \frac{1}{s}\sum_{i=1}^{s}\hat{g}_{t+s+1}^{(i)}, \ldots, \frac{1}{s-1}\sum_{i=2}^{s}\hat{g}_{t+h+2-s}^{(i)}, \frac{1}{s-2}\sum_{i=3}^{s}\hat{g}_{t+h+3-s}^{(i)}, \ldots, \hat{g}_{t+s+h-1}^{(s)}\right) & s < h \\[2mm] \cdots & \cdots \\[2mm] \left(\frac{1}{h}\sum_{i=s-h+1}^{s}\hat{g}_{t+s}^{(i)}, \frac{1}{h-1}\sum_{i=s-h+2}^{s}\hat{g}_{t+s+1}^{(i)}, \ldots, \frac{1}{2}\sum_{i=s-1}^{s}\hat{g}_{t+s+h-2}^{(i)}, \hat{g}_{t+s+h-1}^{(h)}\right) & s \geq h \end{cases} \qquad (7)$$

where $t = N$

For example, Table 1 shows the sequential symbolic forecasts for the horizon $h = 5$. Every single model with starting day s, according to (6), is a vector of dimension h in column s. To calculate the averaging model according to (7), we use the currently available forecasts from the current and previous single models for each day, starting from $t + s$. For instance, at $s = 1$, the prediction (7) is equal to the first single model (the vector in the first column ($s = 1$) of Table 1). For the next day, $s = 2$, we have the first two single models in the first two columns from $t + 2$, so we can average over these predictions in Table 1 to predict the horizon from $t + 2$ to $t + 6$, etc. After $s = h$, we will have the complete vectors of predictions according to the last formula from (7). For example, in Table 1, for the case $s = 5$, the regions covering the terms that are averaged by (7) to obtain the predictions in a new h-dimensional vector from $t + 5$ to $t + 9$ are marked with dashed lines.

Table 1. Forecasts for the case $h = 5$.

t \ s, Model (s)	($s=1$)	($s=2$)	($s=3$)	($s=4$)	($s=5$)	($s=6$)	($s=7$)	($s=8$)	($s=9$)	($s=10$)
$t+1$	$\hat{g}^{(1)}_{t+1}$									
$t+2$	$\hat{g}^{(1)}_{t+2}$	$\hat{g}^{(2)}_{t+2}$								
$t+3$	$\hat{g}^{(1)}_{t+3}$	$\hat{g}^{(2)}_{t+3}$	$\hat{g}^{(3)}_{t+3}$							
$t+4$	$\hat{g}^{(1)}_{t+4}$	$\hat{g}^{(2)}_{t+4}$	$\hat{g}^{(3)}_{t+4}$	$\hat{g}^{(4)}_{t+4}$						
$t+5$	$\hat{g}^{(1)}_{t+h}$	$\hat{g}^{(2)}_{t+h}$	$\hat{g}^{(3)}_{t+h}$	$\hat{g}^{(4)}_{t+h}$	$\hat{g}^{(h)}_{t+h}$					
$t+6$		$\hat{g}^{(2)}_{t+h+1}$	$\hat{g}^{(3)}_{t+h+1}$	$\hat{g}^{(4)}_{t+h+1}$	$\hat{g}^{(h)}_{t+h+1}$	$\hat{g}^{(h+1)}_{t+h+1}$				
$t+7$			$\hat{g}^{(3)}_{t+h+2}$	$\hat{g}^{(4)}_{t+h+2}$	$\hat{g}^{(h)}_{t+h+2}$	$\hat{g}^{(h+1)}_{t+h+2}$	$\hat{g}^{(h+2)}_{t+h+2}$			
$t+8$				$\hat{g}^{(4)}_{t+h+3}$	$\hat{g}^{(h)}_{t+h+3}$	$\hat{g}^{(h+1)}_{t+h+3}$	$\hat{g}^{(h+2)}_{t+h+3}$	$\hat{g}^{(h+3)}_{t+h+3}$		
$t+9$					$\hat{g}^{(h)}_{t+h+4}$	$\hat{g}^{(h+1)}_{t+h+4}$	$\hat{g}^{(h+2)}_{t+h+4}$	$\hat{g}^{(h+3)}_{t+h+4}$	$\hat{g}^{(h+4)}_{t+h+4}$	
$t+10$						$\hat{g}^{(h+1)}_{t+2h}$	$\hat{g}^{(h+2)}_{t+2h}$	$\hat{g}^{(h+3)}_{t+2h}$	$\hat{g}^{(h+4)}_{t+2h}$	$\hat{g}^{(2h)}_{t+2h}$
$\ldots$						$\ldots$	$\ldots$	$\ldots$	$\ldots$	$\ldots$

3.1.3. Framework of the Proposed Strategy

Our proposed strategy involves two main stages:

Stage 1: Generating Initial Models

This is a procedure for building, calibrating, and selecting an initial model based on historical data of type (1) using a dataset of size $N = N_0$. For this purpose, we use known measured values for the dependent Y and independent variables X. The first part of the data for $t = 1, 2, \ldots, N_0 - v$ will serve to train and validate the models, and the last v values are for independent "out of sample" testing. This study uses $v = 31$ or the test sample data for one month. The main result of this stage is the determination of optimal hyperparameters after evaluation of the data from testing and error correction using ARIMA. In this case, the models will become hybrids. A general scheme of the generation of the initial models in stage 1 is shown in Figure 1.

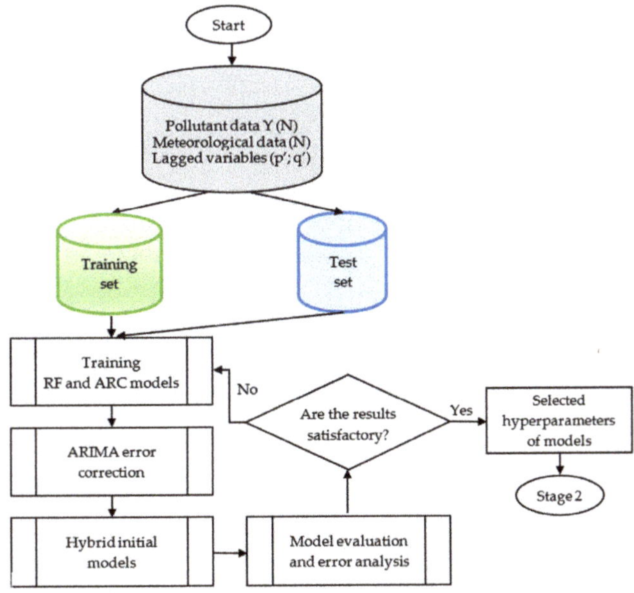

Figure 1. Flowchart of the algorithm of stage 1: Generating initial hybrid models.

When this approach is applied over a long period of time, stage 1 may be periodically initialized to update the hyperparameters.

Stage 2: Multi-Step Ahead Forecasting

This is the core of the proposed approach, which includes the following:

- Construction of single independent models and determining their predictions;
- Calculating averaged predictions (averaging models);
- Evaluation and comparison of the results.

The single independent models are built using the hyperparameters of the ML initial models, obtained in stage 1. The predictors are the measured data for air pollutants and independent time series, their values at previous moments (lagged variables), and forecasted (unmeasured) data for independent variables. For each given time period of horizons $s = 1, 2, \ldots, S$, a separate single model is built and evaluated that predicts h values as described in (4), (6). This is followed by a statistical evaluation of the models and residual diagnostics, including possible error correction with an appropriate ARIMA model.

The corresponding averaging models (5) are obtained by using the known forecasts of single models (6) in (7) up to a given horizon s (see also Table 1). The details of stage 2 are shown in Figure 2.

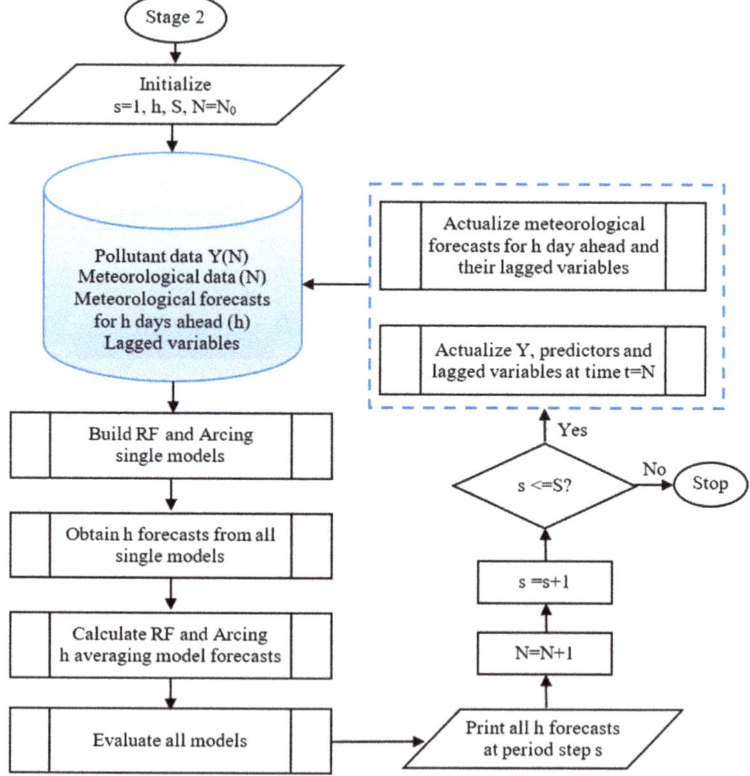

Figure 2. Flowchart of the algorithm of stage 2: Multi-step ahead forecasting.

3.2. Model Assumptions

Each model is built on clearly defined assumptions that determine its limitations for practical application. It complies with

- using the ML regression-type method to construct forecasting models for multivariate time series dependent on predictors;
- predictor variables of qualitative and quantitative type;
- fixed forecasting horizon h.

In our implementation, only a limited number of factors affecting air pollutants are used, limited to those measured by state-certified automatic measuring stations in the Republic of Bulgaria, synchronized with European criteria [46]. In this study, time series of three pollutants and eight meteorological variables were used. In order to account for the influence of the remaining unmeasured factors, lagged variables containing deterministic and stochastic information on unmeasured factors were used. Predicted and unmeasured weather forecasts in the predictor variables are recorded by us day by day for the selected time period. However, such types of forecasts can be freely retrieved from multiple sources on the Internet for any major population location over 3-, 5-, and 10-day weather forecast time intervals.

As can be seen from (4), the approach enables the use of arbitrary predictors and is not limited to meteorological ones as in this study.

3.3. Methods

We will use two ensemble tree methods: RF and Arcing (variant arc-x4) (ARC). ARIMA will also be applied for residual correction to improve model accuracy and adequacy. Ensemble methods are presented and discussed, for example, in [47,48].

- Ensemble Model

An ensemble model is called the linear combination:

$$\overline{f}(x) = \sum_{j=1}^{M} w_j f_j(x). \tag{8}$$

with weights w_j satisfying the conditions

$$\sum_{j=1}^{M} w_j = 1, \quad 0 < w_j \leq 1, \; j = 1, 2, \ldots, M. \tag{9}$$

where $f_j(x)$, $j = 1, 2, \ldots, M$ are singular models created with the same algorithm for different perturbed samples x. In this paper, we will consider methods for which:

$$w_j = \frac{1}{M}. \tag{10}$$

In the case of regression, the final ensemble model is the arithmetic mean of the predictions of its constituent component models.

- Random Forest

The RF algorithm was developed by Leo Breiman in his well-known paper from 2001 [49], after combining his bagging idea with the random subspace method created by Tin Kam Ho in 1995 [50]. It can be briefly characterized as a bagged tree classifier using a majority vote. RF is a high-performance ensemble method with tens or hundreds of unpruned decision trees. Generally, RF applies to regression and classification for cross-sectional and time-series datasets with any type of variable. The same procedure is applied for the construction and training of each individual model (tree) $f_j(x)$ from the ensemble (8). Given an initial sample of size n, the RF algorithm selects a random sub-sample, called out-of-bag (OOB), comprising about one-third of all data to test the model. From the remaining up to n instances onward, perturbed (randomized) samples are formed by subtraction with replacement using bagging [49]. A component tree is built using a recursive binary procedure with the formed sample. The resulting trees $f_j(x)$ are different and independent of each other. An important aspect of the RF algorithm is the random selection of a subset of all available predictors, called *mtry* (typically *mtry* = 3 to 5), when dividing the cases at each current node of the tree. The final RF model of *mtree* = M is found by (8), (10). RF's ability to calculate variable importance for each component tree and the composed ensemble model is useful for regression practice. It should be noted that RF is not particularly sensitive to the phenomenon of multicollinearity and is applicable even with highly correlated variables [51].

The main control hyperparameters set before the start of the RF algorithm are: *mtree*—the number of trees in an ensemble; *nodesize*—the size of the smallest allowable parent node; and *mtry*—the number of predictors randomly selected for splitting at each node. The last of these hyperparameters does not significantly affect the model's results.

- Arcing

In this paper, we will apply the Arcing method (adaptively resample and combine), also known in the literature as Arc-x4. It was proposed and studied by Leo Breiman [52]. The algorithm is classified in the group of boosting methods, but it is relatively rarely used, and its predictive properties have not been sufficiently studied. This applies in particular to its ability to forecast time series. By the way, in [53], the authors show empirically that Arc-x4 outperforms all other algorithms from the boosting class for classification applied to real binary databases.

The algorithm induces an ensemble of sequentially dependent classifiers (models) $C_1, C_2, \ldots, C_k, \ldots, C_T$ for a number of trials T. At the k-th step, the classifier C_k is training on the current resampled set T_k, and runs the original training set T down C_k by updating the probabilities $P^{(k+1)}$ for the next classifier C_{k+1} by the expression

$$P^{(k+1)}(i) = \frac{1 + m(i)^4}{\sum\left(1 + m(i)^4\right)}. \tag{11}$$

where $m(i)$ is the total number of misclassifications of case i by the previous classifiers $C_1, C_2, \ldots, C_k$. Unlike AdaBoost [54], classification is performed with unweighted voting, and in the case of regression, the prediction is averaged with equal weights according to (10). It is established that Arc-x4 reduced both the bias and variance of unstable models [52,53,55].

- Autoregressive Moving Average with Transfer Functions

The autoregressive moving average (ARIMA) is a linear type method, also known as the Box-Jenkins methodology [56], widely used for time series analysis and forecasting in statistics and econometrics. The main requirements for its application are the normality of data and stationarity, i.e., a constant mean and variance of the involved time series. However, in large sample sizes (e.g., where the number of observations per variable is greater than 10), violations of the normality assumption often do not noticeably impact the results [57]. In the more general case, the time series (1) may not be stationary and show a deterministic trend of some order (linear, quadratic, etc., up to some order d). Let us denote the back-shift operator $BZ_t = Z_{t-1}$ with $(1 - B)Z_t$. The transition to a stationary time series could be performed with a preliminary calculation of d finite differences of the series with an operator of this type $(1 - B)^d$. The one-dimensional (univariate) time series ARIMA ($p, d,$ and q) model has the following form:

$$\left(1 - \sum_{j=1}^{p} \phi_j B^j\right)(1 - B)^d Z_t = \left(1 - \sum_{j=1}^{q} \theta_j B^j\right) a_t + c, \tag{12}$$

where $p, d,$ and q are model parameters, with constant non-negative integers for each t. Here, p is the number of autoregressive (AR) terms, d is the order of differencing, q is the number of moving average (MA) terms a_t, and c is an additive constant [56]. In

Equation (12), $\phi_1, \phi_2, \ldots, \phi_p$ are estimates of the autoregressive part (AR) and $\theta_1, \theta_2, \ldots, \theta_q$ are estimates of the moving average (MA).

When predictor time series (called transfer functions (TF)) are also used in the modeling, the method is called ARIMA/TF. Predictors are set with parameters (p, d, and q) of the same type. Model (12) takes the form:

$$\Delta^d Z_t = \frac{MA}{AR} a_t + \sum_{i=1}^{k} \left(\frac{Num_i}{Den_i} \Delta_i^{d_i} B^{b_i} X_{it} \right) + \mu. \tag{13}$$

where X_i, $i = 1, 2, \ldots, k$ are the predictor time series, $\Delta^d = (1 - B)^d$, $\Delta^{d_i} = (1 - B)^{d_i}$, B^{b_i} is a delay term of positive integer order b_i, MA, AR, Num_i, Den_i are difference polynomials, dependent on the predictor's parameters, and μ is a constant [56].

- Hybrid method

Let us denote the generated and validated RF and ARC models at each prediction step s by Bs and their residuals by res_Bs with values

$$res\_Bs_t = Y_t - Bs_t. \tag{14}$$

If the corresponding ARIMA/TF model of res_Bs is Ar_res, built with the actual observations to forecast the entire considered period, then the hybrid model hBs and its residuals are calculated by

$$hBs = Bs + Ar\_res, \; res\_h = Y - h\_Bs. \tag{15}$$

3.4. Evaluation Measures

Let Y be the observed true time series (target) and P be the model prediction, Y_i and P_i ($i = 1, 2, \ldots, n$) are their values, respectively, $\overline{P}$, $\overline{Y}$ are mean values, and n is the sample size. The following well-known statistical measures of accuracy are considered to evaluate the prediction performance of the constructed ML models: Root mean squared error (RMSE), normalized relative mean squared error (NMSE), fractional bias (FB), Theil's forecast accuracy coefficient U_{II} [58], coefficient of determination (R^2), and index of agreement (IA) [59], given by the expressions:

$$RMSE = \sqrt{\frac{1}{n}\sum_{i=1}^{n}(Y_i - P_i)^2}, \quad NMSE = \frac{\sum\limits_{i=1}^{n}(Y_i - P_i)^2}{\sum\limits_{i=1}^{n}(Y_i - \overline{Y})^2} \tag{16}$$

$$FB = 2\frac{\overline{Y} - \overline{P}}{\overline{Y} + \overline{P}}, \quad U_{II} = \frac{\sqrt{\sum\limits_{i=1}^{n}(Y_i - P_i)^2}}{\sqrt{\sum\limits_{i=1}^{n}Y_i^2}} \tag{17}$$

$$R^2 = \frac{\left\{\sum\limits_{i=1}^{n}(P_i - \overline{P})(Y_i - \overline{Y})\right\}^2}{\sum\limits_{i=1}^{n}(P_i - \overline{P})^2 \cdot \sum\limits_{i=1}^{n}(Y_i - \overline{Y})^2}, \quad IA = 1 - \frac{\sum\limits_{i=1}^{n}(P_i - Y_i)^2}{\sum\limits_{i=1}^{n}\left(|P_i - \overline{Y}| + |Y_i - \overline{Y}|\right)^2} \tag{18}$$

RMSE and NMSE are used to assess the model's accuracy. The FB index measures the tendency of a model to over-predict with values close to 2 and under-predict with values close to -2. IA is a dimensionless and bounded measure in $[0, 1]$ with values closer to 1, indicating better agreement between the model and the target variable. The coefficient U_{II} is dimensionless and is used to compare models obtained by different methods and to identify large values. The model is considered to be of good quality when U_{II} is less than 1.

A good predictive model should have a value close to 0 for RMSE, NMSE, and FB and a value close to 1 for R^2 and IA. It should be noted that using the RMSE and coefficient of determination R^2 to compare models and forecasts should be interpreted with care, as this may result in misleading conclusions ([60], Ch. 14). Also, statistical significance may be useful for small validation samples to judge whether accuracy differs among reasonable forecasting methods. For construct validity, the accuracy measures should agree ([60], Ch. 14).

Models and statistical analyses were performed using Salford Predictive Modeler 8.2 (SPM) [61] and IBM SPSS statistics software, version 28.0 [62,63] on a laptop (Acer, Intel Core i7, CPU 1.8 GHz).

3.5. Study Area and Data

The proposed approach from Section 3 was applied to predict the air pollutants in Pernik, a typical medium-sized city in Bulgaria. Pernik is located in western Bulgaria, about 20 km (12 miles) southwest of the capital Sofia, with a population of 70,000 as of 2021. The city is at an altitude between 700 and 850 m (2297 and 2789 feet), has a length of 22 km (14 miles), and is surrounded by three low mountains. Through the city flows the river Struma. The city's territory is crossed by major roads, including Pan-European Corridors VIII and IV, which connect Central Europe and Greece. The climate of Pernik is moderately continental. Economically, the city is an industrial zone with steel production, heavy machinery (mining and industrial equipment), brown coal, building materials, and textiles. The location of Pernik is 42°36′ N 23°02′ E.

A dataset was collected for the concentration of three air pollutants (PM_{10}, SO_2, and NO_2) in the city of Pernik. Figure 3 shows the sequence plots of the pollutants. Daily data are modeled from 1 January 2015 to 9 February 2019. In the first stage, the training set is taken from 1 January 2015 to 21 December 2018 (1450 days), and the test period covers the next 31 days until 21 January 2019. The independent meteorological variables are eight: maximum air temperature (*maxT*, °C), minimum air temperature (*minT*, °C), wind speed (*speed*, m/s), wind direction (*direction$*), atmospheric pressure (*press*, mbar), cloud cover (*cloud*, %), relative humidity (*humidity*, %), and precipitation (*precipi*, mm). All measured data have been gathered from the official site of the automatic measuring station in Pernik [64,65] and the forecast weather data from the official site Sinoptik.bg.

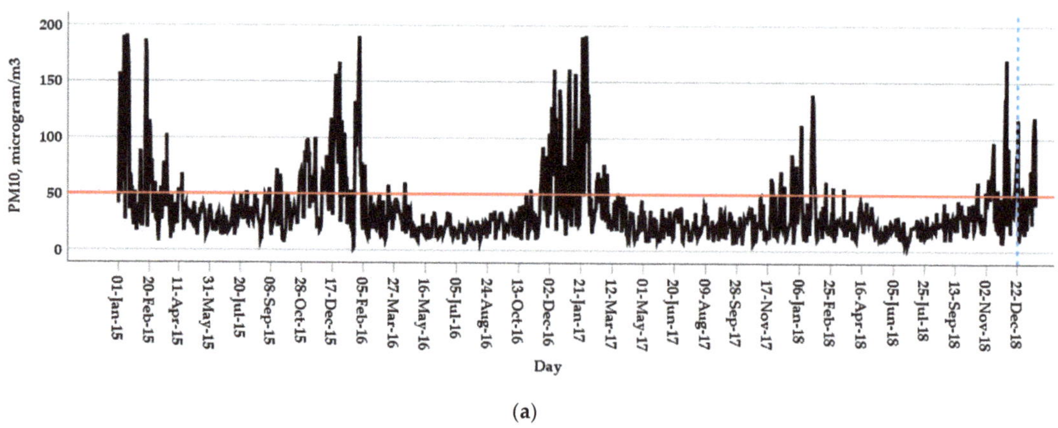

(a)

Figure 3. *Cont.*

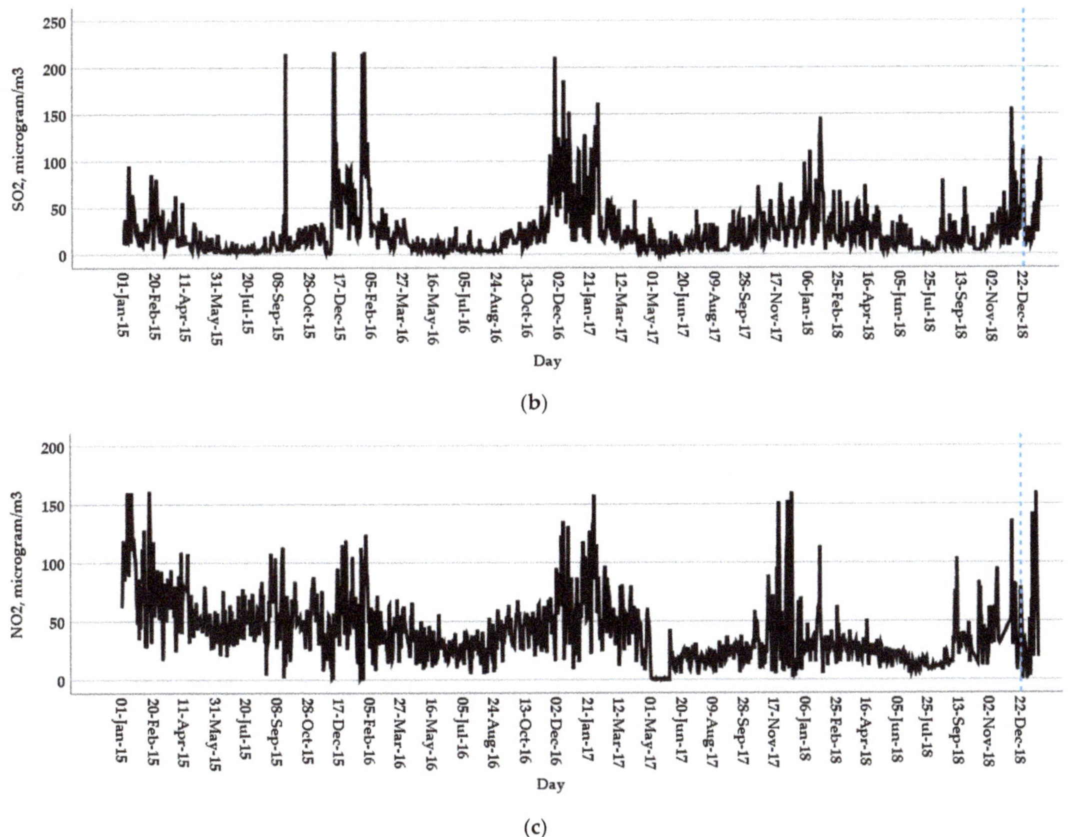

(b)

(c)

Figure 3. Sequence plots of the examined pollutant data: (**a**) PM_{10}, (**b**) SO_2, (**c**) NO_2. The horizontal red line in (**a**) indicates the European and national standard for the upper daily PM_{10} limit of 50 µg/m^3. The blue vertical lines separate the training and test samples.

4. Results

4.1. Preliminary Statistical Processing

The preliminary statistical processing of the data includes descriptive statistics, treatment of outliers and missing data, research on the multicollinearity of variables, and examination for sequence autocorrelation.

Descriptive statistics for the initial sample of n = 1481 cases are given in Table 2. Of these, pollutant data for the last 31 days was used as an independent test sample in building the initial models. This part of the data can be seen in Figure 3 on the right side of the vertical blue lines on 22 December 2018. Missing data are below 5% for all samples. In the analyses, they are replaced by the method of linear interpolation. Also, Table 2 shows large values of the skewness and kurtosis for the three pollutants, speed and precipi. This is a sign that the distribution of these variables is not normal. This could affect the direct application of classical regression methods but not the ML techniques. In Table 2, large values are observed, particularly for PM_{10} and SO_2. To reduce the influence of single spikes, available outliers of less than six cases are replaced by the values of their next largest value. We denote the obtained working variables for the pollutants as *YPM10* (PM_{10}), *YSO2* (SO_2), and *YNO2* (NO_2). Their statistics are presented in the first three columns of Table 2. Figure 4 shows the boxplots of the distributions of these variables, used hereafter as dependents.

Table 2. Summary statistics of the initial data for pollutants and meteorological variables.

Variable / Statistics	PM_{10} ($\mu g/m^3$)	SO_2 ($\mu g/m^3$)	NO_2 ($\mu g/m^3$)	*MaxT* (°C)	*MinT* (°C)	*Speed* (m/s)	*Humidity* (%)	*Pressure* (mbar)	*Cloud* (%)	*Precipi* (mm)
Valid	1411	1431	1434	1481	1481	1481	1481	1481	1481	1481
Missing	70	50	47	0	0	0	0	0	0	0
Mean	36.49	27.06	41.58	17.77	10.04	2.0004	0.694	1017.67	0.3197	1.759
Median	27.00	17.00	35.00	19.00	10.00	1.9400	0.700	1017.00	0.2500	0.000
Std. Deviation	30.309	45.114	28.920	10.527	10.243	0.8576	0.142	7.068	0.2629	4.0538
Variance	918.626	2035.244	836.351	110.815	104.914	0.736	0.020	49.957	0.069	16.433
Skewness	2.623	10.198	1.543	−0.151	−0.186	1.382	−0.088	0.248	0.707	4.284
Kurtosis	8.384	158.460	4.456	−0.925	−0.666	4.127	−0.747	0.463	−0.536	26.605
Minimum	2	1	0	−13	−27	0.28	0.31	990	0.00	0.0
Maximum	219	916	262	38	30	7.50	0.98	1039	1.00	44.0

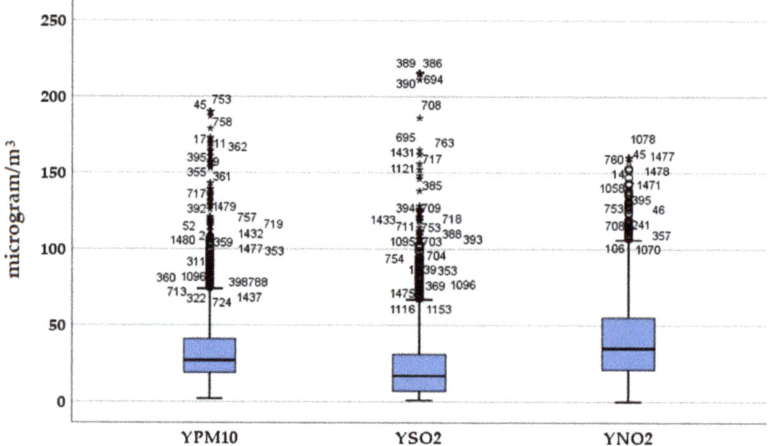

Figure 4. Box-plots of the used variables *YPM10*, *YSO2*, and *YNO2* for PM_{10}, SO_2, and NO_2, respectively.

It is known that the accuracy of regression models could be affected by the presence of multicollinearity between variables. Statistical analysis was performed to check for bicorrelation in the data using the non-parametric Spearman's Rho test. The Rho coefficients were the largest in absolute value only for (*minT*, *maxT*), equal to 0.969. All other Rho coefficients are less than 0.7. Since only 3 to 4 randomly selected predictors are used in the RF and ARC algorithms for each tree node splitting, we can assume that our data have no problematic multicollinearity.

Moreover, the autocorrelation functions (ACF) and partial ACF (PACF) plots of all considered time series showed that they do not exhibit trends. The ACF and PACF of *YPM10* indicated large PACF coefficients for the first 2 to 3 lags, for *YSO2* and *YNO2*—to the second lag, and for meteorological variables, an influence was found only for lag 1. Thus, in the general model (4), in our case, it is obtained $p' \leq 2$, $q' \leq 1$. That is, we will use lagged variables of the dependent variables up to the second order and for all predictors up to the first order.

In addition, in Figure 5 and Table 3, we give an example of a comparison of the measured values and forecasted weather conditions for one horizon of $h = 10$ days used in this study. There are some pretty big inaccuracies in these weather forecasts, except for those about relative humidity.

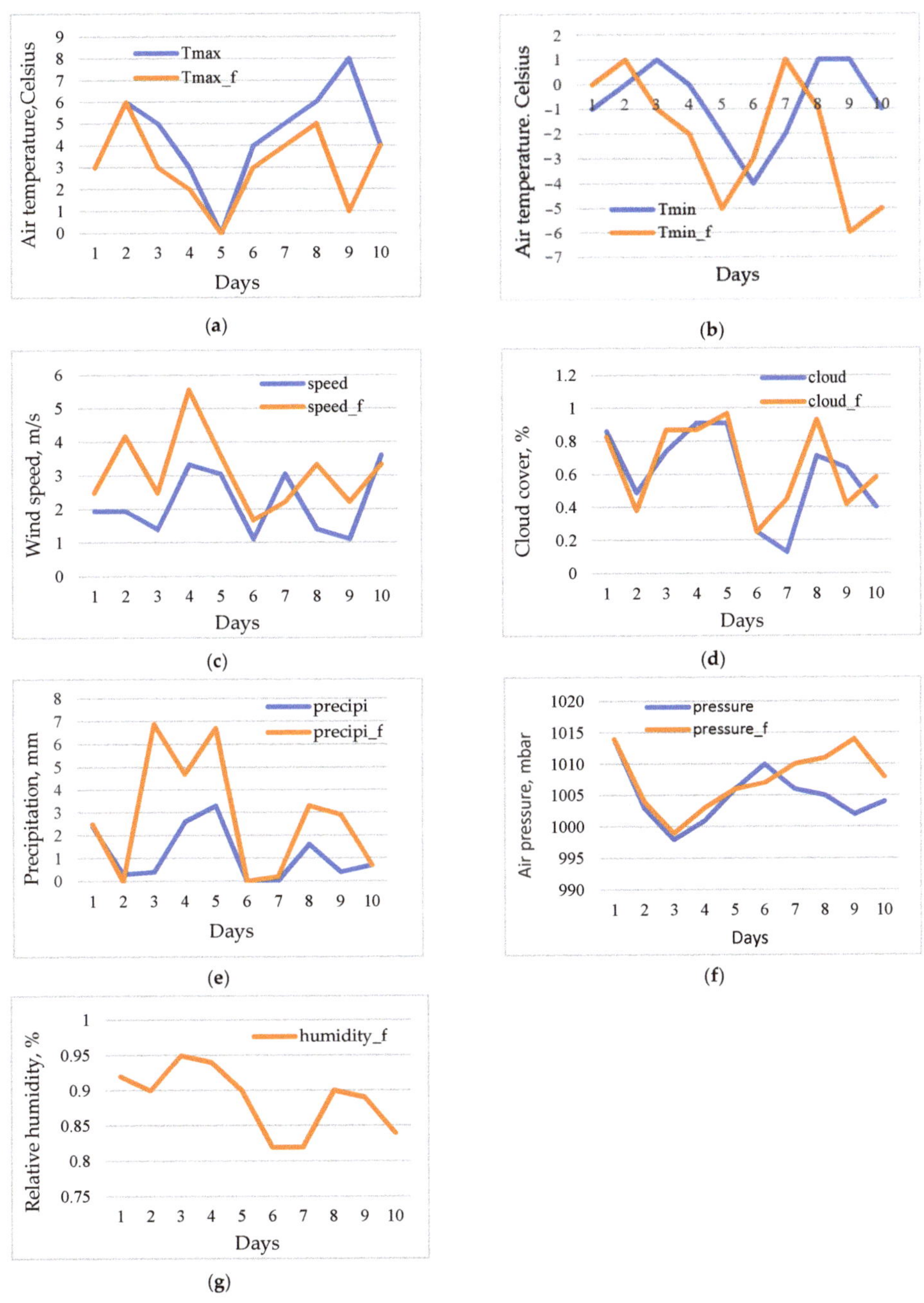

Figure 5. Measured meteorological values and their ex-ante weather forecasts (_f) for a 10-day horizon used in the multi-step procedure (example dataset): (**a**) MaxT, (**b**) MinT, (**c**) speed, (**d**) cloud, (**e**) precipi, (**f**) pressure, and (**g**) humidity.

Table 3. Example data for measured values of wind direction and corresponding weather forecasts.

Day	Direction$	Direction$_f	Day	Direction$	Direction$_f
1	ESE	ESE	6	SW	SE
2	SE	SSE	7	S	SE
3	WSW	NNE	8	S	SSW
4	NE	NNE	9	ESE	W
5	NNW	N	10	SSW	S

4.2. Construction and Evaluation of the Initial Hybrid Models

A basic principle of forecasting is the construction of a model that well explains large historical variations in the dataset [60]. This is our first task. At this stage, the dependent variables *YPM10*, *YSO2*, and *YNO2* of air pollutants PM_{10}, SO_2, and NO_2, respectively, and the eight meteorological variables are used. They cover a period of $n = 1481$ days from 1 January 2015 to 21 January 2019. Of these, the data for the first $N1 = N\text{-}v = 1450$ were used for training and validation, and the last $v = 31$ days were used as a hold-out (out-of-sample) test sample. Two lagged variables each were used for *YPM10*, *YSO2*, and *YNO2*, and one lagged variable each for all predictors was used for all initial ML models.

Multiple RF models were built and tuned varying for different selections of hyperparameters: number of trees in the model (*mtree*) from 100, 200, and 300; minimum number of cases for *nodesize* (5 and 10); and *mtry* = 3 and 4 for the random selection of predictors for splitting from a pool of 19 predictors. The models are trained with OOB procedures. Arcing models (denoted AR or ARC) were selected among models with 20, 30, 40, and 50 trees; a minimum number of cases in parents to child nodes was *m*1:*m*2 = 10:5, *mtry* = 3. ARC models were cross-validated (CV) with standard 5-fold and 10-fold CV. Here we follow the recommendation of [66] to use k-fold cross-validation over hold-out validation. Along with this, for greater precision, the initial models were also tested with a separate hold-out test sample of $v = 31$ days.

The hyperparameters for the RF models for the three pollutants showed close values: *mtree* = 300, *nodesize* = 5, and *mtry* = 3, OOB validation. The ARC models with the best statistics are ensembles with 50 trees, *m*1:*m*2 = 10:5, *mtry* = 3, 10-fold CV scheme.

From the built RF models, three models were selected, labeled *TRF_P*, *TRF_S*, and *TRF_N*, for PM_{10}, SO_2, and NO_2, respectively. Similarly, three ARC models were selected: *TAR_P*, *TAR_S*, and *TAR_N*. After a detailed examination of their residuals, it was found that there were weak autocorrelations. To ensure a lack of fit, ARIMA/TF models of the residuals were built for correction. All predictors were used as transfer functions. The corrections are added to the initial models to construct the hybrid test models using (14)–(15). They are denoted by *hTRF_P*, *hTRF_S*, etc. The basic descriptive statistics of the dependent variables *YPM10*, *YSO2*, and *YNO2* were compared with these hybrid models in Table 4. Reasonably good agreement of the relevant descriptive statistics is observed for the RF and ARC models with *YPM10*, *YSO2*, and *YNO2*, respectively.

Table 4. Descriptive statistics of the initial hybrid models for the test sample vs. measured values [a].

Statistic	Pollutant Variables			Initial Hybrid Models					
	YPM10	*YSO2*	*YNO2*	*hTRF_P*	*hTAR_P*	*hTRF_S*	*hTAR_S*	*hTRF_N*	*hTAR_N*
Mean	36.1249	25.4146	41.3707	36.046	36.306	25.377	25.730	41.283	42.244
Median	27.00	17.00	35.00	28.540	28.056	17.859	17.422	37.640	37.615
Std. Dev.	29.562	29.064	27.973	25.996	27.792	25.190	27.295	23.217	24.390
Variance	873.913	844.717	782.463	675.8	772.38	634.548	745.001	539.031	594.885
Skewness	2.551	2.932	1.281	2.412	2.632	2.355	2.892	1.058	1.241
Kurtosis	7.694	11.985	2.183	6.806	8.178	6.905	11.324	1.562	2.141
Minimum	2	1	0	6.311	8.295	0.379	0.457	0	0
Maximum	190	215	160	176.071	185.111	171.522	202.785	142.038	149.649

[a] the standard error of skewness for all variables is 0.064; the standard error of kurtosis for all variables is 0.127.

The following Table 5 presents the main performance results of the initial hybrid models. In row 4 the parameters of the ARIMA/TF models of the residuals are given. In their estimation, insignificant variables and lags were removed at the significance level $\alpha = 0.05$ In row 5 are the estimated Ljung-Box test statistics for lack of fit applied to the residuals of the ARIMA/TF models [67]. All Ljung-Box statistics are insignificant at level $\alpha = 0.05$, which allows to reject the null hypothesis, indicating that the models exhibit significant autocorrelations. For the six hybrid models in Table 5, the Ljung-Box test was applied to the 24 lags [68]. The last six rows of Table 5 present the statistics from (16)–(18). These show that all hybrid test models perform very well, with the ARC models outperforming the RF models with the exception of fractional bias.

Table 5. Performance statistics of the hybrid RF-ARIMA/TF and ARC_ARIMA/TF initial models.

Statistic	Initial Hybrid Models					
	hTRF_P	*hTAR_P*	*hTRF_S*	*hTAR_S*	*hTRF_N*	*hTAR_N*
Variable	YPM10	YPM10	YSO2	YSO2	YNO2	YNO2
ARIMA/TF	(2,0,14)	(1,0,3)	(1,0,5)	(0,0,11)	(1,0,21)	(2,0,21)
Ljung-Box Sig.	0.231	0.454	0.905	0.304	0.360	0.154
RMSE	8.3182	6.0339	8.9356	7.2069	10.0499	8.9468
NMSE	0.0792	0.0417	0.0946	0.0615	0.1292	0.1024
FB	−0.0006	−0.005	0.001	−0.0123	0.0013	−0.0209
Uii	0.0046	0.0034	0.006	0.0049	0.0052	0.0047
IA	0.99998	0.99999	0.99998	0.99999	0.99997	0.99998
R^2	0.932	0.960	0.932	0.966	0.884	0.905

Figure 6 illustrates the behavior of Ljung-Box coefficient significance values where the underlying process assumed independence (white noise).

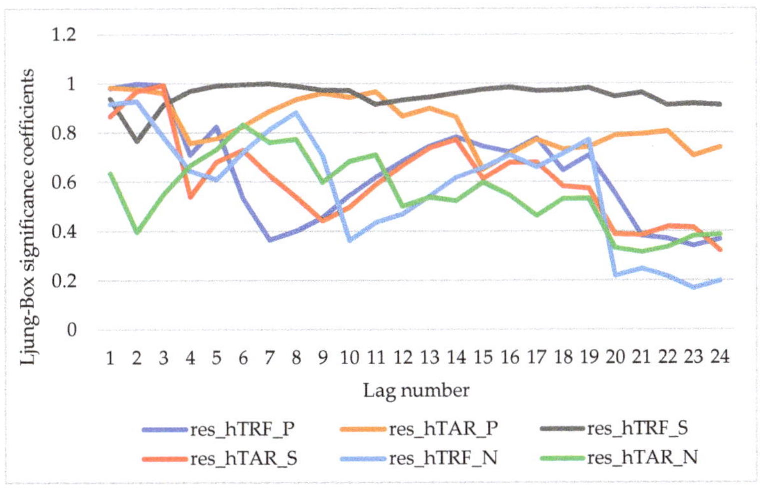

Figure 6. Significance values of Ljung-Box coefficients for residuals of the initial hybrid test models.

Based on the performed diagnostics, we can conclude that the initial hybrid models are adequate and can be used to predict future pollutant values [33,68].

In particular, separately for all three dependent variables (*YPM10*, *YSO2*, and *YNO2*), the corresponding variable importance was established. In all three cases, the results indicated that the lagged variables of the targets, minimal air temperature, and wind speed are among the most important predictor variables for the training process.

4.3. Results from Stage 2—Multi-Step Forecasting

Following the algorithm in Figure 2, the built and calibrated initial models are extended step by step to calculate the h-day forecasts of the unknown concentrations of the three pollutants. All models use the already established hyperparameters from stage 1. A separate model is built according to (6) to predict each future horizon h.

For completeness, in Figure 7, we present the measured values of air pollutants for 17 days, which we further seek to predict. Some outliers are observed in the first seven days.

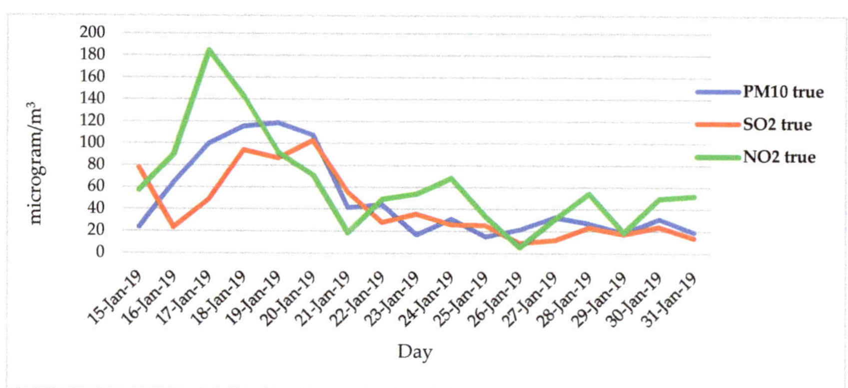

Figure 7. Measured values of the three air pollutants to be predicted.

4.3.1. Construction and Evaluation of the Single Models

For each of the three pollutants, two single hybrid models were built-with RF and ARC. The models are labeled *RF_P* and *AR_P* (for PM_{10}), *RF_S* and *AR_S* (for SO_2), and *RF_N* and *AR_N* (for NO_2), respectively, at each horizon step s, $s = 1, 2, \ldots, 17$. The first prediction horizon ($s = 1$) starts from 15 January 2019 and uses data from 1 January 2015 to 14 January 2019 with known data plus 10 days ahead with forecasted meteorological data. This sets the value of the initial calibration data, where $N_0 = 1474$. The total number of single models needed to forecast 10 days ahead, performing $s = 17$ period steps, is 102.

From the obtained results, Figure 8 (in the left side Figure 8a,c,e,g,i) illustrate the evaluation statistics (16)–(18) of the horizon forecasts from all created single models. It is seen from Figure 8a that the RMSEs of model *RF_P* are smaller than those of model *AR_P*. The same ratios are observed for *RF_N* and *AR_N*. Similar are the results for *RF_S* and *AR_S*, at $s > 6$. The larger error values for $s < 7$ are probably due to the more difficult prediction of large outliers in the original data illustrated in Figure 7. In the case of NMSE in Figure 8c, we have similar results. Even here, the differences are larger in favor of RF models. In Figure 8f, the values of all FBs are in the interval $(-0.65, 0.70)$ without large deviations and with a decreasing trend. The largest range is observed in FB for model *AR_S*. Figure 8g shows for *Uii* the same ratios as for NMSE. All of Theil's *Uii* coefficients are less than 1. This indicates the models' very good predictive performance (see also Section 3.4). The last figure in Figure 8i shows the IAs of the forecasts that vary strongly in the interval $(0.1, 0.8)$. Here, the IA values of the RF models outperform, although less so than the corresponding values of the AR models. We have an exception for *RF_N* at $s > 10$. The overall conclusion is that, despite the better statistical performance of the initial AR models, the RF models do slightly better in predicting ex ante pollutant concentrations, and that is performed with highly changeable predictors.

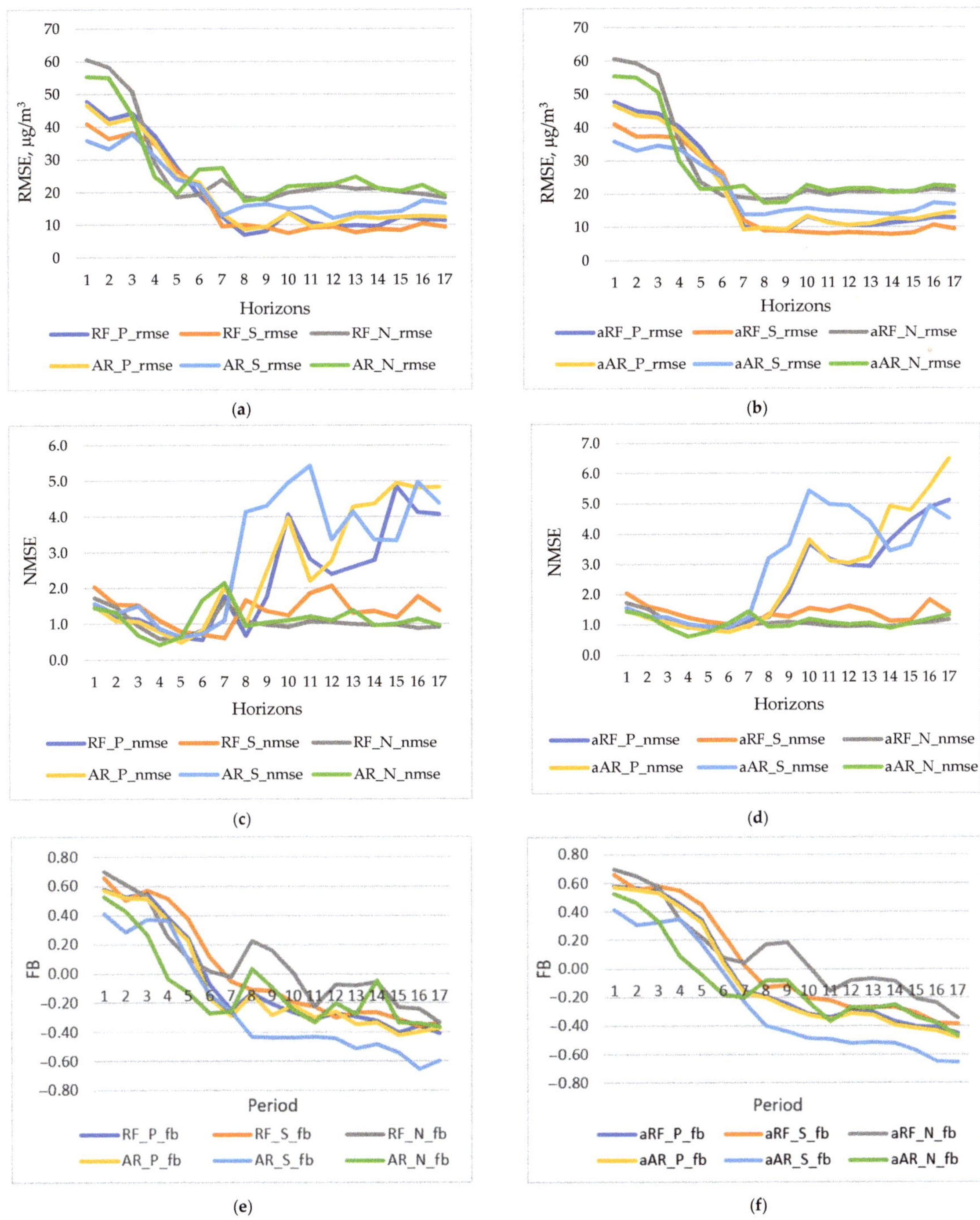

Figure 8. *Cont.*

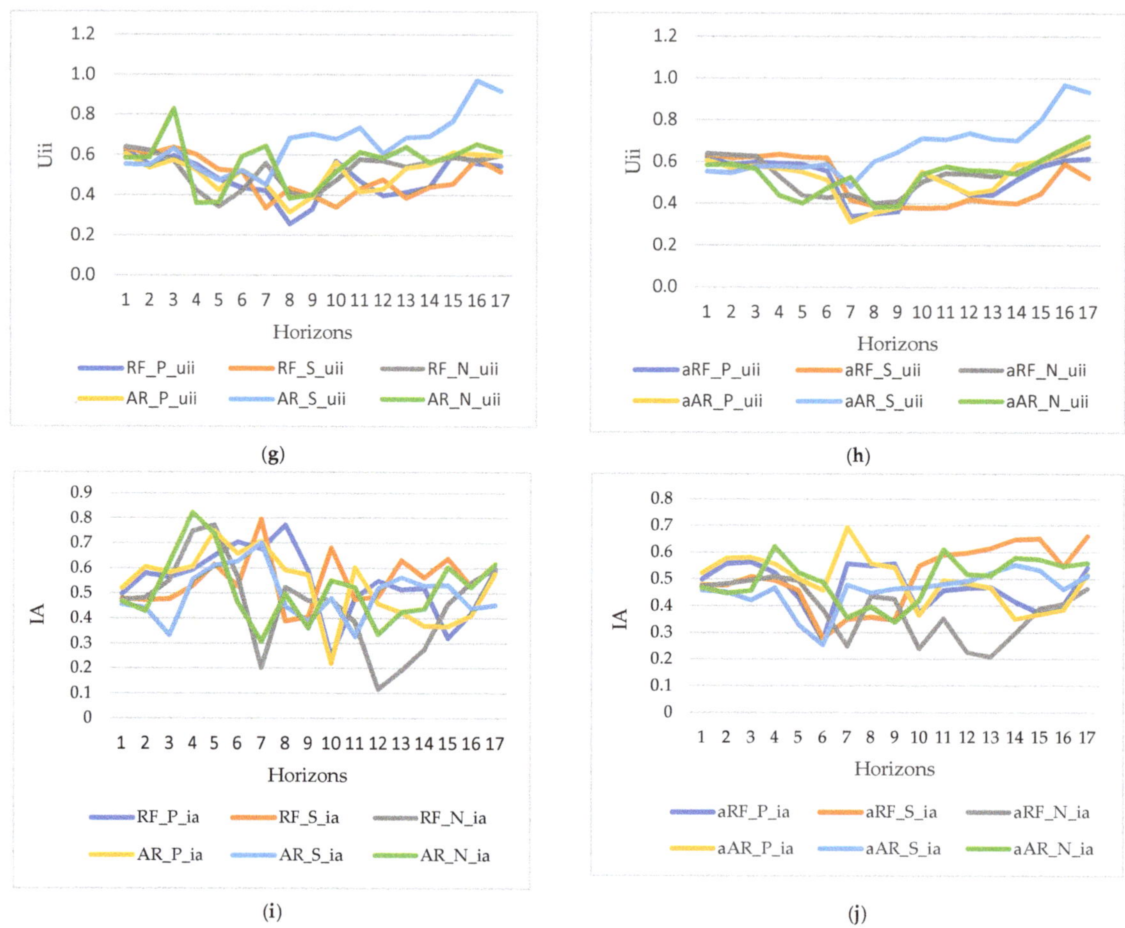

(g)

(h)

(i)

(j)

Figure 8. Comparison of the prediction accuracy statistics of all single models RF_ and AR_ (on the left) and the corresponding averaging models aRF_ and aAR_ (on the right): (**a**,**b**) RMSE; (**c**,**d**) NMSE; (**e**,**f**) FB; (**g**,**h**) Uii; (**i**,**j**) IA.

4.3.2. Construction and Evaluation of the Averaging Models

After computing the 102 single models for each period step s, each with a horizon h, forecasts are obtained. They are averaged for each day by (7). The predictive averaging models are labeled aRF_P and aAR_P (for PM_{10}), aRF_S and aAR_S (for SO_2), and aRF_N and aAR_N (for NO_2). In our case, for horizon $h = 10$, we have calculated the forecast values for $S = 17$ periods.

From the obtained results, Figure 8b,d,f,h,j (right column) illustrate the corresponding evaluation accuracy statistics (16)–(18) for all created averaging models. Figure 8b shows RMSE behavior almost identical to that of single models. Especially for the last 10 horizons, in most cases, the RMSEs of the averaging models are smaller than the corresponding RMSEs of the single models. In particular, for PM_{10} the aRF's RMSE is equal to 13.1 $\mu g/m^3$ vs. 13.8 $\mu g/m^3$. For the NO_2 model, aRF shows 21.5 $\mu g/m^3$ vs. 23.8 $\mu g/m^3$. For SO_2, aAR has RMSE = 17.3 vs. 17.4, and for NO_2, the aAR model has RMSE = 22.7 vs. 27.5 for the single model, respectively. In Figure 8d, at $s > 5$ NMSEs, the averaging models appear more smoothed compared to the corresponding values of single models in Figure 8c. Here there is an exception for $s = 17$ in model AR_P. Fractional bias is within the same limits of $[-0.65, 0.70]$ for all constructed models, as shown in Figure 8e,f. Also, all of Theil's Uii coefficients are less than 1, which indicates a very good predictive ability for averaging models.

Although to a lesser extent, the other comparisons lead to the same general conclusion as for single models: a slightly pronounced superiority of RF models over AR. In the following two subsections, we will conduct statistical tests to check if there are statistically significant differences.

4.4. Comparison of the Accuracy Measures of the Forecasts

In this section, we compare the estimates of the statistical indicators (16)–(18) between the obtained final forecasts of the three pollutant targets ($YPM10$, $YSO2$, and $YNO2$) for the two methods and for the two multi-step-ahead prediction approaches. This does not include R^2 as noted in Section 3.4. For this purpose, we use Kendall tau-b rank correlation for paired samples, a nonparametric measure of the association between two sets of rankings. This statistic is useful for comparing methods when the number of forecasts is small, the distribution of the errors is unknown, or outliers (extreme errors) exist [60]. A higher positive correlation indicates better agreement between methods or models. The statistical significance of the coefficients is at level 0.05.

4.4.1. Comparison among the Two ML Methods

Table 6 presents Kendall's tau-b correlations of accuracy indicators for the pairs of models obtained with RF and Arcing methods. Good agreement among the methods for calculating accuracy measures (RMSE) with coefficients from 0.6 to 0.8 is observed. For NMSE, the correlations are high for PM_{10} predictions (0.838 and 0.926); for the rest of the pairs, they are lower—around 0.4. The highest correlations are for FB for all model pairs (from 0.85 to 1.000). The correlations for AI are also high within the interval 0.5–0.7, except for the NO_2 models. For Uii, medium and high correlation values are obtained for the PM_{10} and NO_2 models. The lower Uii correlations for some models of SO_2 (with low and insignificant correlations) can be explained by the few large outliers (see Figure 7). In general, following [60], it can be concluded that the correlations agree well, so the two methods exhibit almost equal predictive quality.

Table 6. Kendall's correlations for comparison of the forecast accuracy, calculated using the two methods, RF and Arc-x4, for 17 period steps, each one for a prediction horizon of $h = 10$ steps ahead.

Statistic	$RF\_P,$ AR_P	$RF\_S,$ AR_S	$RF\_N,$ AR_N	$aRF\_P,$ aAR_P	$aRF\_S,$ aAR_S	$aRF\_N,$ aAR_N
RMSE	0.897	0.676	0.676	0.912	0.676	0.603
NMSE	0.838	0.382	0.397	0.926	0.368	0.412
FB	0.853	0.941	0.824	1.000	0.926	0.926
Uii	0.662	0.029 [a]	0.368	0.750	0.091 [a]	0.809
IA	0.618	0.471	0.574	0.706	0.647	0.029 [a]

[a] Insignificant coefficients.

4.4.2. Comparison among the Two Multi-Step Ahead Strategies

In Table 7, agreement among each pair of single and averaging models for five different statistical measures (16)–(18) of the forecasts (without R^2) is presented. The correlations for RMSE are between 0.65 and 0.8, except for the NO_2 models. The NMSE coefficients are similar (from 0.6 to 0.83), and a lower coefficient is observed for the NO_2 models (0.309). The FB correlations show high values (0.8–0.99) for all model pairs. The correlations for Uii are medium to high, in the range of 0.49–0.75. The correlations for IA are weak, with an insignificant coefficient, except for 0.544 for (AR_P, aAR_P) and 0.632 for (RF_N, aRF_N). The results show reasonably good agreement among the forecasts of single and averaging models.

Table 7. Kendall's correlations for comparison of the forecast accuracy of single and averaging models for 17 period steps, each one for a prediction horizon of $h = 10$ steps ahead.

Statistic	RF_P, aRF_P	AR_P, aAR_P	RF_S, aRF_S	AR_S, aAR_S	RF_N, aRF_N	AR_N, aAR_N
RMSE	0.794	0.691	0.809	0.809	0.426	0.647
NMSE	0.824	0.794	0.647	0.779	0.309	0.618
FB	0.912	0.794	0.956	0.912	0.987	0.794
Uii	0.603	0.662	0.706	0.632	0.750	0.485
IA	0.338	0.544	0.294	0.088 [a]	0.632	0.324

[a] Insignificant coefficients.

5. Discussion with Conclusions

In this study, we developed a multi-step ahead ex-ante forecasting strategy for time series with stochastic and high-frequency behavior. As shown in the preliminary study of the data (Table 2 and Figures 4 and 5), the examined time series of air pollutants do not exhibit a normal distribution. They are characterized by many outliers that cannot be ignored. For the prediction of this type of data, we selected the ML methods RF and Arc-x4. We have previously explored many other methods to implement the modeling, including CART, MARS, LASSO, CART ensembles and bagging, stochastic gradient boosting, and more. We chose RF and ARC-x4 not only for their high statistical performance but also for their ability to predict new data well. The goal was to determine which ML methods are most suitable for achieving good results in a real-world situation. For the same reason, restrictions and assumptions are imposed on the predictors described in Section 3.2. Here, however, we must pay attention to the fact that lagged dependent variables were used as predictors, which indirectly reflected in a stochastic manner many other measurable and non-measurable factors influencing the pollution level. We have determined the approximate number of lags according to the behavior of the ACF and PACF of the dependent and meteorological variables. On this basis, a general form of the dependence in (4) is proposed. In this paper, we have chosen a short time horizon h of 10 days and repeated the experiments for 17 consecutive horizons (periods). We have yet to specifically investigate the most appropriate horizon length for the proposed strategy. This question remains open.

The developed forecasting strategy consists of two stages. The first stage is very important, with the selection and detailed examination of the candidate predictive models. First, RF and ARC models were created and analyzed, showing very good predictive properties, as can be seen from Table 5. The basic requirements for building models without autocorrelating residuals were carefully checked by examining the relevant ACF and using different statistical tests, including the Ljung-Box portfolio test. Some residuals were found to have values outside the confidence intervals. For this reason, all models had to be hybridized with the correction of their errors. This was done using the ARIMA method. Each hybrid model was calculated as a sum of the ML model and the ARIMA model of its residuals. The residuals of the hybrid methods were re-examined to obtain statistically valid models, checked by tests. Overall, the results on the right side of Table 5 suggest the hybrid initial ARC models outperform the RF models for all three pollutants.

The implementation of the second stage of the multi-step prediction required building a large number of single models for each horizon and each pollutant. The implementation turned out to be laborious. Updating the database should also be taken into account. For the first $s = 1, 2, \ldots, h$ periods, the forecasts are the average value of the available forecasts from the previous and current models. The final averaging models were found using (7). The application of the proposed approach was demonstrated for three different pollutants—PM_{10}, SO_2, and NO_2. The resulting final predictions were evaluated using five accuracy measures. The comparison of errors is illustrated in Figure 8 for both predictions of the single and averaging models. It is seen that the RF models achieve slightly more accurate predictions of tested future data in all cases. In addition, Kendall's correlation was performed to compare the association between the accuracy of the two methods (RF and ARC) and the two strategies (single MIMO and averaging). In general, all indicators agree. Therefore, we can conclude that construct validity was obtained [60] and that both multi-step ahead approaches are alternatives.

Many studies have compared the performance of multi-step ahead strategies. However, due to the variety of modeling methods, accuracy criteria, and data, none of the existing strategies is known to be the best in all contexts. Nevertheless, the proposed approach can be formally compared with other results. For example, while in [37], the independent value prediction (Dir) was studied, in the present work, time series with predictors were used, ARIMA error correction was used, the data sets were updated dynamically, and more new elements were involved. The authors of the recent study [39] have employed all five strategies from Section 2 to forecast $PM_{2.5}$ for 10 days ahead. The best results among all constructed models were achieved using the recursive strategy with LASSO feature selection and forecasting the predictors in future time with the ARIMAX model. In one study, the direct strategy for hourly 1- to 24-step-ahead predictions of the air pollution index in Malaysia is preferred over other approaches [45]. A stacked ensemble with diverse ML modeling techniques using different strategies was adopted for $PM_{2.5}$ prediction in [39]. Existing multi-step ahead forecasting approaches have been thoroughly reviewed and compared empirically using 111 experimental datasets [38]. The authors concluded that multi-output strategies based on MIMO and DIRMO significantly outperform the single-output methods Rec, Dir, and DirRec. Our findings are primarily consistent with the results in [38].

Compared to the five standard multi-step ahead strategies, the proposed approach can be classified as an extension of the MIMO strategy and called MIMO averaging. It can also be noted that a large number of diverse ML methods are used in the subject area. To the best of our knowledge, the ability of Arc-x4 is examined for the first time in our study for multi-step ahead prediction. Although the limitations and assumptions of the models are laid out in this paper, the proposed MIMO averaging strategy is general. It can be applied to many different predictors, including dummy, land-use, or other types of variables. Some of the following questions remain open for further study: choice of horizon length; optimization of the coefficients in front of individual single models in the summation formula (7); the possibility of stacking the forecasts of single models built by diverse ML algorithms, and more.

For our data and the chosen horizon, $h = 10$, the proposed strategy is seen as an alternative to other multi-step ahead prediction methods. It can be used in comparison with or in conjunction with other approaches. Finally, we can conclude that the proposed MIMO averaging ex-ante forecasting strategy has the potential for real-world application and solving tasks of public interest, such as informing the population about the levels of the main air pollutants in a given local area.

Author Contributions: Conceptualization, S.G.-I., A.I. and H.K.; Data curation, A.I. and M.S.-M.; Investigation, S.G.-I., A.I., H.K. and M.S.-M.; Methodology, S.G.-I., H.K. and M.S.-M.; Resources, A.I.; Software, S.G.-I., A.I., H.K. and M.S.-M.; Validation, S.G.-I., A.I., H.K. and M.S.-M. All authors have read and agreed to the published version of the manuscript.

Funding: This study has emanated from research conducted with the financial support of the Bulgarian National Science Fund (BNSF), Grant number KP-06-IP-CHINA/1 (КП-06-ИП-КИТАЙ/1). The authors also acknowledge the support of the Bulgarian National Science Fund, Grant KP-06-N52/9.

Data Availability Statement: The data used in this study are freely available on the official websites provided in references [64,65].

Conflicts of Interest: The authors declare no conflict of interest.

References

1. World Health Organization, Regional Office for Europe. 2021. Review of Evidence on Health Aspects of Air Pollution—REVIHAAP Project: Technical Report. Available online: https://www.euro.who.int/__data/assets/pdf_file/0004/193108/REVIHAAP-Final-technical-report-final-version.pdf (accessed on 9 February 2023).
2. Gibson, J. Air pollution, climate change, and health. *Lancet Oncol.* **2015**, *16*, e269. [CrossRef] [PubMed]
3. Manisalidis, I.; Stavropoulou, E.; Stavropoulos, A.; Bezirtzoglou, E. Environmental and health impacts of air pollution: A review. *Front. Public Health* **2020**, *8*, 14. [CrossRef] [PubMed]
4. Rajagopalan, S.; Al-Kindi, S.; Brook, R. Air pollution and cardiovascular disease: JACC state-of-the-art review. *J. Am. Coll. Cardiol.* **2018**, *72*, 2054–2070. [CrossRef] [PubMed]
5. Tecer, L.; Alagha, O.; Karaca, F.; Tuncel, G.; Eldes, N. Particulate matter (PM 2.5, PM 10–2.5, and PM 10) and children's hospital admissions for asthma and respiratory diseases: A bidirectional case-crossover study. *J. Toxicol. Environ. Health A* **2008**, *71*, 512–520. [CrossRef] [PubMed]
6. Sicard, P.; Augustaitis, A.; Belyazid, S.; Calfapietra, C.; de Marco, A.; Fenn, M.; Bytnerowicz, A.; Grulke, N.; He, S.; Matyssek, R.; et al. Global topics and novel approaches in the study of air pollution, climate change and forest ecosystems. *Environ. Pollut.* **2016**, *213*, 977–987. [CrossRef] [PubMed]
7. Ravindra, K.; Rattan, P.; Mor, S.; Aggarwal, A. Generalized additive models: Building evidence of air pollution, climate change and human health. *Environ. Int.* **2019**, *132*, 104987. [CrossRef]
8. Brasseur, G.P.; Jacob, D.J. *Modeling of Atmospheric Chemistry*; Cambridge University Press: Cambridge, UK, 2017.
9. Barratt, R. *Atmospheric Dispersion Modelling: An Introduction to Practical Applications*; Routledge: London, UK, 2013. [CrossRef]
10. Todorov, V.; Dimov, I.; Ostromsky, T.; Zlatev, Z.; Georgieva, R.; Poryazov, S. Optimized quasi-Monte Carlo methods based on Van der Corput sequence for sensitivity analysis in air pollution modelling. In *Recent Advances in Computational Optimization. WCO 2020. Studies in Computational Intelligence*; Springer: Cham, Switzerland, 2021; Volume 986, pp. 389–405. [CrossRef]
11. Ostromsky, T.; Dimov, I.; Georgieva, R.; Zlatev, Z. Air pollution modelling, sensitivity analysis and parallel implementation. *Int. J. Environ. Pollut.* **2011**, *46*, 83–96. [CrossRef]
12. Liu, Y.; Zhou, Y.; Lu, J. Exploring the relationship between air pollution and meteorological conditions in China under environmental governance. *Sci. Rep.* **2020**, *10*, 14518. [CrossRef]
13. Holst, J.; Mayer, H.; Holst, T. Effect of meteorological exchange conditions on PM10 concentration. *Meteorol. Z.* **2008**, *17*, 273–282. [CrossRef]
14. Veleva, E.; Zheleva, I. Statistical modeling of particle mater air pollutants in the city of Ruse, Bulgaria. *MATEC Web Conf.* **2018**, *145*, 01010. [CrossRef]
15. Tsvetanova, I.; Zheleva, I.; Filipova, M.; Stefanova, A. Statistical analysis of ambient air PM10 contamination during winter periods for Ruse region, Bulgaria. *MATEC Web Conf.* **2018**, *145*, 01007. [CrossRef]
16. Veleva, E.; Georgiev, R. Seasonality of the levels of particulate matter PM10 air pollutant in the city of Ruse, Bulgaria. *AIP Conf. Proc.* **2020**, *2302*, 030006. [CrossRef]
17. Tsvetanova, I.; Zheleva, I.; Filipova, M. Statistical study of the influence of the atmospheric characteristics upon the particulate matter (PM10) air pollutant in the city of Silistra, Bulgaria. *AIP Conf. Proc.* **2019**, *2164*, 120014. [CrossRef]
18. Siew, L.Y.; Chin, L.Y.; Wee, P.M.J. ARIMA and integrated ARFIMA models for forecasting air pollution index in Shah Alam, Selangor. *Malays. J. Analyt. Sci.* **2008**, *12*, 257–263.
19. Veleva, E.; Zheleva, I. GARCH models for particulate matter PM10 air pollutant in the city of Ruse, Bulgaria. *AIP Conf. Proc.* **2018**, *2025*, 040016. [CrossRef]
20. Lasheras, F.; Nieto, P.; Gonzalo, E.; Bonavera, L.; de Cos Juez, F. Evolution and forecasting of PM10 concentration at the Port of Gijon (Spain). *Sci. Rep.* **2020**, *10*, 11716. [CrossRef]
21. Feng, R.; Zheng, H.J.; Gao, H.; Zhang, A.R.; Huang, C.; Zhang, J.X.; Luo, K.; Fan, J.R. Recurrent Neural Network and random forest for analysis and accurate forecast of atmospheric pollutants: A case study in Hangzhou, China. *J. Clean. Prod.* **2019**, *231*, 1005–1015. [CrossRef]
22. Yazdi, D.; Kuang, Z.; Dimakopoulou, K.; Barratt, B.; Suel, E.; Amini, H.; Lyapustin, A.; Katsouyanni, K.; Schwartz, J. Predicting fine particulate matter (PM2. 5) in the greater London area: An ensemble approach using machine learning methods. *Remote Sens.* **2020**, *12*, 914. [CrossRef]
23. Masih, A. Application of ensemble learning techniques to model the atmospheric concentration of SO2. *Glob. J. Environ. Sci. Manag.* **2019**, *5*, 309–318. [CrossRef]
24. Bougoudis, I.; Iliadis, L.; Papaleonidas, A. Fuzzy inference ANN ensembles for air pollutants modeling in a major urban area: The case of Athens. In *Proceedings of the International Conference on Engineering Applications of Neural Networks, Sofia, Bulgaria, 5–7 September 2004*; Springer: Cham, Switzerland, 2014; pp. 1–14. [CrossRef]
25. Zhai, B.; Chen, J. Development of a stacked ensemble model for forecasting and analyzing daily average PM2.5 concentrations in Beijing, China. *Sci. Total. Environ.* **2018**, *635*, 644–658. [CrossRef]
26. Wang, P.; Liu, Y.; Qin, Z.; Zhang, G. A novel hybrid forecasting model for PM10 and SO2 daily concentrations. *Sci. Total. Environ.* **2015**, *505*, 1202–1212. [CrossRef] [PubMed]
27. Dairi, A.; Harrou, F.; Khadraoui, S.; Sun, Y. Integrated multiple directed attention-based deep learning for improved air pollution forecasting. *IEEE Trans. Instrum. Meas.* **2021**, *70*, 3520815. [CrossRef]

28. Sayegh, A.; Munir, S.; Habeebullah, T. Comparing the Performance of Statistical Models for Predicting PM10 Concentrations. *Aerosol. Air Qual. Res.* **2014**, *14*, 653–665. [CrossRef]

29. Sethi, J.K.; Mittal, M. A new feature selection method based on machine learning technique for air quality dataset. *J. Stat. Manag. Syst.* **2019**, *22*, 697–705. [CrossRef]

30. Xu, Y.; Liu, H.; Duan, Z. A novel hybrid model for multi-step daily AQI forecasting driven by air pollution big data. *Air. Qual. Atmos. Health* **2020**, *13*, 197–207. [CrossRef]

31. Pankratz, A. *Forecasting with Dynamic Regression Models*; John Wiley & Sons: New York, NY, USA, 1991.

32. Firmino, P.R.A.; de Mattos Neto, P.S.; Ferreira, T.A. Error modeling approach to improve time series forecasters. *Neurocomputing* **2015**, *153*, 242–254. [CrossRef]

33. Gocheva-Ilieva, S.; Voynikova, D.; Stoimenova, M.; Ivanov, A.; Iliev, I. Regression trees modeling of time series for air pollution analysis and forecasting. *Neural Comput. Appl.* **2019**, *31*, 9023–9039. [CrossRef]

34. Rybarczyk, Y.; Zalakeviciute, R. Machine learning approaches for outdoor air quality modelling: A systematic review. *Appl. Sci.* **2018**, *8*, 2570. [CrossRef]

35. Masih, A. Machine learning algorithms in air quality modeling. *Glob. J. Environ. Sci. Manag.* **2019**, *5*, 515–534. [CrossRef]

36. Ganchev, I.; Ji, Z.; O'Droma, M. A generic multi-service cloud-based IoT operational platform-EMULSION. In Proceedings of the 2019 International Conference on Control, Artificial Intelligence, Robotics & Optimization (ICCAIRO), Athens, Greece, 8–10 December 2019. [CrossRef]

37. Cheng, H.; Tan, P.-N.; Gao, J.; Scripps, J. Multistep-ahead time series prediction. *Lect. Notes Comput. Sci.* **2006**, *3918*, 765–774. [CrossRef]

38. Taieb, S.B.; Bontempi, G.; Atiya, A.F.; Sorjamaa, A. A review and comparison of strategies for multi-step ahead time series forecasting based on the NN5 forecasting competition. *Expert Syst. Appl.* **2012**, *39*, 7067–7083. [CrossRef]

39. Ahani, I.; Salari, M.; Shadman, A. Statistical models for multi-step-ahead forecasting of fine particulate matter in urban areas. *Atmos. Pollut. Res.* **2019**, *10*, 689–700. [CrossRef]

40. Ahani, I.K.; Salari, M.; Shadman, A. An ensemble multi-step-ahead forecasting system for fine particulate matter in urban areas. *J. Clean. Prod.* **2020**, *263*, 120983. [CrossRef]

41. Kang, I.-B. Multi-period forecasting using different models for different horizons: An application to U.S. economic time series data. *Int. J. Forecast.* **2003**, *19*, 387–400. [CrossRef]

42. Liu, H.; Duan, Z.; Chen, C. A hybrid framework for forecasting PM2.5 concentrations using multi-step deterministic and probabilistic strategy. *Air. Qual. Atmos. Health* **2019**, *12*, 785–795. [CrossRef]

43. Vassallo, D.; Krishnamurthy, R.; Sherman, T.; Fernando, H. Analysis of random forest modeling strategies for multi-step wind speed forecasting. *Energies* **2020**, *13*, 5488. [CrossRef]

44. Galicia, A.; Talavera-Llames, R.; Troncoso, A.; Koprinska, I.; Martínez-Álvarez, F. Multi-step forecasting for big data time series based on ensemble learning. *Knowl.-Based Syst.* **2019**, *163*, 830–841. [CrossRef]

45. Mustakim, R.; Mamat, M.; Yew, H.T. Towards on-site implementation of multi-step air pollutant index prediction in Malaysia industrial area: Comparing the NARX neural network and support vector regression. *Atmosphere* **2022**, *13*, 1787. [CrossRef]

46. Air Quality Standards, European Commission. Environment. Available online: https://www.eea.europa.eu/themes/air/air-quality-concentrations/air-quality-standards (accessed on 9 February 2023).

47. Ren, Y.; Zhang, L.; Suganthan, P.N. Ensemble classification and regression-recent developments, applications and future directions. *IEEE Comput. Intell. Mag.* **2016**, *11*, 41–53. [CrossRef]

48. Zhou, Z.H. *Ensemble Methods: Foundations and Algorithms*; CRC Press: Boca Raton, FL, USA, 2012.

49. Breiman, L. Random forests. *Mach. Learn.* **2001**, *45*, 5–32. [CrossRef]

50. Ho, T.K. Random decision forests. In Proceedings of the 3rd International Conference on Document Analysis and Recognition, Montreal, QC, Canada, 14–16 August 1995; pp. 278–282.

51. Strobl, C.; Boulesteix, A.L.; Kneib, T.; Augustin, T.; Zeileis, A. Conditional variable importance for random forests. *BMC Bioinform.* **2008**, *9*, 307. [CrossRef] [PubMed]

52. Breiman, L. Arcing classifiers. *Ann. Stat.* **1998**, *26*, 801–824.

53. Khanchel, R.; Limam, M. Empirical comparison of boosting algorithms. In *Classification—The Ubiquitous Challenge. Studies in Classification, Data Analysis, and Knowledge Organization*; Weihs, C., Gaul, W., Eds.; Springer: Berlin/Heidelberg, Germany, 2005; pp. 161–167. [CrossRef]

54. Freund, Y.; Schapire, R.E. A decision-theoretic generalization of on-line learning and an application to boosting. *J. Comp. Syst. Sci.* **1997**, *55*, 119–139. [CrossRef]

55. Bauer, E.; Kohavi, R. An empirical comparison of voting classification algorithms: Bagging, boosting, and variants. *Mach. Learn.* **1999**, *36*, 105–139. [CrossRef]

56. Box, G.E.; Jenkins, G.M.; Reinsel, G.C.; Ljung, G.M. *Time Series Analysis: Forecasting and Control*; John Wiley & Sons: Hoboken, NJ, USA, 2015.

57. Schmidt, A.F.; Finan, C. Linear regression and the normality assumption. *J. Clinic. Epidem.* **2018**, *98*, 146–151. [CrossRef]

58. Bliemel, F. Theil's forecast accuracy coefficient: A clarification. *J. Mark. Res.* **1973**, *10*, 444–446. [CrossRef]

59. Willmott, C. On the validation of models. *Phys. Geogr.* **1981**, *2*, 184–194. [CrossRef]

60. Armstrong, J.S. *Principles of Forecasting: A Handbook for Researchers and Practitioners*; Kluwer Academic: Boston, MA, USA, 2001.

61. SPM—Salford Predictive Modeler. 2022. Available online: https://www.minitab.com/enus/products/spm/ (accessed on 9 February 2023).
62. IBM SPSS Statistics 29. 2022. Available online: https://www.ibm.com/products/spss-statistics (accessed on 9 February 2023).
63. Yordanova, L.; Kiryakova, G.; Veleva, P.; Angelova, N.; Yordanova, A. Criteria for selection of statistical data processing software. *IOP Conf. Ser. Mater. Sci. Eng.* **2021**, *1031*, 012067. [CrossRef]
64. RIOSV Pernik: Monthly Monitoring of Atmospheric Air: Monthly Report on the Quality of Atmospheric air of Pernik according to Data from Automatic Measuring Station "Pernik-Center". Available online: http://pk.riosv-pernik.com/index.php?option= com_content&view=category&id=29:monitoring&Itemid=28&layout=default (accessed on 9 February 2023). (In Bulgarian)
65. Pernik Historical Weather. Available online: https://www.worldweatheronline.com/pernik-weather-history/pernik/bg.aspx (accessed on 9 February 2023).
66. Yadav, S.; Shukla, S. Analysis of k-fold cross-validation over hold-out validation on colossal datasets for quality classification. In Proceedings of the 2016 IEEE 6th International Conference on Advanced Computing (IACC), Bhimavaram, India, 27–28 February 2016; pp. 78–83. [CrossRef]
67. Ljung, G.; Box, G. On a measure of lack of fit in time series models. *Biometrika* **1978**, *65*, 297–303. [CrossRef]
68. Fischer, B.; Planas, C. Large scale fitting of regression models with ARIMA errors. *J. Off. Stat.* **2000**, *16*, 173–184.

Article

RaKShA: A Trusted Explainable LSTM Model to Classify Fraud Patterns on Credit Card Transactions

Jay Raval [1], Pronaya Bhattacharya [2], Nilesh Kumar Jadav [1], Sudeep Tanwar [1,*], Gulshan Sharma [3], Pitshou N. Bokoro [3,*], Mitwalli Elmorsy [4], Amr Tolba [5] and Maria Simona Raboaca [6,7]

[1] Department of Computer Science and Engineering, Institute of Technology, Nirma University, Ahmedabad 382481, Gujarat, India; 21mced18@nirmauni.ac.in (J.R.); 21ftphde53@nirmauni.ac.in (N.K.J.)
[2] Department of Computer Science and Engineering, Amity School of Engineering and Technology, Research and Innovation Cell, Amity University, Kolkata 700157, West Bengal, India; pbhattacharya@kol.amity.edu
[3] Department of Electrical Engineering Technology, University of Johannesburg, Johannesburg 2006, South Africa; gulshans@uj.ac.za
[4] Private Law Department, Faculty of Law and Political Science, King Saud University, Riyadh 12584, Saudi Arabia
[5] Computer Science Department, Community College, King Saud University, Riyadh 11437, Saudi Arabia; atolba@ksu.edu.sa
[6] Doctoral School, University Politehnica of Bucharest, Splaiul Independentei Street No. 313, 060042 Bucharest, Romania; simona.raboaca@icsi.ro
[7] National Research and Development Institute for Cryogenic and Isotopic Technologies—ICSI Rm. Vâlcea, Uzinei Street, No. 4, P.O. Box 7, Râureni, 240050 Râmnicu Vâlcea, Romania
*   Correspondence: sudeep.tanwar@nirmauni.ac.in (S.T.); pitshoub@uj.ac.za (P.N.B.)

Citation: Raval, J.; Bhattacharya, P.; Jadav, N.K.; Tanwar, S.; Sharma, G.; Bokoro, P.N.; Elmorsy, M.; Tolba, A.; Raboaca, M.S. *RaKShA*: A Trusted Explainable LSTM Model to Classify Fraud Patterns on Credit Card Transactions. *Mathematics* **2023**, *11*, 1901. https://doi.org/10.3390/math11081901

Academic Editors: Snezhana Gocheva-Ilieva, Hristina Kulina and Atanas Ivanov

Received: 12 March 2023
Revised: 14 April 2023
Accepted: 15 April 2023
Published: 17 April 2023

Abstract: Credit card (CC) fraud has been a persistent problem and has affected financial organizations. Traditional machine learning (ML) algorithms are ineffective owing to the increased attack space, and techniques such as long short-term memory (LSTM) have shown promising results in detecting CC fraud patterns. However, owing to the black box nature of the LSTM model, the decision-making process could be improved. Thus, in this paper, we propose a scheme, *RaKShA*, which presents explainable artificial intelligence (XAI) to help understand and interpret the behavior of black box models. XAI is formally used to interpret these black box models; however, we used XAI to extract essential features from the CC fraud dataset, consequently improving the performance of the LSTM model. The XAI was integrated with LSTM to form an explainable LSTM (X-LSTM) model. The proposed approach takes preprocessed data and feeds it to the XAI model, which computes the variable importance plot for the dataset, which simplifies the feature selection. Then, the data are presented to the LSTM model, and the output classification is stored in a smart contract (SC), ensuring no tampering with the results. The final data are stored on the blockchain (BC), which forms trusted and chronological ledger entries. We have considered two open-source CC datasets. We obtain an accuracy of 99.8% with our proposed X-LSTM model over 50 epochs compared to 85% without XAI (simple LSTM model). We present the gas fee requirements, IPFS bandwidth, and the fraud detection contract specification in blockchain metrics. The proposed results indicate the practical viability of our scheme in real-financial CC spending and lending setups.

Keywords: Explainableartificial intelligence; credit card frauds; deep learning; long short-term memory; fraud classification

MSC: 91G45

1. Introduction

Modern credit-card (CC)-based applications are web/mobile-driven, and the customer base has shifted toward electronic payment modes. The online repayment modes for CC bring users flexibility and quality of service (QoS). Still, on the downside, it also opens the doors for malicious intruders to intercept the web channels. Thus, recent statistics have suggested a surge in security attacks in CC ecosystems and payment gateway services [1,2]. These attacks mainly include banking frauds, attacks on credit and debit payments of CCs due to unsecured authentication, expired certificates, web injection loopholes, attacks on payment gateways (third-party gateway services), and many others [3]. A recent report by the Federal Trade Commission (FTC) has suggested that financial fraud on a global scale has exponentially risen from 2018 to 2023. Consumers reported losing more than $5.8 billion to fraud in 2021, which was up more than 70% from the year before, according to a newly released FTC report [4]. Thus, it becomes highly imperative to study the nature of these CC frauds conducted by malicious attackers.

The surge in CC frauds has pushed researchers globally to look at possible solutions that can thwart the attack vectors and secure the boundaries of the CC financial system (network, software, and hardware) [5]. The fraud incidents have forced innovative solutions to secure the network perimeters and present privacy and integrity [6,7], authorization and identity-based [8] and non-repudiation-based solutions [9]. Owing to the complex nature of attacks and zero-day possibilities, it is difficult to build an end-to-end CC fraud detection scheme that addresses financial ecosystems' security, privacy, and accuracy requirements. Traditional crypto-primitives (secured 3D passwords and multi-layer gateway encryption) require overhead due to proxy channels and the requirement of identity control and multi-attribute signatures. It significantly hampers the Quality-of-Service (QoS) for end CC applications [10]. For CC fraud detection, security schemes are proposed of specific nature, and thus, such schemes are not generic and are custom-built to support end applications. Thus, it is crucial to analyze and study the CC attack patterns, the effect, and the disclosure strategy to conceptualize a generic security scheme that can cater to large attack sets.

Lately, artificial intelligence (AI)-based models have been used as a potential tool in CC financial fraud (FF) patterns [11,12]. The CC-FF detection algorithm works on URL detection, phishing detection, behavior-based authentication, and others. Machine learning (ML) and deep learning (DL) models are proposed to increase the attack detection accuracy in financial payment ecosystems [13]. Thus, the AI scope in CC-FF detection has solved challenges of security vulnerabilities of Android/IoS mobile OS, permission attacks, and web-URL attacks [14]. However, owing to the massive amount of available data, and real-time analysis, ML models are not generally considered effective for CC-FF detection. Thus, DL techniques are mostly employed to improve the accuracy and precision of CC-FF detection [15]. A fraudulent transaction closely resembles a genuine transaction, which can be detected by minute-level (fine-grained) pattern analysis. In such cases, the behavioral pattern technique aids in determining the transaction's flow and order. So, the anomaly is quickly identified based on the behavioral trend observed from previous attacks dictionaries.

For small datasets, standard ML techniques employ decision trees, random forests, and support vector machines. For large data, mostly recurrent neural networks (RNNs) and long short-term memory (LSTM) models are considered as they can process data sequences, which is a common feature in financial transactions. These models maintain a memory of past events (unusual patterns in CC transaction histories, spending behavior, unusual withdrawals, deposits, and small transactions to multiple accounts) [16]. Such events are considered anomalous events. Other suitable models include deep belief networks, autoencoders, and gated recurrent unit models. These models have shown promising models, but the performance varies significantly owing to the application requirements and dataset characteristics. In most average cases, RNNs and LSTM perform well [14]. Thus, in the proposed scheme, we have worked on the CC-FF detection based on the decoded–encoded input using the LSTM model.

With LSTMs, the accuracy of the prediction model improves, but it is equally important to understand the factors the model uses to make its predictions. Thus, including explainable AI (XAI) with LSTM is a preferred choice which would help the users understand significant data features the LSTM model uses to predict fraudulent CC transactions [17].

The Explainable Artificial Intelligence (XAI) refers to techniques and approaches in machine learning that enable humans to understand and interpret the reasoning behind the decisions made by AI models. XAI aims to improve AI systems' transparency, accountability, and trustworthiness. It [18] is also used in other domains such as healthcare, education, marketing, and agriculture. For instance, the authors of [19] utilize XAI in an autonomous vehicle where they efficiently interpret the black box AI models to enhance the accuracy scores and make autonomous driving safe and reliable. Furthermore, in [20], the authors use the essential properties of XAI for fall detection using wearable devices. They applied the Local Interpretable Model-Agnostic Explanations (LIME) model to obtain important features from the fall detection dataset and provide better interpretability of the applied AI models. The integrated model of XAI and LSTM is termed an explainable LSTM (X-LSTM) model. It reduces the bias in the data and model, which is essential for validating the obtained results. This approach applies XAI before the LSTM in the X-LSTM model. X-LSTM helps to improve the accuracy of simple LSTM models via the identification of gaps sequences in the data or model that need to be addressed. It can handle regulatory requirements, which improves the visibility and transparency of CC financial transactions.

Once the prediction results are obtained from the X-LSTM model, there is a requirement for transaction traceability and verification. Thus, the integration of blockchain (BC) and smart contracts (SC) makes the CC-FF detection ecosystem more transparent, auditable, and visible for interpretation to all financial stakeholders (banks, users, CC application, and gateway servers) [21–23]. The obtained model results are stored with action sets in SC, and such contracts are published over decentralized offline ledgers, such as interplanetary file systems (IPFS) or swarm networks. The use of IPFS-assisted SC would improve the scalability factor of public BC networks, as only the metadata of the transactions are stored on the public BC ledger. The actual data can be fetched through the reference hash from the BC ledger and mapped with the IPFS content key to obtain the executed SC. This makes the CC-FF scheme distributed among networked users and adds a high degree of trust, auditability, and compliance in the ecosystem.

After going through several studies in the literature mentioned in Section 2, we analyzed that recent approaches in CC-FF detection mainly include rule-based systems, statistical models, and sequence-based models (RNNs, LSTMs), which often need more interpretability. Most approaches do not cater to the requirements of new FF patterns and are tightly coupled to the end application only. Thus, from the novelty perspective, we integrate XAI with the LSTM model (our proposed X-LSTM approach). *RaKShA* addresses the issue of transparency and interpretability of CC-FF detection and further strengthens the power and capability of LSTM models. Secondly, our scheme is innovative as we propose the storage of X-LSTM output in SC, which provides financial compliance and addresses auditability concerns in financial systems. Via BC, the proposed scheme ensures that all results are verifiable, traceable, and tamper-proof, which is crucial in the financial industry. Finally, to address the scalability concerns of the public BC networks, we have introduced the storage of SC and associated data in IPFS and the content hash to be stored as metadata (transaction) in public BC. This significantly reduces a transaction's size, allowing more transactions to be packaged in a single block. This makes our scheme resilient, adaptable to real-time financial systems, and generic in CC-FF detection scenarios. Furthermore, the research contributions of the article are as follows.

- A system flow model of the proposed scheme is presented for the CC-FF datasets considering the X-LSTM model and the storage of prediction results finalized via SC on the BC network.
- Based on the system flow, a problem formulation is presented, and we present a layered overview of our proposed scheme and its associated layers.
- In the scheme, at the AI layer, we design a boosted XAI function on the CC dataset post the preprocessing phase, and the output is fed to the LSTM model, which improves the accuracy. The LSTM output is fed to SC to detect fraudulent CC transactions.

- The performance analysis is completed on testing and validation accuracy, RMSProp optimizer, and XAI variable importance plot. The transaction costs, IPFS bandwidth, and SC contract are evaluated for BC simulation.

The rest of the paper is structured as follows. Section 2 discusses the existing state-of-the-art (SOTA) approaches. Section 3 presents the proposed scheme's system model and problem formulation. Section 4 presents the proposed scheme and details the data preprocessing, the sliding window formulation, the X-LSTM model, and the proposed SC design. Section 5 presents the performance evaluation of the proposed scheme. Finally, Section 6 concludes the article with the future scope of the work.

2. State-of-the-Art

The section discusses the potential findings by researchers for FF detection via AI models and BC as a trusted component to design auditable financial systems. Table 1 presents a comparative analysis of our scheme against SOTA approaches. For example, Ketepalli et al. [24] proposed the LSTM autoencoder, vanilla autoencoder, and random forest autoencoder techniques for CC datasets. The results show high accuracy for LSTM and random forest autoencoders over vanilla autoencoders. The authors in [25] explored the potential of DL models and presented a convolutional LSTM model for CC-FF detection. An accuracy of 94.56% is reported in their work. In some works, probability and statistical inferences are presented. For example, Tingfei et al. [26] proposed an oversampling-based method for CC-FF detection using the LSTM approach. Cao et al. [7] described a unique method for identifying frauds that combines two learning modules with DL attention mechanisms. Fang et al. suggested deep neural networks (DNN) mechanisms for Internet and web frauds. The scheme utilized the synthetic minority oversampling approach to deal with data imbalances [27]. Chen et al. [28] proposed using a deep CNN network for fraud classification.

Similarly, trust and provenance-based solutions are proposed via BC integration in financial systems. Balagolla et al. [29] proposed a BC-based CC storage scheme to make the financial stakeholders operate autonomously. Additionally, the authors proposed an AI model with scaling mechanisms to improve the scalability issues of the BC. Musbaudeen and Lisa [30] proposed a BC-based accounting scheme to automate daily accounting tasks and simplify audit features for a banking system. The authors in [31] researched the imbalanced classification problem. Additionally, the authors presented limitations of CC datasets (labeled data points), which makes it difficult to summarize model findings. Thus, low-cost models are preferred. Tingfei et al. [26] proposed an oversampling strategy based on variational automated coding (VAE) and DL. This technique was only effective in controlled environments. The study results showed that the unbalanced classification problem could be solved successfully using the VAE-based oversampling method. To deal with unbalanced data, Fang et al. [27] suggested synthetic minority oversampling methods.

Zheng et al. [32] presented boosting mechanisms in CC systems. The authors used AdaBoost ML during the training process. The model incorrectly classified many different symbols. Thus, improved TrAdaBoost is presented that updates the weights of incorrectly classified data. Cao et al. [7] presented a two-level attention model of data representation for fraud detection. The sample-level attention learns in a central manner where the significant information of the misclassified samples goes through a feature-level attention phase, which improves the data representation. The dependency between model fairness and scalability is not discussed.

Table 1. Comparative analysis of proposed scheme with SOTA schemes.

Authors	Year	Objective	Algorithms	Dataset	Outcomes	Disadvantages
Proposed work	2023	Integrated XAI with LSTM to improve model interpretability	LSTM	CC fraud dataset	Improved accuracy with XAI	-
Belle et al. [33]	2023	Network-based representation learning	Representation Learning	Real-life CC dataset	Conventional performance and network measures are discussed	Security aided principles are not discussed
Ni et al. [34]	2023	Fraud detection models based on feature boosting mechanism with spiral balancing technique	Feature boosting mechanism	Two CC real-world datasets	Multifactor synchronous embedding mechanism is presented with a spiral method to improve the feature metric	Oversampling of data is not considered
Labanca et al. [35]	2022	An active learning framework and a feedback system-based model to identify fraud involving money laundering	ML with anomaly patterns	A synthetic capital market dataset	Isolation forest is best algorithm for anti-money laundering fraud detection	lack of an intuitive explanation for the anomaly score
Xiuguo et al. [14]	2022	The authors developed a model to detect fraud using textual and numerical data from the annual report	LSTM, and gated recurrent units	5130 Chinese A-share listed companies' annual reports from 2016–2020,	Accuracy could be increased by using textual data	Missing feature selection details
Esenogho et al. [36]	2022	Proposed efficient approach for fraud detection using synthetic minority oversampling technique (SMOTE) with edited nearest neighbor	SMOTE-ENN	CC dataset	90% accuracy of ensemble model	Feature selection is not properly explained
Chen et al. [37]	2022	Hierarchical multi-task learning approach	federated learning and ML	Auto loan dataset of Chinese automobile	Based on its high accuracy and F1-score, machine transfer learning approach performs better than other algorithms for predicting fraud	Feature selection is not presented

Table 1. *Cont.*

Authors	Year	Objective	Algorithms	Dataset	Outcomes	Disadvantages
Ji and Yingchao [38]	2021	Proposed the fraud detection support system using XAI	XAI over ML and DL models	Open CC datasets	DNN model scored 96.84% accuracy compared with random forest	Less emphasis on transparency and interpretability
Ileberi et al. [39]	2021	Proposed ML framework for CC frauds	logistic regression, random forest, extreme gradient boosting, and decision trees	CC fraud dataset	Extreme gradient boosting and Adaboost achieves 99% accuracy	The dataset is oversampled and overfitted
Cao et al. [7]	2021	Combines two modules of learning with DL and attention methods	DL and attention mechanisms	self-defined multiple-fraud dataset	Feature-level attention helps detection models learn more about fraud patterns	Did not discuss the interpretability of the neural network
Cui et al. [40]	2021	Created a model applying the ReMEMBeR Model to address the issue of fraud detection as pseudo-recommender	DL, anomaly detection, ensemble learning	real-world online banking transaction dataset	All applied algorithms are outperformed by the ReMEMBeR Model	Less attribute-related information
Benchaji et al. [41]	2021	Identified fraud in credit card transaction based on sequential modeling of data	LSTM, sequential learning	credit card dataset	The LSTM gives the higher at 96% accuracy compared with other models	Did not discuss the security of the non-fraud data
Balagolla et al. [29]	2021	Proposed a decentralized BC-based fraud detection model	logistic regression, SVM, and random forest	CC dataset	Random forest secured 99% accuracy with public BC	Details of BC implementations are not discussed
Chen et al. [28]	2021	Proposed a deep convolution neural network (CNN) to detect financial fraud	CNNs with mining techniques	real-time CC fraud dataset	The model offers improved detection when compared to the existing models	Feature selection is not determined
Forough et al. [42]	2020	Proposed an ensemble model based on the sequential model to detect credit card fraud.	ANN, LSTM, FFNN, GRU	European cards dataset and The Brazilian dataset	Based on precision and recall, the LSTM performs better than other models	Feature selection and data security methods are not discussed
Tingfei et al. [26]	2020	An oversampling-based VAE is suggested for the detection of credit card fraud	generative adversarial networks, principal component analysis, and VAE	CC fraud dataset	VAE reaches 0.5 times the number of positive cases in original training set	Recall rates did not have much improvement

Table 1. *Cont.*

Authors	Year	Objective	Algorithms	Dataset	Outcomes	Disadvantages
Kumar et al. [43]	2019	Random forest for CC fraud detection	random forest	CC fraud detection	Accuracy of 90% is reported	Feature selection is not discussed
Jiang et al. [6]	2018	Proposed a unique aggregation and feedback mechanism-based fraud detection technique	sliding window for a behavioral pattern of cardholder	CC self-generated dataset	An 80% accuracy is achieved	Did not consider individual time windows

Esenogho et al. [36] observed the nature of typical ML models, which entails a static mapping of the input vector to the output vector. These models are inefficient for the detection of CC frauds. To detect credit card fraud, one author proposed the neural network ensemble classifier and the SMOTE techniques to create a balanced dataset. The ensemble classifier uses the adaptive boosting (AdaBoost) algorithm and LSTM neural network as the base learner. Combining SMOTE-ENN and boosted LSTM classifier methods are efficient in detecting fraud. The research on fraud detection on a dataset of Chinese listed businesses using LSTM and GRU was presented by Xiuguo et al. [14]. A DL model with proposed encoding and decoding techniques for anomaly detection concerning time series is presented by Zhang et al. [16]. Balagolla et al. [29] proposed a methodology employing BC and machine intelligence to detect fraud before it happens. Chen et al. [37] presented research on loan fraud prediction by introducing a new method named hierarchical multi-task learning (HMTL) over a two-level fraud classification system. Chen et al. [28] proposed a deep CNN model (DCNN) for CC-FF with alert notifications, and the model presented high accuracy.

From the above literature, we analyzed that many researchers proposed their solutions concerning CC fraud detection. However, their approaches utilize obsolete feature space that cannot be considered in the current timespan. None of them have used the staggering benefits of XAI that efficiently selects the best features from the given feature space. Additionally, it is also analyzed that once the data are classified using AI algorithms, the data are not overlooked for data manipulation attacks. A broad scope is available to the attackers, where they can tamper with the classified data (from AI algorithms), i.e., from fraud to non-fraud or vice versa. Hence, the amalgamation of XAI with AI algorithms and integration of blockchain is not yet explored by the aforementioned solutions. In that view, we proposed an XAI-based LSTM model (X-LSTM) that seamlessly collected the efficient feature space and then passed it to the AI algorithm for the classification task. Furthermore, the classified data are forwarded to the IPFS-based public blockchain to tackle data manipulation attacks and preserve data integrity.

3. *RaKShA*: System Flow Model and Problem Formulation

In this section, we discussed the proposed scheme, *RaKShA* through a system flow model and presented the problem formulation. The details are shown as follows.

3.1. System Flow Model

In this subsection, we present the schematics of our scheme *RaKShA*, which presents a classification model to identify fraud patterns in the financial ecosystems. Figure 1 presents the proposed system flow diagram. In the scheme, we consider the entity E_U, which denotes the user entity (whose financial data are under scrutiny). In the scheme, we assume there are n E_U, denoted as $\{U_1, U_2, \ldots, U_n\}$.

For any U_n, we consider CC details, denoted by $F(U_n) = \{U_{LB}, U_{BA}, U_{PA}, U_{RS}\}$, where U_{LB} denotes the balance limit of CC, U_{BA} denotes the pending bill amount of the monthly CC billing cycle, U_{PA} denotes the payment amount E_U is liable to make, and U_{RS} denotes the repayment status (Step 1). For the experiment, we select the credit card dataset (U_{CC}) (Step 2). The data are collected into comma-separated values (CSVs), and preprocessing techniques are applied to the collected CSV. The preprocessed data are sent through a sliding window for U_n, denoted as $W(U_n)$ (Step 3). Based on $W(U_n)$, the data are sent to the XAI for feature importance which is denoted as $X(W(U_n))$ (Steps 4, 5). The XAI output is then passed to the LSTM model to classify the fraud patterns of U_n (Step 6). Based on the X-lSTM model output, E_{U_n} executes an SC to notify the user of the genuineness and the safety of investment on U_n (Step 7). The classification details are also stored on local IPFS, where any public user can fetch U_n data based on the IPFS content key (Step 8). Finally, the transaction meta-information obtained from IPFS is stored on public BC (Step 9).

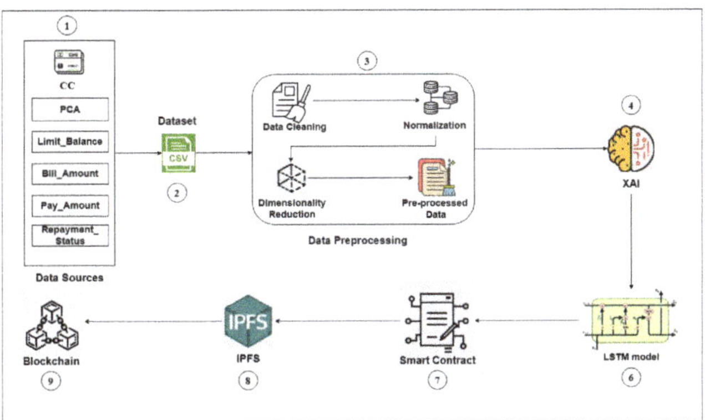

Figure 1. *RaKShA*: The proposed system flow model.

3.2. Problem Formulation

As discussed in the above Section 3.1, the AI-based *RaKShA* scheme is proposed for any n^{th} E_U. The financial resource is collected from the user entity. For simplicity, we consider that each user has a single CC for which fraud detections are classified. Thus, any user $\{U_1, U_2, \ldots, U_n \in E_U\}$ has an associated CC denoted as $\{C_1, C_2, \ldots, C_n\}$. The mapping function $M : E_U \rightarrow C$ is denoted as follows.

$$U_i \longrightarrow C_i \tag{1}$$

Similarly, the scheme can be generalized for many to one-mapping, where any user might have multiple CCs for which fraud detection is applied. In such cases, we consider a user identity U_{id} to be mapped to different CCs offered by respective banks. The mapping $M_2 : U_{id} \rightarrow C_k \rightarrow B_k$ is completed, where any n^{th} E_U is mapped to a subset $C_k \subset C$, which is further mapped to associated banking information $B_k \subset B$, where C denotes the overall CC set, and B denotes the associated banks who have presented these CCs to U_i.

$$U_i \longrightarrow C_k \tag{2}$$

In the model, we consider two types of transactions: normal (genuine) transactions and fraudulent (fraud) transactions. Any U_i uses its CC at multiple shopping venues (online or point-of-sale transactions), money transfers, cash withdrawals, and others. We consider that fake CC transactions are generated by an adversarial user U_r who can exploit the operation of the CC transaction.

$$U_r \notin \{U_1, U_2, \ldots, U_n\} \tag{3}$$

Here, a function F represents a U_r attack on the normal transaction system, which produces a fake transaction T_f in the CC network.

$$F = \left(U_r \xrightarrow{\text{attack}} \left(U_i \xrightarrow[\text{with}]{\text{Transaction}} C_i \right) \right) \tag{4}$$

The goal of the proposed scheme is to detect this malicious T_f from normal transaction sets $T_r = \{T_1, T_2, \ldots, T_l\}$, where $T_l \subset T$, which is proposed by n genuine users. The main goal is satisfied when every transaction is in normal behavior similarly to T_r. In

Equation (5), we present the sum of the maximum count of the normal behavior of the CC transaction.

$$\mathbb{O} = \left(\sum_{i=0}^{l} \text{secure}(T_r) \right) \tag{5}$$

The models work on the detection of T_f and differentiate its anomalous behavior from T_r. The detection mechanism is presented in Equation (6) as follows.

$$\mathbb{Q} = \left(\sum_{i=0}^{l} \text{detect}(T_f) \right) \tag{6}$$

We design an XAI model for the CC dataset, which finds the important features for the classification of T_f. The important features $Imp(F_s)$ are passed as inputs to the LSTM model, which generates the classification output. The goal is to maximize accuracy $A(O)$, which is fed to SC to be stored at the BC layer. In general, the problem formulation P_f aims at maximizing the A_O, $Imp(F_s)$. Secondly, the LSTM model should minimize the training loss T_loss and maximize the validation accuracy $A(Val)$. Mathematically, the conditions for P_f are summarized as follows.

1. C_0: *Maximize $Imp(F_s)$*: To improve the accuracy of the LSTM model, we consider that our XAI approach would maximize $Imp(F_s)$, which would aid in the maximization of $A(O)$.
2. C_1: *Maximize $A(O)$*: The LSTM model post-XAI (X-LSTM) would focus on maximizing $A(O)$, such that T_{loss} is minimized.
3. C_2: *Minimize T_{loss}*: This would help in improving the validation accuracy $A(Val)$.
4. C_3: *Maximize $A(Val)$*: The final condition is to reduce false positives, which would improve $A(Val)$.

The entire problem P_f is then represented as a maximization problem.

$$P_f = max(C_0, C_1, -C_2, C_3) \tag{7}$$

subject to operational constraints as follows.

$$\begin{aligned}
OC_1 &: T \leq T_{max} \\
OC_2 &: T_f \leq T_r \\
OC_3 &: C(T_f) = \{0, 1\} \\
OC_4 &: T_{loss} \leq T_{thresh} \\
OC_5 &: G(C_e) \leq G(Acc) \\
OC_6 &: E(C) \leq \Delta(maxT)
\end{aligned} \tag{8}$$

OC_1 denotes that the LSTM model should respond with output in a finite bounded period, denoted by T, which should not exceed a timeout T_{max}. OC_2 denotes that the scheme is rendered fair when the number of fake transactions exceeds genuine transactions. The scheme would have less accuracy when T_f would exceed genuine transactions in the ecosystem. C_3 talks about a deterministic property of T_f classification $C(T_f)$, that it would always output $\{0, 1\}$, which is a Boolean identifier to classify the transaction as genuine (1) or fake (0). Any other state is not acceptable. OC_4 indicates that T_{loss} should not exceed a threshold training loss, which is decided in real time based on previous inputs and outputs to the model. OC_5 indicates conditions for SC execution, which signifies that SC should be only executed (C_e) when the account wallet has sufficient funds (in terms of gas limit), which are denoted by $G(C_e)$. Thus, it should be less than the total fund in the wallet ($G(Acc)$). OC_6 denotes that the time to add the update of SC execution to IPFS and block mining in BC should again be finite and should not exceed a maximum timeout $\Delta(maxT)$ set by the public BC network.

4. *RaKShA*: The Proposed Scheme

This section presents the working of the proposed system, which is presented as a layered model into three sublayers: the data layer, the AI layer, and the BC layer. Figure 2 presents the systematic overview of the architecture. The details of the layers are as follows.

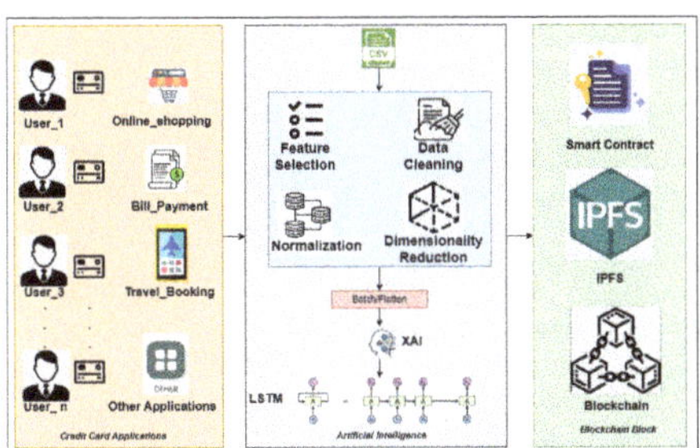

Figure 2. Architectural view of the proposed scheme (*RaKShA*).

4.1. Data Layer

At the data layer, we consider E_U, which have mapped CCs (one-to-one or one-to-many mapping), and these users conduct transactions from their CCs at multiple venues. We consider that the CC firms can track conditions of lost, inactive, or stolen CC, and thus, any transaction made after a complaint lodged by E_U should be marked as T_f. The challenge lies in identifying fraud transaction patterns P_f, which look identical to genuine patterns P_r. The real-time data at this layer are collected and compiled to form the CC transaction dataset, which is added as a CSV file to the AI layer.

We consider that E_U uses different applications (portals) to carry out transactions (both normal and abnormal). We consider transaction instances $\{T_1, T_2, \ldots, T_l\}$ for n users with q CC, with the trivial condition $q \geq n$. We consider any user makes w transactions in the billing cycle from CCs, which are mapped to U_{id}, and the overall amount A is computed at the billing cycle. Thus, the mapping is denoted as follows.

$$U_{id} \xrightarrow{\text{performs}} T_l$$
$$T_l \xrightarrow{\text{maps}} q \qquad (9)$$
$$U_{id} \xrightarrow{\text{bill}} A$$

Specifically, any U_{id} contains the following information.

$$U_{id} = \{CC_{num}, B_{id}, Txn, TA, CC_{lim}, OD_{lim}\} \qquad (10)$$

where CC_{num} denotes the CC number, B_{id} denotes the bank identifier which has issued the CC, Txn denotes the total transactions carried out on CC_{num} in the billing cycle, TA denotes the total amount (debited) in the billing cycle, CC_{lim} denotes the spending limit (different for online transactions and offline transactions), and OD_{lim} denotes the overdraft limit set for U_{id} on CC_{num}.

In the case of genuine transactions T_r, the values of Txn over the billing period are not sufficiently high, which indicates that CC is used frequently. In addition, the location of the CC swipe (online based on gateway tracking and offline based on geolocation) should not be highly distributed (different locations indicate anomaly). Furthermore, TA should not normally exceed the CC_{lim}, and OD_{lim} should not reach the maximum OD set for CC_{num}.

Fake transactions T_f have a high probability of violating any of these conditions, which the AI model captures based on credit histories.

For all users, we collect the transaction details and store them in a CSV file, denoted as CV_d, and T_i represents the transaction data.

$$\forall T_i \in CV_d \tag{11}$$

In the CC fraud detection dataset, there are 31 attributes, where attributes $V_1 - V_{28}$ denote features that resulted from transformation via principal component analysis (PCA) and are numerical values. T denotes the elapsed time between the current transaction and the first transaction, and a class C attribute signifies whether a transaction is T_f or T_r.

$$A = \{\{V_1, V_{28}\}, T, sC\} \tag{12}$$

The prepared CSV file is then sent to the AI layer for analysis.

4.2. AI Layer

At this layer, the CSV file is sent to the XAI module, whose main aim is to reduce the dataset dimensionality and maximize the accuracy of finding the important features $Imp(F_s)$ of the dataset, which in turn would maximize $A(O)$, predicting the required output. The dataset dimension is modeled as $r^{P \times Q}$, where P denotes rows, and Q denotes columns. Thus, the goal is to select $Imp(F_s)$ over Q so that only important features are presented to the LSTM model and it achieves high accuracy.

4.2.1. Data Preprocessing

This sublayer considers the data preprocessing techniques, including data cleaning, normalization, and dimensionality reduction. In data cleaning, we correct or delete inaccurate, corrupted, improperly structured, redundant, or incomplete data from the dataset D obtained from the CSV file. Not applying data preprocessing techniques leads to inefficient accuracies and high loss while classifying CC frauds. For instance, not applying data normalization leads to a range problem, where the particular value of a column is higher or lower than the other value in the same column. Furthermore, missing values are not formally accepted by the AI models; hence, they must be filled with either 0 or central tendency values, i.e., mean value. Similarly, it is essential to find the best features from the dataset; otherwise, the AI model will not be trained efficiently and not improvise the accuracy and loss parameters. Toward this aim, we utilize the standard preprocessing techniques on the CC fraud data. In place of NaN values, 0 is inserted, and then, the label encoding technique is used to transform string values in columns into a numeric representation. Finally, we consider C to denote the different target classes in D, and a group transformation is applied, represented by ω and δ, which divides the data into different timestamps.

$$\delta_l = \omega_l(\delta_{\text{instances} \times \text{features}}) \quad \forall l \epsilon C \tag{13}$$

The NaN data are denoted as $[\varnothing]$. We first use the *isnull()* function to find the overview of NULL values in the dataset, and the operation is denoted by N_s, for NaN Data$[\varnothing]$.

$$N_s = isnull(CV_d) \tag{14}$$

From the data, the NULL values are then dropped using the *drop()* function, which is denoted as D_c. The function is denoted as R_i for a particular row.

$$R_i \longrightarrow D_c \tag{15}$$

Next, all NaN values are updated in the column for which we compute the mean using the *fillna()* function. The model replaces categorical data, whereas the mean and median are used to replace numerical data. The column of data is denoted as c_i. After filling in the empty data, the cleaned data are denoted as C_D.

$$A = \frac{1}{n} \sum_{i=1}^{n} c_i$$
$$C_D \longleftarrow c_i \tag{16}$$

Each target class has a string data type and needs to be transformed using the one-hot encoded vector. Consider y as the original target class column, with Γ as unique classes. y has the shape $(k, 1)$ and the data type string. y is subjected to a single hot encoding transformation.

$$y_{k,\Gamma} = \begin{bmatrix} 1 \\ 0 \\ \cdot \\ 0 \\ 0 \end{bmatrix} \cdots \begin{bmatrix} 0 \\ 1 \\ \cdot \\ 0 \\ 0 \end{bmatrix} \cdots \begin{bmatrix} 0 \\ 0 \\ \cdot \\ 0 \\ 1 \end{bmatrix}$$

Normalization is typically required with attributes of different scales. Otherwise, the effectiveness of a significant and equally significant attribute (on a smaller scale) could be diminished as other qualities have values on a bigger scale. Statistics refers to the process of reducing the size of the dataset so that the normalized data fall between 0 and 1. where $(\forall C_D \in X_{\text{normalized}})$

$$X_{\text{normalized}} = \frac{(X - X_{\text{minimum}})}{(X_{\text{maximum}} - X_{\text{minimum}})} \tag{17}$$

The technique of minimizing the number of random variables or attributes taken into account is known as dimensionality reduction. In many real-world applications, high-dimensionality data reduction is crucial as a stage in data preprocessing. In data mining applications, high-dimensionality reduction has become one of the crucial problems. It is denoted as D_r.

$$D_r = \{x_i, y_i\}$$
$$x \in \mathbb{R}^y \tag{18}$$

4.2.2. XAI Module

In the work, we propose an XAI module that uses a boosting approach, combining several weak classifiers to form a strong classifier. The $r^{P \times Q}$ data function contains 284,808 rows and 31 columns. The XAI function (Ψ) determines the highest priority on Q.

In this work, we used the feature importance technique of XAI to detect any CC fraud. Using XAI algorithms obtains better prediction over the other results. The XAI gives the highest priority feature of the dataset columns (Q). XAI function (Ψ) is applied to the dataset, which is denoted as follows.

$$\zeta = \Psi\{\forall r^{284808 \times 31}\} \tag{19}$$

After applying the XAI function on the dataset, we obtain the important feature, and dimensionality becomes reduced. The new function of XAI is denoted as ζ, and $\mathbb{R}$ is a new dimension of the dataset.

$$\zeta \longleftarrow (\mathbb{R}^{284808 \times 20}) \tag{20}$$

4.2.3. LSTM Module Post-XAI: The X-LSTM Approach

Once XAI selects $Imp(F_s)$, we shift toward sending the features as inputs to the LSTM model. We use a technique of flattening to feed information from multiple vectors into the classification model as a 1D array. The preprocessed data are called CV_p. The parameter is immediately updated after computing the gradient for one training sample in stochastic gradient descent. It is a mini-batch with a batch size of 1. We repeat the two procedures—flattening and mini-batch selection—in all the training samples. Mini-batch is represented as $\mathbb{B}$, which is presented as follows.

$$\hat{y} = \theta^T \mathbb{B} + r \tag{21}$$

The loss function is used to evaluate the proposed algorithm, which predicts the highlighted dataset. It is determined as μ. All preprocessed feature data move on the LSTM block. A hidden LSTM unit has several gates, each completing a certain function. The tanh and sigmoid activation functions manage the gates input and output. Within the LSTM cell, the activation functions sigmoid and tanh are utilized for the input vector x. Figure 3 shows the details of the LSTM cell for processing our XAI output.

$$\mu(\theta, B) = \sum_{i=1}^{n} -y \log(\hat{y}) \tag{22}$$

subject to,

$$\theta_{k+1} = \theta_k - \alpha \nabla J_j(\theta) \tag{23}$$

where θ denotes the weights, and B is the bias value. The actual class is y, and $\hat{y}$ is the predicted class. α is the learning rate and ∇ denotes the partial derivative.

$$CV_p \longrightarrow B_s \tag{24}$$

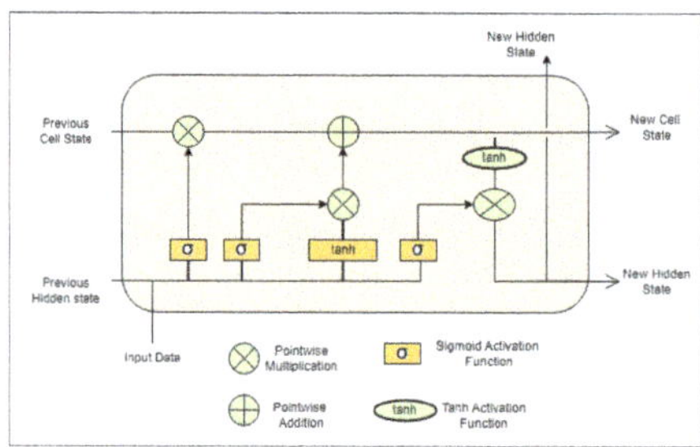

Figure 3. LSTM architecture.

The RMSProp optimizer function is considered, and the loss function is MSE. The algorithm addresses the C_1, C_2, and C_3 conditions of P_f under the operational constraints OC_1, as our proposed model training preprocesses the data. Thus, the training response is in a finite bounded period (does not exceed T_{max}). The algorithm effectively classifies T_f from T_r transactions, and OC_2 is satisfied. A deterministic output $A_y = \{0, 1\}$ is obtained from the LSTM block, which satisfies our OC_3 condition. T_{loss} is under an experimentally observed T_{thresh}, which is obtained from successive process runs on different CC datasets. This satisfies the OC_4 condition.

4.3. BC Layer

At this layer, the classification output A_y obtained from the CC fraud detection dataset with the transaction details is stored in an SC. We consider the transaction details X, where every row corresponds to a user transaction, and the column corresponds to features. The LSTM model outputs A_y, based on the classification function $F(X) = Y$. In the SC<, we consider a function *storeDetails*(X, Y), which takes inputs X and Y from LSTM output. The SC is executed, and the details are published on IPFS, from which we generate a javascript object notation (JSON) file, which is denoted as $JS(X, Y)$. Next, we use the IPFS API to publish $JS(X, Y)$ on the IPFS network, which generates the content key $CK(IPFS)$ and the hash of $CK(IPFS)$, which is denoted as H_{CK}. H_{CK} is stored as a transaction on a public BC network, using the *storeHash(H_{CK})* function.

Algorithm 1 presents the details of the SC. In the case of fraud transaction detection, all nodes of the BC are notified of the account from which it is detected.

Algorithm 1 SC to store fraud transactions in BC network

Input: $\{A_y\}$ LSTM output
Output: A flag F to denote fraud transaction is detected
  procedure STORE FRAUD TRANSACTIONS
      Eth.acc ← *Connect* Ethereum Network
      A_U ← *Call_Procedure*Fraud Notification
      address owner
      Event E FraudDetect (M_s, uint256, T)
      Call constructor()
      owner = M. sender
      U ← *Call_Notify_Fraud_Detected* (M_s)
      Require(M.sender == owner)
      emit FraudDetected(M, block.T)
      if $(W(owner) > min.bal)$ **then**
         Deploy contract
         Notify F ← 1
         Notify *'Fake Transaction detected'*
         Generate JSON file $JS(X, Y)$
         Publish contact on IPFS and generate $CK(IPFS)$
         H_{CK} ← SHA-256($CK(IPFS)$)
         C ← *storeHash(H_{CK})*
      else
         Notify F ← 0
         Notify *'Transaction is genuine'*
         Generate JSON file $JS(X, Y)$
         Publish contact on IPFS and generate $CK(IPFS)$
         H_{CK} ← SHA-256($CK(IPFS)$)
         C ← *storeHash(H_{CK})*
      end if
  end procedure

Initially, we connect to the Ethereum network using Web3.js and send a transaction to SC [44]. Next, an account is created to which the function $FraudNotification()$ has access and message M is added with timestamp T in a block in case function $Notify\_Fraud\_Detected$ returns *true*. In such a case, the required gas fee $G(C_e)$ should be in the owner's address to deploy the contract. This satisfies the OC_5 condition of P_f. Next, the executed contract produces bytecodes, and input data are supplied to the contract. The contract data are also published on the IPFS network, and CK and H_{CK} are generated, which links the published contract with the BC network. Once complete, the function $close()$ closes a connection to the Ethereum network and frees up the EVM memory.

For the experiment, we perform an SC function such as the $getFraudStatus()$ function, which returns a boolean indicating the fraud status of the *cardholder* associated with the Ethereum address that is calling the function. It retrieves the cardholder struct associated with the caller's address through the cardholders mapping and returns the *isFraud* boolean value of the *cardholder* struct. A true value indicates that the cardholder has engaged in fraudulent activities, while a false value indicates that the cardholder has not. $checkFraudTransactionStatus()$ is a public view function in the FraudDetection contract that takes an Ethereum address as input, retrieves the associated *cardholder* struct, and returns a boolean indicating if the cardholder has engaged in fraudulent activities. A true value means that the cardholder has engaged in fraud, while a *false* value means the opposite. *getTransactionsAmounts*() and *getTransactionsLocations*() are public view functions defined in the FraudDetection contract that retrieve and return the transaction amounts and locations, respectively, of the cardholder that is making the function call. Both functions access the *allTransactionAmounts* and *allTransactionLocations* arrays stored in the cardholder struct that is associated with the cardholder's Ethereum address.

5. *RaKShA*: Performance Evaluation

In this section, we discuss the performance evaluation of the proposed scheme. First, we discuss the tools and setup and present the CC datasets (dataset 1 and dataset 2) used for simulation. Then, we present the simulation parameters for the LSTM model and the BC setup, which are followed by X-LSTM performance analysis, SC design, and performance analysis of BC metrics. Finally, the details are presented as follows.

5.1. Experimental Tools and Setup

For the experiment, we used the Google Collab platform with Python and imported the required set of libraries: Numpy for linear algebra, Fourier transforms and matrices, Pandas for ML-related tasks, and Matplotlib for visualizing the data. SC is developed in Solidity programming language on Remix IDE for BC simulation. LSTM with parameters such as epochs, batch size, and loss function is defined. We compared different optimizers for the model's accuracy [45].

5.2. Dataset

Two open-source CC datasets are analyzed for fraud transaction detection [46]. The dataset contains transactions from different CC from September 2013 from European CC users. The dataset is first made balanced, and the explicit features are hidden via PCA, and $\{V_1, V_2, \ldots, V_{28}\}$ features are present. Other features are time (the elapsed time between each transaction and the initial transaction) and transaction amount. This dataset has 0.17% class 1 data for the prediction of futuristic data. There are 284808 data available in the dataset. We experiment with techniques such as XAI data and without XAI data on this dataset to obtain better predictions between the techniques.

Another CC dataset is considered from the UCI repository [47], with CC applications. The attributes and names are hidden (due to privacy preservation and to assure user confidentiality). The dataset contains continuous, nominal, and large values, with 690 instances and 15 attributes. This dataset has attributes that help predict the class labels. There are 22.1% class 1 and 78% Class 0 data for prediction. Here, we also analyze different vectors to understand the behavior of the data. Figure 4 is the visualization of the vector performance concerning the amount. Each point in the scatter plot represents a transaction in the dataset. The amount variable represents the amount of money involved in the transaction, while each V variable is a transformed feature that the model uses to detect fraud. The X-axis represents the values of the V variable, and the Y-axis represents the transaction amount. By plotting the amount against each V variable, we can see if there is any relationship between these variables and the transaction amount. For example, if there is a strong positive correlation between the amount and a particular V variable, transactions with higher values might be more likely to involve larger amounts of money. Conversely, if there is a negative correlation between the amount and a V variable, then transactions with lower values of that variable might be more likely to involve larger amounts of money.

5.3. Simulation Parameters

For predicting the output, parameter selection plays an important role. In work, we have considered two epoch values: 50 and 500 epochs. Furthermore, the batch size is a hyperparameter that defines the number of samples to work through before updating the internal model parameters. When training neural networks, batch size regulates how accurately the error gradient is estimated. The details of the hyperparameters are presented in Table 2. On similar lines, Table 3 presents the BC and SC setup parameters.

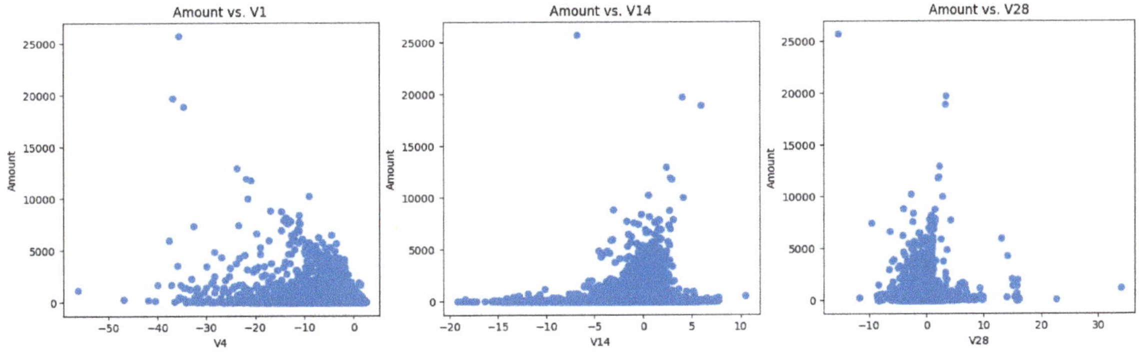

Figure 4. Vector visualization of dataset.

Table 2. Hyperparameters for the LSTM network.

Parameter	Value
Epochs	50 and 500
Batch Size	200
Optimizer	Adam, RMSprop,
Loss Function	MSE
Activation Function	Sigmoid, RELU

Table 3. BC and SC parameters.

Parameter	Value
Solidity Compiler	v0.8.17
Remix IDE	v0.28.1
Number of CC Users	100
Gas Limit	3,000,000
IPFS Key	2048 bits
Hash	256 bits
Consensus	PoW

5.4. X-LSTM Analysis

In this section, we present the simulation results of the proposed X-LSTM network based on the tuning hyperparameters. We first present the details of the XAI feature selection process, which exploits boosting mechanism to create a strong classifier from weak classifiers. We consider that XGBoost handles the relationships between data and associated distribution. Initially, we consider the Shapley addictive explanations (SHAP) model on the CC fraud dataset [46].

To validate the results obtained from the SHAP beeswarm plot, we plot the variable importance plot on the same dataset. Figure 5a presents the details. This plot shows the importance of a variable (attribute) in output classification. Thus, the plot signifies how much accuracy is affected by the exclusion of a variable. The variables are presented in decreasing order of importance. The mean on the x-axis is the mean decrease in the Gini coefficient, and thus, the higher the values of the mean decrease in the Gini score, the higher the importance of the variable in the output prediction. From the figure, it is evident that attributes V_{14}, V_{17}, and V_{12} are more important, and attributes V_{21}, V_6, and V_2 are the least important. The plot closely synchronizes with the SHAP beewswarm plot in most instances, thus validating our cause of selection of important attributes to the LSTM model.

Figure 5b shows the details of the beeswarm SHAP plot. The results show the important features of different features. In the plot, the y-axis represents the features, and the x-axis shows the feature's importance. For example, features V_{14}, V_{17}, and V_{10} have a high SHAP value, which signifies a positive impact on CC fraud prediction. Similarly, features V_{20}, V_8, and V_{15} have a negative impact on the SHAP value and thus are not so important to the output prediction.

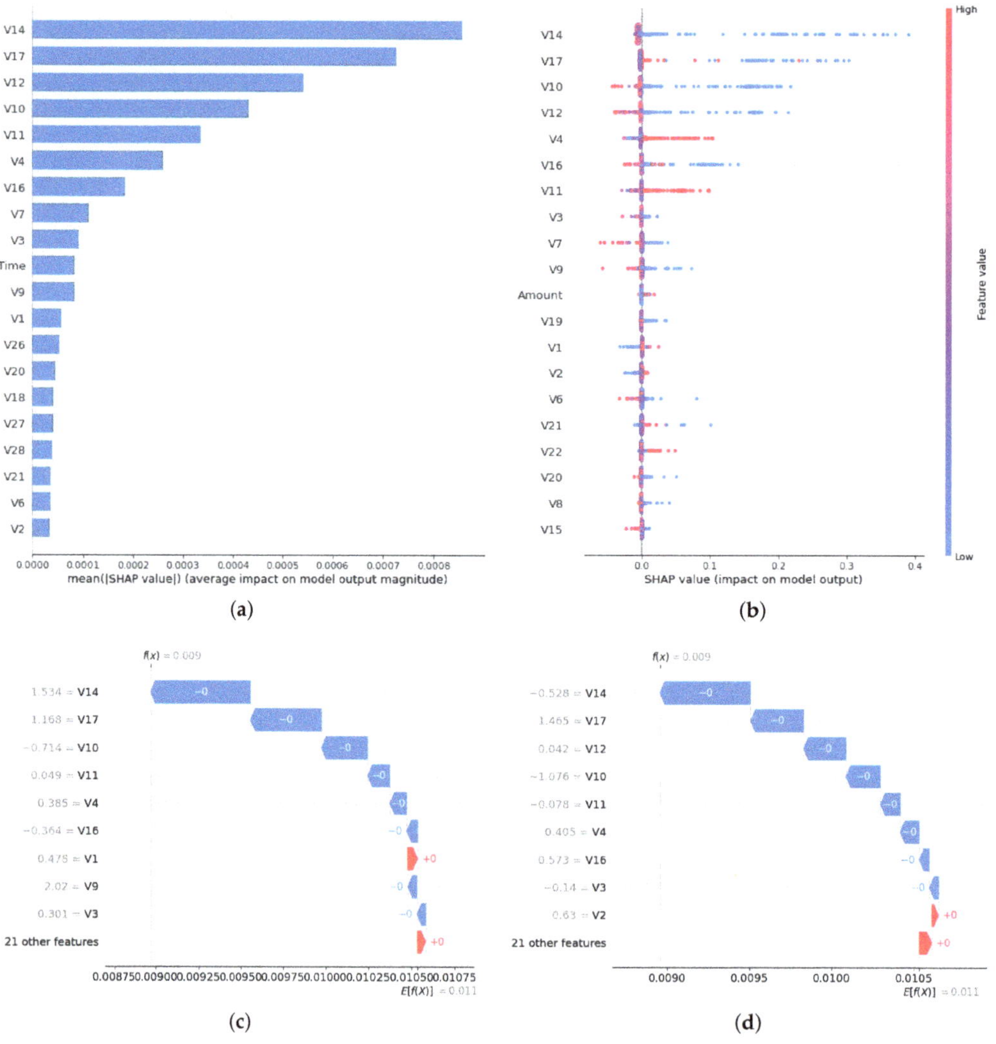

Figure 5. SHAP model performance parameter. (**a**) Variable importance plot on CC-FF dataset. (**b**) SHAP XAI model on CC-FF dataset. (**c**) Waterfall SHAP XAI model on CC-FF dataset. (**d**) SHAP XAI model on CC-FF dataset.

The SHAP model has different types of graphs for feature importance; similar to a waterfall, SHAP works by first computing the baseline value of the output, which is the expected value of the output when all input features have their average or most common values. Then, for each instance to be explained, it calculates the contribution of each feature to the difference between the actual output and the baseline output. In Figure 5c,d, each feature's contribution is represented as a vertical bar that either adds or subtracts from the baseline value. The height of the bar represents the magnitude of the contribution. Figure 6 is a Force SHAP model. It also shows the interaction effects between features [48]. These interaction effects are represented as connections between the features, and the thickness of the connection represents the strength of the interaction.

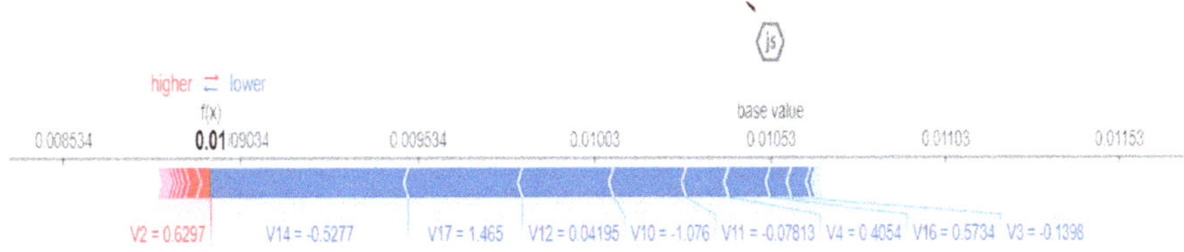

Figure 6. Force SHAP model.

In the study of feature selection, the Eli5 model is also used to present the feature importance of the data. Eli5 stands for Explain Like I'm Five, and it is used for model interpretation and explanation of machine learning models [49]. These methods help to identify the most influential features and how they affect the model's output. To examine and decipher ML classifiers, ELI5 prepares decision trees by weights for tree-based models using the Gini index [48,50]. The tabulated weights determined for each parameter are displayed in Figure 7a. The features are ranked and given weights according to their significance (the most important parameter is at the top).

LIME is a model interpretation and justification method applied to machine learning [48]. Figure 7b presents the LIME graph for CC fraud detection. In the figure, the green color represents the features are positively correlated with the local values, and red color shows the opposite correlation. The fundamental goal is to create a collection of "local surrogate models" that may be used to explain how the original model makes predictions in a specific situation. To accomplish this, LIME first creates a collection of "perturbed" instances that each have slightly different feature values from the original instance. A local surrogate model, such as a linear model or decision tree, is then trained using these perturbed instances to mimic the behavior of the original model in the immediate vicinity of the instance to be explained. It is also a model for presenting the feature importance for better prediction.

5.4.1. LSTM Performance without XAI Input Selection

Firstly, we present the accuracy comparison by directly applying the model without considering the XAI output. For LSTM, we check the accuracy based on the epochs size, such as 50 and 500. In addition, we check the parameters such as the batch size, which is 200. We have applied the LSTM model on both datasets [46,47]. Figure 8a shows the accuracy and loss graphs for LSTM for 50 epochs. A maximum accuracy of 60% is achieved with RMSProp optimizer on the CC fraud detection dataset. For 500 epochs, Figure 8b shows the results. The model gives 85% accuracy with the RMSProp optimizer. Similarly, for the UCI dataset, Figure 8c reports an accuracy of 76% with 50 epochs and 80% accuracy for 500 epochs. Figure 8d demonstrates the results.

5.4.2. LSTM Performance with XAI Input Selection

Next, we present the performance comparison of the model with inputs considered from the XAI output. We ran the model for 50 and 500 epochs on the CC fraud detection dataset [46]. Figure 8e shows the result on the CC-FF dataset for 50 epochs, and Figure 8f shows the result for 50 epochs. Table 4 presents the comparative analysis for the CC-FF-dataset (with and without XAI) for 50 and 500 epochs, respectively. Furthermore, the proposed work is compared with [41], where they used the same dataset to detect CC fraud patterns. However, their work is carried out without applying XAI, which implies that their AI model has not analyzed essential features of CC fraud. Hence, their approach offers 96% training accuracy. Contrary, the proposed work adopts staggering properties of XAI that offer an accuracy of 99.8% without overfitting the LSTM model (as shown in Table 5). In addition, the authors also want to mention that once the AI models classify the data, it requires the data to be secure from data manipulation attacks. Nevertheless, we realize that [41] has not adopted any security feature in their proposed work. On the contrary, we have used an IPFS-based public blockchain for secure storage against data manipulation attacks. This improves the security and privacy concerns of the proposed scheme.

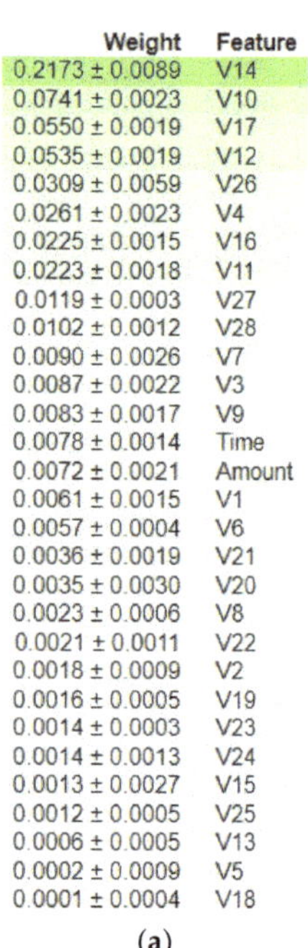

Weight	Feature
0.2173 ± 0.0089	V14
0.0741 ± 0.0023	V10
0.0550 ± 0.0019	V17
0.0535 ± 0.0019	V12
0.0309 ± 0.0059	V26
0.0261 ± 0.0023	V4
0.0225 ± 0.0015	V16
0.0223 ± 0.0018	V11
0.0119 ± 0.0003	V27
0.0102 ± 0.0012	V28
0.0090 ± 0.0026	V7
0.0087 ± 0.0022	V3
0.0083 ± 0.0017	V9
0.0078 ± 0.0014	Time
0.0072 ± 0.0021	Amount
0.0061 ± 0.0015	V1
0.0057 ± 0.0004	V6
0.0036 ± 0.0019	V21
0.0035 ± 0.0030	V20
0.0023 ± 0.0006	V8
0.0021 ± 0.0011	V22
0.0018 ± 0.0009	V2
0.0016 ± 0.0005	V19
0.0014 ± 0.0003	V23
0.0014 ± 0.0013	V24
0.0013 ± 0.0027	V15
0.0012 ± 0.0005	V25
0.0006 ± 0.0005	V13
0.0002 ± 0.0009	V5
0.0001 ± 0.0004	V18

(a)

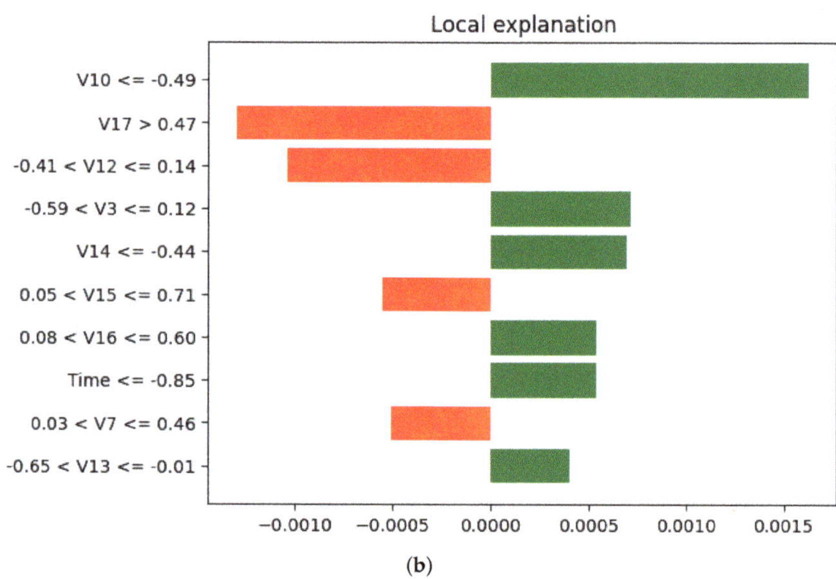

(b)

Figure 7. Comparison of Eli5 and LIME XAI models. (**a**) Eli5 Model. (**b**) Lime XAI Model.

Table 4. Accuracy and loss comparison of X-LSTM.

Epochs	Accuracy	Loss
50 epochs without XAI	60%	47%
500 epochs without XAI	85%	23%
50 epochs with XAI	86.2%	3.6%
500 epochs with XAI	99.8%	1.5%

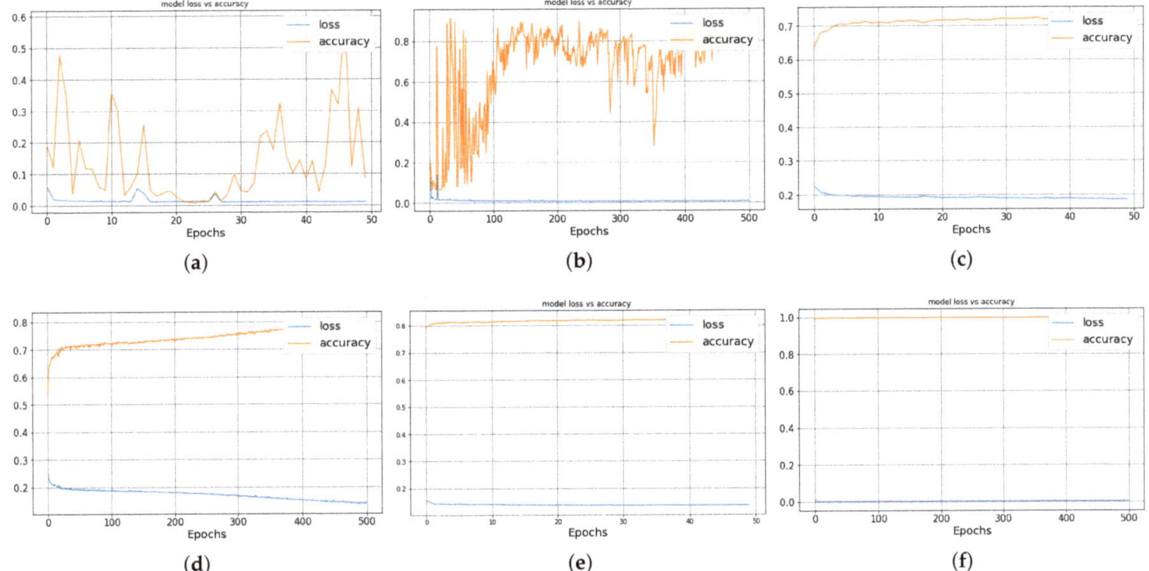

Figure 8. Performance of AI algorithm based on datasets 1 and 2. (**a**) 50 epochs LSTM RMSprop optimizer of dataset 1. (**b**) 500 epochs LSTM RMSprop optimize of dataset 1. (**c**) LSTM 50 Epochs RMSprop Optimizer of dataset 2. (**d**) LSTM 500 Epochs RMSprop Optimizer of dataset 2. (**e**) LSTM and XAI model on 50 epochs of CC-FF dataset. (**f**) LSTM and XAI model on 500 epochs of CC-FF dataset.

Table 5. Performance analysis of XAI models for 500 epochs.

XAI Models	Accuracy	Loss	Precision	Recall
SHAP	99.8%	0.0068%	99%	98%
LIME	98%	0.17%	98%	98%
ELi5	97%	0.18%	93%	96%

5.4.3. Evaluation Metrics

In AI, precision, recall, and accuracy are crucial performance metrics that enable us to quantitatively assess a model's capacity to accurately classify positive and negative instances. These parameters allow us to compare the performance of various models, identify particular areas where a model may need improvement, and are simple enough for both technical and non-technical audiences to comprehend. Overall, important factors that are heavily considered when assessing the effectiveness of binary categorization models include precision, recall, and accuracy.

- Precision ($\mathfrak{P}$): Out of all the positive predictions produced by the model, precision is the percentage of actual positive predictions. In other words, precision assesses the reliability of optimistic forecasts. A high precision number means that the model almost never predicts something that will actually happen.

$$\mathfrak{P} = \frac{\psi}{\psi + \Xi} \tag{25}$$

- Recall ($\mathfrak{R}$): Out of all the real positive instances in the dataset, recall is the percentage of true positive predictions. Recall, then, gauges the model's ability to recognize every positive instance in the dataset. A high recall number means that the model almost never misses any successful examples.

$$\mathfrak{R} = \frac{\psi}{\psi + \xi} \tag{26}$$

- Accuracy ($\mathfrak{A}$): The percentage of accurate forecasts among all the model's predictions is known as accuracy. In other terms, accuracy assesses how well the model can categorize positive and negative instances accurately. A high accuracy rating shows that the model can accurately classify the majority of the dataset's instances.

$$\mathfrak{A} = \frac{\psi + \varsigma}{\psi + \varsigma + \Xi + \xi} \tag{27}$$

where true positive, true negative, false positive, and false negative are represented as $\psi, \varsigma, \Xi, and\ \xi$.

A binary classification model's effectiveness is graphically depicted by the Receiver Operating Characteristic (ROC) curve. At various categorization criteria, it plots the true positive rate (TPR) vs. the false positive rate (FPR). The true positive rate (TPR), often called sensitivity or recall, is the percentage of true positives (positive examples that were classified correctly) among all actual positive instances. The FPR, on the other hand, is the ratio of false positives (negative cases that were wrongly categorized as positive) to all true negative instances. The ROC curve depicts the trade-off between these two rates at different categorization thresholds. The area under the ROC curve (AUC) is a metric that quantifies the overall performance of the model across all possible classification thresholds. The AUC ranges from 0 to 1, where a perfect classifier has an AUC of 1, while a random classifier has an AUC of 0.5. Generally, a higher AUC indicates a better performance of the model. Our model achieves the 0.97 roc_auc shown in Figure 9.

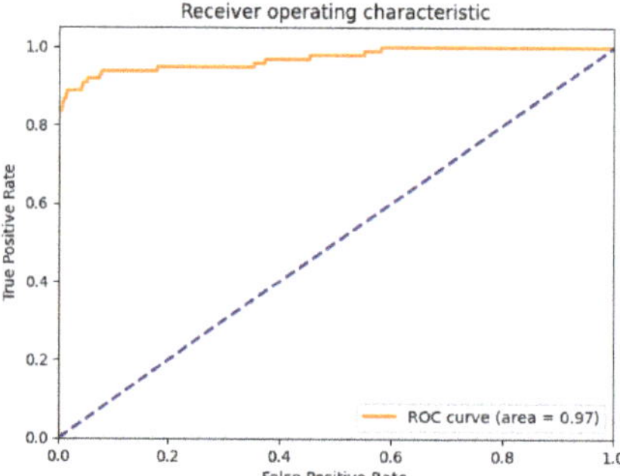

Figure 9. ROC-AUC Graph.

5.5. Smart Contract Design

In the proposed scheme, the LSTM classification output is published via SC, which helps any public user to find whether the new transaction is fake or real. In the SC, we have considered transaction detail, amount, the sender and receiver address, the location of the transaction, and the transaction timestamp. The fraud conditions are kept based on anomalies reported by the X-LSTM model. Figure 10 presents the capture of the fraud transaction (Call_Notify_Fraud_Detected(M_s) function), as depicted in Algorithm 1, and is indicated as RED box in the figure. Some common operating conditions include the execution of a transaction from a new location (not close to the user location), the transaction amount exceeding a specified threshold, and account debits amounting to multiple unknown parties. In the SC, there are two boolean functions *checkFraudTransaction*, which checks the transaction as fraud or not based on the LSTM classification, and *getFraudStatus*, which reports the fake transaction details.

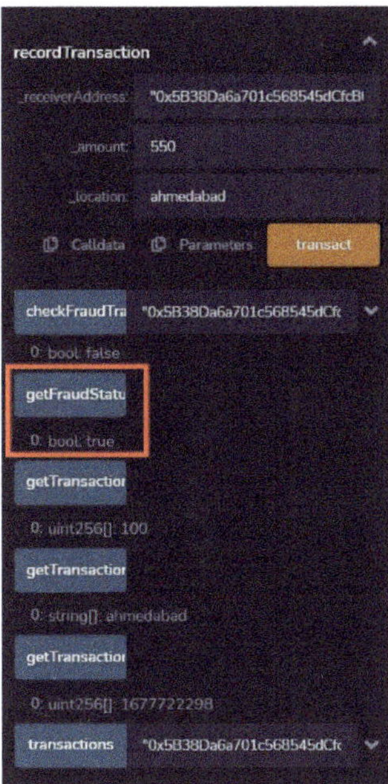

Figure 10. Fraud transaction SC functions.

5.6. BC Performance Metrics

In this section, we discuss the performance of the BC, which stores the information of the SC details. We consider the gas value consideration for the SC design and the IPFS bandwidth for the analysis. The details are presented as follows. We forward the non-attack data to be stored on IPFS and the content hash on public BC post-classification [51]. Financial stakeholders authenticate the non-attack data in the contract, and the contract is executed.

5.6.1. Gas Value for SC

Gas is a unit of measurement for the computing work needed to execute the code in an SC on the BC network. Figure 11a presents the gas cost of transaction and execution. The intricacy of the code within an SC determines how much gas is needed for the contract to function. The quantity of gas a user is ready to pay for the transaction to be carried out is specified when they start a transaction that interacts with a smart contract. The transaction might fail, and all fees paid would be forfeited if the gas limit was too low. Conversely, the user will pay more fees than necessary if the gas limit is too high.

5.6.2. IPFS Bandwidth

IPFS is a peer-to-peer network where the data are stored and exchanged between nodes in the BC network. Figure 11b indicates the IPFS transfer and receive bandwidth over a while. When a user requests data from IPFS, the data are retrieved from the network of nodes rather than from a centralized server. This indicates that the data are dispersed across many nodes, which can speed up data retrieval. However, it also means that bandwidth is an important consideration for IPFS users, as the speed of data transfer will depend on the available bandwidth of the nodes on the network.

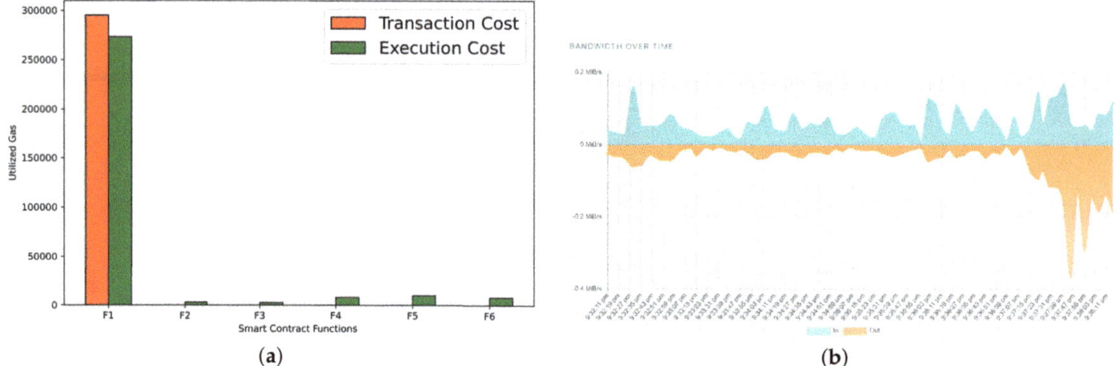

Figure 11. (**a**) Gas cost consumption. (**b**) IPFS bandwidth utilization.

5.6.3. Scalability Graph

The Transactions Per Second (TPS) speed offered by the Blockchain Network (BN) is what determines how scalable a blockchain is. The suggested system's BC (Ethereum) and conventional blockchain (BCN) network scalability comparison graph is shown in Figure 12. The X-axis in this graph shows transaction time in milliseconds, and the Y-axis lists the number of transactions. The suggested method enables more transactions to be added to the BC. Moreover, IPFS can store a lot of data and fetch data much more quickly. Data are kept in IPFS, and IPFS data's hashes are sent to the BC. The proposed strategy using Ethereum Blockchain (EB) outperforms the conventional approach using bitcoin, according to graph visualization. This occurred as a result of bitcoin's lack of advanced technological features offered by the EB.

5.7. Potential Limitations and Future Scope

In this section, we discuss the potential limitations and future improvements of the proposed *RaKSha* scheme. The scheme offers the benefits of CC-FF detection via a proposed X-LSTM approach and then storing the results on SC executed on a public BC network. However, there are some potential limitations that we need to consider in the approach.

Firstly, using public BC for real-time financial data analysis might not be feasible owing to a large amount of real-time data collection (transactions) by financial stakeholders. Secondly, financial data are highly confidential and are subjected to financial laws, and thus, the privacy preservation of the records becomes a critical issue.

Secondly, the proposed approach requires a significant amount of computing power and resources to assure user scalability. Thus, it requires access to cloud servers for resources, which again jeopardizes the privacy and security of data storage. Thirdly, the proposed X-LSTM approach must be resilient to detect emerging CC fraud patterns. In this case, the model needs to continuously train and update itself to recognize the zero-day patterns, which might make the model bulky over time and limit its effectiveness. Thus, the presented limitations must be carefully studied while designing practical solutions for financial ecosystems.

Thus, the presented limitations open up new avenues for the future expansion of the proposed scheme. To address the issue of privacy preservation, the proposed scheme needs to incorporate random noise (differential privacy) to thwart any possible linkage attacks. To address the issue of the X-LSTM model learning and improve the model accuracy, more specific features must be generated by XAI models, which leads to the design of optimized XAI models that could improve the LSTM output. Finally, the proposed SC can be further optimized to improve the IPFS bandwidth, improving public BC networks' transaction scalability.

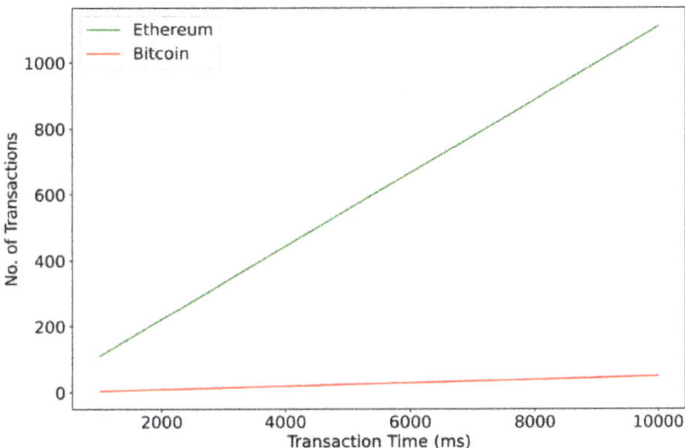

Figure 12. Scalability graph.

6. Concluding Remarks

The paper proposed a novel CC fraud detection scheme, *RaKShA*, in which we proposed an integration of XAI with the LSTM (X-LSTM) model, and the output is verified via SC. The results are stored in IPFS, which is referenced on the public BC network. The proposed approach addressed the limitation of traditional fraud detection by providing model interpretability, improved accuracy, security, and transparency. Modeling X-LSTM augmented the power of the LSTM model in CC-FF detection and made the scheme scalable and adaptable, which helps users to prevent themselves from FF. We validated the proposed layered reference scheme against two CC datasets and presented a comparative analysis of LSTM accuracy and loss (with and without XAI interpretation). For 500 epochs, an accuracy of 99.8% is reported via XAI, which shows an improvement of 17.41% on the simple LSTM model. The use of SC and public BC ensures that the fraud detection data are accessible and verifiable by all users, which makes the proposed scheme a useful CC-FF auditing tool at a low cost.

The presented scheme opens exciting opportunities to improve financial ecosystems' security and transparency barriers. The scheme applies not only to CC frauds but is extensible to insurance, tax evasion, and web transaction frauds. In different use cases, the underlying semantics remain common; however, fine-tuning the proposed scheme according to use case practicality needs to be considered for optimal solutions.

Author Contributions: Conceptualization: J.R., P.B., N.K.J., G.S., P.N.B. and S.T.; writing—original draft preparation: M.E., A.T., J.R., A.T. and M.S.R.; methodology: S.T., G.S., A.T. and P.N.B.; writing—review and editing: S.T., P.B., J.R., N.K.J. and M.S.R.; investigation: M.S.R., S.T., G.S. and M.E.; supervision: S.T., P.N.B. and P.B.; visualization; P.B., J.R., M.E., N.K.J. and M.S.R.; software: A.T., J.R., S.T. and M.E. All authors have read and agreed to the published version of the manuscript.

Funding: This work was funded by the Researchers Supporting Project Number (RSPD2023R681) King Saud University, Riyadh, Saudi Arabia and also funded by the University of Johannesburg, Johannesburg 2006, South Africa.

Informed Consent Statement: Not applicable.

Data Availability Statement: No new data were created or analyzed in this study. Data sharing is not applicable to this article.

Conflicts of Interest: The authors declare no conflict of interest.

References

1. Luo, G.; Li, W.; Peng, Y. Overview of Intelligent Online Banking System Based on HERCULES Architecture. *IEEE Access* **2020**, *8*, 107685–107699. [CrossRef]
2. Srivastava, A.; Singh, S.K.; Tanwar, S.; Tyagi, S. Suitability of big data analytics in Indian banking sector to increase revenue and profitability. In Proceedings of the 2017 3rd International Conference on Advances in Computing, Communication & Automation (ICACCA) (Fall), Dehradun, India 15–16 September 2017; pp. 1–6. [CrossRef]
3. Yildirim, N.; Varol, A. A Research on Security Vulnerabilities in Online and Mobile Banking Systems. In Proceedings of the 2019 7th International Symposium on Digital Forensics and Security (ISDFS), Barcelos, Portugal, 10–12 June 2019; pp. 1–5. [CrossRef]
4. HAYES, A. Blockchain Facts. 2022. Available online: https://www.investopedia.com/terms/b/blockchain.asp (accessed on 2 March 2023).
5. Patel, S.B.; Bhattacharya, P.; Tanwar, S.; Kumar, N. KiRTi: A Blockchain-Based Credit Recommender System for Financial Institutions. *IEEE Trans. Netw. Sci. Eng.* **2021**, *8*, 1044–1054. [CrossRef]
6. Jiang, C.; Song, J.; Liu, G.; Zheng, L.; Luan, W. Credit Card Fraud Detection: A Novel Approach Using Aggregation Strategy and Feedback Mechanism. *IEEE Internet Things J.* **2018**, *5*, 3637–3647. [CrossRef]
7. Cao, R.; Liu, G.; Xie, Y.; Jiang, C. Two-Level Attention Model of Representation Learning for Fraud Detection. *IEEE Trans. Comput. Soc. Syst.* **2021**, *8*, 1291–1301. [CrossRef]
8. Fan, K.; Li, H.; Jiang, W.; Xiao, C.; Yang, Y. Secure Authentication Protocol for Mobile Payment. *Tsinghua Sci. Technol.* **2018**, *23*, 610–620. [CrossRef]
9. Wang, L.; Li, J.; Zuo, L.; Wen, Y.; Liu, H.; Liu, W. T-Tracer: A Blockchain-Aided Symbol Mapping Watermarking Scheme for Traitor Tracing in Non-Repudiation Data Delivery. In Proceedings of the BSCI'22: Fourth ACM International Symposium on Blockchain and Secure Critical Infrastructure, Nagasaki, Japan, 30 May–3 June 2022; pp. 23–34. [CrossRef]
10. Bhatttacharya, P.; Patel, K.; Zuhair, M.; Trivedi, C. A Lightweight Authentication via Unclonable Functions for Industrial Internet-of-Things. In Proceedings of the 2022 2nd International Conference on Innovative Practices in Technology and Management (ICIPTM), Gautam Buddha Nagar, India, 23–25 February 2022; Volume 2; pp. 657–662. [CrossRef]
11. Ferreira, F.G.D.C.; Gandomi, A.H.; Cardoso, R.T.N. Artificial Intelligence Applied to Stock Market Trading: A Review. *IEEE Access* **2021**, *9*, 30898–30917. [CrossRef]
12. Choi, D.; Lee, K. An artificial intelligence approach to financial fraud detection under IoT environment: A survey and implementation. *Secur. Commun. Netw.* **2018**, *2018*. [CrossRef]
13. Chauhan, K.; Jani, S.; Thakkar, D.; Dave, R.; Bhatia, J.; Tanwar, S.; Obaidat, M.S. Automated Machine Learning: The New Wave of Machine Learning. In Proceedings of the 2020 2nd International Conference on Innovative Mechanisms for Industry Applications (ICIMIA), Bangalore, India, 5–7 March 2020; pp. 205–212. [CrossRef]
14. Xiuguo, W.; Shengyong, D. An Analysis on Financial Statement Fraud Detection for Chinese Listed Companies Using Deep Learning. *IEEE Access* **2022**, *10*, 22516–22532. [CrossRef]
15. Alarfaj, F.K.; Malik, I.; Khan, H.U.; Almusallam, N.; Ramzan, M.; Ahmed, M. Credit Card Fraud Detection Using State-of-the-Art Machine Learning and Deep Learning Algorithms. *IEEE Access* **2022**, *10*, 39700–39715. [CrossRef]
16. Zhang, A.; Zhao, X.; Wang, L. CNN and LSTM based Encoder-Decoder for Anomaly Detection in Multivariate Time Series. In Proceedings of the 2021 IEEE 5th Information Technology, Networking, Electronic and Automation Control Conference (ITNEC), Xi'an, China, 15–17 October 2021; Volume 5, pp. 571–575. [CrossRef]
17. Saraswat, D.; Bhattacharya, P.; Verma, A.; Prasad, V.K.; Tanwar, S.; Sharma, G.; Bokoro, P.N.; Sharma, R. Explainable AI for Healthcare 5.0: Opportunities and Challenges. *IEEE Access* **2022**, *10*, 84486–84517.[CrossRef]
18. Tjoa, E.; Guan, C. A survey on explainable artificial intelligence (xai): Toward medical xai. *IEEE Trans. Neural Netw. Learn. Syst.* **2020**, *32*, 4793–4813. [CrossRef] [PubMed]
19. Mankodiya, H.; Obaidat, M.S.; Gupta, R.; Tanwar, S. XAI-AV: Explainable Artificial Intelligence for Trust Management in Autonomous Vehicles. In Proceedings of the 2021 International Conference on Communications, Computing, Cybersecurity, and Informatics (CCCI), Beijing, China, 15–17 October 2021; pp. 1–5. [CrossRef]
20. Mankodiya, H.; Jadav, D.; Gupta, R.; Tanwar, S.; Alharbi, A.; Tolba, A.; Neagu, B.C.; Raboaca, M.S. XAI-Fall: Explainable AI for Fall Detection on Wearable Devices Using Sequence Models and XAI Techniques. *Mathematics* **2022**, *10*, 1990. [CrossRef]
21. Akram, S.V.; Malik, P.K.; Singh, R.; Anita, G.; Tanwar, S. Adoption of blockchain technology in various realms: Opportunities and challenges. *Secur. Priv.* **2020**, *3*, e109. [CrossRef]
22. Gupta, R.; Nair, A.; Tanwar, S.; Kumar, N. Blockchain-assisted secure UAV communication in 6G environment: Architecture, opportunities, and challenges. *IET Commun.* **2021**, *15*, 1352–1367. [CrossRef]
23. Gupta, R.; Shukla, A.; Tanwar, S. BATS: A Blockchain and AI-Empowered Drone-Assisted Telesurgery System Towards 6G. *IEEE Trans. Netw. Sci. Eng.* **2021**, *8*, 2958–2967. [CrossRef]
24. Ketepalli, G.; Tata, S.; Vaheed, S.; Srikanth, Y.M. Anomaly Detection in Credit Card Transaction using Deep Learning Techniques. In Proceedings of the 2022 7th International Conference on Communication and Electronics Systems (ICCES), Coimbatore, India, 22–24 June 2022; pp. 1207–1214.
25. Arun, G.; Venkatachalapathy, K. Convolutional long short term memory model for credit card detection. In Proceedings of the 2020 4th International Conference on Electronics, Communication and Aerospace Technology (ICECA), Coimbatore, India, 5–7 November 2020; pp. 1168–1172.

26. Tingfei, H.; Guangquan, C.; Kuihua, H. Using Variational Auto Encoding in Credit Card Fraud Detection. *IEEE Access* **2020**, *8*, 149841–149853. [CrossRef]

27. Fang, W.; Li, X.; Zhou, P.; Yan, J.; Jiang, D.; Zhou, T. Deep Learning Anti-Fraud Model for Internet Loan: Where We Are Going. *IEEE Access* **2021**, *9*, 9777–9784. [CrossRef]

28. Chen, J.I.Z.; Lai, K.L. Deep convolution neural network model for credit-card fraud detection and alert. *J. Artif. Intell.* **2021**, *3*, 101–112.

29. Balagolla, E.; Fernando, W.; Rathnayake, R.; Wijesekera, M.; Senarathne, A.N.; Abeywardhana, K. Credit Card Fraud Prevention Using Blockchain. In Proceedings of the 2021 6th International Conference for Convergence in Technology (I2CT), Maharashtra, India, 2–4 April 2021; pp. 1–8. [CrossRef]

30. Oladejo, M.T.; Jack, L. Fraud prevention and detection in a blockchain technology environment: Challenges posed to forensic accountants. *Int. J. Econ. Account.* **2020**, *9*, 315–335. [CrossRef]

31. Makki, S.; Assaghir, Z.; Taher, Y.; Haque, R.; Hacid, M.S.; Zeineddine, H. An Experimental Study With Imbalanced Classification Approaches for Credit Card Fraud Detection. *IEEE Access* **2019**, *7*, 93010–93022. [CrossRef]

32. Zheng, L.; Liu, G.; Yan, C.; Jiang, C.; Zhou, M.; Li, M. Improved TrAdaBoost and its Application to Transaction Fraud Detection. *IEEE Trans. Comput. Soc. Syst.* **2020**, *7*, 1304–1316. [CrossRef]

33. Van Belle, R.; Baesens, B.; De Weerdt, J. CATCHM: A novel network-based credit card fraud detection method using node representation learning. *Decis. Support Syst.* **2023**, *164*, 113866. [CrossRef]

34. Ni, L.; Li, J.; Xu, H.; Wang, X.; Zhang, J. Fraud Feature Boosting Mechanism and Spiral Oversampling Balancing Technique for Credit Card Fraud Detection. *IEEE Trans. Comput. Soc. Syst.* **2023**, 1–16. [CrossRef]

35. Labanca, D.; Primerano, L.; Markland-Montgomery, M.; Polino, M.; Carminati, M.; Zanero, S. Amaretto: An Active Learning Framework for Money Laundering Detection. *IEEE Access* **2022**, *10*, 41720–41739. [CrossRef]

36. Esenogho, E.; Mienye, I.D.; Swart, T.G.; Aruleba, K.; Obaido, G. A Neural Network Ensemble with Feature Engineering for Improved Credit Card Fraud Detection. *IEEE Access* **2022**, *10*, 16400–16407. [CrossRef]

37. Chen, L.; Jia, N.; Zhao, H.; Kang, Y.; Deng, J.; Ma, S. Refined analysis and a hierarchical multi-task learning approach for loan fraud detection. *J. Manag. Sci. Eng.* **2022**, *7*, 589–607. [CrossRef]

38. Ji, Y. Explainable AI Methods for Credit Card Fraud Detection: Evaluation of LIME and SHAP through a User Study University of Skövde, School of Informatics 2021. Available online: https://www.diva-portal.org/smash/record.jsf?pid=diva2%3A1626230&dswid=4084 (accessed on 11 March 2023).

39. Ileberi, E.; Sun, Y.; Wang, Z. Performance Evaluation of Machine Learning Methods for Credit Card Fraud Detection Using SMOTE and AdaBoost. *IEEE Access* **2021**, *9*, 165286–165294. [CrossRef]

40. Cui, J.; Yan, C.; Wang, C. ReMEMBeR: Ranking Metric Embedding-Based Multicontextual Behavior Profiling for Online Banking Fraud Detection. *IEEE Trans. Comput. Soc. Syst.* **2021**, *8*, 643–654. [CrossRef]

41. Benchaji, I.; Douzi, S.; El Ouahidi, B.; Jaafari, J. Enhanced credit card fraud detection based on attention mechanism and LSTM deep model. *J. Big Data* **2021**, *8*, 151. [CrossRef]

42. Forough, J.; Momtazi, S. Ensemble of deep sequential models for credit card fraud detection. *Appl. Soft Comput.* **2021**, *99*, 106883. [CrossRef]

43. Kumar, M.S.; Soundarya, V.; Kavitha, S.; Keerthika, E.; Aswini, E. Credit Card Fraud Detection Using Random Forest Algorithm. In Proceedings of the 2019 3rd International Conference on Computing and Communications Technologies (ICCCT), Chennai, India, 21–22 February 2019; pp. 149–153. [CrossRef]

44. Bhavin, M.; Tanwar, S.; Sharma, N.; Tyagi, S.; Kumar, N. Blockchain and quantum blind signature-based hybrid scheme for healthcare 5.0 applications. *J. Inf. Secur. Appl.* **2021**, *56*, 102673. [CrossRef]

45. Afaq, S.; Rao, S. Significance of epochs on training a neural network. *Int. J. Sci. Technol. Res.* **2020**, *9*, 485–488.

46. Credit Card Fraud Detection. Available online: https://www.kaggle.com/datasets/mlg-ulb/creditcardfraud (accessed on 3 January 2012).

47. Credit Approval Data Set. Available online: https://archive.ics.uci.edu/ml/datasets/Credit+Approval (accessed on 3 January 2012).

48. Khanna, V.V.; Chadaga, K.; Sampathila, N.; Prabhu, S.; Bhandage, V.; Hegde, G.K. A Distinctive Explainable Machine Learning Framework for Detection of Polycystic Ovary Syndrome. *Appl. Syst. Innov.* **2023**, *6*, 32. [CrossRef]

49. Khatri, S.; Vachhani, H.; Shah, S.; Bhatia, J.; Chaturvedi, M.; Tanwar, S.; Kumar, N. Machine learning models and techniques for VANET based traffic management: Implementation issues and challenges. *Peer-to-Peer Netw. Appl.* **2021**, *14*, 1778–1805. [CrossRef]

50. Agarwal, N.; Das, S. Interpretable machine learning tools: A survey. In Proceedings of the 2020 IEEE Symposium Series on Computational Intelligence (SSCI), Canberra, ACT, Australia, 1–4 December 2020; pp. 1528–1534.

51. Gupta, R.; Bhattacharya, P.; Tanwar, S.; Kumar, N.; Zeadally, S. GaRuDa: A Blockchain-Based Delivery Scheme Using Drones for Healthcare 5.0 Applications. *IEEE Internet Things Mag.* **2021**, *4*, 60–66. [CrossRef]

 *mathematics*

Article

ELCT-YOLO: An Efficient One-Stage Model for Automatic Lung Tumor Detection Based on CT Images

Zhanlin Ji [1,2], Jianyong Zhao [1], Jinyun Liu [1], Xinyi Zeng [1], Haiyang Zhang [3], Xueji Zhang [4,*] and Ivan Ganchev [2,5,6,*]

[1] Hebei Key Laboratory of Industrial Intelligent Perception, College of Artificial Intelligence, North China University of Science and Technology, Tangshan 063210, China; zhaojianyong@stu.ncst.edu.cn (J.Z.)
[2] Telecommunications Research Centre (TRC), University of Limerick, V94 T9PX Limerick, Ireland
[3] Department of Computing, Xi'an Jiaotong-Liverpool University, Suzhou 215000, China
[4] School of Biomedical Engineering, Shenzhen University Health Science Center, Shenzhen 518060, China
[5] Department of Computer Systems, University of Plovdiv "Paisii Hilendarski", 4000 Plovdiv, Bulgaria
[6] Institute of Mathematics and Informatics—Bulgarian Academy of Sciences, 1040 Sofia, Bulgaria
* Correspondence: zhangxueji@szu.edu.cn (X.Z.); ivan.ganchev@ul.ie (I.G.)

Abstract: Research on lung cancer automatic detection using deep learning algorithms has achieved good results but, due to the complexity of tumor edge features and possible changes in tumor positions, it is still a great challenge to diagnose patients with lung tumors based on computed tomography (CT) images. In order to solve the problem of scales and meet the requirements of real-time detection, an efficient one-stage model for automatic lung tumor detection in CT Images, called ELCT-YOLO, is presented in this paper. Instead of deepening the backbone or relying on a complex feature fusion network, ELCT-YOLO uses a specially designed neck structure, which is suitable to enhance the multi-scale representation ability of the entire feature layer. At the same time, in order to solve the problem of lacking a receptive field after decoupling, the proposed model uses a novel Cascaded Refinement Scheme (CRS), composed of two different types of receptive field enhancement modules (RFEMs), which enables expanding the effective receptive field and aggregate multi-scale context information, thus improving the tumor detection performance of the model. The experimental results show that the proposed ELCT-YOLO model has strong ability in expressing multi-scale information and good robustness in detecting lung tumors of various sizes.

Keywords: lung cancer; tumor; CT image; one-stage detector; YOLO; multi-scale; receptive field

MSC: 68W11; 9404

Citation: Ji, Z.; Zhao, J.; Liu, J.; Zeng, X.; Zhang, H.; Zhang, X.; Ganchev, I. ELCT-YOLO: An Efficient One-Stage Model for Automatic Lung Tumor Detection Based on CT Images. *Mathematics* **2023**, *11*, 2344. https://doi.org/10.3390/math11102344

Academic Editors: Snezhana Gocheva-Ilieva, Atanas Ivanov and Hristina Kulina

Received: 9 April 2023
Revised: 6 May 2023
Accepted: 15 May 2023
Published: 17 May 2023

1. Introduction

Lung cancer is a common disease that has a higher mortality rate than other cancers. It is the main cause of cancer death [1]. According to the American Cancer Society, the number of new lung cancer cases in the United States is expected to reach 238,340 this year, with 127,070 deaths because of this. Computed tomography (CT) imaging is the most commonly employed method for detecting lung diseases [2,3]. Regular CT screening for people at high risk of developing lung cancer can reduce the risk of dying from this disease. Professional doctors can diagnose lung cancer according to the morphological characteristics of the lesions in CT images. However, CT scans produce huge amounts of image data, which increases the difficulty of performing proper disease diagnosis. Furthermore, doctors may make a wrong diagnosis due to long work shifts and monotonous working. In addition, even experienced doctors and experts can easily miss some small potential lesions. Therefore, automatic detection of lung tumors, based on CT images, needs to be further advanced for improving the quality of diagnosis.

Accurate detection of lung cancer is a challenging task. On the one hand, the tumors have complex edge features and may change their position [4]. As illustrated in Figure 1a, showing the CT chest images of patients with lung cancers, the texture, gray scale, and shape of tumors are important for clinical staging and pathological classification [5]. On the other hand, redundant image information causes difficulties in the detection task. For example, the images of abundant blood vessels, bronchi, and tiny nodules in the lung interfere with the unique features of tumors. In addition, tumors have different sizes (Figure 1b) and different types of tumors have different growth rates. For example, the multiplication rate of lung squamous cell carcinoma is lower than that of lung adenocarcinoma. Moreover, tumors of the same type have different sizes at different stages of their development [6]. In addition, a tumor naturally has different sizes in multiple CT scanning slices. The challenge brought by the difference in tumor sizes seriously limits the accuracy of existing methods for tumor detection.

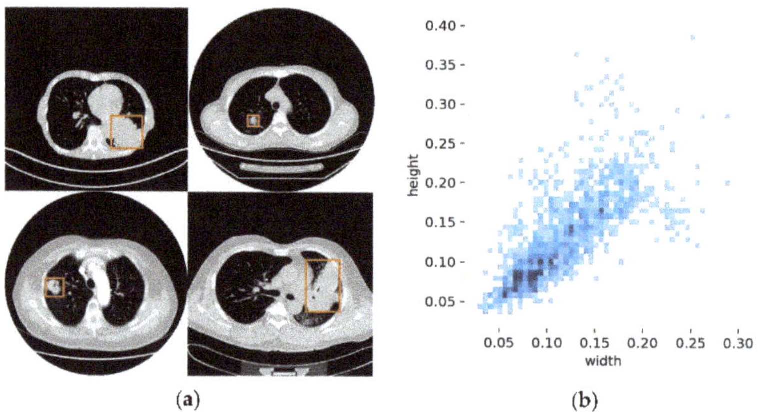

(a) (b)

Figure 1. (**a**) Sample CT chest images of four patients with lung cancer showing round or irregular masses of different size with uniform or nonuniform density; (**b**) tumor size distribution in the dataset, used in the experiments presented further in this paper (the tumor sizes are highly variable, making it difficult to accurately locate and classify tumors).

To date, a lot of work has been done on automatic detection of lung lesions. The early computer-aided lung cancer detection methods mainly relied on an artificially designed feature extractor. Feature extractor can obtain the gray scale, texture and other morphological features of a tumor in an image, which are subsequently fed into a Support Vector Machine (SVM) or AdaBoost for classification. However, the artificially designed features cannot well correspond to the highly variable tumor size, position, and edge, thus limiting the detection ability of these methods [7]. Recently, as deep learning has been increasingly applied in various medical and health care fields, and many researchers have devoted themselves to the study of lung tumor detection based on deep neural networks (DNNs) [8,9]. Unlike traditional methods relying on artificial design, DNNs have a large number of parameters and can fit semantic features better.

Gong et al. [10] used a deep residual network to identify lung adenocarcinoma in CT images, and obtained comparable or even superior outcomes compared to radiologists. Mei et al. [11] conducted experiments on the PN9 dataset to detect lung nodules in CT scans using a slice-aware network. The results showed that the proposed SANet outperformed other 2D and 3D convolutional neural network (CNN) methods and significantly reduced the false positive rate (FPR) for lung nodules. Xu et al. [12] designed a slice-grouped domain attention (SGDA) module that can be easily embedded into existing backbone networks to improve the detection network's generalization ability. Su et al. [13] used the Bag of Visual Words (BoVW) and a convolutional recurrent neural network (CRNN) to detect lung tumors in CT images. The model first segments the CT images into smaller nano-segments using biocompatibility techniques, and then classifies the nano-segments using deep learning techniques. Mousavi et al. [14] introduced a detection approach based on a deep neural network for identifying COVID-19 and other lung infections. More specifically, their method involves using a deep neural network to extract features from chest X-ray images, employing an LSTM network for sequence modeling, and utilizing a SoftMax classifier for image classification. This method shows excellent performance in detecting COVID-19 and can help radiologists make diagnoses quickly. In [15], Mei et al. utilized a depth-wise over-parameterized convolutional layer to construct a residual unit in the backbone network, leading to improved feature representation ability of the network. Moreover, the study also implemented enhancements in the confidence loss function and focal loss to handle the significant imbalance between positive and negative samples during training. It is noteworthy that this method focuses on the efficiency and practicability of the detector. Version 4 of You Only Look Once (YOLO), i.e., YOLOv4, was used as a benchmark for this method but there have been few studies using YOLO to detect lung tumors so far.

Although many processing methods exist for automated detection of lung tumors in CT images, the variability of tumor size is less considered. As indicated above, the size of lung tumors exhibits variability, thus posing challenges for precise tumor detection. As the multi-scale issue constrains the efficacy of prevalent detection methods, some researchers have paid attention to this issue and proposed improvements to the existing methods. Causey et al. [16] utilized 3D convolution in combination with Spatial Pyramid Pooling (SPP) to develop a lung cancer detection algorithm, which enabled reducing the FPR based on the National Lung Screening Trial (NLST) data cohort used for testing, whereby the area under the curve (AUC) value reached 0.892, proving that the detection performance is better than that of using only 3D convolution. Compared with detecting 2D slices one by one, 3D convolution can be used to obtain rich space and volume information in adjacent slices, and models can be generalized to sparsely annotated datasets. However, 3D convolution consumes more computer memory than conventional convolution. Other studies have proposed feature pyramid networks (FPNs), whereby the recognition of small-size tumors depends on features from the shallow network, while the top-level network has more abundant semantic information, which is important for the accurate classification of tumors. The purpose of FPN is to connect the feature maps spanning different layers, so as to restore the low-resolution information of the deep feature map and enhance the semantic information of the shallow feature map. In order to effectively integrate multi-scale information, Guo et al. [17] fused feature maps at different layers. In [18], Guo and Bai construct a FPN to detect multi-scale lung nodules, thus significantly improving the accuracy of small lung nodule detection. In [19], by applying a bi-directional FPN (BiFPN), the feature fusion structure of YOLOv5 was improved, and a fusion path was added between features at the same layer. Some other improvements of feature fusion network have also achieved good results in other tasks [20]. The original FPN structure and its variants adopt complex cross-scale connections to obtain a stronger multi-scale representation ability. Although helpful for improving multi-scale tumor detection, this operation requires more parameters and increases computational expenses, so it is contrary to the general expectation of a highly efficient detector.

Taking inspiration from the previous work, we have considered a real-world hospital scenario where a large volume of CT data is available, but hardware resources are limited. To reduce hardware costs while maintaining the speed of tumor detection, we have selected YOLOv7 as the underlying framework as it can achieve good balance between accuracy and tumor detection speed without requiring generation of candidate boxes, as opposed to the two-stage detection models. In this paper, we propose a novel one-stage detection model, called ELCT-YOLO, based on the popular YOLOv7-tiny network architecture [21], for solving the problem of multi-scale lung tumor detection in CT scan slices. For ELCT-YOLO, firstly, we designed a Decoupled Neck (DENeck) structure to improve the multi-scale feature representation ability of the model. Different from the previous design scheme of feature fusion structure [22,23], we do not stack a large number of basic structures, nor build a complex topology. We propose the idea of decoupling the feature layer into a high-semantic region and low-semantic region, as to reduce semantic conflict in the fusion process. Secondly, we propose a Cascaded Refinement Scheme (CRS), which includes a group of Receptive Field Enhancement Modules (RFEMs) to explore rich context information. Using atrous convolution, we constructed two multi-scale sensing structures, namely a Series RFEM (SRFEM) and a Parallel RFEM (PRFEM). In order to expand the effective receptive field, these serial structures use a series of atrous convolutions with different sampling rates. At the same time, a residual connection was applied to alleviate the grid artifacts as per [24]. The achieved parallel structure can construct complementary receptive fields, in which each branch matches the amount of information based on its own receptive field. In addition, we studied the performance of different cascaded schemes through experiments.

The main contributions of this paper can be summarized as follows:

1. In order to solve the problem of multi-scale detection, a novel neck structure, called DENeck, is designed and proposed to effectively model the dependency between feature layers and improve the detection performance by using complementary features with similar semantic information. In addition, compared with the original FPN structure, the design of DENeck is more efficient in terms of the number of parameters used.
2. A novel CRS structure is designed and proposed to improve the robustness of variable-size tumor detection by collecting rich context information. At the same time, an effective receptive field is constructed to refine the tumor features.
3. It is proposed to integrate the spatial pyramid pooling—fast (SPPF) module of YOLOv5 [25] at the top of the original YOLOv7-tiny backbone network in order to extract important context features by utilizing a smaller number of parameters and using multiple small-size cascaded pooling kernels, in order to increase further the model's operational speed and enrich the representation ability of feature maps.

2. Related Work

Deep learning-based object detection methods have significance value in medical applications, such as breast cancer detection [26], retinal lesion detection [27], rectal cancer detection [28], and lung nodule detection [29]. Many of the methods listed above rely on the YOLO family as their foundation, demonstrating a very fast processing speed. Although the YOLO family has a good speed–precision balance, it is not effective in detecting lesions with scale changes in CT images. In the next subsections, we first introduce the YOLO principles and then introduce the current popular methods to deal with multi-scale problems, namely, the feature pyramids and exploring multi-scale context information [30].

2.1. The YOLO Family

Two major types of deep learning models are currently employed for object detection. The first kind pertains to object detection models that rely on region proposals, such as Regions with CNN (R-CNN), Fast R-CNN, Faster R-CNN, and Mask R-CNN. The second type are object detection models that use regression analysis for detection, such as the YOLO series and SSD series. While the accuracy of two-stage object detection models has improved significantly over time, their detection speed is limited by their structure [31]. The YOLO model [32] was the pioneering one-stage detector in the field of deep learning, as proposed by Redmon et al. in 2015. The main dissimilarity between one-stage and two-stage object detectors relates to the fact that the former do not have a candidate region recommendation stage, which enables them to directly determine the object category and get the position of detection boxes in one stage. Due to YOLO's good speed–precision balance, YOLO's related research has always received much attention. With the introduction of subsequent versions of YOLO, its performance continues to improve.

The second version of YOLO, YOLOv2 [33], uses Darknet-19 as a backbone network, removes the full connection layer, and uses a pooling method to obtain fixed-size feature vectors. A 13×13 feature map is obtained after down-sampling of a 416×416 input image 5 times. YOLOv2 uses the ImageNet dataset and the Common Objects in COntext (COCO) dataset to train the detector and locate the position of objects in the detection dataset, and utilizes the classification dataset to increase the categories of objects recognized by the detector. This joint training method overcomes the limitation of object detection tasks in terms of categories.

To enhance multi-scale prediction accuracy, YOLOv3 [34] introduces a FPN, using the feature maps of C3, C4, and C5 in Darknet-53 and combined horizontal connections. Finally, the model generates prediction maps for three different scales, enabling it to detect objects of various sizes, including large, medium, and small ones. By using a K-means clustering algorithm, YOLOv3 analyzes the information in the ground truth box of the training dataset to obtain nine types of prior bounding boxes, which can cover the objects of multiple scales in the dataset. Each prediction branch uses anchors to generate three kinds of prediction boxes for the object falling into the region, and finally uses a non-maximum suppression algorithm to filter the prediction box set. Compared with the previous two versions, YOLOv3 improves the detection ability and positioning accuracy of small objects.

YOLOv4 [35] uses CSPDarknet-53 as a backbone network, which combines DarketNet-53 with a Cross-Stage Partial Network (CSPNet). The neck of YOLOv4 uses SPP and Path Aggregation Network (PANet) modules. The fundamental concept of the SPP module is to leverage the average pooling operation of different sizes to extract features, which helps obtain rich context information. PANet reduces the transmission path of information by propagating positional information from lower to higher levels. Unlike the original PANet, YOLOv4 replaces the original shortcut connection with the tensor *concat*. In addition, YOLOv4 also uses Mosaic and other data enhancement methods.

Jocher et al. [25] introduced YOLOv5, which is the first version of YOLO to use Pytorch. Due to the mature ecosystem of Pytorch, YOLOv5 deployment is simpler. YOLOv5 adds adaptive anchor box calculation. When the best possible recall is less than 0.98, the K-means clustering algorithm is utilized to determine the most suitable size for the anchor boxes. YOLOv5 uses an SPPF module to replace the SPP module. In Figure 2, SPPF employs several cascaded pooling kernels of small sizes instead of the single pooling kernel of large size used in the SPP module, which further improves the operational speed. In the subsequent neck module, YOLOv5 replaces the ordinary convolution with CSP_2X structure to enhance feature fusion.

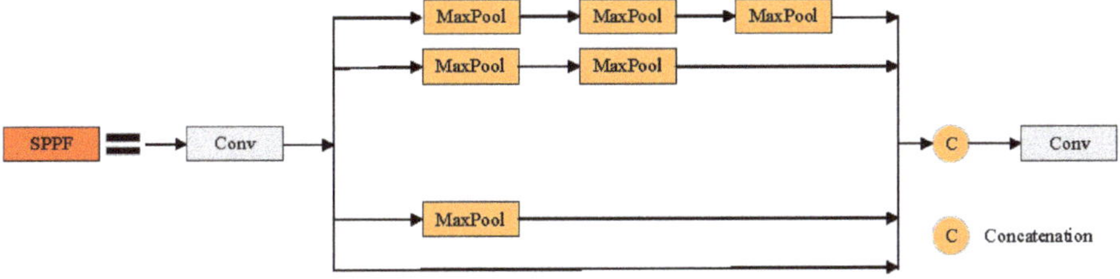

Figure 2. The SPPF module structure.

YOLOv6 [36] also focuses on detection accuracy and reasoning efficiency. YOLOv6-s can achieve an average precision (AP) of 0.431 on COCO and a reasoning speed of 520 frames per second (FPS) on Tesla T4 graphics cards. Based on the Re-parameterization VGG (RepVGG) style, YOLOv6 uses re-parameterized and more efficient networks, namely EfficientRep in the backbone and a Re-parameterization Path Aggregation Network (Rep-PAN) in the neck. The Decoupled Head is optimized, which reduces the additional delay overhead brought by the decoupled head method while maintaining good accuracy. In terms of training strategy, YOLOv6 adopts the anchor-free paradigm, supplemented by a simplified optimal transport assignment (SimOTA) label allocation strategy and a SIoU [37] bounding box regression loss in order to further improve the detection accuracy.

YOLOv7 [21] enhances the network's learning ability without breaking the original gradient flow by utilizing an extended efficient layer aggregation network (E-ELAN) module (Figure 3). In addition, YOLOv7 utilizes architecture optimization methods to enhance object detection accuracy without increasing the reasoning costs, redesigns the re-parameterized convolution by analyzing the gradient flow propagation path, introduces an auxiliary head to improve its performance, and employs a new deep supervision label allocation strategy. The ELCT-YOLO model, proposed in this paper, is based on improvements of the popular YOLOv7-tiny network architecture [21], as described further in Section 3.

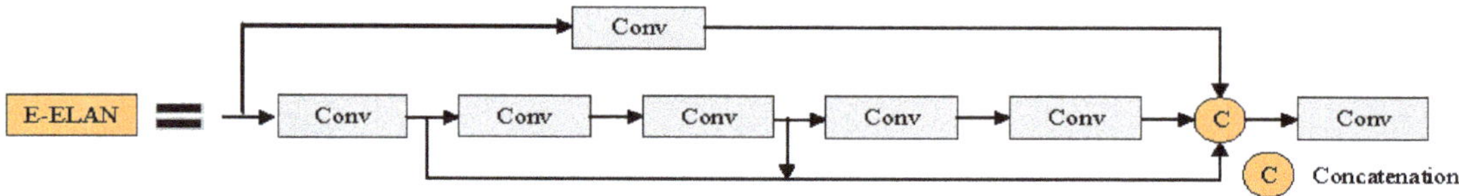

Figure 3. The E-ELAN module structure.

YOLOv8, the latest version of YOLO, has achieved a significant improvement in both detection accuracy and speed, lifting the object detection to a new level. YOLOv8 is not only compatible with all previous YOLO versions, but also adopts the latest anchor-free paradigm, which reduces the computational load and breaks away from the width and height limit of fixed anchor boxes. However, the author of YOLOv8 has not published a paper to explain its advantages in detail.

2.2. Multi-Scale Challenge and FPN

Both the one-stage object detectors and the two-stage object detectors face the challenge of multi-scale detection. As mentioned in the introduction, tumors in different CT images and the focus area in different sections of the same tumor have differences in scale. The existing CNNs have limited ability to extract multi-scale features, because continuous pooling operations or convolution operations with a step size greater than 1 lead to the reduction in the resolution of the feature map, resulting in a conflict between semantic information and spatial information [38]. An approach commonly used to address the challenge of detecting objects at multiple scales is to create an FPN by combining features from different layers.

An FPN architecture that combines the deep feature map with the shallow feature map was proposed by Lin et al. in [39]. They believed that the network's deep features contain strong semantic information, while the shallow features contain strong spatial information. The combination is achieved through multiple up-sampling layers. By utilizing the inherent feature layer of ConvNet, FPN constructs a feature pyramid structure that can greatly enhance the detection network's ability to handle objects of various scales, with minimal additional cost. The use of this network structure has become prevalent for addressing multi-scale problems in the realm of object detection due to its efficacy and versatility.

By integrating a bottom-up pathway with FPN architecture, PANet [40] can effectively enhance the spatial information within the feature pyramid structure. NAS-FPN [22] uses the Natural Architecture Search (NAS) algorithm to find the optimal cross-scale connection architecture. It is believed that the artificially designed feature pyramid structure has limited representation ability. In addition, BiFPN [23] and Recursion-FPN [41] propose weighted feature fusion and detector backbone based on looking and thinking twice, respectively to obtain a strong feature representation. Generally speaking, these methods focus on introducing additional optimization modules to obtain better multi-scale representation. In the ELCT-YOLO model, proposed in this paper, we use a decoupling method to aggregate multi-scale features, which allows to detect lung tumors more accurately without increasing the complexity of the model.

2.3. Exploring Context Information by Using Enlarged Receptive Field

Rich context information is helpful for detecting objects with scale changes [42]. Many studies have explored context information using enlarged receptive field, which are realized mostly through pooling operations or atrous convolution.

PoolNet [43] proposes a global guidance module, which first uses adaptive average pooling to capture picture context information, and then fuses the information flow into the feature map of different scales to highlight objects in complex scenarios. ThunderNet [44] applies average pooling to obtain global contextual features from the highest level of the backbone network, which is then aggregated with features at other layers to increase the receptive field of the model. Generally speaking, in order to obtain abstract information, CNN needs to repeat pooling operations, which results in focusing only on the local region. The lack of position information is detrimental to (intensive) detection tasks. Atrous convolution is a popular solution to this problem.

ACFN [45] and Deeplab-v2 [38] use atrous convolutions with various dilation rates instead of the repeated pooling operation in CNN. This strategy can enlarge the receptive field while preserving complete positional information. Liu et al. [46] have built a multi-sensor feature extraction module, which aggregates multi-scale context information by using atrous convolution with a same-size convolution kernel but different dilation rates. However, while improving the receptive field of the network, atrous convolution also brings challenges because discrete sampling may lose some information and make the weight matrix discontinuous. Furthermore, the irregularly arranged atrous convolution with different dilation rates can aggravate this problem. This situation, called the gridding effect, is analyzed in [24]. Inspired by the above methods, we have designed two types of RFEMs— a SRFEM using a serial combination and a PRFEM using a parallel combination—to sense multi-scale context information, which apply an appropriate dilation rate combination and residual connection to reduce the gridding effect.

3. Proposed Model

3.1. Overview

The proposed ELCT-YOLO model, shown in Figure 4, is based on YOLOv7-tiny, which is a popular and efficient object detector. With an input image size of $512 \times 512 \times 3$, where 512 represents the image's width and height and 3 represents the number of channels, the features are efficiently extracted through a backbone network, which is mainly based on E-ELAN modules. A SPPF module is added at the top of the backbone network to extract important context features. By concatenating feature maps of various scales, the SPPF module enhances the network's receptive field and boosts both the efficiency of detecting defects at multiple scales and the reasoning speed. The output feature maps of $C3$, $C4$, and $C5$, obtained in the backbone at three different scales corresponding, respectively, to 8, 16, and 32 times down-sampling, are inputted to the neck for feature aggregation. As described in Section 2, the neck structure has an important impact on the accurate detection of lung tumors with scale changes. Therefore, we redesigned the original neck structure of YOLOv7-tiny, and called it DENeck, by decoupling the feature pyramid into a high-semantic region and low-semantic region. Further, we propose a CRS structure to enhance the multi-scale feature representation capability by expanding the receptive field of the low-level semantic region. The three detection heads are used for anchor box classification and regression of large, medium, and small objects, respectively. The network performs detection on the feature maps output by the three detection heads P3, P4, and P5, whose corresponding scales are (16, 3, 80, 80, 7), (16, 3, 40, 40, 7), and (16, 3, 20, 20, 7), respectively. The first-dimension value (i.e., 16) in the output of the ELCT-YOLO detection head represents that the model processes 16 images at once. The second-dimension value (i.e., 3) represents the use of k-means clustering to obtain three prior boxes of different sizes. The values 80, 40, and 20 in the third and fourth dimensions represent the detection of images at different granularities, corresponding to receptive fields of 8×8, 16×16, and 32×32, respectively. The fifth-dimension value represents the model's prediction information, including the predicted box information, confidence in the presence of tumors, and classification information for adenocarcinoma and small cell carcinoma.

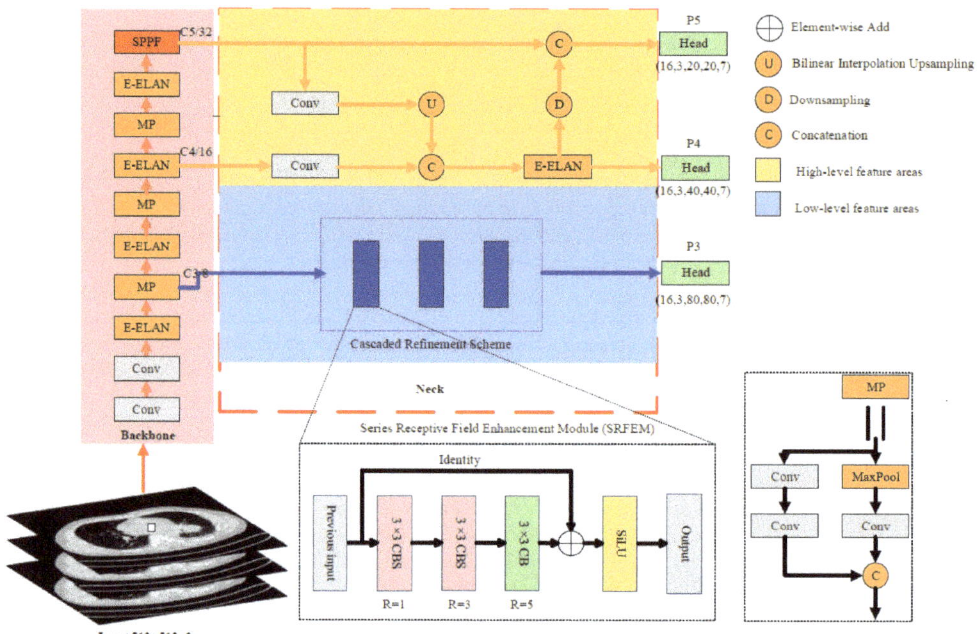

Figure 4. A high-level structure of the proposed ELCT-YOLO model (SRFEM is used for all CRSs as it enables achieving the best results, c.f., Section 4.5).

3.2. Decoupled Neck (DENeck)

3.2.1. Motivation

In YOLOv7-tiny, the neck structure adopts a structure similar to the PANet to cope with difficulty of performing multi-scale object detection. Its core idea is to use the multi-scale expression built in CNN, which is generated by repeated down-sampling or pooling operations. As described in Section 2, PANet first fuses feature information from top level to bottom level, and then constructs a bottom-up secondary fusion path to generate enhanced semantic and detail information. However, this design may not be suitable in each situation.

First of all, this fusion method ignores the semantic differences of features with different scales [47]. In a linear combination of feature layers, the adjacent feature layers are closer in semantic information, while the feature layers that are far away not only bring detailed information in semantics or space, but also introduce confusion information in the process of transmission. Further, we believe that this conflict is more obvious in the process of processing CT images. Unlike natural images, CT images are reconstructed by a specific algorithm based on the X-ray attenuation coefficient. The quality of CT images is limited by specific medical scenarios. Compared with the dataset commonly used in computer vision tasks, CT images have a single background and low contrast [48]. The characteristics of the CT images determine their low-level features, such as the tumor edge and shape, which need to be paid attention to in the process of tumor detection. The semantic confusion will destroy the details of the lesions. Based on this logic, our designed neck network reduces semantic conflicts by a decoupling method. This enhances the model's ability to detect tumors at different scales and emphasizes the tumor region in the CT image.

3.2.2. Structure

We use the backbone of YOLOv7-tiny as a benchmark, where $\{C3, C4, C5\}$ represent the corresponding feature layer generated by the backbone. The corresponding output feature map of the same space size is denoted by $\{P_3^{out}, P_4^{out}, P_5^{out}\}$, and the stride of the feature map relative to the input image is $\{3, 4, 5\}$ pixels.

As shown in Figure 4, the $P3$ branch in the blue area corresponds to low-level semantic information, including details of tumor edge and shape. At the same time, it is noted that canceling the information from $P4$ and $P5$ will lead to insufficient receptive fields of low-level semantic branches, so we propose a CRS structure to increase the receptive fields of low-level semantic region and improve the multi-scale feature representation ability. The $P4$ and $P5$ branches in the yellow area in Figure 4 correspond to high-level semantic information, which is crucial to determine the tumor type. We maintain a cross-scale feature fusion between higher levels because there is less conflict between them.

The designed DENeck feature aggregation method is as follows:

$$P_3^{out} = RFEM(C3) \tag{1}$$

$$P_4^{out} = E - ELAN(concat[B4, resize(C5)]) + C4 \tag{2}$$

$$P_5^{out} = E - ELAN\left(concat\left[B5, down\left(P_4^{td}\right)\right]\right) + C5 \tag{3}$$

where RFEM can be either a Series RFEM (SRFEM) or a Parallel RFEM (PRFEM), both of which were tried in different cascaded combinations for use in the proposed model (c.f., Section 4.5); "+" denotes element-wise addition; $B4$ and $B5$ correspond to $C4$ and $C5$ output by 1×1 convolution, respectively (we use independent 1×1 convolutional layers at different levels to reduce the differences in features between levels); P_4^{td} denotes the feature obtained by fusing $C4$ and $C5$ after *resize* operation, which includes up-sampling in alignment with resolution and 1×1 convolution adjustment dimension; *concat* and *down* denote the tensor splicing operation and down-sampling operation, respectively. E-ELAN is used after *concat* to reduce the aliasing caused by fusion. Batch normalization (BN) and Sigmoid Weighted Liner Unit (SiLU) activation functions are used behind all the convolutional layers in the DENeck structure.

3.3. Cascaded Refinement Scheme (CRS)

While the Decoupled Neck paradigm helps improve detection performance, it leads to loss of receptive fields. Low-level semantic features are short of receptive fields that are large enough to capture global contextual information, causing the detectors to confuse tumor regions with their surrounding normal tissues. In addition, tumors of different sizes in CT images should match receptive fields of different scales.

In response to this, we propose a CRS structure to further improve the effective receptive fields. CRS consists of two types of modules—a SRFEM, shown Figure 5, and a PRFEM, shown in Figure 6. They both use dilated convolutions with different dilation rates to adjust the receptive fields.

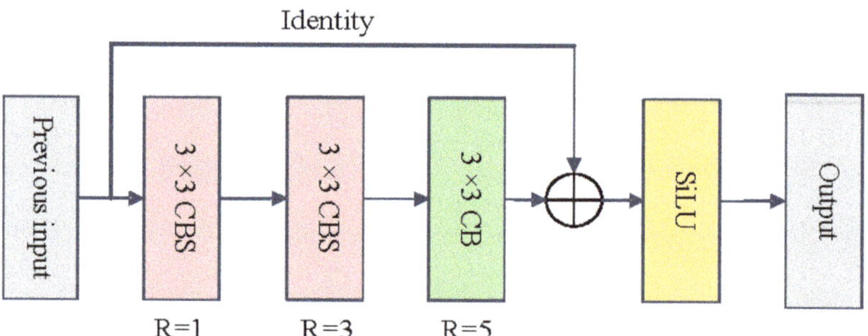

Figure 5. The SRFEM structure.

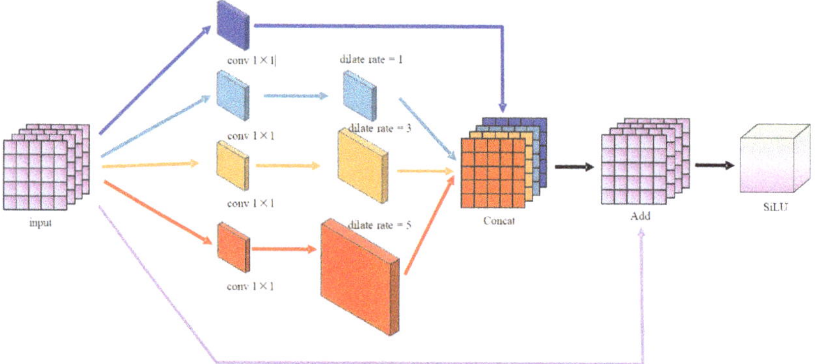

Figure 6. The PRFEM structure.

Different from the normal convolution, in dilated convolution, the convolution kernel values are separated by fixed intervals, which can increase the size of the perception area without changing the parameters [45]. If $x(m, n)$ is the input of the dilated convolution, then its output $y(m, n)$ is defined as follows:

$$y(m,n) = \sum_{i=1}^{M} \sum_{j=1}^{N} x(m + r \times i, n + r \times j) w(i,j) \tag{4}$$

where M and N denote the size of the convolution kernel (the normal convolution kernel is of size $M = 3$, $N = 3$), $w(i, j)$ is a specific parameter of the convolution kernel, and r denotes the dilated convolution sampling rate (i.e., the number of zeros between non-zero values in the convolution kernel). Different values of r can be set to obtain corresponding receptive fields. When $r = 1$, the receptive field is 3×3, and when $r = 2$ and $r = 3$, the receptive field is expanded to 5×5 and 7×7, respectively. The amount of computation is always the same as the normal convolution of $M = 3$, $N = 3$. This operation is often used to expand the receptive fields of the network while preserving the spatial resolution of the feature map.

For the dilated convolution of $k \times k$, the formulae for calculation of the equivalent receptive field (RF) and resolution (H) of the output feature map are the following:

$$RF = (r - 1)(k - 1) + k \tag{5}$$

$$H = \frac{h + 2p - RF}{s} + 1 \tag{6}$$

where p, h, and s represent the padding filling, input feature map resolution, and convolution stride size, respectively.

3.3.1. Series Receptive Field Enhancement Module (SRFEM)

In CT images, tumor detection is prone to the interference of surrounding normal tissues, especially for tumors with small differences in gray levels [49]. The objective of SRFEM is to enlarge the effective receptive field, which helps mitigate the influence of non-lesion regions and emphasize the tumor targets. We also took into account the issue of losing details due to sparsely sampled dilated convolutions, which is more prominent when multiple consecutive dilated convolutions are applied [24].

As shown in Figure 5, SRFEM uses three dilated convolutions with a 3×3 convolution kernel and a shortcut connection to form a residual structure, where the dilation rates of the dilated convolutions are 1, 3, and 5, respectively.

Let the given input feature be x. Then, the SRFEM output is expressed as follows:

$$y = SiLU\left(input + Conv_3^5\left(Conv_3^3\left(Conv_3^1(x)\right)\right)\right) \tag{7}$$

where $Conv_3^1$, $Conv_3^3$, and $Conv_3^5$ denote the dilation rates of 1, 3, and 5 corresponding to a 3×3 convolution, respectively. $Conv_3^5$ applies BN, while both $Conv_3^1$ and $Conv_3^3$ apply BN and SiLU. $Conv_3^5\left(Conv_3^3\left(Conv_3^1(x)\right)\right)$ aims to obtain a feature map with a sufficiently large receptive field, which is added to the shortcut connection to stack deeper networks. The fused features lead to y through a SiLU activation function. Compared to the input features, the number of channels of y remains unchanged.

3.3.2. Parallel Receptive Field Enhancement Module (PRFEM)

PRFEM aims to construct a multi-branch structure, that extracts corresponding spatial scale features with different receptive fields, and then stitches these features together to obtain a complete expression of the image. Chen et al. [38] first used dilated convolution to build a spatial pyramid module, called ASPP, in DeeplabV2. ASPP is a multi-branch structure consisting of four 3×3 convolution branches, whose corresponding dilation rates are 6, 12, 18, and 24, respectively. They can capture richer semantic information. However, when the dilation rate is too large, the acquisition of local semantic information is compromised [50].

The inspiration of PRFEM comes from DeeplabV2. The difference lies in that PRFEM is used to generate uniform receptive fields which adapt to tumors of different sizes shown in Figure 7. More specifically, PRFEM consists of three parallel 3×3 convolution branches with different dilation ratios, one 1×1 convolution branch, and one identity branch. First, for each branch with dilated convolution, we use 1×1 convolution to reduce the channel number of dilated convolution to a quarter of the input feature map, ensuring an even distribution of information across different scales. Then, the 1×1 convolution branch obtains the association of image details and enhanced position information. As an example, for a dilated convolution with a dilation rate of $R = (1,3,5)$ and a convolution kernel of 3×3, the corresponding padding is set to $P = (1,3,5)$, so that the resolution of the feature map remains unchanged, as per formula (6). We stitched together the sampling results from different branches in terms of channel to obtain multi-scale information representation. Finally, the identity connection is used to optimize the gradient information propagation and lower the training difficulty. After each convolutional layer, BN and SiLU are performed.

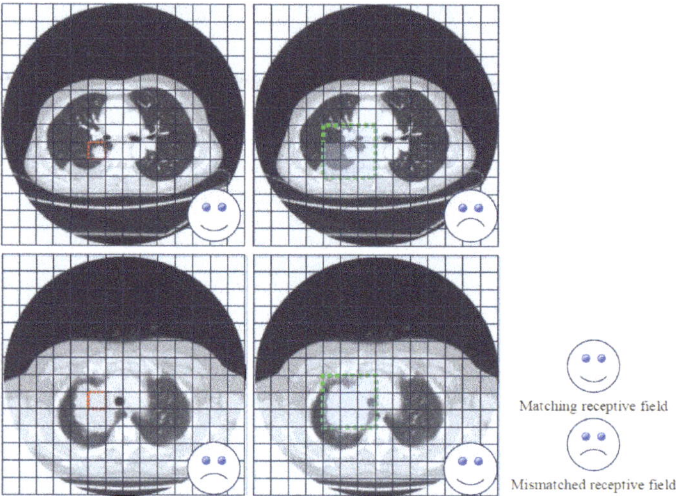

Figure 7. Tumor targets under different receptive fields. Matching small receptive fields with large tumors may lead to inaccurate results for network classification (**bottom-left image**), and matching large receptive fields with small tumors may cause the network to focus more on background information and ignore small-sized tumors (**top-right image**).

4. Experiments and Results

4.1. Dataset and Evaluation Metrics

We randomly sampled 2324 CT images (1137 containing adenocarcinoma tumors and 1187 containing small cell carcinoma tumors) from the CT data provided by Lung-PET-CT-Dx [51] for the training, validation, and testing of the proposed model. These images were collected retrospectively from suspected lung cancer patients. Category information and location information for each tumor was annotated by five experienced radiologists using the LabelImg tool. The CT images provided in the dataset are in the Digital Imaging and Communications in Medicine (DICOM) format. We performed pre-processing on the DICOM format of the CT images to enable their use in the proposed ELCT-YOLO model. The image pre-processing operation flow is illustrated in Figure 8.

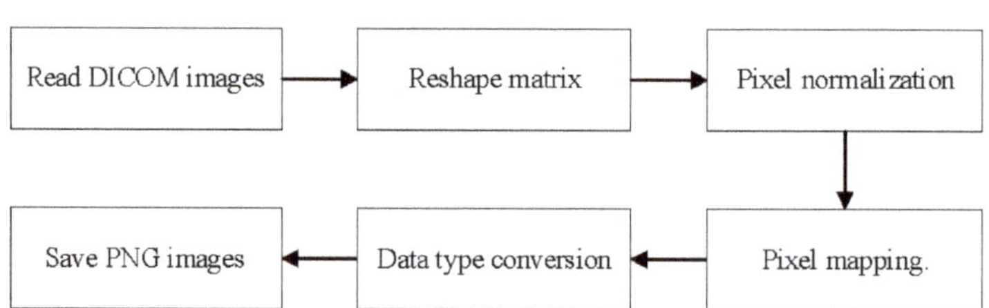

Figure 8. The image pre-processing operation flow.

First, we read the DICOM files to obtain the image data. Next, we used a Reshape operation to adjust the coordinate order and generate a new matrix. Then, we normalized the pixel values by subtracting the low window level from the original pixel values and dividing by the window width to improve contrast and brightness. After that, we used pixel mapping to map the gray values to an unsigned integer pixel value between 0 and 255. Through these steps, we successfully adjusted the pixel values and generated the corresponding PNG images.

The 2324 CT images were split into training, validation, and test sets at a ratio of 6:2:2. The choice of this ratio is based on the size of the utilized dataset, taking into account the experience of previous researchers. Another common ratio is 8:1:1. However, using an 8:1:1 ratio in our case would result in an insufficient number of samples in the validation and testing sets, which may not fully reflect the model's generalization ability on real-world data. Additionally, if the number of samples in the testing set is too small, the evaluation results of the model may be affected by randomness, leading to unstable evaluation results. Therefore, we chose the 6:2:2 ratio.

For performance evaluation of the models compared with respect to tumor detection, we used common evaluation metrics, such as $mAP@0.5$: the mean average precision (IoU = 0.5), *precision* (P), and *recall* (R), defined as follows:

$$P = \frac{TP}{TP + FP} \tag{8}$$

$$R = \frac{TP}{TP + FN} \tag{9}$$

$$AP = \int_0^1 P dR \tag{10}$$

$$mAP = \frac{\sum_{i=1}^N AP_i}{N} \tag{11}$$

where TP, FP, and FN denote the number of correctly detected, incorrectly detected, and missed tumor cases presented in images, respectively. mAP is obtained by averaging the corresponding AP values for each category (in our case, $N = 2$ represents the two considered tumor categories of adenocarcinoma and small cell carcinoma).

4.2. Model Training

ELCT-YOLO is based on the implementation of open-source YOLOv7. Training of the model was conducted on a Linux system running Ubuntu 20.04.1, utilizing an RTX2080Ti GPU for accelerated computation. The model training utilized a batch size of 16, and an input image size of 512×512 pixels was specified. The stochastic gradient descent (SGD) optimizer was adopted in the model training, with the initial learning rate and momentum default value being 0.01 and 0.937, respectively. The following adjustment strategy was used for the learning rate of each training round:

$$lf = 1 - \frac{1}{2}(1 - lrf) \times (1 - cos\frac{i \times \pi}{epoch}) \tag{12}$$

where i denotes the i-th round, lrf denotes the final OneCycleLR learning rate multiplication factor which is set to 0.1, lf denotes the multiplier factor for adjusting the learning rate, and *epoch* represents the current training round We used mosaic enhancements to load images and corresponding labels. In addition, we did not load the weight file trained by YOLOv7 on the MS COCO dataset during the training process. This is because there is a huge difference in the domain between ordinary natural images and medical images, and migration did not result in desired results [52]. To minimize the impact of randomness on the evaluation results, we divided the dataset into five equally sized and mutually exclusive parts. We repeated the experiments five times and selected the highest peak of the average value as the final result. As Figure 9 illustrates, the proposed ELCT-YOLO model achieved stable convergence after 120 rounds of training.

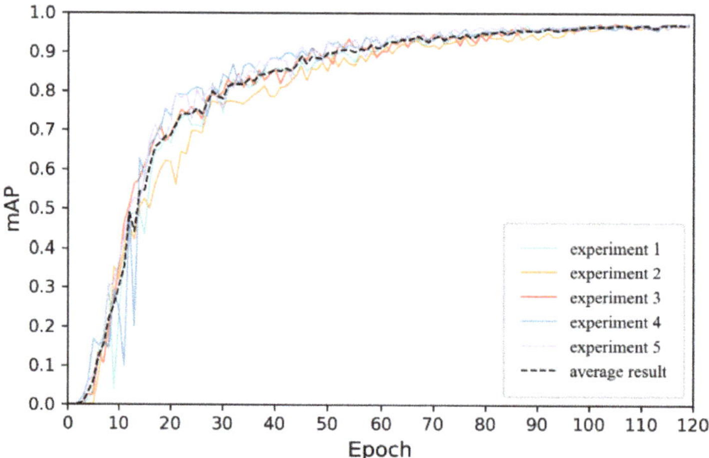

Figure 9. The mAP variation curves during the ELCT-YOLO training.

The loss function (*L*) of the ELCT-YOLO model, used to calculate the loss between the predicted boxes and the labels of the matched grids, was the following:

$$L = \lambda_1 \times L_{obj} + \lambda_2 \times L_{cls} + \lambda_3 \times L_{box} \tag{13}$$

where L_{obj}, L_{cls}, L_{box} denote the coordinate loss, classification loss, and objectness loss, respectively. The values of λ_1, λ_2, and λ_3 are equal to 0.7, 0.3, and 0.05, respectively. L_{obj} and L_{cls} use binary cross-entropy to calculate the objectness and classification probability losses, while L_{box} uses the Complete Intersection over Union (CIoU) to calculate the regression loss of bounding boxes [53]. The CIoU loss function not only considers the aspect ratio, overlap area, and center distance but also includes a penalty term, and is expressed as follows:

$$L_{CIoU} = 1 - IoU + \frac{\rho^2\left(b, b^{gt}\right)}{c^2} + \alpha v \tag{14}$$

where IoU represents the intersection over union between the predicted box b and the ground truth box b^{gt}, $\rho^2\left(b, b^{gt}\right)$ represents the Euclidean distance between the center point of the predicted box and the center point of the ground truth box [54], and αv is the penalty term that ensures that the width and height of the predicted box quickly approach those of the ground truth box. The values of α and v are calculated as follows:

$$\alpha = \frac{v}{(1 - IoU) + v} \tag{15}$$

$$v = \frac{4}{\pi^2}\left(arctan\frac{w^{gt}}{h^{gt}} - arctan\frac{w}{h}\right)^2. \tag{16}$$

where w and h denote the width and height of the predicted bounding box, respectively, while w^{gt} and h^{gt} denote the width and height of the ground truth bounding box, respectively.

The convergence curves of the confidence loss, classification loss, and regression loss during the process of training and validation of the ELCT-YOLO model are presented in Figures 10 and 11. It can be observed that with more training iterations, the losses of ELCT-YOLO on the training set continuously decrease, indicating the model's ability to fit the distribution of the training data. On the other hand, the losses on the validation set reflect the detection model's good generalization ability on unknown data.

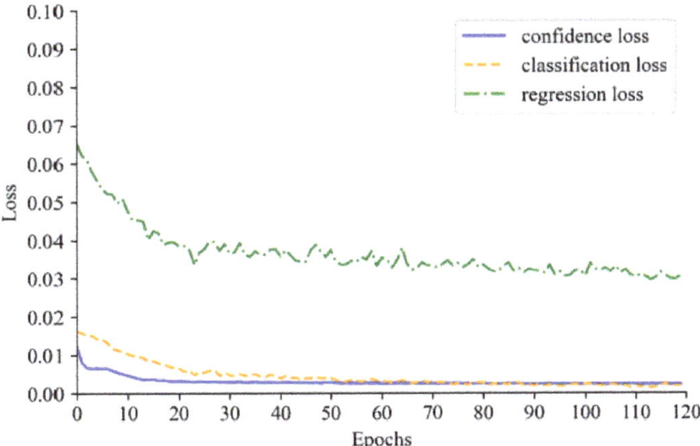

Figure 10. The loss curves during the ELCT-YOLO training.

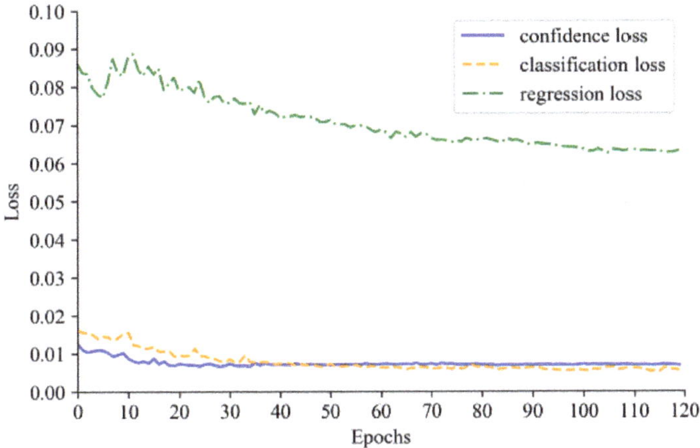

Figure 11. The loss curves during the ELCT-YOLO validation.

4.3. Comparison of ELCT-YOLO with State-of-the-Art Models

We compared the proposed ELCT-YOLO model with six state-of-the-art models, namely YOLOv3, YOLOv5, YOLOv7-tiny, YOLOv8, SSD, and Faster R-CNN. The obtained results are shown in Table 1

Table 1. Performance comparison of models used for lung tumor detection in CT images (the best value achieved among the models for a particular metric is shown in **bold**).

Model	P	R	mAP	FPS	Size (MB)
YOLOv3	0.930	0.925	0.952	63	117.0
YOLOv5	0.949	0.923	0.961	125	17.6
YOLOv7-tiny	0.901	0.934	0.951	**161**	11.8
YOLOv8	**0.967**	0.939	**0.977**	115	21.4
SSD	0.878	0.833	0.906	95	182.0
Faster R-CNN	0.903	0.891	0.925	28	315.0
ELCT-YOLO	0.923	**0.951**	0.974	159	**11.4**

As evident from Table 1, the proposed ELCT-YOLO model is the winner based on *recall*, while also having the smallest size among the models. According to mAP, it takes second place by closely following the winner (YOLOv8, which was also trained for 120 epochs with a batch size of 16) and scoring only 0.003 points less, but its size is almost half the YOLOv8 size. Regarding the achieved *precision*, ELCT-YOLO does not perform so well; it occupies fourth place by scoring 0.044 points less than the winner (YOLOv8). Regarding the FPS, the proposed ELCT-YOLO model takes second place, closely following the winner (YOLOv7-tiny) by processing only 2 frames less per second.

As mentioned in the Introduction, devices used in real medical scenarios are often resource-constrained, so smaller-size models are more appropriate for use. ELCT-YOLO achieves a good balance between accuracy and efficiency in tumor detection. In addition, in terms of *recall*, ELCT-YOLO achieved best results among the models compared, which is conducive to tumor screening, as the higher the *recall* value, the fewer tumors will be missed, and the detector will find every potential lesion location.

Figure 12 illustrates sample images from the test set along with their corresponding detection results. It is evident from the figure that ELCT-YOLO performs well in detecting tumors of varying scales in CT images.

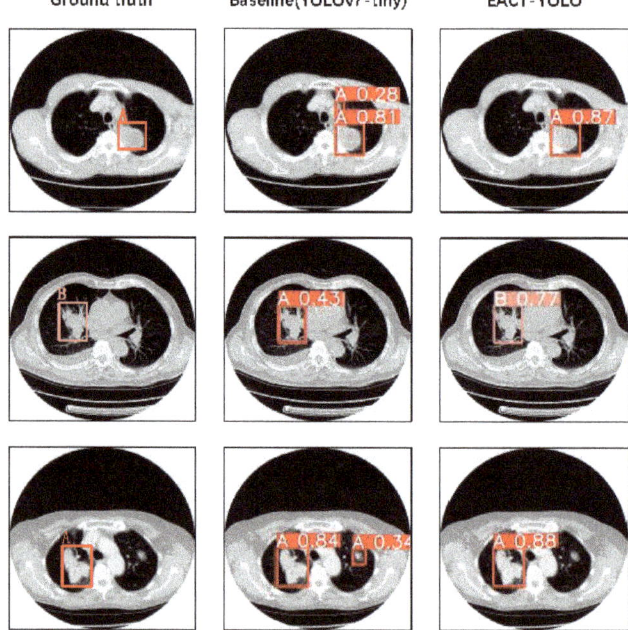

Figure 12. Sample images, extracted from the test set, with lung tumors detection results (label A represents adenocarcinoma, whereas label B represents small cell carcinoma). For irregular tumors with patchy heightened shadows or tumors with obvious pleural traction, EACT-YOLO can effectively reduce the interference of background information and distinguish the tumor target from the background.

4.4. Ablation Study of ELCT-YOLO

To further evaluate the impact of using the designed DENeck and CRS structures, and of integrating the SPPF module [25] into YOLOv7-tiny, we performed an ablation study on these performance improvement components, the results of which are shown in Table 2.

Table 2. Results of the ablation study performed on YOLOv7-tiny performance improvement components, used by ELCT-YOLO (the best mAP and size values achieved are shown in **bold**).

No.	SPPF	DENeck	CRS	mAP	Size (MB)
1				0.955	12.0
2	✓			0.958	**11.2**
3		✓		0.968	**11.2**
4			✓	0.966	12.6
5	✓	✓	✓	**0.974**	11.4

First of all, the SPPF module of YOLOv5 [25], which we introduced at the top of the original YOLOv7-tiny backbone network, did not lead to a significant improvement in the mean average precision (mAP), but the model size was reduced by 7%. Then, using the designed DENeck structure alone enabled improving the mAP from 0.955 to 0.968, while the model size equaled that when using the SPPF module alone. Our belief has been confirmed that in the case of medical images, particularly CT images, precision in lesion detection can be improved by reducing confusing details. Using the designed CRS structure alone did not provide better results than using DENeck alone but led to improving the mAP value from 0.955 to 0.966, compared to the original YOLOv7-tiny model, though increasing the model size. This is because the shallow prediction branch needs effective global information to distinguish tumor regions from the background. When we integrated all three components, the mAP value exceeded that of applying any one of these components alone, while also keeping the model size very close to the minimum reached when using only SPPF or DENeck, which proves the rationality of the design of the ELCT-YOLO model proposed.

4.5. CRS Study

The designed CRS structure, described in Section 3, consists of two modules—SRFEM and PRFEM. In order to achieve a more effective receptive field, we studied the use of different cascade schemes, the results of which are shown in Table 3, where SRFEM and PRFEM are denoted as P and S, respectively. The CRS study was based on *precision, recall,* and the *mAP*.

Table 3. Performance comparison of different cascade schemes (the best value achieved among the schemes for a particular metric is shown in **bold**).

Scheme	P	R	mAP
PPP	0.961	0.929	0.965
SPP	**0.977**	0.893	0.969
SSP	0.958	0.924	0.969
SSS	0.921	**0.957**	**0.974**

As can be seen from Table 3, using different cascade schemes (different P-S combinations) led to different values of the evaluation metrics used for the comparison. The PPP scheme performed worst according to all metrics. This may be due to the lack of receptive fields in low-contrast scenes, which is key to the improvement of detection performance, although PRFEM can capture multi-scale information from CT images to improve the ability to detect tumors. Overall, SSS is the best-performing scheme based on two of the evaluation metrics, i.e., *recall* and the *mAP*, reaching 0.957 and 0.974, respectively. The use of SSS can effectively enhance the receptive field of shallow branches, thereby improving the detection performance. Thus, this scheme was utilized by the proposed ELCT-YOLO model in the performance comparison with the state-of-the-art models (c.f., Table 1).

In addition, we verified the effect of using different dilation rates on the SSS cascaded scheme, in order to further improve the feature map quality. We considered three cascades of dilation rates: Natural numbered Series (NS), Odd numbered Series (OS), and Even numbered Series (ES). In Table 4, $R_{NS} = (1,2,3)$, $R_{OS} = (1,3,5)$, $R_{ES} = (2,4,6)$ represent the values of these three series, respectively. Section 2 mentioned that the sparse sampling of dilated convolutions can easily lead to the loss of details. Therefore, choosing an appropriate sampling rate is also a way to alleviate the gridding effects. The comparison results in Table 4 show that $R_{OS} = (1, 3, 5)$ outperforms the other two schemes, according to all three evaluation metrics.

Table 4. Performance comparison of using different dilation rates in the SSS cascade scheme (the best value achieved among the dilation rates for a particular metric is shown in **bold**).

Dilation Rate	P	R	mAP
$R_{NS} = (1,2,3)$	0.938	0.923	0.958
$R_{OS} = (1,3,5)$	**0.969**	**0.933**	**0.967**
$R_{ES} = (2,4,6)$	0.954	0.921	0.961

The sampling positions of the three consecutive dilated convolutions are visualized in Figure 13. It can be seen intuitively that when the dilation rate is $R_{NS} = (1, 2, 3)$ the SSS module can only obtain less receptive fields and cannot capture global information; when the dilation rate is $R_{ES} = (2, 4, 6)$, the receptive field increases, but the feature information is not continuous, which will lead to the loss of details. The combination of $R_{OS} = (1, 3, 5)$ covers a larger receptive field area without losing edge information. This is consistent with our experimental results.

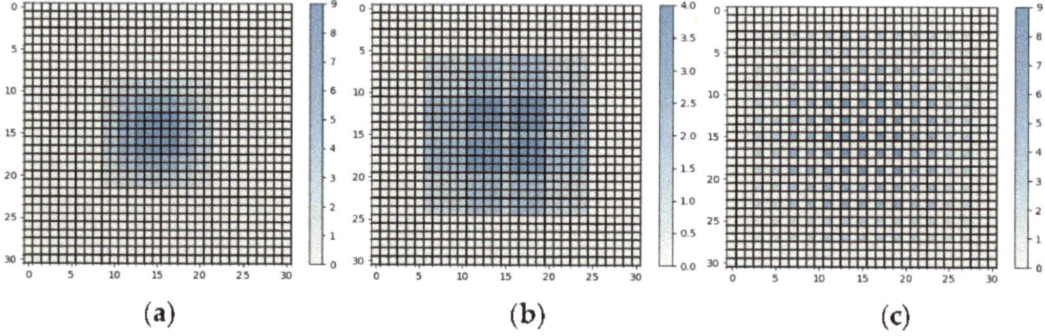

(a)   (b)   (c)

Figure 13. The effective receptive fields generated by different dilation rates in the SSS cascade scheme: (**a**) $R_{NS} = (1, 2, 3)$; (**b**) $R_{ES} = (2, 4, 6)$; (**c**) $R_{OS} = (1, 3, 5)$. The colors depicted at distinct positions within the graphs indicate the frequency at which each location was utilized in computing the receptive field center.

4.6. DENeck Study

To verify the effectiveness of DENeck, we applied it on the YOLOv7-tiny model along with traditional feature fusion methods (each applied separately from the rest). The comparison results are shown in Table 5. The main focus of this experiment was to compare the impact of various feature fusion methods on the detection performance based on different topological structures. The proposed DENeck module achieved the best detection performance among the compared methods. Comparing FPN to PANet and BiFPN, we found that the latter two outperform FPN. This is because the feature fusion in FPN is insufficient, and it is difficult to extract precise localization information of tumors.

Furthermore, in order to demonstrate the generalization ability of the designed DENeck structure under different scale networks, we evaluated its performance for detecting tumors in models with different depths. The obtained comparison results are shown in Table 6. We used three basic networks of YOLOv7: YOLOv7-tiny, YOLOv7, and YOLOv7x. The depth of these networks is gradually deepened in the stated order.

Table 5. Comparisons between DENeck and traditional feature fusion methods (the best value achieved among the methods for a particular metric is shown in **bold**).

Method	mAP	Size (MB)
FPN	0.957	14.6
PANet	0.963	11.7
BiFPN	0.967	**11.2**
DENeck	**0.971**	11.3

Table 6. Performance comparison of combining different scale networks with the designed DENeck structure (the best value achieved among the networks for a particular metric is shown in **bold**).

Network	mAP	Size (MB)
YOLOv7-tiny's	0.965	**11.4**
YOLOv7's	0.967	70.4
YOLOv7x's	**0.971**	128.6

Table 6 shows that increasing the model scale improves the mAP, but the improvement is not significant—only by 0.006 points. This shows that, while the DENeck structure can be utilized by deepened backbones, its usage is more effective on lightweight networks that enable reducing the model size.

5. Conclusions and Future Work

This paper has proposed an efficient one-stage ELCT-YOLO model based on improvements introduced into the YOLOv7-tiny model, for lung tumor detection in CT images. Unlike existing neck structures, the proposed model aims to obtain multi-scale tumor information from the images. Firstly, a novel Decoupled Neck (DENeck) structure has been described for use in ELCT-YOLO to reduce semantic conflicts. More specifically, the model's neck was divided into high-semantic layers and low-semantic layers, in order to generate clearer feature representations by decoupling the fusion between these two semantic types. The conducted experiments proved that DENeck can be integrated well into backbone networks of different depths, while also showing outstanding robustness. Secondly, a novel Cascaded Refinement Scheme (CRS), configured at the lowest layer of the decoupling network, has been described for use in ELCT-YOLO in order to capture tumor features under different receptive fields. The optimal CRS structure was determined through another set of experiments. In addition, the problem of sparse sampling caused by dilated convolution has been considered and the effect of different receptive field combinations on the cascaded modules has been compared by means of experiments. Thirdly, it has been proposed to integrate the SPPF module of YOLOv5 at the top of the original YOLOv7-tiny backbone network in order to extract important context features, further improve the model's operational speed, and enrich the representation ability of feature maps. Extensive experiments, conducted on CT data provided by Lung-PET-CT-Dx, demonstrated the effectiveness and robustness of the proposed ELCT-YOLO model for lung tumor detection.

The presented study has focused on addressing the multi-scale issue of tumor detection using a lightweight model. The model still needs further optimization in reducing both the number of parameters and computational complexity. As a next step of the future research, we will use network distillation techniques and existing lightweight convolutional modules to construct a simpler model, aimed at reducing the inference latency and parameters' number. In addition, the study presented in this paper has only focused on tumor detection tasks based on CT images. In fact, some emerging technologies such as super-wideband microwave reflection measurement are more user friendly and cost effective than traditional detection techniques such as the CT-based ones [55]. In the future, we will also focus on studying emerging technologies for lung cancer detection more in depth.

Author Contributions: Conceptualization, J.Z. and Z.J.; methodology, X.Z. (Xueji Zhang); validation, I.G. and H.Z.; formal analysis, J.Z. and X.Z. (Xinyi Zeng); writing—original draft preparation, J.Z.; writing—review and editing, I.G.; supervision, J.L.; project administration, X.Z. (Xueji Zhang) and Z.J. All authors have read and agreed to the published version of the manuscript.

Funding: This publication has emanated from joint research conducted with the financial support of the S&T Major Project of the Science and Technology Ministry of China under the Grant No. 2017YFE0135700 and the Bulgarian National Science Fund (BNSF) under the Grant No. КП-06-ИП-КИТАЙ/1 (KP-06-IP-CHINA/1).

Data Availability Statement: Not applicable.

Conflicts of Interest: The authors declare no conflict of interest.

References

1. Slatore, C.; Lareau, S.C.; Fahy, B. Staging of Lung Cancer. *Am. J. Respir. Crit. Care Med.* **2022**, *205*, P17–P19. [CrossRef] [PubMed]
2. Nishino, M.; Schiebler, M.L. Advances in Thoracic Imaging: Key Developments in the Past Decade and Future Directions. *Radiology* **2023**, *306*, 222536. [CrossRef] [PubMed]
3. Lee, J.H.; Lee, D.; Lu, M.T.; Raghu, V.K.; Park, C.M.; Goo, J.M.; Choi, S.H.; Kim, H. Deep learning to optimize candidate selection for lung cancer CT screening: Advancing the 2021 USPSTF recommendations. *Radiology* **2022**, *305*, 209–218. [CrossRef]
4. Zhang, T.; Wang, K.; Cui, H.; Jin, Q.; Cheng, P.; Nakaguchi, T.; Li, C.; Ning, Z.; Wang, L.; Xuan, P. Topological structure and global features enhanced graph reasoning model for non-small cell lung cancer segmentation from CT. *Phys. Med. Biol.* **2023**, *68*, 025007. [CrossRef]
5. Lin, J.; Yu, Y.; Zhang, X.; Wang, Z.; Li, S. Classification of Histological Types and Stages in Non-small Cell Lung Cancer Using Radiomic Features Based on CT Images. *J. Digit. Imaging* **2023**, 1–9. [CrossRef] [PubMed]
6. Sugawara, H.; Yatabe, Y.; Watanabe, H.; Akai, H.; Abe, O.; Watanabe, S.-I.; Kusumoto, M. Radiological precursor lesions of lung squamous cell carcinoma: Early progression patterns and divergent volume doubling time between hilar and peripheral zones. *Lung Cancer* **2023**, *176*, 31–37. [CrossRef]
7. Halder, A.; Dey, D.; Sadhu, A.K. Lung nodule detection from feature engineering to deep learning in thoracic CT images: A comprehensive review. *J. Digit. Imaging* **2020**, *33*, 655–677. [CrossRef]
8. Huang, S.; Yang, J.; Shen, N.; Xu, Q.; Zhao, Q. Artificial intelligence in lung cancer diagnosis and prognosis: Current application and future perspective. *Semin. Cancer Biol.* **2023**, *89*, 30–37. [CrossRef]
9. Mousavi, Z.; Rezaii, T.Y.; Sheykhivand, S.; Farzamnia, A.; Razavi, S. Deep convolutional neural network for classification of sleep stages from single-channel EEG signals. *J. Neurosci. Methods* **2019**, *324*, 108312. [CrossRef]
10. Gong, J.; Liu, J.; Hao, W.; Nie, S.; Zheng, B.; Wang, S.; Peng, W. A deep residual learning network for predicting lung adenocarcinoma manifesting as ground-glass nodule on CT images. *Eur. Radiol.* **2020**, *30*, 1847–1855. [CrossRef]
11. Mei, J.; Cheng, M.M.; Xu, G.; Wan, L.R.; Zhang, H. SANet: A Slice-Aware Network for Pulmonary Nodule Detection. *IEEE Trans. Pattern Anal. Mach. Intell.* **2022**, *44*, 4374–4387. [CrossRef] [PubMed]
12. Xu, R.; Liu, Z.; Luo, Y.; Hu, H.; Shen, L.; Du, B.; Kuang, K.; Yang, J. SGDA: Towards 3D Universal Pulmonary Nodule Detection via Slice Grouped Domain Attention. *IEEE/ACM Trans. Comput. Biol. Bioinform.* **2023**, 1–13. [CrossRef]
13. Su, A.; PP, F.R.; Abraham, A.; Stephen, D. Deep Learning-Based BoVW–CRNN Model for Lung Tumor Detection in Nano-Segmented CT Images. *Electronics* **2023**, *12*, 14. [CrossRef]
14. Mousavi, Z.; Shahini, N.; Sheykhivand, S.; Mojtahedi, S.; Arshadi, A. COVID-19 detection using chest X-ray images based on a developed deep neural network. *SLAS Technol.* **2022**, *27*, 63–75. [CrossRef] [PubMed]
15. Mei, S.; Jiang, H.; Ma, L. YOLO-lung: A Practical Detector Based on Imporved YOLOv4 for Pulmonary Nodule Detection. In Proceedings of the 2021 14th International Congress on Image and Signal Processing, BioMedical Engineering and Informatics (CISP-BMEI), Shanghai, China, 23–25 October 2021; pp. 1–6.
16. Causey, J.; Li, K.; Chen, X.; Dong, W.; Huang, X. Spatial Pyramid Pooling with 3D Convolution Improves Lung Cancer Detection. *IEEE/ACM Trans. Comput. Biol. Bioinform.* **2020**, *19*, 1165–1172. [CrossRef] [PubMed]
17. Guo, Z.; Zhao, L.; Yuan, J.; Yu, H. MSANet: Multiscale Aggregation Network Integrating Spatial and Channel Information for Lung Nodule Detection. *IEEE J. Biomed. Health Inform.* **2022**, *26*, 2547–2558. [CrossRef]
18. Guo, N.; Bai, Z. Multi-scale Pulmonary Nodule Detection by Fusion of Cascade R-CNN and FPN. In Proceedings of the 2021 International Conference on Computer Communication and Artificial Intelligence (CCAI), Guangzhou, China, 7–9 May 2021; pp. 15–19.
19. Yan, C.-M.; Wang, C. Automatic Detection and Localization of Pulmonary Nodules in CT Images Based on YOLOv5. *J. Comput.* **2022**, *33*, 113–123. [CrossRef]
20. Zhong, G.; Ding, W.; Chen, L.; Wang, Y.; Yu, Y.F. Multi-Scale Attention Generative Adversarial Network for Medical Image Enhancement. *IEEE Trans. Emerg. Top. Comput. Intell.* **2023**, 1–13. [CrossRef]
21. Wang, C.-Y.; Bochkovskiy, A.; Liao, H.-Y.M. YOLOv7: Trainable bag-of-freebies sets new state-of-the-art for real-time object detectors. *arXiv* **2022**, arXiv:2207.02696.

22. Ghiasi, G.; Lin, T.-Y.; Le, Q.V. Nas-fpn: Learning scalable feature pyramid architecture for object detection. In Proceedings of the IEEE/CVF Conference on Computer Vision and Pattern Recognition, Long Beach, CA, USA, 16–20 June 2019; pp. 7036–7045.
23. Tan, M.; Pang, R.; Le, Q.V. Efficientdet: Scalable and efficient object detection. In Proceedings of the IEEE/CVF Conference on Computer Vision and Pattern Recognition, Virtual, 14–19 June 2020; pp. 10781–10790.
24. Wang, P.; Chen, P.; Yuan, Y.; Liu, D.; Huang, Z.; Hou, X.; Cottrell, G. Understanding convolution for semantic segmentation. In Proceedings of the 2018 IEEE Winter Conference on Applications of Computer Vision (WACV), Lake Tahoe, NV, USA, 12–15 March 2018; pp. 1451–1460.
25. Jocher, G.; Chaurasia, A.; Stoken, A.; Borovec, J.; Kwon, Y.; Michael, K.; Fang, J.; Yifu, Z.; Wong, C.; Montes, D.; et al. *ultralytics/yolov5: v7.0—YOLOv5 SOTA Realtime Instance Segmentation*; Zenodo: Geneva, Switzerland, 2022.
26. Alsaedi, D.; El Badawe, M.; Ramahi, O.M. A Breast Cancer Detection System Using Metasurfaces With a Convolution Neural Network: A Feasibility Study. *IEEE Trans. Microw. Theory Tech.* **2022**, *70*, 3566–3576. [CrossRef]
27. Fang, H.; Li, F.; Fu, H.; Sun, X.; Cao, X.; Lin, F.; Son, J.; Kim, S.; Quellec, G.; Matta, S.; et al. ADAM Challenge: Detecting Age-Related Macular Degeneration From Fundus Images. *IEEE Trans. Med. Imaging* **2022**, *41*, 2828–2847. [CrossRef]
28. Wang, D.; Wang, X.; Wang, S.; Yin, Y. Explainable Multitask Shapley Explanation Networks for Real-time Polyp Diagnosis in Videos. *IEEE Trans. Ind. Inform.* **2022**, 1–10. [CrossRef]
29. Ahmed, I.; Chehri, A.; Jeon, G.; Piccialli, F. Automated pulmonary nodule classification and detection using deep learning architectures. *IEEE/ACM Trans. Comput. Biol. Bioinform.* **2022**, 1–12. [CrossRef] [PubMed]
30. Wu, H.; Zhao, Z.; Zhong, J.; Wang, W.; Wen, Z.; Qin, J. Polypseg+: A lightweight context-aware network for real-time polyp segmentation. *IEEE Trans. Cybern.* **2022**, *53*, 2610–2621. [CrossRef] [PubMed]
31. Wu, X.; Sahoo, D.; Hoi, S.C. Recent advances in deep learning for object detection. *Neurocomputing* **2020**, *396*, 39–64. [CrossRef]
32. Redmon, J.; Divvala, S.; Girshick, R.; Farhadi, A. You only look once: Unified, real-time object detection. In Proceedings of the IEEE Conference on Computer Vision and pattern Recognition, Las Vegas, NV, USA, 26 June–1 July 2016; pp. 779–788.
33. Redmon, J.; Farhadi, A. YOLO9000: Better, faster, stronger. In Proceedings of the IEEE Conference on Computer Vision and Pattern Recognition, Honolulu, HI, USA, 21–26 July 2016; pp. 7263–7271.
34. Redmon, J.; Farhadi, A. Yolov3: An incremental improvement. *arXiv* **2018**, arXiv:1804.02767.
35. Bochkovskiy, A.; Wang, C.-Y.; Liao, H.-Y.M. Yolov4: Optimal speed and accuracy of object detection. *arXiv* **2020**, arXiv:2004.10934.
36. Li, C.; Li, L.; Jiang, H.; Weng, K.; Geng, Y.; Li, L.; Ke, Z.; Li, Q.; Cheng, M.; Nie, W. YOLOv6: A single-stage object detection framework for industrial applications. *arXiv* **2022**, arXiv:2209.02976.
37. Gevorgyan, Z. SIoU loss: More powerful learning for bounding box regression. *arXiv* **2022**, arXiv:2205.12740.
38. Chen, L.C.; Papandreou, G.; Kokkinos, I.; Murphy, K.; Yuille, A.L. DeepLab: Semantic Image Segmentation with Deep Convolutional Nets, Atrous Convolution, and Fully Connected CRFs. *IEEE Trans. Pattern Anal. Mach. Intell.* **2018**, *40*, 834–848. [CrossRef]
39. Lin, T.-Y.; Dollár, P.; Girshick, R.; He, K.; Hariharan, B.; Belongie, S. Feature pyramid networks for object detection. In Proceedings of the IEEE Conference on Computer Vision and Pattern Recognition, Honolulu, HI, USA, 21–26 July 2017; pp. 2117–2125.
40. Liu, S.; Qi, L.; Qin, H.; Shi, J.; Jia, J. Path aggregation network for instance segmentation. In Proceedings of the IEEE Conference on Computer Vision and Pattern Recognition, Salt Lake City, UT, USA, 18–23 June 2018; pp. 8759–8768. [CrossRef]
41. Qiao, S.; Chen, L.-C.; Yuille, A. Detectors: Detecting objects with recursive feature pyramid and switchable atrous convolution. In Proceedings of the IEEE/CVF Conference on Computer Vision and Pattern Recognition, Virtual, 19–25 June 2021; pp. 10213–10224.
42. Liu, Y.; Li, H.; Cheng, J.; Chen, X. MSCAF-Net: A General Framework for Camouflaged Object Detection via Learning Multi-Scale Context-Aware Features. *IEEE Trans. Circuits Syst. Video Technol.* **2023**, 1. [CrossRef]
43. Liu, J.-J.; Hou, Q.; Cheng, M.-M.; Feng, J.; Jiang, J. A simple pooling-based design for real-time salient object detection. In Proceedings of the IEEE/CVF Conference on Computer Vision and Pattern Recognition, Long Beach, CA, USA, 16–20 June 2019; pp. 3917–3926.
44. Xiang, W.; Mao, H.; Athitsos, V. ThunderNet: A turbo unified network for real-time semantic segmentation. In Proceedings of the 2019 IEEE Winter Conference on Applications of Computer Vision (WACV), Waikoloa Village, HI, USA, 7–11 January 2019; pp. 1789–1796.
45. Xu, L.; Xue, H.; Bennamoun, M.; Boussaid, F.; Sohel, F. Atrous convolutional feature network for weakly supervised semantic segmentation. *Neurocomputing* **2021**, *421*, 115–126. [CrossRef]
46. Liu, J.; Yang, D.; Hu, F. Multiscale object detection in remote sensing images combined with multi-receptive-field features and relation-connected attention. *Remote Sens.* **2022**, *14*, 427. [CrossRef]
47. Guo, C.; Fan, B.; Zhang, Q.; Xiang, S.; Pan, C. Augfpn: Improving multi-scale feature learning for object detection. In Proceedings of the IEEE/CVF Conference on Computer Vision and Pattern Recognition, Virtual, 14–19 June 2020; pp. 12595–12604.
48. Bhattacharjee, A.; Murugan, R.; Goel, T.; Mirjalili, S. Pulmonary nodule segmentation framework based on fine-tuned and pre-trained deep neural network using CT images. *IEEE Trans. Radiat. Plasma Med. Sci.* **2023**, *7*, 394–409. [CrossRef]
49. Ezhilraja, K.; Shanmugadivu, P. Contrast Enhancement of Lung CT Scan Images using Multi-Level Modified Dualistic Sub-Image Histogram Equalization. In Proceedings of the 2022 International Conference on Automation, Computing and Renewable Systems (ICACRS), Pudukkottai, India, 13–15 December 2022; pp. 1009–1014.
50. Chen, L.-C.; Papandreou, G.; Schroff, F.; Adam, H. Rethinking atrous convolution for semantic image segmentation. *arXiv* **2017**, arXiv:1706.05587.

51. Li, P.; Wang, S.; Li, T.; Lu, J.; HuangFu, Y.; Wang, D. A large-scale CT and PET/CT dataset for lung cancer diagnosis [dataset]. *Cancer Imaging Arch.* **2020**. [CrossRef]
52. Mustafa, B.; Loh, A.; Freyberg, J.; MacWilliams, P.; Wilson, M.; McKinney, S.M.; Sieniek, M.; Winkens, J.; Liu, Y.; Bui, P. Supervised transfer learning at scale for medical imaging. *arXiv* **2021**, arXiv:2101.05913.
53. Zheng, Z.; Wang, P.; Liu, W.; Li, J.; Ye, R.; Ren, D. Distance-IoU loss: Faster and better learning for bounding box regression. In Proceedings of the AAAI Conference on Artificial Intelligence, vol.34, New York, NY, USA, 7–12 February 2020; pp. 12993–13000. [CrossRef]
54. Wang, C.; Sun, S.; Zhao, C.; Mao, Z.; Wu, H.; Teng, G. A Detection Model for Cucumber Root-Knot Nematodes Based on Modified YOLOv5-CMS. *Agronomy* **2022**, *12*, 2555. [CrossRef]
55. Alamro, W.; Seet, B.-C.; Wang, L.; Parthiban, P. Early-Stage Lung Tumor Detection based on Super-Wideband Microwave Reflectometry. *Electronics* **2023**, *12*, 36. [CrossRef]

Article

Leisure Time Prediction and Influencing Factors Analysis Based on LightGBM and SHAP

Qiyan Wang [1,†] and Yuanyuan Jiang [2,*,†]

1   Leisure Economy Research Center, Renmin University of China, Beijing 100872, China
2   School of Statistics, Renmin University of China, Beijing 100872, China
*   Correspondence: jyy_amy@ruc.edu.cn
†   These authors contributed equally to this work.

Abstract: Leisure time is crucial for personal development and leisure consumption. Accurate prediction of leisure time and analysis of its influencing factors creates a benefit by increasing personal leisure time. We predict leisure time and analyze its key influencing factors according to survey data of Beijing residents' time allocation in 2011, 2016, and 2021, with an effective sample size of 3356. A Light Gradient Boosting Machine (LightGBM) model is utilized to classify and predict leisure time, and the SHapley Additive exPlanation (SHAP) approach is utilized to conduct feature importance analysis and influence mechanism analysis of influencing factors from four perspectives: time allocation, demographics, occupation, and family characteristics. The results verify that LightGBM effectively predicts personal leisure time, with the test set's accuracy, recall, and F1 values being 0.85 and the AUC value reaching 0.91. The results of SHAP highlight that work/study time within the system is the main constraint on leisure time. Demographic factors, such as gender and age, are also of great significance for leisure time. Occupational and family heterogeneity exist in leisure time as well. The results contribute to the government improving the public holiday system, companies designing personalized leisure products for users with different leisure characteristics, and residents understanding and independently increasing their leisure time.

Keywords: data analysis; classification; decision trees; LightGBM; SHAP; leisure time; influencing factors; time allocation

MSC: 68T09

Citation: Wang, Q.; Jiang, Y. Leisure Time Prediction and Influencing Factors Analysis Based on LightGBM and SHAP. *Mathematics* **2023**, *11*, 2371. https://doi.org/10.3390/math11102371

Academic Editors: Snezhana Gocheva-Ilieva, Atanas Ivanov and Hristina Kulina

Received: 3 April 2023
Revised: 8 May 2023
Accepted: 10 May 2023
Published: 19 May 2023

1. Introduction

Individuals have an increasing desire for a better quality of life as the economy develops and tangible prosperity grows. Leisure has steadily become a common way of life and an integral component of individuals' aspirations for a fulfilling existence [1]. Leisure time is an indispensable prerequisite for achieving people's independence and all-round development [2,3]. People are eager for a higher level of material cultural life, a richer leisure and entertainment life, and realizing personal ideals in the fields of politics, economics, culture, and so on [4]. As a result, it is imperative to ensure that all residents have enough leisure time to enrich themselves [5] and succeed in their endeavors. In addition, ample leisure time is required for people to participate in leisure activities and enjoy leisure life [6]. Leisure activities provide opportunities for individuals to engage in leisure consumption, which, in turn, can stimulate innovation in consumption patterns and drive economic growth. Encouraging leisure consumption necessitates the provision of leisure time, as leisure time is a prerequisite for leisure consumption activities [7,8].

However, it appears that "money" and "leisure" have become diametrically opposed existences [9]. While material life has been gradually enriched, "time poverty" exists [10], which is particularly noticeable in China. The "996 working system" sparked a heated debate on the Internet in 2019 [11], with some related topics on the Sina Weibo platform being viewed more than 100 million times. In March of this year, Visual Capitalist released a survey report indicating that China is among the ten countries with the lowest total number of paid leave days, which includes public holidays and paid vacation days [12]. China's current vacation system not only offers a limited number of paid vacation days but also suffers from a low implementation rate. A survey conducted by the Ministry of Human Resources and Social Security of China in 2015 revealed that the implementation rate of paid leave in China is approximately 50%. Furthermore, there exists a certain dissatisfaction among the public towards the current vacation system. In 2019, the Leisure Economics Research Center of Renmin University of China conducted a survey on the satisfaction of Beijing residents with the vacation system. The results showed that 46% of respondents expressed dissatisfaction with the leave-in-lieu policy, and over 50% were unhappy with the current vacation system. These findings suggest that the current vacation system in China is at odds with people's exponentially growing desire for leisure. To address this problem, it is crucial to delve into the various factors that impact leisure time and identify ways to enhance the vacation system to better fulfill people's leisure requirements. Achieving a harmonious balance between work and leisure can yield benefits for both individuals and society, such as improved productivity [3] and overall well-being [13].

Based on this situation, we should concentrate on social reality, explore the causes of the conflict between material abundance and time poverty, and analyze how to provide residents with as much leisure and freedom as possible while maintaining the smooth progress of the comprehensive pursuit of a prosperous society and the construction of a better life. Thus, it is highly important to examine the factors that impact changes in residents' leisure time.

This paper sheds light on the dynamics of leisure time and highlights key factors that affect individuals' leisure time from the perspective of machine learning. Understanding these factors can benefit not only individuals in making informed decisions about achieving a healthy work–life balance, but it can also provide valuable insights for markets to gain insight into consumer needs and for governments to develop policies that support the development of individuals, businesses, and the economy. The main contributions of this paper are as follows. The first is to apply a Light Gradient Boosting Machine (LightGBM) model and the SHapley Additive exPlanation (SHAP) approach based on game theory to analyze the factors influencing leisure time from the standpoint of the nonlinear relationship. The extant literature is primarily based on linear models [14] and lacks the exploration of nonlinear relationships. Second, we conduct thorough data analysis on primary survey data collected in 2011, 2016, and 2021, while most of the previous studies used secondary data. Third, as far as we know, this paper is the first to study the changes in leisure time based on time allocation, demographics, occupation, and family characteristics, as compared to previous research that explored the correlation between a specific factor and leisure time [3,14,15]. Last but not least, based on the conclusions of this paper, we discuss feasible measures to increase and make full use of personal leisure time from three aspects: government policy system, market product supply, and personal leisure demand.

The remainder of this paper is structured as follows. Section 2 provides an overview of relevant research on defining leisure time as well as its macro- and micro-influencing factors. Section 3 describes the LightGBM model and the SHAP approach in summary. Section 4 introduces the data sources. Section 5 demonstrates the LightGBM model construction process and evaluation metrics. Section 6 presents the empirical results of SHAP and delves into the effects of various factors on the changes in leisure time, as well as the interaction effects between the factors. Finally, Section 7 concludes and discusses some measures for increasing personal leisure time.

2. Literature Review

2.1. Definition of Leisure Time

Existing research has not provided a distinct and consistent definition of leisure time. Some scholars consider leisure time as the remaining time after subtracting work time, housework time, and personal care time from total time [16–18]. Some scholars emphasize the importance of "free choice" in leisure time [19]. Leisure time, according to Leitner M.J. and Leitner S.F. (2004), is free or unrestricted time that excludes the time required for work and personal life (such as sleep) [20]. Žumárová (2015) defines leisure time as a period when you can freely choose activities and have a pleasant experience [21]. Some scholars place greater emphasis on personal subjective emotions and believe that leisure time is beneficial to physical and mental health [22–24], so leisure time is different for everyone [25]. According to Seibel et al. (2020), leisure time is time spent away from employment and is subject to personal subjective decision-making [26]. Some scholars define leisure time in terms of the activities they participate in, believing that leisure time is the time to engage in activities that we can choose whether or not to do, and no one else can do the activities for us [27,28].

According to existing studies, leisure time has the following attributes. First, it excludes time spent on work, housework, and personal care. Second, individuals are free to engage in leisure pursuits during leisure time. Third, leisure time can bring pleasant experiences. This paper defines leisure time based on four categories of total time; that is, daily time is divided into four categories based on the attributes of activities: work/study time (including round-trip time), the essential time for personal life (including the time for sleep, meals, personal hygiene, healthcare, and other necessary activities), housework time, and leisure time. Leisure time consists primarily of time spent acquiring cultural and scientific knowledge, reading newspapers, watching television, and engaging in a variety of other leisure activities. The definition in this paper conforms to the three attributes of leisure time mentioned above.

2.2. Micro-Influencing Factors of Leisure Time

With regards to the **time allocation characteristics,** since the total amount of time remains unchanged, leisure time is squeezed out by work/study time within the system (excluding commuting time and overtime), commuting time, essential time for personal life, and housework time [29–32].

With regards to the **demographic characteristics**, the issue of gender inequality in leisure time has received a lot of attention [33]. It is debatable whether there is gender inequality in leisure. While some scholars initially argued that gender equality in leisure could exist [34,35], further studies have shown significant gender inequality in leisure, with men having significantly more leisure time than women being verified by a descriptive statistical analysis of survey data of employed men and employed women in Lithuanian [36], and there is a noteworthy disparity between the quality of leisure time experienced by women and men, with women reporting significantly lower levels based on a multilevel regression of data from the International Social Survey Programme [37]. In-depth interviews with 12 representative mothers show that women adjust their leisure time based on the preferences of their partners and children [38]. A comparative analysis of survey data from Germany and the UK indicates that compared with men, women tend to undertake more housework [39]. Age and marital status have also been identified as factors that affect leisure time [40]. Adolescents and retirees are found to have the most leisure time by using the function of leisure participation [41], while there are also some opinions that leisure time increases with age in adults based on statistical tests [42]. Previous studies have also discovered that there are significant age differences in leisure activity participation [2,43], and the participation rate of leisure activities decreases with age [44]. Furthermore, educational level is also found to be linked to leisure activities [45,46]. Thus, the educational level should also be considered in relation to leisure time.

With regards to **occupational characteristics**, occupational characteristics have been found to correlate with leisure activity participation through a review of a series of representative literature [47]. Occupational characteristics can be considered from multiple perspectives. Occupational category, for example, represents the basic characteristics of the occupation according to occupational classification standards [48]. Enterprise ownership and company size (number of employees), as part of the company's own organizational characteristics [49], reflect the environmental characteristics of the occupation. Furthermore, the weekly rest situation reflects the overtime characteristics of the occupation [50]. Consequently, the aforementioned four features may be correlated with leisure time. For instance, it has been found that individuals in different occupational categories have noticeable differences in both leisure time and leisure activities [47,51,52]. However, as far as we are aware, there have been limited studies looking into the effects of all the aforementioned occupational characteristics on leisure time.

With regards to **family characteristics**, household income has always been a factor of concern to scholars [53]. The exact effect of household income on leisure time is a matter of debate. Lee and Bhargava (2004) argue that household income is a determinant of leisure time [40]. A linear regression of survey data from college students shows that leisure time is positively influenced by household income [54]. However, multiple regression results based on Australian Time Use Survey data indicate that household income has no significant effect on leisure time [6]. Additionally, having someone to care for in the home tends to affect leisure time as well [55]. When the number of children in need of care at home increases, women's time to care for children will increase accordingly [56].

2.3. Macro-Influencing Factors of Leisure Time

Everyone in one area is subject to the same external environment, which comprises macro-influencing factors. Hence, this paper focuses on studying the endogenous influencing factors of leisure time from a micro perspective, that is, concentrating on the effects of residents' personal characteristics on leisure time, with only qualitative analysis of the macro-influencing factors conducted.

Holiday system: The holiday system is a necessary precondition for limiting leisure time. Since China switched from a single day off to a double day off per week on 1 May 1995, Chinese residents' leisure time has grown significantly [57]. In general, the more legal holidays there are, the more leisure time people have. York et al. (2018) find that China's Golden Week holiday system has become an important source of leisure time [58]. The continuous and gradual implementation of paid leave could contribute to further increasing the leisure time of the entire population [59].

Productivity: It has been found that scientific and technological progress and productivity development can increase leisure time within a certain period of time [60]. Dridea and Sztruten (2010) believe that leisure time can serve as an indicator reflecting the productivity of a developed society, and the increase in labor productivity will lead to an increase in leisure time [61]. Min and Jin (2010) claim that the remarkable progress in productivity has liberated people from heavy work and resulted in more leisure time [62].

In summary, despite the extensive literature on leisure time, there are still several limitations. First, studies on changes in Chinese residents' leisure time and factors affecting leisure time at the micro level are relatively scarce [63,64]. Second, the current literature lacks primary data and mainly relies on secondary cross-sectional data. Third, most of the literature is based on descriptive statistics or linear models, which limits the ability to explore the nonlinear relationships between features. To address these issues, this paper utilizes real and effective primary survey data gathered from the Beijing Residents' Time Allocation Survey, which was carried out by the Leisure Economy Research Center of Renmin University of China in 2011, 2016, and 2021. In light of the survey data, we explore the changes in the leisure time of Chinese residents and its main influencing factors from multiple perspectives, including time allocation characteristics, demographic characteristics, occupational characteristics, and family characteristics. To evaluate and describe the nonlinear relationship between leisure time and these factors, a LightGBM model and the SHAP approach are employed.

3. Methods

We utilize LightGBM (Light Gradient Boosting Machine) to classify leisure time into two categories and employ the SHAP (SHapley Additive exPlanation) approach to quantify the effects of the factors influencing leisure time. LightGBM is known for its high efficiency and performance across a range of scenarios [65], including classification, regression, ranking, time-series prediction, and so on [66,67]. SHAP is a game-theory-based method for decomposing model predictions into the aggregate of the SHAP values and a fixed baseline value [68,69], and it is widely used in the explanation of various models [70,71].

3.1. Light Gradient Boosting Machine (LightGBM)

The Gradient Boosting Decision Tree (GBDT) has long been popular in academia and industry [72]. Based on the GBDT algorithm framework, Microsoft created LightGBM (Light Gradient Boosting Machine), a more efficient and precise gradient boosting algorithm framework [73].

Let $\mathcal{X}^p$ be the input space and $\mathcal{G}$ be the gradient space. Suppose we have a training set consisting of n i.i.d. instances $\{(x_1^T,y),\ldots,(x_n^T,y)\}$, where x_i is a vector and $x_i^T = (x_{i1},\ldots,x_{ip})$, p is the number of features. The predicted value $f(x)$ of GBDT for each instance is represented by K decision tree model $t_k(x)$:

$$f(x) = \sum_{k=1}^{K} t_k(x) \tag{1}$$

GBDT learns the approximate function $\hat{f}$ of f by minimizing the expected value of the loss function L:

$$\hat{f} = \underset{f}{\mathrm{argmin}}\, E_{y,x}[L(y,x)] \tag{2}$$

When splitting internal nodes, unlike the information gain utilized in GBDT, the Gradient-based One-Side Sampling (GOSS) algorithm is employed in LightGBM. Denote the negative gradients of the loss function as $\{d_1,\ldots,d_n\}$ in each iteration. Firstly, the data are split in accordance with the absolute values of the gradients. The top-$a \times 100\%$ instances constitute set A, and the remaining samples are randomly sampled to form set B. The size of B is $n \times b \times (1-a) \times 100\%$. Then, divide the node at point m on the set $A \cup B$ according to the variance gain $\widetilde{V}_j(m)$ of feature j:

$$\widetilde{V}_j(m) = \frac{1}{n}\left(\frac{(\sum_{x_i \in A_l} d_i + \frac{1-a}{b}\sum_{x_i \in B_l} d_i)^2}{n_l^j(m)} + \frac{(\sum_{x_i \in A_r} d_i + \frac{1-a}{b}\sum_{x_i \in B_r} d_i)^2}{n_r^j(m)}\right) \tag{3}$$

where $A_l = \{x_i \in A : x_{ij} \leq m\}$, $A_r = \{x_i \in A : x_{ij} > m\}$, $B_l = \{x_i \in B : x_{ij} \leq m\}$, $B_r = \{x_i \in B : x_{ij} > m\}$.

Through the GOSS algorithm, LightGBM only needs to perform computations on small samples, which greatly saves computation time. In addition, LightGBM further improves computational efficiency through the Histogram algorithm and the Exclusive Feature Bundling (EFB) algorithm. In comparison to eXtreme Gradient Boosting (XGBoost), which computes all objective function gains of each feature at all possible split points based on all instances and then selects the feature and split point with the largest gain [74], LightGBM optimizes computation from three aspects: reducing the quantity of possible split points by the Histogram algorithm, decreasing the sample size by means of the GOSS algorithm, and trimming the feature set through the EFB algorithm [73]. The higher efficiency of LightGBM has been verified by experiments [65,75].

3.2. SHapley Additive exPlanations (SHAP)

Although LightGBM has significant benefits in terms of computing efficiency and prediction accuracy, it is essentially a black-box model that can only show the order of importance of features but cannot output the specific impact of features on prediction results. As a consequence, we employ SHapley Additive exPlanations (SHAP) for analysis of the LightGBM results. The SHAP approach is an algorithm framework for the post-hoc explanation of complex black-box models. It can quantify the effects of each feature in shaping the projected outcome [69].

Let f represent the original black-box model to be explained, g represent the explanation model based on SHAP, x represent an instance, and x' represent the simplified input of x; there is a mapping relationship between them such that:

$$h_x(x') = x \tag{4}$$

It should be ensured that $g(z') \approx f(h_x(z'))$ whenever $z' \approx x'$ in local methods. Based on this, the additive model can be utilized to give attributes to the original prediction model:

$$g(z') = \Phi_0 + \sum_{j=1}^{P} \Phi_j z'_j \tag{5}$$

where $z' \in \{0,1\}^P$, P is the number of simplified input variables, and $\Phi_j \in \mathbb{R}$. It can be seen from Equation (5) that SHAP attributes the contribution of feature j to Φ_j, which is the Shapley value of feature j, and Φ_0 is a constant term.

It should be noted that when using LightGBM to make predictions, we cannot directly employ Equation (5) but need to perform logarithmic probability conversion on $g(z')$:

$$\ln \frac{g(z')}{1 - g(z')} = \Phi_0 + \sum_{j=1}^{P} \Phi_j z'_j \tag{6}$$

Let F denote the set including all features and $S \subseteq F$ denote the subset. To calculate Φ_j, $f_{S \cup \{j\}}(x_{S \cup \{j\}})$ and $f_S(x_S)$ should be trained, where $x_{S \cup \{j\}}$ are the values of the features in $S \cup \{j\}$ and x_S are the values of the features in S. Φ_j is then computed [76,77]:

$$\Phi_j = \sum_{S \subseteq F \backslash \{j\}} \frac{|S|!(|F| - |S| - 1)!}{|F|!} \left[f_{S \cup \{j\}}(x_{S \cup \{j\}}) - f_S(x_S) \right] \tag{7}$$

The complexity of calculating Φ_j by Equation (7) is $O(KN2^{|F|})$; in order to improve the computational efficiency, a TreeExplainer method for explaining the decision tree model is proposed [78,79], which reduces the complexity to $O(KND^2)$, where K is the number of trees, N is the peak node count among the trees, and D is the greatest depth of all trees.

Lundberg et al. (2018) [77] calculate pairwise interaction effects by extending SHAP values on the basis of the Shapley interaction index in game theory:

$$\Phi_{j,j} = \sum_{S \subseteq F \backslash \{i,j\}} \frac{|S|!(|F| - |S| - 2)!}{2(|F| - 1)!} \left[f_{S \cup \{i,j\}}(x_{S \cup \{i,j\}}) - f_{S \cup \{i\}} - f_{S \cup \{j\}} + f_S(x_S) \right] \tag{8}$$

4. Data Preparation

4.1. Data Source and Processing

The data we analyzed are from the Beijing Residents' Time Allocation Survey, which was conducted in 2011, 2016, and 2021 by the Leisure Economy Research Center of Renmin University of China. The corresponding effective sample sizes are 1106, 830, and 1597, respectively. We are in charge of questionnaire design, investigation, and data analysis. The sampling method is multi-stage random sampling. The questionnaire adopts a self-filling structure, which consists of a tripartite structure. The first part contains the respondents' fundamental elements, such as gender, age, and educational level. The second part comprises two daily time allocation tables for weekdays and weekends. Each table regards every 10 min as a unit; as a result, a day is divided into 144 time periods, and the respondents are required to fill in the unique items in each time period. The third part collects information about the respondents' involvement in physical exercise, cultural and recreational activities, hobbies, amateur learning, public welfare activities, and tourism in the previous year, including the frequency, companions, and so on. The questionnaire is filled in by the respondents themselves, which is the expression of their real thoughts. Thus, the survey data are ensured to be true, objective, and accurate.

The time allocation features selected in this paper are the average daily time calculated by $\frac{5\times time(\text{on weekdays})+2\times time(\text{on weekends})}{5+2}$. Leisure time is a numerical variable in the questionnaire, with a median of 237.14 minutes per day. In this paper, the survey data from three years are combined, and the "year" feature is introduced to distinguish instances from different years. The efficient sample contains no missing values, and abnormal values are deleted to prevent them from affecting the model's accuracy. First, we eliminate apparent outliers, such as the observation with an extreme age value of 159. Second, we apply the 3σ principle (i.e., outliers are defined as observations with a standardized score higher than three) to eliminate the outliers in the numerical features other than leisure time. Outliers of leisure time are not processed by the 3σ principle as they are processed in two classes during modeling, which can help avoid the influence of outliers. The sample size after outlier processing is 3356, which is utilized for further analysis in this paper. Taking the median of leisure time mentioned above as the boundary, this paper regards the observations less than the median as negative examples and the other observations as positive examples for binary classification, totaling 1639 negative cases and 1717 positive cases.

4.2. Variable Description

The dependent variable is leisure time. According to existing research, leisure time in this paper mainly denotes the time that individuals have at their disposal to engage in activities of their own choosing and bring pleasant experiences, excluding work/study time, essential time for personal life, and housework time. Moreover, leisure time in this paper consists of time for participating in recreational pursuits, including learning about culture and science; reading various forms of written media, including news, books, and magazines; watching TV, movies, and dramas; garden walks; and other leisure activities. The work/study time within the system in this paper refers to the time specified by the company/school [80], which excludes overtime and commuting time. The influencing factors of the residents' leisure time are mainly considered from four aspects: time allocation characteristics, demographic characteristics, occupational characteristics, and family characteristics. Our sample comprises students, current employees, and retirees. Thereby, in terms of the level of education, we divide people into five categories: (1) those who are not working and not students, (2) those who are still in school (students), and those who are current employees, including: (3) those who have been educated for 9 years or less, (4) those who have been educated for 9–12 years, and (5) those who have been educated for more than 12 years. Students and retirees are all classified as "not working" in each occupational characteristic because they are not presently employed. Further details are shown in Table 1.

Table 1. Factors influencing residents' leisure time.

Class	Symbol	Meaning	Variable Type	Remarks
Dependent variable	leisure time	Residents' leisure time	Categorical	0: $\leq$median, 1: >median
Year	year	Year	Categorical	0: 2011, 1: 2016, 2: 2021
Demographic factors	gender	Gender	Categorical	0: Male, 1: Female
	age	Age	Numerical	–
	marital status	Marital status	Categorical	0: Single, 1: Married
	education	Educational level	Categorical	0: Not working, 1: In school; Years of education of current employees: 2: $\leq$9 years, 3: 9–12 years, 4: >12 years

Table 1. *Cont.*

Class	Symbol	Meaning	Variable Type	Remarks
	weekly rest days	Weekly rest days	Categorical	0: Not working, 1: Two days off per week, 2: Fewer than two days off per week
Occupational factors	enterprise ownership	Ownership of the work unit	Categorical	0: Not working, 1: Enterprises owned by the whole people, 2: Collectively owned enterprises, 3: Individual industrial and commercial households, 4: Joint ventures, 5: Wholly owned enterprises, 6: Joint-stock enterprises, 7: Others
	occupation	occupational category	Categorical	0: Not working, 1: Agriculture, forestry, animal husbandry, and fisheries, 2: Industrial and commercial services, 3: Professional technicians, 4: Workers or general staff, 5: Managers; 6: Literary artists, 7: Personal occupation, 8: Others
	company size	Number of employees in the work unit	Categorical	0: Not working, 1: Working in government agencies, 2: 1–29 employees, 3: 30–99 employees, 4: 100–499 employees, 5: $\geq$500 employees
Family factors	care or not	Is there anyone in the family who needs care	Categorical	0: No, 1: Yes
	household income	Annual household income	Categorical	0: <CNY 30,000; 1: CNY 30,000–50,000; 2: CNY 50,000–100,000; 3: CNY 100,000–200,000; 4: $\geq$CNY 200,000
Time allocation factors	system time	Work/study time within the system	Numerical	–
	commuting time	Commuting time to work or to study in school	Numerical	–
	essential time	Essential time for personal life	Numerical	–
	housework time	Housework time	Numerical	–

5. LightGBM Model Construction and Evaluation

5.1. Model Construction

The models utilized in this paper are run in the environment of Python 3.7. The Light-GBM package [73], Scikit-learn package [81], and shap package [79] are applied for model training, evaluation, and explanation. The modeling process involves the following steps:

- Step 1: Encoding the categorical variables. All categorical variables are encoded with integers as shown in Table 1. LightGBM can directly process categorical variables through special algorithms rather than using one-hot encoding.
- Step 2: Splitting the data set. Randomly split the data set into the train, validation, and test sets proportional to 8:1:1.
- Step 3: Training and optimizing. Train the model and optimize the parameters with five-fold cross-validation on the train set and validation set. The final parameters of LightGBM utilized in this paper are n_estimators = 270, num_leaves = 10, and learning_rate = 0.05.
- Step 4: Prediction and evaluation. Predict on the train set and test set and evaluate the model.

5.2. Evaluation Metrics

To evaluate the model's effectiveness, we apply five commonly utilized evaluation metrics for classification models: accuracy, precision, recall, F1-score, and AUC (Area Under Curve). First, we construct the binary classification confusion matrix as presented in Table 2 according to the model prediction results.

Table 2. Confusion matrix for dichotomous model.

	Predicted Value = Negative	**Predicted Value = Positive**
Actual value = Negative	TN	FP
Actual value = Positive	FN	TP

Then, we calculate the following five metrics. Larger values of these metrics indicate better model performance.

$$Precision = \frac{TP}{TP + FP}, \quad Recall = \frac{TP}{TP + FN} \tag{9}$$

$$Accuracy = \frac{TP + TN}{TP + TN + FP + FN}, \quad F1 = \frac{2}{\frac{1}{Precision} + \frac{1}{Recall}} \tag{10}$$

To calculate AUC, we should calculate TRP (True Positive Rate) and FPR (False Positive Rate) first.

$$TPR = Recall = \frac{TP}{TP + FN}, \quad FPR = \frac{FP}{FP + TN} \tag{11}$$

The ROC (Receiver Operating Characteristic) curve is then drawn with FPR as the horizontal axis and TPR as the vertical axis, and AUC is calculated as the area under the ROC curve.

5.3. Model Evaluations

The confusion matrix of LightGBM on the test set is shown in Figure 1. The horizontal axis of Figure 1 represents the predicted value of 0 or 1, the vertical axis represents the actual value of 0 or 1, and the black area represents the number of misclassified instances. The ROC curve is shown in Figure 2, and AUC on the test set can be calculated as 0.91.

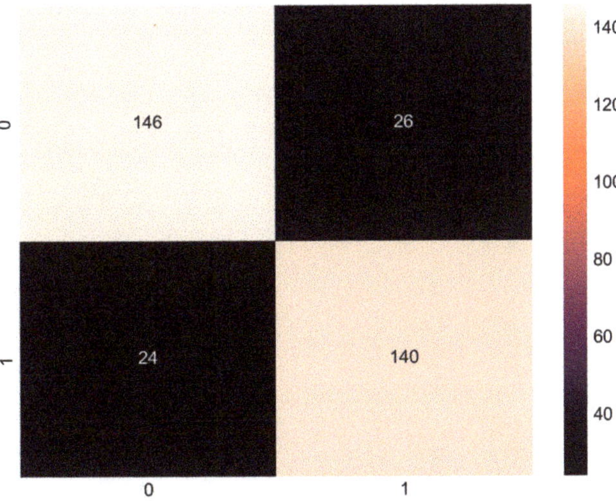

Figure 1. Confusion matrix for LightGBM on the test set.

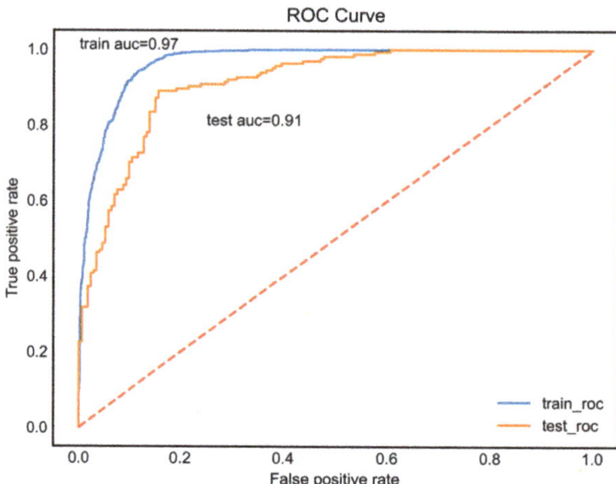

Figure 2. ROC curve for LightGBM on the train set and test set.

In addition, we choose several classic models to compare their performance with LightGBM, including logistic regression (LR), Support Vector Machines (SVM), K-Nearest Neighbors (KNN), Decision Trees (DT), Random Forests (RF), and Deep Neural Networks (DNN). The DNN model is trained by the PyTorch-tabular package [82], and to avoid overfitting, we designed a simple DNN with only two hidden layers containing 64 and 32 neurons, respectively. For the other compared algorithms, we utilize the Scikit-learn package with default parameters. It should be noted that the processing of categorical and numerical features varies when using different models. In particular, when using Decision Trees, Random Forests, and LightGBM models, there is no need to standardize numerical features. However, when using other comparison models, numerical features must be standardized. Additionally, when using LightGBM and DNN models, categorical features only require the label encoder, as the models are capable of processing them on their own. However, for the other comparison models mentioned, categorical features must be converted into dummy variables.

According to the confusion matrix, the average value of accuracy, precision, recall, and F1-score corresponding to all categories on the test set can be calculated, and the results are shown in Table 3. The models in Table 3 are ranked based on their performance from best to worst.

Table 3. Evaluation metrics for LightGBM and competitors on the test set.

Model	Accuracy	Precision	Recall	F1
LightGBM	0.85	0.85	0.85	0.85
LR	0.84	0.84	0.84	0.84
SVM	0.84	0.84	0.84	0.84
RF	0.82	0.82	0.81	0.81
DNN	0.80	0.80	0.80	0.80
DT	0.77	0.77	0.77	0.77
KNN	0.74	0.74	0.73	0.73

Table 3 shows that LightGBM performs the best in terms of accuracy, precision, recall, and F1 score, followed by logistic regression and support vector machines. Although logistic regression is not a black-box model and can directly solve the coefficients of each independent variable, it has a strong assumption (assuming a log-odds relationship between features), and its estimates may still be inaccurate when this assumption is violated. Moreover, logistic regression limits the relationship between features to be monotonic by interpreting the direction and magnitude of the coefficients before the features, whereas the relationship between features is often complex. As we found in the conclusion section of our paper, there is a U-shaped relationship between age and leisure time and an inverted U-shaped relationship between annual household income and leisure time, which logistic regression cannot capture. Furthermore, many statistical theories are based on the assumption that variables are independent of each other, which is difficult to achieve in real-world data. In this regard, tree models may be more suitable than other statistical models. To sum up, the results demonstrate that LightGBM performs well, with favorable scores across multiple metrics, indicating that the selected factors can better explain the changes in residents' leisure time. Further, SHAP is a better choice to analyze the factors influencing leisure time in Section 6 than some other explanation algorithms such as logistic regression.

6. Analysis of the Changes and Influencing Factors of Leisure Time by Using SHAP

The model built in this paper identifies the relationships between the features very well, which was verified by the excellent results of the evaluation metrics. Therefore, based on the train set, the marginal contributions of each feature for the determination of positive and negative cases are calculated according to the SHAP values of each feature so as to find out how each feature affects the dependent variable.

Beeswarm plots are introduced as a tool to analyze the factors. It should be noted that each point in a beeswarm plot represents a single instance. The different colors signify the various values of the current feature, with blue corresponding to small values and red corresponding to large values. The horizontal axis of the plot indicates SHAP values associated with the features. The magnitude of the SHAP value reflects the feature's effects on the outcome. A positive SHAP value indicates that the feature leads to a positive impact on the instance's leisure time, while a negative SHAP value indicates the opposite. Additionally, the higher the SHAP value, the more likely the instance's leisure time exceeds the median.

6.1. Changes in Beijing Residents' Leisure Time over the Last 30 Years

From Figure 3, we find that in the past 10 years from 2011 (blue) to 2021 (red), the SHAP value decreased, indicating that the leisure time of Beijing residents has decreased considerably.

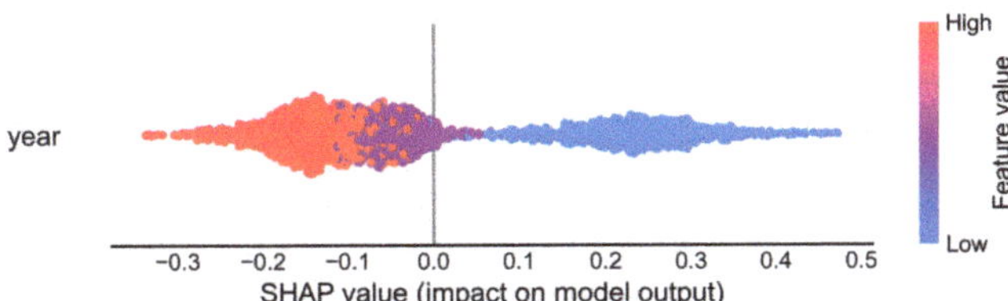

Figure 3. Beeswarm plot of the effects of "year".

In fact, according to the data from the Beijing Residents' Time Allocation Survey in 1986, 1996, 2001, 2006, 2011, 2016, and 2021, we can see noticeable changes in leisure time. This demonstrates a trend in which leisure time grew initially and then decreased over the past 30 years in Figure 4. On 1 May 1995, China started implementing the two-day weekend system, and the implementation of the two-day weekend system greatly increased people's leisure time. Specifically, the average daily leisure time of Beijing residents increased by 1 h and 4 min between 1986 and 1996 thanks to the aforementioned institutional factor. However, under the influence of market factors, the leisure time of residents began to decrease gradually. The average daily leisure time of Beijing residents in 2021 was only 13 min longer than in 1986, while it was 51 min shorter than in 1996.

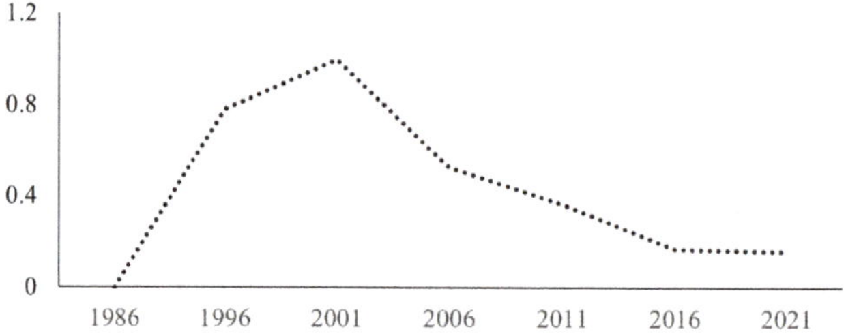

Figure 4. Changes in leisure time over the past 30 years (leisure time has been normalized by Min–Max).

6.2. Analysis on the Influencing Factors of Beijing Residents' Leisure Time

6.2.1. Primary Factors Restricting Leisure Time: Work/Study and Housework

The features in Figure 5 are ordered by their significance as calculated by their mean absolute SHAP values. They reflect how the factors influence leisure time in the process of modeling, resulting in the final prediction result.

As shown in Figure 5, all the time allocation characteristics, including work/study time within the system, housework time, essential time for personal life, and commuting time, substantially decrease the amount of leisure time. Work/study time within the system stands out as the most influential factor. It reveals that there are still deficiencies in the current national holiday system and that longer working hours within the system have put a significant strain on leisure time. According to the data from the "China Labor Statistical Yearbook", the average weekly working hours of Chinese urban employees have been more than 44 h from 2001 to 2020 [83].

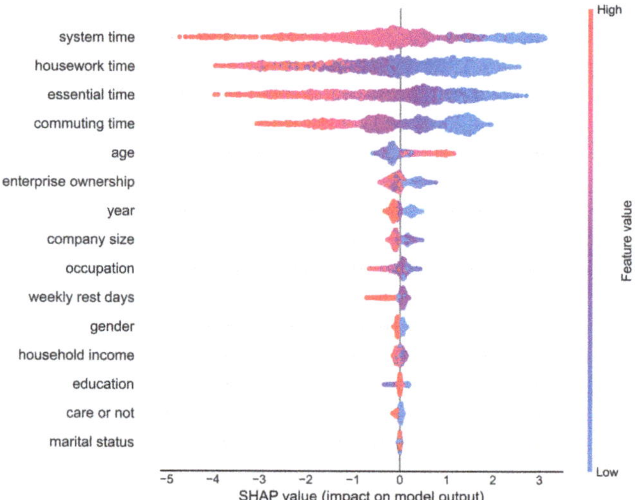

Figure 5. Beeswarm plot of feature importance ranking.

Aside from time allocation characteristics, the second most significant influencing factor is age, which is one of the demographic characteristics. Additionally, occupational characteristics play a crucial role in shaping leisure time as well. Despite ranking lower in the order of feature importance, family characteristics do have an effect on leisure time.

Below is a thorough analysis of how demographic, occupational, and family factors influence leisure time.

6.2.2. Age Differences and Gender Inequality in Leisure Time

Age and gender are the most important influencing factors of demographic characteristics, as depicted in Figure 6.

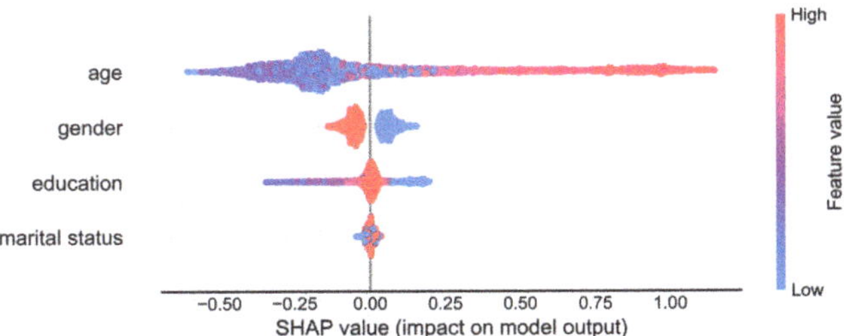

Figure 6. Beeswarm plot of the effects of demographic factors.

Because the elderly are typically retirees, they tend to have more leisure time. Instances in different gender groups are significantly distributed on both sides of the vertical axis, with males (blue) having more leisure time. It is clear that there is gender inequality in leisure time, which is supported by previous study findings [35]. The SHAP values of years of education primarily range between −0.5 and 0.25, implying that it has an effect on leisure time. As the SHAP values of marital status fluctuate around zero, its effect on leisure time is negligible.

6.2.3. Occupational Heterogeneity in Leisure Time

As illustrated in Figure 7, among occupational characteristics, "enterprise ownership" (i.e., the ownership of the work unit) has the largest impact on leisure time. The color from blue to red denotes "not working, enterprises owned by the whole people, collectively owned enterprises, individual industrial and commercial households, joint ventures, wholly-owned enterprises, joint-stock enterprises and others". Persons working in enterprises owned by the whole people or in collectively owned enterprises have considerably more leisure time than those in other enterprises, which has been given little emphasis in the previous research. Regarding company size, employees of small companies (blue and purple) have more leisure time than those of large companies (red). From the perspective of occupational category, SHAP values of occupational category vary between −0.6 and 0.6, showing that different occupational categories have varying impacts on leisure time. For instance, management positions and personal occupations (red) are associated with a detrimental effect on leisure time. Additionally, having fewer than two days off per week (also shown in red) significantly reduces leisure time.

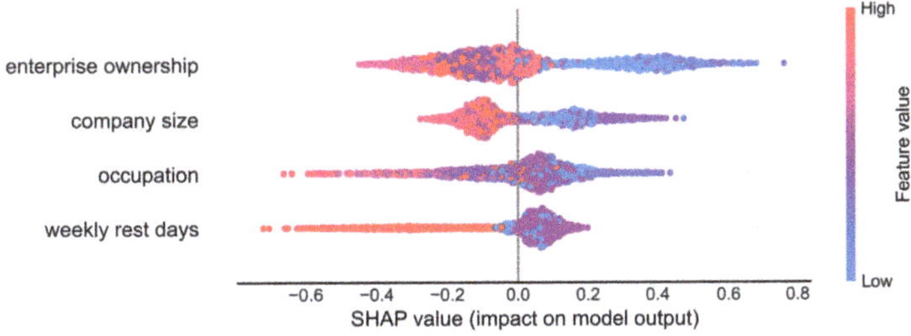

Figure 7. Beeswarm plot of the effects of occupational factors.

6.2.4. High Income and Caring for Others Squeezing Leisure Time

Annual household income is the most important factor among family characteristics. Figure 8 depicts the major effects of annual household income. The horizontal axis represents the values of the feature, and the left vertical axis represents the SHAP values of the feature, which quantifies the feature's influence on the LightGBM model's outcome. The color here has the same meaning as the horizontal axis, namely, corresponding to the feature values.

An upside-down U-shaped curve characterizes the relationship between annual household income and leisure time, as shown in Figure 8. The lowest (blue) and highest income (red) have a significant negative impact on leisure time, presenting a phenomenon of extremely low income and extremely high income accompanied by a lack of leisure time. When the income is less than CNY 30,000, it has a negative impact on leisure time. When the income is between CNY 30,000 and 100,000, it has a positive impact on leisure time, and this positive impact increases with income. However, when the income exceeds CNY 100,000, it begins to have a negative impact on leisure time again, and this influence increases with income.

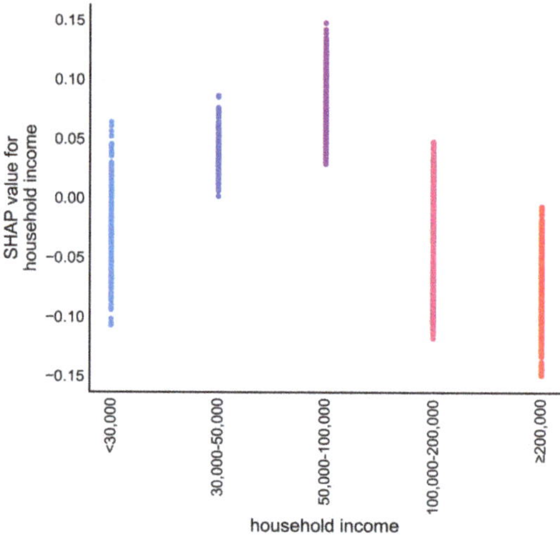

Figure 8. Scatter plot of the effects of annual household income.

As for the factor "care or not", Figure 9 shows that persons without family members to care for (blue) have significantly more leisure time than others. Obviously, when there are people in need of care, it will take up a lot of time. This is consistent with the conclusions of an earlier study that found that when children with chronic diseases need home care, parents' leisure time is reduced accordingly [55].

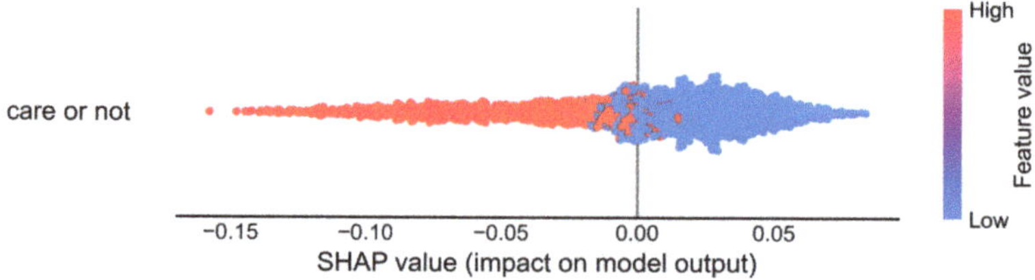

Figure 9. Beeswarm plot of the effects of "care or not".

6.3. Interaction Effects of the Factors Influencing Beijing Residents' Leisure Time

To capture the interaction effects between features, we utilize SHAP's dependency plot for analysis. It can display both the primary and joint impacts of features simultaneously. The interaction effects indicate how two features jointly affect the model's prediction, and they are displayed through the differing color-coded vertical distribution of SHAP values. The horizontal axis in the dependency plot represents the values of the main feature; the left vertical axis represents the SHAP values of the main feature, which describe the contributions of the main feature to the outcome of LightGBM; the right vertical axis is utilized to describe the interaction effects, illustrating the SHAP values of the interaction feature, and the hue transitions from blue to red as the values of the interaction feature change from small to large.

6.3.1. Gender Inequality Shifts over a Decade

It is evident in Figure 10 that leisure time has decreased over the past ten years from 2011 to 2021. In 2011, women's SHAP values (red) were lower than men's (blue), showing that gender inequality was severe with respect to leisure time. In 2016, women's SHAP values (red) were spread out across the entire vertical axis, indicating that there was no significant difference in leisure time between men and women. In 2021, women's SHAP values (red) began to be distributed in the upper part of the vertical axis, showing that women's leisure time had slightly surpassed men's. The improvement from gender inequality to gender equality has depended on the sustained efforts for gender equality in all fields of society [84].

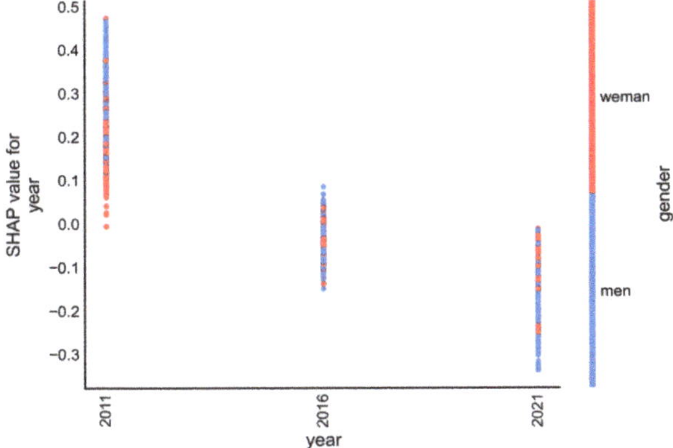

Figure 10. Interaction effects of "year" and "gender".

6.3.2. Gender Inequality Shifts over the Educational Level

It can be seen from Figure 11 that individuals who have graduated but are not currently employed have the most leisure time, while students and current employees have comparatively less leisure time. From the perspective of the fluctuation range of the SHAP values corresponding to the number of years of education, the impact of education level on leisure time shows a decreasing trend with increasing education level, and the direction shows a trend from negative influence to positive influence.

As shown in Figure 11, when the number of years of education is less than nine, women (red) are distributed in the lower half of the vertical axis, indicating that women in this group have less leisure time. When the number of years of education is 9–12, women (red) are uniformly distributed on the vertical axis, showing a tendency toward gender equality. When the number of years of education exceeds 12, most women (red) are distributed in the upper half of the vertical axis, indicating that among highly educated groups, women have more leisure time. This highlights that women have more leisure time as their education level rises. To sum up, education level has a significant moderating effect on gender inequality in leisure time.

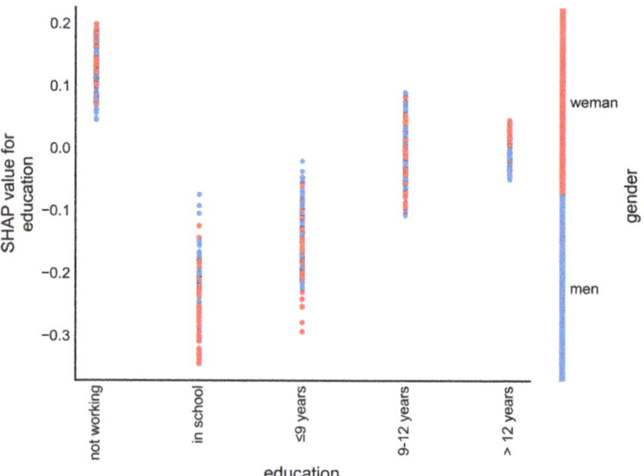

Figure 11. Interaction effects of "education" and "gender".

6.3.3. Leisure Time Changes for Family Caregivers over a Decade

It can be seen from Figure 12 that in 2011, individuals who needed to care for family members (red) were distributed in the lower half of the vertical axis, implying that they had less leisure time. However, these individuals were distributed in the upper part of the vertical axis in 2016 and 2021, indicating that even with family members in need of care, people have begun to have more leisure time. This improvement may be attributed to economic development, technological progress, and an increase in annual household income, which have provided more advanced methods of assisting people in caring for others, such as hiring professional caregivers [85], utilizing AI intelligent nursing systems [86], etc.

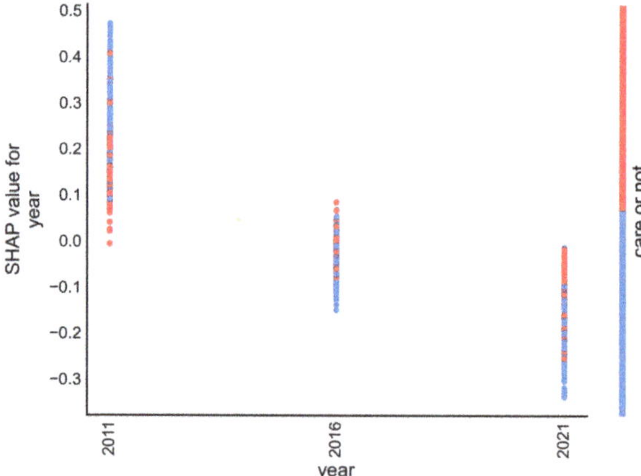

Figure 12. Interaction effects of "year" and "care or not".

6.3.4. Positive and Negative Effects of Weekly Rest Days

Overall, Figure 13 depicts that the impact of age on leisure time follows a U-shaped pattern. Individuals between the ages of 30 and 40 are in the golden stage of striving for dreams, and they have the least leisure time; as they get older, their leisure time steadily increases.

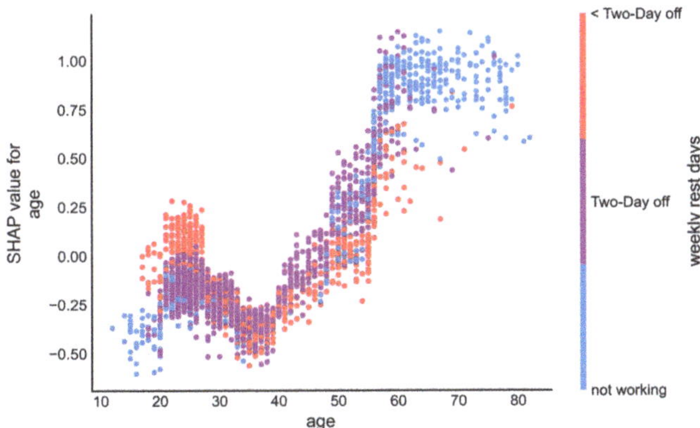

Figure 13. Interaction effects of "age" and "weekly rest days".

From the color distribution of the vertical axis in Figure 13, there is a significant interaction effect between age and the weekly rest days. We have a stereotype that fewer vacation days equal less leisure time, and in general, this inference is correct. However, in some cases, fewer vacation days may contribute to a positive change in leisure time. The results in Figure 13 indicate that people between the ages of 20 and 30 who are unable to guarantee two days off weekly (red) are distributed on the upper vertical axis, meaning that they have more leisure time instead. The reason for this phenomenon may be when they must work overtime on weekends, they will look for leisure compensation at other times, such as seeking "retaliatory leisure" by reducing other time, which leads to an increase in leisure time. People aged 30–60 who are unable to take two days off weekly (red) are distributed at the bottom of the vertical axis, suggesting that being unable to take weekend breaks has a major negative impact on leisure time. In general, the failure to implement two days off weekly exerts a marked detrimental impact on leisure time.

7. Conclusions and Discussions

7.1. Main Conclusions

This paper analyzes the changes in residents' leisure time and the major influencing factors from a machine learning viewpoint in line with the survey data from Beijing residents' daily time allocation. In general, the time allocation characteristics are the most significant influencing factors. Work time within the system and housework time are the primary drivers of the substantial reduction in leisure time.

In terms of **demographic factors**, there are age heterogeneity and gender inequalities in leisure time. A U-shaped connection exists between age and leisure time. In the initial stages of life, in order to accumulate capital, individuals sacrificed more and more leisure time as they grew older. As they reach their 40s and beyond, capital accumulation increases, working hours begin to decline after reaching a peak, and leisure activities become more feasible. People's pursuit of leisure time becomes more urgent as they get older, and as work and life pressures increase, they may consciously increase their leisure time. Gender inequality is evident in leisure time, with men enjoying more leisure time than women. Women may shoulder more housework and caregiving responsibilities, resulting in a continuous erosion of their personal leisure time. Gender inequality has improved considerably over time, and by 2021, there was a trend toward gender equality. Education can reconcile gender inequality, and higher education can serve to promote gender equality.

In terms of **occupational factors**, they also have a significant influence on leisure time, especially in relation to enterprise ownership. Employees of enterprises owned by the whole people or collectively have more leisure time compared to others. This shows the differences in overtime culture under various enterprise systems, such as the long-standing "996" work system in the Internet industry, in which leisure time is severely constrained by the high-intensity work mode. This is consistent with the conclusion that different occupation categories have different leisure time. The impact of company size is also notable, with large companies exhibiting less leisure time. Interestingly, people aged 20–30 may actively create more leisure time if they have fewer than two days off per week, possibly due to "retaliatory leisure" psychology, which is the active creation of leisure time at the cost of other time. However, in general, taking fewer than two days off per week reduces leisure time.

In terms of **family factors**, annual household income exhibits an inverted U-shaped relationship with leisure time, whereby individuals with lower incomes (<CNY 30,000) and higher incomes (>CNY 100,000) experience a decrease in leisure time. In contrast, those with annual household incomes between CNY 30,000 and 100,000 experience an increase in leisure time, and this positive impact increases as the income rises. In addition, when there is someone at home who needs to be cared for, the caregiver's leisure time is consumed. The interaction analysis of joining to "year" shows that with the development of science and technology, the crowding-out effect of taking care of others on leisure time starts to diminish.

7.2. Discussion

Leisure time not only facilitates personal self-development but also stimulates leisure consumption and promotes economic growth. In light of the conclusions of this paper, we put forward the following potential measures to increase personal leisure time.

Reform the current vacation system to ensure the adequate supply of leisure time. The conclusions indicate that leisure time is primarily influenced by working hours. At a national level, the national vacation system determines working hours within the system and serves as the main constraint on the supply of leisure time. The current vacation system can be reformed by the government to increase the overall availability of leisure time. It is important for a country's vacation system to be in sync with its economic progress; thus, on the basis of certain increase in labor productivity, the length of legal holidays could be appropriately increased. Additionally, to prevent the occurrence of leave-in-lieu and alleviate worker fatigue, one potential solution in developed cities is to implement a four-day-week system , with possible adjustments made based on the actual situation of different enterprises or regions. Furthermore, the results show that having fewer than two days off weekly significantly reduces leisure time, highlighting the challenge of implementing the existing vacation system and ensuring an adequate supply of leisure time. The "996 work system" has even become the standard configuration of Internet companies, and it is difficult to implement both paid leave and two days off per week. To address this problem, relevant reward and punishment policies should be issued to encourage the realization of legal holidays.

Provide personalized leisure products to promote the upgrading of leisure consumption. The results of this paper show that demographic characteristics such as age and gender have a significant impact on leisure time. Accordingly, enterprises can perform user clustering based on the characteristics of various groups and provide personalized leisure products to satisfy different consumer demands. At the market level, material guarantees are necessary to meet people's leisure consumption needs. For example, the conclusions of this paper demonstrate that women have less leisure time due to increased family obligations. For these groups with special needs, enterprises should create and develop innovative leisure products by leveraging cutting-edge technologies such as 5G and artificial intelligence, which help pave the way for the transformation and enhancement of the leisure industry. This can drive the evolution of the digital economy and travel consumption as well as provide an extensive variety of online services. The supply of online products such as "cloud music" and "cloud exhibition" can also be increased, enabling people to conveniently engage in leisure activities at any time and from any location. In particular, for elderly adults, community-based programs that provide leisure activities at home can create a fulfilling and enjoyable lifestyle for them in their twilight years.

Advocate a proper perception of leisure and stimulate potential leisure needs. The findings suggest notable dissimilarities in leisure time among people with different occupational characteristics. To alter this professional imbalance in leisure time, the government should first take the lead in enforcing and penalizing practices, providing channels for employees to report violations, and safeguarding employees' rights and interests. Second, we must promote the perception of leisure across society to encourage employees to pursue reasonable leisure time actively. From a demand standpoint, it is essential to provide a basic guarantee to strengthen people's leisure needs. Highlight the fact that leisure time is the guarantee for people to live a happy life and do not put "leisure" and "labor" in opposition. The purpose of "labor" is to free up more time and money for leisure activities, which not only relax the body and mind but also help people achieve self-reflection and self-improvement, allowing them to dedicate themselves to "labor" more effectively. We should enhance public awareness; promote diverse and healthy leisure options; create a favorable environment for high-end leisure, cultural, and tourism activities; and raise awareness of the importance of leisure by organizing leisure conferences and publishing relevant leisure tourism manuals.

Despite conducting a comprehensive analysis of the effects of time allocation factors, demographic factors, occupational factors, and family factors on leisure time from a micro perspective, this paper has several research limitations. Firstly, due to technical constraints, the SHAP approach utilized in this paper provides insight into how features affect LightGBM model predictions, but it may not reveal the true causal relationships between features and outcomes in the real world. Although this does not undermine the conclusions drawn in this paper, we intend to utilize other causal inference methods such as Double Machine Learning to quantify the causal effects and evaluate the intervention effects by making counterfactual predictions in future studies. Secondly, owing to data unavailability, this paper only considers Beijing as a case study, yet leisure time varies across regions. Thereby, in the future, we aim to incorporate more regions for comparative analysis.

Author Contributions: Conceptualization, Q.W.; Software, Y.J.; Validation, Q.W. and Y.J.; Formal Analysis, Y.J.; Investigation, Q.W. and Y.J.; Data Curation, Y.J.; Writing—Original Draft Preparation, Q.W. and Y.J.; Writing—Review and Editing, Q.W. and Y.J.; supervision, Q.W. All authors have read and agreed to the published version of the manuscript.

Funding: This research was funded by the National Social Science Fund of China (grant number: 21ATJ004).

Data Availability Statement: The data underpinning the presented findings are in Chinese and are available by contacting the corresponding author.

Acknowledgments: We would like to express our appreciation for the data assistance provided by the Leisure Economy Research Center of Renmin University of China.

Conflicts of Interest: The authors declare no conflict of interest.

References

1. Bouwer, J.; Van Leeuwen, M. *Philosophy of Leisure: Foundations of the Good Life*; Routledge: New York, NY, USA, 2017.
2. Opić, S.; Đuranović, M. Leisure time of young due to some socio-demographic characteristics. *Procedia-Soc. Behav. Sci.* **2014**, *159*, 546–551. [CrossRef]
3. Cui, D.; Wei, X.; Wu, D.; Cui, N.; Nijkamp, P. Leisure time and labor productivity: A new economic view rooted from sociological perspective. *Economics* **2019**, *13*, 1–24. [CrossRef]
4. Dimitrova, R. Trends Analysis to Use Leisure Time. *Econ. Financ.* **2019**, *6*, 28–38.
5. Anderson, L.S.; Heyne, L.A. Flourishing through leisure: An ecological extension of the leisure and well-being model in therapeutic recreation strengths-based practice. *Ther. Recreat. J.* **2012**, *46*, 129.
6. Bittman, M. Social participation and family welfare: The money and time costs of leisure in Australia. *Soc. Policy Adm.* **2002**, *36*, 408–425. [CrossRef]
7. Cook, D.T. Leisure and consumption. In *A Handbook of Leisure Studies*; Rojek, C., Shaw, S., Veal, A., Eds.; Palgrave Macmillan: London, UK, 2006; pp. 304–316.
8. Stebbins, R. *Leisure and Consumption: Common Ground/Separate Worlds*; Palgrave Macmillan: New York, NY, USA, 2009.

9. Sullivan, O.; Gershuny, J. Inconspicuous consumption: Work-rich, time-poor in the liberal market economy. *J. Consum. Cult.* **2004**, *4*, 79–100. [CrossRef]

10. Vickery, C. The time-poor: A new look at poverty. *J. Hum. Resour.* **1977**, *12*, 27–48. [CrossRef]

11. Lin, K. Tech worker organizing in China: A new model for workers battling a repressive state. In *New Labor Forum*; SAGE Publications Sage CA: Los Angeles, CA, USA, 2020; Volume 29, pp. 52–59.

12. Mapped: Which Countries Get the Most Paid Vacation Days? Available online: https://www.visualcapitalist.com/cp/mapped-which-countries-get-the-most-paid-vacation-days/ (accessed on 28 April 2023).

13. Kuykendall, L.; Boemerman, L.; Zhu, Z. The importance of leisure for subjective well-being. In *Handbook of Well-Being*; DEF Publishers: Salt Lake City, UT, USA, 2018.

14. Yasarturk, F.; Akyüz, H.; Karatas, I.; Turkmen, M. The relationship between free time satisfaction and stress levels of elite-level student-wrestlers. *Educ. Sci.* **2018**, *8*, 133. [CrossRef]

15. Liu, H.; Da, S. The relationships between leisure and happiness-A graphic elicitation method. *Leis. Stud.* **2020**, *39*, 111–130. [CrossRef]

16. Greaney, V.; Hegarty, M. Correlates of leisure-time reading. *J. Res. Read.* **1987**, *10*, 3–20. [CrossRef]

17. Roberts, K. *Leisure in Contemporary Society*; Cabi: Wallingford, UK, 2006.

18. Voorpostel, M.; Van Der Lippe, T.; Gershuny, J. Spending time together—Changes over four decades in leisure time spent with a spouse. *J. Leis. Res.* **2010**, *42*, 243–265. [CrossRef]

19. Shaw, S.M.; Dawson, D. Purposive leisure: Examining parental discourses on family activities. *Leis. Sci.* **2001**, *23*, 217–231. [CrossRef]

20. Leitner, M.J.; Leitner, S.F. *Leisure Enhancement*; Haworth Press: Binghamton, NY, USA, 2004.

21. Žumárová, M. Computers and children's leisure time. *Procedia-Soc. Behav. Sci.* **2015**, *176*, 779–786. [CrossRef]

22. Schulz, J.; Watkins, M. The development of the leisure meanings inventory. *J. Leis. Res.* **2007**, *39*, 477–497. [CrossRef]

23. Iwasaki, Y. Pathways to meaning-making through leisure-like pursuits in global contexts. *J. Leis. Res.* **2008**, *40*, 231–249. [CrossRef]

24. Soyer, F.; Demirel, M.; Kacay, Z.; Ayhan, C.; Demirel, D.H. Examination of the Opinions of University Students on the Meaning of Leisure Time and the Lesson Study Approaches. *Khazar J. Humanit. Soc. Sci.* **2017**, 18–31.

25. Auger, D. The diverse meanings of leisure/Les diverses significations du loisir. *Soc. Leis.* **2016**, *39*, 173–176. [CrossRef]

26. Seibel, S.; Volmer, J.; Syrek, C.J. Get a taste of your leisure time: The relationship between leisure thoughts, pleasant anticipation, and work engagement. *Eur. J. Work Organ. Psychol.* **2020**, *29*, 889–906. [CrossRef]

27. Burda, M.C.; Hamermesh, D.S.; Weil, P. *Total Work, Gender and Social Norms*; NBER Working Papers No. 13000; National Bureau of Economic Research: Cambridge, MA, USA, 2007.

28. Andronis, L.; Maredza, M.; Petrou, S. Measuring, valuing and including forgone childhood education and leisure time costs in economic evaluation: Methods, challenges and the way forward. *Soc. Sci. Med.* **2019**, *237*, 112475. [CrossRef]

29. Clark, B.; Chatterjee, K.; Martin, A.; Davis, A. How commuting affects subjective wellbeing. *Transportation* **2020**, *47*, 2777–2805. [CrossRef]

30. Pepin, J.R.; Sayer, L.C.; Casper, L.M. Marital status and mothers' time use: Childcare, housework, leisure, and sleep. *Demography* **2018**, *55*, 107–133. [CrossRef] [PubMed]

31. Wales, T.J.; Woodland, A.D. Estimation of the allocation of time for work, leisure, and housework. *Econom. J. Econom. Soc.* **1977**, 115–132. [CrossRef]

32. Zuzanek, J. Work, leisure, time-pressure and stress. In *Work and Leisure*; Haworth, J.T., Veal, A.J., Eds.; Routledge: London, UK, 2004; pp. 123–144.

33. Thrane, C. Men, women, and leisure time: Scandinavian evidence of gender inequality. *Leis. Sci.* **2000**, *22*, 109–122. [CrossRef]

34. Becker, G.S. Human capital, effort, and the sexual division of labor. *J. Labor Econ.* **1985**, *3*, S33–S58. [CrossRef]

35. Bittman, M.; Wajcman, J. The rush hour: The character of leisure time and gender equity. *Soc. Forces* **2000**, *79*, 165–189. [CrossRef]

36. Lydeka, Z.; Tauraitė, V. Evaluation of the time allocation for work and personal life among employed population in Lithuania from gender perspective. *Eng. Econ.* **2020**, *31*, 104–113. [CrossRef]

37. Haller, M.; Hadler, M.; Kaup, G. Leisure time in modern societies: A new source of boredom and stress? *Soc. Indic. Res.* **2013**, *111*, 403–434. [CrossRef]

38. Miller, Y.D.; Brown, W.J. Determinants of active leisure for women with young children—An "ethic of care" prevails. *Leis. Sci.* **2005**, *27*, 405–420. [CrossRef]

39. Bauer, F.; Groß, H.; Oliver, G.; Sieglen, G.; Smith, M. *Time Use and Work–Life Balance in Germany and the UK*; Anglo-German Foundation for the study of Industrial Society: London, UK, 2007.

40. Lee, Y.G.; Bhargava, V. Leisure time: Do married and single individuals spend it differently? *Fam. Consum. Sci. Res. J.* **2004**, *32*, 254–274. [CrossRef]

41. Zuzanek, J. Social differences in leisure behavior: Measurement and interpretation. *Leis. Sci.* **1978**, *1*, 271–293. [CrossRef]

42. Dyble, M.; Thorley, J.; Page, A.E.; Smith, D.; Migliano, A.B. Engagement in agricultural work is associated with reduced leisure time among Agta hunter-gatherers. *Nat. Hum. Behav.* **2019**, *3*, 792–796. [CrossRef]

43. Shaw, B.A.; Liang, J.; Krause, N.; Gallant, M.; McGeever, K. Age differences and social stratification in the long-term trajectories of leisure-time physical activity. *J. Gerontol. Ser. Psychol. Sci. Soc. Sci.* **2010**, *65*, 756–766. [CrossRef]

44. Agahi, N.; Ahacic, K.; Parker, M.G. Continuity of leisure participation from middle age to old age. *J. Gerontol. Ser. B: Psychol. Sci. Soc. Sci.* **2006**, *61*, S340–S346. [CrossRef]

45. Andersen, L.B.; Schnohr, P.; Schroll, M.; Hein, H.O. All-cause mortality associated with physical activity during leisure time, work, sports, and cycling to work. *Arch. Intern. Med.* **2000**, *160*, 1621–1628. [CrossRef]

46. Werneck, A.O.; Oyeyemi, A.L.; Araújo, R.H.; Barboza, L.L.; Szwarcwald, C.L.; Silva, D.R. Association of public physical activity facilities and participation in community programs with leisure-time physical activity: Does the association differ according to educational level and income? *BMC Public Health* **2022**, *22*, 279. [CrossRef]

47. Kirk, M.A.; Rhodes, R.E. Occupation correlates of adults' participation in leisure-time physical activity: A systematic review. *Am. J. Prev. Med.* **2011**, *40*, 476–485. [CrossRef]

48. Ganzeboom, H.B.; Treiman, D.J. Internationally comparable measures of occupational status for the 1988 International Standard Classification of Occupations. *Soc. Sci. Res.* **1996**, *25*, 201–239. [CrossRef]

49. Wei, J.; Li, Y.; Liu, X.; Du, Y. Enterprise characteristics and external influencing factors of sustainable innovation: Based on China's innovation survey. *J. Clean. Prod.* **2022**, *372*, 133461. [CrossRef]

50. Aleksynska, M.; Berg, J.; Foden, D.; Johnston, H.; Parent-Thirion, A.; Vanderleyden, J.; Vermeylen, G. *Working Conditions in a Global Perspective*; Research report/Eurofound; Publications Office of the European Union: Luxembourg, 2019.

51. Vandelanotte, C.; Short, C.; Rockloff, M.; Di Millia, L.; Ronan, K.; Happell, B.; Duncan, M.J. How do different occupational factors influence total, occupational, and leisure-time physical activity? *J. Phys. Act. Health* **2015**, *12*, 200–207. [CrossRef]

52. Gu, J.K.; Charles, L.E.; Ma, C.C.; Andrew, M.E.; Fekedulegn, D.; Hartley, T.A.; Violanti, J.M.; Burchfiel, C.M. Prevalence and trends of leisure-time physical activity by occupation and industry in US workers: The National Health Interview Survey 2004–2014. *Ann. Epidemiol.* **2016**, *26*, 685–692. [CrossRef]

53. Firestone, J.; Shelton, B.A. A comparison of women's and men's leisure time: Subtle effects of the double day. *Leis. Sci.* **1994**, *16*, 45–60. [CrossRef]

54. Yasartürk, F.; Akyüz, H.; Gönülates, S. The Investigation of the Relationship between University Students' Levels of Life Quality and Leisure Satisfaction. *Univers. J. Educ. Res.* **2019**, *7*, 739–745. [CrossRef]

55. Hatzmann, J.; Peek, N.; Heymans, H.; Maurice-Stam, H.; Grootenhuis, M. Consequences of caring for a child with a chronic disease: Employment and leisure time of parents. *J. Child Health Care* **2014**, *18*, 346–357. [CrossRef] [PubMed]

56. Fernandez-Crehuet, J.M.; Gimenez-Nadal, J.I.; Reyes Recio, L.E. The national work–life balance index©: The European case. *Soc. Indic. Res.* **2016**, *128*, 341–359. [CrossRef]

57. Shen, H.; Wang, Q.; Ye, C.; Liu, J.S. The evolution of holiday system in China and its influence on domestic tourism demand. *J. Tour. Futur.* **2018**, *4*, 139–151. [CrossRef]

58. York, Q.Y.; Ye, B.H. Research note: Why gold is so stronghold, revealing the mechanism of China's golden week holiday system. *Leis. Stud.* **2018**, *37*, 352–358. [CrossRef]

59. Wang, P.; Wei, X.; Yingwei, X.; Xiaodan, C. The impact of residents' leisure time allocation mode on individual subjective well-being: The case of China. *Appl. Res. Qual. Life* **2022**, *17*, 1831–1866. [CrossRef]

60. Gali, J. Technology, employment, and the business cycle: Do technology shocks explain aggregate fluctuations? *Am. Econ. Rev.* **1999**, *89*, 249–271. [CrossRef]

61. Dridea, C.; Sztruten, G. Free time-the major factor of influence for leisure. *Rom. Econ. Bus. Rev.* **2010**, *5*, 208.

62. Min, J.; Jin, H. Analysis on Essence, Types and Characteristics of Leisure Sports. *Mod. Appl. Sci.* **2010**, *4*, 99. [CrossRef]

63. Rätsel, S. Revisiting the neoclassical theory of labour supply: Disutility of labour, working hours, and happiness. *Work. Pap. Ser.* **2009**.

64. Yaniv, G. Workaholism and marital estrangement: A rational-choice perspective. *Math. Soc. Sci.* **2011**, *61*, 104–108. [CrossRef]

65. Al Daoud, E. Comparison between XGBoost, LightGBM and CatBoost using a home credit dataset. *Int. J. Comput. Inf. Eng.* **2019**, *13*, 6–10.

66. Zhang, L.; Liu, M.; Qin, X.; Liu, G. Succinylation site prediction based on protein sequences using the IFS-LightGBM (BO) model. *Comput. Math. Methods Med.* **2020**, *2020*, 8858489. [CrossRef]

67. Sun, X.; Liu, M.; Sima, Z. A novel cryptocurrency price trend forecasting model based on LightGBM. *Financ. Res. Lett.* **2020**, *32*, 101084. [CrossRef]

68. Molnar, C. Interpretable Machine Learning. Available online: https://originalstatic.aminer.cn/misc/pdf/Molnar-interpretable-machine-learning_compressed.pdf (accessed on 28 April 2023).

69. Lundberg, S.M.; Lee, S.I. A unified approach to interpreting model predictions. In Proceedings of the 31st Conference on Neural Information Processing Systems (NIPS 2017), Long Beach, CA, USA, 4–9 December 2017; pp. 4765–4774.

70. Zhang, J.; Ma, X.; Zhang, J.; Sun, D.; Zhou, X.; Mi, C.; Wen, H. Insights into geospatial heterogeneity of landslide susceptibility based on the SHAP-XGBoost model. *J. Environ. Manag.* **2023**, *332*, 117357. [CrossRef]

71. Wen, X.; Xie, Y.; Wu, L.; Jiang, L. Quantifying and comparing the effects of key risk factors on various types of roadway segment crashes with LightGBM and SHAP. *Accid. Anal. Prev.* **2021**, *159*, 106261. [CrossRef]

72. Friedman, J.H. Greedy function approximation: A gradient boosting machine. *Ann. Stat.* **2001**, *29*, 1189–1232. [CrossRef]

73. Ke, G.; Meng, Q.; Finley, T.; Wang, T.; Chen, W.; Ma, W.; Ye, Q.; Liu, T.Y. Lightgbm: A highly efficient gradient boosting decision tree. In Proceedings of the 31st Conference on Neural Information Processing Systems (NIPS 2017), Long Beach, CA, USA, 4–9 December 2017; pp. 3147–3155.

74. Chen, T.; Guestrin, C. Xgboost: A scalable tree boosting system. In Proceedings of the 22nd ACM Sigkdd International Conference on Knowledge Discovery and Data Mining, San Francisco, CA, USA, 13–17 August 2016; pp. 785–794.
75. Alabdullah, A.A.; Iqbal, M.; Zahid, M.; Khan, K.; Amin, M.N.; Jalal, F.E. Prediction of rapid chloride penetration resistance of metakaolin based high strength concrete using lightGBM and XGBoost models by incorporating SHAP analysis. *Constr. Build. Mater.* **2022**, *345*, 128296. [CrossRef]
76. Shapley, L.S. 17. A Value for n-Person Games. In *Contributions to the Theory of Games (AM-28), Volume II*; Kuhn, H.W., Tucker, A.W., Eds.; Princeton University Press: Princeton, NJ, USA, 1953; pp. 307–318.
77. Lundberg, S.M.; Erion, G.G.; Lee, S.I. Consistent individualized feature attribution for tree ensembles. *arXiv* **2018**, arXiv:1802.03888.
78. Lundberg, S.M.; Nair, B.; Vavilala, M.S.; Horibe, M.; Eisses, M.J.; Adams, T.; Liston, D.E.; Low, D.K.W.; Newman, S.F.; Kim, J.; et al. Explainable machine-learning predictions for the prevention of hypoxaemia during surgery. *Nat. Biomed. Eng.* **2018**, *2*, 749–760. [CrossRef] [PubMed]
79. Lundberg, S.M.; Erion, G.; Chen, H.; DeGrave, A.; Prutkin, J.M.; Nair, B.; Katz, R.; Himmelfarb, J.; Bansal, N.; Lee, S.I. From local explanations to global understanding with explainable AI for trees. *Nat. Mach. Intell.* **2020**, *2*, 56–67. [CrossRef] [PubMed]
80. Lee, S.; McCann, D.; Messenger, J.C. *Working Time around the World: Trends in Working Hours, Laws, and Policies in a Global Comparative Perspective*; International Labour Office: Geneva, Switzerland, 2007.
81. Pedregosa, F.; Varoquaux, G.; Gramfort, A.; Michel, V.; Thirion, B.; Grisel, O.; Blondel, M.; Prettenhofer, P.; Weiss, R.; Dubourg, V.; et al. Scikit-learn: Machine learning in Python. *J. Mach. Learn. Res.* **2011**, *12*, 2825–2830.
82. Joseph, M. Pytorch tabular: A framework for deep learning with tabular data. *arXiv* **2021**, arXiv:2104.13638.
83. Department of Population and Employment Statistic National Bureau of Statistics; Department of Planning and Finance, Ministry of Human Resources and Social Security. *China Labor Statistical Yearbook*; China Statistics Press: Beijing, China, 2021.
84. Alarcón, D.M.; Cole, S. No sustainability for tourism without gender equality. *J. Sustain. Tour.* **2019**, *27*, 903–919. [CrossRef]
85. Seidel, D.; Thyrian, J.R. Burden of caring for people with dementia—Comparing family caregivers and professional caregivers. A descriptive study. *J. Multidiscip. Healthc.* **2019**, *12*, 655–663. [CrossRef]
86. Higgins, O.; Short, B.L.; Chalup, S.K.; Wilson, R.L. Artificial intelligence (AI) and machine learning (ML) based decision support systems in mental health: An integrative review. *Int. J. Ment. Health Nurs.* **2023**. [CrossRef]

 *mathematics*

Article

Detection of Anomalies in Natural Complicated Data Structures Based on a Hybrid Approach

Oksana Mandrikova, Bogdana Mandrikova * and Oleg Esikov

Institute of Cosmophysical Research and Radio Wave Propagation, Far Eastern Branch of the Russian Academy of Sciences, Mirnayast, 7, 684034 Paratunka, Russia; oksanam1@mail.ru (O.M.); esikov.oleg@mail.ru (O.E.)
* Correspondence: 555bs5@mail.ru; Tel.: +8-919-436-12-08

Abstract: A hybrid approach is proposed to detect anomalies in natural complicated data structures with high noise levels. The approach includes the application of an autoencoder neural network and singular spectrum analysis (SSA) with an adaptive anomaly detection algorithm (AADA) developed by the authors. The autoencoder is the quintessence of the representation learning algorithm, and it projects (selects) data features. Here, under-complete autoencoders are used. They are a product of the development of the principal component method and allow one to approximate complex nonlinear dependencies. Singular spectrum analysis decomposes data through the singular decomposition of matrix trajectories and makes it possible to detect the data structure in the noise. The AADA is based on the combination of wavelet transforms with threshold functions. Combinations of different constructions of wavelet transformation with threshold functions are widely applied to tasks relating to complex data processing. However, when the noise level is high and there is no complete knowledge of a useful signal, anomaly detection is not a trivial problem and requires a complex approach. This paper considers the use of adaptive threshold functions, the parameters of which are estimated on a probabilistic basis. Adaptive thresholds and a moving time window are introduced. The efficiency of the proposed method in detecting anomalies in neutron monitor data is illustrated. Neutron monitor data record cosmic ray intensities. We used neutron monitor data from ground stations. Anomalies in cosmic rays can create serious radiation hazards for people as well as for space and ground facilities. Thus, the diagnostics of anomalies in cosmic ray parameters is quite topical, and research is being carried out by teams from different countries. A comparison of the results for the autoencoder + AADA and SSA + AADA methods showed the higher efficiency of the autoencoder + AADA method. A more flexible NN apparatus provides better detection of short-period anomalies that have complicated structures. However, the combination of SSA and the AADA is efficient in the detection of long-term anomalies in cosmic rays that occur during strong magnetic storms. Thus, cosmic ray data analysis requires a more complex approach, including the use of the autoencoder and SSA with the AADA.

Keywords: data analysis; anomaly detection; neural networks; wavelet transform; cosmic rays; space weather

MSC: 62C12; 62L20; 68T05

Citation: Mandrikova, O.; Mandrikova, B.; Esikov, O. Detection of Anomalies in Natural Complicated Data Structures Based on a Hybrid Approach. *Mathematics* **2023**, *11*, 2464. https://doi.org/10.3390/math11112464

Academic Editors: Snezhana Gocheva-Ilieva, Atanas Ivanov and Hristina Kulina

Received: 10 April 2023
Revised: 12 May 2023
Accepted: 24 May 2023
Published: 26 May 2023

1. Introduction

In recent years, methods of data statistical modeling and analysis have been under intensive development in different spheres of human activity [1–3]. Forecasting and analysis methods aimed at the detection of anomalous natural phenomena are of special topicality in the field of environmental sciences [1–4]. The main problems in such tasks are the incomplete knowledge concerning useful signal structures, high noise levels, and the impossibility of suppressing noise completely. The requirements of high accuracy and real-time solutions make the method development more difficult. Strictly mathematical apparatuses are not effective enough, such that the application and development of heuristic approaches and methods are required.

Singular spectrum analysis (SSA) has been successfully applied in data analysis [5,6]. SSA allows for the investigation of data structures, the suppression of noise, and the detection of trends and periodicities [7–10]. For example, in [5], the authors used SSA together with support vector regression (LS-SVR) and a random forest (RF) to make precipitation forecasts. The investigations [5] showed that SSA-based data pre-processing made it possible to improve the performance of the LS-SVR and RF methods. The authors of [6] analyzed the compression of Earth geophysical data using SSA. Based on SSA, they succeeded in distinguishing six-month, twelve-month, and 10.6-year periods in the analyzed data. However, in cases where there is a complicated structure, linear approximation is not always effective, and the best results are obtained through the use of linear estimates [11]. The authors of [5] also noted this fact and plan to consider other ways of processing data, in particular, wavelet transformation.

Wavelets have a wide set of bases, making it possible to detect data that have complicated structures [11–15]. For example, algorithms of matching pursuit [14], such as using greedy algorithms, allow one to obtain quite accurate approximations, even in cases of incomplete data with relatively high levels of noise. In such cases, a signal is estimated by isolating coherent structures [11]. However, matching pursuit algorithms have very high computational complexity. If the energy of the signal is small relative to the energy of the noise, such estimates have very low thresholds [11], and the application of these algorithms does not allow one to obtain good results, as has been confirmed in investigations [16]. However, the flexibility of wavelet constructions makes it possible to combine these algorithms with different methods and adapt them to processed data. Complex hybrid approaches can be developed for complex data analysis using wavelet transforms. In [17], an F-filter [18] was applied together with wavelet transformation to detect low-amplitude periodicities. This allowed for the estimation of process changeability and the detection of hidden regularities in data within an interval under analysis.

In recent years, to approximate and analyze complex data, traditional statistical methods and modern heuristic tools, including elements of artificial intelligence and machine learning, have been combined more often [4,5,16,19]. Such combinations make it possible to improve the quality of data analysis procedures. Their efficiency is provided via the numerical realization of these methods. In this paper, we suggest a hybrid approach based on the combination of the developed adaptive anomaly detection algorithm (AADA) with an autoencoder neural network. It is known that if representative sampling is available, neural networks allow one to obtain approximations of acceptable accuracy when dealing with complex data. In this paper, we apply under-complete autoencoders, which have determinate bases (as a result of the development of the principal component method) that make it possible to approximate complex nonlinear dependencies. They have high adaptive capability and can significantly reduce noise levels [19]. The autoencoder is used in the paper to determine the characteristics of the data structures and to reduce noise. The further application of the AADA provides effective anomaly detection.

The AADA is based on the combination of wavelet transforms with threshold functions. In the AADA, we apply adaptive thresholds, which are estimated in a moving window based on the probabilistic approach. This algorithm is similar to the method described in [17]. It allows for the detection of the nonstationary features of different time–frequency structures.

The efficiency of the suggested approach is illustrated in the use of data taken from neutron monitors, which record cosmic ray (CR) intensity variations. Anomalies in cosmic rays can create hazards for people and space and ground facilities. Thus, the diagnostics of anomalies in cosmic ray parameters is very topical, and research is being carried out by teams from different countries [1–4].

Anomalies in CRs can have the form of sudden short-term increases relative to a characteristic level. Such features often occur before magnetic storms and are used as their predictors [20,21]. During strong magnetospheric storms, anomalies in CR data have a trend form with significant decreases (Forbush decreases [22]). Such anomalies may last for several days. In the background of significant anomalous decreases, short-term sudden peak-like changes, which have complex non-stationary spectra, can be observed. They indicate strong disturbances in the near-Earth space.

The complexity of CR data structures means that the application of classical methods and approaches is ineffective. For example, the application of the principal component method was attempted in [23] to investigate the combined effect of the solar activity level and the inclination of the neutral surface of the interplanetary magnetic field to galactic cosmic ray modulation in the heliosphere. The authors [23] obtained results that confirm theoretical conceptions and drift motions of cosmic rays in the heliosphere. However, the obtained results were not confirmed with the present theory due to the variation complexity of CRs. One of the most successful methods in this field is the station ring method [24]. This method is the most effective when data from high-latitude neutron monitors are used [24]. However, the conditions required for the implementation of the method cannot always be fulfilled due to the random distribution of stations over the globe and the significant impact of natural and man-made noises on the measurement results. It is also difficult to quantify the station ring method and, as a consequence, realize it numerically and estimate its accuracy.

Machine learning methods are also being developed to analyze CRs. For example, the authors of [25] suggest using graph neural networks to investigate the energy spectrum and content of CRs. This approach allows one to reduce time and computational efforts. However, at present, CR data analysis using this method is limited due to the configuration peculiarities of the applied detector [25]. In [26], a hybrid approach was proposed to filter artifacts in experiments focusing on the detection of cosmic rays. The authors [26] applied convolutional neural networks together with adaptive thresholds and Daubechies wavelets to reduce the number of false artifacts. The developed solution [26] made it possible to fully automate the analysis procedure. However, the constructed classifiers are limited in terms of annotator accuracy when recognizing if a hit is a signal or an artifact [26].

Due to the reasons mentioned above, the problem of CR data analysis and anomaly detection is topical and requires the application of a complex of methods and tools. This work continues these investigations [16,19]. The adaptive technique used for the estimation of thresholds in a wavelet space was described in detail in [16]. The authors of [19] showed the efficiency of the combination of wavelet transforms with the autoencoder network. In that paper, the approach was developed, and its efficiency for the near-real-time detection of CR complex-spectrum short-term anomalies, which precede magnetic storm commencement, was confirmed. The proposed method is also compared with the combination of SSA and the AADA. The application of SSA made it possible to detect a CR variation component that has a strong correlation with the geomagnetic activity Dst index [27]. These results confirm the theory [18] and show the importance of taking CRs into account in space weather forecasts.

2. Description of the Applied Methods

2.1. Singular Spectrum Analysis

Based on singular spectrum analysis, the initial time series of F is transformed into a matrix followed by singular decomposition, grouping, and transition to time series components [8]. The algorithm used for the implementation of the method was suggested in [8] and is described below.

1. Transformation of tshe initial one-dimensional series F into a trajectory matrix,

$$X = [X_1, \ldots, X_K] = \begin{bmatrix} f_1 & \cdots & f_K \\ \cdots & \cdots & \cdots \\ f_L & \cdots & f_N \end{bmatrix},$$

where f_i is the initial series element, L is the window length, and N is the initial series length.

2. Singular decomposition of the obtained trajectory matrix X.

Assume that $S = XX^T$, $\lambda_1, \ldots, \lambda_L$ are eigenvalues of S, taken in nonascending order ($\lambda_1 \geq \ldots \geq \lambda_L \geq 0$), and $U_1, \ldots, U_L$ is the orthonormalized system of eigenvectors of the matrix S.

Assume that $d = \text{rank } X = max\{i : \lambda_i > 0\}$ (as a rule, in reality $d = L$) and $V_i = X^T U_i / \lambda_i (i = 1, \ldots, d)$. In these notations, singular decomposition of the trajectory matrix X can be written as follows:

$$X = X_1 + \ldots + X_d,$$

where the matrixes $X_i = \sqrt{\lambda_i} U_i V_i^T$ have the rank of 1 and are called elementary matrixes, $\sqrt{\lambda_i}$ are the singular numbers, which make up the singular spectrum and are the measure of data dispersion. U_i is the left singular vector of the trajectory matrix X, and V_i is the right singular vector of the trajectory matrix X.

Thus, the trajectory matrix X can be represented in the following form:

$$X = \sum_i \sqrt{\lambda_i} U_i V_i^T.$$

3. The grouping of the set d of elementary matrixes from item 2 on m non-intersecting subsets X_{I_i}, $I_i \in \{I_1, \ldots, I_m\}$. Assume that $I_i = \{i_1, \ldots, i_p\}$, then the resulting matrix X_{I_i}, corresponding to group I_i, is determined as $X_{I_i} = X_{i_1} + \ldots + X_{i_p}$.

Thus, the grouped singular decomposition of the trajectory matrix X can be represented as follows:

$$X = X_{I_1} + \ldots + X_{I_m}.$$

4. Matrixes X_{I_i} of the grouped decomposition are Hankelized (are averaged over anti-diagonals). Using the correspondence between the Hankel matrixes and the time series, the recovered series $\widetilde{F}^{(k)} = \left(\widetilde{f}_1^{(k)}, \ldots, \widetilde{f}_N^{(k)} \right)$ are obtained. The initial series $F = (f_1, \ldots, f_N)$ is decomposed into a sum m of the recovered series, where each value of the initial series is equal to

$$f_i = \sum_{k=1}^{m} \widetilde{f}_i^{(k)}, i = 1, 2, \ldots, N.$$

This decomposition is the main result of the SSA algorithm for time series analysis. This decomposition is meaningful if each of its components can be interpreted as either a trend, oscillation (periodicals), or noise.

2.2. Autoencoder Neural Network

The autoencoder is a feed-forward network trained without a teacher but by using the back-propagation method [28]. In the paper, we applied a two-layer autoencoder, where the initial one-dimensional series of F was transformed according to the formula [28]

$$\widetilde{F} = h^{(2)} \left(V^{(2)} (h^{(1)} \left(V^{(1)} F + b^{(1)} \right)) + b^{(2)} \right),$$

where the superscript is (1), (2) is the layer number, $h^{(1)} \in \mathbb{R}^{d \times 1}$ is the non-linear activation function, $V^{(1)} \in \mathbb{R}^{d \times N}$ is the waight matrix, $F \in \mathbb{R}^{N \times 1}$ is the input vector, N is the dimension of the input vector, $b^{(1)} \in \mathbb{R}^{d \times 1}$ is the displacement vector, $h^{(2)} \in \mathbb{R}^{N \times 1}$ is the linear activation function, $V^{(2)} \in \mathbb{R}^{N \times d}$ is the weight matrix, a $b^{(2)} \in \mathbb{R}^{N \times 1}$ is the displacement vector, and $\mathbb{R}$ are real numbers.

If we set the dimension of the network hidden layer to be smaller than the dimension of the input layer and use only linear activation functions, the network will realize the principal component method [28]. When increasing the number of hidden layers and introducing nonlinear activation functions, the network can approximate complex nonlinear relations in data.

The network architecture is illustrated in Figure 1.

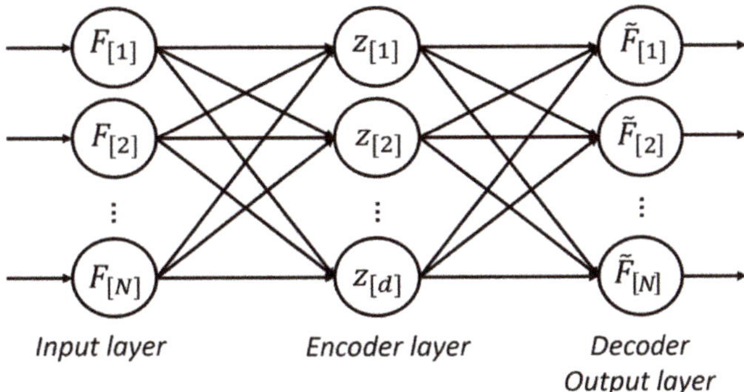

Figure 1. Architecture of the autoencoder NN.

In order to suppress noise, the dimension of the hidden layer architecture was set to be smaller than that of the output layer, $(d < N)$.

2.3. Adaptive Anomaly Detection Algorithm

We proposed the AADA for the first time in [19]. The algorithm includes the following operations:

1. Discrete time series $F[n]$ is represented in the form of the series [29,30]

$$F[n] = \sum_{j=0}^{J} \sum_{k=1}^{K} WF\left(\frac{1}{2^j}, \frac{k}{2^j}\right) \Psi_{jk}[n],$$

where $\Psi_{jk} = 2^{\frac{j}{2}} \Psi(2^j n - k)$ are the basic wavelets, $j, k \in N$, $WF\left(\frac{1}{2^j}, \frac{k}{2^j}\right) = \langle F, \Psi_{jk} \rangle$ are the coefficients of function F decomposition into a series, J is the largest scale of decomposition into a wavelet series, and K is the series length.

2. A threshold function is applied to wavelet coefficients of the time series $F[n]$ decomposition,

$$P_{T_j^l}\left[WF\left(\frac{1}{2^j}, \frac{k}{2^j}\right)\right] = \begin{cases} WF\left(\frac{1}{2^j}, \frac{k}{2^j}\right), & if \left|WF\left(\frac{1}{2^j}, \frac{k}{2^j}\right)\right| \geq T_j^l, \\ 0, & if \left|WF\left(\frac{1}{2^j}, \frac{k}{2^j}\right)\right| < T_j^l, \end{cases}$$

where $T_j^l = t_{1-\frac{\alpha}{2}, l-1} \hat{\sigma}_j^l$, $t_{\alpha, N}$ are α-quantiles of Student's distribution [31], $\hat{\sigma}_j^l$ is the coefficient root-mean-square deviation estimated in a moving window of the length l,

$$\hat{\sigma}_j^l = \sqrt{\frac{1}{l-1} \sum_{m=1}^{l} \left(WF\left(\frac{1}{2^j}, \frac{k}{2^j}\right) - \overline{WF}\left(\frac{1}{2^j}, \frac{k}{2^j}\right)\right)^2}.$$

We obtain a representation of the series,

$$\hat{F}[n] = \sum_{j=0}^{J} \sum_{k=1}^{K} P_{T_j^l}\left[WF\left(\frac{1}{2^j}, \frac{k}{2^j}\right)\right] \Psi_{jk}[n].$$

3. For the detected anomalies, their intensities at the time instant $t = k$ can be estimated as follows:

$$E_k = \sum_{j=0}^{J} P_{T_j^l}\left[WF\left(\frac{1}{2^j}, \frac{k}{2^j}\right)\right],$$

which are positive in cases of function values anomalous increases and negative in cases of function values anomalous decreases.

2.4. Scheme of Method Realization

The proposed approach can be represented in the form of the scheme illustrated in Figure 2. The presence or absence of an anomaly in data is determined by the decision rule,

«There is an anomaly in data if $\varepsilon_k^{NN} > \Pi$ or $\varepsilon_k^{SSA} > \Pi$»,

where $\varepsilon_k^{NN} = \sum_{i=i-l}^{i+l} E_k^{NN}$, $\varepsilon_k^{SSA} = \sum_{i=i-l}^{i+l} E_k^{SSA}$ are summary error vectors estimated in a moving time window of the length l (in the paper, $l = 5$), E_k^{SSA} is the result of the application of SSA with the $AADA$ (scheme), E_k^{NN} is the result of the application of the autoencoder NN with the $AADA$ (scheme), and Π is the threshold value calculated empirically (based on posterior risk) separately for each station, taking into account the anisotropy of CRs and the characteristics of the recording instrumentation.

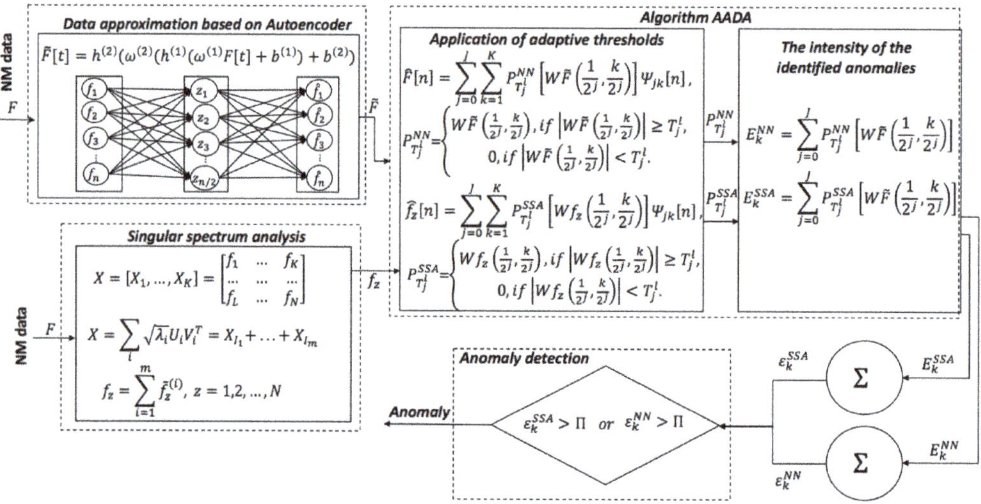

Figure 2. Scheme of method realization.

3. Data Processing Results

In the experiments, we used the minute data taken from the neutron monitor of a high-latitudinal station, Oulu [32] (www.nmdb.eu). Neutron monitor (NM) data reflect cosmic ray intensities (particle counts per minute (cpm)). Particle fluxes recorded by ground NM can be of galactic, solar, and Earth origin. Thus, based on ground NM, solar activity and the Earth's seismic activity are investigated [33]. Neutron monitor data contain regular time variations, anomalous features, and natural and man-made noises [34]. Regular variations contain periodical variations, such as diurnal, 27-day, 11-year, and 22-year solar cycles. Anomalous features have different structures (Forbuch effects of different intensities and durations [22] and strong sudden ground proton increases (GLE-events)) occur in the data during disturbances in the near-Earth space. NM data structures at different stations differ due to anisotropy properties [24]. Weather conditions near a recording device (rain, snow, hail, wind, etc.) and instrumentation errors caused by readjustments also have a significant impact on NM data.

In the experiments, we applied a standard two-layer autoencoder architecture [28] (Figure 1). When constructing NN training sets, the data were selected on the basis of space weather factor analysis. The NN input vector dimension was $N = 1440$ counts, which corresponds to a day (minute data). The NN hidden layer dimension was determined empirically and was taken to be $d = N/2$. To check the adequacy of the constructed NN, the Q-criterion was used [31]. The process of constructing the autoencoder network was described in detail for the problem of anomaly detection in CR data in [19].

Taking into account the diurnal variations, a window length of $L = 1440$ counts (corresponds to a day) was used in the SSA method. Figure 3 illustrates the NM data over four different time intervals and the corresponding seven first components obtained on the basis of SSA (item 2 of the SSA algorithm). An analysis of Figure 3 shows that the initial NM data have a nonstationary structure and contain high noise levels. The detected components include a trend, periodical components, local features, and noise variations (Figure 3).

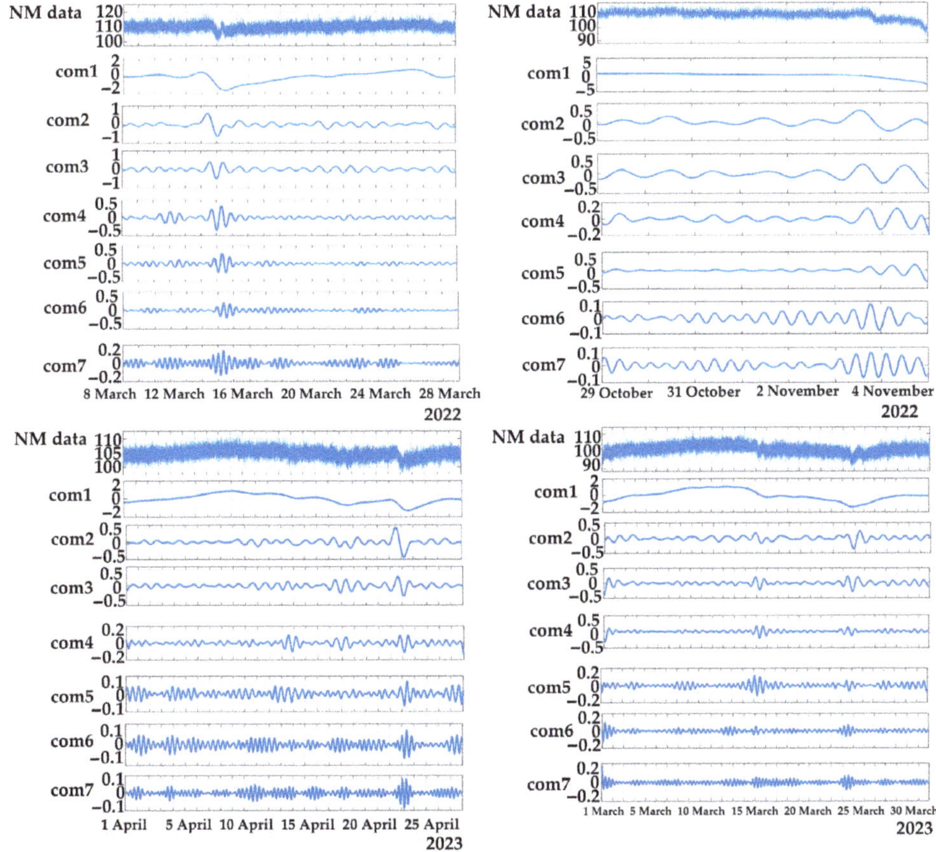

Figure 3. NM data from Oulu station and the corresponding seven first components.

The matrixes grouping in the SSA algorithm (item 3 of the algorithm) was carried out by taking into account the eigenvalues (item 2 of the algorithm) and was based on the estimates of the confined dispersion fraction [28]. The graph of the first 30 eigenvalues is illustrated in Figure 4. The dashed line in Figure 4 separates the eigenvalues, which correspond to the components used in the analysis. The confined dispersion fraction was estimated using the following formula:

$$\frac{\sigma_1^2 + \sigma_2^2 \ldots + \sigma_p^2}{\sigma_1^2 + \sigma_2^2 \ldots + \sigma_p^2 + \ldots + \sigma_d^2}.$$

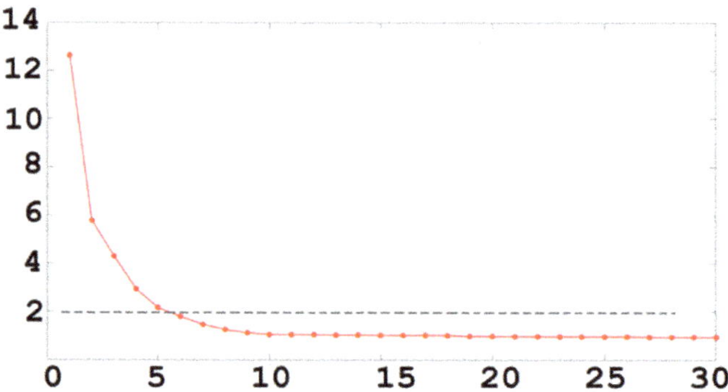

Figure 4. Graph of eigenvalues of the SSA method first 30 components.

The results of the confined dispersion fraction estimates are shown in Tables 1–4. An analysis of Tables 1–4 indicates that the first three components determine the greater fraction of the confined dispersion. The component with the 1st eigenvalue determines the trend, and the components with the 2nd and 3rd eigenvalues include diurnal periodicities in the CR data. The results obtained after the summation of these components are presented below.

Table 1. March 2023.

Component	Confined Dispersion Fraction
com1	0.8942
com1 + com2	0.9288
com1 + com2 + com3	0.9501
com1 + com2 + com3 + com4	0.9607
com1 + com2 + com3 + com4 + com5	0.9655
com1 + com2 + com3 + com4 + com5 + com6	0.9681
com1 + com2 + com3 + com4 + com5 + com6 + com7	0.9703

Table 2. April 2023.

Component	Confined Dispersion Fraction
com1	0.8262
com1 + com2	0.8934
com1 + com2 + com3	0.9247
com1 + com2 + com3 + com4	0.9353
com1 + com2 + com3 + com4 + com5	0.9395
com1 + com2 + com3 + com4 + com5 + com6	0.9427
com1 + com2 + com3 + com4 + com5 + com6 + com7	0.9458

Table 3. 27 October–4 November.

Component	Confined Dispersion Fraction
com1	0.7508
com1 + com2	0.8490
com1 + com2 + com3	0.9074
com1 + com2 + com3 + com4	0.9291
com1 + com2 + com3 + com4 + com5	0.9395
com1 + com2 + com3 + com4 + com5 + com6	0.9470
com1 + com2 + com3 + com4 + com5 + com6 + com7	0.9526

Table 4. March 2022.

Component	Confined Dispersion Fraction
com1	0.6269
com1 + com2	0.7581
com1 + com2 + com3	0.8307
com1 + com2 + com3 + com4	0.8649
com1 + com2 + com3 + com4 + com5	0.8835
com1 + com2 + com3 + com4 + com5 + com6	0.8964
com1 + com2 + com3 + com4 + com5 + com6 + com7	0.9049

In the SSA method, taking into account the presence of diurnal variations, a window length of $L = 1440$ counts was used (corresponding to a day). The components were grouped, taking the eigenvalues into account. The plot of the eigenvalues for the first 30 components is shown in Figure 3. The dotted line in Figure 3 separates the eigenvalues, and these components were used in the analysis. The remaining components were taken as noise. Below are the results obtained by adding the components, corresponding to the 1st, 2nd, and 3rd eigenvalues. The component with the 1st eigenvalue determines the trend, and the components with the 2nd and 3rd eigenvalues include daily periodicities of the CR data.

Results of the Estimates of the Confined Dispersion Fraction

Figure 5 shows the results of the experiments during a strong magnetic storm, which occurred on 4 November 2022. To analyze the near-Earth space state, Figure 5a,b illustrates the data concerning the interplanetary magnetic field (IMF) Bz [35] component and geomagnetic activity Dst index [36], respectively.

Based on space weather data [35], the near-Earth space was calm on 29 October. From 30 October to 1 November, inhomogeneous accelerated fluxes from a coronal whole and a coronal mass ejections were recorded [35]. The disturbances in the near-Earth space were indicated by the increase in Bz fluctuation amplitude in the negative domain (decrease to Bz = −12 nT) (Figure 5a). The Dst index decrease on 1 November up to −36 nT (Figure 5a) denoted the anomalous increase in geomagnetic activity. According to the processed data (Figure 5d,e,g,h), low-intensity anomalies in the CR data were observed during that period. The results of the combinations of the autoencoder and SSA with the AADA are identical that confirms their reliability. The results also show the efficiency of both approaches in detecting low-intensity anomalies in the CR data.

According to the data [35], inhomogeneous accelerated fluxes from a coronal mass ejection were recorded on 3 and 4 November. They caused a strong magnetic storm occurrence at the end of the day on 3 November (at 20:00 UT). The strongest disturbances were observed on 4 November. The Dst index decreased to −105 nT (Figure 5b). The processing results (Figure 5d,e,g,h) show an anomalous increase in CR intensity before the storm and a significant decrease (Forbush decrease in high amplitude) during the strongest geomagnetic disturbances on 4 November. A comparison of the results of the different approaches (Figure 5d,e,g,h) illustrates the high efficiency of the autoencoder with the AADA (Figure 5g,h). The method allowed for the detection of the CR intensity anomalous increases, which occurred before the magnetic storm. The anomaly reached its maximum intensity on 3 November, 8 h before the storm. The results of the SSA and AADA combination (Figure 5d,e) also show positive anomaly occurrence during that period. However, due to the complicated nonlinear structure of the anomaly, the application of SSA turned out to be less effective. The result also points to the importance of taking into account the CR parameters for space weather forecasts.

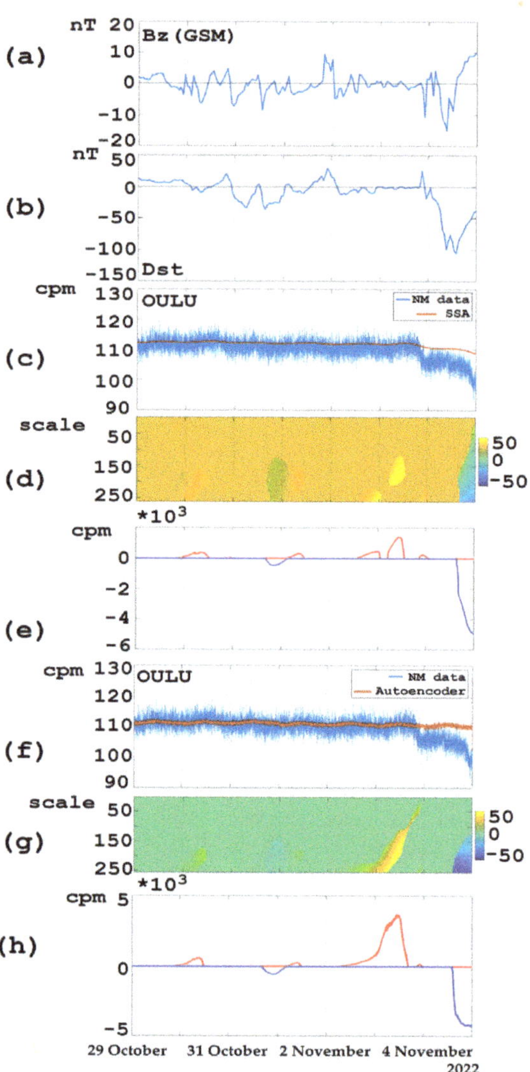

Figure 5. (**a**) Bz (GSM) data, (**b**) Dst index data, (**c**) NM data are shown in blue, their approximation by SSA is in orange, (**d**,**e**) are the result of the AADA algorithm application to the NM signal approximated by SSA, (**f**) NM data are shown in blue, their approximation by the autoencoder is in orange, (**g**,**h**) are the result of the AADA application to the NM signal approximated by the autoencoder.

Figure 6 shows the results of the application of the SSA + AADA method during a strong magnetic storm, which occurred on 23 March 2023. To analyze the near-Earth space state, Figure 6a,b illustrates the interplanetary magnetic field (MMF) Bz [35] component data and geomagnetic activity Dst index data [36], respectively.

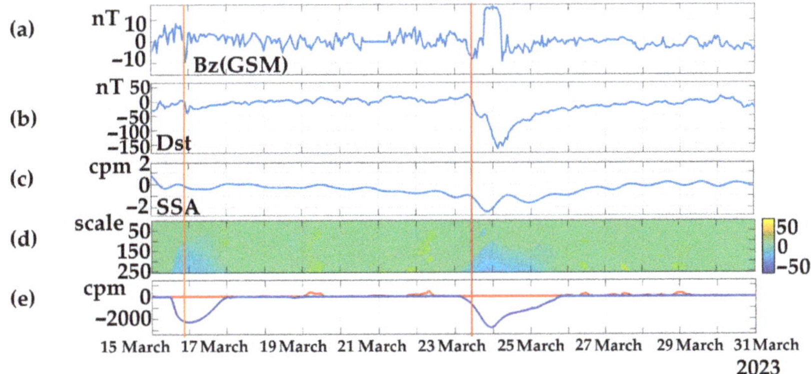

Figure 6. (**a**) Bz (GSM) data, (**b**) Dst index data, (**c**) NM data approximation by the SSA method, (**d,e**) are the result of the AADA algorithm application to the NM signal approximated by SSA.

Based on space weather data [35], an inhomogeneous flux from a coronal whole and a coronal mass ejection arrived on the first half of the day on 15 March. IMF Bz fluctuations increased and reached Bz = −17 nT in the negative domain (Figure 6a). At 20:00 UTC at the end of the day on 15 March, a geomagnetic disturbance was recorded [35]. The Dst index decreased to −38 nT at that time (Figure 6b). The near-Earth space state on 15 March was characterized as being weakly disturbed. The processing results (Figure 6d,e) show an anomalous decrease in CR intensity (Forbush decrease) several hours before the geomagnetic disturbance on 15 March. The anomaly reached its maximum intensity at 12:00 UTC on 16 March.

Further, an inhomogeneous accelerated flux from a coronal mass ejection arrived at 04:00 UTC on 23 March [35]. The GSM fluctuations were intensified (Figure 6a). At 11:00 UTC on 23 March, the geomagnetic storm commencement was recorded [35]. The Dst index value on 24 March decreased to Dst = −162 (Figure 6b). The processing results (Figure 6d,e) show an anomalous decrease in CR intensity (high-amplitude Forbush decrease) several hours before the geomagnetic storm on 23 March. The anomaly reached its maximum intensity at 14:00 UTC on 23 March.

Thus, the SSA + AADA method allowed for the detection of CR intensity anomalous decreases, which occurred several hours before the geomagnetic disturbances. The result also indicates the importance of taking into account the CR parameters for space weather forecasts.

Figure 7 shows the results of the experiments for the period 2–4 March 2023. According to space weather data [35], an inhomogeneous accelerated flux from a coronal whole and a coronal mass ejection arrived at 18:00 UTC on 2 March. At 23:00 UTC on 2 March, an anomalous increase in geomagnetic activity occurred (the Dst index decreased to −39 nT, Figure 7b). Based on the data [35], the magnetic storm commencement (marked by an orange vertical line) was recorded at 18:00 UTC on 2 March. The near-ground space state on 3 March was characterized as being unstable. A comparison of the results of the different methods (Figure 7d,e,g,h) shows the high efficiency of the autoencoder with the AADA combination (Figure 7g,h). The method allowed for the detection of the CR intensity anomalous increases, which occurred at the time of the geomagnetic disturbance commencement. The result of the SSA with the AADA combination (Figure 7d,e) turned out to be ineffective due to the complicated structure of the anomaly and the smoothing effect of the SSA method. The possibility of detecting low-amplitude anomalies through the use of an autoencoder with the AADA combination was studied in detail in [19]. Estimates showed the high sensitivity of that approach for short-period anomalies.

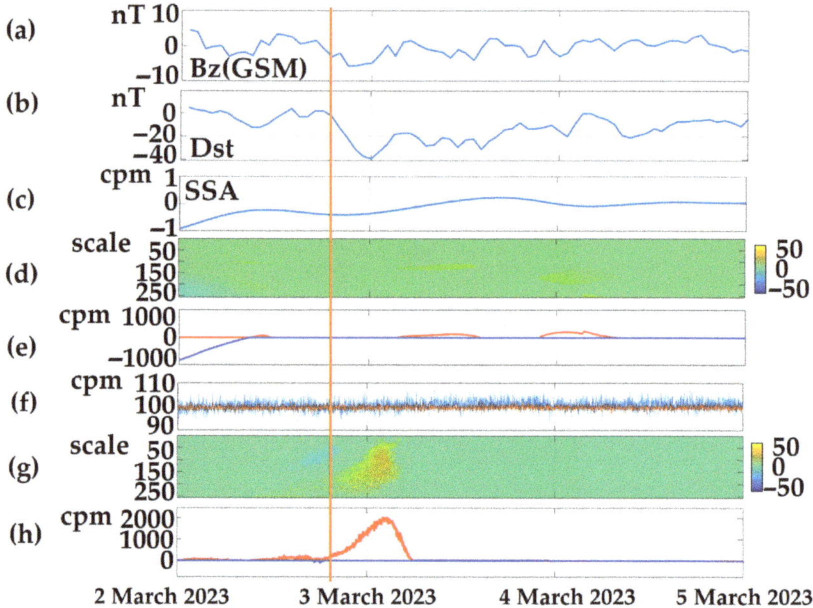

Figure 7. (**a**) Bz (GSM) data, (**b**) Dst index data, (**c**) approximation of the NM data by the SSA method, (**d**,**e**) are the result of the AADA algorithm applied to the NM signal approximated by SSA, (**f**) the NM data are shown in blue, their approximation by the autoencoder is in orange; (**g**,**h**) are the result of the AADA algorithm application to the NM signal approximated by the autoencoder.

Figure 8 shows the results of the data processing for the period from 8 March 2022 to 28 March 2022 [32]. Figure 8a,b illustrates the IMF Bz component data and geomagnetic activity Dst index data, respectively. The orange vertical lines show the times of the geomagnetic disturbances. A red vertical line marks the moderate magnetic storm's commencement.

According to space weather data [35], Bz component fluctuations increased and reached Bz = −10 nT (Figure 8a) on 11 March. The processing results (Figure 8d,e,g,h) show anomalous changes in the CR data during that period. At 23:00 UT at the end of the day on March 11, a weak magnetic storm was recorded [35]. During the storm on 12 March, the Dst index decreased to −51nT (Figure 8b). Based on the processed data (Figure 8d,e,g,h), an anomalous increase in CR intensity occurred during that period. It was clearly detected using the method based on the autoencoder and AADA combination. The next day, at 10:48 on 13 March, a moderate magnetic storm was recorded (minimum Dst = −85) [36]. According to the processed data (Figure 8d,e,g,h), the anomalous decrease in CR intensity (high-amplitude Forbush decrease) began at the time of the magnetic storm.

At the end of the period under analysis on 27 March, an inhomogeneous accelerated flux from a coronal whole and a coronal mass ejection arrived [35]. Bz component fluctuation amplitude increased (Bz = −11 nT, Figure 8a). Based on the data [35], an anomalous increase in geomagnetic activity was recorded at 06:00 UT on 27 March. According to the processed data (Figure 8d,e,g,h), an anomalous decrease in CR intensity (low-amplitude Forbush decrease) occurred 6 h before the geomagnetic disturbance.

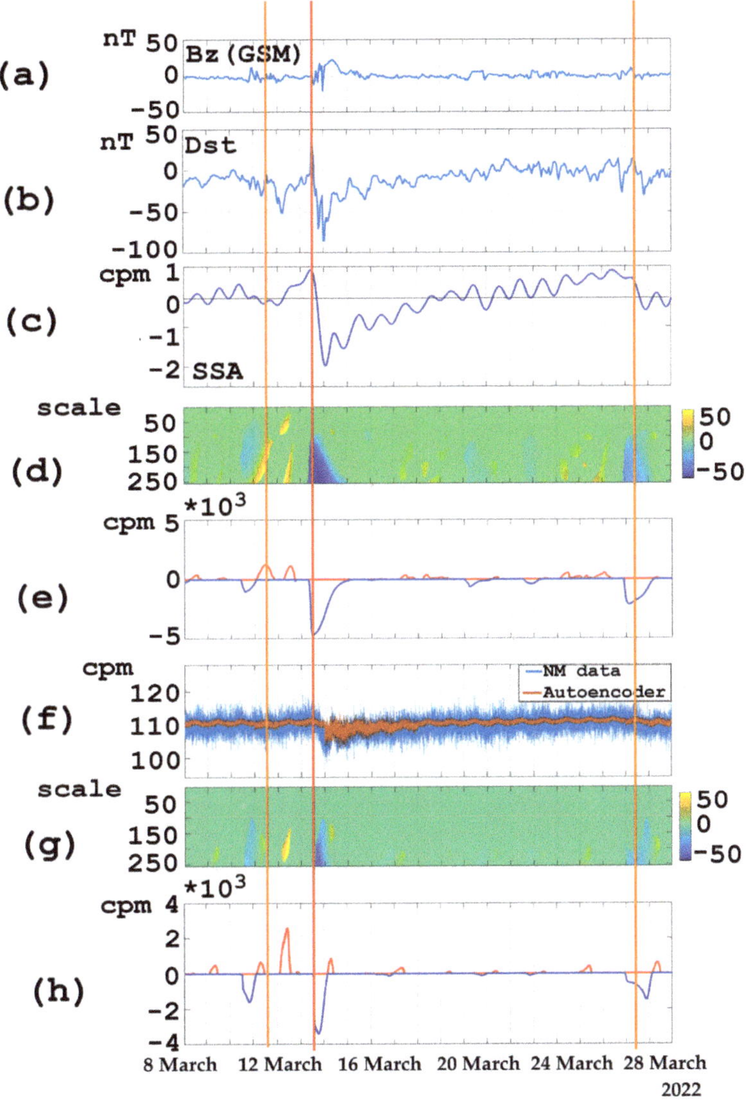

Figure 8. (**a**) Bz (GSM) data, (**b**) Dst index data, (**c**) the NM data approximation by SSA, (**d**,**e**) are the result of the AADA algorithm application to the NM signal approximated by SSA, (**f**) the NM data are shown in blue, their approximation by the autoncoder is in orange, (**g**,**h**) are the result of the AADA algorithm application to the NM signal approximated by the autoencoder.

We should note that the CR variation component, detected using SSA (Figure 8c), has a strong correlation with geomagnetic activity Dst index (Figure 8b) during the period under analysis. This correlation is the most clearly traced during the period that preceded and accompanied the moderate magnetic storm from 8 March 2022 to 23 March 2022. This result is of high applied significance and confirms the importance of taking into account the CR parameters for space weather forecasts. The result also shows the capability of SSA to suppress noises and detect CR variation components.

The results of the estimates of the suggested approach efficiency are presented in Tables 5–7. Table 5 shows the results of the autoencoder + AADA method when different time window dimensions l (item 2 of Section 2.3) were used. Table 6 illustrates the results of this method when different wavelet functions were used. It follows from Tables 5 and 6 that the best result was obtained for the time window $l = 1440$ and Coiflet 2 wavelet function. The efficiency was ~87%. Table 7 presents the results of the SSA + AADA method. The percentage of anomaly detection by this method was ~84%.

Table 5. Estimate of the autoencoder + AADA method efficiency for different time window dimensions.

Period	Number of Geomagnetic Disturbances and Geomagnetic Storms	Wavelet Function	Moving Time Window Dimension	Result
2013–2015, 2019–2020	405	Coiflet 2	$l = 720$	Detected: 64% Undetected: 36% False alarm: 32 events
			$l = 1080$	Detected: 78% Undetected: 22% False alarm: 27 events
			$l = 1440$	Detected: 87% Undetected: 13% False alarm: 27 events

Table 6. Estimate of the autoencoder + AADA method efficiency using different wavelet functions.

Period	Number of Geomagnetic Disturbances and Geomagnetic Storms	Moving Time Window Dimension	Wavelet Function	Results
2013–2015, 2019–2020	405	$l = 1440$	Coiflet 1	Detected: 87% Undetected: 13% False alarm: 29 events
			Coiflet 2	Detected: 87% Undetected: 13% False alarm: 27 events
			Coiflet 3	Detected: 85% Undetected: 15% False alarm: 28 events
			Daubechies 1	Detected: 84% Undetected: 16% False alarm: 29 events
			Daubechies 2	Detected: 86% Undetected: 14% False alarm: 29 events

Table 7. Estimate of the SSA + AADA method efficiency (Coiflet 2 was used, time window length $l = 1440$).

Period	Number of Geomagnetic Disturbances and Geomagnetic Storms	Results of SSA + AADA
2013–2015, 2019–2020	405	Detected: 84% Undetected: 16% False alarm: 35 events

Thus, based on the estimate results (Tables 5–7), the efficiency of the autoencoder + AADA method is higher than that of the SSA + AADA method. However, as shown above (Figure 6), the SSA + AADA method effectively detects the periods of long anomalous changes (from a day and longer) in CRs. Such anomalies are often observed during strong magnetic storms. The application of a more flexible NN apparatus enables the better detection of short-period anomalies (Figures 5, 7 and 8). Thus, a more complex approach is required to improve anomaly detection efficiency. A scheme of such an approach, including the use of SSA and the autoencoder with the AADA, is illustrated in Figure 2.

4. Conclusions

The work results confirmed the efficiency of the autoencoder and AADA combination in the analysis of CR data and the detection of anomalies. The complicated structure of CR data and high noise levels require the application of a complex of methods. The autoencoder makes it possible to approximate CR data time variations and suppress noise. The AADA can detect anomalies that have complicated structures and allows one to estimate their parameters. The algorithm's adaptive capability and high detecting efficiency of wavelets lead to the possibility of detecting anomalies of different amplitude and duration in the presence of noise and the absence of priori data.

The comparison of the results of the autoencoder and SSA with the AADA combinations showed the higher efficiency of the autoencoder and AADA method. The anomaly detection by the method, based on the SSA and AADA combination, was ~84%. The anomaly detection when using this method, based on the autoencoder and AADA combination, was ~87%. Due to the complicatesd nonlinear structure of CR data, their approximation by the autoencoder provides high accuracy. However, the detailed analysis showed that the SSA and AADA method combination is effective when detecting CR long-term anomalies characteristic of strong magnetic storms. The application of a more flexible NN apparatus enables the better detection of short-period anomalies preceding magnetic storm commencement. The application of SSA turned out to be effective in detecting CR variation components when analyzing process dynamics. Thus, in order to improve the quality of CR data analysis, a more complex approach, including the use of SSA and the autoencoder with the AADA, is required.

The work results are of applied significance and confirm the importance of taking into account CR parameters for space weather forecasts. The strong correlation of CR variations with geomagnetic activity Dst index confirmed the theory [2] regarding the possibility of predicting magnetic storms based on CR flux data.

Author Contributions: Conceptualization, O.M.; methodology, O.M. and B.M.; software, B.M. and O.E.; validation, B.M. and O.E.; formal analysis, O.M. and B.M.; writing—review and editing, O.M., B.M. and O.E.; project administration, O.M. All authors have read and agreed to the published version of the manuscript.

Funding: The work was carried out according to the Subject AAAA-A21-121011290003-0 "Physical processes in the system of near space and geospheres under solar and lithospheric influences" IKIR FEB RAS.

Data Availability Statement: Not applicable.

Acknowledgments: The authors are grateful to the institutes that support the neutron monitor stations (http://www01.nmdb.eu/, http://spaceweather.izmiran.ru/) (accessed on 1 March 2022), the data of which were used in the work.

Conflicts of Interest: The authors declare no conflict of interest.

References

1. Kuznetsov, V.D. Space weather and risks of space activity. *Space Tech. Technol.* **2014**, *3*, 3–13.
2. Badruddin, B.; Aslam, O.P.M.; Derouich, M.; Asiri, H.; Kudela, K. Forbush decreases and geomagnetic storms during a highly disturbed solar and interplanetary period, 4–10 September 2017. *Space Weather* **2019**, *17*, 487. [CrossRef]
3. Gocheva-Ilieva, S.; Ivanov, A.; Kulina, H.; Stoimenova-Minova, M. Multi-Step Ahead Ex-Ante Forecasting of Air Pollutants Using Machine Learning. *Mathematics* **2023**, *11*, 1566. [CrossRef]
4. Dorman, L.I. Space weather and dangerous phenomena on the earth: Principles of great geomagnetic storms forcasting by online cosmic ray data. *Ann. Geophys.* **2005**, *23*, 2997–3002. [CrossRef]

5.   Bojang, P.O.; Yang, T.-C.; Pham, Q.B.; Yu, P.-S. Linking Singular Spectrum Analysis and Machine Learning for Monthly Rainfall Forecasting. *Appl. Sci.* **2020**, *10*, 3224. [CrossRef]

6.   Yu, H.; Chen, Q.; Sun, Y.; Sosnica, K. Geophysical Signal Detection in the Earth's Oblateness Variation and Its Climate-Driven Source Analysis. *Remote Sens.* **2021**, *13*, 2004. [CrossRef]

7.   Belonin, M.D.; Tatarinov, I.V.; Kalinin, O.M. *Factor Analysis in Petroleum Geology*; VIEMS: Kaluga, Russia, 1971; p. 56.

8.   Danilov, D.L.; Zhiglyavsky, A.A. *Principal Components of Time Series: The Caterpillar Method*; Presskom: St. Petersburg, Russia, 1997; p. 308.

9.   Broomhead, D.S.; King, G.P. Extracting qualitative dynamics from experimental data. *Phys. Nonlinear Phenom.* **1986**, *20*, 217–236. [CrossRef]

10. Colebrook, J.M. Continuous plankton records—Zooplankton and environment, northeast Atlanticand North Sea. *Oceanol. Acta* **1978**, *1*, 9–23.

11. Mallat, S.G. *A Wavelet Tour of Signal Processing*; Academic Press: San Diego, CA, USA, 1999.

12. Herley, C.; Kovacevic, J.; Ramchandran, K.; Vetterli, M. Tilings of the time-frequency plane: Construction of arbitrary orthogonal bases and feist tiling algorithms. *IEEE Trans. Signal Proc.* **1993**, *41*, 3341–3359. [CrossRef]

13. Chen, S.; Donoho, D. *Atomic Decomposition by Basis Pursuit*; Technical Report; Stanford University: Stanford, CA, USA, 1995.

14. Mallat, S.G.; Zhang, Z.F. Matching pursuits with time-frequency dictionaries. *IEEE Trans. Signal Process.* **1993**, *41*, 3397–3415. [CrossRef]

15. Coifman, R.R.; Wickerhauser, M.V. Entropy-based algorithms for best basis selection. *IEEE Trans. Inf. Theory* **1992**, *38*, 713–718. [CrossRef]

16. Mandrikova, O.; Mandrikova, B.; Rodomanskay, A. Method of Constructing a Nonlinear Approximating Scheme of a Complex Signal: Application Pattern Recognition. *Mathematics* **2021**, *9*, 737. [CrossRef]

17. Kudela, K.; Rybak, J.; Antalová, A.; Storini, M. Time Evolution of low-Frequency Periodicities in Cosmic ray Intensity. *Sol. Phys.* **2002**, *205*, 165–175. [CrossRef]

18. Stamper, R.; Lockwood, M.; Wild, M.N.; Clark, T.D.G. Solar causes of the long-term increase in geomagnetic activity. *J. Geophys. Res.* **1999**, *104*, 325. [CrossRef]

19. Mandrikova, O.; Mandrikova, B. Hybrid Method for Detecting Anomalies in Cosmic ray Variations Using Neural Networks Autoencoder. *Symmetry* **2022**, *14*, 744. [CrossRef]

20. Belov, A.; Eroshenko, E.; Gushchina, R.; Dorman, L.; Oleneva, V.; Yanke, V. Cosmic ray variations as a tool for studying solar-terrestrial relations. *Electromagn. Plasma Process. Body Sun Body Earth* **2015**, 258–284.

21. Papailiou, M.; Mavromichalaki, H.; Belov, A.; Eroshenko, E.; Yanke, V. Precursor Effects in Different Cases of Forbush Decreases. *Sol. Phys.* **2011**, *276*, 337–350. [CrossRef]

22. Forbush, S.E. On the Effects in the Cosmic Ray Intensity Observed during Magnetic Storms. *Phys. Rev.* **1937**, *51*, 1108–1109.10. [CrossRef]

23. Gololobov, P.Y.; Krivoshapkin, P.A.; Krymsky, G.F.; Gerasimova, S.K. Investigating the influence of geometry of the heliospheric neutral current sheet and solar activity on modulation of galactic cosmic rays with a method of main components. *Sol. -Terr. Phys.* **2020**, *6*, 24–28.

24. Abunina, M.A.; Belov, A.V.; Eroshenko, E.A.; Abunin, A.A.; Oleneva, V.A.; Yanke, V.G.; Melkumyan, A.A. Ring of Station Method in Research of Cosmic Ray Variations: 1. General Description. *Geomagn. Aeron.* **2020**, *60*, 38–45. [CrossRef]

25. Koundal, P. Graph Neural Networks and Application for Cosmic-Ray Analysis. In Proceedings of the 5th International Workshop on Deep Learning in Computational Physics, Dubna, Russia, 28–29 June 2021. [CrossRef]

26. Piekarczyk, M.; Bar, O.; Bibrzycki, Ł.; Niedźwiecki, M.; Rzecki, K.; Stuglik, S.; Andersen, T.; Budnev, N.M.; Alvarez-Castillo, D.E.; Cheminant, K.A.; et al. CNN-Based Classifier as an Offline Trigger for the CREDO Experiment. *Sensors* **2021**, *21*, 4804. [CrossRef] [PubMed]

27. Ahn, B.-H.; Moon, G.-H.; Sun, W.; Akasofu, S.-I.; Chen, G.X.; Park, Y.D. Universal time variation of the Dst index and the relationship between the cumulative AL and Dst indices during geomagnetic storms. *J. Geophys. Res.* **2002**, *107*, 1409. [CrossRef]

28. Pattanayak, S. *Pro Deep Learning with TensorFlow: A Mathematical Approach to Advanced Artificial Intelligence in Python*; Apress: Bangalore, India, 2017; p. 398.

29. Chui, C.K. *An Introduction to Wavelets; Wavelet Analysis and Its Applications*; Academic Press: Boston, MA, USA, 1992; ISBN 978-0-12-174584-4.

30. Daubechies, I. *Ten Lectures on Wavelets; CBMS-NSF Regional Conference Series in Applied Mathematics*; Society for Industrial and Applied Mathematics: Philadelphia, PA, USA, 1992.

31. Witte, R.S.; Witte, J.S. *Statistics*, 11th ed.; Wiley: New York, NY, USA, 2017; p. 496.

32. Real Time Data Base for the Measurements of High-Resolution Neutron Monitor. Available online: https://www.nmdb.eu (accessed on 30 March 2023).

33. Kuzmin, Y. Registration of the intensity of the neutron flux in Kamchatka in connection with the forecast of earthquakes. In Proceedings of the Conference Geophysical Monitoring of Kamchatka, Kamchatka, Russia, 20 September–1 October 2006; pp. 149–156.

34. Schlickeiser, R. *Cosmic Ray Astrophysics*; Springer GmbH & Co., KG.: Berlin/Heidelberg, Germany, 2002; p. 519.

35. Institute of Applied Geophysics. Available online: http://ipg.geospace.ru/ (accessed on 30 March 2023).
36. Geomagnetic Equatorial Dst Index. Available online: https://wdc.kugi.kyoto-u.ac.jp/dstdir/ (accessed on 30 March 2023).

MDPI

St. Alban-Anlage 66

4052 Basel

Switzerland

Tel. +41 61 683 77 34

Fax +41 61 302 89 18

www.mdpi.com

Mathematics Editorial Office

E-mail: mathematics@mdpi.com

www.mdpi.com/journal/mathematics